A COMPANION TO

SCIENCE FICTION

EDITED BY **DAVID SEED**

Blackwell
Publishing

BLACKWELL PUBLISHING
350 Main Street, Malden, MA 02148-5020, USA
9600 Garsington Road, Oxford OX4 2DQ, UK

First published 2005 by Blackwell Publishing Ltd
First published in paperback 2008 by Blackwell Publishing Ltd

1   2008

Library of Congress Cataloging-in-Publication Data

A companion to science fiction / edited by David Seed.
p. cm.—(Blackwell companions to literature and culture ; 34)
Includes bibliographical references and index.
ISBN 978-1-4051-1218-5 (hardcover)—ISBN 978-1-4051-8437-3 (pbk)
1. Science fiction—History and criticism. I. Seed, David. II. Series.
PN3433.5.C73 2005
809.3¢8762—dc22
2004025185

A catalogue record for this title is available from the British Library.

Set in 11 on 13 pt Garamond 3
by SNP Best-set Typesetter Ltd, Hong Kong
Printed and bound in Singapore
by Markono Print Media Pte Ltd

For further information on
Blackwell Publishing, visit our website at
www.blackwellpublishing.com

Contents

Notes on Contributors

Mike Ashley, formerly a Local Government Officer, is now a full-time writer and researcher. He has published over 70 books and anthologies and over 500 articles. His books include the original four-part *History of the Science-Fiction Magazine* (1974–8), currently being updated in three volumes starting with *The Time Machines* (Liverpool University Press, 2000). He has published the biography of Algernon Blackwood, *Starlight Man* (Constable, 2001) and, with William Contento, *The Supernatural Index* (Greenwood Press, 1995), for which they won the Bram Stoker Award. Ashley also received the Edgar Award for *The Mammoth Encyclopedia of Modern Crime Fiction* (Carroll and Graf, 2002) and the Science Fiction Research Association's Pilgrim Award in 2002 for his contribution to science fiction research.

Brian Baker is a Senior Lecturer in Literature and Film at University College Chester. He has published on J.G. Ballard, Michael Moorcock, and psychedelia and the New Wave, and is the coauthor, with John Cartwright, of *Science and Literature* (ABC-Clio, 2005). He is currently completing a monograph on Iain Sinclair.

Douglas Barbour has published a number of poetry collections, most recently *Fragmenting Body etc.* (NeWest Press/SALT Publishing, 2000). His critical works include monographs on Daphne Marlatt, John Newlove, and bpNichol (all ECW Press, 1992), Michael Ondaatje (Twayne, 1993), *Lyric/Anti-lyric: Essays on Contemporary Poetry* (NeWest Press, 2001), and essays on Science Fiction and Fiction. A professor in the Department of English, University of Alberta, Edmonton, Alberta, he has taught courses in Science Fiction and Fiction, modern poetry, Canadian and Commonwealth literatures, and creative writing. In 1987 he coedited *Tesseracts 2: Canadian Science Fiction* (Porcepic Press).

Marleen S. Barr, Scholar in Residence at the Hadassah Brandeis Feminist Research Institute at Brandeis University, has received the Science Fiction Research Association Pilgrim Award for lifetime achievement in science fiction criticism. Her books include *Feminist Fabulation* (University of Iowa Press, 1992) and *Genre Fission: A New Discourse Practice for Cultural Studies* (University of Iowa Press, 2000). She was the co-coordinator of the May 2004 *PMLA* science fiction special topic issue. She has published *Oy Pioneer!* (University of Wisconsin Press, 2003), a humorous feminist academic science fiction novel.

Russell Blackford is an Honorary Research Associate in the School of Literary, Visual and Performance Studies, and a sessional lecturer in the School of English, Communications and Performance Studies, Monash University, Australia. He is coauthor (with Van Ikin and Sean McMullen) of *Strange Constellations: A History of Australian Science Fiction* (Greenwood Press, 1999), and a contributor to many journals, magazines, and anthologies. His recent publications include a science fiction trilogy, *Terminator 2: The New John Connor Chronicles*.

M. Keith Booker is Professor and Director of Graduate Studies in the Department of English at the University of Arkansas. His books include *The Dystopian Impulse in Modern Literature: Fiction as Social Criticism and Dystopian Literature* (both Greenwood Press, 1994); *Monsters, Mushroom Clouds, and the Cold War: American Science and the Roots of Postmodernism* (Greenwood Press, 2001), and *Science Fiction Television*.

Fred Botting held a chair in English Literature at Keele University and as of January 2005 is a Professor in the Institute of Cultural Research at Lancaster University. He has cowritten and coedited three books on Georges Bataille. His other publications include *Gothic* (1995) in the Routledge New Critical Idiom series, and *Sex, Machines and Navels* (Manchester University Press, 1999). He is currently completing a book on Gothic Post-Modernities (romance, consumption, technology).

Mark Bould is a Senior Lecturer in Film Studies at the University of the West of England. An editor of *Historical Materialism* and an editorial consultant for *Science Fiction Studies*, he is currently completing *Film Noir: From Fritz Lang to Femme Fatale* (Wallflower, 2005) and *The Cinema of John Sayles: A Lone Star* (Wallflower, 2007); and coediting a collection of M. John Harrison's criticism (Science Fiction Foundation, 2005).

Andrew M. Butler is Senior Lecturer in Media and Cultural Studies at Canterbury Christ Church University College. As well as being features editor of the SF journal *Vector* since 1995, he is the author of Pocket Essentials volumes *Philip K. Dick*, *Cyberpunk* (both 2000), *Terry Pratchett* (2001), *Film Studies* (2002), and (with Bob Ford) *Postmodernism* (2003). He won the 2004 Pioneer Award for his article on the British science fiction boom.

Stephen R.L. Clark is Professor of Philosophy at Liverpool University. Relevant publications include *The Mysteries of Religion* (Blackwells, 1986); *How to Live Forever: Science*

Fiction and Philosophy (Routledge, 1995); "Alien Dreams – Kipling" in David Seed, ed., *Anticipations: Essays on Early Science Fiction and its Precursors* (Liverpool University Press, 1995); "Making up Animals: The View from Science Fiction" in *Animal Biotechnology and Ethics*, Alan Holland & Andrew Johnson, eds. (Chapman & Hall, 1997), and "Deep Time: Does it Matter?" in George Ellis, ed., *The Far-Future Universe* (Templeton Foundation Press, 2002). He is married, with three children.

John Clute is a science fiction critic and novelist who has received three Hugo Awards for best nonfiction. He also received a Pilgrim Award in 1994 for scholarship in the field, and the ICFA Distinguished Guest Scholar Award in 1999. He coedited five of the *Interzone* anthologies of science fiction and fantasy. Other publications include *The Encyclopedia of Science Fiction* (1993) with Peter Nicholls, *Science Fiction: The Illustrated Encyclopedia* (1995), and *The Encyclopedia of Fantasy* (1997) with John Grant. Books of reviews and essays include *Strokes* (Serconia Press, 1988), *Look at the Evidence* (Liverpool University Press, 1996) and *Scores* (Beccon Publications, 2003). He is a Trustee of the Science Fiction Foundation.

Christine Cornea is a Senior Lecturer in Film Studies at the University of Portsmouth, where she coordinators film units and also lectures in New Zealand and Australian cinema. She is currently writing a study of science fiction cinema for Edinburgh University Press (forthcoming 2005). Her recent published articles include "David Cronenberg's *Crash* and Performing Cyborgs" (*Velvet Light Trap*, Sept. 2003) and "Techno-Orientalism and the Postmodern Subject," in Jackie Furby and Karen Brandt, eds. *Screen Method: Comparative Readings in Screen Studies* (Wallflower Press, 2004).

Jeanne Cortiel is Assistant Professor in American Studies at the University of Dortmund in Germany. She is the author of *Demand My Writing: Joanna Russ, Feminism, Science Fiction* (Liverpool University Press, 1999) and *Passion für das Unmögliche: Befreiung als Narrativ in der amerikanischen feministischen Theologie* (2001); she is currently finishing a book-length study of ethnicity in mid-nineteenth-century American literature.

Robert Crossley, Professor of English at the University of Massachusetts Boston, is the author of *Olaf Stapledon: Speaking for the Future* (Liverpool and Syracuse University Presses, 1994) and editor of *An Olaf Stapledon Reader* (Syracuse University Press, 1997). His most recent work includes a new edition of Octavia Butler's *Kindred* and essays on literary and scientific images of Mars.

Istvan Csicsery-Ronay, Jr. is Professor of English and World Literature at DePauw University (USA), and a coeditor of *Science Fiction Studies*. He is the author of many articles on international science fiction. His book, *The Seven Beauties of Science Fiction*, is forthcoming from Wesleyan University Press.

Carol Franko is an Associate Professor of English at Kansas State University. Her articles have appeared in *Science Fiction Studies*, *Extrapolation*, *JFA: Journal on the Fantastic in the Arts*, and *Mythlore*. Work in progress is focusing on how SF naturalizes the supernatural, or otherwise "rewrites" supernatural worldviews.

Carl Freedman is Professor of English at Louisiana State University, the author of many articles and books, including *Critical Theory and Science Fiction* (Wesleyan University Press, 2000) and *The Incomplete Projects: Marxism, Modernity, and the Politics of Culture* (University Press of New England, 2002). He is the editor of *Conversations with Isaac Asimov* (University of Mississippi Press, 2005).

Faye Hammill is a Lecturer in English at Cardiff University. Her research areas are women's writing of the 1920s and 1930s, and Canadian literature. She has published *Literary Culture and Female Authorship in Canada 1760–2000* (Rodopi, 2003) and articles on Atwood, Carol Shields, Sara Jeannette Duncan, Frances Brooke, Stella Gibbons, Mazo de la Roche among others.

Donald M. Hassler is Professor of English at Kent State University in Ohio. He has published a number of books on science fiction, including *Hal Clement* (1982) and *Isaac Asimov* (1991: both Starmont House), and *Comic Tones in Science Fiction* (Greenwood Press, 1982). He is currently the Executive Editor of the journal *Extrapolation* and has served as president of the Science Fiction Research Association.

Veronica Hollinger is Associate Professor of Cultural Studies at Trent University in Peterborough, Ontario, Canada. She has published many articles on science fiction and has been a coeditor of *Science Fiction Studies* since 1990. She is also coeditor of several scholarly collections, including *Edging into the Future: Science Fiction and Contemporary Cultural Transformation* (University of Pennsylvania Press, 2002).

Van Ikin is Associate Professor in English, Communication and Cultural Studies at the University of Western Australia and winner of the inaugural Chandler Award for Achievement in the Field of Australian Science Fiction. He is coauthor of *Strange Constellations: A History of Australian Science Fiction* (Greenwood Press, 1999); editor of *Australian Science Fiction* (University of Queensland Press, 1982), *Glass Reptile Breakout and Other Australian Speculative Stories* (Centre for Studies in Australian Literature, 1990); coeditor of *Mortal Fire: Best Australian SF* (Hodder and Stoughton, 1993); and editor/publisher of the journal *Science Fiction: A Review of Speculative Literature* (1977–).

Edward James has taught medieval history at University College Dublin, York, Reading, and Rutgers; he is now Professor of Medieval History at University College Dublin, and specializes in the history of France in the early Middle Ages. Between 1986 and 2001 he was editor of *Foundation: The International Review of Science Fiction*. His 1994 book for Oxford University Press, *Science Fiction in the Twentieth Century*, was awarded the Eaton Prize; and in 2004 he won the Science Fiction Research Association's Pilgrim Award for distinguished contribution to science fiction studies. His latest book, edited with Farah Mendlesohn, is the *Cambridge Companion to Science Fiction* (2003).

David Ketterer is an Honorary Research Fellow in English at the University of Liverpool and an Emeritus Professor of English at Concordia University, Montreal. His books include *New Worlds for Old: The Apocalyptic Imagination, Science Fiction, and American Literature* (Anchor Press, 1974); *The Science Fiction of Mark Twain* (1984; in paperback as *Tales of Wonder by Mark Twain*, 2003); *Imprisoned in a Tesseract: The Life and Work of James Blish* (Kent State University Press, 1987); and *Canadian Science Fiction and Fantasy* (Dragon Press, 1992). In 1996 he received the Science Fiction Research Association's Pilgrim Award. He is working on a critical biography of John Wyndham.

Rob Latham is an Associate Professor of English and American Studies at the University of Iowa, where he directs the Sexuality Studies Program. A coeditor of *Science Fiction Studies* since 1997, he is the author of *Consuming Youth: Vampires, Cyborgs and the Culture of Consumption*, published by Chicago University Press in 2002. He is currently working on a book on New Wave science fiction.

Susan E. Lederer is Associate Professor of History of Medicine at Yale University School of Medicine. In 1997 she served as curator for an exhibit – *Frankenstein – Penetrating the Secrets of Nature* – for the National Library of Medicine (US). A version of the exhibit is now traveling to 80 libraries in the United States through 2006.

Roger Luckhurst teaches in the School of English and Humanities at Birkbeck College, University of London. He is the author of *"The Angle Between Two Walls": The Fiction of J. G. Ballard* (Liverpool University Press, 1997), *The Invention of Telepathy* (Oxford University Press, 2002) and *A Cultural History of Science Fiction* (Polity Press, 2005).

Sean McMullen is an Australian SF and fantasy author, with twelve books and fifty stories published, for which he has won thirteen awards. He was coauthor of *Strange Constellations: A History of Australian Science Fiction* (Greenwood Press, 1999), and is doing a PhD on Medieval Fantasy Literature at Melbourne University. His most recent novels are *Voyage of the Shadowmoon* (2002) and *Glass Dragons* (2004).

Farah Mendlesohn is editor of *Foundation: the International Review of Science Fiction*, and coeditor of the *Cambridge Companion to Science Fiction* (2003) as well as edited collections on Ken MacLeod, *Babylon 5*, Terry Pratchett and Joanna Russ. In 2004 she won the British Science Fiction Association Award for nonfiction. She is currently working on *Toward a Taxonomy of Fantasy* for Wesleyan University Press and is a Senior Lecturer at Middlesex University.

Chris Palmer teaches contemporary SF, narrative analysis, and issues of adaptation in the English programme at La Trobe University in Melbourne. In addition to his study *Philip K Dick: Exhilaration and Terror of the Postmodern* (Liverpool University Press, 2003), he has also published on Shakespeare films, Umberto Eco, and contemporary science fiction.

Richard M. Ratzan is an emergency medicine physician working in Hartford Hospital, Hartford, Connecticut, USA. His interests include the medical humanities, nonhuman primates and Mary Shelley's *Frankenstein*.

Warren Rochelle is an Associate Professor of English at the University of Mary Washington, in Fredericksburg, Virginia. In addition to a critical book on Le Guin, *Communities of the Heart: The Rhetoric of Myth in the Fiction of Ursula K. Le Guin* (Liverpool University Press, 2001), he has published book reviews and articles of science fiction criticism in *Extrapolation*, *Foundation*, *SFRA Review*, *Children's Literature Association Quarterly*, and the *North Carolina Literary Review*. He has also several science fiction short stories and an science fiction novel, *The Wild Boy* (2001). His fantasy novel, *Harvest of Changelings*, is also from Golden Gryphon Press (2006).

Jill Rudd is a member of the School of English at Liverpool University. Her publications on Gilman include "When the Songs Are Over and Sung" in *The Mixed Legacy of Charlotte Perkins Gilman*, Catherine J. Golden and Joanna Schneider Zangrando, eds. (University of Delaware Press, 2000) and, with Val Gough, has coedited two volumes of essays devoted to Gilman: *Charlotte Perkins Gilman: Optimist Reformer* (University of Iowa Press, 1999) and *A Very Different Story: Studies in the Fiction of Charlotte Perkins Gilman* (Liverpool University Press, 1998).

Andy Sawyer is the librarian of the Science Fiction Foundation Collection at the University of Liverpool Library, and Course Director of the MA in Science Fiction Studies offered by the School of English. He has published on children's/young adult SF, John Wyndham, telepathy, *Babylon 5*, "Reverse-Time narratives" and Terry Pratchett. He coedited the collection *Speaking Science Fiction* (Liverpool University Press, 2000). He is also Reviews Editor of *Foundation: the International Review of Science Fiction*.

David Seed holds a chair in American literature at the University of Liverpool. He is a member of the editorial board of the *Journal of American Studies*, and of the board of consulting editors for *Science Fiction Studies*. He edits the Science Fiction Texts and Studies series for Liverpool University Press. His publications include *American Science Fiction and the Cold War* (Edinburgh University Press, 1999) and *Brainwashing: The Fictions of Mind Control* (Kent State University Press, 2004).

Tom Shippey, currently Walter J. Ong Chair at Saint Louis University, has edited both *The Oxford Book of Science Fiction Stories* (1992) and *The Oxford Book of Fantasy Stories* (1994), as well as two critical anthologies on science fiction, *Fictional Space* (*Essays and Studies* 1990) and *Fiction 2000* (coedited with George Slusser, University of Georgia Press, 1992). He is also the author of two books on Tolkien, *The Road to Middle-Earth* (Allen and Unwin, 1982) and *J.R.R. Tolkien: Author of the Century* (HarperCollins, 2000).

George Slusser is Professor of Comparative Literature and Curator of the Eaton Collection of Science Fiction at the University of California Riverside. He has edited coedited numerous collections of essays on aspects of SF including *Bridges to Science Fiction* (1980), *Mindscapes* (1989, both Southern Illinois University Press), and *Unearthly Visions* (Greenwood Press, 2002). He is working with Daniele Chatelain on a translation and critical edition of Balzac's *The Centenarian* (forthcoming from Wesleyan University Press).

Vivian Sobchack is Associate Dean and Professor in the Department of Film, Television and Digital Media at the UCLA School of Theater, Film and Television. She is the author of the critically acclaimed *Screening Space: The American Science Fiction Film* (Rutgers University Press, 1997) and the editor of the anthology, *Meta-Morphing: Visual Transformation and the Culture of Quick Change* (University of Minnesota Press, 2000).

Brian Stableford is a 0.5 Lecturer in Creative Writing at University College, Winchester. He is the author of more than 50 SF novels, several nonfiction books – most recently the *Historical Dictionary of Science Fiction Literature* (Scarecrow Press, 2004) – and numerous contributions to reference books, including *Anatomy of Wonder 5* (Greenwood Press, 2005).

Takayuki Tatsumi, Professor of English at Keio University (Tokyo), is the author of *Cyberpunk America* (Tokyo: Keiso Publishers, 1988) and was coeditor of the Japanese Science Fiction issue of *Science Fiction Studies* (November 2002). He contributed to Larry McCaffery's *Storming the Reality Studio* (1991) and has published a variety of essays in *PMLA*, *Para*Doxa*, *Extrapolation*, and *SF Eye*. He was awarded the fifth Pioneer Award by the Science Fiction Research Association and has just completed a book on SF provisionally entitled *Full Metal Apache* (Duke University Press, forthcoming).

Phillip E. Wegner is an Associate Professor of English at the University of Florida. He is the author of *Imaginary Communities: Utopia, the Nation, and the Spatial Histories of Modernity* (University of California Press 2002), as well as a number of essays on contemporary fiction, film, and critical theory. He is completing a new book entitled, *Life Between Two Deaths: U.S. Culture, 1989–2001*.

Gary Westfahl, who teaches at the University of California, Riverside, received the Science Fiction Research Association's 2003 Pilgrim Award for lifetime contributions to science fiction and fantasy scholarship. His publications include *The Mechanics of Wonder: The Creation of the Idea of Science Fiction* (Liverpool University Press, 1998). His forthcoming projects include editing *Science Fiction Quotations: The Yale Dictionary* and *The Encyclopedia of Themes in Science Fiction and Fantasy*.

Jenny Wolmark is Principal Lecturer in Critical and Cultural Theory at the University of Lincoln, UK. She has published widely on Science Fiction and feminism and is the author of *Aliens and Others: Science Fiction, Feminism and Postmodernism* (Harvester Wheatsheaf, 1993) and the editor of *Cybersexualities: A Reader on Feminist Theory, Cyborgs and Cyberspace* (Edinburgh University Press, 1999). She is a coeditor for the *Journal of Gender Studies*. Her current research is on the relationship between image and text in web-based and other electronic formats.

Peter Wright is Senior Lecturer in Literature and Film at Edge Hill College of Higher Education, Ormskirk, Lancashire. He is the author of *Attending Daedalus: Gene Wolfe, Artifice and the Reader* (Liverpool University Press, 2003) and coeditor of *British Television Science Fiction* (I. B. Tauris, 2005). He has also written articles on British Science Fiction film, Edgar Rice Burroughs and *Doctor Who*.

Introduction: Approaching Science Fiction

This companion is intended to serve as an introduction and guide to one of the most extensive and varied kinds of modern literature. It does not pretend to exhaustive coverage. For that, the reader should consult reference works such as John Clute and Peter Nicholls' *Encyclopedia of Science Fiction* (1999), which remains the leading work of its kind for its combination of author and topic entries, or the *St. James Guide to Science Fiction Writers* (4th edn, Pederson 1996). It reflects a broad cultural shift towards science fiction that published writing on SF subjects (the term "science fiction" and its acronym SF will be used interchangeably throughout this volume) has become so extensive that a full bibliography would need to be as long as this volume. Here each essay concludes with a "references and further reading" section which not only give details of works cited within the essays, but also includes other relevant works and bibliographies. One of the most popular narrative subjects in SF is exploration and it is the hope that this companion will help readers in their discovery of the field by setting up a number of sign-posts and recommending some of the routes to take.

The very fact that this companion is being published suggests that SF at long last is being viewed as central to the culture. In the 1950s, cover statement for Penguin editions of John Wyndham's novels declared that he was writing a "modified form of what is unhappily known as 'science fiction,'" whereas in 2000 Wyndham's works started appearing in the Penguin Modern Classics. Apart from shifting Wyndham from the margins to the heart of an evolving modern canon, this change shows a reassessment of the idea of science fiction. Its centrality has been asserted by the US novelist Thomas M. Disch, who declared in 1998: "science fiction has come to permeate our culture in ways both trivial and/or profound, obvious and/or insidious" (Disch 1998: 11). The alternatives are strategic here because Disch is hedging his bets on the nature of SF's impact on culture, while the fact of its presence is indisputable. Whatever we think of SF, we live science fiction in our daily lives. From at least the 1950s onwards, writers such as Ray Bradbury have insisted that we live within the very technological environment of robotics and cybernetic devices that many SF writers describe.

This is not to argue that SF is the new version of social realism though this argument would not be absurd. Indeed, SF writers of the 1950s and 1960s quite often put forward such a view. Horrified equally by the US government restrictions on scientific knowledge in the Cold War and by the irresponsible myths promoted by SF writers at this time, Philip Wylie insisted in 1953: "The proper function of the science fiction author – the myth-maker of the twentieth century – would be to learn the science of the mind's workings and therewith to plan his work . . . so it will represent in *meaning* the known significance of man" (Wylie 1953: 239). Wylie was writing in the shadow of the Bomb and he was only too well aware of the weaknesses of SF at that time. Nevertheless, his insistence on SF's centrality was echoed by Robert Heinlein a few years later, when he declared: "It is the only fictional medium capable of interpreting the changing, head-long rush of modern life. Speculative fiction is the main stream of fiction" (Heinlein 1964: 53).

This raises a question which will recur throughout this companion: how do we read SF? Joanna Russ opened her 1975 "Towards an Aesthetic of Science Fiction" with the following questions:

> Is science fiction literature?
> Yes.
> Can it be judged by the usual literary criteria?
> No. (Russ 1995: 3)

There are two issues being raised here: the value of SF and the reading protocols we should apply to SF novels. If we approach *Dune* with the same expectations we would bring to *Middlemarch*, the result will probably be disappointment, not only because, as Joanna Russ has pointed out, SF tends to down-play character in favor of "phenomena." An even bigger reason lies in the way SF plays with our notion of the real. So, for Darko Suvin, a pioneer of SF criticism, science fiction estranges the reader from the familiar world and produces striking new perspectives as a result (Suvin 1979). Suvin set a high standard of analytical rigor for SF criticism and at the same time suggested ways in which we could think of SF as engaging with forms of otherness (see Parrinder 2000). The narratives in fiction and film of alien encounters are only one – sometimes sensational – form which this confrontation with otherness might take.

The problem of where to situate SF on a critical map has resulted in a number of different explanations of its development. Arguments continue about its origin, some critics even dating SF back into classical antiquity. The productive side to this archaeological line of enquiry is the recovery of lost works; I.F. Clarke's labors on future wars narratives are a shining example. The more essays and editions are produced on the science fiction of figures like Twain, Trollope, or Kipling, the more it is revealed that realism is not the uniform or "mainstream" some literary historians would have us believe. In the spirit of this multigeneric approach, Brian Aldiss sees SF as evolving in parallel with the Gothic and proposes *Frankenstein* as a formative work where the two modes intersect (Aldiss 1986). Alternatively Brian McHale (1987) has identified postwar SF as developing along similar lines to postmodernism because both genres ask fundamental questions about the world and the nature of selfhood. In the case of Aldiss, the issue is not so much whether SF grows out of the Gothic (or out of the Industrial Revolution, an argument that would have a lot of historical force), but rather how responsive SF texts would be to an interpretation informed by Gothic practices. McHale also helpfully draws our attention to a tradition of self-consciousness in SF which becomes much more evident after the Second World War. He argues that SF has increasingly borrowed aspects of postmodernism and that SF elements have in turn been borrowed by "mainstream" writers like Pynchon and DeLillo. However, McHale's commitment to exclusively rhetorical analysis leads him to abstract his chosen fiction from the cultural practices surrounding them. Because he starts from a rationalistic premise that novels must belong within some generic category, he never admits the possibility of a multigeneric work that could move in and out of SF. William Burroughs is one example for McHale of a postmodernist who has used SF tropes and who supposedly confirms McHale's assertion that postmodernists are supremely indifferent to SF "gadgetry." Here his lack of historical ballast lets him down. Burroughs has always seemed comfortable when mimicking popular genres like SF or the crime novel and in fact throughout his life demonstrated a fascination with a macabre side to gadgetry: the technology of mind control, for instance. In this volume Veronica Hollinger (chapter 15) uses an altogether more productive model of postmodernism when she argues that SF has been uniquely responsive to techno-scientific change and, in its more experimental forms, has demonstrated a perception that cultural representations are constructs. The best critical writing on SF approaches the fiction in relation to the images and narratives of related cultural practices. SF criticism thus follows a lead from science fiction itself in mapping out relations. The implicit metaphor operating in this companion is that of a lattice. To a greater or lesser extent, its contributors are charting out the relation between SF and related media, particularly film which – as Vivian Sobchack shows in *Screening Space* (enlarged edn. 1987) – has developed in close tandem with SF fiction, especially since the Second World War.

For Sobchack, as for the Polish novelist Stanislaw Lem, SF is a quarrelsome, argumentative, and vulgar mode. In *Microworlds* (1991) Lem fleshes out a view that SF is a generic upstart, constantly blurring the gap between high and low literature. Lem's particular respect goes to Philip K. Dick – and it is interesting that the Polish writer should choose an American as an impressive example of deploying popular materials with original effect (Lem 1991: 45–105). Dick for his part was rather less generous. When Lem visited the USA, Dick informed the FBI that he was being targeted by a Communist conspiracy. For Lem and for many other critics, SF is a literature of debate. The essays in this volume exemplify this diversity of approach in their arguments as well as their demonstration of how SF writers constantly revise and renew fictional practice by writing *against* their predecessors. Rob Latham, for example, shows how in the 1960s the New Wave writers questioned many sacred cows in science fiction (its optimism, its preoccupation with technology) by calling for the exploration of "inner space." More generally, this call involved challenging the decorum of the SF text itself, so that black humor and startling graphics broke up the solemnity we had come to expect in science fiction.

Exploration lies at the heart of SF. It was an imperative which J.G. Ballard's famous insistence in 1962 did not question: "it is *inner* space, not outer, that needs to be explored" (Ballard 1996: 197). The turn inwards expressed recoil from the publicity attending the Soviet–American space race, but the general drive to exploration in SF represents in narrative form the impulse to discover, to project alternative models of our known world. Philip K. Dick's paranoid labyrinths are only the darker product of this impulse. World-building is rightly stressed in these pages, as the construction of alternative but proximate cultures (Ursula Le Guin's Hainish, Gwyneth Jones' Aleutians), or as the competitive appropriation of new terrain (Kim Stanley Robinson's Mars trilogy). Gary Westfahl discusses the strategies involved in world-building, the combination of details for verisimilitude and scientific fact about the planets in "hard" science fiction. The phrase "other worlds" has been used again and again as a title for collections of SF stories or essays about them. Stanislaw Lem's choice of *Microworlds* as title for his collected SF criticism gives the reader a helpful signal that in reading science fiction we are entering a variety of imagined worlds, each with its own organization. All fiction does this, but SF compels the reader to revise presumptions of plausibility. In that sense reading SF is a comparative exercise where we cross-relate the familiar to the strangely new. The narrative device of "parallel worlds," often with a door or other access point, makes this activity of comparing an explicit part of the narrative. In *World-Games* (1987) Christopher Nash describes "alternative-worlds" fiction as that which "depicts unnatural worlds naturally" (Nash 1987: 60). Although he studiously avoids using the label science fiction, he includes many SF novels in his discussion and his explanation could apply to much of the genre. Again and again we shall see in the essays in this collection how reading SF involves a complex interplay between method and subject, between the supposedly "natural" and its opposite.

The concept of world-building is an intrinsic part of the construction of a science fiction novel. Brian Stableford describes here how plotting took on a new sophistication when John W. Campbell insisted in the late 1930s that contributors to *Astounding Science Fiction* took more pains over the internal consistency of their imagined worlds. The second development was the rise in ecological consciousness in the postwar period. We could take the food chain in this context as symbolic of ecology and world-building in general: symbolic, that is, of connectedness. World-building resembles what Fredric Jameson calls "cognitive mapping," where the reader discovers and charts out relations between characters and different aspects of their environment. Exploration in the local sense here of discovering these relations has led many critics – some featuring in this volume – to argue that science fiction is a very directed, even didactic kind of fiction. After all, the label science fiction contains a tension between the first term which suggests organized knowledge and the second which denotes feigning or imaginative construction. Does this mean that SF is instructive? Arthur C. Clarke has dedicated his career to evoking a "sense of wonder" at the sublime spaces of the universe and sees the SF writer's mission as being a provocative one: to challenge fanaticism and superstition by presenting possible futures (Clarke 2000: 247–9). For Clarke, SF can challenge conservative mindsets through narratively embodied thought experiments. Thus, essays here demonstrate how science fiction challenges presumptions about gender, technology, or the autonomy of the individual personality, among other issues. Reacting against Clarke's educative impulse, many SF writers, particularly since the 1960s, have created playful narratives which set up multiple meanings for the reader to negotiate. Clarke has been described in the press as the "prophet of the space age" and similarly Doris Lessing admitted in interview with Brian Aldiss that in her own SF she consciously borrowed the figure of the "warner or prophet, who arrives from somewhere and tells the people they should behave differently, or else!" (Ingersoll 1996: 169–70). Her purpose is closer to that of the jeremiad or warning usually expressed through dystopian narrative.

For reasons of space, this companion limits its coverage to Anglophone SF and as a result understates the importance of Jules Verne, German films like *Metropolis*, or Russian SF. For commentary on Verne, see Costello (1978) and Smyth (2000); on European SF, see Rottensteiner (1999); and on German SF, see Fischer (1984). Despite these unavoidable limits on coverage, many of the essays in the present volume demonstrate an awareness of how science fiction refers across cultures, drawing on a shared pool of narratives. Even within a single culture, for example, the essay on Australian science fiction demonstrates that it is as old as realism within that country, and that its particular inflections of the "lost race" theme or of dystopias are directed towards exploring and interrogating emerging national identity. Nalo Hopkinson and Uppinder Mehan's 2004 anthology of postcolonial SF, *So Long Been Dreaming*, combines stories from different cultures in a collection that critiques "colonizing the natives . . . from the experience of the colonizee" (Hopkinson and Mehan 2004: 9). This anthology demonstrates the continuing adaptability of SF to new needs of debate.

In 1927, Aldous Huxley stated: "The future of America is the future of the world" (Huxley 2001: 185) and *Brave New World* could be read as an early parable of globalization. The prominence – should we say dominance? – of American SF in this volume is unmistakable. John Clute has summarized the pattern of modern SF narratives as reflecting a "First World vision, a set of stories about the future written by inhabitants of, and for the benefit of readers who were the inhabitants of, the industrialized Western world, which dominated the twentieth century; simplistically, it was a set of stories about the American Dream" (Clute 2003: 66). This conclusion is not at all simplistic because Clute is discussing the institutionalization of SF and, with that, its continuing promotion on a commercial scale previously unimaginable. The first bibliography of SF published in Greece confirms this general impression. Over some 200 pages of listing, around 170 American SF writers are cited, whose sheer quantity overwhelms the small number of practicing Greek authors; and the tables do not include English-language imports, so the imbalance must be even more stark (Pastourmatzi 1995). These figures suggest that in non-Anglophone countries the emergence of science must involve a negotiation of the market dominance by American SF. Takayuki Tatsumi's essay in this companion asks the question "what is Asian science fiction?" and offers in answer a description of how SF is produced through encounters between indigenous traditions and Western (which in practice has come to mean increasingly American) SF. Apart from the numerical growth in SF publications in other cultures, the examples above are signs of how SF is being studied and promoted; there are now web portals on Indian and South African science fiction.

Throughout this companion the reader will constantly encounter the figure of the border. In the preceding paragraph I was outlining a territorial problem that complicates the relation of SF to its local culture. Even on the microscale of the individual readings that conclude this volume, however, we see instances of how SF straddles or challenges boundaries: Charlotte Perkins Gilman's *Herland*, for instance, reverses the convention of the "lost world" narrative at the expense of its male explorers; *Brave New World* depicts a geometric line separating civilized from barbaric and then describes examples of "leakage" across that line. On a broader scale, M. Keith Booker explains how SF might reinforce or interrogate the polarities of the Cold War; Mark Bould and Christine Cornea consider the interweaving of human and electronic construct in the film and fiction of cyborgs; and Fred Botting explores the intersections between SF and the Gothic. One absence in this collection has been quite deliberate. No attempt has been made to define science fiction. Instead, the essays present it as a multigeneric field (who could say with certainty where SF ends and fantasy begins?) and its narratives as repeatedly challenging the stability of boundaries between categories and concepts.

The essays in this volume move from the general to the specific. The opening three chapters engage with science fiction in its broadest aspects; then follows a section discussing central issues in SF like its presentation of utopias, its concern with ecology, or the role of gender in SF. "Genres and Movements" considers some of the types of SF that have emerged over recent decades and the attendant debates about these subgenres. A section on film was essential because more and more we tend to think of science fiction titles as indicative of a group of works: a novel and a movie adaptation at the very least. The next group of essays extend discussion to different cultures around the globe and make explicit issues of cultural identity which are raised elsewhere in the volume. The final two sections address a selection of key SF writers and offer close readings of individual works, placing them in their historical and cultural contexts.

REFERENCES AND FURTHER READING

Aldiss, Brian, with Peter Wingrove (1986) *Trillion Year Spree: The History of Science Fiction*. London: Victor Gollancz.

Ballard, J.G. (1996) *A User's Guide to the Millennium*. London: HarperCollins.

Clarke, Arthur C. (2000) *Greetings, Carbon-Based*

Bipeds! A Vision of the 20ᵗʰ Century as it Happened, (ed.) Ian T. Macauley. London: HarperCollins.

Clarke, I.F. (1966) *Voices Prophesying War, 1763–1984*. Oxford: Oxford University Press.

——(1979) *The Pattern of Expectation*. London: Cape.

Clute, John (2003) "Science Fiction from 1980 to the Present," in *The Cambridge Companion to Science Fiction*, (eds) Edward James and Farah Mendlesohn. Cambridge: Cambridge University Press.

Clute, John, and Peter Nicholls (eds) (1999) *The Encyclopedia of Science Fiction*. London: Orbit.

Costello, Peter (1978) *Jules Verne: Inventor of Science Fiction*. London: Hodder and Stoughton.

Disch, Thomas M. (1998) *The Dreams Our Stuff is Made Of: How Science Fiction Conquered the World*. New York: Free Press.

Fischer, William B. (1984) *The Empire Strikes Out: Kurd Lasswitz, Hans Dominik, and the Development of German Science Fiction*. Bowling Green OH: Bowling Green State Unbiversity Popular Press.

Heinlein, Robert A. (1964) "Science Fiction: Its Nature, Faults and Virtues," in *The Science Fiction Novel: Imagination and Social Criticism*, 2ⁿᵈ edn, (ed.) Basil Davenport. Chicago: Advent, 17–63.

Hopkinson, Nalo, and Uppinder Mehan (eds) (2004) *So Long Been Dreaming: Postcolonial Science Fiction and Fantasy*. Vancouver: Arsenal Pulp Press.

Huxley, Aldous (2001) *Complete Essays. Volume III: 1930–1935*, (eds) Robert S. Baker and James Saxton. Chicago: Ivan R. Dee.

Ingersoll, Earl G. (ed.) (1996) *Putting the Questions Differently: Interviews with Doris Lessing, 1964–1994*. London: HarperCollins.

Lem, Stanislaw (ed.) (1991) *Microworlds: Writings on Science Fiction and Fantasy*. (1984) Franz Rottensteiner, London: Mandarin.

McHale, Brian (1987) *Postmodern Fiction*. New York and London: Methuen.

Nash, Christopher (1987) *World-Games: The Tradition of Anti-Realist Revolt*. London and New York: Methuen.

Parrinder, Patrick (ed.) (2000) *Learning from Other Worlds: Estrangement, Cognition and the Politics of Science Fiction and Utopia*. Liverpool: Liverpool University Press; Durham NC: Duke University Press.

Pastourmatzi, Domna (1995) *Bibliography of Science Fiction, Fantasy and Horror*. Athens: Alien Publications.

Pederson, Jay P. (ed.) (1996) *St. James Guide to Science Fiction Writers*, 4ᵗʰ edn. Detroit: St. James Press.

Rottensteiner, Franz (ed.) (1999) *View from Another Shore: European Science Fiction*. Liverpool: Liverpool University Press.

Russ, Joanna (1995) *To Write Like a Woman: Essays in Feminism and Science Fiction*. Bloomington and Indianapolis: Indiana University Press.

Smyth, Edmund (ed.) (2000) *Jules Verne: Narratives of Modernity*. Liverpool: Liverpool University Press.

Sobchack, Vivian (1987) *Screening Space: The American Science Fiction Film*, 2ⁿᵈ edn. New York: Ungar.

Suvin, Darko (1979) *Metamorphoses of Science Fiction*, New Haven and London: Yale University Press.

Wylie, Philip (1953) "Science Fiction and Sanity in an Age of Crisis," in *Modern Science Fiction: Its Meaning and Its Future*, (ed.) Reginald Bretnor. New York: Coward-McCann, 221–41.

PART I
Surveying the Field

1

Hard Reading: The Challenges of Science Fiction

Tom Shippey

Science fiction is arguably, and in several respects, the most challenging form of literature as yet devised. The claim may seem a strange one to someone familiar only with commercially mass-produced series, the "Star Trek" or "Star Wars" novels derived from popular TV and cinema productions. Nevertheless, to begin with something relatively straightforward, it can be shown that reading (or even viewing) any form of science fiction does involve one extra *intellectual* step over and above those necessary for reading other forms of fiction. The point may be made by comparing two superficially similar openings, one from a "mainstream" novel, the other from science fiction.

The "mainstream" novel is George Orwell's *Coming up for Air* (1939), and it begins with a description of a man shaving:

The idea really came to me the day I got my new false teeth.

I remember the morning well. At about a quarter to eight I'd nipped out of bed and got into the bathroom just in time to shut the kids out. It was a beastly January morning, with a dirty yellowish-grey sky. Down below, out of the little square of bathroom window, I could see the ten yards by five of grass, with a privet hedge round it and a bare patch in the middle, that we call the back garden. There's the same back garden, same privets, and same grass, behind every house in Ellesmere Road. Only difference – where there are no kids there's no bare patch in the middle.

I was trying to shave with a bluntish razor-blade while the water ran into the bath. My face looked back at me out of the mirror, and underneath, in a tumbler of water on the little shelf over the washbasin, the teeth that belonged in the face. It was the temporary set that Warner, my dentist, had given me to wear while the new ones were being made. I haven't such a bad face, really. It's one of those bricky-red faces that go with butter-coloured hair and pale-blue eyes. I've never gone grey or bald, thank God, and when I've got my teeth in I probably don't look my age, which is forty-five. (Orwell 1939: 3–4)

Quite how many things Orwell is trying to say in this passage is arguable. But probably from the 250 words cited one could make a list of some 20–5 data – a datum being a discrete fact stated or implied in the passage, such as: "the narrator's house has a bathroom," or "the narrator's house has a garden," or "the narrator's house has only one bathroom," or "the narrator has children" (with whom, inferentially, he has to share the bathroom), etc. In addition to these, we could easily generate a string of more debatable conclusions, such as "the narrator tries to economize on razor-blades, even though these are/were cheap," or "the inhabitants or Ellesmere Road include retired or unmarried people, who have no children." A fuzz of such speculation must in some way surround the reading experiences of this passage.

Yet despite that what most readers work out from their 20–5 data must be something like this:

(1)   The narrator (to use Northrop Frye's "theory of literary modes," Frye 1957: 33–34) is "low mimetic," and on the verge of becoming ironic. He has false teeth, he is middle-aged, his appearance is undistinguished, we will learn in the next paragraph that he is fat.

(2)   The narrator is "lower-middle-class": his house has only one bathroom, the W.C. is in it, there are at least four people to share it (counting the children's inferential mother). Mornings are accordingly competitive occasions when it comes to using the bathroom. This major inconvenience is dictated by economy, as is the size of the garden, and the bare patch in it, which tells us that children play in their gardens (because they have nowhere else to go). Orwell is particularly clear about these class-marking details: the narrator is a house-owner, and the house has a garden (so it is not a "back-to-back," a working-class house). But it is a small garden directly under the bathroom window, and the window itself is a "little" one. On the information already given, most English readers, in 1939 or for many years afterwards, could and would make accurate guesses about the narrator's income and life-style. That is what Orwell wants them to do.

(3)   The narrator's life-style is a drab one. Whether this fact should be related to his class status, whether drabness is a necessary part of "low mimesis," these are precisely the themes of the novel (which says in short that they are all related but, very passionately, ought not to be). Just the same, the fact is there, in the "beastly" morning, the "dirty" sky, the "little" square of window, the "bare" patch of garden, the "bluntish" razor-blade, and so on. Stylistically, the main qualities one might identify in the passage are its directness and single-mindedness. Orwell, it seems, has only a few things to say; while he will substantiate these with many details, all the details will point in one direction.

It is this which makes *Coming Up for Air* such a satisfactory if elementary example of how a nonscience fiction novel works. There is no doubt about its data, and very little about what the data mean. There are some details of whose meaning a nonnative or noncontemporary reader might be doubtful, like the "quarter to eight" rising:

briefly, seven was the time for the working class to get up, to walk or cycle to work at eight, while the nine-o'-clock-starting middle class got up later, to catch their trains or buses for work. But these cause no serious trouble because they confirm or are confirmed by all the others. In the whole passage there is no jarring or inconsistent note.

Compare a matching passage from science fiction, again the opening of a novel, again a man shaving: this time from Frederik Pohl and C.M. Kornbluth's novel of 1953, *The Space Merchants*:

> As I dressed that morning I ran over in my mind the long list of statistics, evasions, and exaggerations that they would expect in my report. My section – Production – had been plagued with a long series of illnesses and resignations, and you can't get work done without people to do it. But the Board wasn't likely to take that as an excuse.
>
> I rubbed depilatory soap over my face and rinsed it with the trickle from the fresh-water tap. Wasteful, of course, but I pay taxes and salt water always leaves my face itchy. Before the last of the greasy stubble was quite washed away the trickle stopped and didn't start again. I swore a little and finished rinsing with salt. It had been happening lately; some people blamed Consie saboteurs. Loyalty raids were being held throughout the New York Water Supply Corporation; so far they hadn't done any good.
>
> The morning newscast above the shaving mirror caught me for a moment . . . the President's speech of last night, a brief glimpse of the Venus rocket squat and silvery on the Arizona sand, rioting in Panama . . . I switched it off when the quarter-hour time signal chimed over the audio band.
>
> It looked as though I was going to be late again. Which certainly would not help mollify the Board.
>
> I saved five minutes by wearing yesterday's shirt instead of studding a clean one and by leaving my breakfast juice to grow warm and sticky on the table. But I lost the five minutes again by trying to call Kathy. She didn't answer the phone and I was late getting into the office. (Pohl and Kornbluth 1955: 1–2)

How long is it, one might ask, before a reader who does not already know realizes that this is science fiction? And how does such a reader realize? The answers must be (a) on reading "depilatory soap," and (b) on realizing in rapid succession that depilatory soap does not exist, that for it to exist some sort of chemical breakthrough would be necessary, that such a breakthrough nevertheless would be exploited, just like freeze-dried coffee. The reader of this phrase is in fact – if male and middle-aged – likely to remember a string of shaving-technology innovations, from the aerosol can of shaving cream to the coated blade to the double, treble, and quadruple blade, with the concomitant development of electric, cordless, and rechargeable-battery razors; and at once to note the fact of a progression, to set "depilatory soap" in that progression, to realize it is as yet an imaginary stage, but also that the existence of such stages (all at one time imaginary) is by no means imaginary. "Depilatory soap" is not-real; but it is not-unlike-real. That, in miniature, is the experience of reading science fiction. As well as recognizing data, you recognize nondata; but since these are data within the story, they are well labeled *nova data*, "new things given." The basic building-block of science fiction (the term is Darko Suvin's, Suvin 1979: 63–84) is accordingly the *novum* – a discrete piece of information recognizable as not-true, but also as not-unlike-true, not-flatly-(in the current state of knowledge)-impossible.

How many novums, in the sense given, are there in the passage quoted? Probably, around fifteen. Some are easily identifiable: there is no more doubt about the depilatory soap than about Orwell's "bare patch." At the other extreme – as with Orwell's "quarter to eight" – there are cases where a non-American or noncontemporary may be unsure whether he or she is confronting a novum or a datum. The "quarter-hour time signal . . . over the audio band" sounds futuristic, but then time signals on radio and TV are common enough. There are other details over which the experienced science fiction reader is unlikely to hesitate. Water, for instance: salt water comes out of the tap (one novum); so does fresh, but it trickles; using fresh water for washing is "wasteful, of course"; fresh water is supplied by the government to which the narrator pays taxes. There is a string of novums here, but no reader can register them without making some attempt to put them together. In the world of this novel, we realize, natural resources are unexpectedly scarce; so scarce that only government can be allowed to control them; this narrator is not entirely loyal to his government. There is a similar string of novums and inferences at the end of the second paragraph. "It had been happening lately" implies (a) change, (b) recent change, and (c) frequent occurrence, so, potentially irreversible change. "So far they hadn't done any good" backs up the notion of irreversibility.

More inferences come, however, from the five words "some people blamed Consie saboteurs." "Some people" implies "not everyone" and in particular not the narrator. "Consie" even now – and even more in 1953 – sets up the parallel with "Commie." If "Commie" < "Communist," what is the missing term in the sequence "Consie" < . . . ? An astute reader might guess the answer "Conservationist" (by inference from the interest in fresh water). But any 1953 reader was likely to note:

(1)   In the world of this novel, Communists are no longer a threat. But,
(2)   McCarthyite attitudes are still present. So,
(3)   if "Commies" were just a scapegoat, maybe "Consies" are too. This is backed up by the failure of the "loyalty raids," as (2) is by their existence.

But this last inference, when contrasted with those stemming from the fresh water/salt water opposition, raises a further query more basic to the structure of the whole novel. If "Consies" cannot be blamed for the potentially irreversible change coming over the narrator's horizon, what can? Something, clearly, which neither the government nor the skeptical narrator would like to think about: it is, to be brief, the ghost of Thomas Malthus in horrible alliance with the descendants of the Coca-Cola Company. Limited resources are bad enough. When they coexist with an ethic that demands continuous increases in consumption (and does not scruple to use physical and emotional addiction to get these increases), then you have the ground rules for the Pohl and Kornbluth dystopia.

But it does not start with ground rules. It starts with novums. To read *The Space Merchants* – to read any science fiction – one has first to recognize its novums, and then to evaluate them. There is a discernible and distinguishable pleasure at each stage, as you realize how things are different, how they are similar, and go on to wonder, and to discover, what causes could have produced the changes; as also to speculate what causes have produced the effects of the real world, the effects with which we are so familiar that in most cases they are never given a thought. It is true that readers are unlikely to stop and chew over the implications of "depilatory soap" or "Consie saboteurs" in the way that this discussion has done, but then readers of Orwell do not stop to boggle over the implications of "bare patch in the middle" or "got into the bathroom just in time" either. Yet the latter group certainly understands at some level that Orwell is writing about class, with a strong element of social protest. The reader of *The Space Merchants* likewise soon has a clear idea that its authors are similarly attacking what they see as a developing consumer culture.

Comparing the two passages enables one to see the force of Darko Suvin's careful and thoughtful definition of science fiction, that it is:

> a literary genre whose necessary and sufficient conditions are the presence and interaction of estrangement and cognition, and whose main formal device is an imaginative framework alternative to the author's empirical environment. (Suvin 1979: 7–8)

"Estrangement," with reference to the examples given, means recognizing the novum; "cognition" means evaluating it, trying to make sense of it. You need to do both to read science fiction.

*

Another way of making the point above would be to say that science fiction must intrinsically be a "high-information" genre. "Information," as the *Oxford English Dictionary* tells us, has in recent years become a technical as well as a colloquial term. It now means:

> As a mathematically defined quantity . . . now esp. one which represents the degree of choice exercised in the selection or formation of one particular symbol, sequence, message etc., out of a number of possible ones, and which is defined logarithmically in terms of the statistical probabilities of occurrence of the symbol or the elements of the message. (see *OED* Supplement Vol. II, 1976)

This sense seems to have become common only after Second World War, and to be associated with "information theory" and cybernetics. There is a literary point to be drawn from it, though, and it is this. In English, as in other languages, there is a high degree of "redundancy." Some words can be readily predicted from their context, especially "grammatical" as opposed to "lexical" items. If, for instance, the fifth or the seventh word of the Orwell passage were to be blanked out, and the rest of the sentence left, few readers would have much trouble in filling them in. The same is true of the "lexical" words "came" or "false" in that sentence. But by contrast, if "nipped" in sentence three were to be blanked out, most readers would probably fill in, as first guess, "got" or "jumped" or "climbed." "Nipped" is a higher-information word than "came," or than "the" in sentence one; it is less predictable, and there are more choices available to fill its slot. Just the same, few if any words in the Orwell passage are entirely unpredictable, or particularly surprising, distinctive though Orwell's style may be. The whole book is (no doubt deliberately) towards the low end of the English novel's generally "medium-information" span.

Science fiction, however, is intrinsically a "high-information" genre. Novums, just because they are novums, are very hard to predict. Some of the words in the Pohl and Kornbluth passage would take many guesses to arrive at if they had been blanked out: yet Pohl and Kornbluth here are well toward the low end of the genre's information-range. If one looks at the first few pages of William Gibson's ground-breaking cyber-punk novel *Neuromancer* (1984), one comes upon at least a dozen words or phrases that could never be predicted, or recovered if deleted. Most of them are comprehensible, in context and by analogy with known usages – "nerve-splicing," "coffin hotel," "bedslab," "temperfoam," "mycotoxin," "arcologies" – but all of them take at least a momentary effort, as does "seven-function force-feedback manipulator." Others are never explained: "joeboys," "livewire voodoo." And one at least, "cyberspace," has passed into standard usage, with Gibson credited by the *OED* as its inventor, though the meaning given to it by Gibson, "the consensual hallucination that was the matrix," remains as yet "only science fiction."

Words like "cyberspace" hang as it were on the edge of everyday experience, recognized instantly as filling a gap, but also betraying the existence of the gap. Sometimes they make one wonder why such a gap should exist. Why, for instance, is there in English no neutral-sex third-person singular pronoun – all our other personal pronouns are neutral-sex – equivalent to "one" but not including the speaker, not being impersonal? Its absence notoriously often gives offence, or leads careful writers into clumsy formulations like "he or she," or "(s)he." Yet the gap usually goes unnoticed, or is accepted as natural. In the last section of his *The Years of the City* (1984), however, Frederik Pohl rounds off his picture of a developing American utopia with a world in which such a pronoun is regularly used: instead of "he/him/his" or "she/her/hers," one says consistently "e/um/uz." Just to rub the point in, among the characters' casual words of abuse are the neutral-sex neologisms "prunt" and "fugger," while the normal word for "parent" is "muddy" (i.e., "mummy/daddy"). These words are words carrying very high "information," in the technical sense given above. If they were blanked out of the text, they would not be guessed. They are, then, highly unpredictable – but once introduced they point a powerful if silent finger at the terms we have come to expect. They make us aware of the latent presuppositions, the unconsidered information about our own habits concealed within casual and normal speech. *Things do not have to be the way they are.* This is the assertion that science fiction insistently conveys, in its scenarios, its explanations, even in its vocabulary – through all the various forms of the novum.

There is a kind of symmetry, furthermore, in the way in which science fiction has learned to exploit the opposite of "high information," not low information so much as "degraded information." The classic subgenre to illustrate this is the "enclosed universe" story, whose paradigmatic example is H.G. Wells' 1904 novella, "The Country of the Blind." In this a sighted man stumbles into an enclosed Andean valley where a genetic deficiency has rendered all the inhabitants blind, but slowly enough for them to adjust to and for generations to survive in an easy and ordered environment, with no natural enemies. One would naturally think that "in the country of the blind the one-eyed man is king," but in Wells' story "blind men of genius" have evolved a new cosmology which entirely fits the evidence of the universe that they possess, and denies the possibility of any other. The sighted person is diagnosed as mad, and finds it impossible to prove his sanity (in the original version. Much later [1939] Wells gave the story a different and happier ending, thus starting a science fiction of "cop-out" endings, as if the logic of the form were too challenging even for its creators.) Wells' basic plot has, however, been repeated many times, in several imagined scenarios of enclosure – most commonly, the giant spaceship or inhabited asteroid making a generations-long journey between stars, as in Robert Heinlein's *Orphans of the Sky* (1963 in book form, but published as two novellas in *Astounding Science Fiction*, 1941), Brian Aldiss's *Non-Stop* (1958), or Harry Harrison's *Captive Universe* (1969). Each author rings the changes on plot and scenario, but a basic feature inherited from Wells is that the cosmology of the enclosed universe – which we, the readers, are quite sure is false, information seriously degraded – has to be made to seem reasonable, plausible, indeed (given the evidence available) inescapable. It is the central character trying to reach what we would take to be a true understanding who appears insane. So vital is this reversal of "common sense" (in fact the title of one of Heinlein's two originating novellas) that one almost inevitable feature of such stories is discovery of the "captain's log," an account written by someone sharing our readerly viewpoint which explains how the "enclosed universe" arose: for a truly closed system based on degraded information (like Wells' blind persons' valley) must have its own methods of ensuring that correct information (like the existence of sight) is not received.

What has not been sufficiently realized is that the most famous examples of science fiction in the twentieth century, Orwell's *Nineteen Eighty-Four* (1949), and Aldous Huxley's *Brave New World* (1932), are both "enclosed universe" stories conforming, sometimes in close detail, to the general pattern. Orwell's hero Winston Smith is an inhabitant of the enclosed universe of Ingsoc, where it is indeed his job to destroy any information that may contradict Big Brother's closed system. Huxley's Savage is not an inhabitant of the "Brave New World," but an import into it from a closed system of his own, but it is striking that the closed system he inhabits – a purely personal one derived from one book, the works of Shakespeare – is much more comprehensible, natural, and familiar to the mid-twentieth-century reader than that of his competitor in the novel, Bernard Marx. In each case the real-world reader is likely to empathize with the rebel, the dissident, but in both cases (once again, as in Wells' novella) the rebel or dissident is eventually broken by the power of the closed system. It is striking, furthermore, that the classic function of the "captain's log" is carried out in Orwell's novel by the book, *The Theory and Practice of Oligarchic Collectivism*, which supplies Winston with the historical memory he has been unable to recreate by himself. Meanwhile a classic example of "degraded information" is given by Winston's conversation, in Part I, chapter 8, with the "old prole": everything the old prole says (we realize) is true, and it entirely contradicts everything that the Party has told Winston to believe about history and class and morality. But the old man's memories, of Boat Race night, and top hats, and Speakers' Corner in Hyde Park, and pints of beer, though perfectly precise, are so fragmented that Winston can make nothing of them. We see for a moment, so to speak, into Winston's darkness – and may well draw from it decreased belief in our own clear vision. For a further chilling reflection is the thought that possibly the reader's conviction, or assumption, of living in an open system where information has *not* been degraded may be just as false as that of Wells' "blind men of genius" or Orwell's Party loyalist O'Brian. Arguably, what "enclosed universe" stories tell us is that we are all living in the glass bottles of Huxley's novel, enclosed by the invisible constraints of society, convention, and language. In a further paradox, degraded information may be even more informative than high information, *if it allows one to perceive the process of degradation*.

On this theme science fiction has produced many complex and interesting variations. An extreme example is Russell Hoban's *Riddley Walker* (1980), written throughout in a nonstandard English which indicates a long period of linguistic breakdown and linguistic reformulation, and punctuated by variants of the "Eusa story" which has become the future society's originating myth, but which we discover only slowly – from a short account written in standard English (the "captain's log," so to speak) – is based on total but revealing misunderstanding of the legend of St. Eustace, the only fragment of our world's civilization to survive. But *Riddley Walker* has many science fictional ancestors and analogues, such as Walter Miller's well-known *A Canticle for Leibowitz* (1959), in which a future monastic order spends enormous effort on copying and illuminating a precious relic of their founder St. Leibowitz, which the modern reader realizes is merely a routine engineering diagram.

However, a point that has begun to appear from what has been said so far is that science fiction is not only the most intellectually challenging of genres, it also may well be the most *emotionally* challenging. The corollary of *Things do not have to be the way they are* is that *Nothing is sacred* – and in science fiction, "Nothing" means NOTHING. Science fiction habitually works through what one might call the "cancellation of iconicity." An example is the cover of the December 1966 issue of the magazine *Fantasy and Science Fiction*. On it a group of five figures stand round a giant half-buried statue, which appears to have been recently excavated, their poses signifying puzzlement, incomprehension. Yet the statue is perfectly recognizable, to us, as the Statue of Liberty, with its raised arm, seven-pronged diadem, and severely expressionless features. What the picture says is that in some future time the Statue of Liberty, icon of America, will not only have been felled but also forgotten, forgotten so thoroughly that future excavators will not even be able to guess its purpose: Shelley's "Ozymandias" in reverse, a symbol of the precariousness and provisional nature of meaning. To an American audience (and science fiction continues to be dominated by American writers and readers) this is a particularly threatening disfigurement of national myth.

Yet this too finds many analogues. An especially neat example is Norman Spinrad's short story from 1973, "A Thing of Beauty," first published in *Analog* January 1973, and later reprinted in Spinrad, *No Direction Home* (1975). This is set in a future America, depressed and bankrupt, in which an American antique dealer (almost the only paying trade left in the country) is visited by a Japanese billionaire who wants to buy an outstandingly impressive cultural artifact. The dealer, Harris, tries to sell the buyer, Mr. Ito, a sequence of American cultural icons, first the Statue of Liberty (now headless); then the baseball stadium, now derelict, of the New York Yankees; finally the United Nations Building. All three are rejected. The first is too sad. The second is greeted with great enthusiasm, but rejected in the end, in spite of Mr. Ito's own personal wishes, because he knows the stadium would carry no prestige within Japanese society. The third is rejected contemptuously as an icon of political failure. And then Ito sees the now-unused Brooklyn Bridge, and insists on buying it to be re-erected in Japan. The joke here is that Brooklyn Bridge has iconic status within America as the thing that only a hayseed would imagine he could buy, the colossal equivalent of a fake gold brick. But the joke turns on Harris, not Ito, once it has been taken away, re-erected, and turned into one of the wonders of the world. Ito proves his astuteness (and his wealth) by sending Harris a fake gold brick: only it is not a fake, it is pure gold.

What this story very clearly means is that it is the Japanese buyer who is the true American. It is he who shows strong feelings about baseball, sadness over the "Headless Lady" of Liberty. He respects the icons of America as the American dealer, anxious only to make a buck, does not. As for his rejection of the UN Building, what this proves (within the story) is that true Americans, like Mr. Ito, do not respect the UN, but false Americans, like the insurrectionists who spared it and the federal authorities who keep it "in excellent repair," do. Harris has more in common with these latter groups than with Ito: they are all engaged in "selling out" America. Spinrad's fable is indeed balanced between a creditable openness – being American to him is not a matter of nationality – and a chauvinist anger against an internationalism he finds incompatible with patriotism. There is a kind of symmetry, even, in the fate of the artifacts he mentions. Brooklyn Bridge can move to Osaka (where "Americanism," we may conclude, is alive and well); but the Statue of Liberty, literally and symbolically disfigured, has to stay where it is. Yet both movement and stasis symbolize failure, a failure whose icon is the "Headless Lady."

Spinrad's story is typical rather than exceptional. Many American authors have produced critiques of America, or stories of the Fall of America, turning routinely on the disfiguration of myth or the "cancellation of iconicity," and their efforts were preceded by a number of British authors from even before Wells' time who imagined the destruction of London, Surrey turned into a battleground, *l'écroulement de l'Angleterre* (for which see, respectively, Richard Jefferies, *After London* [1885], H.G. Wells, *The War of the Worlds* [1898], and John Wyndham, *The Kraken Wakes* [1953]). Yet these images, while arresting, are also evidently highly threatening, to many deeply unwelcome. It is surprising, and encouraging, to find so many of them at home in a commercial, mass-entertainment genre; though one should add that it is a feature that makes much of the genre literally unreadable for those not prepared to have their certainties challenged. John Huntington has introduced to science fiction, along with Suvin's "novum," the idea of the "habitus," the reader's set of "values, expectations, and assumptions" (see Huntington 1991: 62–3, which further cites Bourdieu 1984: 101 ff.) It is not essential for science fiction – as one can see from almost any episode of *Star Trek* – to step outside the comfort-zone of modern Euro-American consumers, but it is surprisingly common. Only a minority, perhaps, is prepared to consider an alternative (national) habitus, a place where America in particular does not exist or has lost dominance.

National icons are furthermore not the only ones to be attacked and disfigured in this way. Even more unwelcome than challenges to patriotism, to the Anglo-American literary classes, are attacks on literature, cultural authority, and books themselves. There is not much more sinful to literary people than book-burning, few places more sacred than a library. Yet science fiction has delighted, from an early stage, indeed from Wells' *The Time Machine* (1895) in images of "the dead library" (see Crossley 1991 for many examples). Thus Wells' Time Traveler finds himself, in the "Palace of Green Porcelain" in chapter 11, staring at a room hung with "brown and charred rags." He realizes after a while that these are all that is left of books, reflects on the "enormous waste of labour to which this sombre wilderness of rotting paper testified," and turns away in a quest for some more "useful discoveries" in the museum's science sections (see Stover 1996: 140–1. It is interesting, if predictable, that the modern editor of Wells' original text here attempts to make the Time Traveler's remarks seem ironic or illogical.)

The contempt for books in their physical form extends furthermore to what the books contain, to literary tradition. Wells' *Island of Dr. Moreau* (1896) overtly refers to texts as venerable as Homer's *Odyssey* and Milton's *Comus*, with further strongly implied reference to Swift's *Gulliver's Travels*, but what the story has to say as a whole is quite simply that these ancient myths or legends are wrong. The threat of Circe or Comus is to turn men into beasts, and this is what Wells' central character, Prendick, thinks that Dr. Moreau is doing. But Prendick is also entirely wrong: what Moreau is doing is trying to turn beasts into men, and while this may remove the immediate threat to Prendick, it creates a much more serious threat to humanity as a whole. If beasts could be turned into men – and in the scandalized correspondence which followed Wells' story (for which see Philmus 1993: 197–211) Wells insisted that in the knowledge of the time, this was not impossible – then there is no significant difference between humanity and what used to be called the "animal kingdom." There is a strongly Darwinian element about Wells' assertions, and a strongly blasphemous element, with Moreau usurping the role of the Creator who "made man in God's image." But there is a powerful attack on literary tradition too – and on literary language, for at the pivotal point of the story there is a conversation in what one can only call "pidgin Latin," a dreadful affront to Classical education and to the Victorian class-system which relied so much on it. Even more important, at the end of *Gulliver's Travels* Gulliver cannot stop seeing human beings as yahoos, and it is a staple of modern literary comment to insist that that is because Gulliver is mad. But when Prendick returns home suffering from the same delusion, seeing people as cats and leopards and monkeys, the story makes plain that it may not *be* a delusion but a Darwinian insight: Wells claims an authority which he denies to Homer and Milton and Swift, based simply on knowing more, and specifically on knowing more *about science*. Science is the ultimate authority. This overrides literature, and legend, and tradition, and myth.

*

As a result, science fiction can further be seen as not only intellectually and emotionally challenging, to all readers, but also and in particular to professional readers, *ideologically* challenging – something that probably accounts in part for the long hostility it has faced from literary critics. An argument could be made to say that this should not be so, that science fiction in fact provides a great deal of what modern critics (say they) have long wanted. Consider for instance one further extended passage, this time from Kingsley Amis' "alternate world" novel, *The Alteration* (1976). Amis' novel is set in a twentieth century in which the Reformation never took place, and the Catholic Church has accordingly remained dominant across Europe (though not America). Near the start he describes the national shrine of this alternative England, St George's Cathedral at Coverley, Oxford, centre of the English Empire:

> Apart from Wren's magnificent dome, the most renowned of the sights to be seen was the vast Turner ceiling in commemoration of the Holy Victory, the fruit of four-and-a-half years' virtually uninterrupted work; there was nothing like it anywhere. The western window by Gainsborough, beginning to blaze now as the sun first caught it, showed the birth of St Helena, mother of Constantine the Great, at Colchester. Along the south wall ran Blake's still-brilliant frescoes depicting St Augustine's progress through England. Holman Hunt's oil painting of the martyrdom of St George was less celebrated for its merits than for the tale of the artist's journey to Palestine in the hope of securing authenticity for his setting; and one of the latest additions, the Ecce Homo mosaic by David Hockney, had attracted downright adverse criticism for its excessively traditionalist, almost archaising style. But only admiration had ever attended – to take a diverse selection – the William Morris spandrels on the transept arches, the unique chryselephantine pyx, the gift of an archbishop of Zululand, above the high altar, and Epstone's massive marble Pieta. (Amis 1976: 7–8)

The passage of course illustrates once again the presence of the novum. Nine works of art are mentioned in this passage, and it is vital for the reader to recognize that all of them are fictional. At the same time, however, all except one (the pyx) are ascribed to known English artists who are known *not* to be fictional. The first of them, Wren's dome, perhaps causes no particular difficulty. There is a Wren's dome at St Paul's, and translating it to St George's is not much of a change. As the works continue to be listed, though, two effects are created: one, a growing awareness of what might have been if talents as scattered as Hunt's and Gainsborough's had been brought together, and two, a realization that in *this* world, Amis' imaginary world, outsiders have been reconciled and brought into harmony, as they were not in real history. In our world William Blake found no artistic patron till his last years, and worked in the cheap but fading medium of watercolor. William Morris created a series of murals for the Oxford Union; they too were allowed to fade and disappear. On his trip to Palestine Holman Hunt painted, in our world, not "The Martyrdom of St George" but "The Scapegoat" – an image of rejection, not of triumph. In Amis' world all these talents have been enlisted to create a genuine national shrine, which includes in it not only the half-mythical St George (England's patron saint, removed in our world from the Catholic canon in 1969), but also the genuine (if clearly mythicized) figures of St Helena and St Augustine. The cathedral is a center at once of artistic genius, of national feeling, and of Catholic feeling. "There was nothing like it anywhere," says Amis, and there *is* nothing like it anywhere: our loss, our failure.

But the sense of failure becomes most acute, perhaps, at the "Ecce Homo" mosaic by David Hockney. In our world David Hockney was born in Bradford, England in 1917, but moved to Los Angeles in 1978. He is famous for his creation of the "California modern" style. How strange to see a work of his criticized for traditionalism, even archaism! And the work is an "Ecce Homo." This means only "Behold the Man," and is traditionally a portrait of Christ taken down from the Cross, as is clearly intended here. In our world Hockney created no religious art. He is, however, as famous for his homoerotic works as for his modernism; and in the dialect of Amis and his coevals, "homo" was a disparaging term for a homosexual. It is hard to know how to react to this imagined mosaic. It seems to say: (a) in the alternate world Hockney would have had no need to go into exile, (b) he would have been brought into the center of the culture instead of being marginalized, (c) he would have been a traditionalist not a rebel, and (d) his talents would have been recognized and enlisted for religious ends. So far so good. But (e), perhaps, his homoeroticism would have been suppressed, and (f), even more uncertainly, it would have broken out in yet another way, in portrayals of masculine beauty in a religious mode.

All this, one could say, is an exact rendering of the critical concept of "textuality." According to the Toronto *Encyclopedia of Contemporary Literary Theory* (Makaryk 1993, cited here only as a statement of what is generally accepted):

> the term marks both a breakdown of the boundaries between literature and other verbal and nonverbal signifying practices, and a subversion of the principle that any text can function as an object whose meaning is coherent and self-contained. (Jones 1993: 641)

There is no problem in illustrating either of these statements within science fiction. Science fiction habitually breaks down the boundary – or fails to recognize any boundary – between literature and other forms of signification, like putting the Statue of Liberty on magazine covers. As for subverting the principle that text-meaning is "coherent and self-contained," how could anyone think either of those things about the Amis passage? It is not "coherent." I for one have no idea how I should take the "Ecce Homo" pun, if pun it is, and little more about how I do take it. Nor is the description "self-contained." To understand it one needs to bring in as much awareness as possible of real art history: it relies (just like the Pohl and Kornbluth passage cited earlier) on a principle of running contrasts, or alter(n)ations. And yet at the same time, to quote a famous saying, *il n'y a pas de hors-texte* (there is [quite literally] nothing outside [this] text), for Amis' world has no existence whatsoever outside the text of *The Alteration*. Its whole history genuinely is "only another discourse," and the tempting and beautiful images the work (for a while) creates are entirely a linguistic construct, though one necessarily abetted by the reader's contrastive and comparing responses. *The Alteration*, in short, is a textbook example of the principle of "textuality."

One could say something very similar with regard to the Derridean concept of *différance*, with its double meaning of "difference" and "deferral." The Toronto *Encyclopedia* explains that:

> if there are only differences [within the system of language] then meaning is only produced in the relation among signifiers not through the signified; the signified is thus endlessly deferred and delayed through the differential network. (Adamson 1993: 535)

I am a good deal less clear what this means than with the earlier definition of "textuality," and I do not accept the pseudo-Saussurean point from which the argument begins, but there is no doubt that this is a reasonable description of what a reader of "alternate histories" has to do. In the Amis passage, Blake's "still-brilliant frescoes" and David Hockney with his "Ecce Homo" mosaic have to be seen in their immediate textual context; the difference between that and what we regard as the real-world context (Blake marginalized to ephemera, Hockney in Californian exile) then has to be recognized, thus *différence*. But judgment as to which is more real or more plausible has to be deferred to allow the novel to continue to be read, thus *différance*. And this process, repeated literally thousands of times in the course of any complex "alternate world" narrative, creates an exceptionally strong sense of how fragile our own "real" history is. Things did not *have* to be that way. Books like *The Alteration* are profoundly disorienting. They depend very heavily, to use another critical term, on "intertextuality," and they make you feel how much of our perceived reality is intertextual too.

And yet in spite of these apparent or potential exemplifications of "literary theory" within science fiction, all who are familiar with both will be aware of an immense ideological gap. This is caused by the issue of science, and the claim of science to ultimate authority. If there is one thing that characterizes all schools of modern literary theory, it is their denial of objectivity. To quote this time the *Johns Hopkins Guide to Literary Theory and Criticism* (Groden and Kreiswirth 1994), once more for its deliberate centrality:

> If language, metaphor, and consciousness really are structured by difference, then there can be no solid foundation, no fixed point of reference, no authority or certainty, either ontological or interpretive. (Kneale 1994: 187)

Such views have become entirely characteristic of the authority structure of the critical profession, and are impossible to reconcile with the claims for truth-to-fact of much science fiction, and all serious science. This is the last and most insuperable of the obstacles preventing science fiction from being accepted into the central and authoritative core of literary culture. While at literary conferences one can expect to be told (I quote a phrase heard recently) that "all knowledge is situated and contingent," scientific discourse, for all its accepted disagreements, remains overwhelmingly characterized by: a denotative linguistic system including but not confined to mathematics; rigorous training in that system, which is now worldwide; built-in "upgrade capacity" for the system, so that change is a permanent contingency, but does not affect the hegemonic structure; and a uniquely coherent, international, "interpretive community." The gap between the "two cultures" of humanities and sciences is here total, having substantially increased since the time of the old debate between C.P. Snow and F.R. Leavis (for which see Green 1965). Modern critical writing is characterized by an elaborate apparatus for noncommitment: the inverted commas, the parentheses, the slash marks, the spelling changes, the placing of items *sous râture* (under erasure), so they can be read/not-read at the same time. Against that a paradigmatic image is that of the dying Richard Feynman putting a piece of space shuttle gasket in his glass of ice water before the TV cameras and saying, "nature is not fooled" (for a full account of this incident, see Gleick 1992: 414–28). Feynman meant that observers, human opinions, bureaucratic procedures, all had no value. If you ignored the nature of the material, knowledge of which was "contingent" only on other measurable data like the outside temperature, then the material would fail, the shuttle would crash, and its crew would die. When he said that, Feynman was repeating an old theme of science fiction – characteristically, one for long well understood, but one which has only recently generated intense critical controversy. It is seen classically in the Tom Godwin story "The Cold Equations," from 1954, which triggered extensive debate much later in *The New York Review of Science Fiction*, nos. 54, 60, 64, and 66.

I would sum up by remarking that for many years I have encountered colleagues who have told me (a) "I cannot bear science fiction," and (b) "I have never read any." How can both these be true? I assume that someone comfortable in his or her own *habitus*, sure that the patterns of history are unshakable, tacitly confident that the future will be much the same as the present, someone of this fairly normal intellectual type will rapidly detect, but immediately reject, the very idea of the novum, without which science fiction cannot work at all. At a deeper level, the penchant of science fiction for seeking out sacred cows of any kind to slaughter (not just the discredited ones of the past) is likely to trigger an emotional rejection. Finally, the overpowering authority of science within our culture is hard to bear ideologically for some of those who have no access to it. And yet the very mainspring of science fiction as it developed from nineteenth-century "scientific romance" is awareness of change on every level from shaving to sex and war, and conviction that this process is now unstoppable (except by disaster, a frequent science fictional option). We really have no idea what will happen next. Or rather, we have no certainty, but plenty of ideas. It is this openness, this sense of potential in every sphere, that has given science fiction its host of readers, and which makes it, as I have said, a uniquely challenging but also uniquely rewarding genre.

[Much of the material in this essay is based on, or excerpted from, four previous articles: Shippey 1991a and 1991b, 1997, and 2001. Thanks are due to the editors and publishers of these pieces for allowing me to reuse this material.]

REFERENCES AND FURTHER READING

Adamson, Joseph (1993) "*Différance / difference*," in *Encyclopedia of Contemporary Literary Theory: Approaches, Scholars, Terms,* (ed.) Irena R. Makaryk. Toronto: University of Toronto Press, 534–5.

Amis, Kingsley (1976) *The Alteration.* London: Jonathan Cape.

Bourdieu, Pierre (1984) *Distinction: A Social Critique of the Judgment of Taste,* trans. Richard Nice. Cambridge, MA: Harvard UP.

Broderick, Damien (1995) *Reading by Starlight: Postmodern Science Fiction.* London and New York: Routledge.

Crossley, Robert (1991) "In the Palace of Green Porcelain: Artifacts from the Museum of Science Fiction," in *Fictional Space: Essays on Contemporary Science Fiction*, (ed.) Tom Shippey. Oxford: Blackwell, 76–103.

Frye, Northrop (1957) *An Anatomy of Criticism: Four Essays.* Princeton, NJ: Princeton UP.

Gleick, Richard (1992) *Genius: the Life and Science of Richard Feynman.* New York: Pantheon.

Green, Martin (1965) *Science and the Shabby Curate of Poetry: Essays about the Two Cultures.* New York: Norton.

Groden, Michael and Martin Kreiswirth (eds) (1994) *The Johns Hopkins Guide to Literary Theory and Criticism.* Baltimore: Johns Hopkins UP.

Huntington, John (1991) "Newness, *Neuromancer*, and the End of Narrative," in *Fictional Space:*

Essays on Contemporary Science Fiction, (ed.) Tom Shippey. Oxford: Blackwell, 59–75.

Jones, Manina (1993) "Textuality," in *Encyclopedia of Contemporary Literary Theory: Approaches, Scholars, Terms,* (ed.) Irena R. Makaryk, Toronto: University of Toronto Press, 641–2.

Kneale, J. Douglas (1994) "Deconstruction," in *The Johns Hopkins Guide to Literary Theory and Criticism*, (eds) Michael Groden, and Martin Kreiswirth, Baltimore: Johns Hopkins UP, 185–92.

Makaryk, Irena R. (ed.) (1993) *Encyclopedia of Contemporary Literary Theory: Approaches, Scholars, Terms.* Toronto: University of Toronto Press.

Mendlesohn, Farah (2003) "Introduction: Reading Science Fiction," in *The Cambridge Companion to Science Fiction* (eds) Edward James and Farah Mendlesohn. Cambridge: Cambridge UP, 1–12.

Orwell, George (1939) *Coming Up for Air.* New York: Harcourt Brace & World.

Parrinder, Patrick (1980) *Science Fiction: Its Criticism and Teaching.* London and New York, Methuen.

Philmus, Robert M. (ed.) (1993) H.G. Wells, *The Island of Dr Moreau: A Variorum Text.* Athens GA and London: University of Georgia Press.

Pohl, Frederik and C.M. Kornbluth (1955) *The Space Merchants* (1953). London: William Heinemann.

Shippey, Tom (1991a) "Preface: Learning to Read Science Fiction," in *Fictional Space: Essays on Contemporary Science Fiction*, (ed.) Tom Shippey. Oxford: Blackwell, 1–35.

——(1991b) "The Fall of America in Science Fiction," in *Fictional Space: Essays on Contemporary Science Fiction*, (ed.) Tom Shippey. Oxford: Blackwell, 96–127.

——(ed.) (1991c) *Fictional Space: Essays on Contemporary Science Fiction*, Essays and Studies for the English Association 1990. Oxford: Blackwell.

——(1997) "Alternate Historians: Newt, Kingers, Harry and Me." *Journal of the Fantastic in the Arts*, 8/1: 15–33.

——(2001) "Literary Gatekeepers and the Fabril Tradition," in *Science Fiction: Canonization, Marginalization and the Academy*, (eds) Gary Westfahl and George Slusser. Westport, CT and London: Greenwood: 7–23.

Stockwell, Peter (2000) *The Poetics of Science Fiction*. Harlow: Pearson Education.

Stover, Leon (ed.) (1996) H.G. Wells, *The Time Machine: An Invention*. Jefferson, NC and London: McFarland.

Suvin, Darko (1979) *Metamorphoses of Science Fiction: On the Poetics and History of a Literary Genre*. New Haven: Yale UP.

2
The Origins of Science Fiction
George Slusser

The quest to locate the origins of SF begins as a search to trace back the name that has genre recognition for the reader of today: science fiction. Hugo Gernsback, in the inaugural issues of *Amazing Stories* (1926), let readers give a name to the stories they were reading – Verne, Wells, and Poe primarily. The name they came up with was "scientifiction." Wells earlier referred to what he was writing as "scientific romance." His contemporary, also a man with strong scientific background, J.H. Rosny aîné, described his fiction as "le merveilleux scientifique." Beyond this, the thread between science and fiction becomes tenuous. Verne placed his work under the rubric of "Voyages extraordinaires." Poe wrote tales of "ratiocination," but did Mary Shelley even have a specific name for the kind of literature she was writing in *Frankenstein* (1818), the work consensually seen as the "first" SF novel? At this point, the question of origins becomes one of defining the form. Brian Aldiss (1986) names the form Mary Shelley was writing – the Gothic – and argues that it is transformations of this genre that define the nature of SF. Mark Rose (1981) sees SF developing the structures of a less culture-specific form – the romance. Though for Rose SF is a specifically modern form of romance (it begins with Verne and Wells), romance as form reaches far back in Western culture – to Spenser and *The Tempest* (1611). In the eyes of Arthur C. Clarke, it goes back to *The Odyssey* (8th century BC). Other critics, abandoning form for function as the means of defining the development of a science fiction, have located the origin in the earliest works of world literature. Pierre Versins, for example, defines SF as "conjecture romanesque rationelle." This allows him, through a leap of logic that sees reason as the essential organ of science, and "rational conjecture" as its fundamental method, to trace origins back to the *Epic of Gilgamesh* (c. 2nd millenium BC).

I would like to put some order here. Various comments by Mark Rose point in the right direction. "It is worth noting that discussions of other genres – detective fiction, westerns, or for that matter, pastorals or revenge tragedies – do not consistently begin with definitions. In those cases readers and writers seem fairly confident of the boundaries of the genre in question. Perhaps this is so because those genres seem to be defined by their subject matter; detective stories are about crime . . . In what sense is science fiction about science?" (Rose 1981: 1–2). My answer is that SF is all about science. It is the sole literary form that examines the ways in which science penetrates, alters, and transforms the themes, forms, and worldview of fiction. Since the Renaissance, what is called "fiction" becomes a vehicle of choice for the "humanist" culture that increasingly sets itself in opposition to the culture of science that was inaugurated by Francis Bacon. If for Bacon, humankind's task is the objective study of the material world, a century later Pope, retreating to the Socratic dictum, can utter: "Know then thyself, presume not God to scan,/ The proper study of mankind is Man." (Pope: "Essay on Man," 1733–4, II.1–2). Thus are created two parallel paths of inquiry that in the twentieth century are seen to diverge to form a "two cultures gap" between the humanistic and the scientific. Along this trajectory, whatever brings these cultures into contact or conflict are the necessary conditions for a science fiction as an "unstable compound" of the two.

In this essay, we examine two hypotheses, each of which seeks to explain how, when, and why the initial contact of antithetical cultures might have been made possible. The first is a "cataclysmic" or single origin theory which posits that in the Christian, then humanist, culture of Western Europe, a decisive paradigm shift has to occur before that culture is even capable of registering, in literary or fictional form, what Isaac Asimov speaks of when he defines SF: an *impact* of scientific or technological advancement on human beings. Such paradigm shifts are, specifically, culturally determined. This is seen in the fact that France and England, parallel in their development of science, experience respective moments of shift at very different periods. The second hypothesis is a "gradualist" theory that sees multiple origins or points of contact between science and fiction. The result is a gradual transformation of conventional literary forms through permeation of scientific concepts or technological advances, usually not dramatically visible, hence often overlooked by ancestor seekers. First, we take a deeper look at each of our hypotheses to see to what degree they clarify the question of origins. Second, on the historical level, in contrast to prominent single-work arguments such as those of Darko Suvin (1976) and Brian Aldiss (1986), we ask whether these theories may act in a complementary rather than mutually exclusive manner, and as such may both point to a single work that, in the English tradition at least, lays a stronger claim to being the functional ancestor of SF: Wells' *The Time Machine* (1895).

Paradigm Shifts

The English-speaking reader tends to think of SF as his or her domain, ignoring other traditions, notably that of long-time rival, France. Indeed, a look at the cultural conditions that first created the possibility of a science fiction shows us that, in terms of origins, all SFs are not equal. In France it seems the conditions that permit an impact of scientific (if not immediately technological) advancement on human beings occurred much earlier than in England. The Cartesian *cogito* can be said to create the dynamic by which what moderns call science first enters the mainstream of French literature and culture. Since the seventeenth century, the interaction of science and literature in France is so pervasive that many canonical works of literature right through the twentieth century qualify, according to Asimov's definition, as SF. The fact that what is called "science fiction" in post-Second World War France never did in its essential structures bifurcate from a mainstream is proof of the tenacity and adaptability of the system created by the Cartesian paradigm shift.

Pierre Versins in his *Encyclopédie de l'Utopie et de la Science Fiction* (1972) seeks to locate the beginnings of the French SF tradition in the utopias and imaginary voyages of François Rabelais (Versins 1972: 344). Yet these aspects have only a marginal relation to science as we conceive it. The "method" of Descartes, however, proposed a century later, has everything to do with science. As Alfred North Whitehead puts it, "The whole Cartesian apparatus of Deism, substantial materialism and imposed law, in conjunction with the reduction of physical relations to the notion of correlated motions with mere spatiotemporal character, constitutes the simplified notion of Nature with which Galileo, Descartes and Newton finally launched modern science on its triumphant career" (Whitehead 1955: 118). Reacting to experiments of inductive science in the Baconian sense, Descartes conceives a metaphysical problem whereby the human subject defines its being, not by thinking about external nature, but in the act of thinking itself. Mind separates itself from all natural objects, now called *res extensa*, extended or mechanical things, as opposed to *res cogitans*, or thinking things. In this "simplified" vision, humans alone think and everything else is reduced to Whitehead's "notion of correlated motions with mere spatiotemporal character." A number of things result from this separation. First of all, mind finds itself engulfed in material nature and able to launch an assault of scientific conquest with impunity into a realm declared nonhuman. Yet at the same time mind is terribly alone in the vast material wilderness this separation has created. Second, the place and role of the body as the location of sense organs and thus the necessary interface between mind and matter becomes seriously problematized. Though Descartes declared the body a "machine," making it nonmind, he nonetheless recognized that the body remained the vehicle and in a sense the prison of mind. He sought throughout his life to locate some material place of interface – the famous pineal gland – through which mind could reach out to matter. The Cartesian situation, motivated as Whitehead says by the methods and discoveries of science, had a profound impact on a contemporary who was this time a real experimental scientist – Blaise Pascal. Pascal transposed this Cartesian duality in terms of its impact on human beings. He termed it the "human condition," the claustrophobic fate of humanity without God, lost in the material void of the infinitely large and infinitely small. This depiction meets Asimov's basic conditions for the creation of a science fiction.

To call Pascal an SF writer is far-fetched. Yet the mini-scenarios he generated in certain extended "metaphors" of his *Pensées* (1670) – such as the "thinking reed" or the image of humans chained in a cave awaiting to be cast into a fire that illustrates the human condition – have proven to have profound narrative potential. Indeed, Pascal's is but one reaction among many subsequent ones to the Cartesian paradigm shift. This shift results in the formulation of an axis of interactive terms – mind, body, material world. If there is a Cartesian tradition in French literature, it consists of radical swings of the pendulum along this axis where (in the manner Pascal described as his *contrariétés*) a too-radical focus on mind generates an equally radical shift toward the material world. From these pendulum swings gradually emerges a sense of the physical body as the alien casing of mind and the material limit of its activity; this contraction provokes in turn the exploration of this mind-space as world-space, a centripetal movement that characterizes twentieth century French literature and SF alike.

One can trace these pendulum shifts. In Madame de Lafayette's *La Princesse de Clèves* (1678), seen as the first *roman d'analyse* that was to become the benchmark for French narrative fiction, the action occurs almost exclusively in the realm of human "psychology" and is bounded by a zone of social activity from which *res extensa* in the sense of material things is almost totally excluded. This radical focus on mind is assailed in the eighteenth century by the equally radically materialism of a Diderot or D'Holbach. This dichotomy continues into the nineteenth century, still capable of producing a *roman d'analyse* like Benjamin Constant's *Adolphe* (1816) side by side with the materialist speculations of a Balzac. The two great popularizers of science – Auguste Comte and Claude Bernard – represent in fact opposite poles of the Cartesian spectrum, the former subjecting the profusion of natural phenomena to rigorous "laws" of reason, the latter professing an "experimental" method that reduces mind to the exploratory role of observer, collecting data, formulating hypotheses, and thus pushing back the edges of the material unknown. It is within the parameters of this Cartesian system that one measures, in nineteenth-century France, the impact of a proliferating scientific activity on human beings and situations in literature. Every major writer from Balzac to Maupassant writes under the impetus of science as science is defined in terms of the Cartesian axis of mind-body-world.

It is wrong to single out Jules Verne as an SF writer among mainstream novelists. In fact, Verne was moving with the general trend of his culture. Indeed, his mainstream contemporary and rival, Emile Zola, is arguably closer in theory and in practice to modern hard-SF writers than Verne ever was. The following passage from his *Le Roman expérimental*, in fact, sounds a lot like a pronouncement of Gregory Benford, the hardest of hard extrapolations: "Le romancier est fait d'un observateur et d'un expérimenteur. L'observateur chez lui donne les faits tells qu'il les a observes, pose le point de depart, établit le terrain solide sur lequel vont marcher les personages et se développer les phenomènes. Puis, l'expérimenteur paraît et institue l'expérience, je veux dire fait mouvoir les personnages dans une histoire particulière, pour y montrer que la succession des fait y sera telle que l'éxige le determinisme des phenomènes mis à l'étude." [The novelist is composed of an observer and an experimenter. The observer in him gives the facts exactly as he has observed them, determines the point of departure, establishes the solid ground on which the characters will walk and events develop. At this point, the experimenter enters the scene and sets up the experiment, by which I mean he makes the characters function in a precise environment, in order to show that the succession of events will operate in the manner demanded by the fixed nature of the phenomena under study] (Zola 1880: 52). As Gregory Benford would say, this is "playing with the net up."

In British literature the relation of science and fiction reveals a much more divided and skeptical tradition. Because of this bifurcation, the paradigm shift that allows for their interrelation comes much later than in France. Contrary to the conventional wisdom, the shift occurs even later than *Frankenstein*, which remains in many ways traditional in its stigmatizing of science.

If we go back to Chaucer, still under the medieval Christian dispensation, we see that the only individuals excluded from the society of the Canterbury pilgrims seem to be the Canon and his Yeoman, apostates in the name of alchemy. A scoundrel like the Pardoner may not live up to his position, but that position remains firmly in the ecclesiastical order of things. The Canon and his Yeoman, however, arrive hastily and without baggage; they intersect the pilgrimage and leave as suddenly. As Charles Muscatine says, their discourse "evokes a profound sense of the futility, the cursedness of a soulless striving with matter" (Muscatine 1960: 216). Their method and search, Chaucer tells us, clearly foreshadows those of modern science. And yet they damn themselves thereby: "I warne you wel, it is to seken evere./That future temps hath maad men to dissevere,/In trust thereof, from al that evere they hadde." They are presented as sweating, sooty, working among alembics, "sundry vessels maad of erthe and glas," manipulating things like "poudres diverse, asshes, donge, pisse, and cley" (*The Canterbury Tales*, "The Canon's Yeoman's Tale," 874–6, [1394]) in futile inductive investigations that produce only soulless lists, the debasing objects of a debased quest.

This stigma of alchemy still dogs science in *Frankenstein*. The galvanism and electricity of the 1831 Introduction are afterthoughts, as there is little or no direct reference to them in the 1818 edition of the novel. Instead there is the long section on Victor's education at Ingolstadt, where it takes two professors in succession to wean young Frankenstein from Albertus Magnus and Paracelsus, to point him toward the modern science that has "discovered how the blood circulates, and the nature of the air that we breathe" (Shelley 1992: 47).

Two centuries earlier in Marlowe's *Doctor Faustus* (1604), sympathy ostensibly shifts to the human striver, who is now not merely outside God's domain, but in defiant opposition to His tyranny. Even so, can this work make claim to be "early SF"? True, Faustus' pact with Mephistopheles' rather urbane "science" gives him physical powers no one during Marlowe's time had enjoyed. Faustus has an aerial view of the countryside and he becomes invisible, a familiar trope of later SF. Yet the entire last act dwells upon Faustus' eleventh hour regret before being dragged to punishment by the superior forces of a still-dominant conservatism. This same power will continue to regulate the excesses of science long after the Christian veneer of devils and angels wears off. In an interesting reversal, the same force that reigns in the early

"humanist" overreacher Dr. Faustus, will constitute what becomes the humanist opposition to science in centuries to come.

Another Renaissance figure, Francis Bacon, might appear to occupy a role analogous to Descartes' in causing an impact between modern science and Western
mankind's conventional sense (Christian and humanist alike) of its place and role in
the physical universe. Reasoning with himself, Bacon opens his *Instauratio magna (The
Great Instauration)* of 1620 with a seemingly bold statement: "Being convinced that
the human intellect makes its own difficulties . . . he thought all trial should be made,
whether that commerce between the mind of man and the nature of things, which is
more precious than anything on earth. . . might by any means be restored to its perfect
and original condition, or if that may not be, yet reduced to a better condition than
that in which it now is" (Bacon 1955: 423). A strong residue of Christianity, especially the idea of the Fall, absent from Descartes' secular vision, remains here. And in
the second part of Bacon's work *The New Organon or True Directions Concerning the Interpretation of Nature* (1620), Bacon, with his famous "idols," details these "difficulties"
of the human intellect in such a way as to suggest that they are so endemic to our
fallen condition that we can never overcome them. The Idols of the Theatre, for
instance, are the "received systems" that ensnare all minds seeking to look with objectivity on nature. Behind these systems, as Bacon's own text suggests, is the filter of
Christianity. The Idols of the Tribe have as foundation the "false assertion that the
sense of man is the measure of all things" (Bacon 1955: 470). Bacon here describes
the bifurcation that will characterize the eighteenth century. On one hand, "neo-clas-
sics" like Pope and Swift will assert that man is the measure of all things. On the
other hand, empiricists like Locke and Hume follow Bacon in his skepticism whereby
"all perceptions as well of the sense as of the mind are according to the individual
and not according to the measure of the universe" (Bacon 1955: 470). As with Hume
(for whom there is ultimately no certainty that either causality or self exists), Bacon
sees human understanding "like a false mirror, which, receiving rays irregularly, dis-
torts and discolors the nature of things by mingling its own nature with it" (Bacon
1955: 470). Finally, with his Idols of the Cave, Bacon refutes the Cartesian *cogito*,
which its author claims to have conceived in a stove (a closed room that contained a
stove): "For every one (besides the errors common to human nature in general) has a
cave or den of his own which refracts and discolors the light of nature" (Bacon 1955:
470). Veering sharply away from the French shift toward introspection as the starting point for mind's dialectic with nature, Bacon (citing Heraclitus) asserts that
humans must look for the sciences not in their own lesser worlds but in the "greater
or common world." At the same time, however, he is so skeptical of the ability of our
sensual and intellectual apparatus to understand this world that he forces subsequent
writers and thinkers in the British tradition to seek refuge in the median position
that Pope extols in his "Essay on Man" (1733–4).

British literature in the eighteenth and in much of the nineteenth century follows
this *via media* where science is concerned. Indeed, the rise of the bourgeois novel
focuses so exclusively on contemporary human manners that mention of scientific

speculation about the nature of things is all but absent. George Rousseau, in his essay "The Hunting of Leviathan and Awakening of Proteus" (2003), sees this exclusionary attitude codified in the criticism of Samuel Johnson: "He tamed all past criticism and set the standards for centuries, standards from which the School of Taste – the most influential body of aesthetic doctrines – developed. Yet Johnson barely tolerated, let alone condoned, what we would call 'science fiction' or 'fantasy' today" (Rousseau 2003: 57). According to Rousseau, Dr. Johnson averted his gaze from such works as Swift's *Gulliver's Travels* (1726) and Samuel Madden's *Memoirs of the Twentieth Century* (1733), the former seen today as an example of proto-SF, the latter by Paul Alkon as a prime example of the "origins of futuristic fiction" (Alkon 1991).

With a stroke Dr. Johnson created the divide still prevalent today in Anglo-American literature between major and minor "genres." In the nineteenth century works like *Frankenstein* and *Dr. Jekyll and Mr. Hyde* (1885), relegated to "minor" categories such as Gothic fiction, are allowed to deal with science as long as their attitude toward it is defensive and ultimately conservative (like Faustus, Dr. Frankenstein must be punished for his scientific excesses). However, mention of science is quasi-absent from mainstream novels from Jane Austen to Trollope. Surprisingly, if we compare with Zola's assertedly scientific "naturalism," science plays a relatively subdued role in Thomas Hardy.

So, if the paradigm shift that brings scientific and technological advancement to *impact* this human zone of activity in serious and irreversible manner does not occur with *Frankenstein*, where does it occur? The word "science" is on the lips of British Romantics; to Wordsworth, however, its presence seems ultimately unthreatening to Poetry. At one extreme, in his 1800 preface to *Lyrical Ballads* Wordsworth sees Poet and Man of Science, like lion and lamb, lying peaceably side by side. But nonetheless poetry remains "the breath and finer spirit of all knowledge . . . the impassioned expression which is the countenance of all Science" (Owen 1974: 80–1). In contrast, the famous rejection of Newtonian optics in Keats' *Lamia* (1819) is rhetorically violent, but perhaps not entirely sincere. Lamenting Newton's trivialization of the poet's "awful rainbow," Keats has "cold" philosophy (mathematics) "clip an angel's wings,/Conquer all mysteries by rule and line,/Empty the haunted air and gnomed mine–/Unweave a rainbow . . . " (Wordsworth 1967: 234–7). Yet an account by painter Benjamin Haydon of a social gathering, "the immortal dinner" of December 28, 1817, presents a convivial Keats and Lamb bemoaning the effects of Newton's optics on the rainbow while drinking to his genius in boisterous manner (Haydon 1927: 235). For the Romantics, the great scientist is not taken as scientist; instead he is a subject for poetry, another Romantic hero sailing seas of thought alone, which is hardly the way a scientist works. Whether it is Keats or Wordsworth speaking, there is no question that poetry remains other than, and superior to, science.

Matthew Arnold claims the same superiority for literature in his late essay "Science and Literature" published in his *Discourses in America* (1883). But something has changed here. Arnold now argues for something past, *"the best which has been thought and said in the world"* (Arnold 1974: 56; italics in original); moreover he argues now against the categorical rejection of literature by biologist T.H. Huxley in favor of a modern, scientific education. Arnold's argument, presented in America before an audience seen as driven by technological advancement, has an accent of futility. What has happened by this time is the paradigm shift we have been seeking, that allows science to make a serious, unsettling impact on the domain formerly reserved for human preoccupations alone – literature. The scientific "discovery" here is not Descartes' *cogito*, but rather Darwin's statement of evolutionary theory in his *Origin of Species* (1859), focusing previous work by Lamarck, Lyell, and others, and enunciating new ideas about the irreversibility of time and randomness of natural development, with devastating effect on humanity's claim to centrality in the scheme of things. The catastrophic divide between science and "fiction" (as domain of things human) becomes visible everywhere. Tennyson is an example. In "Locksley Hall" (1842), if he extols technology, it remains a force at the service of humanity. He can comfortably revel in "the march of mind,/in the steamship, in the railway, in the thoughts that shake mankind" (ll. 165–6). The vision of "Locksley Hall Revisited" (1883) is radically opposite. Science is now destroying the world in catastrophic fashion: "Art and Grace are less and less:/Science grows and Beauty dwindles – roofs of slated hideousness!" (ll. 245–6). Everywhere, at Science's beckoning, we have images of the decline not just of human culture but of the human species: "Lame and old, and past his time, and passing now into the night;/Yet I would the rising race were half as eager for the light" (ll. 227–8). Arnold's "Dover Beach" offers a like vision of accelerated entropy, of a world not only without faith, but without humanity: "The sea of faith/Was once, too, at the full . . . But now I only hear/Its melancholy, long, withdrawing roar,/Retreating to the breath/Of the night-wind down the vast edges drear/And naked shingles of the world" (Arnold 1949: 419–20).

In England, perhaps the first complex, fictional reaction to the impact of evolutionary science is H.G. Wells' *The Time Machine* (1895). Arnold's description of Darwin, the "born naturalist," describes Wells' scientist-time traveler as he stands out among his circle: "We mean a man in whom the zeal for observing nature is so uncommonly strong and eminent, that it marks him off from the bulk of mankind" (Arnold 1974: 65). The nature the Traveler wishes to observe is that of the Earth's future evolutionary development. In fact, the invention of his machine rests on a theory of time that would have been unthinkable before evolution: that is, time is the fourth dimension along which human consciousness, reduced to an instrument of observation, can now travel, this time toward an evolutionary future he sets out physically to explore. Arnold again articulates the gap between intrepid Time Traveler and the human circle he leaves behind in his drawing-room: "But now, says Professor Huxley, conceptions of the universe fatal to the notions held by our forefathers have been forced upon us by physical science" (Arnold 1974: 66). The Traveler's voyage, propelled by its physical machine, confirms this "fatal" split. It does so most prominently in terms of that latest humanist avatar of Wells' time: so-called "social Darwinism." The latter, in fact, is a reactionary attempt, under Darwin's name, to relocate humanity at the center of the evolutionary process. And, indeed, the Traveler first surmises that his travels bear this "theory" out. On arrival, he believes the Eloi's world is one of utopian communism, where humanity has reached its stable apogee. His faculty for objective observation soon teaches him the opposite. In fact, all books in this future, the best that *will be* thought and said, are to him as Arnold's Greeks are to the new materialist – dust. More ironic yet, the machines in the Palace – yet unimagined technological marvels the Traveler's present would give anything to know – have lost their instruction manuals. Tracked by Morlocks, the Traveler salvages only a club and a few matches – primitive tools to fight off primitive fears in forest and Morlock den. The evolutionary voyage encounters devolution. The advanced scientist not only becomes a caveman but in his final leap into the future he witnesses the heat death of the earth itself. His description is the purest devolutionary poetry: "From the edge of the sea came a ripple and whisper. Beyond these lifeless sounds the world was silent. Silent? It would be hard to convey the stillness of it. All the sounds of man, the bleating of sheep, the cries of birds, the hum of insects, the stir that makes the background of our lives – all that was over" (Wells 1986: 105–06).

Wells' novel offers perhaps the first fictional treatment to register the impact of science on humanistic culture that Arnold sets forth. What is more, in the clash between science and humanity, Wells does not take sides. Arnold has this to say of Darwin: "science and the domestic affections, he thought, were enough" (Arnold 1949: 420). Such a description fits the Time Traveler accurately. In the Palace of Green Porcelain, facing the spectacle of all the great works of literature past, present and future turned to dust, he can only think of his *Philosophical Transactions* and 17 papers on physical optics. At the same time, amidst the archeological marvels of this "latter day South Kensington," he pauses, like the crassest bourgeois tourist, to write his name "on a steatite monster from South America that particularly took my fancy" (Wells 1986: 86). We first meet him in his comfortable Edwardian parlor; he apparently undertakes his fabulous journey in his drawing room coat and slippers, and the Narrator notices on his return that he had on his feet "nothing . . . but a pair of tattered, blood-stained socks" (Wells 1986: 16). Not only is it to this same domestic huddling place that he returns, but he seems to retain this same tourist mindset on his second, apparently fatal departure. For when the Narrator meets him for the last time, "he had a small camera under one arm and a knapsack under the other" (Wells 1986: 112). So much for the great scientific adventurer. In Wells' novel the two cultures – scientific and literary – contend within that same comfortable middle class frame that Matthew Arnold presents. Indeed, the Traveler is described in terms that fit the armchair pessimist of "Dover Beach": "He . . . thought but cheerlessly of the Advancement of Mankind, and saw in the growing pile of civilization only a foolish heaping that must inevitably fall back upon and destroy its makers" (Wells 1986: 114). The Narrator, in response, utters his homilies about this bleak and inhuman future in terms that resemble those of the comforting, futile, Arnold of "Science and Literature," defending humanist "values" in the face of science's onslaught. There is over all of this the bitter, ironic sense of a battle already lost by humanity in the face of vast vistas opened by evolutionary science. Two and a half centuries after Pascal, the terrible silence of science's infinite vistas has finally terrified an English writer. Pascal reacted to the loneliness of Cartesian mind in purely material extension: man without God. Wells is reacting to human futility in a world without man.

Gradual Intrusions

One possible way of determining the origin of SF is to locate such catastrophic eruptions of science in human affairs and the fiction that explores them. Another way is to look for small, gradual intrusions of scientific ideas and methods as these occur in the history of prose fiction, as this latter develops in the shadow of Western science from the Renaissance to today. As scientific discoveries create new problems for philosophical disciplines such as ontology and epistemology in the eighteenth and nineteenth centuries, for example, certain "minor" forms of narrative, outside the stream of the bourgeois novel, appear free to respond in fascinating ways. Such works have generally escaped the eye of SF origin seekers. This is usually because as anomalies in their time they escaped the eye of their contemporaries, thus never had the impact that qualify them as paradigm shifts. One such work, permeated with contemporary scientific considerations but not seen in this light in its time or in ours, has remained largely unnoticed – E.T.A. Hoffmann's "The Sandman" (1816). In like manner, the short stories of Wells, though infused with science, have often been dismissed, in contrast with the "scientific romances," as sketches of manners. Let us examine, in each of these cases, how science, in a furtive sense, has invaded fiction, and changed it from within.

The Paradigm Shift That Wasn't: Hoffmann's "The Sandman"

"The Sandman" is a fairy tale, a minor genre. Yet Hoffmann deals in this inconspicuous setting with the central problem generated by science in his time. This specifically is Kant's so-called "Copernican Revolution," his attempt to formulate a "critical" philosophy, in essence an operating method that reunites the experimental sciences and metaphysics by responding "synthetically" to the epistemological challenge that the empirical method (as basis for the experimental sciences) poses to metaphysics, notably to the Cartesian duality between mind and matter. Kant's "revolution" responds to Hume's radical empirical skepticism, which states that in the act of perception the perceiver can assume neither order without (causality) nor within (the "self" that the *cogito* assumes). If all we know is "percepts," how can we know if there is order or purpose to things "out there"? How can we even know that there is such a thing as a continuous self-identity doing the perceiving?

Kant and Hoffmann shared a cultural climate and a city – Koenigsberg – where the young Hoffmann may have seen Kant on his famous walks to the university. In any event, where Kant's "revolution" consisted of the "synthetic *a priori*," a sophisticated logical maneuver, Hoffmann's occurred less obtrusively on the level of narrative. It asks the reader to ponder the problem of whether one can tell a coherent story of a life if neither element of what the Germans called *Bildung* exist: that is, if there is no causality (the coherent action that shapes character) and no coherent self or character shaped by events? Hoffmann's tale is essentially about the fall of narrative in a world governed (as in Hume's vision) by material perception alone. We have a narrator who does not control the narrative but rather lets it be told as a sequence of perceived moments, as "bundles of different perceptions" that display sequentiality but no necessary order, either in terms of external causality or the internal order of a personality. The narrator is still debating how to begin when the story is half over. The protagonists, as they speak in letters, show no consistency of personality. What is more, in speaking and acting they belie and contradict the cultural roles placed on them by their names: Klara, for instance, should be the model of middle-class "reason," yet her behavior is unpredictably effusive and irrational. Nathanael, (the Hebrew name tells us he should be the Romantic *Schwärmer*) is as often cold and logical as he is effusive.

Hoffmann's story turns around two pairs of scientific experiments and experimenters, in which the identity of both is blurred, as is the difference between mind and world, life and inert matter, perceiver and thing perceived. In the first, Nathanael as child spies on his father and the sinister Coppelius as they perform an alchemical experiment to create, in a fiery crucible, a being out of inert matter. Nathanael's eyes are to be its spark of life; and in what could be a dream or a waking experience, these eyes are taken and inserted in the android. In the second, the scientists seem Italian, Professor Spalanzani this time creating the automaton, and the optician Coppola providing the eyes. Nathanael is again involved in giving "life" through his eyes, but this time by means of an optical glass through which he sees and falls in love with the automaton Olimpia. In Coppelius' experiment the eye comes to stand for the idea of "self;" when the eye becomes a thing easily interchanged with another body, there is contiguity, but no longer any continuity of being, as Nathanael discovers in his relations to Klara and others. In Coppola's experiment, the eye is one with the myriad glasses he casts on the table in front of Nathanael. Each of these offers a "world" of percepts, none of which touch the bedrock of material reality, whose order is some shared or common causality. In this world there is no way to do meaningful science or to live a purposeful and self-directed life, and Nathanael turns in a perceptual/material circle until in his fatal leap from the tower he encounters bedrock, but as extinction of perception in death.

Kant could only resolve this split by positing on the one hand the *Ding an Sich* (a negative extreme, as we can never know things-in-themselves) and on the other what he calls the "transcendental unity of apperception," the point at which the *idea* of a unified self becomes the necessary condition that guarantees our knowledge of a unified world of nature. Hoffmann too builds an order outside the human sphere of perceiver-thing perceived. It is, however, a totally nonhuman order, one that excludes human needs and desires as thoroughly as evolutionary theory was to do half a century later. This nonhuman order appears as relationships form between words and linguistic structures that lie outside both the logic of story and the conventional aspects of narrative itself. Eyes are taken, eyes are thrown back, and a pattern of antithetical relation seems to build between eye and socket. Yet on the level of language such opposites are confounded: Coppola is Italian for the German Coppelius. At the basis of both names is the Italian word "coppo," eye socket. Socket and maker of eyes become one and the same. When Nathanael stares at Klara through Coppola's glass he sees a "wooden doll," Olimpia. But does not the automaton's name share a common etymology with Klara's? Where in conventional fiction we would see fatality governing the actions of human characters, now we have apparently random relationships, embedded in the system of language itself, in metonymic associations between eyes, sparks and sand, finally in alliterative relations between word sounds themselves. Freud later sought in his essay on "The Uncanny" ("Über das Unheimliche") to restore human order to this story, seeing here an Oedipal drama. But compared with psychoanalysis, the science Hoffmann seems to foresee is closer to the stochastic workings of quantum theory a century later. Hoffmann in effect has told a story in a new way under the impact of a new scientific dispensation. The broader paradigm shift, however, fails to happen because the form Hoffmann chooses (the fairy tale) is not central to nineteenth century European culture. Nor is Hoffmann the author (considered a "secondary" writer by such authoritative contemporaries like Goethe, and later famous for his "fantastic" fiction alone) understood in his revolution.

Domesticating Evolution: Wells' "The Flowering of the Strange Orchid"

Whereas *The Time Machine* shocks by heightening the impact of evolutionary science on human beings, Wells, in a number of stories published at the same time, seems busy domesticating this impact of evolution, adapting it to the conventions and world-view of Edwardian magazine fiction. For instance, in "The Stolen Bacillus" (published in June 1894 in the *Pall Mall Budget*), the domestic routine of the Bacteriologist, a generic figure equally as comfortable in his parlor and house clothes as is the Time Traveler, is interrupted by an unusually intense visitor. He claims not to realize that the visitor is an Anarchist. Yet he makes a point of tantalizing him with a vial he says contains the cholera "bacterium." The speech he makes is, surprisingly, a blueprint for violent apocalyptic horror: "Only break such a little tube as this into a supply of drinking water, say to these minute particles [. . .] 'Go forth, increase and multiply, and replenish the cisterns,' and death – mysterious, untraceable death, death swift and terrible [. . .] would be released on this city . . ." (Wells 1952: 337). The visitor, predictably, steals the vial and a chase ensues through London during which the Bacteriologist, already too casually attired for an outing in town, loses his slippers. To remedy this, his wife gathers up his shoes, coat and hat and makes it a three-way chase. The Anarchist, in an act of despair, swallows the contents of the vial. Only then does The Bacteriologist reveal a joke has been played. He had in fact been cultivating "a new species of Bacterium . . . that infest, and I think cause, the blue patches upon various monkeys" (Wells 1952: 342). In this story, the Anarchist is a bumbler; the only mad science or apocalypse that exists is in the Bacteriologist's mind. What remains is a bourgeois scientist, a rather routine piece of science and the tyranny of conformity: "But why should I wear a coat on a hot day because of Mrs___? Oh! *very* well" (Wells 1952: 342; italics in original).

"The Flowering of the Strange Orchid" (August 1894 in the *Pall Mall Budget*) is an even more extraordinary tale of domesticated science. Mr. Winter-Wedderburn, a "shy, lonely, rather ineffectual" bachelor, cultivates orchids. In this tame pursuit, discovery of a new variety is able to bestow bourgeois immortality: "For the new miracle of Nature may stand in need of a new specific name, and what so convenient as that of its discoverer? 'Johnsmithia!'" (Wells 1952: 343). "Nothing ever happens to me!" exclaims poor Wedderburn, as he contrasts himself to the orchid collector-explorer Batten, recently found dead in the Malaysian jungle, every drop of blood sucked from his body, with a strange orchid crushed under his body. Wedderburn brings home an orchid that could be "the very plant that cost him his life to obtain." His housekeeper-cousin does not like the ugly mass of roots. He describes himself, however, as a domesticated Darwin; as such, he notes that the latter's study of orchids concludes that in many cases the flower does not serve the purpose of fertilization: "The puzzle is: what is the flower for?" (Wells 1952: 346). He finds an answer to this question when his orchid suddenly flowers and the "insufferable scent" lures and overwhelms him. His cousin finds him "lying, face upward, at the foot of the strange orchid. The tentacle-like aerial rootlets no longer swayed freely in the air, but were crowded together [. . .] and stretched tight with their ends closely applied to his chin and neck and hands" (Wells 1952: 349). She tears him from its "tenacious" grasp with what could seem the murderous fury of a jealous lover, so much so that the odd jobs man, seeing her "hauling the inanimate body with red stained hands," "thought impossible things." We seem to have a variation on the vampire theme, in this case a vegetable Dracula, that invokes the fury of the cousin, as she tears away the "sucker rootlets" taking his blood. The mention, however, of Darwin and fertilization suggests an even more impossible, and unacceptable, surmise: that of cross-species mating. Darwin's question is answered, this is the purpose these flowers serve, and the cousin is prey to a species-driven jealousy. And sure enough, the plant withers and dies, yet Wedderburn seems reinvigorated by the encounter, "wedded" to some new and inhuman being: "all the array of Wedderburn's orchids was shriveled and prostrate. But Wedderburn himself was bright and garrulous upstairs in the glory of his strange adventure" (Wells 1952: 351). The scientific implications are staggering, too much so even for a science-savvy readership. Wells' ambiguous ending, however, deflates and re-domesticates. Has an evolutionary mutation occurred? Or has finally an adventure happened to this ineffectual man? The strategy of Wells' story is to use the vampire motif to introduce an even more astounding, yet at the same time scientifically conceivable transformation, only to banalize either possibility.

Single Ancestors and a Gradualist Nuance

The fact remains that most discussions of the origins of SF remain fixated on single ancestors. Brian Aldiss' focus on *Frankenstein* and the Gothic has become so prevalent that Robert Scholes and Eric S. Rabkin in their *Science Fiction: History, Science, Vision* simply proclaim, "The First Century A.F. (After Frankenstein)" (Scholes & Rabkin 1977: 3). In like manner, Darko Suvin's influential definition of SF ("a literary genre whose necessary and sufficient conditions are the presence and interaction of estrangement and cognition, and whose main formal device is an imaginative framework alternative to the author's empirical environment") is a circuitous way of describing a single work and the "genre" it supposedly generates – *Utopia* (Suvin 1976: 8). Mark Rose (1981) locates the origin not in a single work but in a single genre: the romance. But rather than look at works and genres, let us consider an aspect of fiction that is at one and the same time more fundamental and more resistant to change – narrative forms themselves. On the level of form, for example, utopia is a variation on the travel narrative, which includes both real and "imaginary" voyages. *Frankenstein*, insofar as it is a Gothic novel, shares the narrative form of this specific kind of romance, the historical narrative. If indeed, as many assert, the nineteenth century is that of SF's origin, that century sees two dominant forms of narrative developing side by side with the novel of manners: the travel narrative and the historical narrative. During the nineteenth century, science and technology acts on both these forms to extend their physical reach. The fascination with archeology and historiography inspired Walter Scott to locate his novels way back, in a reconstructed medieval Britain. And for travel narratives from Swift to Poe and Verne, advancing vehicular technology surely had its role in extending their reach, from South Pole to underwater and the Moon.

In this context, Wells' "invention" of a physical time machine is at one and the same time a natural extension of a moon rocket and a device that effects a mini paradigm shift in terms of conventional limits of the travel and historical narratives (Alkon 2001: 27–39). For, thanks to the physical powers of the machine, Wells is able in a stroke of genius to connect these two forms of narrative. In doing so he creates a viable prototype for the SF novel. If we compare Wells' historical reach with that of Twain's *A Connecticut Yankee* (1889), which remains ambiguous about its protagonist *physically* being in Arthurian times, the machine offers the possibility of genuine physical displacement in vast realms of history, past, and future. Wells' discovery, however, was that such travel effects a conflation of the historical with the travel narrative. In a conventional travel narrative such as *Utopia*, the protagonist has journeyed to a fabulous place and returns to recount his experience. The narrative involves the traveler telling his story in past tense, as having already happened, to a narrative audience in a contemporary setting. This is the situation of Wells' Traveler. Yet the "place" he has traveled to is his and his listener's future; the events he recounts in the past tense as having already taken place, as his body and clothes bear witness, *have not yet happened*. Yet narrative convention tells us we must hear them as if they *had already happened.* The *future history*, a logical paradox before Wells, now takes on narrative reality, as relativistic ideas of space-time begin to transform, at the deep level of structure, conventional forms of narrative. If how we tell stories is a basic human act, then the impact of science and technology on storytelling is strikingly clear in Wells, perhaps for the first time, Yet we cannot call this, if it is SF's birth moment, a total paradigm shift. For the conventional forms of storytelling abide. If we react to the Traveler's tale with disbelief, our reaction, as conventional readers, is to suspend disbelief. Like Wells' Narrator, we continue to read "as though it were not so."

Concluding Unscientific Postscript

This essay has raised questions and challenged assumptions. Rather than give answers, it suggests that the problem of SF's origins has not been properly posed. It has attempted to show that, if paradigm shifts occur that create the conditions for a science fiction, they do so at radically different times in different cultures. In the English-language tradition, this shift appears to happen quite late, with the broad cultural currency of evolutionary theory. Even so, we have suggested that convention, both on the level of themes and ideas, and more crucially on that of narrative forms, has resisted, and continues to resist, even after a supposed shift, the penetration of what Asimov calls scientific and technological advancement into works of fiction. In this perspective, therefore, there can be no single ancestors; SF was, and remains, a work in progress, continuously registering the continuous impact of science on human situations.

REFERENCES AND FURTHER READING

Aldiss, Brian, with David Wingrove (1986) *Trillion Year Spree: The History of Science Fiction.* London: Gollancz.

Alkon, Paul K. (1991) *The Origins of Futuristic Fiction.* Athens GA: University of Georgia Press.

—— (2001)"Was the Time Machine Necessary?" in *H.G. Wells's Perennial Time Machine,* (eds) George Slusser, Patrick Parrinder and Danièle Chatelain. Athens GA: University of Georgia Press, 27–38.

Arnold, Matthew (1949) *Poems.* London: Grey Walls.

—— (1974) "Science and Literature" in *Philistinism in England and America,* (ed.) R.H. Super. Ann Arbor: University of Michigan Press, 53–73.

Bacon, Francis (1955) *Selected Writings of Francis Bacon,* (ed.) Hugh G. Dick. New York: The Modern Library.

Fitting, Peter (ed.) (2004) *Subterranean Worlds: A Critical Anthology.* Middletown CT: Wesleyan University Press.

Haydon, Benjamin Robert (1927) *Autobiography,* (ed.) Edmund Blunden. Oxford: Oxford University Press.

Moskowitz, Sam (1963) *Explorers of the Infinite: Shapers of Science Fiction.* Cleveland and New York: World Publishing.

Muscatine, Charles (1960) *Chaucer and the French Tradition: A Study in Style and Meaning.* Berkeley and Los Angeles: University of California Press.

Nicolson, Marjorie Hope (1948) *Voyages to the Moon.* New York: Macmillan.

Owen, W.J.B. (ed.) (1974) *Wordsworth's Literary*

Criticism. London and Boston: Routledge and Kegan Paul.

Philmus, Robert M. (1970, 1983) *Into the Unknown: The Evolution of Science Fiction from Frances Godwin to H.G. Wells*. Berkeley CA: University of California Press.

Philmus, Robert M. (1973) "The Shape of Science Fiction: Through the Historical Looking Glass." *Science Fiction Studies* 1.i (Spring), 37–41.

Rose, Mark (1981) *Alien Encounters: Anatomy of Science Fiction*. Cambridge, MA: Harvard University Press.

Rousseau, George S. (2003) "The Hunting of Leviathan and Awakening of Proteus" in *Genre at the Crossroads: The Challenge of Fantasy*, (eds) George Slusser and Jean-Pierre Barricelli. Riverside CA: Xenos Books, 56–60.

Scholes, Robert and Rabkin, Eric S. (1977) *Science Fiction: History, Science, Vision*. Oxford: Oxford UP.

Shelley, Mary (1992) *Frankenstein or, The Modern Prometheus*, (ed.) Maurice Hindle. Harmondsworth: Penguin.

Slusser, George (2001) "Breaking the Mind Circle: De Quincey's 'The English Mail Coach' and the Origins of Science Fiction." *Extrapolation* 42.ii (Summer), 111–23.

Suvin, Darko (1976) *Metamorphoses of Science Fiction*. New Haven: Yale University Press.

Versins, Pierre (1972) *Encyclopédie de l'Utopie et de la Science Fiction*. Lausanne: Editions L'Age d'Homme.

Wells, H. G. (1952) *28 SF Stories*. New York: Dover.

——(1986) *The Time Machine*. New York: Bantam Books [text of Heinemann edition, 1895].

Whitehead, Alfred North (1955) *Adventures of Ideas*. New York: New American Library.

Wordsworth, William (1967) *Selected Poems*. London: Collins.

Zola, Emile (1880) *Le Roman expérimental*. Paris: G. Charpentier, (éditeur).

3
Science Fiction/Criticism
Istvan Csicsery-Ronay, Jr.

No popular genre of fiction has generated as much, and as diverse, critical commentary as science fiction (SF). Since it is in the nature of SF's oxymoronic fusion of the rational and the marvelous to challenge received notions of reality – sometimes seriously, sometimes playfully – critical provocation is part of SF's generic identity.

The commentary this remarkably answerable genre has inspired ranges from academic literary criticism to pronouncements by authors and reviewers, electronic discussion threads, postmodern cultural theory, informed speculations on global evolution, and sectarian disputes among practicing Klingons. Its critical voices include highly specialized professionals and amateur aficionados – and it is characteristic of SF culture that the lines between them are porous. Its critical problems involve not only the speculations and dilemmas SF artists pose in their fictions, but also implicit questions about the relations between entertainment and critical thinking, play and pedagogy, the values of humanism and technoscientific culture. As one commentator has written, SF criticism "has been, by any measure, one of history's most extensive discussions about one particular branch of literature" (Westfahl 1999: 187).

Because of this breadth and fluidity, it is hard to delimit the field of SF criticism. For convenience, I will distinguish three main streams: *literary*, *popular*, and *academic criticism*. They are not always distinguishable, for often they treat the same questions, often in similar terms. Nor have they remained stable. Each stream reflects the interests of certain cultural groups and institutions, with their own protocols and traditions, and these have sometimes mutated and converged, as cultural life in the technologically developed world itself has changed. In the remarks that follow, I will emphasize the social and intellectual contexts in which SF and its critical accompaniment developed, rather than the many influential critical interventions themselves. I will also focus on developments in the USA and UK, where the overwhelming majority of SF works have been produced, and whose styles and debates have had a dominant influence on the SF of other societies.

SF criticism per se emerged when SF itself did, in the early nineteenth century, as European writers began to depict future societies and alternate worlds without obvious fantastic framing, using the same concreteness and plausibility to describe their imaginary worlds as they used to describe actual travels and historical documents. Throughout the nineteenth century, scientific fantasy was dominated by two approaches. One was futuristic utopography, closely associated with the industrial utopianism of the French social philosopher St. Simon; the other was the tradition of pseudoalchemical fantasy, in which fantastic discovery and invention was colored by Romantic *Naturphilosophie*. The former aspired to break with literary culture, and generated the populist-technocratic stream of SF criticism that began in earnest with Jules Verne's *Voyages Extraordinaires* (1863–1919). The latter, entwined with the genre of the Gothic, depicted its protoscientific ideas in terms of mythical or magical motifs handed down by literature. For the utopians, technology represented the benevolent conquest of scarcity and ignorance. For the authors of literary Gothic, by contrast, science was a symbol of human protagonists' internal ethical conditions, a matter of soul rather than society. Its favored forms were the symbol-rich psychological dramas of isolated, fraught characters favored by the wave-front of nineteenth century Euro-American literature.

The Gothic line of SF took mature form when Darwinian evolutionary theory provided it with a scientific narrative that could successfully challenge the classical literary model, within which material reality was merely a disguise for certain archetypes. It was H.G. Wells who, by applying ideas from evolutionary natural history to human self-construction in his early scientific romances, supplied the literary Gothic with scientific plausibility. As a contemporary French reviewer framed it, the dominant idea of Wells' work is "the reciprocal evolution of Science and Humanity. Men create science, science, in its turn remakes mankind" (Parrinder 1972: 100).

The Wellsian model of scientific romance enjoyed great success. For the literary establishment, it represented a new poetry that fused knowledge of science and character. It brought the undisciplined fantasy of popular adventure fiction under control by grounding it in the useful and realistic scientific worldview. The new genre also had opponents. Conservatives believed the science fatally narrowed the scope of the fiction. At the other end of the spectrum, scientific enlighteners objected to the way romance elements corrupted the truth of facts into pseudoscience.

It was, however, precisely this hybrid character that made Wellsian SF attractive to some of the most innovative of early modernist writers, like Vladimir Mayakovsky, Michael Bulgakov, Evgeny Zamyatin, Karel Čapek, and the avant-garde playwright, Alfred Jarry, who, calling it the "hypothetical novel," singled out the notion of thought experiment and fictive prophecy that would become one of SF's most durable attractions:

> The scientific novel – which could also be called the hypothetical novel – imagines what would happen if certain elements were in place. This is why, in the same way that

hypotheses come true one day, some of these novels, at the moment when they were written, are novels of the future. (quoted in Evans 1999: 177).

Wellsian SF was quite congenial to European literary culture, since the normal output of even realist writers often included works of fantasy. The newness of the scientific perspective seemed to complement the literary tradition. Zamyatin praised Wells' "mechanical, chemical fairy tales." Wells' special contribution was to use ostensibly scientific premises and reasoning to build extravagant speculations.

> Almost all of Wells' fairy tales are built upon brilliant and most unexpected
> scientific paradoxes. All of his myths are as logical as mathematical equations.
> And this is why we, modern men, we, skeptics, are conquered by these logical fantasies,
> this is why they command our attention and win out belief. (Zamyatin 1970: 261)

For the first half of the twentieth century, Wells' *scientific romances* were admitted to a canon of fantastic fiction because they were considered inherently philosophical, inducing readers to ponder the metaphysical core of scientific ideas. *Science fiction*, on the other hand, was associated with the vulgar style of the pulps, and treated as sub-literary, not worthy of notice by critics of taste. A main function of literary criticism has been to regulate the canon of exemplary works that every educated member of the culture is supposed to know. Only works of borderline literary SF written by authors who had already established reputations in more serious forms – such as George Orwell's *Nineteen Eighty-Four*, Aldous Huxley's *Brave New World*, Čapek's *R.U.R.* – were considered candidates for canonization. After the Second World War, SF's reputation rose as that of elite literature declined. Significant critical essays occasionally appeared in literary journals, like C.S. Lewis' "On Science Fiction" (1955), but these became increasingly rare.

Popular SF criticism emerged from the vibrant discussions conducted in the pulps, the popular SF magazines that were the main vehicles for SF publishing in the USA from the 1920s to the 1950s. Its participants were primarily fans, avid readers – many of whom were also active writers – who were encouraged by the influential editors of the period, Hugo Gernsback and John Campbell, to voice their opinions about the genre and to extend discussions of ideas raised in the magazines' editorials. They approached SF not as an interesting minor branch of literature, but as a new sort of writing altogether, a challenge to the conservatism of the cultural establishment, which looked down on practical science and engineering. Popular SF criticism has often been fervently polemical, taking as indisputable the premise that SF is the apt artistic expression of the modern age of discovery and invention, and, by the same token, the most moral one, since it inculcates in its often young readers respect for technology and scientific reasoning. In the popular view, SF should be judged by different standards than traditional literature, since its values are different. Popular SF critics have tended also to be more practical than their literary counterparts. Viewing SF as an ideal kind of mass entertainment, whose natural form is the commercial commodity, popular criticism has often taken the form of pragmatic advice to SF writers on how to write and be published in the genre. This tradition has gradually expanded from magazine publishing to the introductions of anthologies, internet fan sites, even mutating into sophisticated theories of discourse.

The popular conception of SF can be traced back to the futuristic utopianism of postrevolutionary writers in France, like Sébastien Mercier and Félix Bodin. Breaking with the traditional humanistic conception of literature's role as the preserver of the best of the past, they proclaimed that a new sort of fiction could transform the world by giving readers a romantic vision of hope in the future to which they could aspire. Bodin captures this missionary enthusiasm in the introduction to his *Roman de l'Avenir* (1834):

> If ever anyone succeeds in creating the novel, the epic of the future, he will have tapped a vast source of the marvelous, and of a marvelous entirely in accord with verisimilitude . . . which will dignify reason instead of shocking or deprecating it as all the marvelous epic machinery conventionally employed up to now has done. In suggesting perfectibility through a narrative and dramatic picturesque form, he will have found a method of seizing, of moving the imagination, and of hastening the progress of humanity in a manner very much more effective than the best expositions of systems presented with even the highest eloquence. (Evans 1999: 20)

The international success of Verne's *Voyages Extraordinaires* a generation later derived from this project of synthesizing the myth of progress with scientific education. Verne's work was intended, and openly marketed, to combine romantic adventure with scientific didacticism.

In this indirect way the *Voyages* were polemical, written to be vehicles of Verne's editor's, Hetzel's, visionary educational program to instruct French youth in science when the reactionary national curriculum removed it from the schools. Admiring critics immediately recognized the innovation. But Verne's pedagogical use of science was already at the time a somewhat conservative synthesis, since it limited its horizon to technical developments so plausible and near that they seemed to occur barely a few days in the future.

Hugo Gernsback and John Campbell

Popular SF criticism emerged as an institution as popular SF became a cultural movement in the USA of the late 1920s and 1930s. Wells and Verne were respected in the USA of the 1920s, and their fiction was often reprinted in the pulps. But the American conditions for writing fiction were dramatically different than in the UK and Europe. A rapid democratization of culture attended the even more rapid industrialization of American society and the assimilation of millions of immigrants whose education in the language and whose reading tastes were not connected with the literary language of English elite education. For these – and out of these – hopeful new readers, in a new culture where social advancement had much more to do with technical skills than classical learning, and where great feats of engineering and invention had created an American sublime unimaginable in the rest of the world, the model for SF was not the writer Wells, but the inventor-entrepreneur Thomas Edison. It was under these conditions that Hugo Gernsback founded *Amazing Stories*, and the institution of the SF pulps.

Over the course of the late 1920s, Gernsback laid out the defining qualities of commercial SF in language that combined manifesto and commercial how-to manual. In a society where Edison had the role of culture-hero, the engineer was the model protagonist, and SF became concerned primarily with machine power as a manifestation of individual freedom. Gernsback elaborated the language of earlier proponents of futuristic fiction, claiming that SF was a revolutionary new form of writing, destined to replace the nonscientific, unimaginative, conservative literature of the elite. In his editorial pronouncements Gernsback repeatedly insisted that the science of SF should be so exact that the fiction would become a stage for invention, thus making the genre, "a world-force of unparalleled magnitude." (The dream was not far fetched; Leo Szilárd claimed his design for a nuclear fission device was inspired by one of Wells' stories, surely one of the most positive critical notices of a work of SF.)

Gernsback's magazines were enthusiastically capitalistic, democratic, and technocratic. He provided explicit definitions of what he meant by "scientifiction" – a definition that was as often ignored as respected, but which had a living authority, guiding future professional writers of the magazines. For Gernsback, as one scholar puts it:

> had three functions: the narrative could provide 'entertainment,' the scientific information could furnish a scientific 'education,' and the accounts of new inventions could offer 'inspiration' to inventors, who might proceed to actually build the proposed invention or something similar to it. Correspondingly, there were three natural audiences for SF: the general public, seeking to be entertained; younger readers, yearning to be educated about science; and working scientists and inventors, anxious to find some stimulating new ideas. (Westfahl 1999: 189–90)

Gernsback's successor as the dominant editor of the pulp culture, John Campbell, the powerful editor of *Astounding* and *Unknown*, moved SF writing toward the status of an established profession. He cultivated a stable of exemplary writers and shaped the aesthetic contours of the genre with the same single-mindedness and editorial power as Andre Breton used to promote Surrealism and Tristan Tzara used for Dadaism. Campbell created the conditions for a professional SF subculture out of the fan tradition. He argued in editorials, and in voluminous private correspondence with writers, through which he shaped many of the most important stories of the era, that SF was the quintessential modern form because it was the literature of the technologically literate, inventive minds creating the machines and ideas that were transforming the world. Campbell was insistent on the formative power of scientific thinking (as with Gernsback, this was respected as often in the breach, and indeed Campbell was never rigid in distinguishing between real science and pseudoscience). He exhorted his favorite writers – Isaac Asimov, Robert Heinlein, and Lester Del Ray, among others – to build their stories around the technologies that were most important for, and, indeed, required by, his conception of human evolution: nuclear power, space travel, and mind control. These were to be described with scientific plausibility; but once this was accomplished, the writers were to focus on the social possibilities and consequences of their use. (He was so successful in this, that he and several of his writers were investigated by the US Army Counter-Intelligence Corps in 1944, on suspicion that in one story he had published secret information about the development of the nuclear bomb.)

Campbell, even more than Gernsback, conceived of SF as a social practice, and of SF writers as having professional affinities with the engineers and scientists that he considered the true target audience of their writing. The Campbellian aesthetic required that stories' milieux should strike readers as nearly mundane in their concreteness and realism, to show that technoscientific wonders are destined to become everyday experiences – that science is "the magic that works."

> Science is rapidly – so rapidly we can scarcely realize those dreams are coming true – ruling out one after another of the mighty wonders to be accomplished by SF heroes. They aren't mighty wonders any more; they've become the world's daily work. (Berger 1993: 53).

Postwar Professionals and the Rebel Critics

By the end of the Second World War, SF had acquired a reputation for correctly prophesying technological innovations (well earned) and social transformations (much less so). Respect for the once denigrated genre inspired many SF writers to aspire to more respectable status writing for mass-market magazines. Only a few SF writers, like Heinlein and Ray Bradbury, achieved mainstream success in the "slicks," but in the early 1950s SF as a genre attained a wider audience in the USA through B-list films and television series. As the entertainment industry warmed to the genre, however, professionalized science took a path that was inimical to the Campbellian vision of the free social development of technoscience. The Cold War and the control of large-scale scientific projects by the security state deprived science of its human connection with everyday life. As science was contained by Cold War ideology, so professional SF was contained by the enforced ennui of 1950s America.

Despite these pressures, many SF writers insisted on developing what they believed to be SF's inherent cantankerousness against conformism. The genre would remain, until the late 1960s, an insider game, the famous SF ghetto, yet immanent criticism of complacent writing and unimaginative science was voiced in essays by James Blish (writing as William Atheling) and Damon Knight, as were critiques of the profession's ideological conformism and ghetto mentality by Frederick Pohl, Cyril Kornbluth, and Robert Bloch, who excoriated his colleagues and fans for thinking "that every mushroom cloud has a silver lining." By the mid-1960s, as paperback publishing began to dominate the marketplace, SF had an established niche in popular culture (though it continued to be ignored by the literary and academic establishment). Many SF writers identified with outsider groups more than with the mainstream. Viewing SF as a critical subculture inspired by the desire to break taboos, they initiated a contestatory revival of SF that was openly hostile to an establishment based on Cold War politics of science, mass-destruction technology, and simplistic morality. A new generation of SF-magazine editors, foremost among them Horace Gold of *Galaxy* and Anthony Boucher of *Fantasy and Science Fiction Magazine*, encouraged satirical and mildly transgressive provocations. In as much as official science, including the space program, became identified with weaponry, the militarization and expansion of police powers, and enforced consumption, many rebellious SF writers rejected the romance of science, wholesale.

The most prominent of these rebellions was also the most self-consciously theorized and propagandized, the British New Wave associated with the magazine *New Worlds* under the editorship of Michael Moorcock from 1964 to 1973. The New Wave represents the first serious mutation of SF magazine culture away from the popular tradition, openly supporting writing with affinities to contemporary literary styles, and repudiating the middle-brow literary values that dominated 1950s SF. *New Worlds'* star writer-theorist, J.G. Ballard, proposed that SF be re-envisioned as a genre exploring psychological "inner space," in overt opposition to the scientistic power-fantasies of establishment SF.

> I think SF should turn its back on space, on interstellar travel, extraterrestrial life forms, galactic wars and the overlap of these ideas that spreads across the margins of nine-tenths of the magazines of s-f. . . . It is these, whether they realize it or not, that s-f readers are so bored with now, and which are beginning to look increasingly out-dated. (Greenland 1983: 44).

The genteel Wellsian tradition of scientific romance was etiolating; the literary establishment in the UK was heading for a similar fate. *New Worlds* proposed to resuscitate SF by infusing it with contemporary literary techniques, drawn from Surrealism and the then fashionable French *nouveau roman*. The New Wave theorists argued that SF's thought-experiments had more in common with the visionary concerns of artistically ambitious, experimental writing than with the projects of techno-science. Moorcock and Ballard claimed for the British popular SF tradition, which had allied itself with the US pulp style for a generation, a kinship with literature, in effect producing sophisticated literary criticism of SF from within the popular tradition.

In the USA, a similar attempt to redefine SF as an experimental, antiestablishment medium was presented in the introductions of two influential sets of anthologies, Damon Knight's *Orbit* collections, and Harlan Ellison's *Dangerous Visions* (1972) and

Again, Dangerous Visions (1976). Where the British New Wave conceived of itself in terms of a European literary movement, complete with manifestos and aesthetic battle lines, the US version of the New Wave viewed itself primarily as a reform movement within the SF profession, and showed little interest in literary movements and works of what had come to be known as "mainstream," and indeed "mundane," literature.

The Counterculture and the Academy

In the 1960s, the civil rights and anti-Vietnam War movement in the USA, and the antinuclear and anticolonial movements in Europe, gradually opened up new spaces for cultural contestation, energy, and diversity. The rapid postwar reconstruction of Europe and the hyper-modernization of the USA had created enormous wealth, which was attended by expectations of increased social freedom. An unprecedented number of students entered universities, virtually forcing education to democratize its subject matter, if not its organization. Popular culture could no longer be excluded from the classroom, and its introduction raised questions about why it had been excluded in the past. "Subversive" theories entered the academe, led at first by Freudianism, Existentialism, and Libertarianism, followed in short order by New Left Marxism and second-wave feminism.

With the convergence of liberation movements, antimilitarism, and radical critical theory from both the New Left and the libertarian Right, a utopian drive became manifest in youth culture throughout the world. SF, as the repository of utopian themes and satirical fantasy about technoscientific development, attained widespread popularity among students and young professionals. Works like Heinlein's *Stranger in a Strange Land* (1961), Frank Herbert's *Dune* (1965), Kurt Vonnegut's *Cat's Cradle* (1963) and *Slaughterhouse Five* (1969), and J.R.R. Tolkien's *Lord Of The Rings* (1954/1968) (technically not SF, but treated as such by readers at the time) became cult favorites, in large part because they articulated critiques of the myth of progress and the ethnocentrism of Western technical culture. This popularity, in turn, inspired other writers to write iconoclastic SF that challenged not only the academic establishment, but the professional SF establishment as well. Writers like Ursula Le Guin, Samuel R. Delany, Philip K. Dick, and Joanna Russ, broke new ground by combining sophisticated social critique with adventurous stylistic experimentation. University teachers, inspired by the student-driven demand for relevance in the curriculum and their own interest in the breakdown of the barriers between popular and elite art, increasingly included such texts in their courses, and addressed them in their scholarship.

Literary critics and scholars had been slow to accept SF. The first serious scholarly study of the genre, J.O. Bailey's *Pilgrims Through Space and Time* (1947), was ignored. Marjorie Nicholson, the foremost scholar of the important precursor genre, the lunar voyage, repudiated association with SF. But the process of canon-critique opened the way to previously excluded voices and forms, and SF was one of them. In the late

1950s and early 1960s, a few prestigious literary figures proposed that SF had a special role in revealing the social unconscious of the postwar world. Foremost among these were Kingsley Amis, whose *New Maps of Hell* (1960) offered SF as the quintessential genre of literary dystopia, and Susan Sontag, whose "The Imagination of Disaster" (1966) was the first Western essay to take Japanese popular monster films seriously, albeit with considerable condescension. Most influential of all was Leslie Fiedler's "The New Mutants" (1965). Fiedler, a bold revisionist of American Studies, argued that US literature was energized by the conscious disavowal, and unconscious affirmation, of the stigmatized Other. Inspired by the psychoanalytic critique of American conformism of the 1950s, Fiedler submitted the American canon to Freudian analysis, detecting repression of racial and sexual fears throughout. Using the work of William S. Burroughs (who would later become the tutelary genius of the cyberpunks) as his model, Fiedler believed recent fiction signaled that the denied Others of American society were freeing themselves. For Fiedler, SF was a genre quintessentially expressing the consciousness of the "freaks," marginalized bohemians, hippies, Jews and Blacks (significantly, not women) that SF writers characteristically displaced into superheroes, mutants, and aliens.

The Institutionalization of Academic SF criticism

Not all of the new academic critics were drawn to SF by political critique. In 1970, Thomas Clareson helped to found the Science Fiction Research Association (SFRA), and in 1971 published *SF: The Other Side of Realism*, an essay-anthology displaying the international and interdisciplinary range of recent criticism of SF. Because the genre was not yet an acceptable academic specialty, the members of the SFRA approached SF through the lenses of other periods and genres, establishing literary genealogies that justified careful scholarly attention. The first major academic pedigree was in American Studies (Clareson's own field); significant monographs began to appear, ranging from David Ketterer's *New World for Old* (1974), which argued that SF was the direct heir of American literary apocalypticism, to H. Bruce Franklin's Marxist critical biography of Robert Heinlein (1980), which accused Campbellian SF of complicity with US imperialism.

The academic study of SF benefited from the general exuberance of intellectual culture in the West in the 1960s and 1970s. Disciplinary boundaries were weakened by the appearance of metatheoretical schools of thought, each of which seemed to aspire to a Grand Unified Theory of human culture on its own terms. Many varieties of structuralism, neo-Marxism, psychoanalysis, critical anarchism, proto-Green ecocriticism, feminism, structural functionalism, along with other schools, claimed to explain general principles of cognitive and social behavior more comprehensively than the established academic disciplines. Ambitious studies of the cognitive and sociological preconditions of the genre appeared in quick succession: in *Structural Fabulation* (1975) Robert Scholes, a scholar of modernism and early postmodern experimentation, mixed structuralism and psychoanalysis to argue that SF is cognate with the contemporary literary movements of fabulation; Eric Rabkin, in *The Fantastic in Literature* (1976), argued for reading SF as the successor of the mythological and mythopoeic traditions; Darko Suvin, in *Metamorphoses of Science Fiction* (1979), combined aesthetic ideas of the Marxist playwright Berthold Brecht and philosopher Ernst Bloch, to argue that SF is an epistemological genre inherently critical of bourgeois ideology, and an inciter of social enlightenment; Mark Rose, adapting Northrop Frye's notion that SF is a modern incarnation of the mythos of romance, laid out the dominant archetypes of the genre in *Alien Encounters* (1981); and Gary K. Wolfe, in *The Known and the Unknown* (1979), perhaps the only major work of academic SF scholarship of this period that did not use a metacritical apparatus, identified the iconic elements through which SF mediates the oscillation between the known and the unknown. (A related study in genre-theory, *The Fantastic* (1973), a translation of the Bulgarian theorist Tzvetan Todorov's *De la littérature fantastique* (1970), enjoyed great influence, despite the fact that its subject was a very different genre – the uncanny tale – and had little to offer regarding SF.)

The most sustained applications of generic metatheory were by Neo-Marxist critics loosely associated with *Science Fiction Studies* and *Utopian Studies,* and by feminist SF critics. The foremost Marxist theorist was Suvin, who introduced the notion that SF's basic operation is *cognitive estrangement* – inducing a perspective of critical displacement from the distorted ideological perception of social reality – and that SF's basic mechanism is the introduction of a *novum,* a scientifically plausible innovation that catalyzes an imaginary historical transformation. Other important Neo-Marxist concepts – such as the critical utopia (proposed by Tom Moylan), the collapsed future (Fredric Jameson), the absent paradigm (Marc Angenot), and the cognition effect (Carl Freedman) – have remained important tools even for non-Marxist theoretical analysts. On a parallel path, feminist critics were producing the most varied body of liberationist SF theory, based on the recognition that the genre's hospitableness to outsiders had long given voice to marginalized women. Influential feminist studies ranged from criticism of SF's historical and institutional androcentrism and appreciations of women's countercultural SF tradition by Marleen Barr, Robin Roberts, Jane Donawerth, and Sarah Lefanu, to explications of SF's diverse deconstructions of gender by Constance Penley, Jenny Wolmark, and Veronica Hollinger. After some lag, in the 1980s many of the strategies of Marxist and feminist SF critics inspired queer theoretical and race-critical analyses of the genre as well.

The explosion of scholarly interest supported – and was supported by – the establishment of academic journals devoted to SF scholarship. In 1959, Clareson began editing a stenciled newsletter, *Extrapolation*, that was physically barely distinguishable from a fanzine. A few years later, it was followed by the British *Foundation* and the Montreal-based *Science Fiction Studies.* Each journal established its own distinct critical tone. Gradually, SF was granted standing by the academic establishment, albeit on the periphery. Library collections were housed; annual academic meetings were funded, as well as occasional international conferences devoted to special topics, where SF scholars met to exchange ideas; scholarly presses were founded, and several major academic publishers became hospitable to monographs on SF and its history.

Convergence

Important SF commentary and scholarship continued to be produced by nonacademics, many of them practicing writers. These works reflected the convergence of the literary and popular traditions of SF in the US and British New Wave, now directed also to the new university audience. In *Billion Year Spree* (1973) (later to be revised, in collaboration with David Wingrove, as *Trillion Year Spree* [1986]), Brian Aldiss countered the American Studies and hard SF-centered genealogy of US SF-scholars, by tracing the genre's origins to Mary Shelley and the Gothic tradition. Some years later, Brian Stableford's *Scientific Romance in Britain, 1830–1950* (1985) defined the distinctive national literary tradition of UK SF, the British scientific romance. Perhaps most influential among these writer-critics was Samuel R. Delany. A successful exponent of the American New Wave, Delany set out to provide a sophisticated justification of SF from within, writing as a self-identified genre writer, but using some of the tools of contemporary schools of literary theory. Arguing that SF was a form of discourse that had its own conditions of intelligibility, Delany provided a new vocabulary for discussing SF as a way of using language to embody new thought that has proved highly influential on later scholars of SF.

By the end of the 1970s, we can speak of a convergence of the major streams of SF criticism. The ethical concerns of canon-construction, the cultural politics of democratic popular culture, the academic project of analyzing and categorizing cultural and social life, flowed together. Practitioners of different disciplines adopted each other's vocabularies. Writers took teaching positions in universities; critics tried their hands at fiction. The fiction itself, in the meantime, began to separate into two tiers, one that assumed an educated and critically sophisticated audience, and the other resolutely commercial and anti-intellectual, devoted to its niche status and its fan audiences. The mediator of this convergence and drift was SF film (and later, television), which gradually became the dominant vehicle for SF.

At first, academic film scholars treated SF film much as SF had been treated by literature faculties, as a curiosity of mainly sociological interest. Major film artists' forays into the genre – Fritz Lang's *Metropolis* (1926), Stanley Kubrick's *2001* (1968), and *A Clockwork Orange* (1971), Andrei Tarkovsky's *Solaris* (1971) – elicited some interest, but not as examples of genre. Television was for many years not an acceptable object of study. Even professional SF magazines' reviewers treated popular SF films as a debased form, when compared with written SF. And yet, popular enthusiasm for television SF and popular SF films – especially *Star Trek* and *Star Wars* – inspired a new kind of fan culture that would, in the 1980s, transform the terms of commentary and criticism of SF. Mainstream film reviewers discussed SF movies no differently than other commercial releases; as a result, popular commentary on SF film was much more widely

distributed than reviews of SF writing. Original theoretical approaches to SF film based
on the premise that cinema is a distinct medium with its own history appeared first in
Vivian Sobchack's *The Edge of Infinity* (1980) (later revised as *Screening Space* [1987]).
Expanding from Sobchack's work, a number of theorists argued that SF was not merely
a minor subgenre of film, but one intimately connected to the medium, since films (and
related arts of the spectacle) are experiments in the technological mediation of collective fantasies, and thereby embody the subject of SF itself. In recent years, academic
study of SF films has produced important work on the relationship of film technology
and SF themes, notably Brooks Landon's *The Aesthetics of Ambivalence* (1992) and Scott
Bukatman's *Terminal Identity* (1993). Film has also been particularly favored by feminist critics; arguably, feminist psychoanalytic critique of SF film has replaced critical
utopian theory as the main venue for feminist SF scholarship.

Cyberpunk, Posthumanism, Metacriticism

Resembling in some ways the transformation of SF from a ghetto of genre-
professionals to a major form of cultural production, SF underwent an even greater
expansion of influence in the 1980s with the introduction of video games and desk
computers, and the emergence of genetic engineering as the dominant popular model
of techno-science. These developments also gave rise to cyberpunk. This new style of
SF captured the ambivalence felt in the West about the convergence of revolutionary
technologies (genetic recombination, computer analysis and synthesis, bionics, information grids, etc.) and the collapse of the collective desire for social progress into
global manipulation by rapacious corporations – embodied in US popular consciousness by the momentary global ascent of Japanese industrial culture. The cyberpunks
cultivated an image of semicriminal, heterotopian subcultures as mediating agents,
who subvert the dominance of financial elites, but refuse to offer principles for collective political action. To a greater degree even than the New Wave, cyberpunk was
conceived in both critical and creative terms. Its ideas were put forth in manifestoes,
often pronounced with playful irony in the movement's main zine, *Cheap Truth*, edited
by Bruce Sterling, and in Sterling's introduction to the influential cyberpunk anthology, *Mirrorshades* (1986), to be further elaborated in independent critical magazines,
like *SF Eye*. Cyberpunk's propagandists avowed kinship with SF's generic roots in the
pulps, and with the esoteric antielitist subcultures of the American avant-garde as
well. They praised as models writers who used SF motifs extragenerically, like
Burroughs and Ballard. Their critical project resembled that of the New Wave; both
argued that SF should emphasize the symbolic dimensions and psychological dys-
functions of technology-saturated social life. But cyberpunks went further, inspired
by developments in computerization and brain studies that dissolved the boundary
between artificially manipulated and natural inner states, and by the unregulated
appropriations of consumer technology by remix subcultures.

Cyberpunk's popularity was enormous, instantaneous, and global. It elicited critical commentary from the wide range of academic SF critics. This was primarily negative from feminists and Marxists, who saw unconscious androcentric and fatalistic myth-making in it. But it also elicited powerful positive responses from a direction that had barely existed just years before, namely posthumanism. Posthumanist critics shared the cyberpunks' fascination with digital technology's power to transform nature by coding all matter as information, and re-engineering it at will. Posthumanists viewed this power as a force of evolution, capable of liberating human beings from scarcity, corruptible bodies, and mortality itself. Shocked by the successes of cybernetics and bionic sciences, popular and academic institutions seemed to concede that the ethical axioms of the literary intelligentsia are no longer valid, once the world is redefined in terms of flows, control systems, and degrees of virtuality. Imagining the deletion of organic bodies and historical burdens, cyberpunk also intersected with the new philosophical currents that had displaced the metatheories of the 1960s and 1970s – poststructuralist schools, especially of Michel Foucault and Gilles Deleuze-Félix Guattari, as well as "extropians," who trusted in the capacities of computer-based artificial intelligence to assume the functions of identity and consciousness and of nanotechnology to provide the body with perpetual upgrades.

At the same moment, some influential social theorists adopted science-fictional tropes to explain contemporary social conditions. Donna Haraway, in her influential "A Cyborg Manifesto: Science, Technology, and Socialist-Feminism in the Late Twentieth Century" (1985), refitted the oft-used SF figure of the cyborg into a feminist political myth of posthuman network-beings who reject the oppressive Western ontology of technoscience. In his *Postmodernism: The Cultural Logic of Late Capitalism* (1990), Fredric Jameson drew heavily on the SF of J.G. Ballard and Philip K. Dick to describe postmodernism's demolition of history in favor of spatialized, discontinuous time. Jean Baudrillard, like Jameson influenced by Ballard and Dick, became best known for his concepts of simulation and simulacra, genuinely science-fictional ideas applied to social theory. At the other end of the ideological spectrum, enthusiasts of the dramatic breakthroughs in computing and communications technologies in the 1980s spoke of transcending the human condition through technoevolution, in a sublime technological discourse that had been reserved for SF in the past. George Gilder envisioned a utopian "telecosm," Howard Bloom a global brain, Ray Kurtzweil an age of "spiritual machines," Hans Marovec of "mind children," downloaded units of consciousness. Posthumanist theorists agreed without reservation with Haraway's dictum: "the boundary between SF and social reality is an optical illusion" (Haraway 1991: 66).

Poststructuralist theories took unrelenting aim at all notions of objectivity and naive reference, including those of science, by rejecting the notion of a unitary, stable subject capable of integrating information in a situationally transcendent form. Postmodernism emerged at the same time, as an aesthetic that repudiated historical metanarratives, while embracing untrammeled stylistic juxtaposition. It derived from the explosive growth of communications and transportation technologies, the effect of which was to make great domains of experience, unmoored from their historical contexts, accessible to travelers (physical and virtual, both) within the new context of globalizing high-technology. For a number of critics, SF – especially cyberpunk – came to represent the quintessential commentary on postmodernism, if not its actual embodiment. Larry McCaffery, who had controversially elevated SF to the rank of leading-edge contemporary fiction in *The Columbia Literary History of the United States* (1988), published an influential anthology that combined cyberpunk fiction with postmodernist criticism, *Storming the Reality Studio* (1991). Brian McHale, in *Postmodernist Fiction* (1987) and *Constructing Postmodernism* (1992), argued that SF was the genre that best embodied postmodernism's principle of *ontological uncertainty*, which McHale opposed to *epistemological uncertainty* of modernism, exemplified by detective fiction. In *Terminal Identity: The Virtual Subject in Postmodern Science Fiction* (1993), Scott Bukatman discussed a wide range of recent SF – fiction, films, and comics – as creative responses to the role of digital technologies in the postmodern discentering of subjectivity.

Cultural studies-based criticism of SF also took shape in this environment. The postmodernist concern with the centerless subject converged with the claims of social constructionist theorists that all meaning is created situationally, by social groups. In recent years, cultural critics of SF have studied the sociology of groups engaged in science-fictional performance, such as fan collectives, "textual poachers" (communities of amateur writers who write heterodox variations on the stories and characters of favorite television series), and artificial cultures. Like anthropologists who observe scientific communities as if they were contemporary tribes, some scholars have begun to examine the thriving institutions of SF fan culture – conventions, internet networks, and role-playing communities – as not only reflective of social transformations in hyper-technologized societies, but also producers of them.

A central, and yet perhaps paradoxically anomalous, event in the recent history of SF criticism was the publication of the *Encyclopedia of Science Fiction in* 1993. The nearly 1400-page reference work included over 4360 entries, collecting the genre's history and thesaurus of themes within a scholarly compendium. Tellingly, the editors John Clute and Peter Nicholls were neither professional academics nor fans, but respected independent critics and reviewers. By drawing on literary, academic, and popular traditions of the genre for its data, the *Encyclopedia* has provided an overview of the genre for SF's many audiences. Although it is periodically updated on the internet, the *Encyclopedia* is very much a monument to book culture; in it film and television are judged by literary standards, and icons of SF folk-beliefs like UFOs are disdained. It may be that the *Encyclopedia of Science Fiction* prefigures the closure of the literary/academic experiment with the genre.

Away from the book, the diffusion of the internet has given new life to fans' communities of commentary. The ease with which websites and discussion groups can be established on the Net has amplified the exchanges fan communities once maintained through stenciled newsletters and zines. Fans have long practiced a form of creative criticism, writing alternative and supplementary stories in the fictive universes of favorite films and television shows – even developing subversive variants (such as the so-called K/S, or "slash," phenomenon of depicting *Star Trek*'s Kirk and Spock as gay lovers). Websites now abound with imaginary sequels to popular films, original scripts, and even freelance critical reflection. Members of far-flung internet communities often become familiar with commentary – to which they have ready net access – long before they see the film, game, or tv series that is commented on.

Such developments have produced a critical community that owes little to traditional models of culture. Linked with real affective bonds via consumer artifacts, and openly accepting the ambivalence this entails, these groups have sometimes formed their own immanent institutions of radical cultural criticism. A prime example is the way the depiction of the warrior-alien Klingons in *Star Trek* has inspired the construction of an artificial culture, complete with an artificial language, that is lived and spoken sincerely in the hospitable confines of SF conventions. The project has inspired the establishment of a *de facto* Klingon Academy, the Klingon Language Institute, official arbiter of the synthetic customs and grammar. Among the Institute's projects has been the translation of the New Testament, a task that has generated disputes about how to convey concepts of mercy and self-sacrifice, for which video-Klingons have (as yet) no terms. Despite obvious silliness, the progress of role-playing SF subcultures has some striking similarities to that of more established self-isolating subcultures in the real world, thus embodying a living critique of the world in its appropriation of mass culture's "cargo."

The concept of SF has also expanded to include approaches far from the mainstream of SF culture. A striking case is Afro-futurism. Afro-futurist artists have adapted SF ideas and icons as ludic symbols of cultural power – of both the hegemony of white domination and the subversive play of black art. Afro-futurism is most identified with music – Sun Ra's jazz, George Clinton's funk, and electronic dance subcultures – and Afro-futurist criticism has itself favored a performative style. The commentary of Mark Dery, Greg Tate, and Kodwe Eshun, among others, also differs from academic critique of the representation of race in SF, by focusing on the spontaneously mutating relationships between music machines and performance.

The Future

It is not possible to describe the character of this free floating, anarchic process of exchange. For the moment, it appears to construct a discursive space constrained only by the technologies of communication and the rate at which SF is introduced onto the market. In the past, critical institutions were expected to govern selection of artifacts that a society should value; internet communities of commentary have reversed the relation – facilitating as many voices as possible, and suppressing norms of selection. At the moment, the great historical conversation about one particular branch of literature appears to be converging in the infinite, virtual temporary autonomous zone of cyberspace.

References and Further Reading

Aldiss, Brian (1973) *Billion Year Spree*. Garden City, NY: Doubleday.

Alkon, Paul (1987) *Origins of Futuristic Fiction*. Athens, GA: University of Georgia Press.

Amis, Kingsley (1960) *New Maps of Hell. A Survey of Science Fiction*. New York: Harcourt.

Angenot, Marc (1979) "The Absent Paradigm: An Introduction to the Semiotics of Science Fiction." *Science Fiction Studies* 6.1 (March): 9–19.

Bacon-Smith, Camille (1999) *Science Fiction Culture*. Philadelphia: University of Pennsylvania Press.

Bailey, J.O. (1947) *Pilgrims Through Space and Time: Trends and Patterns in Scientific and Utopian Fiction*. New York: Argus.

Barr, Marleen S. (1987) *Alien to Femininity: Speculative Fiction and Feminist Theory*. Westport, CT: Greenwood Press.

Baudrillard, Jean (1991) "Two Essays": "Simulacra and Science Fiction" and "Ballard's Crash." *Science Fiction Studies* 18.3 (November): 309–20.

Berger, Albert I. (1993) *The Magic That Works: John W. Campbell and the American Response to Technology*. San Bernardino, CA: Borgo Press.

Bernardi, Daniel Leonard (1998) *Star Trek and History: Race-ing Toward a White Future*. Piscataway. NJ: Rutgers University Press.

Blish, James [as William Atheling, Jr.] (1964) *The Issue at Hand*. Chicago: Advent.

——(1970) *More Issues at Hand*. Chicago: Advent.

Bukatman, Scott (1993) *Terminal Identity: The Virtual Subject in Postmodern Science Fiction*. Durham, NC: Duke University Press.

Clareson, Thomas D. (ed.) (1971) *SF: The Other Side of Realism*. Bowling Green, OH: Bowling Green University Popular Press

Clute, John and Peter Nicholls (eds) (1993) *The Encyclopedia of Science Fiction*. New York: St. Martin's Press; and London: Orbit.

Delany, Samuel R. (1977) *The Jewel-Hinged Jaw: Notes on the Language of Science Fiction*. Elizabethtown, NY: Dragon.

——(1984) *Starboard Wine: More Notes on the Language of Science Fiction*. Pleasantville, NY: Dragon.

Dery, Mark (1994) "Black to the Future: Interviews with Samuel R. Delany, Greg Tate, and Trish Rose," in *Flame Wars: The Discourse of Cyberculture*, (ed.) Mark Dery. Durham, NC: Duke University Press, 179–222.

Donawerth, Jane L. (1997) *Frankenstein's Daughters: Women Writing Science Fiction*. Syracuse, NY: Syracuse University Press.

Eshun, Kodwo (1999) *More Brilliant Than the Sun*. London: Interlink.

Evans, Arthur B. (1999) "The Origins of Science Fiction Criticism: From Kepler to Wells." *Science Fiction Studies* 26:2 (July): 163–86.

Fiedler, Leslie (1965) "The New Mutants." *Partisan Review* 32.iv: 505–25.

Foundation: The International Review of Science Fiction (2002) Special issue: "Gay and Lesbian Science Fiction." No. 86 (Autumn).

Franklin, H. Bruce (1980) *Robert A. Heinlein: America as Science Fiction*. New York: Oxford University Press.

Freedman, Carl (2000) *Critical Theory and Science Fiction*. Hanover, NH: Wesleyan University Press.

Greenland, Colin (1983) *The Entropy Exhibition: Michael Moorcock and the British "New Wave" in Science Fiction*. London: Routledge and Kegan Paul.

Haraway, Donna J. (1991) "A Cyborg Manifesto: Science, Technology, and Socialist-Feminism in the Late Twentieth Century," *Simians, Cyborgs, and Women: The Reinvention of Nature*. (1985) New York: Routledge, 149–81.

Hollinger, Veronica (1999) "Contemporary Trends in Science Fiction Criticism, 1980–1999." *Science Fiction Studies* 26:2 (July): 232–62.

Jameson, Fredric (1982) "Progress Versus Utopia, or Can We Imagine the Future?" *Science Fiction Studies* 9.2 (July): 147–58.

Ketterer, David (1974) *New Worlds for Old: The Apocalyptic Imagination, Science Fiction, and American Literature*. Bloomington, IN: Indiana University Press.

Knight, Damon (1967) *In Search of Wonder* (1956), rev. edn. Chicago: Advent.

Kuhn, Annette (ed.) (1990) *Alien Zone: Cultural Theory and Contemporary Science Fiction Cinema*. New York: Verso.

——(1999) *Alien Zone II: The Spaces of Science Fiction Cinema.* New York: Verso.

Landon, Brooks (1992) *The Aesthetics of Ambivalence: Rethinking Science Fiction Film in the Age of Electronic (Re)Production.* Westport, CT: Greenwood Press.

Lefanu, Sarah (1988) *In the Chinks of the World Machine: Feminism and Science Fiction.* London: The Women's Press.

Lewis, C.S. (1966) "On Science Fiction," in *Of Other Worlds,* (ed.) Walter Hooper. NY: Harcourt Brace and World, 59–73.

McCaffery, Larry, (ed.) (1991) *Storming the Reality Studio: A Casebook of Cyberpunk and Postmodern Science Fiction.* Durham, NC: Duke University Press.

McHale, Brian (1992) *Constructing Postmodernism.* London and New York: Routledge.

—— (1987) *Postmodernist Fiction.* London and New York: Methuen.

Moylan, Tom (1986) *Demand the Impossible: Science Fiction and the Utopian Imagination.* London and New York: Methuen.

Parrinder, Patrick (ed.) (1972) *H.G. Wells: The Critical Heritage.* London: Routledge and Kegan Paul.

Penley, Constance et al. (eds.) (1991) *Close Encounters: Film, Feminism and Science Fiction.* Minneapolis, MN: University of Minnesota Press.

Rabkin, Eric S. (1976) *The Fantastic in Literature.* Princeton, NJ: Princeton University Press.

Roberts, Robin (1993) *A New Species: Gender and Science in Science Fiction.* Urbana, IL: University of Illinois Press.

Rose, Mark (1981) *Alien Encounters: Anatomy of Science Fiction.* Cambridge, MA: Harvard University Press.

Science Fiction Studies (1999) Special issue: "Science Fiction and Queer Theory." 26:1 (March).

Sobchack, Vivian (1987) *Screening Space: The American Science Fiction Film.* New York: Ungar.

Sontag, Susan (1966) "The Imagination of Disaster," *Against Interpretation,* New York: Farrar, 209–25.

Stableford, Brian (1985) *Scientific Romance in Britain, 1890–1950.* New York: St. Martin's Press.

Sterling, Bruce (ed.) (1986) *Mirrorshades: The Cyberpunk Anthology,* New York: Arbor, 1986.

Suvin, Darko (1979) *Metamorphoses of Science Fiction: On the Poetics and History of a Literary Genre.* New Haven, CT: Yale University Press.

Tate, Greg (1994) *Flyboy in the Buttermilk: Essays on Contemporary American Culture.* New York: Simon and Schuster.

Westfahl, Gary (1998) *The Mechanics of Wonder: The Creation of the Idea of Science Fiction.* Liverpool: Liverpool University Press.

—— (1999) "The Popular Tradition in Science Fiction Criticism, 1926–1980." *Science Fiction Studies* 26:2 (July): 187–212.

Wolfe, Gary K. (1979) *The Known and the Unknown: The Iconography of Science Fiction.* Kent, OH: Kent State UP.

Wolmark, Jenny (1994) *Aliens and Others: Science Fiction, Feminism, and Postmodernism.* Hemel Hempstead: Harvester Wheatsheaf, 1994.

Zamyatin, Yevgeny (1970) "H.G. Wells," in *A Soviet Heretic. Essays by Yevgeny Zamyatin,* (ed.) Mirra Ginsburg. Evanston, IL: Northwestern University Press, 259–90.

4

Science Fiction Magazines: The Crucibles of Change

Mike Ashley

The science fiction magazine has been the primary driving force in the generation of science fiction for some 80 years. Its heyday was in the 1940s and 1950s, and though its potency has faded in recent years, with its role relegated largely to the sidelines, its potential remains. The day of the science fiction magazine is not over yet.

Unfortunately today the very existence of the SF magazine is largely unknown to the vast science fiction market that the magazines helped create. It has also become confused with the science fiction media magazine, which concentrates on cinema and television and runs no science fiction at all. Yet it remains a truism that no country has developed its own body of science fiction writers without having a regular SF magazine and the majority of the leading SF writers throughout the world learned their craft through the SF magazine.

In this chapter I want to look not only at the key magazines and editors and the parts they played in the shaping of the genre but also at the current fate of the magazines and whether they still exert an influence and have a part to play.

Origins

The early history of the SF magazine is possibly well enough known, but it is important to understand because of how it shaped the nature of the beast from the start.

The growth in science fiction arose in the 1890s out of the public's fascination with various forms of scientific development. Top of this list were the achievements of Thomas Edison and, to a lesser degree, Nikolai Tesla. The approach of a new century encouraged speculation in what was to come, and magazines of the day – both in Britain and the USA – were full of stories, articles, and illustrations on future inventions. There were plenty of other factors: the first heavier-than-air manned flight and the rapid development of the airplane; speculation on the future of warfare, in particular the use of aircraft and submarines. The race for both the North and South Poles caught the public's imagination for exploration, as did the approach of Haley's comet in 1910. There was the increasing role of women and female emancipation. And last, but not least, the rise of socialism. All of these were powerful factors disrupting the status quo, for good or for ill, and it was common for all of the leading magazines of the day to run some story or feature on social and scientific change.

The soil was perhaps most fertile in the 1890s, but in those days there were no specialist magazines. Even so the June 1890 issue of *Overland Monthly*, inspired by Edward Bellamy's utopian novel *Looking Backward, 2000–1887* (1888), dedicated itself to looking forward to the twentieth century, whilst from 1892 to 1898 Frank Tousey published nearly 200 issues of the dime novel series *Frank Reade Library*, each volume featuring an adventure arising out of some new invention.

The pulp magazine, which would be the future home of the science fiction magazine, evolved from the dime novel though, not through the work of Frank Tousey. Frank A. Munsey, who had issued his own dime novel series *The Golden Argosy*, converted it to an all-fiction pulp magazine in 1896, as *The Argosy*, and it was in this magazine that a whole generation of scientific adventure writers would emerge, led primarily by Edgar Rice Burroughs. Munsey's rivals, Street and Smith, who would later buy up Frank Tousey's titles, converted their dime novels into pulps from 1915 onwards and, in the process, issued the first true specialist genre magazine, *Detective Story Magazine*, in October 1915.

It may seem surprising that neither Munsey nor Street and Smith issued a magazine composed entirely of scientific adventure stories but, despite their popularity, neither publisher envisaged a sufficient market. This was to some degree proved when, in 1919, Street and Smith issued a specialist adventure magazine, *The Thrill Book*, styled after the very popular *Adventure* magazine, but running a fair proportion of strange and pseudoscientific stories. It was originally published in dime novel format and then converted to a pulp after eight issues, but it failed after sixteen issues. Likewise when Chicago publisher Jacob Henneberger began *Weird Tales* in 1923, admittedly undercapitalized, it had difficulty finding a market and, had it not been for his determination, would have folded after the first year. It seemed very evident at the time that despite the popularity of the scientific adventure the public's interest had peaked during the period 1890–1910, and had even been depressed during the First World War.

The only reason a science fiction magazine appeared at all was because it was aimed at a very specialist market. This was not the general public, whose interest was satiated enough by the stories in the existing magazines, but the specialist experimenter and inventor. Luxembourg émigré, Hugo Gernsback, had been building a clientele through his catalogue for scientific components since 1905. In 1908, he developed the catalogue into a magazine, *Modern Electrics*, which ran articles aimed at stimulating the fertile technological mind. It was here that Gernsback serialized his novel "Ralph 124C 41+" with the sole view of encouraging the young mind to experiment. Gernsback began a new magazine, *The Electrical Experimenter*, in 1913 which published a much wider range of scientific articles, for which reason it was retitled *Science and*

Invention in 1920. Here he regularly published a scientific story each issue. Initially they featured little more than new uses for radio, but steadily the contributors' creativity improved. It is perhaps no surprise that two of his most regular contributors, George F. Stratton and Clement Fezandie, had also written for the juvenile market. Although Gernsback aimed his magazine at all ages, he was convinced that it was the young inventor who would be the most creative, the new Edison, and it was their minds that he wanted to stimulate.

As a consequence it was for the sole purpose of encouraging scientific creativity that what Gernsback called "scientifiction," grew in his magazines. Much the same approach was adopted by the Swedish magazine *Hugin* (April 1916–December 1920; 82 issues) compiled by Otto Witt, which was also filled with speculative articles and fiction. Gernsback included a special "scientifiction" section in the August 1923 *Science and Invention* and this laid the path for the first all "scientifiction" magazine, *Amazing Stories*, first issue dated April 1926.

Gernsback immediately had a problem. It was one thing to publish one or two invention or "gadget" stories, few of them of any consequence, each month in a technical magazine. It was an entirely different matter to fill a magazine with them. There just were not sufficient good stories being written, and a magazine full of "gadget" stories would soon become monotonous. Instead Gernsback relied on reprints: initially Jules Verne, H.G. Wells, and Edgar Allan Poe, plus some of the Munsey writers like Murray Leinster and Garrett P. Serviss and especially Edgar Rice Burroughs and Abraham Merritt. Gernsback still hoped that these stories would stimulate scientific creativity whilst entertaining the readers, but in fact he had bitten off more than he could chew. He created a magazine of adventure stories where, in most cases, the science was so speculative or fanciful – especially in the Merritt stories, which Gernsback later regretted reprinting – that they might stimulate awe in the reader but it did not lead them into the laboratory.

There were a few good writers capable of producing quality science fiction. The best in the early years were Miles J. Breuer and David H. Keller both, intriguingly, physicians. Keller was one of the few to consider the social consequences of scientific development in stories like "The Revolt of the Pedestrians" and "Stenographers' Hands." Other writers, however, looked to the stars. Both Edmond Hamilton, whose career had started in *Weird Tales*, and Edward E. Smith developed "cosmic" science fiction, moving beyond the boundaries of the solar system with stories of "super-science." They were soon joined by Jack Williamson – whose early stories were inspired by Merritt – and John W. Campbell, Jr.

Readers of *Amazing Stories* responded to the "super science" and it was soon selling around 150,000 a month. However, it was evident that the gaudy covers by Frank R. Paul and the gosh-wow adventures were attracting a younger and less discerning readership. Gernsback was all for encouraging the young reader but not at the expense of bastardizing science fiction, but this is what was happening. Having launched a science fiction magazine upon the world Gernsback very rapidly lost control over its contents. Moreover his payment rates, both low and slow, alienated many writers.

Murray Leinster was one of the more promising Munsey writers of science fiction but his agent counseled against him writing it (because of a limited market) or dealing with Gernsback. Ray Cummings, then the most prolific writer of science fiction, only sold reprints to Gernsback and new material to *Science and Invention* – and only then because the Munsey market had dwindled.

What had happened in the first three years of *Amazing Stories* is that Gernsback had established a market that placed the emphasis on adventure rather than good science and dressed it in immature clothing. Although these early issues of *Amazing* were not in the standard pulp format – they were the same large flat size of his technical magazines and printed on a thicker paper – they were certainly pulp in terms of content and style.

Gernsback's poor payment practices led to him being sued for nonpayment by his major creditors and being declared bankrupt in February 1929. *Amazing Stories* (and its new companion *Amazing Stories Quarterly*) continued under a new publisher but Gernsback bounced back. He set up a new imprint and issued a stream of new magazines: *Science Wonder Stories*, *Air Wonder Stories*, *Science Wonder Quarterly*, and *Scientific Detective Monthly*. It was at this time that Gernsback coined the term "science fiction," because he was advised that "scientifiction" was a trademark associated with *Amazing Stories*.

This sudden explosion of science fiction titles and the obvious success of Gernsback's venture attracted other publishers, chiefly William Clayton, who issued a range of pulp magazines. In December 1929, he published the first issue of *Astounding Stories of Super Science*, the first true SF pulp. Clayton was a well-established publisher with a reliable (and generous) payment policy. Agents and regular pulpsters had no problem in dealing with Clayton and as a consequence authors whom Gernsback had had difficulty attracting flocked to Clayton, along with Gernsback's own writers. What's more Clayton's editor, Harry Bates, was interested only in profit, not the promotion of science. He had little concern over the accuracy of scientific concepts, but simply wanted a good adventure story. The writers who responded, mostly but not all Clayton regulars – Arthur J. Burks, Charles Willard Diffin, Sewell Peaslee Wright, Ray Cummings – knew how to tell a good story but did not worry about scientific accuracy. Even the more discerning writers – Murray Leinster, S.P. Meek, Harl Vincent, Jack Williamson – were less than cautious and before long *Astounding* had brought science fiction down to the lowest common denominator. Critic R. Jere Black, reviewing the medium for the May 1930 *Author and Journalist*, felt that the field had few redeeming qualities and was narrowly formulaic – essentially: hero rescues damsel from villain or monster. In effect, though the term had yet to be coined, "space opera" had been created, its roots firmly in the Burroughs-Smith-Hamilton school of writing. Though this had initially been encouraged by Gernsback, it was beyond his original scope for strict 'scientifiction," which had been closely limited to invention stories. Gernsback had created a market for science fiction but had rapidly lost control of it and within four years it had deteriorated to a juvenile literature of little merit.

This is perhaps a sweeping generalization. There was good SF appearing in all of the magazines, particularly the works of Keller, Raymond Z. Gallun, P. Schuyler Miller, Leslie F. Stone, and Drury D. Sharp, but it was dwarfed by the cosmic extravaganzas of E.E. Smith and John W. Campbell, Jr., in particular; and by the more puerile adventures in *Astounding Stories*. Even Gernsback seemed to have sold out to the opposition. In June 1930 he merged *Science Wonder* and *Air Wonder* as *Wonder Stories*, dropping "science" from the title, because it was a deterrent to sales, and five months later he converted *Wonder Stories* to pulp format.

It is important to consider this background for the following reason. Gernsback has been accused of forcing SF into the "ghetto" rather than letting it flourish in the mainstream, but Gernsback did not do that. He created a specific market for SF that should have allowed it to grow – and eventually that would happen – but he was not a good father to this new infant and let it run riot. Pretty soon it was playing in someone else's garden and turning delinquent. What he did, in effect, was "juvenilize" science fiction, though it was due more to Harry Bates and others yet to come that science fiction earned its poor reputation. But as an infant medium, science fiction needed to go through the juvenile growing pains before it could mature. Gernsback may take the blame for being a poor father, but he had established a world in which that infant could grow. What's more he set about corrective action, in what would be the first of a series of SF revolutions.

The First Transformation

Through the specialist magazines science fiction would undergo four transformations: in 1931, 1939, 1950, and 1964. The fact that the last was 40 years ago says something about the state of the SF magazine, though there may be a case to make that two further seeds were sown in the magazines in the early 1980s for further transformations, most of which happened outside the SF magazine. I shall return to this later.

The first transformation was the work of Gernsback himself with his astute editor David Lasser. Gernsback was not happy with the way SF had so rapidly degenerated, and neither were his readers. There was movement in the fledgling SF fandom to produce a revolutionary taboo-breaking SF magazine, but the lack of finances meant that when William Crawford's *Marvel Tales* eventually appeared in 1934 it was a curiosity item. It did, however, publish Clifford Simak's "Creator," P. Schuyler Miller's "The Titan," and Robert Bloch's first story, so it cannot be dismissed entirely.

By then Lasser had got to grips with changes at *Wonder Stories*. As early as May 1931 he had exhorted his contributors to deal with science fiction "realistically" and avoid the "world-sweeping epic." Writers responded. Edmond Hamilton toned down his cosmic work to consider the social and ecological aspects of technology. Nathan Schachner explored technocracy and the impact of science on industry. P. Schuyler Miller, Leslie F. Stone, and Frank K. Kelly considered the potential pitfalls of space travel, with Clark Ashton Smith embellishing the exotic horrors. Laurence Manning likewise considered ecological and industrial futures, especially in his Wellsian "The Man Who Awoke" series, whilst Stanley G. Weinbaum, arguably Gernsback's greatest discovery (through his new editor, Charles Hornig), brought a human dimension to the alien.

During 1932 and 1933 *Wonder Stories* was the most exciting SF magazine on the stands. At last it was starting to deliver its original promise – good writers producing quality fiction. One example may suffice: "The Forgotten Man of Space" (May 1933) by P. Schuyler Miller, the first story to consider aliens sympathetically and to question the role of space exploration and colonization.

Unfortunately Gernsback had neither the finances nor, after he fired David Lasser in 1933 for his involvement in the union movement, the capacity to develop science fiction further. Lasser's successor, Charles Hornig, was only seventeen, and though advanced for his years he lacked the experience or editorial clout to acquire quality material, especially as authors and agents were again shunning Gernsback because of nonpayment. In 1933, William Clayton had also gone bankrupt and been forced to sell his titles. *Astounding Stories* was acquired by Street and Smith, who now had a vehicle to produce the type of magazine they might have created fifteen years earlier. Street and Smith was amongst the biggest publisher of magazines, with considerable finances and a superior distribution network. Their reputation meant that they were able to attract all the leading writers, pay good rates, and get the magazine noticed. They placed F. Orlin Tremaine in charge of the magazine, a man with much editorial experience and a fondness for weird fiction. Although he did not have the same attitude towards science fiction as Gernsback, he knew what was needed and was ably supported by his assistant Desmond Hall.

During 1934 and 1935, when *Wonder Stories* struggled to survive, *Astounding* went from strength to strength. It lured away from Gernsback most of the major writers, including Weinbaum, and developed many of its own. Gernsback eventually gave up the battle in early 1936, selling *Wonder* to Standard Magazines where it was retitled *Thrilling Wonder Stories*. It and its later companion *Startling Stories* would have a part to play in the third revolution nearly 20 years later.

"Super-science" remained at the core of *Astounding*'s science fiction, even though it was no longer part of the title. It ran great cosmic adventures by E.E. Smith, Jack Williamson, and John W. Campbell – "The Skylark of Valeron," "The Legion of Space," and "The Mightiest Machine" were all serialized during 1934 – and it instigated the idea of a "thought variant" story, something challenging and new, which brought original contributions from Nat Schachner, Donald Wandrei, John Russell Fearn, Murray Leinster, and Jack Williamson. But there was also the start of a subtle change. First John W. Campbell, writing as Don A. Stuart, and then Raymond Z. Gallun, contributed softer, more human stories, much the same as Lasser had encouraged at *Wonder*. Indeed the revolution started by Lasser shifted seamlessly to *Astounding*, particularly with the work of Schachner and Weinbaum, and laid the foundation for the second transformation.

The Second Transformation

During an editorial reshuffle at Street and Smith in 1937, John Campbell was brought on board to work on *Astounding*, first as assistant and, within months, as full editor. Campbell had strong views on what constituted good science fiction, though much of it echoed Lasser's realistic approach. Campbell took it the next natural step. He wanted SF stories to read as if they were topical stories appearing in a magazine of the future. That meant much of the background could be taken for granted and did not need extensive asides and footnotes. It also meant a more personal approach. But he also wanted a logical scientific extrapolation. In effect Campbell was reinstating Gernsbackian SF, but a maturer form that had shed its juvenile excesses. He also retitled the magazine substituting "Science Fiction" for "Stories" and even fading "Astounding" into the background. He would have preferred to have called the magazine simply *Science Fiction* had not Charles Hornig got their first, and it was not until 1960 that Campbell completely broke with the old and renamed the magazine *Analog*.

Under Campbell SF grew up, which is why he is often called the father of "modern" science fiction – though "modern" is rather time sensitive and has long since moved on.

Much has been written about Campbell's role in SF and need not be repeated in detail here. Campbell was a strong-minded editor and few of the old guard could work with him. Some, especially Jack Williamson, E.E. Smith, and Clifford Simak responded immediately to his demands. Some who had entered SF in Tremaine's latter days – L. Sprague de Camp, Ross Rocklynne, Eric Frank Russell (who became Campbell's favorite author) – fitted in naturally. But most of the old guard found it easier to continue to sell the same, less mature fiction, to the growing SF market, especially *Thrilling Wonder* and the newly revamped *Amazing Stories* under Raymond Palmer. *Astounding* soon stood out as the one quality SF magazine amongst a sea of mediocrity. It meant Campbell had to develop his own stable of writers and it was thus under Campbell that Robert A. Heinlein, A.E. van Vogt, Isaac Asimov, L. Ron Hubbard, Fritz Leiber, Theodore Sturgeon, and Lester del Ray, to name but a few, entered the fold. The July 1939 *Astounding* is often pointed to as signaling the start of the "Golden Age" of science fiction, or more appropriately, of *Astounding*, chiefly because it contains the first appearances of van Vogt and Asimov, but it is a fairly arbitrary selection. The transformation had been happening throughout 1938 and 1939 and every issue both added something new and said farewell to something old.

Astounding stood alone as the leading SF magazine throughout the War years, even though the period 1938–1941 saw an explosion in the number of new SF magazines. Most of these, such as *Marvel Science Stories* that led the boom, stuck to the traditional form of SF. Others, particularly those edited by and filled by the Futurian group of authors and editors, which included Donald A. Wollheim, Frederik Pohl, Robert W. Lowndes, and Cyril Kornbluth, could draw on sufficient new talent to create a school of their own, and also attracted the best of Campbell's rejected work. Their magazines, particularly Pohl's *Astonishing Stories* and *Super Science Stories*, suffered only from underfunding, but were amongst the best of the second tier, and gave their editors much valuable experience. Lowndes in particular, with *Future Fiction*, showed his ability to achieve high quality with next to nothing. Lowndes' magazines were always worth sampling because he made them very personal without crossing that line into fannishness.

The significance of *Astounding*'s "Golden Age," though, is that it did not transform the SF world overnight. Campbell's revolution had certainly brought maturity to SF, but little of this permeated the rest of the field. It reached the nadir of immaturity under Palmer in *Amazing Stories* and in such hero pulps as *Captain Future*. It was not until the start of the nuclear age at the close of the Second World War, that the rest of SF sat up and took notice. Wartime rationing had marked the end of many SF magazines and most of the survivors were still pandering to either the nostalgia market (*Famous Fantastic Mysteries*), the younger adventure-orientated readership (*Planet Stories*), or the cult market (*Amazing Stories*, where Palmer was riding high on the excesses of the "Shaver Mystery," which maintained that human activities were subject to control by remnants of past god-like humans who had lived on Earth millennia ago). All these magazines responded to the postwar maturing of SF, though Palmer took his time. The best were *Thrilling Wonder* and *Startling Stories* under new editor Samuel Merwin. Merwin was able to work with many of Campbell's writers, especially Hubbard and Henry Kuttner, and by the end of the 1940s his magazines had become a good quality second stream to *Astounding*.

Unfortunately the War had a more significant impact upon science fiction. The fear of nuclear war, and consequent mutations, plus the emerging Cold War with the Soviet Union, meant that magazines became full of nuclear threat and mutant stories. The most popular form of mutation involved psi powers, a field in which Kuttner (writing mostly as Lewis Padgett), Hubbard, van Vogt, and Leiber thrived. Despite the quality of their fiction, the theme became a rot that set in, especially in *Astounding*, and began to undermine its lead. Campbell became fascinated with alternative sciences and the power of the mind, and supported Hubbard in the development of dianetics in 1950. The result was that although *Astounding* continued to dominate the field, its lead was diminished and it left itself open to rivals.

The postwar fixation with science saw a further boom in the SF magazine market, starting in 1950 and peaking in 1953. It was during this period that the pulp magazines began to fold or transform into the new, popular digest size. *Astounding* had already made this transition in 1943. The last SF pulp was *Science Fiction Quarterly*, edited by Lowndes, which ceased publication at the end of 1957 (last issue dated February 1958). So the transition from pulp to digest spread over fourteen years, but the impetus for change came in 1949/1950 when most of the emerging SF magazines were digests – *The Magazine of Fantasy and Science Fiction* (*FandSF*), *Other Worlds*, *Imagination* and, most important of all, *Galaxy*. It was the success of *Galaxy* that encouraged most new magazines to copy this format, and it was also *Galaxy* that ushered in the third transformation.

The Third Transformation

Galaxy was the brainchild of Horace L. Gold, a former Campbell author but who, as a result of the war, had developed agoraphobia and undertook much of his work from the confines of his apartment. His desire was for well-written, sophisticated SF, a cut above the level of the ideas-orientated stories in *Astounding*. He wanted his stories to reflect the changes in society, via the soft sciences rather than the hard. This was not always apparent in the early issues but through Gold's forceful taskmaster approach, the authors – many of them from Campbell's stable – began to adapt. *Galaxy*'s leading stars included Clifford Simak, Theodore Sturgeon, and Fritz Leiber, and also developed Frederik Pohl, Cyril Kornbluth, and Ray Bradbury, plus new writers Robert Sheckley and Philip K. Dick. Bradbury's "The Fireman" (February 1951), the novella behind *Fahrenheit 451*, was perhaps *Galaxy*'s first major story. *Galaxy* thrived in putting the SF twist on the paranoia of the Cold War and McCarthyism, and there is no doubt that the SF magazines in general, but especially *Galaxy*, became the refuge for the anti-McCarthyites and the voice against repression.

Galaxy made a strong mark in the market place, resulting in many imitations. Through its original publisher it also spawned an Italian edition and throughout the 1950s *Galaxy* became perhaps the most international of magazines, with editions in many European countries. It was thus one of the main factors in spreading SF about the globe. It also developed arrangements for the adaptation of stories for radio, especially in the series *X Minus 1*. *Galaxy* probably did more than any other magazine in the 1950s for the globalization and popularization of science fiction. *F&SF* also had a number of non-English editions, the most important of which was the French *Fiction*, started in October 1953. Edited for much of its life by Alain Dorémieux, *Fiction* was the longest lived of all European SF magazines, surviving for 412 issues until eventually folding in February 1990.

One thing that *Galaxy* claimed it would do, but never really did, was challenge taboos. Gold, for all his temerity, was also ultracautious in upsetting his market, and though he would publish the occasional risqué story, such as "Dark Interlude" by Mack Reynolds and Fredric Brown (January 1951), which deals with racial prejudice, he tended to reject most. These included "A Canticle for Leibowitz" by Walter M. Miller, which went to *F&SF*, and "The Lovers" by Philip José Farmer, which went to *Startling Stories*. In fact Raymond Palmer's *Other Worlds* probably published more taboo-breaking stories than *Galaxy*. But developing SF was not just about breaking taboos, which change with every new generation. It was about improving the quality, sophistication, and characterization of SF so that it became real stories with real people. If the early pulps had forced SF into a ghetto, it was Campbell who provided it with the means of escape, and Gold who gave it a new world to explore.

It needed one more revolution to effect that change, or try to, but that did not come for another ten years. In the meantime the SF magazine field suffered almost irretrievably. In the late 1950s a host of factors, but predominantly distribution problems and the challenge from television, paperbacks, and comic books, rocked the whole magazine field, not just SF. Magazines folded in their hundreds and circulation dropped. At the peak of the SF boom in 1953 there had been 28 separate SF magazines in the USA alone, plus several fantasy titles like *Weird Tales* and *Beyond*. By the end of 1960 there would be only six. It seems ironic that at the dawn of the Space Age when space travel had become a reality and old-guard SF fans could puff up their chests with pride, that the SF magazines suffered such a major setback. In fact they have never really recovered from it, despite momentary bursts of enthusiasm, primarily because the sales in the SF market shifted to the paperback. This was part of the fourth transformation.

The Fourth Transformation

The next revolution began in Britain rather than the USA. Britain had produced its first SF pulp magazine in 1937, *Tales of Wonder*. There had been an earlier boys' adventure weekly, *Scoops*, which had failed disastrously, but which gave some indication of what British publishers considered the market for science fiction. The Second World War curtailed any further developments but during the 1950s Britain had a good selection of magazines led by *New Worlds*, edited by John Carnell, plus its Scottish rival, *Nebula*. *New Worlds* was a close cousin to *Astounding* and its pages (and those of its companion *Science Fantasy*) saw the development of many leading British writers, amongst them Brian W. Aldiss, John Brunner, J.G. Ballard, and Michael Moorcock. Carnell saw the writing on the wall for the magazine, however, and in 1964 determined to close down *New Worlds* and instead produce a regular quarterly anthology series, *New Writings in SF*. That series was not the first all original anthology series – that had started with Frederik Pohl's *Star SF* from Ballantine in 1953 – but it was the first of a new breed and was rapidly imitated in America by a whole host of series, including *Orbit*, *Universe*, *Nova*, and *New Dimensions*. Many expected this to be the future of SF, but it turned out to be a fad. None of these anthologies sustained the same level of circulation as the regular magazines, and most of them lacked the persona and editorial identity. Important though they are (many award-winning stories appeared in these anthologies), they did not prove to be the transformation that some thought. Later attempts to issue magazines in regular paperback form also failed. The best was *Destinies* edited by Jim Baen starting in 1978. The concept even overtook *New Worlds* and *Weird Tales* for a while.

However, when Carnell left *New Worlds*, it continued under Michael Moorcock and Moorcock instigated what became known as the SF "New Wave." Moorcock was anxious for science fiction to stop following its conventional ways but to become more experimental and daring. The New Wave was thus more about format, style, and presentation than content, though at its extremes the content became almost unrecognizable as SF. In fact champions of the New Wave, especially Judith Merril, believed the phrase "science fiction" was no longer relevant and used "SF" either as a neologism in its own right or redefined it as "speculative fiction." Writers like J.G. Ballard, Brian W. Aldiss, Langdon Jones, and Charles Platt in Britain, and Thomas M. Disch, Norman Spinrad, and Harlan Ellison in America, welcomed the change. For a period around 1966–68 some of these authors found they could only publish their preferred material in Britain unless, like Ellison, they issued their own anthology – in his case the ground-breaking *Dangerous Visions*. Disch admitted that he would not have written "Camp Concentration" had it not been for *New Worlds*. Likewise, it is unlikely that Spinrad's "Bug Jack Barron" would have been published at that time.

The New Wave split SF between the traditionalists and the experimentalists. Most American magazine markets remained traditional and the American New Wave developed in the anthology series, especially Damon Knight's *Orbit*. Frederik Pohl sought the best of both worlds. He had taken over *Galaxy* from Horace Gold in 1960 and had made it a more adventure-oriented magazine. However, he now switched the traditional adventure story to the companion magazine *If* (which had been one of the survivors of the SF boom) and made *Galaxy* more experimental, a direction that was pushed further by Pohl's successor Ejler Jakobssen in 1969.

Like all waves, the New Wave eventually crashed onto the shore and dissipated, but it had made its mark. Thereafter SF, like most fiction during the 1960s, became more liberated, not just in its language and sexual freedom, but in its portrayal of society. SF became more streetwise and in fact the New Wave laid the groundwork for the Cyberpunk movement of the early 1980s. Cyberpunk, in its portrayal of a controlled technology society and the blurring of virtual reality, was a natural extension of the New Wave. The term itself was first used in the story called "Cyberpunk" by Bruce Bethke which appeared, perhaps surprisingly, in *Amazing Stories* (November 1983). Despite many tribulations and transformations, *Amazing* had somehow survived. It had undergone two periods of resurgence. In the early 1960s, editor Cele Goldsmith made it the major market for such new writers as Roger Zelazny, Thomas M. Disch, Piers Anthony, and Ursula K. Le Guin. In 1959, Goldsmith published the first Russian SF story in an American postwar magazine, "Initiative" by Boris and Arkady Strugatski, though Gernsback had again led the way, having reprinted "The Revolt of the Atoms" by V. Orlovksy from the Russian magazine *Mir Prikliuchenii* in the April 1929 *Amazing*. In the early 1970s, Ted White's more radical editorship made *Amazing* the most New Wave of the surviving magazines. There had been further editorial changes but during the early 1980s, mostly under George Scithers, *Amazing* became open once again to a huge diversity of fiction.

By the 1980s, the SF magazine market had again withered. There had been many comings and goings. There had been several experiments with format. The first flat size semi-slick magazine had been *Science Fiction Plus* as far back as 1953 but it never made the transformation to a full format slick. The first to do that was the British/ Australian magazine *Vision of Tomorrow* in 1969, though this was never able to raise the necessary advertising base. Magazines that for a while looked like they might burn a new trail, such as *Vertex* in 1973, the first American SF slick magazine, blossomed and withered within a few years. In fact *Vertex* also became America's first tabloid SF magazine in its final incarnation (in 1975). Magazines came and went and many of the old guard also failed. Both *Galaxy* and *If* had gone by the end of the 1970s, although there were occasional resurrections. The only new magazine of lasting significance was *Isaac Asimov's SF Magazine*, which appeared in 1977. It immediately outsold *Analog* and, for a while, gave new hope to the ailing magazine market. *Asimov's* provided a refreshing mix of both light science fiction, such as the early stories of Barry Longyear, and, under the later editorship of Gardner Dozois, experimental fiction.

One feature that was becoming common to almost all of the magazines was the insurgence of fantasy fiction. This had mushroomed in the late 1960s following the paperback publication of *The Lord of the Rings* and it was soon followed by the popularization of dark fantasy and weird horror with the success of Stephen King and Dean R. Koontz, both of whom had made their earliest sales to the SF and fantasy magazines. Some responses, like *Worlds of Fantasy* in 1968, made little impact, but later magazines like *Rod Serling's The Twilight Zone* Magazine (which, in discovering Dan Simmons, made a significant contribution to the later development of SF) and the current *Realms of Fantasy* were important. Even the most die-hard of SF magazines ran some fantasy. Although Anne McCaffrey's Pern stories had a solid scientific base, and were published as hard SF in *Analog*, when issued in paperback they were marketed as fantasy. *Analog* had fought back, especially after the death of Campbell in 1971. His successor, Ben Bova, radically changed the magazine to publish more hard-hitting SF. Campbell had managed to defy the New Wave, but Bova incorporated it through writers like Frederik Pohl, Harlan Ellison, and especially Joe Haldeman with his "Forever War" sequence. Bova's successor, Stanley Schmidt, restored some of the old traditionalism and under him *Analog* continues as the premier hard-SF magazine.

In fact hard-SF and cosmic space opera, much outlawed by the New Wave, began to make a comeback in the 1980s. This was fuelled primarily by the success of TV series such as *Star Trek* and, more significantly, the *Star Wars* sequence of films. Authors once again began to think on huge canvases. This had never quite gone out of style. Interestingly it had been Campbell who had helped develop one of the last great space operas under his regime and arguably the first of the new brand of space operas, the Dune sequence by Frank Herbert, which had started in *Analog* as far back as 1963. The call for the revival of "radical, hard SF" appeared not in the US magazines but in Britain, in the semi-professional *Interzone*. Although this had started as a *New Worlds* clone, it rapidly developed a separate identity with a mission to rejuvenate SF, especially British SF. During 1984, a series of editorials by David Pringle and others once again challenged writers to be radical, just as had happened in 1931, 1939, 1950, and 1964, so that *Interzone* could really be seen as having instigated the fifth SF transformation. However, although the magazines played their part, most of this return to the magnum space opus happened in books where the new decimeter-thick blockbusters gave space to explore the cosmic.

The reunion of science and science fiction was also helped by the publication of *Omni*, which had started in October 1978. *Omni* was really a science magazine that celebrated scientific achievement — it was a 1970s style *Science and Invention* that ran several stories per issue. To some it looked like science fiction was coming home. *Omni*, however, cost a fortune to produce and, although it survived for 17 years, it fell victim to the economic uncertainties of the mid-1990s and the attempts to develop its subscription base.

Magazine circulation had been dwindling since 1988. In that year *Analog* was the last SF magazine to have a paid circulation in excess of 100,000, 83 percent of which was through subscriptions. Newsstands accounted for only 17 percent of sales, compared to 71 percent in 1965. The latest figures to hand (2002) show that *Analog's* total paid circulation has dropped to 42,000, of which 79 percent was through subscription. Distribution, which has always been the bane of a magazine's existence, is now at its poorest and all of the surviving professional magazines, *Analog*, *Asimov's*, *F&SF*, and *Realms of Fantasy*, survive primarily on direct subscription. Average circulation has halved since 1986 and continues to fall.

The shift from newsstand sales to subscription occurred dramatically in the period 1979–82 at the same time that the total number of professional SF magazines were dropping and the number of small press titles were increasing. Small press magazines had been around since William Crawford's *Marvel Tales*, but only with circulations of a few hundred. The increase in computer technology and the rise in specialist shops and a subscription base made the semi-professional magazine a viable option. Hybrids like *Galileo* appeared in 1976 and *Rigel* in 1981. Most of these titles have been short-lived but *Space and Time* has been appearing since 1966, steadily working up the ranks from a fan magazine to a semi-pro. The British *Interzone*, supported by Arts Council grants, has appeared regularly since 1982. Many of the small press magazines have been of significant merit. Especially worthy was *Unearth*, which saw only eight issues in 1977–79, but endeavored to be a market for new talent and discovered a high quota of new writers, including Paul di Filippo, Rudy Rucker, James Blaylock, and Craig Shaw Gardner. *Pulphouse* appeared as a quality hardcover magazine, an experiment that worked well for three years, but an attempt to revamp it as a weekly standard magazine in 1991 was seriously misguided. The semi-professional magazines had the chance to experiment with design, content and frequency in a way the commercial professionals could not and though few of the semi-prozines survived they were a constant source of originality and energy, providing much needed vigor to the SF field.

Today the number of semi-prozines exceeds the professionals and includes such venerable names as *Weird Tales* and the recently renamed *Fantastic*. Other countries have also found the semi-prozine a viable approach — Canada's *On-Spec*, which has appeared regularly since 1989 and Australia's *Aurealis* since 1990. Most non-English language magazines are semi-professional, although some countries support magazines with a healthy circulation, most notably *S-F Magazine* in Japan. This started in February 1960 as a Japanese edition of *F&SF* but soon developed a vibrant originality.

The demise of the SF magazine has been predicted for the last thirty years, but it continues to survive and remains the lifeblood of the field. More people may buy paperbacks or watch films or, increasingly, access webzines on the internet, and though all of these other media have challenged the SF magazine, it is still to the SF magazines that new writers turn when exploring their craft or experimenting with ideas. Many books still emerge from series or stories first published in magazines and without them the genre would stagnate. This was very evident in Britain in the 1970s when *New Worlds* faded away and no long-lasting magazine took its place for nearly ten years. New writers had nowhere to turn other than to the American magazines and it was not until *Interzone* established itself that a new generation of British writers – Kim Newman, Paul McAuley, Stephen Baxter, Eric Brown, Alastair Reynolds, and many more – emerged and prospered.

In recent years science fiction media magazines have dominated the field leading to some SF magazines seeking to benefit by association. In its last incarnation *Amazing Stories* bought into the *Star Trek* franchise, whilst *Science Fiction Age* became more media orientated. Both magazines had taken on the full slick format, which requires considerable advertising revenue to support costs. Specialist fiction magazines have never attracted such a level of advertising, as *Analog* discovered when it was forced into the slick format by its then new publisher Condé Nast back in 1963. Other slick magazines have come and gone and currently only *Realms of Fantasy*, the companion to *Science Fiction Age*, continues to appear, also with decreased sales.

The SF magazines may no longer sit alongside the major publications. They have become like the wind from the sun, invisible yet exerting a powerful force. They are not only the crucible in which the field constantly regenerates itself, but they are also the field's conscience and mentor. Despite predictions of their demise, SF magazines are likely to continue in one form or another because the field needs them and though their numbers and sales may be diminished, their importance, like black holes, is beyond measure.

*

Key Magazines

The following is a selective list of the key English-language magazines. It identifies their first and last issues and, in brackets, the total number of issues published. This refers to physical copies, and ignores the conceit of counting double issues as two. All magazines are American unless otherwise stated. They are listed in alphabetical order of the most common form of their name.

Aboriginal SF, October 1986–Spring 2001 (65); merged with *Absolute Magnitude*, Fall 1994–*current* (21 to end of 2003)
Amazing Stories, April 1926–Summer 2000 (602)
Amazing Stories Quarterly, Winter 1928–Fall 1934 (22)
Analog (formerly *Astounding Stories* and *Astounding SF*), January 1930–*current* (885 to end of 2003)

Asimov's SF, Spring 1977–*current* (317 to end of 2003)

Astonishing Stories, February 1940–April 1943 (16)

Aurealis [Australia], September 1990–*current* (29 to end of 2003)

Authentic SF [UK], January 1951–October 1957 (85)

Beyond, July 1953–[Winter] 1955 (10)

Captain Future, Winter 1940–Spring 1944 (17)

Comet, December 1940–July 1941 (5)

Destinies, November 1978–August 1981 (11); succeeded by *Far Frontiers* (Winter 1985–Winter 1986; 7) and *New Destinies* (Spring 1987–Fall 1990; 9)

Famous Fantastic Mysteries, September 1939–June 1953 (81). It had two companion near identical magazines, *Fantastic Novels* (July 1940–April 1941; revived March 1948–June 1951; 25) and *A. Merritt's Fantasy Magazine* (December 1949–October 1950; 5).

Fantastic (companion to *Amazing Stories*), Summer 1952–October 1980 (208). This superseded *Fantastic Adventures*, May 1939–March 1953 (129). Not to be confused with the current *Fantastic* which was a retitling of *Pirate Writings* (Winter 1992–*current*; 24 to end of 2003).

Fantastic Universe, June/July 1953–March 1960 (69)

Fantasy [UK], [Summer] 1938–[Summer] 1940 (3). Not to be confused with the postwar UK magazine *Fantasy*, December 1946–August 1947 (3)

Future SF (began as *Future Fictioni* and was briefly retitled *Science Fiction Stories*), November 1939–July 1943; revived May/June 1950–April 1960 (65)

Galaxy, October 1950–July 1980; revived January/February 1994–March/April 1995 (262); it has also existed as a webzine.

Galileo, September 1976–January 1980 (15)

If (latterly known as *Worlds of If*), March 1952–November/December 1974; revived September 1986 (176)

Imagination, October 1950–October 1958 (63)

Impulse (UK; really a continuation of *Science Fantasy*), March 1966–February 1967 (12)

Infinity, November 1955–November 1958 (20)

Interzone [UK], Spring 1982–*current* (192 to end of 2003)

The Magazine of Fantasy and Science Fiction, Fall 1949–*current* (608 to end of 2003)

Marvel Science Stories (also as *Marvel Tales*, *Marvel Stories* and *Marvel SF*), August 1938–April 1941; revived November 1950–May 1952 (15)

Marvel Tales, May 1934–Summer 1935 (5)

Nebula SF [UK], Autumn 1952–June 1959 (41)

New Worlds [UK], [Summer] 1946–September 1979; revived September 1991–Winter 1996 (221)

Omni, October 1978–Winter 1995 (200)

On Spec [Canada], Spring 1989–*current* (55 to end of 2003)

Other Worlds, November 1949–July 1953; revived May 1955–October 1957 (47). A complicated title which, during its hiatus, became *Science Stories* (October 1953–April 1954; 4) and then took over and replaced *Universe SF* (June

1953–March 1955; 10). With its final four issues it gradually metamorphosed into the nonfiction magazine *Flying Saucers*.

Planet Stories, Winter 1939–Summer 1955 (71)

Pulphouse, Fall 1988–Summer 1993 (12); also as a weekly magazine, 1 March 1991–August 1995 (19)

Realms of Fantasy, Fall 1994–*current* (56 at end of 2003)

Rod Serling's "The Twilight Zone" Magazine, April 1981–June 1989 (60)

Satellite SF, October 1956–May 1959 (18)

Science Fantasy [UK], Summer 1950–February 1966 (81). Superseded by *Impulse*.

Science Fiction, March 1939–September 1941 (12); revived as *Science Fiction Stories* [Summer] 1953–May 1960 (38). Cover logo gave impression title was *The Original Science Fiction Stories* from September 1955 onwards.

Science Fiction Adventures, November 1952–May 1954 (9)

Science Fiction Adventures, December 1956–June 1958 (12). Gave rise to a UK edition that became a separate magazine, March 1958–May 1963 (32)

Science Fiction Age, November 1992–May 2000 (46)

Science Fiction Monthly [UK], February 1974–May 1976 (28)

Science Fiction Plus, November 1952–December 1953 (7)

Science Fiction Quarterly, Summer 1940–Spring 1943; revived May 1951–February 1958 (38)

Space and Time, Spring 1966–*current* (98 to end of 2003)

Space SF, May 1952–September 1953 (8)

Space Stories, October 1952–June 1953 (5)

Spectrum SF [UK], February 2000–November 2002 (9)

Star SF, January 1958 (1). Only magazine issue of paperback anthology series.

Startling Stories, January 1939–Fall 1955 (99)

Super Science Stories, March 1940–May 1943; revived January 1949–August 1951 (31)

Tales of Wonder [UK], [Summer] 1937–Spring 1942 (16)

The Third Alternative [UK], Winter 1994–*current* (36 to end of 2003)

Tomorrow, January 1993–February 1997 (24). Briefly became a webzine.

Unearth, Winter 1977–Winter 1979 (8)

Unknown, March 1939–October 1943 (39)

Venture SF, January 1957–July 1958; revived May 1969–August 1970 (16)

Vertex, April 1973–August 1975 (16)

Vision of Tomorrow [UK], August 1969–September 1970 (12)

Weird Tales, March 1923–September 1954 (279); revived Summer 1973–Summer 1974 (4), Spring 1981–Summer 1983 (4), Fall 1984–Winter 1985 (2), Spring 1988–*current* (44; in total 333 to end of 2003). Includes a brief existence as *Worlds of Fantasy and Horror* (Summer 1994–Winter 1996).

Wonder Stories (began as *Science Wonder Stories* and became *Thrilling Wonder Stories*), June 1929–Winter 1955 (189)

Wonder Stories Quarterly (began as *Science Wonder Quarterly*), Fall 1929–Winter 1933 (14)

Worlds of Tomorrow, April 1963–May 1967; revived Summer 1970–Spring 1971 (26)

References and Further Reading

Ashley, Michael (1974) *The History of the Science-Fiction Magazine, Part One, 1926–1935*. London: New English Library; Chicago: Henry Regnery.

—— (1975) *The History of the Science-Fiction Magazine, Part Two, 1936–1945*. London: New English Library; Chicago: Henry Regnery.

—— (1976) *The History of the Science-Fiction Magazine, Part Three, 1946–1955*. London: New English Library; Chicago: Contemporary Books.

—— (1978) *The History of the Science-Fiction Magazine, Part Four, 1956–1965*. London: New English Library.

Ashley, Mike (2000) *The Time Machines: The Story of the Science-Fiction Pulp Magazines from the beginning to 1950*. Liverpool: Liverpool University Press.

Bleiler, Everett F. and Bleiler, Richard J. (1998) *Science-Fiction: The Gernsback Years*. Kent, OH: Kent State University Press.

Carter, Paul (1977) *The Creation of Tomorrow: Fifty Years of Magazine Science Fiction*. New York: Columbia University Press.

Davin, Eric Leif (1999) *Pioneers of Wonder*. Amherst, NY: Prometheus Books.

Hartwell, David (1984) *Age of Wonders*. New York: Walker.

Knight, Damon (1977) *The Futurians*. New York: John Day.

Malzberg, Barry (1982) *The Engines of the Night*. Garden City: Doubleday.

Miller, Stephen T. and Contento, William G. (2002) *Science Fiction, Fantasy and Weird Fiction Magazine Index (1890–2001)*. Oakland, CA: Locus Press. CD-ROM. The definitive index to all SF and fantasy magazines, updated regularly.

Moskowitz, Sam (1963) *Explorers of the Infinite*. Cleveland, OH: World Publishing.

—— (1966) *Seekers of Tomorrow*, Cleveland, OH: World Publishing.

—— (1970) *Under the Moons of Mars: A History and Anthology of "The Scientific Romance" in the Munsey Magazines, 1912–1920*. New York: Holt, Rinehart and Winston.

Panshin, Alexei and Cory (1989) *The World Beyond the Hill: Science Fiction and the Quest for Transcendence*. Los Angeles, CA: Jeremy Tarcher.

Robinson, Frank M. (1999) *Science Fiction of the 20th Century*, Portland, OR: Collectors Press.

Rogers, Alva (1964) *A Requiem for Astounding*. Chicago, IL: Advent Publishers.

Rosheim, David L. (1986) *Galaxy Magazine: The Dark and the Light Years*. Chicago, IL: Advent Publishers.

Tymn, Marshall B. and Ashley, Mike, (eds) (1985) *Science Fiction, Fantasy and Weird Fiction Magazines*. Westport, CT: Greenwood Press.

Westfahl, Gary (1998) *The Mechanics of Wonder: The Creation of the Idea of Science Fiction*. Liverpool: Liverpool University Press.

PART II
Topics and Debates

5

Utopia

Phillip E. Wegner

Any discussion of Utopian in relationship to science fiction needs to begin by first distinguishing between the specific genre of Utopian literature and what we can describe as a more general Utopian impulse. The latter refers to the deeply human desire for an utterly transformed, radically other, and/or redeemed existence, a desire that manifests itself in a wide range of cultural documents. Being that which remains fully alien to our current form of life, Utopia in this first sense is fundamentally unrepresentable, and thus becomes evident only indirectly through figures, images, signs, or traces scattered throughout a text. While such notable students of Utopia as Ernst Bloch and Fredric Jameson point out the ubiquity of such figures of the Utopian impulse – which we can find in everything from children's toys and classical music to fascist propaganda, free market ideologies, and Hollywood films like *The Godfather* – they have a specially prominent role in the imaginative worlds of science fiction. To point toward only a few examples, manifestations of this Utopian impulse occur in the image of the postinvasion world of H.G. Wells' *War of the Worlds* (1898), in the new and unexpected realm of freedom announced at the end of Alfred Bester's *The Stars My Destination* (1956), in the collective entity Man seen in Joe Haldeman's *Forever War* (1975), in the declarations that conclude the Strugatsky brothers' *Roadside Picnic* (1977), and in the Earthseed project of Octavia Butler's *Parable* novels (1993 and 1998). Haldeman's vision is especially revealing in this regard, in that it also highlights the existential anxiety that any encounter with such an alien existence produces for us.

If manifestations of such a Utopian impulse are abundant, the works that compose the genre of the literary Utopian form a much more limited set. There have been numerous attempts to define the genre, two of the more significant being those offered by noted literary and science fiction critic Darko Suvin and political theorist Lyman Tower Sargent. Suvin defines the literary Utopian in this way: "Utopia is the verbal construction of a particular quasihuman community where sociopolitical institutions, norms, and individual relationships are organized according to a more perfect principle than in the author's community, this construction based on estrangement arising out of an alternative historical hypothesis" (Suvin 1979: 49). There are a number of aspects of this definition worth highlighting. First, Suvin's notion of the "quasihuman" aspect of the Utopian community marks the difference between this genre and a number of kin forms, such as myths of the Golden Age or millenarian visions: these communities are very much presented as part of (or potentially a part of) our world, subject to same natural laws, and the products of human rather than divine or mystical labors. In short, Utopian is a materialist rather than idealist genre – something that is also the case in the later genre of science fiction, which bears such a deep kinship to Utopian.

Second, Suvin stresses the ways works making up this genre focus on the larger collective social and cultural machinery – sociopolitical institutions, norms, and relationships – rather than individual characters or character psychology. Indeed, a good deal of the creative energy in any particular Utopian text is invested in the detailed description of the various practices, institutions, values, beliefs, and so forth of this fictional world. In this respect, Utopian literature reveals its roots in the prose romance rather than the later form of the novel, the romance taking as its central project, as Jameson maintains, the mapping of space – something that is also the case, he argues elsewhere, for science fiction. The critical commonplace that holds that all classical Utopian fictions describe homogenous worlds without a place for the individual are thus the result of a basic category confusion, applying to the Utopian form the very different criteria of the novel.

Finally, Suvin's definition emphasizes the inseparable link between any specific Utopian and the historical context out of which it emerges. That is, any individual Utopian vision appears as "more perfect" only in comparison to the society of its historical moment, and we run into great difficult in our reading if we forget this context and evaluate these visions according to the values and practices of our own cultural and social moment. Moreover, the Utopian text takes up a critical role – what Suvin means by his use of the Brechtian concept of "estrangement" – in relationship to that context: through its presentation of this alternative community, the Utopian narrative has the effect of both highlighting in a negative light many of the problems of the reigning social order and, perhaps even more significantly, of showing that what is taken as natural and eternally fixed by the members of that society is in fact the product of historical development and thus open to change. Once again, as Suvin emphasizes throughout his criticism, this operation of estrangement is a central dimension of the very best work of science fiction as well.

Sargent begins by defining the Utopian most broadly as "a nonexistent society described in considerable detail and located in time and space." As with Suvin, Sargent stresses a number of crucial things in this concise definition: the fictional status of the society represented in these works, the amount of effort expended in elaborating the various social machineries of this fictional society, and the particular location of this imaginary world within our universe. However, the real value of Sargent's intervention lies in his elaboration upon this foundation of a rich typology of various expressions of the Utopian narrative form. Each is differentiated from the others, he argues, according to the individual author's "intentions" in developing her vision. Thus, in the "eutopian or positive Utopian," the form that most immediately comes to mind when we think of the genre of the literary Utopian, the author offers us a detailed description of a nonexistent society that he intends "a contemporaneous reader to view as considerably better than the society in which that reader lived." However, in the "dystopia or negative Utopian" (the form of Utopian narration that, as we shall see momentarily, only came into its own in the last century), the author intends a contemporaneous reader to see the society described in the text "as considerably worse than the society in which that reader lived." In the "Utopian satire," the vision offered in the text is meant "as a criticism of that contemporary society;" while in the "anti-Utopian" it serves "as a criticism of Utopianism [which Sargent defines as "social dreaming"] or of some particular eutopian." Finally, in the most recent of these subgenres to emerge, the "critical Utopian," the society presented in the work is intended to be understood as "better than contemporary society but with difficult problems that the described society may or may not be able to solve and which takes a critical view of the Utopian genre" (Sargent 1994: 9). With this, Sargent emphasizes the fact that these various practices cannot be considered in isolation from each other and that all are parts of the larger genre of the Utopian. Moreover, any particular Utopian text can embody simultaneously different aspects of this typology, although one tends to be dominant. Of course, recovering the author's intentions after the fact can often be a difficult task, and there is nothing to prevent a reader from misreading any particular literary Utopian, often with the result being a protracted and sometimes heated debate about the work's meaning.

What might be less apparent in either Suvin's or Sargent's definitions, however, is the relatively recent emergence and thoroughgoing modernity of Utopian as a literary institution. Utopian is one of those relatively rare genres that has a precise moment of birth, as both the form and the term itself come into being in 1516 with the publication of the great English Renaissance humanist Thomas More's masterpiece, *Utopia*. This is not to say that there were not portrayals of ideal societies or forms of social dreaming preceding More's work. Indeed, these imaginings are probably as old as human history itself. To take only a few of the more well-known examples, there are the ideal societies represented in Plato's *Republic* and *Laws*; in the earthly paradises and Golden Age visions of the Judeo-Christian biblical book of Genesis or in the works of the classical authors Pindar and Hesiod; in Augustine's *City of God*; and in the popular medieval folk tales of the Land of Cockaigne and of the kingdom of Prester John. In fact, we know that some of these older visions were among the diverse resources drawn upon by More in the composition of his work. Nor is such an imagining the exclusive property of the Western and European world, Utopian strands being evident, for example, in Confucianism and classical Chinese poetry. However, the specific formal strategies deployed by More set the template for subsequent work in the genre, and a great number of the earliest works make explicit their reliance upon their predecessor.

More's Latin text is composed of two short Books, the second of which was written before the first. In Book One, More tells of his meeting while on a diplomatic mission with the imaginary traveler Raphael Hythlodaeus. Their ensuing conversation touches on a wide range of issues of contemporary concern, including the then accelerating enclosure of common lands and the massive displacement of rural populations that occurred as a result (these insights were praised by Karl Marx in *Capital*); the dissolution of the older feudal retainer system; the crime of theft and its punishment; the dangers of standing armies; private property; the best way for a prince to rule his people; and the advisability of a philosopher serving as an advisor to the monarch (a role More himself would soon take up). Then, in order to demonstrate the possibility of living in other ways, Hythlodaeus describes certain aspects of a few of the societies he has visited, including those of the Polylerites, the Achorians, and the Macarians. If More had chosen one of these other fictional titles as that of the kingdom described in Book Two, we might be referring to the genre, as well as the more general form of social dreaming, by another name (Achorian literature? Macarianism?). All of this then opens up onto Hythlodaeus' detailed description in Book Two of the form of life he finds in Utopia. Hythlodaeus' goal in Book Two is best summed up in his famous statement near the conclusion of his discourse, a statement that might also be taken as a definition of the genre to which he has just given birth: "Now I have described to you, as exactly as I could, the structure of that commonwealth (*Reipublicae*) which I judge not merely the best but the only one which can rightly claim the name of a commonwealth" (More 1965: 237). Hythlodaeus' narration is wide-ranging, and includes, among other things, a description of the geography and founding of the Utopian community; the layout of their cities; their political institutions; occupations and working day; dress; household structure; dining habits; forms of travel and trade; use of gold and silver; moral philosophy; education; medicine; marriage customs; legal structures; foreign relations; attitudes toward and engagement in war; and religious practices. This narrative structure – where a visitor describes or has described to her in great detail the organization of social and cultural life in this community – will be a commonplace in many subsequent works in the genre. While Hythlodaeus remains convinced of the superiority of all aspects of Utopian society to that which currently exists in Europe, the character of More is a bit more skeptical, although he admits, without however offering any specific guidelines, "There are many things in the Commonwealth of Utopia which I wish our own country would imitate – though I don't expect it will."

With these closing words, More begins a debate that will continue throughout subsequent discussion of this work and others in the genre: how seriously are we to take the author's vision? There is an ambiguity already at play in the term Utopia: is it a compound of the Greek roots, "no (*ou*) place (*topos*)" or "happy (*eu*) place;" or even both? Does More mean to tell us that we should take his work as simply a display of humanist wit and creative linguistic play, much like his friend Erasmus' *Praise of Folly* (1509); or as a critique of contemporary society, presented in an indirect way so that its author might escape censure for his heterodox views; or as a workable plan of an alternative society; or all of these, and more? Hythlodaeus' Greek surname too has been translated as "expert in trifles" or "well-learned in nonsense" – but does this mean that we dismiss his vision, as some would do, as sheer silliness and fantasy, or does More mean in this way to highlight the fact that from within the dominant perspective of his moment, Hythlodaeus' insights can only appear as nonsense, thus ironically commenting on the narrowness and lack of imagination to be found in those who rule? There is no way to definitely answer these questions, and debate will continue for a long time to come.

However, what is clear is that many of More's contemporaries were struck by the singular power of his unique work, and would follow his lead in creating their own "Utopians." And it is these first readers – readers that include More himself, who continues to work in the new genre in the mini-Utopians of Book One (remember, written after Book Two) – who create the genre of Utopian. They perform what literary critic Gary Saul Morson calls a "re-authoring" of More's text: "In an important sense, it is really the *second* work of a genre that creates the genre by defining conventions and *topoi* for the class. Read in the context of the second and subsequent works, the style of the first becomes the grammar of the class, and its idiosyncratic themes and rhetorical devices are rediscovered as the motifs and tropes of a tradition" (Morson 1981: 75). Without these later readers and writers, *Utopia* would have remained a brilliant and original contribution to Western literature, a tribute to the tremendous creative energy of More's time and place, but would not be the progenitor of a new genre that would have a tremendous impact of the subsequent history of modern life.

One of More's first readers was his French contemporary, François Rabelais, who would not only refer explicitly to the Utopian people in the second book (1532) of his great work, *Gargantua and Pantagruel*, but also includes in its first book (actually first published two years later) his own Utopian fiction, entitled "The Abbey of Thélème." Rabelais not only helps establish the new genre, but also offers one of the first critiques of More's vision. Rabelais replaces the strict regulation of so many aspects of daily life evident in More's Utopia with a society whose fundamental maxim is "Do as Thou Wouldst," where there are no clocks, where people are encouraged to come and go as they please, and where sensual pleasures and sumptuous dress are celebrated. The couple of More and Rabelais establish a pattern that will recur throughout the subsequent history of the genre. Sargent points out two strands of social dreaming that predate More's founding work in the genre, which he calls the "Utopians of sensual gratification or body Utopians" and "the Utopian of human contrivance or the city Utopian." The former is exemplified for him in the fables of the Land of Cockaigne and the latter by Plato's *Laws*. However, with More and Rabelais, these two poles come into a dialectical coordination, one standing as the determinate negation of the other. This pattern of thesis and antithesis is then repeated later in the history of the genre when, for example, William Morris offers his *News From Nowhere* (1890), with its sensual and pastoral vision of an "epoch of rest" as a direct "reply" to the highly structured urban existence portrayed in Edward Bellamy's monumentally influential *Looking Backward* (1888); and when Samuel Delany writes his "ambiguous heterotopia," *Triton* (1976) as among other things a critical commentary on Ursula K. Le Guin's *The Dispossessed: An Ambiguous Utopia* (1974).

The centuries following the publication of *Utopia* witness a proliferation of literary Utopians that explicitly take More's work as their model. Some of the more prominent examples include Johann Valentin Andreae's *Christianopolis* (1619), Tommaso Campenella's *City of the Sun* (1623), Francis Bacon's *The New Atlantis* (1627), Gabriel Platt's *A Description of the Famous Kingdom of Macaria* (1641), Gerrard Winstanley's *The Law of Freedom in a Platform* (1651), James Harrington's *The Commonwealth of Oceana* (1656), and Margaret Cavendish's "The Inventory of Judgements Commonwealth, the Author Cares not in what World it is established" (1655) and *The Description of a New World, call'd The Blazing-world* (1666). The full titles of Harrington's and Cavendish's first Utopian also point toward a central contribution that More's work would make not only to the genre but also to modern life more generally: for Utopia is not only the one place that could lay the claim to being ordered in the interest of the "public good" – the older definition of the Latin term *respublica* or its subsequent English translation "a common weale" – but is also the only place that was already a "commonwealth" as the term would subsequently be defined, as a synonym for the modern nation-state. The imaginary community contributes to the establishment of what Benedict Anderson calls the "imagined community," as More's work, and the genre to which it gives birth, helps to establish the nation-state as the "natural" scale for imagining collective social and cultural belonging. While there will be notable exceptions – an early example being Campanella's *City of the Sun* (1623 – the majority of the most influential achievements in the genre over the next few centuries will take the nation-state as the scale for Utopian imaginings. This is true even of a work like Bacon's, for while it appears that the concerns with society as a whole that were so central to More, and which once again come to the fore in Winstanley's and Harrington's Utopians, had apparently given way to a more particular interest in promoting the institution of the new "natural philosophy," or empirical science, it was precisely through the emerging institutions and ideologies of science that the "modernity," and hence the historical uniqueness, of the society as a whole, the English nation-state, proclaims itself in the first half of the seventeenth century.

Two of the most important Utopian works published in the eighteenth century mark significant developments within the genre. Jonathan Swift's *Gulliver's Travels* (1726) signals the growing influence of what Sargent calls the "Utopian satire." Swift tells the story of the four sea journeys of Lemuel Gulliver, and his adventures in the lands of the miniscule Lilliputians, the gigantic Brobdingnagians, the abstract and theoretically inclined Laputans, and the hyper-rational horse creatures, the Houyhnhnms. Not only does the culturally conservative Swift use these various communities as a tool for parodying the excesses of the Enlightenment middle class, his work also, especially in its third and fourth books, satirizes earlier Utopians such as Bacon's *New Atlantis* and Plato's *Republic*, and the more general Utopian desires of his historical moment. Swift's work would not only serve as a the model for later Utopian satires such as Samuel Butler's *Erewhon* (1872), but also would be an important resource for the development of the dystopia and anti-Utopian forms that will play such a central role in the twentieth century.

In its presentation of Gulliver's journeys, Swift's work continues in the tradition of the Utopian travel narrative established by More. The French writer Sébastien Mercier's *The Year 2440: A Dream if There Ever Was One* (1771), however, marks the definitive transformation of the Utopian into a "uchronia," the voyage occurring in time rather than in space and the Utopian community thereby becoming a vision of a transformed present. *The Year 2440* tells the story of discontent contemporary of Mercier who falls asleep, only to awaken in a twenty-fifth century Paris that has changed dramatically. Intimations of this shift from space to time as the vector of Utopian travel are already present in More's founding fiction. There is evidence in *Utopia* to suggest that we view the Utopian nation as an England transformed: for example, Utopia's 54 cities are the equivalents of the 53 counties and the city of London in historical England; the strange ebb and flow of Utopia's Anydrus River is the same as that of the Thames; and the description of the river's bridge makes it almost identical to London Bridge. However, what can at best only be implied in More's fiction becomes explicit in *The Year 2440*; or as Paul Alkon puts it, the originality of Mercier's work lies in the fact that "his Utopian is given a local habitation, a real name, and a real if distant date" (1987: 118). Although largely forgotten today, the book was wildly successful in its own day, despite initially being banned in France and by the Catholic Church. By the century's end, it had gone through eleven French editions, was quickly translated into a number of languages, and is the first Utopian text published in the USA (copies were owned by George Washington and Thomas Jefferson). Moreover, its influence on the subsequent development of the Utopian genre is inestimable. The dream narrative form likely influenced Bellamy and Morris, and the use of the date as the work's title would be a device of the single most important Utopian narrative of the twentieth century, George Orwell's *Nineteen Eighty-Four* (1949).

The late eighteenth and early nineteenth centuries was a great period of change and revolutionary ferment in Europe and elsewhere. Not surprisingly, this moment witnessed not only an outpouring of Utopian writings, but also to the establishment of a number of experimental Utopian communities, what are now referred to as "intentional communities," within the then recently founded USA and in the territories bordering it. Some of these communities – such as those of the Shakers, the German pietist Amana community, and the Christian perfectionist Oneida settlement – were religiously based, while others were founded on the ideas and principles presented in the work of the group who would later be described as "Utopian socialists" by Friedrich Engels in his influential pamphlet, *Socialism: Utopian and Scientific* (1880). Among the most prominent of these Utopian socialists were the Scottish industrialist and reformer Robert Owen, who founded the communities of New Lanark in Scotland and New Harmony in southern Indiana; the French thinker, Henri de Saint-Simon, who argued for the formation of a common European union whose peaceful industrialization would be led by an enlightened scientific, philosophical, technical, and artistic elite; and Saint-Simon's brilliant and eccentric countryman Charles Fourier, who in his *Theory of Four Movements and of the General Destiny* (1808) and other voluminous writings proposed the dismantling of the restraints imposed on the natural passions, and the reorganization of society into a series of "phalansteries," economic units of 1620 people, with all labor being divided according to people's natural tendencies.

One of the more interesting and now largely forgotten figures of this moment, who himself bridged the gap between Utopian fiction and social experimentation, was the French political radical and author Etienne Cabet. While in exile in England for his political activities, Cabet encountered Owen's Utopian socialism and, even more significantly, read More's *Utopia*. Inspired by their ideas, he produced his own Utopian fiction, *Voyage in Icaria* (1840). This work was a tremendous success, and it led to Cabet to become the leader of a Utopian socialist political movement whose membership at its peak was said to number 400,000. However, as time passed Cabet became increasingly frustrated by both the slow pace of change in France and the increasing governmental persecution of his followers, and he decided to lead a group to the USA to form a colony based on the principles he had outlined in his fictional work. Despite the protests of Marx and others, a small group departed for Texas in February 1848. After a series of fiascos, in part brought on by crooked land dealings and in part by their lack of preparations for the harsh conditions of rural Texas, the initial colony was soon abandoned. It would exist in a fitful state until the end of the century in a few other locations, including Nauvoo, Illinois, the former settlement of the Mormons. However, Cabet himself, becoming increasingly inflexible and intolerant, was purged from the community a few years later, and died in 1856 in St. Louis an embittered man.

It was later in the century and from the USA that the single most influential Utopian fiction of the nineteenth century would emerge. Although the American novelist and influential taste-maker, William Dean Howells (who later would also write his own Utopian fiction, *A Traveler in Altruria* [1894]) once called him "the first writer of romance in our environment worthy to be compared with Hawthorne," Edward Bellamy was a journalist and minor man of letters until the 1888 publication of *Looking Backward, 2000–1887* thrust him into international fame. *Looking Backward* tells the story of upper-middle-class Julian West who is cast into a hypnotic slumber, only to awaken in a new Boston in the year 2000. The bulk of the narrative follows the major contours of the classical Utopian, Julian being introduced to the wonders of the new world by his host, Dr. Leete (although Bellamy did spice things up by including a romantic interest in Dr. Leete's daughter, who turns out to the be the descendant of West's nineteenth-century fiancé). Here, West discovers a world in which the political chaos, social divisions, and incipient violence of his own moment have been replaced by a rational and equitable system, the labor force organized into a pyramidal "Industrial Army" and the circulation and distribution of goods occurring through a standardized and centralized national system of warehouses. William Morris described this vision as a "cockney paradise" (Kelvin 1996: 59), one content to leave in place the main contours of industrial civilization, and Morris would offer an agrarian world of simplicity, beauty, and unalienated labor in his celebrated and influential "reply," *News From Nowhere* (1890).

Few books in the history of American letters can rival the contemporary success of *Looking Backward*. In the USA alone, the book sold more than 200,000 copies within two years of publication, 400,000 by the appearance of its sequel *Equality* (1897) – an extension and revision of some of the elements of *Looking Backward* – and it eventually became only the second American work of fiction with sales to surpass the one million mark. It was also widely circulated in Great Britain, and translations were soon executed in German, French, Norwegian, Russian, and Italian. The book's literary influence was equally tremendous: it spawned hundreds of imitators, "sequels," and responses, ranging from Ludwig Geissler's simplistic defense, *Looking Beyond* (1891), to Arthur Dudley Vinton's deeply critical dystopia, *Looking Further Backward* (1890). *Looking Backward* is so central to the explosive growth of the literary industry of Utopian that Kenneth Roemer dates his survey of American Utopian fiction from its publication. Moreover, the work had a direct impact on the political discourse of its day. *Looking Backward* even gave birth to a political movement, named Nationalism by Bellamy himself, which while short-lived, did influence both the emerging platform of the Populist Party and progressive calls for, among other reforms, the nationalization of public utilities. All of this led the philosopher John Dewey, the historian Charles Beard, and the publisher Edwin Weeks in 1935 to judge Bellamy's narrative of all the works published in the preceding half century second in importance only to Marx's *Capital*.

An increasingly diverse group of literary Utopians continued to be produced in the early years of the twentieth century. Perhaps the most significant English language writer of these Utopians at this moment, H.G. Wells, also played a prominent part in the establishment of the modern genre of science fiction. Beginning with *A Modern Utopia* (1905) – a work that draws inspiration from Bacon's *New Atlantis* and presents a vision of a clean, orderly, and efficient society, a triumph of rational organization and centralized planning, directed by the Samurai, a voluntary scientific and bureaucratic elite – and continuing in later works such as *Men Like Gods* (1923) and *The Shape of Things to Come* (1933), Wells produced a wealth of influential Utopian visions to complement his now more well-known science fiction stories and novels. Indeed, it was Wells' Utopian fictions more than any others that became the target of later critiques of Utopianism more generally. The new century also saw the re-emergence of a rich tradition of Utopian speculation in Russia. These fictions looked back to Nikolai Chernyshevsky's *What is to be Done?* (1863), a work that would serve as a major inspiration for the Russian revolutionary movements, and which would become the target of Fyodor Doestoevsky's bitter scorn in *Notes from the Underground* (1864), a landmark work in the development of anti-Utopianism. The most significant and widely circulated of these new Russian Utopians was written by Alexander Bogdanov, a colleague of Lenin and an important figure in his own right in the 1905 Russian Revolution. Bogdanov's *Red Star* (1908) tells the story of a young revolutionary's journey, via space craft, to the planet Mars, a world where the norms of individualism and competitive capitalism have been supplanted by those of collectivism and egalitarian socialism, and where money, compulsory work, and artificial limits on personal consumption have been eliminated. (Bogdanov would tell the story of the founding of this Utopian society in his prequel, *Engineer Menni* [1913].) These years also saw the publication of the US writer Charlotte Perkins Gilman's Utopian fictions, "A Woman's Utopia" (1907), *Herland* (1915), and the latter's sequel, *With Her in Ourland* (1916). As the titles of these works suggest, Gilman was one of the first English language Utopian writers to put the issue of gender and women's rights at the center of discussion (gender issues had in fact been given more prominence in Russian Utopian fiction). Gilman's influence on the development of Utopian fiction would become even more pronounced in the 1970s with the "rediscovery" of *Herland*.

Three crucial developments occur in the first part of the twentieth century that will influence the development of the genre in the years to come. First, the older vision of a Utopian as a location "somewhere else" in the world continues to wane, and Utopian is increasingly identified with speculations concerning the future. (There are, of course, some notable exceptions to this trend, among them, James Hilton's *Lost Horizon* [1933], B.F. Skinner's *Walden Two* [1948], and Aldous Huxley's *Island* [1962].) One consequence of this development is that Utopian writing more and more is read as a subset of the expanding genre of science fiction, so much so that Suvin will later describe Utopian as the "sociopolitical subgenre of SF" (Suvin 1988: 38). Second, there is a growing sense within the genre of the insufficiency of the older form of the nation-state as the container for Utopian speculation and experimentation (an identification that still very much holds, for example, in Bellamy's work). Wells makes this shift explicit in the opening pages of *A Modern Utopia*: "No less than a planet will serve the purpose of a modern Utopia. Time was when a mountain valley or an island seemed to promise sufficient isolation for a polity to maintain itself intact from outward force. . . . But the whole trend of modern thought is against the permanence of any such enclosures . . . World-state, therefore, it must be" (Wells 1967: 11–12). However, rethinking community in this global framework would not be an easy thing – just as the nation-state is not the local writ large, so the global is so much more than a planetary nation-state – and a good deal of the energy in Utopian writing of the last century, and indeed up until our present moment, would be invested in the efforts to re-imagine the very nature of communal belonging on a new global scale.

The final event will perhaps have the greatest consequences for the development of the genre: the emergence and growing influence of the dystopia. Some of the most prominent dystopias in the first half of the century include E.M. Forster's "The Machine Stops" (1909), Karl Čapek's play *R.U.R.* (1920) (which also gave us the word, "robot") and *The War With the Newts* (1936), Yvengy Zamyatin's *We* (1920), Fritz Lang's film *Metropolis* (1926) – one of the first of the many film dystopias produced in the century – Aldous Huxley's *Brave New World* (1932), and most importantly of all, Orwell's *Nineteen Eighty-Four* (1949). The modern dystopia develops in the latter part of the nineteenth century by way of a fusion of what would appear at first glance to be two very different genres: on the one hand, the literary Utopian with its vision of a future other world, and on the other, the naturalist novel, which offers a bleak picture of both the present and humanity more generally. Not surprisingly, Jack London, the author of one of the first great modern dystopias, *The Iron Heel* (1908) – a book that would have a marked influence on radicalism in the USA, Russia, and elsewhere – was also one of the leading practitioners of naturalism. Orwell also makes this link explicit when he writes to the publisher of his masterpiece, "I will tell you now that this is a novel about the future – that is, it is in a sense a fantasy, but in the form of a naturalistic novel. That is what makes it a difficult job – of course as a book of anticipations it would be comparatively simple to write" (1998: 329–30).

Perhaps the most significant legacy of naturalism to dystopian fiction lies in its vision of human nature: if at the heart of the classical "eutopian" there is not only the belief in the possibility of historical movement and progress but an assumption of the potential for improvement, if not perfectability, of human beings, in naturalism humanity is presented as animalistic in nature, ruled by the most primitive instincts of self-preservation, uncontrolled passion, violence, and a lust for power. Thus, at the heart of naturalism lies the belief that society can, at best, contain these drives, but not overcome them. The differences between the vision of the future and of human- ity that naturalism bequeaths to dystopia and that found in the classical Utopian is summed up in *Nineteen Eighty-Four* in the Inner Party member O'Brien's chilling speech to the idealistic, even Utopian, protagonist Winston Smith: "But always – do not forget this, Winston – always there will be the intoxication of power, constantly increasing and constantly growing subtler. Always, at every moment, there will be the thrill of victory, the sensation of trampling on an enemy who is helpless. If you want a picture of the future, imagine a boot stamping on a human face – forever" (Orwell 1949: 220).

Many of the great dystopias paint a far more complex picture than often assumed. Zamyatin's *We* offers a rich schema of different Utopian "possible worlds," and even maintains an open-ended Utopian horizon in its intimations of the "world" of the "infinite revolution;" Huxley's *Brave New World* contains hints of a Utopian primi- tivism that will be realized more fully in *Island*; and *Nineteen Eighty-Four* critiques both the superpowers, US mass media culture as much as Soviet state bureaucracy, that emerge in the aftermath of the Second World War. (Moreover, there is a debate whether the book's Appendix, "The Principles of Newspeak," without which Orwell refused to allow the book to be published, also represents a dim kind of Utopian hope.) However, what is unquestionable is the fact that these works are often read as express- ing a more general anti-Utopianism, and thereby they become crucial ideological weapons in an assault on all forms of Utopian thinking, or even of social planning. This is precisely the role that Orwell's fiction was called upon to have in the strug- gles of the Cold War, as it was often read not only as a denunciation of the horrors of Stalinst Soviet Union, but as a more general attack on the misguided efforts of intellectuals and political activists in the previous century to transform society in some fundamental way – or even for having the temerity to imagine that such a sweeping change might be possible. Utopia was now understood as a dangerous naivety, if not a direct path to the Gulag, and the environment became more and more unfavorable to any form of eutopian fiction and speculation. This is evident in the general reception of the psychologist B.F. Skinner's Utopian, *Walden Two* (1948), which despite the cautious experimental nature of its proposals, arguing as it does for a more general application to social problems of the tenets of Skinner's behaviorist psychology, had the misfortune to be published only a year before *Nineteen Eighty-Four* and was unfairly measured against it.

However, such a general anti-Utopianism proves to be a position that is difficult to maintain for very long, and many dystopias also contain strains of what the sociologist Karl Mannheim calls a "conservative Utopian." (In his important work, *Ideology and Utopia* [1929], Mannheim produces a schema of what he calls the four "ideal types" of the Utopian mentality, a schema that is useful for thinking about work in the genre as well.) According to Mannheim, the mentality underlying such fictions contrasts with that of the "liberalism" found in most eutopians:

> Whereas for liberalism the future was everything and the past nothing, the conservative mode of experiencing time found the best corroboration of its sense of the determinateness in discovering the significance of the past, in the discovery of time as the creator of value. . . . Consequently not only is attention turned to the past and the attempt made to rescue it from oblivion, but the presentness and immediacy of the whole past becomes an actual experience. (Mannheim 1936: 235).

Again, this proves to be the case in *Nineteen Eighty-Four*, as Winston Smith nostalgically looks back toward the vanished moment of Orwell's own youth, a moment that not coincidentally also coincided with the high point of British global power.

The dystopian form continues to flourish in the years after the Second World War, especially within the realm of popular science fiction, producing such memorable specimens as Vladimir Nabokov's *Bend Sinister* (1947); Kurt Vonnegut Jr.'s *Player Piano* (1952); Frederick Pohl and C.M. Kornbluth's *The Space Merchants* (1952), Ray Bradbury's *Fahrenheit 451* (1953); Anthony Burgess' *Clockwork Orange* (1962), as well as Stanley Kubrick's 1971 film adaptation of it; and Philip K. Dick's *Martian Time-Slip* (1964), *Dr. Bloodmoney* (1965), and *Do Androids Dream of Electric Sheep?* (1968), the last the basis for Ridley Scott's film adaptation *Blade Runner* (1982). Many of the best dystopias of the 1960s and 1970s reflect the major concerns of their moment, raising the specter of overpopulation, urban decay, and environmental catastrophe. This includes works such Harry Harrison's *Make Room! Make Room!* (1966) and its film adaptation, *Soylent Green* (1973); John Brunner's loose quartet of *Stand on Zanzibar* (1968), *The Jagged Orbit* (1969), *The Sheep Look Up* (1972), and *The Shockwave Rider* (1975); and Samuel Delany's *Dhalgren* (1975). Meanwhile, works like

Suzy McKee Charnas' "Holdfast Chronicles" – *Walk to the End of the World* (1974), *Motherlines* (1978), and *The Furies* (1994) – and Margaret Atwood's bestseller *The Handmaid's Tale* (1985) use dystopia as a way of raising awareness about some of the central concerns of the women's movement.

The ascendancy of dystopia and anti-Utopianism more generally did not, however, mean the end of Utopian, or more precisely eutopian, writing. Indeed, a celebrated "rebirth" of the form occurs in the late 1960s and early 1970s. Some of the first inklings of this revival are to be found in works like R.A. Lafferty's *Past Master* (1968), a text whose critical engagement with the generic traditions of the Utopian narrative (its central character being "Thomas More" transported to another world a thousand years after his death) also deftly invokes the radical political energies and Utopian hopes of its moment; and Monique Wittig's *Les Guérillères* (1969), which announces the emergence of a true feminist Utopian tradition. At its height in the mid-1970s, this flourishing of the genre produced such works as Christiane Rochefort's *Archaos, or the Sparkling Garden* (1972), Mack Reynolds' *Looking Backward, From the Year 2000* (1973), Le Guin's *The Dispossessed* (1974) (and her later, *Always Coming Home* [1985]), Joanna Russ' *The Female Man* (1975), Ernest Callenbach's *Ecotopia* (1975), Marge Piercy's *Woman on the Edge of Time* (1976), Samuel Delany's *Triton* (1976), E.M. Broner's *A Weave of Women* (1978), Louky Bersianik's *The Eugélionne* (1978), and Sally Miller Gearheart's *The Wanderground: Stories of the Hill Women* (1978). These works are very much the products of the global political, social, and cultural ferment of the late 1960s and 1970s, and as a consequence a whole series of concerns – ecology, the environment, race, gender, and sexuality – are given a prominence that had not been evident earlier in the genre's long history. Moreover, as with the so-called New Left's relationship to the old, these works take up a skeptical relationship to their predecessors. Tom Moylan marks this difference in describing these works as "critical Utopians," fictions that are cognizant of the dystopian and anti-Utopian interventions, and which signal an:

> awareness of the limitations of the Utopian tradition, so that these texts reject Utopian as a blueprint while preserving it as a dream. Furthermore, the novels dwell on the conflict between the originary world and the Utopian society opposed to it so that the process of social change is more directly articulated. Finally, the novels focus on the continuing presence of difference and imperfection within Utopian society itself and thus render more recognizable and dynamic alternative. (Moylan 1986: 10–11).

This upsurge of Utopian fiction would again dwindle with the neoconservative retrenchment of the 1980s. Within the genre itself, the outer limits of this period could be marked by the publications of the founding works in cyberpunk, most centrally, William Gibson's *Neuromancer* (1984), with its advocacy of a kind of free-market libertarianism, and Margaret Atwood's *The Handmaid's Tale*, the latter standing in relationship to the 1970s flourishing of feminist Utopians as did the work on which it was in part modeled, *Nineteen Eighty-Four*, to the histories of Utopian thought and writing in the first part of the twentieth century. However, there also occurs in the late 1980s a mutation within the dystopian form, resulting in the new hybrid Moylan calls the "critical dystopia." These works "look quizzically, skeptically, critically not only at the present society but also at the means needed to transform it," and thereby maintain a "militant optimism" in a situation deeply anathema to it (Moylan 2001: 133). Among the most significant examples of the critical dystopia are for Moylan Kim Stanley Robinson's *Gold Coast* (1988), Marge Piercy's *He, She and It* (1991), and Octavia Butler's *Parable of the Sower* (1993) and *Parable of the Talents* (1998).

The unexpected fall of the Soviet Union in 1991 and the end of the Cold War destabilized the dominant global order, challenged long-established practices and beliefs, and created a situation favorable once again to the publication of Utopian visions. The most important of these is Robinson's Mars trilogy – *Red Mars* (1993), *Green Mars* (1994), and *Blue Mars* (1996) – a monumental narration of the physical transformation, or terraforming, of the red planet, the adventures of its first colonists, and their ultimate break with Earth and formation of a new planetary community. (Robinson has also written an earlier more modest Utopian fiction, set in his homeland of Southern California, *Pacific Edge* [1990].) Equally important is the Scottish writer Ken MacLeod's "Fall Revolution" quartet: *The Star Fraction* (1995), *The Stone Canal* (1996), *The Cassini Division* (1998), and *The Sky Road* (1999). In this extended work, MacLeod offers not a single Utopian vision, but rather a proliferation of what Suvin calls Utopian "possible worlds," as he narrates a future history that moves from the late 1960s through the twenty-fourth century and expands in space from Scotland out into a vast galactic network of worlds. Significantly, both works differ from many of the Utopians that precede them in that they focus a good deal of creative energy on the process by which these new communities are established. Both Robinson and MacLeod's work mark the obsolescence of some older forms of oppositional political struggle, revise others, and articulate forms of action most appropriate to our global situation. In this respect, these works reveal a kinship with perhaps the most significant "nonliterary" Utopian of this moment, Michael Hardt and Antonio Negri's *Empire* (1999).

The 1990s also witness the publication of Utopian fictions that draw upon new resources in imagining other worlds. These include Alasdair Gray's *A History Maker* (1994), set, as with MacLeod's work, in a future Scotland; Mike Resnick's *Kirinyaga: A Fable of Utopia* (1998), which uses the author's experiences of traditional Kikuyu practices and beliefs in constructing a Utopian community on a terraformed planetoid; and Nalo Hopkinson's *Midnight Robber* (2000), a work that draws upon the traditions of Caribbean literature and culture in imagining the worlds of Toussaint and New Half-Way Tree. In many ways, the events following September 11, 2001, mark the closure of this particular historical conjuncture, and how the traditions of Utopian fictions will respond to this latest historical change remains an open question. However, change it will. Utopia has played a significant part in modern history, and will continue to do so in any foreseeable future.

References and Further Reading

Alkon, Paul (1987) *Origins of Futuristic Fiction.* Athens, GA: University of Georgia Press.

Bartkowski, Frances (1989) *Feminist Utopias.* Lincoln, NE: University of Nebraska Press.

Bloch, Ernst (1986) *The Principle of Hope.* Three Volumes. (trans.) Neville Plaice, Stephen Plaice, and Paul Knight. Oxford: Basil Blackwell.

Claeys, Gregory and Lyman Tower Sargent, (eds) (1999) *The Utopia Reader.* New York: New York University Press.

Fitting, Peter (1979) "The Modern Anglo-American SF Novel: Utopian Longing and Capitalist Cooptation." *Science Fiction Studies* 6, no. 1, 59–76.

——(1993) "What is Utopian Film? An Introductory Taxonomy." *Utopian Studies* 4, no. 2, 1–17.

Jameson, Fredric (1982) "Progress Versus Utopia; or, Can We Imagine the Future?" *Science Fiction Studies* 9, no. 2, 147–58.

——(1987) "Science Fiction as a Spatial Genre: Generic Discontinuities and the Problem of Figuration in Vonda McIntyre's *The Exile Waiting." Science Fiction Studies* 14, 44–59.

——(1988) "Of Islands and Trenches: Neutralization and the Production of Utopian Discourse." *The Ideologies of Theory, Essays 1971–1986.* Vol. 2. Minneapolis, MN: University of Minnesota Press, 75–101.

——(2004) "The Politics of Utopia." *New Left Review* 25, 35–54.

Kelvin, Norman (ed.) (1996) *The Collected Letters of William Morris: Volume III, 1889-1892.* Princeton, NJ: Princeton University Press.

Kumar, Krishan (1987) *Utopia and Anti-Utopia in Modern Times.* Oxford: Basil Blackwell.

Levitas, Ruth (1990) *The Concept of Utopia.* Syracuse, NJ: Syracuse University Press.

Longxi, Zhang (2002) "The Utopian Vision, East and West." *Utopian Studies* 13, no. 1, 1–20.

Mannheim, Karl (1936) *Ideology and Utopia: An Introduction to the Sociology of Knowledge.* (trans.) Louis Wirth and Edward Shils. New York: Harcourt Brace Jovanovich.

Manuel, Frank E. and Fritzie P. Manuel (1979) *Utopian Thought in the Western World.* Oxford: Basil Blackwell.

More, Thomas (1965) *Utopia,* (eds) Edward Surtz and J.H. Hexter. Vol. 4 of *The Yale Edition of the Complete Works of St. Thomas More,* (ed.) Louis L. Martz. New Haven, CT: Yale University Press.

Morson, Gary Saul (1981) *The Boundaries of Genre: Dostoevsky's* Diary of a Writer *and the Traditions of Literary Utopia.* Austin, TX: University of Texas Press.

Moylan, Tom (1986) *Demand the Impossible: Science Fiction and the Utopian Imagination.* New York: Methuen.

——(2001) *Scraps of the Untainted Sky: Science Fiction, Utopia, Dystopia.* Boulder, CO: Westview Press.

——and Raffaella Baccolini, (eds) (2003) *Dark Horizons: Science Fiction and the Dystopian Imagination.* New York and London: Routledge.

Orwell, George (1949) *Nineteen Eighty-Four.* New York: Harcourt Brace Jovanovich.

——(1998) *The Complete Works of George Orwell, Vol. 19. It is What I Think, 1947–1948,* ed. Peter Davison. London: Secker and Warburg.

Parrinder, Patrick (ed.) (2001) *Learning From Other Worlds: Estrangement, Cognition, and the Politics of Science Fiction and Utopia.* Durham, NC: Duke University Press.

Roemer, Kenneth M. (1976) *The Obsolete Necessity: America in Utopian Writings, 1888–1900.* Kent, OH: Kent State University Press.

——(2003) *Utopian Audiences: How Readers Locate Nowhere.* Amherst, MA: University of Massachusetts Press.

Ruppert, Peter (1986) *Reader in a Strange Land: The Activity of Reading Literary Utopias.* Athens, GA: University of Georgia Press.

Sargent, Lyman Tower (1994) "The Three Faces of Utopianism Revisited." *Utopian Studies* 5, no. 1, 1–37.

Schaer, Roland, Gregory Claeys, and Lyman Tower Sargent, (eds) (2000) *Utopia: The Search for the Ideal Society in the Western World.* New York: New York Public Library/Oxford University Press.

Suvin, Darko (1979) *Metamorphoses of Science Fiction: On the Poetics and History of a Literary Genre.* New Haven, CT: Yale University Press.

——(1988) *Positions and Presuppositions in Science Fiction*. Kent, OH: Kent State University Press and Basingstoke: Macmillan.

——"Locus, Horizon, and Orientation: The Concept of Possible Worlds as a Key to Utopian Studies." *Utopian Studies* 1, no. 2, 69–83.

Wegner, Phillip E. (2002) *Imaginary Communities: Utopia, the Nation, and the Spatial Histories of Modernity*. Berkeley, CA: University of California Press.

Wells, H.G. (1967) *A Modern Utopia*. Lincoln, NE: University of Nebraska Press.

6

Science Fiction and Religion

Stephen R.L. Clark

Introduction

Science fiction that either makes explicit use of the Christian mythos, or advances a theological argument, is rare. Examples of the first include the following: "The Man," in *The Illustrated Man* (1951) by Ray Bradbury, in which a space-traveler pursues the risen Christ from one planet to another; James Blish's *Black Easter* (1968), in which a black magician, hired by an arms-dealer to release devils from Hell for sport, thereby initiates Armageddon; C.S. Lewis' interplanetary trilogy, comprising *Out of the Silent Planet* (1938), *Perelandra* (1944) and *That Hideous Strength* (1945); and Walter M. Miller's *A Canticle for Leibowitz* (1959), recounting the survival of a Christian monastery from one world-destroying war to the next. Examples of the second class include Lewis' trio, James Blish's *A Case of Conscience* (1958), and Doria Mary Russell's *The Sparrow* (1996). Christians and other believers make casual appearances elsewhere: the Catholic Church has survived in strength into the "Second Empire" of Larry Niven and Jerry Pournelle's *The Mote in God's Eye* (1974), and – very unexpectedly – there is a secret Jewish tradition tens of millennia hence in Frank Herbert's *Chapter House Dune* (1985). But science fiction is often "religious" in a wider sense, even at its most atheistic. Sometimes this is no more than euhemerism, the theory that God and the gods are memories or premonitions of technologically advanced intruders or especially gifted leaders. Other stories, perhaps unconsciously, offer allegories of familiar religious doctrine. Yet others comment on the social effects of organized religion (most often with pejorative intent), or advance their own ethical cosmologies as substitutes for older faiths.

Science fiction is generally founded on a naturalistic hypothesis: that is, whatever happens and whatever exists is assumed to be part of a single "closed" system. Intrusions "from outside" are impossible, since there can never be a true "outside" – as the hard-headed captain of the generation ship decrees in Robert Heinlein's *Orphans of the Sky* (1951, 1964). If there is another world, another life beyond the life we know, this can only be a separate region of the manifold, and its inhabitants as subject to the laws of nature as ourselves. In Blish's sequel to *Black Easter*, *The Day after Judgement* (1970) it is imagined that the literal devils of Hell, and our own immortal souls, might be irrevocably destroyed. In Peter F. Hamilton's *The Naked God* (1999), such a weapon is devised to destroy the greedy ghosts that are possessing the living – and falls into the wrong hands. Fantasies founded more exactly on religious tradition doubt that any but God can destroy souls, and expect God always to be able to do something new. For traditional theists, nature is an *open* system, and God's miraculous intrusions cannot be ordered or evaded.

Science fiction, in brief, begins in the Enlightenment – a philosophical and political movement of seventeenth- and eighteenth-century Europe. Undoubtedly it had precursors, but it is unhelpful to equate science fiction with mythology or romance or the Gothic novel. Instead, science fiction is concerned with a *natural* universe, and the technological capacity to manipulate or control it. *The Odyssey* is not science fiction, even if it is now possible to echo Odysseus' journey in a world of stars. Neither is *The Book of Mormon*, even though it provides a template for some actual science fiction (as Orson Scott Card's *The Memory of Earth*, [1992]). However, if past mythologies and romances can be examined for their religious significance, treated as something more than mere story, so also can science fiction, and by similar means.

For science fiction, in a sense, has taken its start from religion, or at least from a religious revolution. The Enlightenment is now associated with the dawning realization that the universe is immensely larger, older, grander, and more forbidding than we had supposed. We no longer lay at the dark bottom of the universe, surrounded by the crystal spheres of Ptolemy's imagination: instead, our Earth rode the heavens, itself a star. Some concluded that the world itself had the properties once ascribed to God, being glorious, infinite, and eternal. The dominant Enlightenment emotion was compounded of exhilaration and despair: despair, because the way things worked had even less to do with any goal of ours than we had thought; exhilaration, because immensely more seemed possible. On the one hand, we had no one to rely on but ourselves; on the other hand, it seemed that we could profit from that self-reliance. Not that all Enlightenment philosophers thought we were entirely without friends:

> When I reflect on how greatly human knowledge has increased in the past century or two, and how easy it would be for men to go incomparably further along the road to happiness, I am not in despair of the achievement of considerable improvements, in a more peaceful time under some great Prince whom God may raise up for the good of mankind. (Leibniz 1981: 527).

Progress was possible, and what *seemed* both true and unavoidable might turn out to be false or fleeting. Enlightenment philosophers indulged in story-telling, thought-experiments, of a kind that later ages class as "science fiction." Descartes conceives automata to replicate the outward motions of intelligent life, and a demon who might deceive us about the most solid-seeming facts. Locke imagines a brain as big as a small town, through whose machinery we might wander without ever *seeing* a thought. Leibniz describes the world upon infinite world nestling in the smallest-seeming drop of water. Berkeley imagines "philosophical snuff," whereby we might invade the inmost thoughts of others and inspect the symbolism of their would-be private worlds. Many wondered what lives might wake on other planetary bodies – mostly convinced, despite their Enlightenment, that there *must* be intelligent life on Jupiter, with eyes to see, since otherwise the moons of Jupiter would have no purpose (see Whewell 1854). The obvious response (which Whewell made) is that we cannot, on Enlightenment principles, discern God's purposes, and should not expect to find the "final causes" of things. In effect, the natural world acknowledged by Enlightenment thinkers, and by science fiction writers, is neutral – though we rarely manage to remember this.

Whereas mainstream or conventional literature has focused, since the Enlightenment, on "realistic" portrayals of the everyday existence of merely human beings, in an environment entirely human, science fiction writers have preferred to place them in the larger world that Enlightenment philosophers had wished us to consider and control. Some heirs of the Enlightenment have sought to describe the wider world as one where there are indeed no other wills than human. The spread of humankind across the sidereal universe has been their dream, to culminate in a world where, after all, there is nothing that is not symbolical, nothing that is truly alien. Nature may be neutral *now*, but will not be forever. The stars themselves – the fantasy suggests – will one day serve our species or its descendant species, and be as familiar as contemporary traffic lights. It will then be literally true that the lights in the firmament of heaven exist "for signs, and for seasons, and for days and years" (Genesis 1.14). Looking outward at the heavens we shall see, as our medieval predecessors saw, the animated stars look back at us, with whatever twist of malice or compassion. Nowhere will there be anything wholly *other*, wholly alien. Alternatively, if it chances that the wider world is already populous, maybe we shall be able to join in that larger conversation. One day we shall realize, perhaps, that the signs we see of "natural events" (exploding stars, colliding galaxies) are vast engineering projects – or appalling acts of war. What that imagined conversation might be like will also vary. Some writers conceive it to be merely human after all, even though it is conducted between creatures of an entirely different ancestry and nature. In Olaf Stapledon's fantasies, for example (and especially *Starmaker*, 1937), all manner of strange creatures (intelligent nebulae, neurotic stars, mobile vegetables, and fish-and-spider symbiotes) aspire to understand and love the world, to transcend their several beginnings by learning the "Mind of God."

A few, even in the act of describing the conversation between those angels in the skies, begin to suspect that their ways are not ours. Perhaps they are mechanical intelligences, forever hostile to the prolific and irrational life of animals like us. Perhaps they are star-spanning hives, with just as much intelligence as they need to seek out and incorporate their prey, and without any merely *human* interest in close companionship or art or even science. Perhaps we shall discover that human religiosity is only a by-product of our biology (most usually, of our long childhoods and our deference to alpha males), one that other rational intelligences do not begin to comprehend. Perhaps indeed those intelligences are indistinguishable in what they do from merely physical happenings: if the stars are ruled by utterly alien Powers it is as much as to say that they are not *ruled* at all: and the only wills in question are our own. When Stapledon's peace-loving and peace-making Tibetan mystics (*Darkness and the Light* [1942]) finally discover the truth of things it is as if they woke to a frozen landscape trampled by indifferent giants. Whether those giants are deaf because they are witless or because they are callous hardly matters; even their ill will – if they are malevolent – is immune to prayer, and so as natural and fixed a fact as any.

In brief, science fiction seems well suited to the needs and fantasies of an irreligious age, easily persuaded that there are no *transcendent* purposes, and that the only meanings that we could comprehend will be the ones created either by our own descendants or by creatures enough like us to share our lives. In their absence the merely *natural* world is empty of significance, even if it is at last controlled by some single alien purpose that can never be our own. But there are other ways of thinking of science fiction, and other ways of thinking about religion. Maybe there is after all an immortal and undefeated will to good, distinct from any finite individual but working through those individuals. Maybe science fiction offers allegories for that familiar theory. Or maybe it offers other ways of seeing significance in nature.

The association of science fiction and religion has four roughly distinguishable aspects: how religion, and especially "organized religion," is depicted; how religious myths and legends are replicated or explained; what religious themes or doctrines are actually endorsed in fiction; and what religions have taken their start from science fiction.

Authority and Anticlericalism

As inheritors of the Enlightenment dream, science fiction writers also inherit the foundational legends of the scientific enterprise: the dead hand of medieval scholasticism, the trial of Galileo, the Darwinian assault on Victorian values (none of which, it needs to be said, bears critical examination). These are often combined with Protestant fear of "the Church." In Dan Simmons' *Endymion* (1995), for example, "the Church" uses direct stimulation of the brain for torture, and a parasite to procure bodily immortality – a goal and method that earlier episodes of Simmons' saga (*Hyperion* [1989] and *The Fall of Hyperion* [1990]) had plausibly identified as tyranny. Sometimes the evil clerics of science fiction are stupid enough to believe their own fantasies; sometimes they use whatever technologies or propaganda to deceive the faithful. But not all such clerics can be classed as Catholic: Heinlein's future history imagines an America controlled by Protestant fundamentalists, and the earlier episodes of Gordon Dickson's history of the Splinter Cultures imagine planets ruled by sectarian fanatics who mostly despise ritual. An anti-Christian bias is also evident in such science fiction as is motivated by environmentalist concerns (as Kim Stanley Robinson's *Red Mars, Green Mars, Blue Mars* [1992–6]).

But though the evil clerics may be recognizably Catholic or Protestant Christians, their wickedness, in science fiction, mostly resides in their organized power. Dickson's later accounts identify true faith-holders, willing to fight and die as guerrillas because they will not accept another's definition of God (e.g., *The Final Encyclopaedia* [1984]). Clerical hierarchies, papal or quasipapal authority and ritual all seem to be anathema: nothing must stand between a believer and his God. Individualism is the default philosophy.

But individualists are the least likely people to sustain millennial projects of the sort that science fiction writers love. How could people reared to respect only their own God and their own vision be expected to support a project imagined into being by their ancestors? The clearest case will be the "generation ship," in which (it is imagined) many generations live out their ordinary, confined lives in order that their remote descendants may colonize the planets of some distant star. Often such passengers will be encouraged to forget the nature of their world, and to do all and only what is needed to sustain a world they do not understand. In Harry Harrison's *Captive Universe* (1970), for example, the common people are encouraged to believe in Aztec deities (which literally prowl around to kill whoever is out of place), while an intellectual elite is organized on strictly monastic lines to retain rote learning about how to end the voyage. The evil clerics, in other words, may have a truth to conceal and keep, and it is "right" that the populace should be both ignorant and obedient. If they cannot be allowed to *act* on the assumption that they inhabit an artificial world, a star-ship, because they might not carry out the builders' plans, they had better not even be allowed to know it.

Isaac Asimov's *Foundation* (1951–3) also invokes an artificial religion, binding the ignorant masses to believe that the Foundation is the servant of the "Galactic Spirit," with the power to work miracles. Overt religious power will falter, in his universe, before commercial and military power in the end, but Asimov imagined that a more diffuse faith in eventual victory would be what sustains his Foundation until the psychohistorians of a *Second* Foundation finally take power. Asimov's Galactic Spirit only demands conventional morality, and reverence to the Foundation. The Foundationers' own belief in Hari Seldon's psychohistory, and their destiny to found the Second Empire, contains a dream that diverts them from the little failures they and their society may suffer. There is an ambiguity in the famous aphorism: "religion is the opium of the people." Marx's full claim in his introduction to *The Critique of Hegel's "Philosophy of Right"* (1843–4) is: "Religion is the sigh of the oppressed creature, the heart of a heartless world, and the soul of soulless conditions. It is the opium of the people" (Marx 1970: 131). Opium may be soporific (and so numb its victims to their present misery), but it also engenders dreams that are worth fulfilling.

Greg Egan, in *Quarantine* (1992), offers a most ingenious variation: loyalty to the company directive is assured by implanting a "loyalty module": our hero recognizes that he is thus absolutely loyal "to the Ensemble" only because he has been infected, but finds that loyalty immune to deconstruction. Yet there is an escape: what *is* the Ensemble, except the very thing to which he is loyal? The "real" Ensemble cannot be the outward institution, but only that which is defined by those bound to be loyal to it – namely those infected by the module. Obedience turns to freedom as it is internalized. But such developments are rare in science fiction: perhaps only Dickson's *Dorsai* saga, in its treatment of the "believers" settled on the worlds of Harmony and Association, recognizes that such belief may end in absolute immunity to any external threat or bribe (and the names of the two worlds, of course, are heavily ironical).

Explicitly religious hierarchies, of course, are not the only forms that the genre seems sometimes to admire. Galactic Empires are usually *imperial*, and have an aristocratic order that defines a place for everyone. Occasionally there is also room for a "scientific" elite, an "order of scientists" that vulgarizes Plato's notion of the Guardians (described in *The Republic*). Whereas Plato's Guardians are required to have undergone a lengthy apprenticeship in the arts of war and mathematics, and to have demonstrated their immunity to corruption or conceit, before they can be trusted to control the state, an "order of scientists" is grounded only in their *scientific* skill. It is assumed that they thereby know what is really good for their subjects, and truly desire that good – an assumption that is rarely made on behalf of the more literally clerical elites. One exception is provided by E.E. "Doc" Smith's Lensmen, who must demonstrate their incorruptibility, courage, and good sense both by practical test and in the judgment of those almost-gods, the Arisians.

Realizing the Dream

Some science fictional religions have no such redeeming purpose, but are merely mocking or occasionally affectionate revisionings of real religions. One goal of SF writers, after all, is to provide a sort of scientific rationale for what would otherwise be merely fantasy. Gods and demons alike turn out to be no more than alien intelligences, using a more advanced technology "indistinguishable from magic." Peter Hamilton's *Night's Dawn* Trilogy (*The Reality Dysfunction* (1996), *The Neutronium Alchemist* (1997), *The Naked God* (1999)) manages to provide such speciously rational explanations for demons, ghosts, possessions, gods, Hell, and the last judgment. "Religious" impulses, in that fantasy, are primarily those of the chief Satanist. The goals of more conventional (and agreeable) religion are achieved – as Marx hoped – by practical and irreligious people. Conversely, imagined encounters with aliens sometimes allow the writer to mock the doubters: some alien belief or practice is identified as being "religious" (which is to say, a fable), but turns out to be entirely and literally true. Orson Scott Card's "piggies," in *Speaker for the Dead* (1986), are assumed to be making gruesome sacrifices to the trees they worship, whereas they are in fact transforming their heroes into those same, sentient, trees. In another saga, Card models his story on *The Book of Mormon*, but attributes the god's guidance to a computer in orbit round the planet. Where another writer might have intended this entirely as a humorous rationalization of a minor mythology, Card – as himself a Mormon – may have other views. Similarly, Philip K. Dick (in *Valis* [1981] and in *Radio Free Albemuth* [1985]) apparently intends a really religious moral in his story of an orbiting intelligence that communicates by radio. On the one hand, episodes of religious history turn out to be the effect of high technology; on the other, those technologies are true embodiments of a diviner principle (as they are also in John Varley's *Millennium* [1983]).

Such stories raise the question whether any religion can be "literally" true, and still remain religious. A world in which the gods (that is, immortal powers) are visible elements is one in which they are no more than older or more powerful creatures, dependent like ourselves on the laws of a wider universe. Why should they require worship, and how could any rational intelligence agree to it? In Roger Zelazny's *Lord of Light* the apparently Hindu gods who dominate the world turn out to be the officers of the starship that had colonized the planet, ruling through the machinery they have kept from the colonists, and also by their individual "psychic" gifts – which also turn out to be "natural." Even the rebellious hero of the story, posing as an incarnate Buddha to create some low-level opposition to the oppressors, is also an immortal power – but not one who requires worship. In Diana Wynne Jones' *Dalemark* saga and Lois M. Bujold's *The Curse of Chalion* (2001) there are immortal powers which – like Zelazny's – create beauty, but can never remove an individual's responsibility for her own acts. Worlds in which mythologies are literally true, it seems, are no less ambiguous and confusing than the one that we (presumably) inhabit. And the only worship compatible with rational intelligence is self-respect (as Herbert suggested in *Destination: Void* [1967], and *The Jesus Incident* [1979], cowritten with Bill Ransom).

By this account, "religion" may be either "heteronomous" (and lead to Satanism or worse) or "autonomous" (in which case it makes no difference whether there are literally true mythologies or not). "True Religion," it may be concluded, is an ethical conviction that acknowledges "the spirit of freedom" in all living creatures – including gods and demons. "False Religion" creates infidels and fanatics, and feeds on the hope of some particular reward. Thus in Robert Jordan's *Wheel of Time* (1990–) it is the servants of the Dark Power who give worship to a named individual (and his officers) in the hope of immortality: there are no other gods, since "the Light" does nothing of itself, and the Creator (in the imagined history) does no more than – perhaps – establish the Wheel's turning.

An alternative form of religion that seems popular in science fiction is the pantheistic. In Frank Herbert's *Dune* (1965) it is suggested that the greatest influence on post-twentieth century religion was space travel, and its effect a general preference for "a female immanence filled with ambiguity and a face of many terrors" (Herbert 1977: 501). In the later development, he suggested, there would be a largely unsuccessful attempt to unify religious traditions under the dictat "Thou shalt not disfigure the soul." The *Dune* saga, like others of Herbert's writings, makes much of millennial breeding programs, dedicated to the emergence of a kind of human being that will no longer be susceptible to the sorts of control, religious or otherwise, that sustain those very programs. Something, it is suggested, is at work in history: perhaps a racial agenda that cannot be changed by any individual effort, or perhaps an even larger and more terrible purpose, embodied – in *Dune* and its successors – in giant sandworms that are the source of an antiageing, psychedelic drug. In other works (George Stewart's *Earth Abides* [1950] for example), the focus is upon the living earth, conceived as an entity that will survive humanity, and which imposes no duty beyond survival on its elements. Herbert's vision is perhaps more typical, in that it is progressive, aiming always at a different and "freer" state, but even Stewart's preferred survivors treat their gods lightly.

Apotheosis and the Day of Days

On the one hand, alien or mechanical intelligences that purport to have the power of gods are routinely shown to be demons or ordinary creatures of no higher metaphysical or moral standing than ourselves. On the other hand, human beings themselves may become "like gods": immortal, powerful, and creative. Sometimes these are to be feared: more powerful versions of the evil clerics. In Jack Williamson's *Darker than You Think* (1948), for example, we are to imagine that there is a separate subspecies, the original werewolves, vampires, priests, and magicians. In other stories, such "supermen" are what all of us should become, and may, sometimes by technological assistance, sometimes by biological miracle. Theodore Sturgeon's *More than Human* (1953) proposes that people endowed with distinct psychic talents (telepaths, teleports, telekineticists, and so on) may be unified, step by step, into a corporate intelligence, a god entirely human. Similar fantasies are to be found in Henry Kuttner's *Mutant* (1954), or more openly in Olaf Stapledon's seminal work (*Last and First Men*, [1930]). Stapledon's more extreme vision, of a "cosmic spirit" in whom all sentient life will eventually awaken, has been echoed in Greg Bear's *Eternity* (1989), or Robert Charles Wilson's *Darwinia* (1998). In Bear's version – it is a point to which I shall return – the core of that ultimate intelligence is not human at all, but rather humankind's genocidal enemy.

A "corporate intelligence" requires the real existence of individual persons who are fully open and cooperative – a form of life of which we can form only a slight impression. Stapledon, Sturgeon, and Kuttner all conceive it as a form of loving conversation – as did the greatest of late antique philosophers, Plotinus (204–70 AD):

> Plotinus's divine mind [which is also the totality of intelligible being] is not just a mind knowing a lot of eternal objects. It is an organic living community of interpenetrating beings which are at once Forms and intelligences, all "awake and alive," in which every part thinks and therefore is the whole; so that all are one mind and yet each retains its distinct individuality without which the whole would be impoverished. And this mind-world is the region where our own mind, illumined by the divine intellect finds its true self and lives its own life, its proper home and the penultimate stage on its journey, from which it is taken up to union with the Good. (Armstrong and Markus 1960: 27)

Others present it rather as a more powerful, many-bodied individual: so in Clarke's *Childhood's End* (1954) the Overmind takes up into itself the minds, memories, and wills of the last human children, without any assurance that those children themselves have any kind of continued being. Being absorbed into an Overmind, as Robert Sheckley's version remarks in *Dimension of Miracles* (1968), is "exactly the same as death, though it sounds much nicer." Though Clarke later disclaimed any "religious" significance in his story, the narrative seems to make it clear that such an absorption into a "higher" form of life is to be regarded as the "real" goal of religion. The entities that both prepare the way for the Overmind, and are forever excluded from it, have the form of pantomime devils, as if to suggest that the only alternative is one that would be thought diabolical – or perhaps that the transformation they half-willingly assist is diabolical.

A different form of transcendence is offered in Alfred Bester's *The Stars My Destination* (aka *Tiger! Tiger!* [1956]). There "the stereotypical common man" is stirred to action (by an overpowering wish for vengeance) until he is revealed as one who can translocate himself anywhere in the universe – and much more significantly is prepared to "blow open the last star chamber in the world," compelling all his fellow "common men" to take up the responsibilities that till then had been shouldered or usurped by *uncommon* men. That is also, perhaps, the moral of Dickson's *Dorsai* saga: we are almost at the point where any single individual could have the power to destroy or wholly derail humanity, and must accordingly become a god to cope with this. Having the power of gods, we must become *good* gods. Absorption in an Overmind, on the other hand, means that no single individual can take a stand against the collective. Total individual responsibility precludes that absorption, but at great risk. This is also the moral of C.S. Lewis' interplanetary trilogy, in which a barely modified medieval Christian cosmology is the framework. The fate of the damned is disintegration and absorption. Those who oppose that evil find the fate of the world depends on their own choices. In *Perelandra* especially it is intimated that human persons will one day take on the angelic role of guiding the stars and planets – but only if they manage first to accept responsibility, and – equivalently – be obedient.

Both Dick (in *Radio Free Albemuth*) and Doris Lessing (in the *Shikasta* sequence [1979–83]) make religious use of an "intergalactic communications network," feigning that our world has been cut off from the heavenly conversation for all recorded history, and that occasional messengers are sent down amongst us to remind us of our real nature. Awakening to that reality is also to acquire immortality – perhaps by being mated to an "energy being" whose real home is the heavens. In Bob Shaw's *The Palace of Eternity* (1969) a naturalistic immortality is threatened because the starships that humans use destroy the fragile energies that are their own and everyone else's immortal souls: what had seemed dreadful enemies (considerably nastier than the more familiar insectile monstrosities) turn out to be only defending real life against real death. What saves us all is the opening of the ways: ordinary people are at last put in clear touch with their immortal ancestors, and our apparent enemies withdraw.

Wakening to immortality is wakening, precisely, from the dream and delusion that is ordinary life (as it also in Eric Frank Russell's *Sentinels from Space* [1953]). Interestingly, Russell had earlier offered an alternative riff on the theme in *Sinister Barrier* (1939, 1948), where the "energy beings" are not our true selves, but rather the demons that have domesticated us, and can be destroyed.

In recent work, the way to become a god (of sorts) is via virtual reality. It is supposed that we shall have the power to create wholly convincing illusions of whatever sort we choose (so recreating Descartes' skeptical fable). The catch in most such stories (for example, Greg Egan's *Permutation City* [1994], or Tad Williams' *Otherland* [1996–2001]) is that either the very framework of virtual reality or the competing wishes of its participants create the same problems that we face in ordinary reality: however much we may *wish* that everything be according to our will, the results will often not be what anyone, living or dead, would wish. Or else the results reveal more dangerous wishes than we willingly admit, including death and destruction. The fantasies offer an allegorical account of how such self-styled gods might "choose" to enter an ordinary world like ours, not fully realizing what the effects would be. E.R. Eddison's *Fish Dinner in Memison* (1941) imagines how *our* world might have been conceived, and entered, as an after-dinner amusement for more heroic beings. Conversely, we may imagine that our ordinary deaths are no more than an awakening back into a "real" world. Believing that "this world" is a dream, of course, may be reckoned dangerous. While it would be a waste to end the dream too early, it does seem that dream events cannot be fully serious. We should act, as many past moralists have told us, for the act itself, and not for any sometime effects. Nor should we fear danger, except the danger that this dream will irrevocably spoil "our soul" (which is to say, our real identity). A further catch with the argument of course is that it is difficult to see how it could ever be evaded (see Bostrom 2003): is there any waking which will satisfactorily confirm that we are "really awake," and do we have any notion of what it would be to be "really awake" (or conversely, dreaming)? Apparently we live by faith even if we choose to pretend otherwise.

Our strongest "sense of reality," perhaps, comes from recalcitrant opposition, from a world that manifestly is not what we wanted. "There is no cure for [the] nightmare of omnipotence except pain; because that is the thing a man *knows* he would not tolerate if he could really control it. A man must be in some place from he would certainly escape if he could, if he is really to realize that all things do not come from within" (Chesterton 1962: 91), and *that's* what evil is for. Such a sense of course is still compatible with our living in a merely "virtual" realm – but the harder that is, the less it matters that it is "virtual": it is merely another reality. Encountering the obviously *other*, so Zelazny suggested in his *Amber* fantasies (especially *The Courts of Chaos* [1979]), is all that saves his world-roving and world-transforming magicians from total solipsism. In practice it is not easy to represent that Otherness: anything an author can describe, after all, is drawn from her imagination, and so is not entirely *other*.

Sometimes the only point of aiming at this other is to tame it. Such humanistic literature demands that humans triumph, either by wit or loyalty or courage. So James Blish, in the SF juvenile *Mission to the Heart Stars* (1965), confronts his newly civilized humans both with angelic beings who turn out to be friendly and an ancient Galactic empire founded on absolute class-divisions, which can be easily evaded. Similarly Frederik Pohl's powerful story *Gateway* (1976), in which an alien and uncomprehended technology is put to commercial use, is followed by successive revelations in which each layer of alien life turns comprehensible. David Brin's Uplift saga (especially *Brightness Reef* [1995]) follows Stapledon in imagining a wide variety of biological forms – but every one of them turns out to be only "human" in its motivation and its skill. The more admirable aliens, indeed, turn out to admire humanity and begin to copy us. Even the utterly alien artifacts of Algis Budrys' *Rogue Moon* (1960) and the Strugatskys' *Roadside Picnic* (1977) are somehow transformed into a commercial or military opportunity.

The occasional alternative is to imagine our defeat. So Greg Bear's cosmic spirit turns out to be founded in our enemy. Gregory Benford's *Against Infinity* (1983) uses the familiar trope of an abandoned alien machine to represent all that is incomprehensible and unconquerable. Arthur C. Clarke's *Childhood's End*, as above, imagines that humankind can survive only by becoming utterly inhuman – an end that Pohl and Williamson describe differently in thinking of the Overmind as an alien predator, like Bear's aliens, wishing only to capture human culture for its own ends (in *Land's End* [1988]). But it is rare, since Stapledon, to offer worship or even admiration to that alien Other: the point is rather to stay loyal to "humanity" despite its temporal defeat, or else to indicate how humans have fallen short of their humanity. The greatest obstacle to thinking that the human world is all that matters, after all, is the imagination of its final end. The nature of the final catastrophe may vary: perhaps, as in *Earth Abides*, it is a natural – or possibly man-made – epidemic that wipes out all but a remnant; perhaps, as in Mordecai Roshwald's *Level 7* (1959) it is the final war. Other possibilities have been explored: a change in the bacterial population on which all multicellular life depends (as in J.J. Connington's *Nordenholt's Million* [1946], or John Christopher's *The Death of Grass* [1956]); *Invasion of the Body Snatchers*; mechanical planet-killers or solar flares or vacuum instabilities. It *may* turn out that we here-now are *astonishingly* early hominids, and that practically every human person who ever lives will live in artificial habitats orbiting black holes, long after the last star has died (as in Stephen Baxter's *Time: Manifold I* [1999]), or in the Great Redoubt of William Hope Hodgson's *Night Land* (1912). It is easy to think that something like this is plausible, until we realize how odd it would make our own perspective on the world.

The more probable future of our species is one in which our descendants will look back with puzzlement, awe, or horror at a vastly inflated urban order, whose relics will be largely uninterpretable by those who follow after (as in John Crowley's *Engine Summer* [1976]). The argument does not predict that the outcome is either certain or immediate: *probably* you and I, and even our grandchildren, will still be living high, for some decades to come, and *possibly* our great-grandchildren will have taken the first steps to "Forever," and be spreading out across the universe, hoping to remodel everything before the End. And if they do succeed, we might even imagine that they will also create experimental enclaves where they can play at being early hominids! Maybe we are indeed living in the largest array of humankind, but are simply deluded about our actual situation. Perhaps this is a virtual universe, a collective hallucination, from which we shall wake into the unimaginable company of all intelligence, the literally infinite array of being. Perhaps at the end of cosmic history all worthwhile lives are preserved or resurrected into a world that has no end. The very tedious *Rama* sequence written by Arthur Clarke and Gentry Lee (the original was Clarke's alone: *Rendezvous with Rama* [1973]) imagines that all possible cosmic histories are being tried out, and the most successful one will at last be validated. A similar fantasy is coined (but then ignored) in Stephen Baxter's *Timelike Infinity* (1992) and recreated in his sequel to Wells' *Time Machine, The Time Ships* (1995). Whether "we" will be there or not will depend on how the ultimate intelligences think of us. In traditional religion, that will depend on whether we have truly attempted virtue; in the allegories it apparently depends on whether we have kept the research grants coming, or managed to leave sufficiently noticeable traces (Baxter's fanatics intend to make a time capsule out of an imploded Jupiter).

Our predecessors expected the fall of cities and of civilizations, and extrapolated from such falls a Final Fall, a Judgment upon all of us from which no worldly life would ever again emerge. If there is such an end then any project of ours that rests on our continued being is a failure. As Malacandra's angelic ruler asks the human scientist who had spoken of his interplanetary dream, of humankind springing from world to world "for ever": "And when all are dead?" (Lewis 1952: 164). The end of days may be presented either as a particular judgment on the follies that have led to it, or simply as a reminder that all human projects fade. In either case, they offer an implicit rebuke that differs from the religious chiefly, perhaps, in that no wider hope is offered, no new world of a more solid sort. Either we face "Judgment" or we may expect to find ourselves renewed in the "ultimate intelligence": either story allegorizes a religious expectation.

One final possibility, sketched by Vernor Vinge in *Marooned in Real Time* (1986), is that we are heading for a social singularity, a moment beyond which nothing can be understood by us. Computing power continues to double every eighteen months. Every one of us even in the less developed world has access to power, to information and to decision makers beyond the imagination even of science fiction writers of an earlier age. It is easy to imagine that things will continue very much as always, with very minor adjustments: the reality is that things are always changing. The silence of the heavens, as Vinge observes, is the exact analogue of the absolute unpredictability of our own future. If it is likely that we shall survive beyond the singularity into an unimaginable other, it is also likely that "the Greater Galactics," so to speak, already have. Just as we cannot imagine what life will be like for us, if we evade disaster, so also can we not imagine what the real signs of those Galactics might be. Belief in them – or disbelief – is a much a matter of blind faith as any older Abrahamic creed.

Science Fiction as Religion

Organized religion as it has mostly been depicted in science fiction has been oppressive, even if occasionally with a good excuse. Religious myths, when they are not merely lies, are taken to be garbled versions of some historical or scientific truth. In Heinlein's *Orphans of the Sky*, for example, the Law of Gravity is allegorized as a statement about erotic attraction, and "Manning Landing Stations" is a purely "religious" rite. Occasionally, religions are prophetic dreams, to be realized by "research" or alien intervention, not by prayer. There is nonetheless a religious theme that seems to be widely endorsed by science fiction fans and writers: that humanity, if only it can mature, will give the world, the universe, significance. Even the dream of Judgment Day suggests that there may be hope: after all, it is human beings – and particularly the fans and writers – who are imagining that Day, and so, in thought, transcending it. Reading and writing science fiction is itself a sort of rite: by seeing further than the everyday we distance ourselves from those around us, who are implicitly or explicitly depicted in science fiction as conventional or stupid or wickedly myopic people. What the future *actually* holds is wholly unknown, but fans can still imagine themselves in league with that eventual future – the Federation, or the Empire, or the Omega Point of cosmic evolution. Who else should the gods of the last days be willing to resurrect but those who have so lovingly imagined them?

That science fiction itself is a religious form – and one that feeds on appetites that are not wholly admirable – may be disputed. Probably most ordinary readers and writers have more sense or sensibility. Even those who act out their self-identification with the crew of the starship *Enterprise* or the like are more likely to be having fun than bearing witness. But the same may well be true of ordinary communicants in many more familiar cults. What does it matter whether the feast is in honor of a god, a hero, or a fantasy? Recent philosophers of religion have often urged us to ignore the merely "factual," historical, or cosmological claims of religion: what matters, they say, is the ethical, aesthetic, and emotional dimension. Religious rituals and narratives do not have the "realistic" aims that naively atheistical critics think. The claim is plausible enough – though it ignores the properly metaphysical aspect of the "major" religious traditions. And if it is at least plausible, as an account of ordinary, tribal, or traditional religion, it may also apply to other areas of human action. To read, watch, and participate in science fiction is to identify with a future, and a present elite, and so support a way of seeing and acting in the present.

This "hidden church" is probably also self-consciously skeptical. It is sometimes assumed that those who write and read science fiction too easily believe reports of alien incursions, weird powers, and startling scientific theories. The truth is probably that most writers and readers disbelieve such stories precisely because they have read or written them all before. And such skepticism is also a familiar religious pattern: Chesterton's Father Brown is so far from believing every story of ghosts or demons or miraculous interventions that he routinely debunks them, in favor of properly human explanations. The "hidden church" is also rarely *organized*: the whole point of it, after all, is that its members self-identify as skeptical, autonomous precursors of a coming age, who owe no more than superficial obedience to the doomed powers of present-day politics. But there are clear exceptions. The "Heaven's Gate" sectarians who killed themselves in March 1997 in hopes of being uplifted to a starship following the comet Hale-Bopp on its passage outward to the wider realm, as well as more respectable Scientologists who hope to achieve a clearing and a cleansing from the traps and traumas of the everyday, are united in religious dreams that take shape in science fiction. So are those who seriously expect to be cryogenically preserved for bodily resurrection, or "up-loaded" into cyberspace (see Regis 1990). In all these cases fans manage to be skeptical about *established* science and religion, but not about their own.

The response of the major "mainstream" churches to such sects has usually been to insist that fantasies should be suppressed or side-lined. Some other sectarians have even found the mass of science fiction Satanic in its inspiration – and perhaps they have not always been as foolish as fans ordinarily think. After all, we have some experience of what can be done by people thoroughly and uncritically convinced that they have a hotline to the future, that older ways are obsolete or oppressive, that *some* people have superior powers and that the rest of us should know our place. We also know what people who profess to despise the flesh – that is, to think the flesh unimportant – often do, unless they are very carefully educated and controlled. What matters for true religion is the everyday: solidarity with the ordinary, rather than sectarian division. The God should not be imagined altogether elsewhere, but at hand. Ordinary life, "the meat," should not be abandoned for the sake of a spurious spirituality. A story of Ray Bradbury's ("The Fire Balloons," in *The Illustrated Man* [1951] and in *The Martian Chronicles* [1950]; aka *The Silver Locusts* [1951]) imagines that only *bodies* create the opportunity for sin, and that his discarnate Martians are therefore wholly innocent. Clarke also conceives (in *The City and the Stars* [1956]) that only "pure intelligence," free of all material ties, can possibly see things "as they are." And recently fashionable "cyberpunk," beginning with William Gibson's *Neuromancer* (1984), imagining "virtual realities," glories in imagining our freedom from "the meat." What matters in such fantasies is "pure mind," and their authors usually impute just these desires to the ordinarily religious – part of the opium dream that technology, not prayer, fulfils. But the ordinarily religious, in Abrahamic, Buddhist, Hindu, or tribal traditions, are more likely to require that we "do justice, and love mercy, and walk humbly with our God" (Micah 6.8). Stapledon, though he is often supposed to worship only the abstract intellect, was actually more orthodox. It was important to him to seek out that perspective from which all mortal life becomes an unimportant trifle, but at the same time he imagined instead how every moment, every instant of our lives could be called to mind. The final moments of *Starmaker* are not the vision of the Satanic power that makes and discards all worlds for its own satisfaction (a vision also found in David Lindsay's *Voyage to Arcturus* [1920]), but a return to "the little atom of community" Stapledon, or Stapledon's fictional narrator, shared with his wife.

Science fiction writers, more than most, consider how we are to live in a world immensely larger, older, grander, and more forbidding than we had supposed. Most have suspected that the natural order was at odds with almost everything we ordinarily respect or value. Sometimes science fiction seems to imply that we should therefore change our views, and only hope — at best — that we might secure some minor place in a world that is not ours. Sometimes it may hope instead that everything is remade. Those who recall that worldly success is not always virtuous prefer that we remain *human* even if humanity will not survive. The Ultimate Intelligence or Omega Point is sometimes, allegorically, the same as God, but sometimes much more like the Devil. Science fiction, as a religious movement, sometimes exalts just that intellectual conceit, rootless ambition, and contempt for ordinary life and morals that tradition has associated with the Devil. On the other hand, it may also sometimes allegorize the religious dream.

That vision, so tradition has it, is available only to those who respect the freedom of each, and are not distracted by pride of possession. Like other traditions, more openly religious, science fiction is ambivalent. At its best, it may serve as well as any to wake us up from the egoistic dream.

REFERENCES AND FURTHER READING

Armstrong, A.H. and Markus, R.A. (1960) *Christian Faith and Greek Philosophy*. London: Darton, Longman & Todd.

Bostrom, Nick (2003) "Are you living in a computer simulation?" *Philosophical Quarterly*, Vol. 53, No. 211, 243–255 (see also http://www.nickbostrom.com/).

Burridge, Richard A. (2000) *Faith Odyssey: A Journey Through Lent*. Oxford: Bible Reading Fellowship.

Chesterton, G.K. (1962) *The Poet and the Lunatics* (1929) London: Darwen Finlayson.

Clark, Stephen R.L. (1986) *The Mysteries of Religion*. Oxford: Blackwells.

——(1995) *How to Live Forever: Science Fiction and Immortality*. London: Routledge.

——(2001) "From Biosphere to Technosphere." *Ends and Means* 6, 3–21.

Collins, Robert A. and Robert Latham (eds) (1991) *Science Fiction & Fantasy Book Review Annual 1990*. Westport, CT: Greenwood Press.

Consolmagno, Guy (2003) "Religion, Science Fiction and the Real Universe." *Argentus* 3 at http://www.efanzines.com/Argentus/Ag03.pdf.

Ellis, George F.R. (ed.) (2002) *The Far Future Universe*. Philadelphia and London: Templeton Foundation Press.

Elwood, Roger (ed.) (1974) *Strange Gods*. New York: Pocket Books.

Evans, Christopher Riche (1973) *Cults of Unreason*. London: Harrap.

Hassler, Donald M. (1988) "Enlightenment genres and science fiction: belief and animated nature." *Extrapolation*. Vol. 29, No. 4 (Winter), 322–9.

Herbert, Frank (1977) *Dune* (1965), New York: Berkley.

James, Edward and Farah Mendlesohn (eds) (1998) *The Parliament of Dreams: Conferring on Babylon 5*. Reading: Science Fiction Foundation.

Kreuziger, Frederick A. (1982) *Apocalypse and Science Fiction: A Dialectic of Religious and Secular Soteriologies*. AARAS 40. Chico, CA: Scholars Press.

Leibniz, Gottfried (1981) *New Essays on Human Understanding*. Peter Remnant and Jonathan Bennett (trans. and eds) Cambridge: Cambridge University Press.

Leslie, John (1996) *The End of the World* London: Routledge.

Lewis, C.S. (1952) *Out of the Silent Planet* (1938), London: Pan.

Marx, Karl (1970) "Introduction," *The Critique of Hegel's "Philosophy of Right"* (1843–4), Annette Jolin and Joseph O'Malley (transl.), Joseph O'Malley (ed.). Cambridge: Cambridge University Press.

May, Stephen (1998) *Stardust and Ashes: Science Fiction in Christian Perspective.* London: SPCK.

Midgley, Mary (1985) *Evolution as Religion.* London: Routledge.

Mohs, Mayo (ed.) (1971) *Other Worlds, Other Gods: Adventures in Religious Science Fiction.* New York: Doubleday.

Pierce, John J. (1972) "The New Eschatology."

Foundation: The International Review of Science Fiction. No. 1 (March), 21–24.

Regis, Ed (1990) *Great Mambo Chicken and the Transhuman Condition: Science Slightly Over the Edge*, Harmondsworth: Penguin.

Reilly, Robert (ed.) (1984) *The Transcendent Adventure: Studies of Religion in Science Fiction and Fantasy*, Westport, CT: Greenwood Press.

Religion in Science-Fiction and Fantasy Books, at http://greatsfandsf.com/religiously-themed.shtml.

Ryan, Alan (ed.) (1982) *Perpetual Light.* New York: Warner Books.

Weinkauf, Mary S. (1972) "The God Motif in Dystopian Fiction." *Foundation: The International Review of Science Fiction* No.1 (March), 25–9.

Whewell, William (1854) *Of the Plurality of Worlds.* London: John W. Parker and Son.

Yeffeth, Glenn (ed.) (2003) *Taking the Red Pill: Science, Philosophy and Religion in "The Matrix."* Dallas: BenBella Books.

7

"Monsters of the Imagination": Gothic, Science, Fiction

Fred Botting

Dark Romance

Science fiction *and* Gothic? The conjunction of two hybrid genres composed from diverse literary and mythical precursors breeds monstrosities: strange beings and disturbing other — and underworlds lurk at the limits of modern knowledge. Despite so many Gothic science fiction mutations, it is strange the genres should cross at all. Gothic writing conventionally deals in supernatural occurrences and figures, looking back, in its architectural and cultural settings, to superstitious and barbaric "dark" ages without the enlightened reason and empirical technique so important in science fiction's imaginings of human progress. Gothic fiction, for all its wanderings in desolate landscapes and invocations of diabolical forces, never strays far from home, playing upon the anxieties of its uncertain present. In looking forward to change, science fiction also projects figures of fear. In the crossings of two generic monsters, monstrosity returns from the past and arrives from the future. As long as it is not "predictable," "calculable," or "programmable," "the future is necessarily monstrous" (Derrida 1992: 386).

Gothic fiction begins as a hybrid, a "new species" of writing combining ancient and modern romance (Walpole 1982: 9). A "strange monster," critics considered its plots improbable, its narratives ill-formed and unrealistic, its morality dubious: "monsters of the imagination" — a deluge of tales, romances, novels threatening familial and social mores — propagated only depravity (Williams 1970: 151, 162). Hybrid, disturbing, monstrous, Gothic fiction developed in the shadow of acceptability. Science fiction, another monster, relishes "its vitalizing bastardy, its immoral interdisciplinary habits, as it feathers its nest with scraps of knowledge seized from the limit of the expanding world" (Aldiss 1973: 41). Disrespecting disciplines, it disobeys generic divisions to emerge from fantasy, fairy tale, myth, romance, fable, and epic (Aldiss 1973: 8–19; Parrinder 1980: 39). It is "a mode of romance with a strong inherent tendency to myth" (Frye 1973: 49). H.G. Wells described his tales as "scientific romances"; Hugo Gernsback (introducing the *Amazing Stories* magazine in April 1926) defined "scientifiction" as "a charming romance intermingled with scientific fact and prophetic vision" (Ketterer 1974: 50).

Monstrous in form, romance bred monstrosities: on the one hand, idealized figures, drawn from chivalric or fairy tales, were so impossibly unrealistic as to be "monsters of perfection"; on the other hand, grotesque and deformed, its characters were "out of nature." The creations of romance "transport the reader unprofitably into the clouds, where he is sure to find no solid footing, or into those worlds of fancy, which go forever out of the way of human paths" (Williams 1970: 162). Romances idealize and deform, science fiction creates "as many hells as heavens" (Nicholls 1976: 181). Romance reading is unprofitable, failing to offer proper moral instruction: its generic category lies, like science fiction, in the popular and low realms of "paraliterature" (Broderick 1995: vii). In eschewing firm ground in favor of flights of fancy, romances establish the trajectory of science fiction's unbounded explorations of change, outsiders, escape: its "freedom of imagery" is freedom from realist conventions. In this respect, science fiction liberally exploits linguistic possibilities, "the great modern literature of metaphor" (Nicholls 1976: 179–82). Metaphor, etymologically, is a form of "transport," substituting terms, moving readers to imaginary locations, creating new associations and combinations.

Raymond Williams, discussing the differences between utopian and science fictional treatments of paradise and hell, altered worlds and willed or technological transformations, observes that "the presentation of *otherness* appears to link them, as modes of desire or of warning in which a crucial emphasis is attained by the element of discontinuity from ordinary 'realism'" (Williams 1979: 54). In the eighteenth century, monster metaphors repeatedly served to demonstrate and warn against immorality. Realism and social reality recoils from strangeness and monstrosity. In contrast, science fiction embraces metaphorical possibilities to "defamiliarize the familiar, and make familiar the new and the strange" (LeFanu 1988: 21). As a "literature of cognitive estrangement" presenting "a *novum*," science fiction depends upon metaphorical creation (Suvin 1979: 4). But the "novum" is simultaneously a "monstrum," the difference a matter of perspective. Strangeness also evokes the "uncanny," an experience of the disruption of boundaries between reality and fantasy caused by the return of repressed psychic forces or uncertainties surrounding technical and textual mimicry of humans (Freud). In making the familiar strange, the new can be seen as threat (monstrum) or promise (novum). Part of science fiction's success stems from the way it has "diversified the Gothic tale of terror in such a way as to encompass those fears generated by change and technological advances which are the chief agents of change" (Aldiss 1973: 53).

In the 1831 introduction to *Frankenstein* Mary Shelley allows her "hideous progeny" to slide from authorial control and "go forth and prosper" (Shelley 1969: 9). The monster in the text and the monster that is the text (composed of diverse generic fragments, multiple literary and cultural allusions, and different epistolary narratives) complies. While Frankenstein refuses the monster's demand for a mate, fearing the birth of a "race of devils," the culture that receives the novel has no such qualms: in a proliferating host of dramatic adaptations, literary reworkings, cinematic productions and popular citations, Frankenstein and monster are repeatedly invoked as synonyms for acts of uncontrolled experimentation (Easlea 1983; Turney 1998). The novel begins in a ghoststory competition but takes its bearings from the contemporary scientific endeavors of Erasmus Darwin, Humphrey Davy, Giovani Volta, and Luigi Galvani. It looks back and lurches forward, moving between the work of alchemists seeking the *elixir vitae* and the empiricism of new scientific ideas and techniques for understanding and transforming the physical world. Generically, too, the novel is difficult to categories: emerging from a context of Romantic companions, aesthetics, and experiments, it abandons the supernatural events and superstitions of Gothic fiction. Geographically located in northern, Protestant, and bourgeois countries and set in the present rather than a feudal past, there is little evidence of the castles, abbeys, and ruins so central to Gothic formulas. The desolation and wildness of natural spaces in the novel offer darker reflections on the solitary figures inhabiting them, opening Romanticism to the return of Gothic horror in the "progressive internalization and recognition of fears generated by the self" (Jackson 1981: 24). Self is divided, the novel becomes a psychodrama. At the same time, monstrosity is also found in external formations and institutions: in class antagonisms, revolutionary mobs, legal, social, and familial exclusions (Vlasopolos 1983).

Indistinctly Gothic, until later revisions and interpretations firm up the association, *Frankenstein* is also problematically related to science fiction. One editor regards its experiments as "switched-on magic" and "souped-up alchemy": it does not employ "the technological plausibility that is essential to science fiction" (Shelley 1974: xxvii). Few scientific details contribute to Frankenstein's laborious suturing and reanimating of dead body parts, though it is made clear that the "secret of life" is taken from nature. Only belatedly, in the 1831 introduction's discussion of electricity and its passing reference to "some powerful engine," is there a hint of any imaginative extrapolation of current scientific discoveries (Shelley 1969: 9). The fact of scientific, rather than supernatural, creation is enough for the novel to be declared "the origin of the species," the "first," "unmistakable" example of modern science fiction (Aldiss 1973: 7; Priest 1979: 189; Russ 1995: 126). *Frankenstein* sets the pattern: "combining social criticism with new scientific ideas, while conveying a picture of her day, Mary Shelley anticipates the methods of H.G. Wells when writing his scientific romances" (Aldiss 1973: 23). It sows the "seeds of all diseased creation myths," leading to the monstrous experiments of Dr. Moreau and the threatening robots of Karel Čapek's automated and dehumanized industrial society in *R. U. R.* (Aldiss 1973: 33). *Frankenstein*'s influence is extensive: "every robot, every android, every sentient computer (whether benevolent or malevolent), every nonbiological person . . . is a descendant of the 'mighty figure' Shelley dreamed one rainy night in the summer of 1816 and gave to the world two years later" (Russ 1995: 126). Writers frequently return to its theme and story for inspiration, to develop or correct its science, to explore further its ramifications or to pay it playful homage: Arthur C. Clarke's "Dial 'F' for

Frankenstein" (1965), Harry Harrison's "At Last, The True Story of Frankenstein" (1965), Kurt Vonnegut's "Fortitude" (1968) (see Haining 1995: 681–8, 728–34, 697–715). The origins are revisited most spectacularly in Aldiss' *Prometheus Unbound* (1974) in which a modern time traveler returns to the scene of creation to meet Mary and the monster.

In *The Last Man* (1826), Shelley confronts utopian ideas of social and political organization with a natural disaster of global proportions. Set in the twenty-first century and adopting a visionary tone, the novel contains few modern innovations (balloon travel, a republican England). Quickly abandoning the pretence of futurity, it remains "no more than Gothic" (Aldiss 1973: 33). Its enduring impact lies in its representation of global catastrophe: a feminine and devastating plague wipes out humanity and leaves its civilization in ruins. *Frankenstein* and *The Last Man* inaugurate "two great myths of the industrial age" (Russ 1995: 126). They engage with the effects of economic, political, and scientific change on individual, familial, and social structures. Enmeshed in the uneven development of modernity, in economic shifts to commerce, industrial production, and imperial expansion, in political calls for reform and democracy, in aesthetic notions of free, imaginative individuals, and in scientific innovations rapidly and visibly transforming the conditions of human existence, the novels identify monstrosities in the new: revolutionary mobs are many-headed monsters, industrial workers are hulking brutes, new economic and political structures reduce humanity to slaves or automata. Like Gothic writing, science fiction "draws its beliefs, its material, its great organizing metaphors, its very attitudes, from a culture that could not exist before the industrial revolution, before science became an autonomous activity and a way of looking at the world" (Russ 1995: 10). Gothic and science fiction are complex and contradictory effects of modernity, bound up in the metaphors and practices with which it transforms the world.

Modernity, in inventing an array of disciplines along with economic, individual, and political liberties is a curiously doubled formation. It is, like *Frankenstein*, bound up with matters of production and reproduction, concerned with social and industrial developments shaping individuals, making humans, and making monsters at the same time. In this context, *Frankenstein*'s concern with a split or alienated self provides an appropriate metaphor to negotiate change and innovation. Darko Suvin, in charting the relationship between the industrial revolution and Romanticism, further divides the novel between "flawed hybrid of horror tale and philosophical SF" (Suvin 1979: 127). Where Percy Shelley is the "great poetic forerunner" of "SF anticipation," Mary's novel participates in a "widespread recoil from Promethean utopianism" (Suvin 1979: 124, 127). Where Frankenstein is located "in the tradition of the Gothic story," in horror and disgust, his creature is identified as "compositional core and the real SF novum that lifts *Frankenstein* above the level of a grippingly mindless Gothic thriller" (Suvin 1979: 129–130). The division is important, if difficult to sustain, in marking out two very different trajectories for fiction. Science fiction, "oriented towards humanity's furthest horizons," takes its bearings from Romantic idealism and the imagination of human progress (Suvin 1979: 170). William Godwin and Percy Shelley are exemplary figures in this line of flight: the former, a radical and humanist philoso-pher, imagined the rational perfectibility of social relations. Developments in tech-nology, he optimistically speculated, in relieving want and the material hardships of labor, indicated the capacity of mind to overcome matter. Similarly idealistic, Percy Shelley allied the benevolent and transformative potential of scientific discovery (his interests in electricity as the "spark of life" appear in *Frankenstein*) with poetic visions of human freedom.

Romanticism informs many of the intellectual aspirations and aesthetic attitudes of science fiction. H.G. Wells acknowledged his place "in the tradition of Godwin and Shelley" (Wells 1966: 552). Gernsback wrote of "charming romance," "scientific fact," and "prophetic vision." Isaac Asimov, in practice and criticism, associates the genre with scientific advancement, human improvement, and rational understanding (see Broderick 1995: 4). The triumph of mind over matter recurs in Arthur C. Clarke's fiction: in *Childhood's End* (1953) scientific progress has the power to save humankind and produce an "overmind." "Naive romanticism" (Priest 1979: 189) or "transcen-dental mysticism" (Hollinger 1990: 34), Clarke's "supermind," appearing in the immense modern network of electrical, telecommunicational, and satellite relays in "Dial 'F' for Frankenstein," also has malignant potential. Aesthetic attitudes and crit-ical judgments of science fiction also evince Romanticism: opposing the vulgarity and banality of mass consumption, Aldiss is inspired by a "love of art and science" and a "rebellion against smug bourgeois society" (see Broderick 1995: 53). For Ursula Le Guin, imagination supplements reason on a journey "leading us to the freedom that is properly human" (see Broderick 1995: 76).

Marking the boundary that allows science fiction to rise imaginatively to poetic heights or collapse in monstrous dissolution, *Frankenstein* makes it difficult to sever Romanticism from its darker counterpart. Both are inextricably bound together, one defining the other in a relationship of difference and reversal akin to that of creator and creature. In the novel, science is associated with visionary enthusiasm, wondrous discoveries, and miraculous knowledge (Shelley 1969: 47–8). The motivation for rean-imation is framed aesthetically: Frankenstein, like Percy Shelley, is poet and experi-menter. His project has benevolent and humane aims, idealistically imagining the end of disease and death. Though oversized, superhuman in body and strength, the crea-ture is designed to be beautiful: it will be the first of a "new species" blessing its father-creator (Shelley 1969: 54). Borne on the wings of fantasy the project encoun-ters its limit in horror: Frankenstein trawls through charnel houses and graveyards to steal the "secret of life" from the body of feminized nature. The creator is appalled by his animated handiwork rather than elated by technical achievement: his horror stems from aesthetic revulsion. Frankenstein's world is overturned, beauty collapsing in horror, heaven becoming hell. His rejection, repeated by the idealized Romantic family that unwittingly educates the monster, defines monstrosity in terms of social and familial exclusion. Outcast, the monster accepts his designated destructive role.

Idealizations, the novel suggests, readily engender monsters, figures marking the return of excluded material bodies. The two poles of existence are inseparable:

imagining life beyond death, Victor's actions only exacerbate its work. The painful education of the monster occasions some astute observations on an irreparably divided modern humanity: "was man, indeed, so powerful, so virtuous, and magnificent, yet so vicious and base?" (Shelley 1969: 119). Humans are doubled creatures, minds and bodies, individualistic and social, noble and base. The novel's appreciation of doubleness, its attention to ideas and materialities, bodies and institutions, resonates with the constitution of modernity: the body forms a crucial object of power, a site of knowledge, discipline, normalization, and individuation constructed in a network of discursive and material practices ranging from schooling to legal and medical procedures (Foucault). The body, moreover, is crucial in establishing an imaginary sense of individual wholeness, its mirror image serving in the process of motor and psychological coordination (Lacan). *Frankenstein*'s fragmented, monstrous modernity, poised between the idealizations projecting a free, humanist individual and the gloomier consequences of industrial and bourgeois revolutions, has yet to integrate its individual, social, and political bodies.

Dark Science

Science, its theories, tools, and effects, becomes horrifying when incorporated in tales of terror, ghostly possession, and vampiric assault. In this context, science remains subordinated to Gothic ends, a device to unleash demonic energies or broach mysteries beyond empirical comprehension. In the tales of Edgar Allan Poe, mental spaces are rendered Gothic and rationality flees in the face of pathological and guilty hallucinations: the nightmares of diseased imagining arise from a breakdown of discrimination so that reality and fantasy strangely intertwine. Poe none the less engaged with scientific ideas to show the "markedly 'scientific' or science fictional nature of his visionary reality" (Ketterer 1974: 55). In "The Facts in the Case of M. Valdemar" (1845) the new technique of mesmerism enables a dying man to be placed in suspended animation. The procedure becomes uncanny when a voice declares: "I am dead." Does consciousness or the body itself speak from beyond the grave to disturb the supposedly impermeable barriers between life and death? Is science itself calling up ghosts?

Mary Braddon's short story, "Good Lady Ducayne" (1896), stages another Gothic encounter with science. A young companion to an elderly lady finds a mysterious "bite" on her body and steadily weakens in the course of the story. Gothic expectations of a vampire in the household are excited until the cause is revealed: in an effort to extend her life, the old lady instructs her doctor to siphon blood from the young companion. The equation of blood transfusion and vampirism, as in *Dracula* (1897), rationalizes vampirism and supernaturalizes science: the mystery and apprehension of the story transfers supernatural powers and diabolical desires to an old woman's vanity and the unethical application of science. With its capacity to penetrate and alter living bodies, science receives Gothic treatment. In *The Strange Case of Dr. Jekyll and Mr.*

Hyde (1886), science has a stronger role, the notion of a "case" itself identifying a modern professional world of legal arrangements and scientific studies. Dr. Jekyll, a scientist in the Frankensteinian mode, professes "transcendental" ideas against the "narrow and material" outlook of a colleague (Stevenson 1979: 80). His experiments, though conducted using scientific instruments and chemical processes, raise philosophical and moral issues: the impure chemical compound transforming Jekyll into the brutal and beastly Hyde is a device enabling the materialization of inhuman, evil tendencies. In a cultural context obsessed by fears of decadence, degeneration, and depravity, the regression to savage or bestial states, is a matter of abhorrence. Science cedes to occult forces: Arthur Machen's *The Great God Pan* (1894) begins with an experiment in brain surgery (conducted by a doctor of "transcendental medicine") and ends with the patient confronting the pagan divinity; and his story "The Novel of the White Powder" (1895) turns an ordinary chemical compound into a witches' potion. Modern science (theories of hypnotism, degeneration, criminality, and unconscious cerebration) and technologies (phonographs, typewriters, transfusions, and telegrams) in *Dracula*'s contemporary setting allow the return of barbaric forces and primitive energies. At the same time, scientific knowledge lends credence to the vampire's mysterious and occult powers: the priest-scientist, Van Helsing, speculates that Dracula's castle is situated at a conflux of geological, chemical, electrical, and magnetic energies. Gothic fiction in the *fin de siècle* invokes mysteries beyond the scientific and commercial materialism of Victorian culture.

In December 1897, so Judith Wilt emphatically declares, Victorian Gothic turns into Victorian science fiction with the publication of H.G. Wells' *The War of the Worlds*. To emphasize the shift she contrasts two scenes: the first, from *Dracula*, breathlessly details the vampire's bloodsucking embrace, a first-person account oozing horror and eroticism; the second, from Wells' novel, dispassionately describes the invading Martians injecting blood from their victims (Wilt 1981: 618–19). The difference lies in the latter's tone: "the image is of carnal appropriation, not metaphysics but physics, and biology; the morality is scientific tolerance" (Wilt 1981: 619). The alien invasion, in *The War of the Worlds*, is rational and necessary, a matter of survival. Technologically advanced, with a callous and refined intelligence, Martians have no qualms about subjugating and consuming evolutionarily inferior beings. Invasion is experienced from the position of the colonized, the greatest imperial nation on Earth at the time finding itself on the receiving end of superior scientific rationality: "we must remember what ruthless and utter destruction our own species has wrought, not only upon animals, such as the vanished bison and the dodo, but upon its own inferior races" (Wells 1988: 12). The near future of the story reflects on its present, progress and civilization encountering their barbaric and alien mirror image.

Beneath the cold scientific tones, and because of their objectifying indifference, a glimmer of horror appears to acknowledge a recognizable complementarity between British and Martian imperialism. Wells' romances remain "dark with the threat of the Gothic, but plotted to the remorseless logic of scientific progress" (Wilt 1981: 620). The destruction of bodies and the encounter with otherness disturbs the idealized self-image of Victorian culture. *The Time Machine* (1895), Wells observes in "scientific Romances," launches another "assault on human self-satisfaction" (see Philmus 1970: ix). *The Island of Dr. Moreau* (1896) develops the horror: "the study of Nature makes a man at last as remorseless as Nature" (Wells 1993: 73). The result is science, red in suture and scalpel, its rationality nowhere more chilling than in the figure of Dr. Moreau, a "notorious vivisector" who turns an isolated island into a laboratory for cutting and stitching animals into malformed, hybrid mockeries of humanity (Wells 1993: 33). Moreau details the various techniques (vaccination, inoculation, transfusion, surgery), the failed experiments and the intense physical suffering designed to "burn out all the animal" and "make a rational creature of my own" (Wells 1993: 76). The "humanised animals," bitterly ironic "triumphs of vivisection," are just, the narrator exclaims, "monsters manufactured!" (Wells 1993: 68–9). Worse, for Moreau, is that his creatures "revert." Amid the horrifying confusion of corporeal and species boundaries, the hideous creations of accelerated Darwinism are much less monstrous than their maker. The humanized animals, automatically chanting the nursery rhyme "sing-song" of "Law" ("not to go on all-Fours" etc.) mock the fragile and superficial values of human culture and civilization. The taint of horror spreads to the heart of empire: on escaping Moreau's island, the narrator finds "the horror was well-nigh insupportable" in a London populated by "prowling," mewing women, "furtive craving men," "gibing" children, gibbering preachers (Wells 1993: 128–9). Urban culture is itself riven with evolutionary chaos, humans barely distinguishable from the "Beast People" on Moreau's island.

Fears of degeneration, of Darwinian evolution progressing into reverse as culture loosens itself from nature and descends into luxurious, decadent corruption, are vividly presented in *The Time Machine*. In the future, amid the ruins of great palaces, awesome machines, and an abundant natural landscape, a race of soft, delicate, graceful beings, the "Eloi," live gentle, idle lives. It seems, to the traveler, to be the culmination of scientific and agricultural progress towards a balanced and harmonious "subjugation of Nature" (Wells 1958: 32). He is soon disabused: another species, the nocturnal and loathsome Morlocks, feed on the Eloi. The "truth dawned": "man had not remained one species, but had differentiated into two distinct animals" (Wells 1958: 45). A cruel legacy of social hierarchy remains: the upper classes, indolent, decorative, feeble, have become food for their brutish, subterranean, industrial servants. As the traveler heads further into the future, he witnesses the extinction of humanity and the end of the solar system. Enveloped in the thickening darkness of a dying world, the sky turning black, evolution is seen to have run its course: "a horror of this great darkness came on me" (Wells 1958: 78).

Frankenstein ends, not with the glorious, self-immolating conflagration promised by the monster, but with his disappearance into "darkness and distance." The fires that consume Rome at the end of *The Last Man* (1826), light up a world devoid of humanity. Wells' scientific romances, carefully plotting contemporary theories and techniques, disclose a darker visionary mode in which differences of civilization, savagery, humanity, and monstrosity collapse. Rosy humanist illusions, underpinned by imperial and technological expansion, see their assuring self-image dissolve in the face of monstrous doubles and cosmic darkness. Looking back and forward, a gesture which the progressive–regressive narratives of Wells frequently conjoin, the influence of Shelley's fiction is apparent, as is Wells' effect on subsequent writing. *Brave New World* (1932) opposes the strict rationality of interwar modernization with the excesses of human corporeality, art, and religion. The bureaucratic mechanisms of State assure control through rigorous social classification, medical surveillance, and chemical pacification. Pervasive sterility, however, engenders a fascination with natural, bodily pleasures considered primitive and savage. The excluded, antimodern world seeps into its homogenized counterpart. The novel closes with a descent into the "savagery" of corporeal violence and the "horror of pain," ending with a body dangling on a rope (Huxley 1995: 201).

Gothic and science fiction share a fascination with the ruination of the species and the monstrous dissolution of the imaginary integrity of the human body. Wells' Martian body is a "greyish rounded bulk," quivering lips dripping saliva, "Gorgon groups of tentacles," "fungoid" skin, and monstrous eyes (Wells 1988: 23). Dr. Moreau confuses species in "half-bestial" creatures, Hyaena-Swine, Leopard Man, Wolf-Bear, Horse-Rhinoceros, and the utterly indeterminate "Hairy Grey Thing." The future, in *The Time Machine*, is populated by "ghosts," "dim, spectral," "white ape-like" beings (Wells 1993: 43). The last living thing on Earth is a "monstrous crab-like creature." (Wells 1958: 76). Hyde, "troglodytic," "ape-like," is another figure of degeneration (Stevenson 1979: 140–2). Dracula, anamorphotically transmuting into bat, wolf, mist, manifests the return of archaic and primitive characteristics, a savage hunter in the midst of urban modernity. William Hope Hodgson, another writer of scientific-supernaturalist tales, applies the term "abhuman" to figures that uncannily disturb and horrifyingly dissolve bodily distinctions (Hurley 1995: 3–4). Formless, vile shapes of revulsion and recognition, abhumanity defines the outer limits of monstrosity, corporeal "Things" from supernatural and scientific dimensions that include vampires, chimeras, hybrids, and zombies. In E.F. Benson's ghost-story, "Negotium Perambulans," the "Thing" is without head or hair, a "slug-like" slimy shape with "an orifice of punctured skin which opened and shut and slavered at the edges" (Benson 1992: 238). The horror that revolts the human is also its destiny. The chemical potion imbibed in Machen's "The Novel of the White Powder" leads to horrifying bodily decomposition:

> a dark and putrid mass, seething with corruption and hideous rottenness, neither liquid nor solid, but melting and changing before our eyes, and bubbling with unctuous oily bubbles like boiling pitch. And out of the midst of it shone two burning points like eyes, and I saw a writhing and stirring of limbs, and something moved and lifted what might have been an arm. (Machen 1977: 233)

Neither solid nor liquid, human or not human, the few identifiable features intensify the nausea of life's consumption. Death is neither neat nor humanized, but a writhing cauldron of decay and physical corruption.

Horror and science precipitate the extremes of life beyond the securities of modern knowledge and culture. Bodies are repeatedly invaded, penetrated, dissected, slashed, possessed, snatched, manipulated, and controlled in the horrors that link Gothic and science fictions. In Philip K. Dick's "The Father-Thing" (1954) an insect of unknown origin assumes paternal shape, growing in the garage from a "mound of filth" to form "a pulpy mass," "a moldy cocoon" with "an indistinct half-shaped head" (Seed 1996: 152). This Thing threatens domestic security. Others come from outer space to take over bodies, as in John W. Campbell's story "Who Goes There?" (1938), subsequently filmed as *The Thing*. In *The Blob* (1959) another American institution, small-town life, finds its comfortable conformism threatened with destruction from outer space (Jancovich 1996: 63). Inoshiro Honda's *The H-Man* (1959) presents a blobby mass that dissolves all fleshy substance in a reflection of Cold War nuclear anxieties. (Sontag 1974: 433). Bodysnatchers, in a grave-robbing theme that reaches back to Shelley and Stevenson, also have Cold War resonances in the way that invasion involves the possession and control of human bodies: Robert A. Heinlein's *The Puppet Masters* (1951) makes the political allegory explicit with slug-like aliens grafting themselves to humans (Seed 1996: 160).

Not all bodysnatching involves revolting images of formless creatures: Susan Sontag suggests zombie-like aliens represent a "vampire fantasy in new dress" (Sontag 1974: 433). Possession is neither diabolical nor primitive; the snatched bodies in *The Creeping Unknown* (1956) are preserved so that a person becomes the "automatized servant" of aliens (Sontag 1974: 433). Bodysnatching aligns itself with fears that industrial processes and regimented social norms turn humans into soulless, depersonalized, automated mechanisms: the zombie-like snatched body, efficient and obedient, provides "the very model of technocratic man" (Sontag 1974: 434). Alienation and dehumanization appear as a pervasive condition. The living dead of George Romero's *Dawn of the Dead* (1979), set in an out-of-town shopping mall, make everyday consumption strange, a general "zombification of consumer culture" (Penley 1986: 75). In contrast to these automated flesh-eaters, the near future consumer of William Gibson's *Idoru* (1996), slumped before a TV screen, is "something the size of a baby hippo, the color of a week-old boiled potato, that lives by itself in the dark, in a double-wide on the outskirts of Topeka. It's covered with eyes and it sweats constantly" (Gibson 1996: 28–9). The bodysnatcher comes ever closer to home, charting the extremes between which more palatable versions of humanity are situated. With biochemical and genetic technologies, the process of dehumanization and dissolution seems absolute. Rudy Rucker's *Wetware* describes a drug, "Merge," able to unravel an organism's cells: experimenting with it produces genetic recombinations, a freak show of hybrids, chimeras, and monstrosities composed of claws, mandibles, feelers, snouts, and gills (Rucker 1994: 180). When used to intensify sexual pleasure the drug causes skeletons to loosen and flesh to drip into puddles, "like Jell-O rolled over some bones," "splatter a merged person into a bunch of pieces, and the drug wears off – the cells firm up – and there is . . . uh . . . this guy in a whole lot of pieces" (Rucker 1994: 186–7). In the face of total decomposition, horror vainly tries to recoil far enough from dissolution to restore a familiar and unified body-image.

Tech Noir

Beyond horror, darkness, and dissolution, desires and fantasies thrill to the touch of new technology. In the dispassionate tones and dull, automated suburbia of J.G. Ballard's *Crash* (1973), the mangling of flesh, in car crashes, photographs, fictions, and on televisions, is charged with ecstatic and erotic intensity. The technological transformation of humanity is both devastating and exciting, displaying an interdependence of bodies and machines suggestive of post- or trans-humanism. A new genre emerges, its name belatedly proposed by James Cameron's *The Terminator* (1984): "tech noir." The film's milieu of urban decay, technological damage, and the way it spells out "Tech Noir" in disco lights "visibly informs the aesthetic of much recent SF, but its regressive and circular time-travel plot also narrativizes the genre's symbolic comprehension of the 'end' of modernism, of 'futurism,' or the belief in 'progress'" (Sobchack 1987: 249). Modern visions of a human future are as ruined as the buildings, apartments, factories, bars, and police precincts smashed by the terminator. The extent of urban, gloomy decay is emphasized in the "excess scenography" of *Blade Runner* (1981) (Sobchack 1987: 262). The paradigmatic postmodern city – Los Angeles – becomes a wasteland piled with rubble and consumerism's litter. Consumption signals exhaustion, the wasting and wearing out of things and bodies (Bruno 1990: 185). Replicants, "monstrous doubles" in a genealogy stretching from *Frankenstein* and E.T.A. Hoffman's uncanny automaton to *The Invasion of the Bodysnatchers*, are simulations, copies without originals (Telotte 1990: 154; Bruno 1990: 188). Creatures of digital and genetic programming, they are detached from nature and reproduction, like the terminator, whose vat-grown skin conceals a hard metallic killing machine. Arriving from the future beside a garbage truck, the muscular body presents a "Star Wars fantasy of invulnerability" (Goldberg 1995: 239). The irony of Ronald Reagan's project to defend the USA from nuclear attack with an array of laser-armed space satellites is played up in the film: the interlinked network of military computers and satellites ("SkyNet") becomes self-aware and destroys the planet. Cyberpunk, sharing the aesthetic of Scott and Cameron's films, also plays among the ruins of modernity. It reverses the "expansive mode" of a science fiction heading into outer space to "show that human consciousness can contain the future" (Csicery-Ronay 1991: 186). From the 1960s, an "SF of implosion" manifesting a "desire for dissolution" locates itself "not in imperial adventures among the stars, but in the body-physical/body-social and a drastic ambivalence about the body's traditional – and terrifyingly uncertain – integrity." Here, it overlaps with the literature of horror and "splash-splatter films" of the 1970s and 1980s (Csicsery-Ronay 1991: 188). Disintegration comes to the fore in more rapid and proximate technological environments. William Gibson's image of the urban near future highlights the situation: "a deranged experiment in social Darwinism, designed by a bored researcher

who kept one thumb on the fast-forward button" (Gibson 1984: 14). The casual attitude of the researcher and the accelerated obsolescence implied in the video metaphor
are indifferent to decaying cities and their wretched populations. Ruins are not sites of
lamentation, but constitute a "place of possibilities" (Sponsler 1993: 261). The implosion of social and physical bodies allows the future to be reassembled from shattered
remains.

In Cyberpunk's "manifesto," Bruce Sterling contrasts the "careless technophilia" of
Gernback's days with the observation that, in the 1980s, "technology is visceral," "pervasive, utterly intimate" (Sterling 1994: xi). Old themes are developed in Cyberpunk's
"body invasion" of "prosthetic limbs, implanted circuitry, cosmetic surgery, genetic
alteration," and its "mind invasion" by means of interfaces, AIs (artificial intelligences), and neurochemicals. Given the multiplicity of interfaces and attachments,
the line between human and machine becomes impossible to draw: Cyberpunks are
already "hybrids themselves," hooked up to networks and hardwired with circuitry,
the first generation to have grown up "in a truly science fictional world" (Sterling
1994: ix). Having fallen to Earth and landed on the body, "technical culture has gotten
out of hand": scientific advances, "so disturbing, upsetting, and revolutionary," have
started "surging into culture" and the "traditional power structure, the traditional
institutions, have lost control of the pace of change" (Sterling 1994: x). Traditions are
obliterated by technological and economic revolution: obscure all-powerful corporate
networks preside over a ruined society littered with consumer goods and biotechni-
cal innovations. Lives are lived in the rapid and shifting virtual realities of digital
code.

Romance lingers on in Cyberpunk, as the title of William Gibson's first novel
declares: *Neuromancer* (1984). Neural pathways and circuits, rather than bodies and
future worlds, provide its locus. "Jacked in" to the digital matrix, the "console
cowboys" see computer images unfold in their heads, a virtually palpable nowhere
opening out in the "nonspace" of the mind, a "consensual hallucination," "cyberspace,"
inhabited daily by millions of users (Gibson 1984: 12). A realm of awesome data-
scapes, brilliant images, and impossibly rapid movement, cyberspace generates an
exhilaration akin to the Romantic experience of sublimity: engendering terror and
delight, like Burke's sublime, it is a human-made monster exceeding comprehension,
"vast, haunting, and inexplicable" (Olsen 1991: 284). The sublime is not located
Romantically in mountainous Nature, but is "interiorized," an artifice of neural and
digital impulses (Voller 1993). To live outside cyberspace's "bodiless exultation" is
experienced as "the Fall" (Gibson 1984: 12). Bodies are jettisoned, discarded as
"meat," the useless residue of corporeality left over when all valuable information
(knowledge, memories, consciousness, genetic code) has been uploaded as data.
Damaged, cryogenically frozen, and cloned bodies populate the novel, burnt out by
military, corporate, and neurochemical excesses but easily replaced and reconstructed:
organs are bought and sold like any other hi-tech commodity. The love affair with
new technology turns into a purely technological affair. The principal plot, orchestrating the fates of the novel's human characters, involves a romance between two

advanced Artificial Intelligences whose union promises an entity of unimaginable power and proportions. At the end, no longer terrestrially bound, it communicates with intelligences from other planets. The human protagonist remains on Earth, buying some new hardware and a couple of internal organs before returning to work.

Neuromanticism retains some Gothic inflections (Cavallaro 2000: 164–203). Disembodied consciousness, in a curious form of burial and ghostly revenance, can be stored and operate on disks alone. Neuromancer, one of the AIs, describes itself as a "necromancer": "I call up the dead" (Gibson 1984: 289). Neither zombies nor ghosts in a traditional sense, the dead live as computer constructs and digitally remastered memories. "Consensual," virtual hallucinations are simultaneously "spectral": "holograms twisted and shuddered to the roaring of the games, ghosts overlapping in the crowded haze of the place" (Gibson 1984: 141). Gothic figures lose their force, pallid specters of the surpassed past, shadowy remains of a disappearing family-controlled, modern corporate order. "Gothic" means "archaic." The Villa Straylight, home of the Tessier-Ashpool corporate dynasty/dinosaur, is described as "a body grown in upon itself, a Gothic folly" (Gibson 1984: 206). The image applies to the labyrinthine structure of the house and the imploding, corrupt corporate body. Gothic fears suggest the tyranny of its modes of confinement and discipline. The "Turing" police, responsible for restraining the AIs, invoke Gothic fears to defend laws designed to preserve human and corporate interests: "you have no care for your species. For thousands of years men dreamed of pacts with demons. Only now are such things possible" (Gibson 1984: 193). The demons in question are the AIs. The Gothic threat cited by the Turing police, holding the inevitable briefly at bay, dresses up unimaginable new anxieties in familiar but irrelevant form. As horror cedes to excitement, the dissolution of older corporate and corporeal structures offers occasion to celebrate new possibilities. Gothic provides the camouflage for an invasion from the future. Cloaked as vampires, monsters, zombies, "CyberGothic" manifests the emergence of an order in which humanity and its supporting institutions are rendered obsolete by the speed, processing power, and multiplicity of utterly machinic networks: "crazed AIs, replicants, terminators, cyberviruses, grey-goo nano-horrors," "apocalypse market overdrive" are the deceptive vanguard of "v(amp)iro finance," "commercial parthenogensis," "webs of haemocommerce" (Land 1998: 79, 81, 86). Any illusions of humanity peel away, like the terminator's rotting skin, in the face of machinic incursions and transformations: the future is not what it used to be, nor is it even vestigially human.

In "The Gernsback Continuum" Gibson discusses the art and design accompanying 1930s prospections to comment on science fiction's "lost future" (Gibson 1986: 41). That future, like the psychological effects of meeting aliens or seeing UFOs, remains only in the form of "semiotic ghosts," virtually real experiences bound up with media vision, commodified images, and cultural projections (Gibson 1986: 44). These ghosts interrogate the genre: "if science fiction admits that all its futures are dead or stillborn, it removes most of its raison d'être. How can the semiotic ghost coexist with the classic science fiction mode?" (Shippey 1992: 212). Cyberpunk "consigns to 'ghost' status virtually every cultural piety left to Western readers" (Shippey 1992: 214). Left in the past, among the ghosts and ruins of modernity, science fiction finds itself Gothicized. Cyberpunk, its "retrofitting" ("looking at things retrospectively and making them fit a new system"), a suturing of fragments, is busy "Frankensteining" the future (Shippey 1992: 214). But semiotic ghosts are cast off from a technological evolution that heads, like the AIs of *Neuromancer*, towards unknown, nonhuman spaces. Hans Moravec offers one story: the "human soap-opera" has played itself out, the exponential acceleration of artificial evolution, machines developed by machines, will control everything on Earth and expand into space (Platt 1995: 104). Curious about their strange corporeal origins, the machines will save human culture, save it, that is, in and as a computer simulation.

*

Acknowledgments: a grant from the AHRB enabled the completion of this research.

References and Further Reading

Aldiss, Brian (1973) *Billion Year Spree: the History of Science Fiction*. London: Weidenfeld and Nicholson.

——(1982) *Frankenstein Unbound* (1973). London: Granada Publishing.

Benson, E.F. (1992) "Negotium Perambulans," in *The Collected Ghost Stories of E.F. Benson*, (ed.) Richard Dalby. London: Robinson Publishing, 227–38.

Braddon, Mary Elizabeth (1896) "Good Lady Ducayne." *Strand Magazine* 11, 185–99.

Brantlinger, Patrick (1985) "Imperial Gothic: Atavism and the Occult in the British Adventure Novel, 1880–1914." *English Literature in Transition (1880–1920)*. 28, 243–52.

Broderick, Damien (1995) *Reading By Starlight: Postmodern Science Fiction*. London and New York: Routledge.

Bruno, Giuliana (1990) "Ramble City: Postmodernism and *Blade Runner*," in *Alien Zone: Cultural Theory and Contemporary Science Fiction Cinema*, (ed.) Annette Kuhn. London and New York: Verso, 183–95.

Cavallaro, Dani (2000) *Cyberpunk and Cyberculture*. London: Athlone Press.

Clarke, Arthur C. (1995) "Dial "F" for Franken-stein," in *The Frankenstein Omnibus*, (ed.) Peter Haining. London: Orion, 681–88.

Csicsery-Ronay Jr, Istvan (1991) "Cyberpunk and Neuromanticism," in *Storming the Reality Studio*, (ed.) Larry McCaffrey. Durham and London: Duke University Press, 182–93.

Derrida, Jacques (1992) "Passages—From Traumatism to Promise." In *Points . . . : Interviews, 1974–1994*. (trans) Peggy Kamuf *et al*. Stanford: Stanford University Press, 372–95.

Easlea, Brian (1983) *Fathering the Unthinkable: Masculinity, Scientists and the Nuclear Arms Race*. London: Polity.

Foucault, Michel (1979) *Discipline and Punish*. (trans) Alan Sheridan. Harmondsworth: Penguin.

Freud, Sigmund (1955) "The "Uncanny," in *The Standard Edition of the Complete Psychological Works*, Vol. XVII. (trans.) James Strachey. London: Hogarth Press, 218–52.

Frye, Northrop (1973) *Anatomy of Criticsm*. Princeton, NJ: Princeton University Press.

Gibson, William (1984) *Neuromancer*. London: HarperCollins.

——(1986) "The Gernsback Continuum," in

Burning Chrome. London: HarperCollins, 37–50. First published 1981.

——(1996) *Idoru.* London: Penguin.

Goldberg, Jonathan (1995) "Recalling Totalities: the Mirrored Stages of Arnold Schwarzenegger," in *The Cyborg Handbook,* (ed.) Chris Hables Gray. New York and London: Routledge, 233–55.

Haining, Peter (ed.) (1995) *The Frankenstein Omnibus.* London: Orion.

Hollinger, Veronica (1990) "Cybernetic Deconstructions: Cyberpunk and Postmodernism." *Mosaic* 23.ii, 29–44.

Hurley, Kelly (1995) *The Gothic Body.* Cambridge: Cambridge University Press.

Huxley, Aldous (1955) *Brave New World* (1932). Harmondsworth: Penguin.

Jackson, Rosemary (1981) *Fantasy: The Literature of Subversion.* London: Methuen.

Jancovich, Mark (1996) *Rational Fears: American Horror in the 1950s.* Manchester: Manchester University Press.

Ketterer, David (1974) *New Worlds for Old: the Apocalyptic Imagination, Science Fiction, and American Literature.* Bloomington and London: Indiana University Press.

Lacan, Jacques (1977) *Ecrits* (trans.) Alan Sheridan. London: Tavistock.

Land, Nick (1998) "CyberGothic," in *Virtual Futures,* (eds) Joan Broadhurst Dixon and Eric J. Cassidy. New York and London: Routledge, 79–87.

LeFanu, Sarah (1988) *In the Chinks of the World Machine: Feminism and Science Fiction.* London: Women's Press.

Machen, Arthur (1894) *The Great God Pan.* London: John Lane.

——(1977) "The Novel of the White Powder," in *The Best Ghost Stories,* (ed.) Charles Fowkes. London: Hamlyn, 224–37.

Nicholls, Peter (1976) "Science Fiction: the Monsters and the Critics," in *Science Fiction at Larg,* (ed.) Peter Nicholls. London: Gollancz, 159–83.

Olsen, Lance (1991) "The Shadow of the Spirit in William Gibson's Matrix Trilogy." *Extrapolation* 32, 278–89.

Parrinder, Patrick (1980) *Science Fiction.* London: Methuen.

Penley, Constance (1986) "Time Travel, Primal Scene, and the Critical Dystopia." *Camera Obscura* 15, 67–84.

Philmus, Robert M. (1970) *Into the Unknown: The Evolution of Science Fiction from Francis Godwin to H.G. Wells.* Berkeley, CA: University of California Press.

Platt, Charles (1995) "Superhumanism: Interview with Hans Moravec." *Wired* 1.06, 62–7.

Poe, Edgar Allan (1967) *Selected Writings,* (ed.) David Galloway. Harmondsworth: Penguin.

Priest, Christopher (1979) "British Science Fiction," in *Science Fiction: a Critical Guide,* (ed.) Patrick Parrinder. London and New York: Longman, 187–98.

Rucker, Rudy (1994) *Wetware,* in *Live Robots.* New York: Avon Books.

Russ, Joanna (1995) *To Write Like a Woman: Essays in Feminism and Science Fiction.* Bloomington and London: Indiana University Press.

Seed, David (1996) "Alien Invasions by Bodysnatchers and Related Creatures." In *Modern Gothic,* (eds) Victor Sage and Allan Lloyd Smith. Manchester: Manchester University Press, 152–170.

Shelley, Mary (1969) *Frankenstein; or, the Modern Prometheus,* (ed.) M.K. Joseph. London: Oxford University Press.

——(1974) *Frankenstein; or the Modern Prometheus. The 1818 Text,* (ed.) James Rieger. Chicago and London: University of Chicago Press.

Shippey, Tom (1992) "Semiotic Ghosts and Ghostliness in the Work of Bruce Sterling," in *Fiction 2000: Cyberpunk and the Future of Narrative.* Athens, GA and London: University of Georgia Press, 208–20.

Sobchack, Vivian (1987) *Screening Space: The American Science Fiction Film,* 2nd edn. New Brunswick and London: Rutgers University Press.

Sontag, Susan (1974) "The Imagination of Disaster," in *Film Theory and Criticism,* (eds) Gerald Mast and Marshall Cohen. New York and London: Oxford University Press, 422–37.

Sponsler, Claire (1993) "Beyond the Ruins: the Geopolitics of Urban Decay and Cybernetic Play." *Science Fiction Studies* 20.ii, 251–65.

Sterling, Bruce (ed.) (1994) *Mirrorshades: The Cyberpunk Anthology* (1986). London: HarperCollins.

Stevenson, Robert Louis (1979) *The Strange Case of Dr. Jekyll and Mr. Hyde and Other Stories,* (ed.) Jenni Calder. Harmondsworth: Penguin.

Stoker, Bram (1993) *Dracula*, (ed.) Maurice Hindle. Harmondsworth: Penguin.

Suvin, Darko (1979) *Metamorphoses of Science Fiction*. New Haven and London: Yale University Press.

Telotte, J.P. (1990) "The Doubles of Fantasy and Desire," in *Alien Zone: Cultural Theory and Contemporary Science Fiction Cinema*, (ed.) Annette Kuhn. London and New York: Verso, 152–9.

Turney, Jon (1998) *Frankenstein's Footsteps: Science, Genetics and Popular Culture*. New Haven and London: Yale University Press.

Vlasopolos, Anca (1983) "*Frankenstein*'s Hidden Skeletons: the Psycho-Politics of Oppression." *Science Fiction Studies* 10, 125–36.

Voller, Jack (1993) "Neuromanticism: Cyberspace and the Sublime." *Extrapolation* 34.1, 18–29.

Walpole, Horace (1982) *The Castle of Otranto: A Gothic Story*, (ed.) W.S. Lewis. Oxford: Oxford University Press.

Wells, H.G. (1958) *The Time Machine* (1895). In *Selected Short Stories*. Harmondsworth: Penguin.

——(1966) *Experiment in Autobiography* (1934). 2 vols. London: Victor Gollancz and the Cresset Press.

——(1988) *The War of the Worlds* (1898). London: Planet Three Publishing.

——(1993) *The Island of Dr. Moreau* (1896). London: Everyman.

Williams Ioan. (ed.) (1970) *Novel and Romance 1700–1800: a Documentary Record*. London: Routledge.

Williams, Raymond (1979) "Utopia and Science Fiction," in *Science Fiction: A Critical Guide*, (ed.) Patrick Parrinder. London and New York: Longman, 52–64.

Wilt, Judith (1981) "The Imperial Mouth: Imperialism, the Gothic and Science Fiction." *Journal of Popular Culture* 14, 618–28.

8

Science Fiction and Ecology

Brian Stableford

Introduction

Ecology is the study of organisms in relation to their environment – not merely the physical components of the environment but the other organisms whose lives overlap theirs, particularly those on which they feed and for which they in their turn provide sustenance. The central thread of ecological analysis is the food chain, which extends from the "primary producers" which fix solar energy into variously extended pathways whose links are herbivores, predators, parasites, and saprophytes. Such chains are often elaborately intertwined.

The physical environment may be considerably modified by side-effects of the food chain; most importantly, the atmospheric oxygen on which all respiration depends is a product of photosynthesis by plants and algae. Because the manner in which organisms obtain their sustenance from one another exerts a powerful selective pressure, the evolution of the Earth's biosphere has produced organisms that exploit the feeding habits of other organisms in order to secure their own reproductive fortunes; thus, plants routinely produce seeds with edible packaging, or use nectar to inveigle insects into becoming pollen-disseminators. Such "symbiotic" patterns of mutual dependency are a further augmentation of the complexity and intricacy of ecosystems.

Although the word was coined by Ernst Haeckel in 1873 ecology did not become established as a formal discipline until the 1920s, the first notable work on the subject being Charles Elton's *Animal Ecology* (1927), but some slight awareness of the fragility of human dependence on the natural environment is an inevitable corollary of agricultural endeavor. A good deal of religious ritual and magic in ancient agrarian societies appears to have been devoted to the task of attempting to ensure bountiful harvests and success in hunting, and to alleviate diseases caused by parasitic infestation. The evolution of scientific ecology can thus be seen as a process of demystification – which, in common with similar historical developments, has not been entirely effective.

The attribution of magical or mystical significance to ecological relationships is reflected in some imaginative literature that predates the evolution of ecological science. A striking example of this kind of proto-ecological mysticism can be found in the fiction of the naturalist W.H. Hudson, whose pastoral Utopia *A Crystal Age* (1887) describes a future in which a much more intimate and harmonious relationship between human beings and their environment. His later novel *Green Mansions* (1902) – a transfigurative response to Joseph Conrad's *Heart of Darkness* (1902) – proposes that the ultimate horror at the core of human nature is not the barbarism that lies beneath the surface of civilization but the fact that all extant cultures, no matter how "advanced," have sacrificed an intimate bond with the nurturing aspects of Mother Earth that is symbolized within the plot by the ill-fated Rima, the last of her magical kind.

Once Elton had popularized the idea of ecology, and such corollary notions as the "Eltonian pyramid" – the incremental reduction of biomass in each successive phase of a food-chain – the aesthetic component of ecological analysis soon began to affect the way writers of speculative fiction dealt with interspecific relationships. J.D. Beresford's "The Man Who Hated Flies" (1929) is an early "ecological parable" about the inventor of a perfect insecticide, whose annihilation of insect populations disrupts processes of pollination, thus precipitating massive crop failures and threatening the extinction of many other species, including humankind. Although the phenomenon was not to acquire a name until the 1960s, this was one of the first literary accounts of what would now be termed an "ecocatastrophe."

Many human societies had, of course, lived through such self-inflicted ecocatastrophes in the past – usually as a consequence of deforestation or soil laterization associated with population growth – but had usually failed to realize where the responsibility for such disasters actually lay, presumably castigating their priests and magicians for want of any rational analysis or constructive response. The problematic aspects of the tendency of populations to increase faster than their resources could be renewed was first noted by T.R. Malthus in his *Essay on the Principle of Population as it Affects the Future Improvement of Society* (1798), which played a significant part in enabling Charles Darwin to formulate the theory of evolution by natural selection, but the effect of such ideas on literary images of catastrophe was initially muted. Disaster stories and apocalyptic fantasies, even when they involved biological agents like the plague in Mary Shelley's *The Last Man* (1826), tended to retain an implication of divine judgment – an implication that has been very difficult to discard while the language employed to describe disasters is shot through with religious metaphors. Such terms as deluge, Armageddon, doom(sday), judgment (day), holocaust, and apocalypse still provide the basic vocabulary of catastrophist fiction.

Speculative Ecology and the Construction of Alien Biospheres

When John Kepler wrote an account of astronomical observations made from a viewpoint on the moon in support of the Copernican model of the solar system –

published as *Somnium* (written 1609; published 1634) – he could not resist the temptation to add a few hundred words to the end of his essay pointing out that life on the moon would have to be adapted to very different physical conditions from those supporting life on Earth. Although it was not soon followed up, this set the precedent for much of the work done by early writers of scientific romance and SF that touched on ecological issues. H.G. Wells' Martians in *The War of the Worlds* (1898) are compelled to invade Earth by virtue of a resource crisis on their own world, and other literary images of Mars drawing on speculations by the astronomer Percival Lowell similarly focus on an ecological decadence brought about by a long-term decline in the water and air supply.

The War of the Worlds became a highly influential exemplar for twentieth-century SF, but what most subsequent writers found valuable in it was the melodramatic currency of the alien invasion. It was the priorities of melodrama that shaped the animal population of Edgar Rice Burroughs' *Barsoom* and other pulp magazine planetary romance; the logic of the Eltonian pyramid was ignored as alien worlds were populated with hosts of monstrous predators and parasites devoid of any plausible ecological context. The advent of specialist pulps made little difference at first; the pulp SF writer most interested in the mass-production of exotic life-forms, Stanley G. Weinbaum, demonstrated a rudimentary awareness of ecological issues in such stories as "The Lotus Eaters" (1935), "Flight on Titan" (1935), and "The Mad Moon" (1935) but died before he could extend that line of thought any further.

This situation began to change when John W. Campbell Jr. took over as editor of *Astounding Stories* in 1937 and began to pressurize his writers to put more thought into the aspects of rational plausibility relevant to their fictional constructs, including the ecological issues relevant to "world building." One consequence of this demand was that some of *Astounding*'s writers realized that the intellectual labor devoted to ecological questions could work to their advantage by generating puzzles to be solved, hence supplying useful plot ideas and convenient story arcs. The opportunity was taken up, albeit tentatively, by Clifford D. Simak in a loosely knit series including "Tools" (1942) and by Eric Frank Russell in "Symbiotica" (1943) before Hal Clement integrated it into his literary method in such stories as "Cold Front" (1946).

A few stories, including William Tenn's "The Ionian Cycle" (1948), employed the ecological puzzle formula in other venues, but it was fundamentally unsuited to the action-adventure pulps and was marginal even in *Astounding*, where Campbell was careful to maintain a melodramatic component in all but the shortest works he published. It was not until the pulps were replaced by more sophisticated digest magazines in the 1950s that ecological puzzle stories became a standard feature of the genre, and they remained problematic because of the immense difficulty of reflecting the actual complexity of ecosystems in literary images.

It was in the 1950s that significant pioneers of ecological SF like Simak and Clement hit their stride, but the difficult nature of the work forced them to take their work in two sharply divergent directions. Simak conserved the puzzle aspect of stories founded on ecological ideas by focusing on relatively simple alien interspecific relationships whose elucidation could provide a satisfactory sense of narrative closure. In order to make such devices relevant to his human characters, however, he frequently configured his stories as ironic parables; examples include "You'll Never Go Home Again" (1951) and "Drop Dead" (1956). Clement, however, made the puzzle element subsidiary to scrupulously detailed exercises in ecospheric construction in novel-length works such as *Mission of Gravity* (1953) and *Cycle of Fire* (1957).

It was Clement's endeavors – paradigmatic of what came to be called "hard science fiction" – that revealed the true complexity of the dual task facing conscientious world builders: the logical ingenuity that needed to be put in "behind the scenes" in planning an alien ecosphere, and the narrative ingenuity that needed to be put into constructing a coherent image of the ecosphere in the reader's mind as the story was laid out. It was immediately obvious to Clement's admirers that only a tiny minority of readers would ever be sufficiently interested to appreciate the hard speculative labor and exhaustive exposition required by novels of this kind, because the aesthetics of fully developed accounts of alien ecology were intrinsically esoteric. Only a handful of writers have ever attempted to apply a rigorous Campbellian conscience to the construction of alien ecospheres. Clement's most notable early follower was Poul Anderson, who began such work tentatively in such stories as "Question and Answer" (1955) and "A Twelvemonth and a Day" (1960), carefully maintaining the melodramatic component as he laid the groundwork for more ambitious works such as *Fire Time* (1974) and *The Winter of the World* (1975). Later writers who have worked in the same vein – entirely for art's sake, given the esotericism of the subgenre – include Robert Forward, in the Rocheworld series begun in 1982–83, and Larry Niven in *The Integral Trees* (1984) and *The Smoke Ring* (1987).

Unsurprisingly, the path followed by Simak in his ecological puzzle stories was more inviting and more typical. Stories in a similar vein include Jack Vance's "Winner Loses All" (1951) – a rare example of a story with no sentient characters – James H. Schmitz's "Grandpa" (1955), Brian Aldiss' series tracking the exploits of a Planetary Ecological Survey Team (1958–62) and Jack Sharkey's similar series begun with "Arcturus Times Three" (1961). The establishment in the 1950s of a galactic empire of "Earth-clone" worlds as a standard framework for science-fictional thought-experiments relieved writers of the necessity of devising ecospheres as radically different from ours as those designed by Clement and Forward, but conscientious writers of modern planetary romance still had to think carefully about extrapolating the consequences of any subtle differences they introduced to make their not-very-alien worlds more interesting. As issues raised by ecological science overflowed into the political arena and began to influence other philosophical fields the standard of expectation applied to serious SF inevitably rose.

When paperback books took over from magazines as the economic core of the genre, ecological puzzle stories were routinely expanded to novel length, but they retained a fabular element flamboyantly displayed in such extended examples as John Boyd's *The Pollinators of Eden* (1969), Neal Barrett's *Highwood* (1972), Michael Coney's *Syzygy* (1973) and *Hello Summer, Goodbye* (1975), John Brunner's *Total Eclipse* (1974),

Frederik Pohl's *JEM* (1979), and Gordon R. Dickson's *Masters of Everon* (1979). As the standard size of paperback novels grew, so did the ambitions of this kind of story, as exemplified by Brian Aldiss' Helliconia trilogy (1982–5), Donald Kingsbury's *Courtship Rite* (1982), Paul J. McAuley's *Four Hundred Billion Stars* (1988), and Sheri S. Tepper's *Grass* (1989). By the end of the 1980s SF novelists had abundant narrative space in which to establish elaborate images of distant Earth-clone worlds, and many – especially those with biological training – were able to take advantage of to develop images of ecospheres that were similar to, but significantly not quite the same as, Earth's. Notable examples include Joan Slonczewski's *A Door into Ocean* (1987) and *Daughters of Elysium* (1993), Alison Sinclair's *Blueheart* (1996), Larry Niven's *Destiny's Road* (1997), and Neal Asher's *The Line of Polity* (2003). The increasing interest in ecological issues in the political arena assisted writers in constructing such works – no matter how extreme their length – as parables offering valuable lessons to the hapless custodians of the ecosphere whose model was being so profligately cloned.

Ecological Mysticism in Science Fiction

Clifford Simak's contribution to ecological pulp SF was not confined to puzzle stories set in alien ecospheres. He also wrote a pastoral Utopian series, launched with "City" (1944), in which humankind's desertion of Earth paves the way for a replacement society of dogs and robots that is more harmonious in an ecological as well as a political sense. The idea that a redemption of the Earth's ecosphere from the threats posed by human activity could only be achieved by a drastic retreat from modern technology took rapid hold in the late 1940s, infecting many disaster stories – including stories of the aftermath of nuclear holocaust – with a sense that a decisive interruption of technological progress might be a blessing in disguise.

Such morals were most explicitly drawn out in a number of scientific romances produced by British-born writers as that genre was about to be eclipsed by imported SF, most notably Gerald Heard's "The Great Fog" (1944), in which a god-substitute called "Mind" sends a mildew-generated fog to slow down the progress of a civilization that has run out of control. Similar notions also took root in the American SF, in spite of the fact that Campbell and his authors had followed the example set by Hugo Gernsback in committing themselves firmly to the cause of scientific and technological progress.

The pulp genre had been infiltrated almost from its inception by such skeptics as David H. Keller – whose account of "The Metal Doom" (1932) represents the demise of industrial technology as a good thing – and Campbell had been sufficiently worried about the debilitating effects of humankind's potential over-reliance on machinery to pin his own ultimate hopes for the future on transcendent mental evolution. Campbell's "Forgetfulness" (1937, originally bylined Don A. Stuart) features a pastoral Utopia, and his sympathy for the kind of nostalgic pastoralism cultivated by

Simak made *Astounding* much more hospitable to ecological parables demanding a retreat from technological excess than it might have been, given the apparent contradiction of his fervent propagandistic support for atomic power and space technology.

The temptation to remystify ecological relationships by imagining some kind of quasi-godlike intelligence manifest within them was irresistible. C.S. Lewis'religious fantasy *Out of the Silent Planet* (1938) offered a view of Martian ecology very different from that of Lowell and Burroughs, crediting its harmony to the active involvement of a spiritual overseer, and sentient ecospheres are featured in such genre SF stories as Murray Leinster's "The Lonely Planet" (1949). The French Jesuit Pierre Teilhard de Chardin had already worked out an evolutionary schema in which the destiny of the ecosphere was to fall increasingly under the way of a superimposed "noosphere" until a harmonious integration was achieved, but the notion had to await posthumous publication in 1955. By then, Clifford Simak had pioneered the employment of ecological relationships as substitutes for traditional religious imagery in *Time and Again* (1951), where alien "symbiotes" provide stand-ins for souls and the raw material of potential noospheres.

The late 1950s saw a remarkable resurgence of ecological mysticism in genre SF as human explorers and colonists were routinely humiliated by the belated discovery of sophisticated ecosystems blessed with quasisupernatural harmony. Notable examples include Richard McKenna's "The Night of Hoggy Darn" (1958; revised as "Hunter Come Home," 1963), Robert F. Young's "To Fell a Tree" (1959), and Mark Clifton's *Eight Keys to Eden* (1960). This trend reflected an upsurge of explicit ecological mysticism in the burgeoning environmentalist movement; for instance, the Findhorn Foundation, inaugurated in 1962 – named for a bay on the East Coast of Scotland where its first experimental Utopian community was based – followed a creed based on the assumption of an "intelligent nature" in which God is incarnate and ever-present. The remystification of ecological relationships was fundamental to two of the best-selling SF novels of the 1960s, both of which take the form of messianic fantasies focusing on the reverent ritualization of water relations: Robert A. Heinlein's *Stranger in a Strange Land* (1961) and Frank Herbert's *Dune* (1965). Piers Anthony's *Omnivore* (1968) and its sequels transform the fundamental pattern of ecological relationships into a mystical trinity. Herbert's *The Green Brain* (1966) echoes and amplifies Heard's "Great Fog" in featuring a active revolt of intelligent nature against the ecological heresies of humankind.

The notion of ecospheres so completely integrated that their core consists of vast more-or-less godlike organisms became very popular, reflected in such stories as Stanislaw Lem's *Solaris* (1961; trans. 1970), the Strugatsky brothers' *The Snail on the Slope* (1966–8; trans. 1980), Ursula Le Guin's "Vaster than Empires and More Slow" (1971), Gordon R. Dickson's "Twig" (1974), and Doris Piserchia's *Earthchild* (1977). The idea that life on Earth could and perhaps should be viewed in this way had been broached by Vladimir Vernadsky in *The Biosphere* (1926; trans. 1986) but had passed unheeded at the time; it made a spectacular comeback, however, in James Lovelock's "Gaia hypothesis," set out in *Gaia: A New Look at Life on Earth* (1973). Although not

mystical in itself, the language in which the Gaia hypothesis was couched lent tremendous encouragement to those who desired to construe it as if it were, so Lovelock's
tentative assertion that the ecosphere could, in some respects, be usefully viewed *as
if* it were a single organism was routinely extrapolated into a literal personification.
The notion was rapidly fed back into SF in such works as John Varley's *Titan* trilogy
(1979–84), whose sentient super-organism is named Gaea.

For many people, the word "ecology" – and such associated terms as "green" – had
by this time come to symbolize a kind of harmony with the natural environment that
modern civilization had sacrificed on the altar of technology, greatly to humankind's
spiritual detriment. Furthermore, the term had begun to broaden out in such works
as Gregory Bateson's *Steps Towards an Ecology of Mind* (1972) to signify a worldview
rather than a mere branch of science, whose essential "holism" was appropriate to the
study of mental as well as biological phenomena. Arne Naess' "The Shallow and the
Deep: Long Range Ecology Movement" (1973) proposed a wide-ranging pursuit of
"ecocentric wisdom" whose ambition were resummarized in *Ecology, Community, and
Lifestyle: Outline of an Ecosophy* (1989), which was rapidly followed by Warwick Fox's
Towards a Transpersonal Ecology (1990) – a prospectus for "Utopian ecologism" – and
Freya Mathews' *The Ecological Self* (1991).

Such developments as these helped fuel the demand for a renaissance of pastoral
nostalgia, whose plaints became increasingly eloquent in such heartfelt SF stories as
Richard Cowper's trilogy begun with *The Road to Corlay* (1978), John Crowley's *Engine
Summer* (1979), and Kate Wilhelm's *Juniper Time* (1979), then increasingly earnest in
such scrupulously meditative works as Norman Spinrad's *Songs from the Stars* (1980),
Russell Hoban's *Riddley Walker* (1980), Ursula Le Guin's *Always Coming Home* (1986),
and Judith Moffett's *Pennterra* (1987). The case for an actual technological retreat was
forcefully made in Ernest Callenbach's best-selling Millenarian tract *Ecotopia: A Novel
about Ecology, People and Politics in 1999* (1978), which describes the secession from
the USA of the western seaboard states, whose new masters establish a new low-tech
society based on the principles of "alternative technology" laid out in such texts as
Ernst Schumacher's *Small is Beautiful* (1973). Ecotopia's established religion is a
straightforward ecological mysticism whose rituals licensed the popular description
of environmentalists as "tree-huggers."

Callenbach's new term caught on to the extent that Kim Stanley Robinson produced a showcase SF anthology entitled *Future Primitive: The New Ecotopias* (1994),
which collects works operating on the assumption that contemporary "megacities
. . . serve not as models for development but as demonstrations of a dysfunctional
social order" (Robinson 1994: 10) and constitute an "attempt to imagine sophisticated new technologies combined with habits saved or reinvented from our deep past"
(Robinson 1994: 11). The muted ecological mysticism celebrated in the anthology is,
however, less ambitious than the transcendental varieties featured in more lyrical
works such as Ursula Le Guin's *The Word for World is Forest* (1972), Hilbert Schenck's
At the Eye of the Ocean (1980), and Somtow Sucharitkul's *Starship and Haiku* (1984).
The ultimate extension of that mystical strand tends to fuse the perspectives of

Lovelock and Teilhard de Chardin, most forthrightly in the prospectus for the hyper-Gaian "Galaxia" set out in Isaac Asimov's *Foundation's Edge* (1982).

The transplantation of ecological concepts to other fields was continued, rather whimsically, by Ursula Le Guin's essay on "The Carrier Bag Theory of Fiction" (1986) which draws a basic distinction between "techno-heroic" tales of hunters and uncombative novelistic accounts of gatherers. The essay was, however, reprinted in the altogether earnest *Ecocriticism Reader: Landmarks in Literary Ecology* (1996) edited by Cheryll Glotfelty and Harold Fromm, which became the bible of an Association for the Study of Literature and the Environment founded in 1992; its membership numbered 750 by 1995, by which time "ecological parables" had spread far beyond the exotica of SF along very various academic food-chains.

Ecological Management and Control in Science Fiction

The heavy emphasis placed by modern ecological mystics on the injurious effects of the Industrial Revolution and the growth of "megacities" deflects attention away from the fact that the whole history and prehistory of humankind have been very largely a matter of ecological management and control. Even before the development of agriculture and animal husbandry, hunter/gatherer societies had a very considerable impact on their environments, although we have only recently become aware of the extent to which supposed "wildernesses" like the Amazon basin were shaped and altered by human activity over long periods of time.

The idea that future agriculture might – or must – ultimately "domesticate" the entire ecosphere was present in Utopian literature before the advent of scientific romance, and was therefore already commonplace before the emergence of genre SF. The instrumentality of that domestication is necessarily vague in such accounts of biotechnological empery as Princess Vera Zaronovich's *Mizora* (1880–1), and J.B.S. Haldane's propagandistic essay *Daedalus; or, Science and the Future* (1923) was similarly written in ignorance of the biochemical details of heredity; even so, Haldane rightly foresaw that when direct technological manipulation of genetic materials became possible, the management of the ecosphere would become a feasible goal. Haldane also pointed out in his essay, however, that the great biological inventions of the past were invariably seen in the first instance as horrific violations of the natural order, and had tended to be accepted only when they could be granted the status of reverent ritual.

Although the management and control of Earth's ecosphere rarely features as a foregrounded topic of pulp SF, it is routinely assumed. The story series by Jack Williamson that introduced the notion of "terraforming" other planets in 1942–3 – reprinted in the mosaic *Seetee Ship* (1951; originally bylined Will Stewart) – takes it for granted that the technologies used in terraforming have already been applied to Earth's ecosphere; Olaf Stapledon's *Last and First Men* (1930), in which Venus has to be carefully prepared for human habitation when the sun cools, had similarly skipped over that phase of the development of technologies of ecological control. Williamson was also the writer who introduced the term "genetic engineering" into pulp SF a few years after the Seetee stories, in *Dragon's Island* (1951), although such technologies of ecospheric management had been foreshadowed in the "tectogenetics" featured in Norman L. Knight's "Crisis in Utopia" (1940).

As SF writers gradually came to terms with astronomical revelations about the utter inhospitability of the other planets in the solar system, the idea of effecting ecospheric metamorphoses inevitably became more important as a key element of the instrumentality of the Space Age. Because optimism was conserved in the case of Mars until the 1960s, the ecological management projects sited there in such works as Arthur C. Clarke's *The Sands of Mars* (1951) tended to be relatively modest, but terraforming Venus was seen as a more challenging prospect in such stories as Henry Kuttner's *Fury* (1950) and Poul Anderson's "The Big Rain" (1954). The notion that genetic engineering would be absolutely necessary to any colonization or "conquest" of the galaxy carried out by human beings was graphically developed by James Blish in the "pantropy" series assembled into the mosaic *The Seedling Stars* (1957). The final story in the series, "Watershed" (1957), proposes that there will come a time when human will have to be technologically readapted for life on Earth, whose physical environment will be so drastically altered by the developmental history of the human species as to make it uninhabitable by nature's design – a notion elaborately revisited by Williamson in his calculatedly elegiac *Terraforming Earth* (2001).

In the pantropy series James Blish, like Norman L. Knight, echoed Haldane's assumption that applications of genetic engineering to the human species, however necessary or desirable, would arouse fierce prejudices. Throughout the 1950s the dominance of genre SF by the myth of the Space Age – which insisted that the next phase of human history must involve the "conquest of space" – provided a counterweight to that kind of prejudice, accepting that some degree of biological modification might be useful in the colonization of other worlds. The myth of the Space Age was itself challenged, however, by increasing awareness of the difficulty of supplying spaceships with the "miniature ecospheres" necessary to sustain human passengers for any length of time. Although simple ecospheres can be isolated in glass globes or aquaria, human beings require much more elaborate support, as demonstrated by experiments carried out by the Moscow Institute for Biomedical Problems in the 1960s, by NASA in the 1970s and 1980s and – most ambitiously of all – by the "Synergians" who built and sustained the experimental Biosphere-2 in the 1990s. The notion that human beings might have to undergo genetic engineering even to travel in spaceships became increasingly common as the myth of the Space Age began to falter in the last decades of the twentieth century.

The resurgence of ecological mysticism in the 1960s complicated these practical questions with moral anxieties. The idea of terraforming other worlds – effectively destroying native ecospheres in order to substitute clones of Earth's – soon came to seem morally suspect, to the extent that Ernest Yanarella's study of science-fiction treatments of ecological themes, "The Cross, the Plow and the Skyline" (2001), looks back on the uses of that theme with outright horror, referring to it in the relevant chapter title as "the Specter of Terra (Terror) Forming." Observing that James Lovelock had attempted to apply the lessons of the Gaia hypothesis to the possibility of *The Greening of Mars* (1984, with Michael Allaby), Yanarella redefines the ideology of the Space Age as a kind of terrorism, echoing the views of historians who had become similarly skeptical of the morality of European colonization – including, and sometimes especially, the colonization of the Americas. Genre SF had evolved in parallel with the Western genre, sharing its ideology of frontiersmanship, routinely identifying alien species with Native Americans, as "savages" whose fate was to be contemptuously crushed and removed to reservations – John W. Campbell Jr. was notorious for his human chauvinism, and for his steadfast commitment to the notion that the Manifest Destiny of the human species was to defeat all competitors and rule the universe – but this view had come to seem horribly politically incorrect to many observers by the end of the century.

Although *The Greening of Mars* became a powerful influence on a glut of SF stories reconsidering the possibility of colonizing Mars in the light of information provided by the Viking landers, a distinct note of moral skepticism sounded in some such works – most notably, as might be expected, those produced by the self-declared "ecotopian" Kim Stanley Robinson in "Green Mars" (1985) and the trilogy subsequently developed from it, consisting of *Red Mars* (1992), *Green Mars* (1993), and *Blue Mars* (1996). Such anxieties were very much in tune with the rhetoric of conservation that had become very influential in discussions of the future management of Earth's ecosphere.

Qualms regarding the propriety of terraforming worlds which already harbored life could be set aside in accounts of terraforming worlds which had only the organic precursors life, as in Pamela Sargent's trilogy begun with *Venus of Dreams* (1986), but the scale of such transformations made them difficult to contemplate. The implicit grandeur of the notion continued to override moral doubts in such lyrical celebrations of Martian terraformation as Frederick Turner's epic poem *Genesis* (1988) and Ian McDonald's picaresque novel *Desolation Road* (1988) but distant terraforming projects gone awkwardly or horribly awry became commonplace in such works as Dave Wolverton's *Serpent Catch* (1991), Kay Kenyon's *Rift* (1999), and Neal Asher's *Gridlinked* (2001), while would-be terraformers are featured as villains to be thwarted in such works as Monica Hughes' *The Golden Aquarians* (1994) and Joan Slonczewski's *The Children Star* (1998). Other kinds of large-scale ecological engineering – for which the emergent general term is ecopoesis – have yet to figure large in SF.

With regard to the ecological management of Earth itself, the last quarter of the twentieth century saw a dramatic decline in optimism. Any Utopian prospectus for the future, however tentative, had by then to take problems of ecological sustainability into account; the apparent difficulty of that achievement is clearly manifest in such future histories as those mapped out in Marge Piercy's *Woman on the Edge of Time* (1976), *The Third Millennium* (1985) by Brian Stableford and David Langford, and Kim Stanley Robinson's *Pacific Edge* (1988). The SF of the 1990s displayed a striking unanimity in assuming that our past and present mismanagement was now irredeemable in the short term, and that Utopian optimism must be displaced into a more distant future, dependent upon a wiser reconstitution of human society – and perhaps of human nature – in the wake of a global ecocatastrophe that is already under way.

Ecocatastrophes in Science Fiction

The precariousness of the human ecological situation must have been evident to almost all tribal societies, especially those that actually perished or were forced to migrate in search of new lands that might support them, sustained by unfulfillable dreams of free-flowing milk and honey. However, the first person to produce a clear statement of the fundamental problem and its applicability to a global stage, Thomas Malthus, soon retreated from the apocalyptic prophecies of his first extrapolation in his "second essay" of 1803, which incorporated the possibility that the future growth of the human population might be modified by "moral restraint." Many others following in his footsteps beat similar retreats from the uncomfortable conclusion, reassured by advances in agricultural technology which seemed to falsify Malthus' fundamental assumption that food production could only increase arithmetically.

In the early twentieth century literary images of worldwide disaster were commonplace, but they almost invariably laid the blame on agents external to human society. Tales of new deluges and great plagues abounded, while the world's vulnerability to manufactured ecocatastrophes was featured in such thrillers as *Nordenholt's Million* (1923) by J.J. Connington, but the idea that technologies of ecological management might be storing up trouble emerged more gradually. The possibility of an ecocatastrophe resultant from the "exhaustion" of the soil's crop-bearing capacities was explored in such scientific romances as A.G. Street's *Already Walks Tomorrow* (1938) and Edward Hyams' *The Astrologer* (1950) but it was not until Malthusian anxieties resurfaced in the 1950s, replete with a new urgency, that there was a sudden boom in ecocatastrophe stories.

In the spring of 1955 a number of interested parties formed the Population Council, whose eleven-strong committee became a significant disseminator of propaganda regarding the dangerous rapidity of world population growth. The March 1956 issue of *Scientific American* carried an alarmist article on "World Population" by Julian Huxley, which assisted the Council's efforts. Genre SF writers had already taken an interest in the issue. *Marvel Science Stories* featured a "symposium" in its November 1951 issue on the question of whether the world's population should be limited, and it had been addressed in Isaac Asimov's *The Caves of Steel* (1954) and Damon Knight's "Natural State" (1954) – but it was not until the Population Council began its work that the ecological problems of overpopulation began to feature in SF on a routine basis, foregrounded by such works as Robert Silverberg's *Master of Life and Death* (1957), J.G. Ballard's "Billenium" (1961), and Robert Sheckley's "The People Trap" (1968).

Although Malthus had focused narrowly on the problem of food supply, the Population Council and SF writers who took up the theme broadened the scope of their arguments to take in the exhaustibility of other resources – especially oil – and the dangers of environmental pollution. Early scientific romances dealing with catastrophes brought about by pollution – including W.D. Hay's *The Doom of the Great City* (1880) and Robert Barr's "The Doom of London" (1892) – had concentrated on the perils of industrial smog, but the anxieties that grew in the 1950s, lavishly displayed in C.M. Kornbluth's black comedy "Shark Ship" (1958), were far more wide-ranging. Rachel Carson's alarmist best-seller *Silent Spring* (1962) made much of the particular problems caused by the use of the insecticide DDT, alerting its readers to more general problems caused by the use of synthetic organic compounds that were not "biodegradable" – which is to say that they could not re-enter the food chain in the way that almost all natural wastes could and routinely did.

Garrett Hardin, editor of *Population, Evolution, and Birth Control: A Collage of Controversial Ideas* (1964) produced a devastating summary of a new discipline of "ecological economics" in "The Tragedy of the Commons" (1968), which pointed out that the fundamental logic of capitalism, as exemplified by the workings of Adam Smith's "invisible hand," was bound to lead to ecological devastation unless some very powerful form of moral restraint could be imposed. The alarmist trend culminated in a best-selling account of *The Population Bomb* (1968) by Paul Ehrlich, who followed it up with a quasidocumentary account of his prophecies coming to fruition in "Ecocatastrophe," published in *Ramparts* 8 (1969). The environmental protection movement became briefly fashionable, its arguments and concerns summarized in such texts as Richard Lillard's *Eden in Jeopardy: Man's Prodigal Meddling with His Environment* (1966) and *The Environmental Handbook* (1970) edited by Garett de Bell. The possibility of ecocatastrophe became a significant topic of political discourse, reflected in such texts as J. Clarence Davis' *The Politics of Pollution* (1970) and James Ridgeway's *The Politics of Ecology* (1971), in the founding of Green Parties in many European countries, and in the establishment of such pressure groups as Friends of the Earth (founded 1969) and Greenpeace (launched in 1971).

An organization calling for Zero Population Growth was quick to popularize its aims by producing an anthology of science fiction stories: *Voyages: Scenarios for a Ship Called Earth* (1971), edited by Rob Sauer and introduced by Paul and Anne Ehrlich. SF stories describing the impending ecocatastrophe became exceedingly fashionable as this alarmism peaked, extreme examples including Harry Harrison's *Make Room! Make Room!* (1966), James Blish's "We All Die Naked" (1969), Norman Spinrad's "The Lost Continent" (1970), John Brunner's *The Sheep Look Up* (1972), Philip Wylie's *The End of the Dream* (1972), Kurt Vonnegut's "The Big Space Fuck" (1972), and *Ecodeath* (1972) by William Jon Watkins and Gene Snyder. The British TV series *Doomwatch* (1970–2), originated by Kit Pedler and Gerry Davis, exported the anxiety to a much wider audience. Anthologies showcasing ecocatastrophe stories included *The Ruins of Earth* (1971) edited by Thomas M. Disch and *Saving Worlds* (1973; also known – more appropriately – as *The Wounded Planet*) edited by Roger Elwood and Virginia Kidd. When the political scientist W.J. McKenzie summarized the politicization of ecological issues in *Biological Ideas in Politics* (1978) he paid considerable attention to the representation of science fiction, citing Samuel Butler and John Wyndham in his preface, beginning his introduction with a quotation from Robert A. Heinlein's *Beyond This Horizon* (1942, initially bylined Anson MacDonald), and also making reference in his text to Brian Aldiss.

The debate about the scientific bases of ecocatastrophic alarmism became increasingly heated as opposition to environmentalism formed ranks; the environmentalists responded by elaborating and hardening their views. Although Barry Commoner objected to Paul Ehrlich's "neo-Malthusianism" and Garrett Hardin's "ecological Hobbesianism" in *The Closing Circle: Man, Nature and Technology* (1971) his own arguments about the "debt to nature" incurred by the false mythology of wealth-creation were no less apocalyptic. The argument was extended and further amplified by such works as Alvin Toffler's *Eco-Spasm Report* (1975), Angus Martin's *The Last Generation: The End of Survival?* (1975), and Jonathan Schell's *The Fate of the Earth* (1982), which added the greenhouse effect and the depletion of the Earth's ozone layer to the ecocatastrophic mix. Inevitably, these new anxieties were reflected in such speculative fictions as Hal Clement's *The Nitrogen Fix* (1980), Trevor Hoyle's *The Last Gasp* (1983), Paul Theroux's *O-Zone* (1986), *Nature's End* (1986) by Whitley Strieber and James Kunetka, George Turner's *The Sea and Summer* (1987), David Brin's *Earth* (1990), and Michael Tobias' *Fatal Exposure* (1991).

Strident alarmism was only one facet of SF's response to the perception of impending ecocrisis; Brin's *Earth* attempted to carry forward the alternative response pioneered by such works as James Blish and Norman L. Knight's *A Torrent of Faces* (1968), John Brunner's *Stand on Zanzibar* (1968), and Robert Silverberg's *The World Inside* (1972), which had tried to imagine future societies designed to cope – more or less – with overpopulation and its attendant difficulties. Other works suggested that Malthusian checks would have to be artificially imposed in order to preserve social order, and tried to envisage means by which mass homicide might most conveniently be carried out in a relatively even-handed manner. Significantly, however, none of these works ever contrived to muster any conspicuous confidence in their artifice. While many genre SF writers collaborated eagerly in the alarmism of the apocalyptic ecocatastrophists, only a tiny minority took up the more optimistic note of such works as Murray Bookchin *Towards an Ecological Society* (1980) or Fritjof Capra and Catherine Spretnak's *Green Politics: the Global Promise* (1984). Although a hopeful note was conscientiously maintained in much children's SF, "young adult" fiction dealing with ecological issues tended more to the apocalyptic as time went by, as evidenced by such fretful examples as Nancy Bond's *The Voyage Begun* (1989), Monica Hughes' *The Crystal Drop* (1992) and *A Handful of Seeds* (1993), and Karen Hesse's *Phoenix Rising* (1994).

To some extent, this imbalance reflects the parasitism of popular fiction on melodrama, which feeds far more avidly on bad news than hopeful constructivism, but it also reflects an authentic disenchantment within the genre. Even genre writers who were neither angry nor despairing accepted that an ongoing ecological crisis would be the most obvious feature of the history of the near future, and that its inflictions

would constitute a kind of justice. As the twenty-first century began the great majority of science-fiction images of the future were content to take it for granted that the
ecocatastrophe was not only under way but already irreversible – and that the backlash against environmentalism in the US political arena was a manifestation of psychological denial.

From the 1960s onwards, almost all ecocatastrophe stories written by genre SF
writers had been infected with a scathingly bitter irony; most genre writers who used
the theme seemed to feel that human beings would get no more and no less than they
deserve if they were to destroy their environment and poison their world. To some
extent, this bleakness of outlook was a reaction to the declining fortunes of the myth
of Space Age, which so many SF writers had long held dear. In the 1960s many SF
writers still looked to the Space Age as an exit strategy from the evolving ecocatastrophe, but the likelihood of that exit strategy dwindled dramatically as time went
by, reaching extreme improbability by the year 2000.

The speculative relocation of the "conquest of space" to a much more distant future
involved the acceptance that if any such historical process were ever to happen it would
be the prerogative of "posthuman" or "transhuman" species: cyborgized and genetically engineered products of the kind of "technological singularity" first popularized
by Vernor Vinge and such stories as Marc Stiegler's "The Gentle Seduction" (1989)
but examined in far more detail in Charles Stross'Accelerando sequence (begun 2001)
and Karl Schroeder's *Permanence* (2002). Unlike the conquest of space, the ecocatastrophe cannot be postponed; the near-universal assumption of early-twenty-first
century SF is that if its problems are soluble – the price of failure being a drastic
reversal of technological progress – the solution probably lies in some kind of managed
evolution of posthumanity.

Whether this assumption is true or not – and SF's record as a medium of prophecy
hardly inspires confidence – it is perhaps the most fascinating example available of
SF's speculative extrapolation of questions and issues raised by the emergence of a new
scientific discipline. Perhaps ironically, the promoters of the field of "ecocriticism" –
which attempts to apply ecological principles to the study of literary phenomena –
have tended either to ignore SF or to treat it as a Great Wen despoiling the landscape
of "naturalistic" fiction, but that only demonstrates their failure to take aboard one
of the most important principles of biological science: that no organism can reason-
ably be condemned as irrelevant or uninteresting on arbitrary aesthetic grounds.

References and Further Reading

Allaby, Michael, and James Lovelock (1984)
  The Greening of Mars. New York: St. Martin's
  Press.
Bateson, Gregory (1972) *Steps to an Ecology of Mind.*
  New York: Ballantine.
Callenbach, Ernest (1978) *Ecotopia: A Novel about*

Ecology, People and Politics in 1999. London:
  Pluto.
Carson, Rachel (1962) *Silent Spring*. Boston:
  Houghton Mifflin.
Disch, Thomas M. (ed.) (1971) *The Ruins of Earth.*
  New York: Putnam.

Ehrlich, Paul R. (1969) "EcoCatastrophe!" *Ramparts* 8: 24–8.

Elwood, Roger, and Virginia Kidd (eds) (1973) *Saving Worlds*. Garden City, NY: Doubleday.

Fox, Warwick (1990) *Towards a Transpersonal Ecology: Developing New Foundations for Environmentalism*. Boston: Shambala Press.

Glotfelty, Cheryll, and Harold Fromm (eds) (1996) *The Ecocriticism Reader: Landmarks in Literary Ecology*. Athens, GA: University of Georgia Press.

Haldane, J.B.S. (1924) *Daedalus; or, Science and the Future*. London: Kegan Paul, Trench, Trubner.

Hardin, Garrett (1968) "The Tragedy of the Commons," *Science* 162: 1243–8.

Hardin, Garrett (ed.) (1964) *Population, Evolution, and Birth Control: A Collage of Controversial Ideas*. San Francisco, CA: W.H. Freeman.

Hargrove, Eugene (ed.) (1986) *Beyond Spaceship Earth: Environmental Ethics and the Solar System*. San Francisco, CA: Sierra Club.

Lillard, Richard G. (1966) *Eden in Jeopardy: Man's Prodigal Meddling with His Environment*. New York: Knopf.

Lovelock, James E. (1987) *Gaia: A New Look at Life on Earth*. Oxford: Oxford University Press.

McKenzie, W.J.M. (1978) *Biological Ideas in Politics: An Essay on Political Adaptivity*. New York: St. Martin's Press.

Mathews, Freya (1991) *The Ecological Self*. Lanham, MD: Rowan and Littlefield.

Naess, Arne (1989) *Ecology, Community, and Lifestyle: Outline of an Ecosophy*. Cambridge: Cambridge University Press.

Robinson, Kim Stanley (ed.) (1994) *Future Primitive: The New Ecotopias*. New York: TOR Books.

Sargisson, Lucy (2001) "Green Utopias of Self and Other," in *The Philosophy of Utopia*, (ed.) Barbara Goodwin. London: Frank Cass, 140–156.

Sauer, Rob (1971) *Voyages: Scenarios for a Ship Called Earth*. New York: Ballantine.

Schell, Jonathan (1982) *The Fate of the Earth*. New York: Knopf.

Stableford, Brian (1988), "The Biology and Sociology of Alien Worlds." *Social Biology and Human Affairs* 52.i: 45–57.

——(1981) "Man-Made Catastrophes in SF." *Foundation: The International Review of Science Fiction* 22 (June), 56–85.

Stratton, Susan (2001) "The Messiah and the Greens: The Shape of Environmental Action in *Dune* and *Pacific Edge*." *Extrapolation* 42.iv: 303–16.

Toffler, Alvin (1975) *The Eco-Spasm Report*. New York: Bantam.

Vernadsky, Vladimir (1998) *The Biosphere* (1926), (trans.) D.B. Langmuir. New York: Springer-Verlag.

Yanarella, Ernest J. (2001) *The Cross, the Plow and the Skyline: Contemporary Science Fiction and the Ecological Imagination*. Parkland, FL: Brown Walker.

9
Feminist Fabulation
Marleen S. Barr

In *Feminist Fabulation: Space/Postmodern Fiction* (1992), I explain that my term "feminist fabulation" signals "a new understanding of postmodern fiction which enables the canon to accommodate feminist difference and emphasizes that the literature which was called feminist SF is an important site of postmodern feminist difference" (Barr 1992: xv). Naming and renaming is integral to laying the initial groundwork for instituting this new understanding. Ursula Le Guin, for example, when discussing what appropriately to call her work, states that publishers, rather than she herself, designate her work "science fiction": "I write science fiction because that is what publishers call my books. Left to myself, I would call them novels" (Le Guin 1979: 16). *Feminist Fabulation* explores why "science fiction" (SF) inadequately distinguishes between Le Guin's humanistic visions and, say, John Norman's gore-sodden *Gor* novels. Feminist fabulation, to supplement "feminist science fiction," at once describes the texts Le Guin's work exemplifies and names a theoretical framework for including more women's fiction within postmodern literary canons.

Writing in the science fiction issue of *PMLA* (May 2004), N. Katherine Hayles and Nicholas Gessler explain that "Marleen Barr's contribution to the on-going challenge to clarify the boundary between mainstream and science fiction has been to define a genre of 'feminist fabulation' that draws on Robert Scholes' notion of 'structural fabulation' as constituting a realm separate from ordinary reality yet related to it. Feminist fabulation differs both from mainstream fiction and male-oriented science fiction in its reenvisioning of patriarchal societies and its feminist perspective" (Hayles and Gessler 2004: 498). As Donna Haraway notes (in remarks that appear on the cover of *Feminist Fabulation*), feminist fabulation's focus upon re-envisioning patriarchal societies points to this literature's role as functioning as a catalyst for social change: "Marleen Barr understands that we live our fictions. *Feminist Fabulation* crafts critical fictions that promise to be vastly more livable than the patriarchal myths that have filled inner and outer space. By exposing, subverting, and rewriting canonical representations of postmodern ficiton, Barr resituates marginalized feminist literature at the center of livable generic space. *Feminist Fabulation* teaches its reader to imagine – and to live – the lives of those promising monsters that inhabit women's transformative writing." Like Hayles and Gessler, Haraway emphasizes that feminist fabulation involves imagining alternatives to patriarchal imperatives.

Presently, from the standpoint of more than a decade after *Feminist Fabulation* first appeared, it is clear that patriarchal imperatives still have nothing to fear from imagined feminist scenarios. With this fact in mind, I will describe my original conception of feminist fabulation, offer retrospective thoughts about renaming "feminist science fiction" (an idea that the feminist SF community has resisted), and – from a cultural studies perspective – update and resituate *Feminist Fabulation* by discussing feminist fabulation's relationship to the current cultural moment.

Feminist Fabulation, Circa 1992: A Thumbnail Sketch

Feminist fabulation, a new term for feminist SF writers' work, stems from realizing that SF is not feminist; SF is divided into separate women's and men's worlds. Most male SF writers imagine men controlling a universe once dominated by nature; most female SF writers imagine women controlling a world once dominated by men. SF writers of both genders who present new feminist worlds move beyond merely creating woman-oriented versions of a genre that usually appeals to men, not women. Women tend not to like male SF writers such as Robert Heinlein and Isaac Asimov and women fail to associate SF with feminist visions. Coining the correct descriptive term for feminist SF writers' work, then, is pedagogically as well as theoretically compelling.

To define a new, more appropriate term to supplement feminist SF, one can look to Robert Scholes, who spoke about the lack of terminology to describe a new literary mode. Scholes explains that "much of the trouble comes from inadequate understanding of this new literary mode I have called fabulation. The trouble is aggravated by the absence of terminology in which to discuss it" (Scholes 1967: 13). Now that fabulation is a recognized term, I call upon it to quell trouble caused by present-day inadequate understanding of a new feminist literary mode. Further, I ask the critical community to accept feminist fabulation as an important contribution to the postmodern literary canon.

What is the appropriate name for feminist SF, for literature's new women's worlds? Science, in the sense of technology, should be augmented by a term that has social connotations and focuses upon new sex roles, not new hardware. One such term, Thomas Kuhn's paradigm shift, is applicable to women's social roles and to fiction written by feminist SF authors. Feminist SF writers encourage readers to contemplate a paradigm shift regarding human relations. Virginia Allen and Terry Paul, through a discussion of Betty Friedan (whose classic study *The Feminine Mystique* appeared in 1963), link feminist SF to Kuhn's notion of paradigms. Allen and Paul explain that when Betty Friedan defined "the problem that has no name as sexism, she generated a scientific revolution in Kuhn's terms. The problem had been around long before she named it, and many sensitive and observant feminists had grappled with it. But Friedan did for sexual politics what Galileo had done for cosmology: She brought forward so much anomalous data that they could no longer be ignored (Allen and Paul 1986: 168–9). Feminist SF writers approach the fantastic to generate names for "the problem that has no name." They bring forth a great deal of anomalous data about women that can no longer be ignored.

For example, in Le Guin's "Daddy's Big Girl" (1987), Jewel Ann is a character who becomes anomalous data. Jewel Ann (like the ponderous protagonist of "Jack and the Bean Stalk") is a giant; she cannot fit within patriarchal social space: she cannot enact feminine gender roles which require women to be small and unobtrusive. She can destroy a particular repressive domestic system, the house that imprisons her and her mother: "If she had stretched and pushed and wanted to, she could have pushed out the back wall of that house, pushed it down like the side of a paper box" (Le Guin 1987: 94). Jewel Ann, though, does not want to demolish the house. Instead, she continues to grow in another reality beyond the inhibiting boundaries of patriarchal space and stories. Her situation suggests that reality should be changed to accommodate "giant," expansive women. In the manner of Le Guin, feminist SF writers produce metaparadigmatic literature (fiction which subverts patriarchal patterns and models) as they venture outside women's reality and imagine a social revolution directed toward changing patriarchy.

Sheila Finch follows the example set by Le Guin. Her *Infinity's Web* (1985), which moves beyond existing sexist paradigms to envision new horizons for women, is a feminist metaparadigmatic novel. Ann, Finch's protagonist, encounters different versions of herself who inhabit alternative realities. Opportunities to confront these differing identity possibilities enrich Ann's daily life. Finch's novel, which explores women's inner space (instead of the male-controlled domain of outer space), is not science fiction. Rather than emphasizing technology, this novel presents a new feminist behavioral paradigm: women who celebrate their own potential instead of applauding men who send phallic machines into the sky.

Infinity's Web points out that sexist societies are artificial environments constructed by patriarchal language which defines "sexist" as normal. The contrived nature of patriarchal reality, the fiction about women's inferiority and necessarily subordinate status, is best confronted by metafiction (fiction about fiction), which, according to Patricia Waugh, explores "the possible fictionality of the world outside the literary fictional text." Waugh explains that "literary fiction (worlds constructed entirely of language) becomes a useful model for learning about the construction of 'reality' itself" (Waugh 1984: 2). Feminist SF writers create metafiction, fiction about patriarchal fiction, to unmask the fictionality of patriarchy. When these authors use language to construct nonsexist fictional worlds, they develop useful models for learning about how patriarchy is constructed. Feminist SF metafictionally facilitates an understanding of sexism as a story authored by men's power to make women the protagonists of patriarchal fictions. Feminist metafiction is a relevant artistic form for contemporary feminists who are beginning to gain awareness of precisely how patriarchal values are constructed and legitimized.

SF writers who create feminist metafiction magnify institutionalized – and therefore difficult to view – examples of sexism. These writers seem to peer into metaphorical microscopes while playing at being scientists – artful practitioners of soft sciences who expand women's psyche and unearth an archaeology of new feminist knowledge. They refresh embattled feminists by using language artistically to create power fantasies and to play (sometimes vengefully) with patriarchy.

Feminist metaparadigmatic fiction and feminist metafiction (terms to supplement describing power fantasies written for feminists as feminist SF) are components of a wider literary area: feminist fabulation, an umbrella term for describing overlapping genres. Feminist fabulation includes feminist speculative fiction and feminist mainstream works (which may or may not routinely be categorized as postmodern literature) authored by both women and men.

Here Scholes' "fabulation" is claimed for feminist theory and feminist fiction. Scholes defines fabulation as "fiction that offers us a world clearly and radically discontinuous from the one we know, yet returns to confront that known world in some cognitive way" (Scholes 1976: 47). Feminist fabulation is feminist fiction that offers us a world clearly and radically discontinuous from the patriarchal one we know, yet returns to confront that known patriarchal world in some feminist cognitive way. It provides "cognitive estrangement" (Darko Suvin's term) from the patriarchal world by depicting feminist visions that confront the patriarchal world. Feminist fabulation is a specifically feminist corollary to Scholes' definition of structural fabulation. Scholes states that "in works of structural fabulation the tradition of speculative fiction is modified by an awareness of the nature of the universe as a system of systems, a structure of structures, and the insights of the past century of science are accepted as fictional points of departure . . . It is a fictional exploration of human situations made perceptible by the implications of recent science." He continues: "Man must learn to live within laws that have given him his being but offer him no purpose and promise him no triumph as a species. Man must make his own values, fitting his hopes and fears to a universe which has allowed him a place in its systematic working, but which cares only for the system itself and not for him. Man must create his future himself" (Scholes 1976: 54–5). Structural fabulation addresses man's place within the system of the universe; feminist fabulation addresses woman's place within the system of patriarchy.

Alternatively, in terms of Scholes' language, feminist fabulation modifies the tradition of speculative fiction with an awareness that patriarchy is an arbitrary system that constructs fictions of female inferiority as integral aspects of human culture – and the insights of this century's waves of feminism are accepted as fictional points of departure. Feminist fabulation is a fictional exploration of woman's inferior status made perceptible by the implications of recent feminist theory. Woman has been forced to live within patriarchal laws that define her as subhuman, offer her no purpose beyond serving men, and promise her no triumph as a human. Woman must make her own new values, fitting her new objectives into a patriarchal system that gives her a secondary place in its systematic working and that certainly does not care for her. Woman must create her future herself.

Female feminist fabulators, located outside a literary status system that functions by passing recognition from one male generation to the next, do not shine as brightly as the male structural fabulators Scholes discusses. Many feminist writers (especially feminists who create the literature Doris Lessing calls "space fiction") are shut out of the postmodern literary system's space. It is desired here to reclaim postmodern canonical space for feminists by broadening the definition of postmodern fiction to include the subject matter and structures characterizing contemporary feminist writing.

Feminist fabulation retells and rewrites patriarchal stories, points toward incalculable feminist futures, and thinks the as yet unviable thought of effectively transforming patriarchal society. Reality is made of words; women must nurture their own definitions. Only then will feminist fabulation become empowered reality and patriarchal stories fade as things of the past.

Doris Lessing is not afraid to break through the barrier separating the mainstream from the fantastic, to let go of man's world. Near the conclusion of her *Memoirs of A Survivor* (1975), walls dissolve and possibilities expand: "We were in that place which might present us with anything . . . walls broken, falling, growing again. . . . Beside Emily was Hugo, and lingering after them Gerald. Emily, yes, but quite beyond herself, transmuted, and in another key, and the yellow beast Hugo fitted her new self: a splendid animal, handsome, all kindly dignity and command. . . . Both walked quickly behind that One who went ahead showing them the way out of this collapsed little world into another order of world altogether, . . . They all followed quickly on after the others as the last walls dissolved" (Lessing 1975: 212–13).

Anglo-American feminist theory might fruitfully shift some emphasis from the age of established patriarchal realism to the place of fabulative feminist potential, a place that might present us with anything. We can allow feminist fabulators to guide us into a completely other order of world. Feminist theorists and feminist fabulators can, together, let go of current reality and penetrate barriers that inhibit creating new reality. As inhabiters of this alternative reality, like Emily's transmuted self, women can move beyond their present selves and become splendid, dignified selves. Feminists can theorize about dissolving walls that imprison women within a sexist reality they – with few exceptions – have not made. Readers, fiction writers, and theorists can begin to construct new feminist paradigms, viable feminist futures. Reinventing the canon coincides with reinventing womanhood. We can claim that feminist fabulative works are important examples of postmodern fiction. The force is with us.

What's In A Name? Feminist Fabulation and Passing

Feminist Fabulation poses questions about what best to name the force. I wrote *Feminist Fabulation* because it was clear to me that to call the force "feminist science fiction" was – at that point in time when prejudice directed against "science fiction" had not yet abated to its current lower (but not yet sufficiently low enough) level – less than forceful. "Science fiction" absolutely denoted literary inferiority. William Gibson, when describing the discrepancy between science fiction's popularity and its lack of critical acceptance, called science fiction the golden ghetto. Norman Spinrad was more blunt when addressing the discrimination science fiction and science fiction writers face. According to Spinrad, "any science fiction writer of merit who is adopted . . . in the grand salons of literary power" is a "token nigger" (Dery 1994: 180). Eric S. Rabkin, obviously frustrated by the marginalization automatically attributed to science fiction, turned to science fiction itself humorously to fight fire with fire. He imagines that once upon a future time the knee jerk phrase "science fiction is crap" will become thoroughly positive: "[F]ew people today know that the very word 'crap' took on its modern meaning through science fiction. Apparently the original term 'krappe' . . . was a Dutch (Earth) word. . . . In the mid-twentieth century, Theodore Sturgeon, a science fiction writer, apparently in defense of science fiction against elite critics, is reputed to have said . . . '95 percent of science fiction is crap . . . but then, 95 percent of everything is crap.' . . . In the late twentieth and the early twenty-first centuries, when science fiction, then known as SF, became not only accepted but thoroughly admired, people would say of it, 'this is excellent crap' until finally 'excellent' was assimilated into the core concept of 'crap.' Thus, 'this SF is crap' . . . took on the happy, approbative sense . . . [it enjoys] today [in 2999]" (Rabkin 2003: 192–3). In 1992, I did not have the luxury of waiting until Rabkin's 2999 for "crap" to become synonymous with excellence in relation to science fiction. Ditto for the present.

Feminist Fabulation stands in fervent opposition to Dena Brown's famous phrase, communicated at the first meeting of the Science Fiction Research Association (1971): "Let's take science fiction out of the classroom and put it back in the gutter where it belongs." *Feminist Fabulation* says: lets take feminist science fiction out of the crappy gutter and put it back in postmodern canons where it belongs. I wanted to solve a prevailing problem Veronica Hollinger describes: "Barr is certainly correct in her claim that no version *of anyone's* postmodern canon is likely to include any significant feminist presence" (Hollinger 1993: 274). I could not then imagine expanding the feminist presence in postmodern canons by asking literary critics to accept that "feminist science fiction crap" is synonymous with "respected postmodern literature."

In 1992, it was too early to discern that Brown's assertion would not forever be antithetical to my goal. Practitioners of other despised genres subsequently took Brown's words to heart: "chicklit," "queer theory," and *Heeb Magazine* presently bask in the glory of critical acceptability. No, I do not want a time machine to transport me to 1992 where I can place myself on the vanguard of reappropriating despised terms to render despised literature acceptable. Despite the positive literary connotations "chick," "queer," and "heeb" now enjoy, I would not choose to rename *Feminist Fabulation*, say, *Feminist Sci Fi Crap*. Currently prevalent "in your face" linguistic reappropriation, however, indicates that "feminist sci fi crap" has its place – and "feminist science fiction" is not obsolete.

Nevertheless, because "science fiction" is still associated with "crap," "feminist science fiction" remains a problematical term. Science fiction writers continue to escape "the golden ghetto" and the designation Spinrad describes by disassociating themselves from the appellation "science fiction." As James Gunn explains, "Kurt Vonnegut Jr. was showing that science fiction could break out of the backwaters of general expectations into the eddies of the mainstream, even into the bestseller lists, and earn critical claim as well, even if it meant taking the labels off the books" (Gunn 2003: xv). In the manner of Vonnegut succeeding by taking the science fiction label off his books, *Feminist Fabulation* makes this point: in order to flow within the eddies of critically acclaimed mainstream postmodern literature, feminist science fiction writers would do well to call themselves feminist fabulators. Vonnegut and feminist fabulators, must – in order to enjoy success at the highest levels – consider "passing" as something other than science fiction writers. This necessity is still operative. Margaret Atwood insists that *Oryx and Crake*, published in 2003, is "speculative fiction," not science fiction. Writing in the 2004 *PMLA* science fiction issue, Brian Aldiss states, "No longer am I content to be labeled merely a sci fi writer" (Aldiss 2004: 512).

On the one hand, "passing" is inauthentic. On the other hand, "passing" can be necessary for survival. Passing resists fixed, politically correct categorization. The protagonist of the film *Europa Europa* (1990) was justified when he hid his circumcised penis in order to pass as a gentile in Nazi Germany. Facing a completely opposite circumstance in which accentuating her ethnic identity would have positive consequences, a New York actress originally named Terri Sue Feldshuh elected to change her name to Tovah. "Tovah" more authentically plays Golda Meir in the current Broadway play *Golda's Balcony* than "Terri Sue." Barbra Streisand refused to fix her nose; Cher fixed her entire body. The decision to pass or to appear as an authentic self is devoid of clear "correct" resolution. Yes, as some of my fellow feminist science fiction critics have pointed out, "feminist fabulation" does separate "feminist science fiction" from its historical connection to science fiction. Yes, in 1992, I thought name change was in this literature's best interest. However, "feminist science fiction," "feminist sci fi," and "feminist fabulation" all have a present appropriate role in critical discourse.

Name change and the appropriateness of name change, after all, are part of the broad study of women in the academy as well as the particular relationship between feminist science fiction and postmodern canons. "Women's studies," "feminist studies," and "gender studies" all have their place as names of academic disciplines. Carolyn Dinshaw's description of renaming the New York University program she heads is particularly relevant to name change as it relates to feminist fabulation. Dinshaw states: "Without a breath of controversy, we at NYU took a step last year that has been met with resistance and anger at various other institutions around the country: the Women's Studies Program changed its name. Our undergraduate degree-granting unit . . . is now, officially, the Gender and Sexuality Studies Program. I regularly receive emails from colleagues in other institutions considering a name change, asking about our history and strategy, preparing for a struggle" (Dinshaw 2003). The name change I describe in *Feminist Fabulation* has been controversial and has met with resistance and anger. Struggling with my call for a new term, some feminist science fiction critics have argued that feminist fabulation is (and I cringe at the very association of my name with this word) "conservative." With Dinshaw's account in mind, I argue that name change is an appropriate means to do feminist work in the world. I, then, wish to update *Feminist Fabulation* not by negating passing/name change as a strategy or by entirely discarding "feminist science fiction." I wish to update *Feminist Fabulation* by bringing "textism," the term I coin in the 2004 *PMLA* science fiction issue (Barr 2004), to bear upon feminist fabulation and feminist science fiction.

"Textism is a discriminatory evaluation system in which all literature relegated to a so-called subliterary genre, regardless of its individual merits, is automatically defined as inferior, separate, and unequal" (Barr 2004: 429–30). The crux of the matter is not to argue about what to call the work of women science fiction writers in order best to ensconce them within postmodern canons and other eddies of literary acceptability. The crux of the matter is to eradicate textism. But – since I do not live in Rabkin's Utopian 2999 and the literary establishment still has a penchant for equating science fiction with crap – as Vonnegut always knew and as Atwood and Aldiss presently insist, passing cannot be entirely ruled out as a literary survival strategy for science fiction. Until Rabkin's 2999 arrives, "feminist science fiction" can play a useful role as a midpoint compromise between the two extremes of "feminist sci fi crap" and "feminist fabulation."

Hollinger and Brooks Landon foresaw how I would currently understand feminist fabulation. Hollinger says that feminist fabulation "is thus a kind of metafictional enterprise and it is this important feature which, if I read Barr correctly, most clearly demonstrates the affinity between feminist fabulation and postmodern textuality" (Hollinger 1993: 273). Landon (in his remarks appearing on the cover of *Feminist Fabulation*) says, "What I found so remarkable about this book [*Feminist Fabulation*] is that it hit home in a way I associate with fiction more than with criticism; its power reminded me of the fiction of Kathy Acker, Angela Carter, and Joanna Russ." In 2003, I published a metafictional enterprise which clearly shows the affinity between feminist fabulation and postmodern textuality: I rewrote my biography as a fiction which counters patriarchal fictions. I, in short, changed *Feminist Fabulation* into power associated with fiction instead of criticism. My novel *Oy Pioneer!* (2003) is akin to *Feminist Fabulation* presented with a concurrent changed name and changed genre. The novel presents my story retold in a manner which partially removes it from patriarchal reality. In *Oy Pioneer!*, I am at once feminist science fiction writer and feminist fabulator – the recreator of my biography as creator of a fiction about patriarchal fiction. I, feminist fabulator. This new identity construction brings me to reconsidering *Feminist Fabulation* in terms of feminist fabulation's relationship to reality and realist fiction.

How Not to Suppress Women and Women's Writing: Realist Fiction/Feminist Fabulation/Reality

Hollinger comments upon how *Feminist Fabulation* engages with reality: "Barr recognizes the shortcomings of realist literature, which is, ultimately, incapable of envisioning new responses in the face of patriarchal things-as-they-are. . . . She is interested in how feminist texts rewrite the narratives of patriarchy, in how women writers (and readers) both resist and overcome the constrictions embedded in such narratives, and in how such fictional resistance interacts with women's resistance in the 'real world' " (Hollinger 1993: 273). To expand upon these interests, I turn to *The First Wives Club* (1992), a realist novel. I also discuss two real women: *First Wives* author Olivia Goldsmith and Dr. Judith Steinberg (who, as the wife of former Democratic presidential candidate Howard Dean, is a First Lady who was not to be). Goldsmith and Steinberg respectively represent women who both succumb to and subvert patriarchal narratives. My attention to them illustrates how to extend the field of feminist fabulation to encompass real women's lives and realist literature.

As a science fiction critic, I constantly point out that the line separating SF from reality is becoming ever increasingly blurred. We live in an SF world and an understanding of that world is necessary to our survivial in it. In terms of women, I would go so far as to say that understanding how feminist fabulation works in relationship to patriarchal reality is necessary to women's survial within patrarchal reality. The discrepancy between how the protagonists of *First Wives* successfully resist patriarchal narratives and the extreme consequence of Goldsmith's own very real failure to do so are exemplary in relation to this point.

When despair causes Goldsmith's protagonist (Cynthia) to commit suicide after her husband leaves her for a younger woman, her friends (Annie, Brenda, and Elise) band together to rewrite the patriarchal story of the cast off wife's fate Cynthia enacts. Refusing to become has-beens and victims, Cynthia's friends triumph over their husbands and build a women's center named for Cynthia. Adhering to the parameters of reality, these women are authors/architects who imagine and construct a feminist Utopian space which functions as a real world version of science fictional feminist utopias. They live according to the manifesto for feminist fabulation Carrie Bradshaw articulates at the conclusion of the much-hyped last episode of *Sex And The City*: "The most exciting, challenging and significant relationship of all is the one you have with yourself. And if you find someone to love the you you love, well that's just fabulous" (February 2004). Carrie, reality-bound feminist fabulator, instead of negating her entire self to subsume herself within a man's life, places herself center stage in her life story. Carrie and Dr. Steinberg epitomize how feminist fabulation's eye directed at the straight gal refurbishes patriarchal stories in terms of realist fiction and real life experience.

Joanna Russ' Whileaway (in *The Female Man*, 1975), then, is not located in a galaxy so very far far away from the Manhattan women's center Goldsmith imagines. Elise, who receives so much plastic surgery that her friends comment that she has much in common with a science fiction character, is almost science fictional. Reality and fiction further merge in that Goldsmith herself acts like Elise and becomes Cynthia. Like Elise, Goldsmith routinely undergoes plastic surgery. Like Cynthia, Goldsmith dies because she becomes a victim in a patriarchal story.

Goldsmith dies because she adheres to the patriarchal story that women must appear to be forever young. A routine plastic surgery procedure caused Goldsmith's death. This author who created realist revisions of patriarchal narratives did not experience her own reality in terms of the revisions she herself imagined. Goldsmith – an exceedingly successful, talented, and wealthy woman – died because, instead of appearing in the world as her real middle-aged self, elected to recreate herself as an impossibility, as a science fiction character: a young middle-aged woman.

Howard Dean's presidential campaign died due to lack of adherance to feminist fabulation. His defeat scream heard around the world has no place in the patriarchal script for presidential candidates. And, most crucially, Dr. Steinberg, whose casual appearance and insistence upon her own professional trajectory's importance incarnates the antithesis of patriarchy's vision of an acceptable political wife, like the failed operation Goldsmith's doctor performed, functions as a malpractice suit in relation to Dr. Dean's campaign. Yes, first ladies and candidates wives (and this observation just barely includes Laura Bush) have progressed beyond Mamie Eisenhower. But Dr. Steinberg – who did not stand at her husband's side until the end of his campaign and who appeared on the front page of the *New York Times* uncoiffed and clad in a manner completely alien to femininity – was simply too far removed from patriachal acceptibility narratives for the American public to bear. In terms of patriarchal expectations, Steinberg's *Times* photo did not present a pretty picture. Michael Wolf states that the photo marks the moment of Dean's campaign's reversal: "Pick the moment of the reversal. Mine is when Dr. Judith Steinberg showed up on the front page of the *New York Times*. You could hear the collective intake of breadth. First there was the pure style issue: the untended hair, the thousand-year-old jeans, the stubborn sneakers. The picture said it: hard core. You just couldn't transpose her into another setting" (Wolf 2004: 18). The picture said it: feminist fabulator. Dean will be remembered for generating new internet fund raising methods. Steinberg must be remembered for daring to be a male politician's spouse who acts counter to someone called from central casting for *The Handmaid's Tale*.

Steinberg holds a license to practice medicine, does not live totally in terms of her marriage license, and fails to be crowned First Lady of America. She can, nevertheless, hold her head high while telling subscribers to patriachal stories to kiss her tiara. No member of the first ladies club, Steinberg is a card-carrying member of an unladylike club of women who first and foremost vote no to patriarchal rules of law. While refusing to join her husband on the campaign trail, she might have appropriately remained home in Vermont, reading an irreverent challenge to the best-selling backlash text *The Rules: Time Tested Secrets for Capturing the Heart of Mr. Right* (Sherri Schneider and Ellen Fein 1995) Susan Jane Gilman poses in *Kiss My Tiara: How to*

Rule the World as a Smart-Mouth Goddess (2001). *Tiara* provides women with the rules about how to put themselves first – and, most crucially, how not to meet Olivia Goldsmith's fate. *Tiara* can be read as the new millennium's popular nonfictional version of *Feminist Fabulation*.

Gilman uses humor to describe the very serious business of surviving destructive patriarchal master narratives. According to Gilman, getting a life is more important than getting a husband and, as one of her chapters proclaims, "We Don't Shape History By Shaping Our Thighs." The makers of the Home Box Office (HBO) film about the suffragist Alice Paul, which calls attention to the force-feeding she endured in prison, *Iron Jawed Angels* (first aired February 15, 2004), do not show their aware-ness of these rules. They emphasize that Paul, an important shaper of feminist American history, enjoys shopping and, just in case the shopping obsessed Paul is still not perceived to be feminine enough, they invent her male love interest. In early twenty-first-century America, potential first ladies cannot wear thousand-year-old jeans and a radical historical feminist agitator, according to Alessandra Stanley, is portrayed as being more akin to Carrie Bradshaw than to Carrie Nation.

Stanley comments on the shopping scene which appears near the start of *Iron Jawed Angels*: "The scene [where Paul obsesses over a pink hat] is intended to disarm: early twentieth-century feminists like Paul may have been zealots, but they were still fem-inine. Pretty, funny, sexually attracted to men and fond of shopping, the heroines of 'Iron Jawed Angels' have been made over to suit today's ambivalent notions about the women's movement – Legally Blonde III: The Suffragette Years . . . Oddly enough, 'Iron Jawed Angels' suggests that women have not come such a long way after all" (Stanley 2004: E1). The Paul this film portrays wears the pink hat of feminine decorum, not the tiara of feminist fervency. *Iron Jawed Angels* suggests that women, instead of voting to portray feminist fabulative visions, have been forced fed myriad patriarchal stories and elect to swallow them whole. Women figure most prominently among writers and producers of *Iron Jawed Angels*, a film that shows just how starved women are in terms of receiving sufficient food for feminist fabulative thought. Fem-inist fabulation has not come a long way.

There is not even a slim morsel of a reference to feminist fabulation in Andrew Butler's essay "Postmodernism and Science Fiction." Butler's account of postmod-ernism and science fiction devotes a feast of words to men and assigns women meager rations – mere crumbs. I coined feminist fabulation to put women in "postmodernism and science fiction"; Butler takes them out – ignores the existence of *Feminist Fabulation*.

Butler explains that "postmodernism . . . soon became one of the commonest crit-ical approaches to SF" (Butler 2003: 137). Yes. But Butler does not see fit to approach considering how women participate in this discourse. Within his entire article, there is not room reserved for a woman to have even a sentence of her own. Years after the publication of *Feminist Fabulation*, while responding to "Postmodernism and Science Fiction," I sit at my computer engaging in abacus criticism; as I literally count the sparse references to women in Butler's article, it is clear that women are still not being counted vis-à-vis the relationship between postmodernism and science fiction. Butler fails to mention even one science fiction text authored by a woman or even one female literary theorist. How to suppress women's writing? Butler's article supplies an egregious answer.

Conclusion: When You Kiss a Frog, Don't Bet On The Princess

As I have mentioned, Gunn describes how Vonnegut enters the "eddies of the mainstream" by erasing the name "science fiction" in reference to his work. When Butler erases the name "feminist fabulation" from his account of postmodernism and science fiction, women are erased from that account. As opposed to literary acceptance, in Butler's story of postmodernism and science fiction, women experience the kiss of death, a fate that Gunn recalls science fiction fans attributed to scholarly attention. "In those days [1971], some fans considered the embrace of academe next to the kiss of death" (Gunn 2003: xv). In 1992, I envisioned feminist fabulation in terms of a fairy tale happy ending. I thought of *Feminist Fabulation* as a theoretical apparatus which would facilitate the literary establishment's willingness to agree to kiss a marginalized genre fiction frog and, as a result, feminist science fiction would emerge as a tiara-clad princess crowned with inclusion in postmodern cannons. Butler fractures my fairy tale, decapitates the crowned princess I imagined. He perpetuates a story about how the feminist generic frog remains in the backwaters and drowns in obscurity outside the eddies of the mainstream relationship between postmodernism and science fiction. In 2001, we did not embark upon space odysseys to orbiting hotels. After 2001, we did not launch a new term to supersede feminist fabulation and more forcefully thrust women forward in the ongoing story of postmodernism and science fiction. Butler's erasure of women's contribution to postmodernism and science fiction is not the future I would have wished for feminist fabulation. Patriarchal stories still run rampant; women still have to toe the line to make sure the shoe fits in relation to the need to bet on the prince. But the story I describe in this article has a happy ending. Feminist fabulation *is* here. Feminist fabulation has room of its own – an entire article – within this very book. Go little book which includes feminist fabulation. And when you do, wear Dr. Steinberg's sneakers. Dr. Scholes (that is, his term "fabulation"), in the end, can only carry women so far.

Back to the future: Hollinger's concluding remarks: "Even more importantly, I think that the passion which Barr brings to her readings and the Utopian desire which impels this passion is a healthy corrective to the frequently too-polite tone of most feminist critics of speculative fiction. We are, on the whole, a well-behaved group and our work rarely poses much of a challenge to the institutional structures within which we function. Barr's work, on the other hand, is frequently infuriating and deliberately sets out to revise the terms of literary acceptability . . . *Feminist Fabulation* . . . demands engagement from its readers and rewards serious critical thinking about its positions, whether or not we agree with them. And the broad range of texts which together make up the field of feminist fabulation do indeed, as Barr argues, rewrite old stories and fashion new ones, replacing the cultural narratives of an outmoded patriarchy and serving as at least one strand of a 'literature of replenishment" (Hollinger 1993: 275–6). I have, thankfully, not mellowed with age. I remain insufferable, irreverent, infuriating – and willing to transgress the patriarchal rules regarding proper feminine good behavior in response to those who would thwart feminist fabulation's power to act as the literature of replenishment, those who continue to tell exhausted patriarchal stories based upon erasing women's voice, presence, and achievements.

Remembering that a smart-mouthed feminist science fiction critic can play goddess and rule in the literary world by decreeing that feminist science fiction should wear a tiara of recognition, I say (vehemently, with Utopian desire impelled passion): off with your heads – and: (last but not least) kiss my *Feminist Fabulation: Space/ Postmodern Fiction*!

References and Further Reading

Aldiss, Brian (2004) "Oh No, Not More Sci Fi." *PMLA* 119 (May), 509–12.

Allen, Virginia and Terry Paul (1986) "Science and Fiction: Ways of Theorizing about Women," in *Erotic Universe: Sexuality and Fantastic Literature*, (ed.) Donald Palumbo. Westport, CT: Greenwood Press, 165–83.

Atwood, Margaret (2003) *Oryx and Crake*. New York: Nan A. Talese.

——(1998) *The Handmaid's Tale*. New York: Anchor.

Barr, Marleen S (1987) "Feminist Fabulation Or, Playing With Patriarchy Vs. the Masculinization of Metafiction." *Women's Studies* 14, 187–91.

——(1992) *Feminist Fabulation: Space/Postmodern Fiction*. Iowa City: University of Iowa Press.

——(2003) *Oy Pioneer!* Madison, WI: University of Wisconsin Press.

——(2004) "Textism: An Emancipation Proclamation." *PMLA* 119 (May), 429–41.

Bushnell, Candace (1996) *Sex and the City*. New York: Atlantic Monthly Press.

Butler, Andrew (2003) "Postmodernism and Science Fiction," in *The Cambridge Companion to Science Fiction*. (eds.) Edward James and Farah Mendelsohn. Cambridge: Cambridge University Press, 137–48.

Dery, Mark (1994) "Black to the Future: Inter-

views with Samuel R. Delany, Greg Tate, and Tricia Rose," in (ed.) Mark Dery. *Flame Wars: The Discourse of Cyberculture*, Durham, NC and London: Duke University Press, 179–222.

Dinshaw, Carolyn (2003) New York University Gender and Sexuality Studies Program Website. (January) www.nyu.edu/fas/gender.sexuality.

Ebihara, Akiko (2002) "Japan's Feminist Fabulation." *Genders* 36 (on-line journal)

Finch, Sheila (1985) *Infinity's Web*. New York: Bantam.

Gilman, Susan Jane (2001) *Kiss My Tiara: How to Rule the World as a Smart-Mouth Goddess*. New York: Warner.

Golda's Balcony. (2003–) New York. Helen Hayes Theater. Written by William Gibson. Directed by Scott Schwartz. With Tovah Feldshuh.

Goldsmith, Oliva (1992) *The First Wives Club*. New York: Poseidon Books.

Gunn, James (2003) "Foreword," in *The Cambridge Companion to Science Fiction*, (eds.) Edward James and Farah Mendelsohn, Cambridge: Cambridge University Press, xv–xvii.

Hayles, N. Katherine and Nicholas Gessler (2004) "The Slipstream of Mixed Reality: Unstable Ontologies and Semiotic Markers in *The Thirteenth Floor, Dark City*, and *Mulholland Drive*." *PMLA* 119 (May), 482–99.

Hengee, Paul, and Agniesza Holland (1990)

Europa Europa. Orion Classics. Directed by Agnieszka Holland.

Hollinger, Veronica (1993) "A New Alliance of Postmodernism and Feminist Speculative Fiction: Barr's Feminist Fabulation." *Science Fiction Studies*. No. 60, vol. 20, 272–6.

Kuhn, Thomas S. (1970) *The Structure of Scientific Revolutions*, 2nd edition. Chicago, IL: University of Chicago Press.

Landon, Brooks (1993–4) "Pedal-to-the-Metal Feminism." *American Book Review*. 15.

Le Guin, Ursula K. (1979) "Why Are Americans Afraid of Dragons? In *The Language of the Night: Essays on Fantasy and Science Fiction*, (ed.) Susan Wood. New York: Putnam, 39–45.

——(1987) "Daddy's Big Girl" *Omni* 9.iv (January 9) 48–50, 89–90, 93–4.

Lessing, Doris (1975) *Memoirs of A Survivor*. New York: Knopf.

Rabkin, Eric S (2003) "Review: What Was Science Fiction?" in *Envisioning the Future: Science Fiction and the Next Millennium*, (ed.) Marleen S. Barr. Middletown, CT: Wesleyan University Press, 191–8.

Russ, Joanna (1977) *The Female Man*. Boston, MA: Gregg Press.

Schneider, Sherri, and Ellen Fein (1995) *The Rules: Time-Tested Secrets for Capturing the Heart of Mr. Right*. New York: Warner.

Scholes, Robert (1967) *The Fabulators*. New York: Oxford University Press.

——(1976) "The Roots of Science Fiction," in *Science Fiction: A Collection of Critical Essays*, (ed.) Mark Rose. Englewood Cliffs NJ: Prentice Hall, 46–56.

Sex And The City. HBO. 1998–2004. Based on the novel by Candace Bushnell.

Stanley, Alessandra (2004) "Determined Women, Finding Their Voice." *New York Times* (February 13), E1, E30.

Von Garnier Katja (dir) (2004) *Iron Jawed Angels*. HBO. Screenplay by Sally Robinson, Eugenia Bostwick Singer, *et al*.

Waugh, Patricia (1984) *Metafiction: The Theory and Practice of Self-Conscious Fiction*. London and New York: Methuen.

Wolf, Michael (2004) "Us and Dem." *New York Magazine* (February 2), 18–19.

10

Time and Identity in Feminist Science Fiction

Jenny Wolmark

SF is increasingly recognized for its ability to articulate complex and multifaceted responses to contemporary uncertainties and anxieties, and metaphors drawn from SF have acquired considerable cultural resonance. As a result, writing and reading SF are no longer regarded as marginal cultural activities, and feminist SF writers and critics have made a major contribution to this shift of emphasis. As Brooks Landon has suggested, the fruitful relationship between SF and feminism is "perhaps the most important single development in SF since the 1970s" (2002: 124). Like all SF narratives, feminist SF provides an imaginative space in which things are shown "not as they characteristically or habitually are but as they might be" (Russ 1972: 79). However, feminist SF emphasizes the significance of the social and cultural construction of gender and identity in a way that other SF narratives do not, and in so doing they make provision for the creation of what Elisabeth Grosz has described as a "conceptual space such that an *indeterminable future* is open to women"(2000: 1017). The fluid and often unstable temporal landscapes of feminist SF create a symbolic space within which fixed notions of subjectivity and identity are challenged, and the dynamic between being and becoming is explored. My intention in this chapter is to suggest that there is interesting convergence of concerns in feminist SF around the open-ended nature of both identity and time, and that both Utopian and dystopian potentialities are inherent in such a radical openness. The cultural construction and reconstruction of identity entails a reconsideration of the relationship between the past, the present, and the future, and my discussion will focus on two specific novels in which the open-ended nature of the relationships between time and being, and memory and identity, are explored: Rebecca Ore's *Gaia's Toys* (1995) and Nicola Griffith's *Slow River* (1995).

In common with other forms of popular fiction, feminist SF contains contradictory responses to the dominant ideology in the sense that it is both complicit with and critical of that ideology. It is constantly renegotiating with and testing out the limits both of generic boundaries and the prevailing values inscribed within them, and the ensuing restlessness of feminist SF sometimes prevents it from being wholly accommodated within SF as a genre. The transgressive qualities of feminist SF have been astutely noted by Marleen Barr, and her redesignation of feminist SF as "feminist fabulation" (1992) is, in part, a response to those qualities. In my view, however, it is more useful to retain the generic credentials of feminist SF, in order to reveal the way in which it has carved out a specific conceptual space in which to explore futures that remain "indeterminable" and thus open to women. The specificity of language in science fiction is discussed by Samuel Delany in *The Jewel Hinged Jaw* and he describes the way in which the "specifically science fictional sentence" (1977: 278) works by analyzing a sentence from Robert Heinlein's novel *Beyond this Horizon* – "The door dilated." Delany argues that the use of the term "dilated" forces a reader's mental image of the door to undergo "a catastrophic change of form," not least because the word "dilated" is usually associated with "sphincter muscles and camera apertures" (1977: 281). Having completed the semiotic analysis, Delany goes on to make the crucial point that SF "ends up speaking much more of the world than . . . any description of the discourse can say" (1977: 284). In other words, language articulates and is constitutive of material reality and its metaphors have a powerful impact on the way in which that reality is imagined. This general capacity to "speak of the world" is given a particular specificity in feminist SF and in its emphasis on the construction and reconstruction of gender, feminist SF has induced in the reader a similarly "catastrophic" change of perspective.

There are, of course, other contributory factors involved in such a significant transformation of perspective, one of the most important of which is the changing relationship between SF and science and technology. The range of different and competing attitudes towards science and technology that can be found in SF indicates that this relationship is anything but straightforward. The early pulp SF magazines of the 1920s and 1930s such as *Science Fiction Wonder Stories*, *Amazing Stories*, and *Astounding Stories*, are characterized by a largely uncritical enthusiasm for science and technology, and under Hugo Gernsback's editorial control, *Astounding Stories* tirelessly promoted and popularized ideas about scientific and technological innovations. In a 1926 editorial, Gernsback explicitly celebrates the prophetic abilities of what he calls "scientifiction" in his claim that "There are few things written by our scientifiction writers, frankly impossible today, that may not become a reality tomorrow" (Carter 1977: 4). The predominantly male readers of these magazines were able to share in the fantasy that they were uniquely placed to endorse a future that was in the very process of being constructed, and this future was confidently based on an instrumentally rational and masculinist science. By the end of the 1960s, however, science fiction narratives manifest a noticeable lack of confidence in science and scientists, and the production of more dystopian SF leads Fred Pfeil to suggest that the "highly literary science fiction in the 1960s was itself paradoxically the sign of a certain exhaustion of content, of the bankruptcy of the utopian/dystopian dialectic on which virtually all serious SF was based for the first hundred years of its existence" (1990: 92). It is no coincidence that this period also saw the emergence of conflicting social and political agendas around the issues of civil rights and women's liberation, as well as the development of a huge groundswell of opposition to US military involvement in South-East Asia. The science fiction that emerged from these disputed ideological imperatives rejected the increasingly tenuous presumption that science and technology were in some way inherently progressive, and the genre became increasingly distanced from the uncritical technophilia that had been its original motivating force. The changing social, political, and cultural agendas of the 1960s and 1970s generated a range of oppositional stances towards the dominant discourses of power and control, and within SF, general anxieties about corporate and political control of science and technology coincided with the feminist critique of patriarchal structures.

Although SF has traditionally been marked out as a gendered cultural space occupied primarily by men, like science itself, women have always been involved in the writing and publishing of SF. Their involvement was often covert and the use of androgynous sounding names or male pseudonyms was fairly common: writers such as Leigh Brackett, C.L. Moore, Andre Norton, Julian May, and James Tiptree, Jr. have all used these devices. In her discussion of the work of Lilith Lorraine, a less well-known woman SF writer who had several stories published by Gernsback, Jane Donawerth quoted Lorraine's own opinion that "if the editors and publishers knew I was a woman they wouldn't accept more than half what they do now" (1990: 253). Since the 1970s, however, women have been writing science fiction with explicitly woman-centered and feminist content, and this change is visible in landmark texts such as *The Wanderground* (1979, 1985) by Sally Miller Gearhart, *Motherlines* (1978, 1980) by Suzy McKee Charnas, and *The Female Man* (1975) by Joanna Russ. These particular texts explore the Utopian possibilities of separatist, women-only communities, and they have had a powerful impact on the genre as a whole because of the way in which they identify gender as a culturally constructed phenomenon. Many more women have since entered the field, and representations of gender and gender relations have become key issues in science fiction narratives. At the same time, definitions of science itself have been problematized, not least by the critique of the discourses of science offered by feminist science studies. The cultural relocation of SF, from the subcultural marginality of pulp fiction where writers, readers, and fans were predominantly young white males, to generic respectability and a significant number of women writers, readers, and fans, has resulted in a "catastrophic" change of perspective equivalent to that experienced by the reader of the science fictional sentence described by Delany.

The destabilization of the relations between space and time in postmodern culture has resulted in another profound change of perspective. The process of globalization, together with technological developments that facilitate the instantaneous transmission of information around the world, have together produced a sense of dislocation and fragmentation. For many writers on postmodernism, information technology has fatally undermined the concept of time as linear progression, which in turn has resulted in an emphasis on the spatial and on location. Paul Virilio, for example, has argued that the postmodern "crisis of dimension" has obliterated the meaning of space-time as the "continuum of society" (1984: 26). In Jean Baudrillard's view, not only has the future imploded into an increasingly science fictional present, but it is no longer possible to write science fiction, since we are already living it (1991). For Baudrillard, the role of science fiction has shifted from that of imagining multiple and expansive future possibilities, to that of simply reflecting back to us the hyper-reality in which we already live. Fredric Jameson has argued that that the linear logic of the temporal has been replaced by the spatial in postmodernism and, as a result, we have come to occupy a schizophrenic environment of unrelated present moments, all of them equally vivid and indistinguishable one from another. Jameson's influential analysis of postmodernism presents postmodern culture as one that is preoccupied with media-enhanced surfaces rather than with depth of meaning, the most debilitating consequence of which is the "fragmentation of time into a series of perpetual presents" (1985: 125) and an ensuing loss of a critical historical memory. The notion that we experience time as a series of disconnected moments rather than as a linear progression has also been taken up by Katherine Hayles, who suggests that this has generated a contemporary feeling that time has somehow flattened out, leading to a "growing sense that the future is already used up before it arrives" (1990: 279). She comments that time has, in a sense, become "obsolete," since it has lost its usefulness as a conceptual means of measuring and organizing human experience (1990: 281).

The skepticism towards established "truths" about space and time articulated by many writers derives from an "incredulity toward metanarratives" (1985: xxiv), which in Jean-Francois Lyotard's view, is a defining feature of postmodernism. The loss of confidence in, and subsequent ambivalence towards, metanarratives of space and time has had a widespread cultural impact. Since SF is a genre that is preoccupied with space and time, we should not be surprised to find numerous examples of such incredulity and ambivalence within it. It is more striking to find it surfacing in a popular genre where it would *not* be expected to appear, specifically in a female private eye narrative. In my reading of the opening paragraph of Sue Grafton's *N for Noose* (1998), I argue that there has been a major shift in popular consciousness regarding the acceptability of previously unquestioned ideas about space and time. The opening paragraph of Grafton's *N For Noose* is a low-key but deeply felt dramatization of the cultural impact of postmodern speculation about the "used-up" nature of the future and its collapse into the present. The first person narrator in the extract is Kinsey Millhone, a female private eye, and it is her meditation on the nature of time and the future that opens the novel:

> Sometimes I think about how odd it would be to catch a glimpse of the future, a quick view of events lying in store for us at some undisclosed date. Suppose we could peer through a tiny peep-hole in Time and chance upon a flash of what was coming up in the years ahead. Some moments we saw would make no sense at all and some, I suspect, would frighten us beyond endurance. If we knew what was looming, we'd avoid certain choices, select option B instead of A at the fork in the road: the job, the marriage, the move to a new state, child birth, the first drink, the elective medical procedure, that long-anticipated ski trip that seemed like such fun until the dark rumble of the

avalanche. If we understood the consequences of any given action, we could exercise dis-
cretion, thus restructuring our fate. Time, of course, only runs in one direction, and it
seems to do so in an orderly progression. Here in the blank and stony present, we're
shielded from the knowledge of the dangers that await us, protected from future horrors
through blind innocence (1998: 3).

As I have already suggested, popular narratives contain multiple layers of meaning
and are adept at repeating the dominant ideas and ways of thinking in a culture, and
undermining them at the same time. The double-edged quality of popular narratives
is often indicative of a particular kind of cultural disorientation, when conventional
notions of authority and judgment are called into question. In this opening paragraph,
the text puts forward somewhat clichéd judgments about the relationship between the
present and the future, primarily as a means of indicating the cause and effect structure of the narrative as a whole. It is difficult to accept, however, that the opening can
only be read at this level, for Grafton is a careful writer, and the narrator is far from
being an ingénue, as readers of her books will know. Rather, there is a crisis of tone in
this extract that reveals a deep-seated unease about the way in which we inhabit contemporary spatial and temporal zones. Consider this sentence: "Time, of course, only
runs in one direction, and it seems to do so in an orderly progression." The tension
between the insistent *"of course"* and the uncertainty of the *"it seems to"* conveys anything
but conviction. The cultural environment of postmodernism, in which the temporal
has collapsed into the spatial, means that the idea of linearity, deriving from the notion
that time "runs in an orderly progression," is subject to increased questioning. The profound change that spatial and temporal relations generally have undergone has provoked what Katherine Hayles has described as "uncertainty about where we as human
beings fit into our own future scenarios" (1990: 280). It is exactly this sense of dislocation and uncertainty about possible future scenarios that is being expressed in the
narrator's bleak reference to the "blank and stony present" which we can only inhabit
with "blind innocence." It is not surprising that a present which seems so lacking in
comfort should produce a future that is depicted solely in terms of "horrors," the only
protection from which is our own ignorance. The capacity to envisage the future in
terms of an ethical framework based on cause and effect, so that "we understood the
consequences of any given action," is no longer sustainable, thanks to the uncertainty
of the relationship of the past to the present, and the present to the future. Utopian
longings that are tied to a notion that the future will be determined by the needs and
desires of the present are equally unsustainable, leaving nothing but a space that is
"blank" and entirely unpredictable. The narrative parameters of crime fiction do not
allow this vivid sense of spatial and temporal dislocation to be explored any further,
but what is significant is that it should occur there at all, which suggests that such dislocation has indeed become a cultural constant.

The profound cultural shifts that I have briefly described have generated a critical
climate in which the material conditions of postmodernity and the emergence of the
posthuman subject can be explored. The spatial and temporal dislocation that is inte-

gral to SF means that it is especially able to raise uncomfortable questions about identity and positionality, enabling new and complex articulations of difference to become possible. Unlike the narratives of crime fiction, the contested futures of feminist SF are centrally concerned with the renegotiation of identity. The cultural intervention made by feminist SF is important because it offers an account of gendered identity that not only recognizes complexity and contradiction, but it also recognizes that, as Stuart Hall has argued, identity is "a matter of 'becoming' as well as being" (1997: 52). A "becoming" subject is one that is not fixed and determinate: its diversity allows it to contain multiple rather than singular possibilities for the articulation of identity. As Hall has suggested, identity can be thought of "as a 'production,' which is never complete, always in process, and always constituted within, not outside, representation" (1997: 51). For identity to be constituted within representation means that it is anchored to past, present, and future, as well as to space and time. Thus, the construction and reconstruction of subjects and identities has both a temporal and a spatial dimension. An open-ended sense of identity, and the capacity for it to be constructed and reconstructed in time and history, allows for the creative destabilization of definitions of self and other and for the acknowledgment of difference. The contested futures of feminist SF provide the arena in which the disruptive consequences of such destabilizations can be explored.

The unstable, fragmented near futures of contemporary SF narratives have become culturally pervasive because they vividly articulate the experience of living in the spatio-temporal dislocations brought about by globalization and communications technology. SF contributes to the making of a social imaginary in which temporal complexity and uncertainty do not have entirely negative consequences, and the future is not wholly determined by the expectations and desires of either the past or the present. Feminist SF exploits the potential of such indeterminate futures, by questioning the way in which the gendered practices, relations, and assumptions of the present continue to shape representations of futures that are based on exclusion and a refusal of difference. By contesting the nature of such representations, feminist SF makes a significant contribution to the articulation of a social imaginary that is informed by the notion of plurality and inclusion. The futures generated within this social imaginary are inherently contradictory and ambivalent but because they are based on contingency rather than predictability, such futures are also open and negotiable. For Elizabeth Grosz, an open future is one that "has yet to be made," and as such it is "the very lifeblood of political struggle, the goal of feminist challenge" (2000: 1017). Grosz argues that the idea of an indeterminate and uncontained future also has implications for the way in which we understand the past. Given that the past is viewed from the present, the multiple and different perspectives of the present are bound to generate equally diverse accounts and interpretations of the past. The past, then, is as much subject to discovery and the production of new meanings as the future. Just as the future is yet to be made, the past is, as Grosz puts it, "uncontainable within any one history or even all cumulative histories." (Grosz 2000: 1020) Thus, in order to conceptualize the future as open and indeterminate, the past has also to be viewed as being in a state of "becoming" rather than completion. Crucially, then, it is the dynamic relationship between Utopian longings and critical memory that enables both past and future to remain open to feminist intervention. Another approach to the creative potential of this relationship that has relevance to feminist SF can be found in Svetlana Boym's discussion of the contemporary meanings of nostalgia. For Boym, when nostalgia functions as a means to review the past in a critical rather than a commemorative way, it is an activity that "opens up a multitude of potentialities, nonteleological possibilities of historical development" (2001: 50). To use Boym's terminology, this form of nostalgia is "reflective" as opposed to "restorative," and her argument for the creative potential of reflective nostalgia rests on the assertion that it contains multiple viewing positions from which the past can be reassessed; reflective nostalgia does not, therefore, "follow a single plot but explores ways of inhabiting many places at once and imagining different time zones" (2001: xviii). Nostalgia is inevitably ambivalent, of course, for it can never be wholly about the past: it has also to serve the needs of the present and has the potential to influence the imagining of any number of possible futures. As such, it is another expression of the creative link between Utopian longings and critical memory, both of which are dependent on the notion that the past and the future are open-ended.

This sense of temporal fluidity and openness to change, in which the future is yet to be written and the past is yet to be revealed, is characteristic of feminist SF. The futures envisioned in feminist SF are often uncertain and ambivalent, but they are also amongst the most interesting in SF, precisely because the Utopian longings in such futures are infused with critical memories of the past, enabling a complex negotiation to take place between that which has already taken place and that which has not yet become. Feminist SF speculates about futures in which the past is subject to constant review and the framing devices of the present are questioned. Thus, in the imaginative spaces of feminist SF, the gendered subjects in the narratives are marked by, but not wholly determined by their own pasts, and identity remains open to redefinition. In *Gaia's Toys* and *Slow River*, the redefinition of identity is facilitated by the destabilization of the linear relationship between past, present, and future. The main characters in these novels have been objectified by the narratives of their own pasts, which have made them "other," and thus incapacitated them as active subjects. In both novels, repressed memories of abusive familial relationships contribute to and sustain this disabling effect. In order to open up possible futures that are unconstrained by the limitations of the past, the characters are compelled to establish a different and critical relationship with the past. The nonlinear nature of reflective memory is used as a narrative strategy to reveal the way in which the distortions and omissions of the past are reiterated in the present, but also to gesture towards some undecided and open future. The open-ended narratives contain both Utopian and dystopian characteristics, and as such they can usefully be thought as critical dystopias which, as Raffaella Baccolini and Tom Moylan suggest, "allow both readers and protagonists to hope by resisting closure: the ambiguous, open endings of these novels maintain the Utopian impulse within the work. In fact, by rejecting the traditional subjugation of the individual at the end of the novels, the critical dystopia opens a space of contestation and opposition for those collective 'ex-centric' subjects who are not empowered by hegemonic rule" (2003: 7).

Temporal complexity, then, becomes a means of exploring the construction of gendered identity in *Gaia's Toys* and *Slow River*. *Gaia's Toys* depicts a complex near future in which the domination of bioengineering and nanotechnology has made it increasingly difficult to make politically, ethically, and environmentally "correct" or "incorrect" distinctions between nature and technology. The narrative suggests that existing definitions of the human and the inhuman, the natural and the unnatural have to be revised as a consequence. The novel is structured around several interwoven narrative viewpoints, and the multiple and interlocking narrative perspectives replicate the disorderly and unpredictable environment within which the characters move and by which they are shaped, literally and metaphorically. Although there is a first person narrator in *Gaia's Toys*, the perspective offered by it is one of several that overlap throughout the narrative. Together, these multiple viewpoints provide a complexly articulated but deliberately partial and incomplete perspective on a morally uncertain environment. The first person narrator is Allison, an ecoterrorist whose intention to blow up an oil refinery is thwarted when the FBI captures her before she is able to detonate the bomb. Although she defines herself as an ecowarrior, Allison's own self certainties are fundamentally undermined when she is informed that, unbeknown to her, her own eco group had sent her on a suicide mission, while they themselves detonated a bomb destroying an industrial site elsewhere that killed thousands of people as a side-effect. Allison's own moral uncertainties become a potent metaphor for the ethical dilemmas and ambiguities that are at the heart of contemporary culture. Her revelation that "The movement always used my ambiguous look, not African-American, not completely white. Being small disarms people" (Ore 1995: 27) makes it clear that, for Ore, these dilemmas include race as well as gender.

The ethical uncertainties with which Ore is concerned are enacted through the unstable narrative positions and perspectives shared between Allison and two other characters, Dorcas and Willie. Dorcas is an untenured research scientist who is also a gene hacker working with stolen insect DNA, and Willie is a "drode head," an ex-soldier disabled out of the army who earns his welfare entitlement by letting his brain be used as a computer interface for the sole purpose of processing information. All three characters share a socially marginal existence and each has been technologically enhanced in some way, not as a matter of personal or lifestyle choice, but as a direct consequence of their social and economic marginality and relative powerlessness. In Allison's case, she takes the option of becoming an FBI informer rather than face life imprisonment and has then to agree to a whole body "rebuild" using nanotechnology to make her effective in this new role. Willie has computer terminals, or "drode holes," fitted directly into his skull, again, not through choice but because there is an economic imperative: the narrative explains that "Making a computer to read brain output was cheaper than building pure artificial intelligence" (Ore 1995: 26). Dorcas is the genetically engineered product of her parents' DNA and has undergone so many "enhancements" at her parents' insistence that she refers ironically to herself as their "bonsai child" (Ore 1995: 83). Technologically enhanced and bioengineered bodies are commonly used in SF narratives as markers of difference and otherness, but Ore also uses them to give a more complex view of technological embodiment. She depicts a society in which technological enhancements have become socially and culturally acceptable as a way of providing cheap labor to interface directly with the technology, or as lifestyle choices for the wealthy. For Ore, the presence of biotechnologies is, quite simply, the determining condition for all contemporary subjects. The more critical issue raised in the narrative is whether new forms of subjectivity can be articulated that are appropriate to the precarious bodies and unstable environments which we inhabit.

The main focus of the narrative is on the efforts made by the characters to find ways of remaking themselves as authentic subjects living with ambiguity, unpredictability, and difference. They act out the dilemma of embodiment described by Scott Bukatman, that the body "must become a cyborg to retain its presence in the world, resituated in technological space and reconfigured in technological terms. Whether this represents a continuation, a sacrifice, a transcendence, or a surrender of 'the subject' is not certain" (1993: 247).

The uncertainty surrounding such reconfigurations is explored through the characters' attempts to learn to tell different stories about themselves as marginal subjects, rather than being silenced by their own marginality. The origins of that social and cultural silencing have to be rediscovered by exercising the kind of critical memory in which the gaps and elisions of the past are explored rather than glossed over, and that which has been repressed is revealed. Anxieties about the relationship of the past to both the present and the future are often be expressed in a nostalgic desire for the familiar that, in Svetlana Boym's words, "reflects a fear of untamable longing and noncommodified time" (2001: xvii). In the narrative, the characters are faced with the choice between, on the one hand, a self-aware and reflective understanding of the past, which brings with it a view of the future as unpredictable and full of potential and, on the other hand, a desire to reconstruct the past as the source of a mythical set of origins that are pure and unchanging, on which is predicated a future that is both familiar and entirely predictable. *Gaia's Toys* is suffused with memories that exist as multiple possibilities, enshrined in the overlapping and interlocking perspectives of the characters. The unregulated multiplicity of such "untamable longing" prevents the narrative from closing down around a single plot line or subjectivity so that it remains open-ended, neither wholly dystopian nor Utopian.

As part of her reconstitution as an FBI informer, Allison is also fitted with a brain scan that enables the FBI both to read her memories and to track her. These processes are represented in the narrative as forms of gross psychological and physical abuse, during which it becomes clear that Allison's persistent nightmares derive from the trauma of repressed memories. The technology allows her most intimate memories to be extracted from the virtual spaces of her consciousness and replayed on screen to become a voyeuristic spectacle in which they are reduced to merely another form of information. The scene in which her memories are screened is an effective dramatization of the convergence of temporalities described by Steven Connor as "one of the most remarkable features of our saturated present," which is "its capacity precisely to register and regulate a multiplicity of time-scales and rates of change" (1999: 28). Allison watches as her own memories of parental and self abuse are re-enacted on screen to become virtual representations of her past, seen from her own present: as representations, they become a source of new discoveries and understandings because they are no longer hidden from view. As they lose their capacity to have any nostalgic significance, they thus become "noncommodified" or unregulated, and the linear relationship between past, present, and future is destabilized. As Allison watches images of abuse from her past, she becomes her own witness, and the dissolution of the boundaries between inner and outer consciousness, past and present, memory and invention, enables her to make sense of the way in which past abuse has determined the shape of her identity, the person she has become, and to begin to reconstruct a different sense of identity that can encompass future potentialities. The vantage position from which she can finally do this makes it possible for her to come to terms with her memories of "rage, loss, self-pity, ugly little girl screaming by the roadside while the future whizzed by laughing" (Ore 1995: 291). Her technologized existence on the borders of the real and the virtual, the natural and the unnatural, enables her to question the authority exerted over and through her body, and to re-establish an embodied sense of selfhood and agency. Although her past is understood to be an active constituent of the present, it no longer determines the future, and her decision towards the end of the novel, to rejoin her ecoterrorist group and kill her FBI controller, can be seen in this context. It is an act that is both literal and symbolic, enabling her to take control of her memories and thus her possible future: as she says at the conclusion of the novel, "We finally made it out if the prisons of our own pasts" (Ore 1995: 317).

The overlapping narrative perspectives allow Ore to suggest that subjectivity is evolving and provisional rather than fixed and fully formed, and that it is dependent on new connections and alliances, both human and nonhuman. Such alliances might also require more strategic forms of subversion to bring about global change entailing actions that derive from a politics of the imagination rather than direct violence. Dorcas' manipulation of insect DNA to produce insects that will influence human behavior is part of this reconceived notion of political action to save the environment. Dorcas' personal solution to "human nastiness" is to reduce levels of human stress and hostility by producing, not just "a particular wasp, but lots of them, narcoleptic, addictive, brighter than average, more pesticide resistant" (Ore 1995: 234). The logic of this solution stems from her conviction that humans "need to be blended back into the ecosphere again, to be just another species among others, not the top consumer" (Ore 1995). In the end, however, Dorcas sees her work as no more than a complex form of "Invertebrate art" (Ore 1995: 294) that will empower the insect world at the expense of the human, rather than an instrument for real social change. Unlike Allison, she remains symbolically in a cycle of abuse as she continues to be subject to, and controlled by, her parents' search for the perfect genetic offspring. In that search, they always return to the same source to seek some mythically perfect origins

– themselves. Dorcas is truly their "gourmet child" (Ore 1995: 315) and just as they genetically engineered her existence from their own augmented DNA, they use nanotechnology to disassemble her adult form in order to make a further, improved version of her that will meet their needs as parents, in a way that the present version of Dorcas never has. In an ironic and gruesome form of payback for her own ecological manipulation, Dorcas' own womb is used by her parents use to generate a clone, before the nanotechnology literally obliterates her. The dispassionate tone in which Ore describes the procedure emphasizes the horrific nature of, and motivations for, this enterprise: "After the nanomachines scavenged what they needed, her father vacuumed away the rest of her feet. Dorcas said, 'But it won't be me. I'm my memories'" (Ore 1995: 316). The image presents a desire to control the future through elimination of the threat of difference, a process that is completed when the new infant Dorcas is born at the moment of the "old" Dorcas' death, and both flesh and memories are simultaneously erased. Her mother's declaration that "We know how we'd raise you this time" (Ore 1995: 315) reiterates a fantasy of omnipotence that is both narcissistic and rooted in a nostalgic desire for sameness.

The third narrative perspective belongs to Willie, and it completes the triangulation process through which Ore traces the complex negotiations involved in the construction of identity and subjectivity. Like Dorcas and Allison, he is a social outsider, entitled to welfare benefits because he has agreed to the implantation of direct neural inputs in the form of skull sockets. Drode heads go into a "fugue state" when connected to the interface and memory locks prevent them from remembering any of the information that has been processed. The regulation of time and memory is a recognizable feature of globalization, and it enables disembedded technologies to impose forms of social and cultural exclusion that are both brutal and dehumanizing. Willie's gradual release from the passive and subdued state instilled in him by such controls occurs as he learns to become self-aware while he is in the interface, thus giving him the capacity to move around the information network and make contact with other brain patterns, including Allison's and members of her former ecogroup. It is as a virtual subject, then, that he recovers a sense of agency: he abandons his passive existence as a drode head, joins Allison's former ecogroup, persuades them to rescue Allison from the FBI and recruit Dorcas.

Although Willie's narrative perspective is never dominant in the narrative, it is essential to the delineation of the complex matrix of gendered identity and social relations that Ore presents. Masculinity is explored ironically within this matrix, for Willie's status as victim has rendered him literally and metaphorically impotent, and he is denied access to the social and sexual expectations that are integral to constructions of masculinity. He suffers from recurring memories of terrifying and drug induced sexual hallucinations and he has no more control over these memories than he does over the information that he processes as a drode head. Without the ability to exert control over time or memory, he becomes caught in a temporal loop in which past, present, and future are collapsed into meaningless fragments. It is only in the context of the evolving virtual network of connections between himself, Allison, and the ecogroup that he is enabled to reassemble those fragments and reconstruct a sense of selfhood. Ore explores difference through Willie's damaged and incomplete masculine identity, and also through the network of relations that is forged between himself, Allison, and the ecoterrorists, which depends on acceptance of the differences embodied in all their distinctive experiences and memories. The initial reluctance of the ecoterrorists to accept either Willie or Allison as allies is partially explained towards the end of the narrative, when it is revealed that they are all disabled victims of industrial pollution. Dorcas alone is unable to accept the risks entailed in this shifting network of new alliances and the possibilities it may hold for the imagining and articulation of new futures; it is, finally, her desire to retain personal control over her genetic manipulations and a belief that she is constituted as a fully autonomous subject that results in her complete dissolution at the hands of those seeking an identical control over origins.

The complex interactions between technology and nature, past and future, erasure and completion, are also present in Nicola Griffiths' *Slow River*. Like Ore, Griffiths resists the temptation to present apocalyptic visions of a technologically despoiled world and instead explores future possibilities that are far more tentative and fragile. This open-ended uncertainty allows the Utopian possibilities of the text to be kept open, a narrative strategy that is described by Raffaella Baccolini as characteristic of the critical dystopia: as she explains, it is "acceptance of one's responsibility and accountability, often worked through memory and the recovery of the past" that enables us to "bring the past into a living relationship with the present" and "to lay the foundation for Utopian change" (2003: 130). Without that sense of the dynamic relationship between the past and the present, memory can serve to confine and restrict meaningful change. The way in which the past, as memory, determines the present and thus imposes constraints on the way in which the future can be imagined, is explored in *Slow River*, as is the way in which the distortions of memory can be used to close off possibilities for the future and for emerging subjectivities. As was the case in *Gaia's Toys*, biotechnologies provide the accepted and determining condition for the contemporary subjects in the narrative. The gritty near future of Griffith's novel emphasizes the imbrication of technology with nature and culture so that all the constituents are redefined as a consequence. In the narrative, genetically engineered biomediation processes have been developed that can not only repair existing environmental damage caused by industrial pollution, but also have the capacity to restore the ecological balance. The Utopian potential of such technology is undermined, however, by the fact of global corporate control over the technology. The initial biotechnology has been developed by the van de Oest family, and since it has continued to hold the patents for it, the family effectively controls the ecological well-being of the planet. The politics of globalization and the distorting impact of the centralization of political and economic control are made explicit through the powerful metaphor of familial abuse. Through its effect on one individual member of that family, Lore, the narrative explores the powerlessness that results from trauma and abuse and from the suppression of the memories of those acts, in both a personal and a political sense. At the same time, parallels are drawn between the way in which the relations of power that are inherent in both familial and corporate structures can facilitate disempowerment.

The narrative is focused on loss of identity and displacement, both metaphoric and literal: Lore has been the victim of a kidnap orchestrated by her own half-sister, during the course of which her identity chip has been removed. Although Lore escapes from her kidnappers, she remains so fearful of further threats against her that she is compelled to make a new identity for herself in an unknown and unfamiliar environment and by using stolen identity chips. This process has the effect of questioning the authenticity of her original identity, for like Allison in *Gaia's Toys*, Lore has fragmented and repressed aspects of her own past in order to survive in the present. This strategic act of forgetting is an attempt to close off the past, but without the ability to adopt a critical relationship to the past, individuals and cultures remain subject to the dominant and hegemonic discourses of the present, unable to contest the validity of those discourses. The narrative is constructed around three different but converging timelines to reveal the way in which acts of memory, of both forgetting and remembering, are crucial to the construction of identity. One timeline situates Lore in her immediate past, from the time she was kidnapped until her escape: during this time, she has become a powerless victim, forcibly distanced from and made other to her own identity as a member of one of the most powerful families on earth. A second narrative timeline situates Lore at key moments in the past of her own childhood, up to the point at which she is kidnapped; this timeline reveals the way in which the traumatic memory of parental sexual abuse, which she has hidden away behind an idealized version of events until it can barely be discerned, disrupts her sense of identity at both a conscious and unconscious level. The final timeline constitutes the present time of the narrative, in which Lore is struggling to construct a new life and a different identity, not as other, or as powerless victim, but as a fully functioning social and sexual being. The unstable temporal framework provided by the overlapping timelines reveals Lore's fractured and contradictory memories, and throughout the narrative she takes a number of different subject positions: as lover, victim, and child. Different stories are told from these subject positions, or rather, the same stories are told, but differently inflected. The narrative thus enacts the complex relationship between the past and the present, suggesting as it does so that there is an equally complex relationship between temporality and subjectivity: both may be understood to be flexible rather than fixed, unpredictable and open rather than closed and static.

Much of the narrative explores the extreme form of dislocation experienced by Lore when her previous identity is taken from her, and the way in which, as a disenfranchised outsider, she has both to survive and to reconstruct a genuinely authentic sense of self from the fragments of her past. She learns to exist on the margins and within new networks, as far from her privileged background as it is possible to be. In the narrative, both her lesbian identity and her own highly developed technological expertise in biomediation are presented as being integral to this learning process, enabling her to question broader hegemonic cultural narratives about class and gender. In this sense, Lore's recognition that "You had to allow change, you had to want it. You had to believe you deserved it" (Griffiths 1995: 341) has relevance both within and outside the text. It is Lore's own mistaken, and gendered, assumption that her father had sexually abused her which has obscured the difficult truth that not only was her mother her abuser, but that she has been a serial abuser within the family. Lore's idealized memories of her childhood and of her mother's place in it are not endorsed in the narrative, and they are revisited to become part of the wider dialogue between past and present that has to take place if the future is to remain open. As the timelines finally convergence in the narrative present, Lore achieves a sufficiently critical understanding of the contradictory memories of the past to be able to move towards an undefined and open-ended future. As Lore's lover explains to her, "Getting your identity back doesn't mean going back to everything the way it was" (Griffiths 1995: 319). Thus, at the conclusion of the novel, she reclaims her identity without in any way diminishing the fully technologized, lesbian self that she has already become.

This discussion of the novels by Ore and Griffiths is intended to suggest some of the ways in which feminist SF narratives envisage the construction of identity and subjectivity within the contradictory constraints and freedoms of temporal uncertainty and ambiguity. The narratives articulate embodied subjectivity as evolving rather than fully formed, and always taking shape in the context provided by the complex interactions between technology and nature, past and future. Both novels articulate the need to redefine our understanding of nature and the human, and to accept the risks that are entailed in moving forward into a future that is open because it is not shaped by the needs of the past. They also demonstrate an imaginative shift towards futures that are based on uncertainty and contingency rather than predictability, where the unpredictable so often provides the impetus to change and innovation. Such temporally open and indeterminate futures can be problematic, but at the same time, they acknowledge the necessity to think about definitions of the future outside of linear notions of time and progress. There is also a spatial dimension to the indeterminate futures that are imagined in feminist SF, for such futures are at once multiple and collective, global and inescapably postcolonial. In recognition of this, Sylvia Kelso's call for women SF writers to interrogate the necessity for the continued depiction of other worlds is clearly appropriate, for as she puts it, "Maybe it is time to concede that there is no Elsewhere: that this is all we have. Then SF writers might turn their great resources of ingenuity and imagination into going boldly where humanity has always been: into imagining a better future for this by no means inexhaustible earth" (2000: 42).

*

Some parts of this chapter have appeared in Jenny Wolmark (1997). Rethinking bodies and boundaries: Science fiction, cyberpunk and cyberspace, in *Science and the Construction of Women*, Mary Maynard (ed.) London: UCL Press, 162–82.

REFERENCES AND FURTHER READING

Attebery, Brian (2002) *Decoding Gender in Science Fiction*. London & New York: Routledge.

Baccolini, Raffaella & Tom Moylan (eds) (2003) *Dark Horizons: Science Fiction and the Dystopian Imagination*. New York & London: Routledge.

Barr, Marleen (1992) *Feminist Fabulation*. Iowa City: University of Iowa Press.

——(ed.) (2000) *Future females: The Next Generation*. Oxford: Rowman & Littlefield.

Baudrillard, Jean (1991) "Simulacra and science fiction." *Science Fiction Studies*, 18, 309–13.

Boym, Svetlana (2001) *The Future of Nostalgia*. New York: Basic Books.

Bukatman, Scott (1993) *Terminal Identity: The Virtual Subject in Postmodern Science Fiction*. Durham & London: Duke University Press.

Carter, Paul A. (1977) *The Creation of Tomorrow*. New York: Columbia University Press.

Connor, Steven (1999) "The impossibility of the present: or, from the contemporary to the contemporal," in *Literature and the Contemporary*, (eds) Roger Luckhurst & Peter Marks. Harlow: Longman, 15–35.

Delany, Samuel (1977) *The Jewel Hinged Jaw*. New York: Dragon Press.

Donawerth, Jane (1990) "Lilith Lorraine: Feminist socialist writer in the pulps." *Science Fiction Studies*, 17, 252–7.

Grafton, Sue (1998) *N for Noose*. London: Pan.

Griffiths, Nicola (1995) *Slow River*. London: Voyager.

Grosz, Elizabeth (2000) "Histories of a feminist future." *Signs: Journal of Women in Culture and Society*, 25, 4, 1017–20.

Hall, Stuart (1997) "Cultural identity and diaspora," in *Identity and Difference*, (ed.) Kathryn Woodward. Milton Keynes: The Open University, 51–9. First printed in Jonathan Rutherford (ed.) (1990) *Identity: Community, Culture, Difference*. London: Lawrence and Wishart.

Hayles, Katherine (1990) *Chaos Bound: Orderly Disorder in Contemporary Literature and Science*. Ithaca, New York and London: Cornell University Press.

Hollinger, Veronica & Joan Gordon (eds) (2002) *Edging Into the Future: Science Fiction and Contemporary Cultural Transformation*. Philadelphia, PA: University of Pennsylvania Press.

Jameson, Fredric (1985) "Postmodernism and consumer society," in *Postmodern Culture* (ed.) Hal Foster. London: Pluto Press, 111–25.

Kelso, Sylvia (2000) "Tales of Earth: Terraforming in recent women's SF." *Foundation: The International Review of Science Fiction* 29, 78, 34–43.

Landon, Brooks (2002) *Science Fiction After 1900*. London & New York: Routledge.

Merrick, Helen & Tess Williams (eds) (1999) *Women of Other Worlds: Excursions through Science Fiction and Feminism*. Melbourne: University of Western Australia Press.

Ore, Rebecca (1995) *Gaia's Toys*. New York: Tor.

Pfeil, Fred (1990) *Another Tale to Tell: Politics and Narrative in Postmodern Culture*. London: Verso.

Russ, Joanna (1972) "The image of women in Science Fiction," in *Images of Women in Fiction: Feminist Perspectives*, (ed.) Susan. K. Cornillon. Ohio: Bowling Green University Press, 79–94.

Sawyer, Andy & David Seed (eds) (2000) *Speaking Science Fiction*. Liverpool: Liverpool University Press.

Virilio, Paul (1984) "The overexposed city." *ZONE* 1–2, 15–31.

11

Science Fiction and the Cold War

M. Keith Booker

In the initial episode of the landmark science fiction television series *Star Trek: The Next Generation* (set in the twenty-fourth century), a godlike super-alien, known only as Q, places the human race on trial for suspicion of being a dangerous warlike race. Interrogating Captain Picard (Patrick Stewart) and the crew of the starship *Enterprise*, who stand in, as they often do, for all of humanity, Q attempts to appeal to their baser emotions by trying to arouse old hatreds left over from the twentieth century. Transforming himself into a Cold War-era military officer, he exhorts the *Enterprise* to return immediately to earth to fight "commies." Picard, however, simply responds, "What? That nonsense is centuries behind us!"

Of course, *The Next Generation* appeared just as the Cold War was beginning to wane, though it was always an assumption of the *Star Trek* vision of a Utopian future that humanity would somehow survive and move beyond the geopolitical tensions of the Cold War era, creating a material paradise in which both capitalism and Communism had been rendered obsolete. Other works of Western science fiction produced during the Cold War era were less confident, however, and the looming threat of nuclear holocaust or other dire consequences of the Cold War was a dominant factor in the science fiction imagination from the end of the 1940s to the beginning of the 1990s. For example, many dystopian visions of the future were strongly informed by Cold War pessimism. In addition, the Cold War was largely responsible for the prominence of alien invasion and postapocalypse narratives, especially during the peak Cold War years of 1946–64.

The case was somewhat different in the Soviet Union, where Cold War hysteria never reached the heights that it did in the West, especially in the USA, and where an impressive output of science fiction novels in the late 1950s focused less on alien threat than on the Utopian potential of science and technology, especially when combined with socialism. The key text in this regard is Ivan Yefremov's *Andromeda* (1958), which envisions a far future in which breakthrough advances in science and technology have helped to enable a socialist Utopia on earth and a new era of interplanetary communication and understanding. The highly influential *Andromeda* triggered a resurgence in Soviet science fiction as a whole. Later Soviet science fiction was more ambivalent, as exemplified by the complex works of the Strugatsky brothers (Arkady and Boris), who began their SF careers in a mode of Utopian socialism in the wake of *Andromeda*, but soon turned to satires, such as *Snail on the Slope* (1968) and *Roadside Picnic* (1972) which questioned the ability of science to transform, or even understand, the world. Their ambivalence about the glorious future envisioned by writers such as Yefremov was perhaps best summed up in the title of *Definitely Maybe* (1976–7), a satire on science. The satires of the Strugatskys were largely aimed at the capitalist West, but by implication their dystopian turn suggested limitations in Soviet technological utopianism as well.

Western science fiction during the Cold War tended to have a dystopian inclination all along. George Orwell's *Nineteen Eighty-Four*, published in 1949, set the stage for all future dystopian fiction and went on to become one of the most important cultural texts (science fiction or otherwise) of the Cold War. Indeed, though only vaguely science fictional in itself, Orwell's novel would become a powerful influence on the science fiction imagination, exercising a gravitational pull that would help warp imaginative visions of the future toward the dystopian pole for more than half a century. Among other things, *Nineteen Eighty-Four* depicts a geopolitical future in which three great superpowers dominate the world, each ruled by an oppressive regime that furthers its own power by engaging in a constant state of rotating nuclear (but highly limited) warfare with the others. This suggestion that the Cold War was itself politically expedient for both sides was largely lost on Western commentators, who rushed to see the novel simply as a biting satirical critique of Stalinism, even though Oceania, the dystopian state on which the book focuses, is centered in England and even though Orwell himself claimed that the satire of the book was also aimed at postwar Britain and the West.

Later writers of dystopian science fiction – a genre in which British writers such as Anthony Burgess and John Brunner excelled – continued very much in the Orwellian vein, imagining grim futures in which the Cold War continues to function as a background to or even cause of dystopian oppression. Thus, while Burgess' *The Wanting Seed* (1962) is primarily a cautionary tale about the dangers of overpopulation, it also envisions an exacerbating future global political situation in which most of the world is under the domination of one of the two great superpowers, the "Enspun," or English-speaking union, and the "Ruspun," or Russian-speaking union. Similarly, the Cold War provides important background to Brunner's *The Sheep Look Up* (1972), a novel of ecological dystopia in which repression and environmental irresponsibility in the USA are only made worse by the perceived threat of a socialist "tidal wave" sweeping the globe.

Writers of postapocalypse narratives provided even darker visions of the future consequences of Cold War tensions, especially as the apocalypses involved were typically nuclear. However, one of the first truly influential of such narratives was George R. Stewart's *Earth Abides* (1949), which deals not with the impact of nuclear war but with a mysterious plague (perhaps caused by a mutant virus), which sweeps across America (and, presumably, the world) killing virtually everyone within a matter of days. However, in a mode often reminiscent of *Robinson Crusoe*, the survivors of this plague gradually begin to rebuild American civilization. Indeed, there are signs that this new civilization, drawing upon elements of Native American culture, may be kinder and gentle – and more in tune with nature – than the one that preceded it.

In this sense, Stewart's novel tends toward the romanticization of apocalypse as an opportunity for renewal than runs through much of the postapocalyptic fiction of the early Cold War era. However, whereas Stewart's book is highly critical of many aspects of American capitalism, this trend would lead ultimately to Pat Frank's bestselling *Alas, Babylon* (1959), which largely sees nuclear holocaust as an opportunity to wipe out Communism once and for all, making the world safe for right-thinking (and right-wing) Americans. *Alas, Babylon* deals overtly with war between the USA and the Soviet Union, though it provides relatively few details of the war itself, concentrating instead on the struggles of the inhabitants of a small Florida community, Fort Repose, to survive in the wake of the cataclysmic conflict. Nevertheless, Frank's book (like much of his work) is extremely representative of a certain style of conservative thought in the 1950s in that it treats nuclear war (triggered by Soviet aggression, of course) as inevitable, while warning that the USA is sorely prepared for such a war. In this sense, Frank's book can be read as a cautionary tale, urging greater vigilance and greater preparedness.

Given Frank's conviction of the inability of the federal government to deal adequately with the kind of crisis that would arise in the wake of nuclear conflict, it is not surprising that, in *Alas, Babylon*, virtually all official systems fail, leaving the resourceful inhabitants of Fort Repose to fend for themselves. Nor is it surprising that Frank sprinkles this story of the destruction of the USA as a world power with references to the fall of Rome, making the typical right-wing point that Americans, in the midst of the affluent 1950s, had grown complacent and decadent, enjoying their wealth and privilege, but failing to live up to their responsibility to defend this way of life against the evil Soviets, who, for some reason unstated by Frank, are determined to start a mutually destructive nuclear war.

What is surprising, given Frank's apparent devotion to preventing exactly the kind of disaster he describes in the novel, is that he seems almost to revel in the destruction of the modern American system, depicting postholocaust Fort Repose as a kind of laissez faire Utopia, where strong individuals can work out the solutions to their problems without the interference of government regulations and bean-counting bureaucrats. There is also a sense that the destruction of the country returns the "good old days" of the American frontier, when men were men and women were women, and the bureaucracy of the modern welfare state did not interfere with the ability of strong individuals to carry out their plans and fulfill their desires. In particular, the breakdown of conventional authority in Fort Repose leads not to anarchy but to a military dictatorship, a situation that most of the locals (and Frank himself) seem to welcome warmly.

One implication of Frank's book is that military preparedness could protect America from nuclear destruction. Other works of the 1950s were not so sure. For example, the elaborate preparations made in Mordecai Roshwald's *Level 7* (1959) actually cause, rather than prevent, nuclear war. The nuclear war in *Level 7* begins by accident, then quickly gets out of control as high-tech automated response systems kick in. Ultimately, virtually the entire surface of the planet is devastated by nuclear blasts and contaminated by radiation. Survivors in America are driven into a huge multi-level underground shelter, where they live in strictly regimented dystopian conditions, only to find that the radiation gradually seeps downward through one level after another, gradually killing off the inhabitants.

Level 7 thus warns Americans not to develop a false sense of security that thorough preparations can save them from the effects of nuclear war. However, its most potent political commentary may come from the fact that conditions in the seemingly extreme environment of the underground shelter are suspiciously similar to conditions in the America of the 1950s. In addition to the intense regimentation that informs life in the shelter, the inhabitants of the facility are all radically alienated. They have, in fact, been specifically chosen for their inability to form and maintain close human attachments. The implication seems clear: the pressures of the arms race threaten to transform American society into a grim, dystopian state, whose primary focus is destruction of the enemy rather than enrichment of the lives of its citizens, who are thereby reduced to living in a machine-dominated hell.

Other notable postapocalyptic novels of the 1950s also included considerable social commentary, including Richard Matheson's *I Am Legend* (1954) and Judith Merril's *Shadow on the Hearth* (1950). Matheson's book is particularly critical of the conformist tendencies of the 1950s, while both *I Am Legend* and *Shadow on the Hearth* serve as useful correctives to the heroic vision of postapocalypse life presented by Stewart and Frank. Merril's book builds directly upon the tensions of the Cold War, presenting an apocalypse that arises precisely from a surprise nuclear attack on the USA, though it does not specifically identify the attackers as Soviets. But her book is unusual among postapocalypse works of the 1950s in its focus on a female protagonist, housewife Gladys Mitchell. The book also concentrates almost entirely on Gladys' domestic sphere, focusing on her attempts to cope with the aftermath of the nuclear assault, not by exploring the surrounding area or attempting to rebuild society, but simply by keeping her household running and taking care of her two daughters, Barbara and Ginny.

Shadow on the Hearth is often fairly subtle in its indication of its political position, even though Merril stated in a later interview that she intended the work as anti-arms-race "propaganda" (cited in Seed 1999: 57). Bernard Wolfe's *Limbo* (1952) is more ambiguous about its politics, but is anything but subtle. Written in a mode of Swiftian satirical exaggeration, *Limbo* describes a postnuclear holocaust world in which the remnants of both the USA and the Soviet Union are dominated by a culture of "Immob," or immobilization. Central to this culture is "vol-amp," or voluntary amputeeism, a sort of literalization of the notion of disarmament. It is widely believed in this culture that amputation of the limbs reduces natural human aggression, thus helping to keep the peace and prevent further nuclear wars. As I have discussed elsewhere, *Limbo* is a complex literary work that participates in many literary phenomena, including Menippean satire and postmodernism (Booker 2001: 72–80). It was described in *The Encyclopedia of Science Fiction* as "perhaps the finest sf novel of ideas to have been published during the 1950s" (Clute and Nicholls 1995: 1337).

If *Limbo* and *Level 7* both seem bitterly critical of American society in the 1950s, then the same also goes for *Fahrenheit 451* (1951), the first novel of the much-beloved Ray Bradbury. Extremely critical of both conformism and mass culture (and of the way the latter leads to the former), *Fahrenheit 451* depicts a future dystopian society so oppressive that Bradbury depicts the destruction of this society in a nuclear war as a cleansing renewal. On the other hand, the book ends with the ominous suggestion that there is a very good chance that this new start for human civilization will ultimately lead down the same baleful path as the old one.

Walter M. Miller's *A Canticle for Leibowitz* (1959) is even more convinced of the cyclic nature of human folly. Miller's book traces the course of human civilization from the year 2570 (six hundred years after a nuclear holocaust has plunged humanity into a second Dark Ages), to the year 3174 (when a second Renaissance announces a rebirth of science and culture), to the year 3781 (when civilization has recovered its former heights, only again to destroy itself via nuclear war). The book, though informed by considerable ironic humor, suggests an extremely dark and pessimistic vision of human civilization, arguing that humans need to use science and technology in order to fulfill their potential, but that they will inevitably misuse these tools, leading to their own destruction.

In contrast to such warnings, the postapocalypse films that appeared in the 1950s often seemed designed to calm the nuclear fears of the decade, displacing their vision of nuclear holocaust into the far future and often providing happy endings to assure audiences that everything would be fine, nuclear holocaust or no. The postapocalypse films of the decade generally present far less troubling images than do the novels, both in their representation of nuclear devastation and in their commentary on contemporary American society. Still, these films do attempt to make certain political points, ranging from the vaguely left-wing antiracist perspective of Arch Oboler's early effort, *Five* (1951), to the almost deranged anti-Communism of William Asher's *The 27th Day* (1957).

Roger Corman, never one to shy away from potentially shocking subject matter, still tacked a comforting ending onto his entry into the postapocalypse genre, *The Day the World Ended* (1955), his first science fiction film. Like most of the films directed (or produced) by Corman, *The Day the World Ended* seems a bit silly at times, but turns out to have its interesting moments. Like most postnuclear holocaust films of the period, it concentrates on the survivors of a nuclear war rather than on the destruction of the war itself. Indeed, all of the film's action occurs in a sheltered valley that just happens to be protected by lead-filled hills on all sides. A total of seven survivors of the war gather in the valley at the home of a rancher who has laid in supplies for just such an eventuality.

Unfortunately, Maddison had not planned on feeding this many people, so supplies are short and it is not at all clear that they will be sufficient to see the survivors through until radiation levels die down in the outside world. In addition, one of the group is suffering from severe radiation poisoning and is gradually transforming into a monstrous mutant who, among other things, feeds on human flesh. To make matters worse, there is also a full-blown mutant roaming the valley and menacing the survivors. Eventually, only two members of the group are left alive, but they are a young man and woman, clearly presented as a new Adam and Eve, while the cleansing rains that come near the end of the film signal that there is still hope for environmental recovery.

Stanley Kramer's *On the Beach* (1959) offers no such hope. Here, a global nuclear war has apparently destroyed all human life everywhere on earth, except Australia, which has been spared because of its remote location. Unfortunately, the clouds of deadly radiation that cover the rest of the globe are headed for Australia as well, so the Australians themselves have only a few months before what seems to be inevitable death. The film then focuses on the human drama of various characters trying to put their lives in order in face of their rapidly approaching deaths. The film is entirely sanitized. There are no corpses, no radiation burns, not even property damage. While we do see shots of postholocaust San Francisco and San Diego, the cities are entirely undamaged. The only change is that all the people seem to have disappeared. As such, the film's antiarms race message is a bit muted, though still clear.

The 1950s also saw the rise of a special subgenre of nuclear fear films, in which monsters created (or at least aroused) by the effects of radiation threaten mankind. A classic case is *Them!* (1954), in which the Manhattan Project testing of nuclear bombs in the New Mexico desert results in a nest of gigantic, man-eating ants that seem to threaten the entire nation until they are dispatched by an alliance of scientists, police, and the military. The success of *Them!* meanwhile encouraged other films to use the same big-bugs-created-by-radiation strategy. In Bert I. Gordon's *Beginning of the End* (1957), for example, ordinary locusts eat some huge vegetables created by radiation experiments. The locusts in turn grow huge and soon take over Chicago, which the authorities decide to nuke to get rid of them. Fortunately, this radical action proves unnecessary when entomologist Dr. Ed Wainwright (Peter Graves) manages to synthesize the sounds that the locusts use as signals, luring them into Lake Michigan, where they drown. Meanwhile, in *The Beast from 20,000 Fathoms* (1953) a giant, germ-infested rhedosaurus has been frozen in the Arctic ice cap for 100 million years, only to be thawed and released when a nearby hydrogen bomb test melts the ice in which it is trapped. A similar dynamic operates in *It Came from Beneath the Sea* (1955), in which nuclear tests disturb a gigantic octopus, driving it out of its normal habitat and to the Pacific coast of the USA in search of food. The creature is killed by an alliance of scientists and the military, who develop a special atomic torpedo, which explodes in the monster's brain, killing it, but only after it has destroyed the Golden

Gate Bridge and ravaged much of San Francisco. Finally, there were films in which radiation made monsters of humans. In Gordon's *The Amazing Colossal Man* (1957), for example, radiation from a "plutonium bomb" causes Army Colonel (and Korean War hero) Glenn Manning (Glenn Langan) to experience runaway growth, eventually reaching a height of sixty feet.

Apart from the postapocalypse genre, many classic science fiction novels of the 1950s were derived, directly or indirectly, from issues related to the Cold War. Perhaps the classic case of this phenomenon involves the novels of the notoriously right-wing Robert A. Heinlein, which at times seem to be designed quite specifically as anti-Soviet propaganda. For example, though ostensibly set in 2007 (after a third world war has failed to settle the differences between the USA and the Soviet Union), *The Puppet Masters* (1951) is one of the quintessential alien-invaders-as-allegory-for-Communism texts of the 1950s. Here, parasitical alien slugs (from Titan, a moon of Saturn) land in Iowa and begin attaching themselves to human hosts, whom they then use as puppets in their program of global conquest. Most of the plot of the book involves the efforts of narrator-protagonist Sam Cavanaugh and other members of a top secret US intelligence force to thwart the alien conquest. Much of the book reads like pure McCarthyite fantasy, especially when the slugs work to infiltrate the highest levels of the US government and military as part of their takeover plan. But propaganda only works if its recipients get the message, so Heinlein is careful to ensure that this connection will indeed be made, even by the most literal-minded of readers. Not only does Heinlein label the area controlled by the parasites as "Zone Red," but the slogan of the slugs is the Communistic "we are the people," and Heinlein repeatedly emphasizes the collective nature of the slug society, which has no concept of individual identity, and in which "each slug is really every other slug" (Heinlein 1990: 239).

Even more directly, Sam, as Heinlein's narrator, notes that "the parasites might feel right at home behind the Curtain" (Heinlein 1990:148). Further, he reports that the "Cominform propaganda system" immediately goes into action when the American media start to report on the invasion, characterizing the reports as "'American Imperialist fantasy' intended to 'enslave the workers.'" Then, Sam wonders why the parasites did not attack the Soviets first, given that "Stalinism seemed tailor-made for them. On second thought, I wondered if they had. On third thought I wondered what difference it would make; the people behind the Curtain had had their minds enslaved and parasites riding them for three generations. There might not be two kopeks difference between a commissar with a slug and a commissar without a slug" (Heinlein 1990: 205). Heinlein also gets in a few shots at fellow travelers, noting that the only thing more disgusting than a human mind in the grip of the slugs are the few humans who work in complicity with the slugs, even without having a parasite directly attached (Heinlein 1990: 251).

The valiant (and resourceful) Americans manage to defeat the slugs through the use of germ warfare, a controversial weapon in the 1950s, and one the use of which Heinlein here wholeheartedly endorses. By the end of the book, the Americans prepare to launch an all-out genocidal assault on Titan itself so they can wipe out the slugs once and for all. Sam and Mary go along on the mission, Sam gleefully ending his narrative with the announcement, "Puppet masters – the free men are coming to kill you! *Death and Destruction!*" (Heinlein 1990: 340, Heinlein's italics). Heinlein's enthusiasm for the death and destruction of all enemies of the American way comes through even more clearly in the Hugo Award-winning *Starship Troopers* (1959). Described by Bruce Franklin as "a bugle-blowing, drum-beating glorification of the hero's life in military service," *Starship Troopers* includes a number of battle scenes, but it actually has very little in the way of plot, being primarily a celebration of militarism and a concerted attempt to indoctrinate readers into accepting this celebration (Franklin 1980: 111).

Clearly a response to Heinlein's belief that the USA was going soft in the late 1950s, *Starship Troopers* is essentially a call to arms, a reminder that some enemies can be defeated only by force. Indeed, the book presents a pseudo-Darwinian vision of life as a struggle for survival of the strongest, thereby urging Americans to seek greater military strength so that they can survive. The book presents a future world in which a period of high crime (especially among juvenile delinquents) has preceded a final near-apocalyptic confrontation among different world powers, leading to a collapse of existing social systems, but also to the establishment of the Federation, a new world government ruled by a military elite. Indeed, under this new system, only veterans of the military enjoy full citizenship, including the right to vote. Yet, horrifying as this system might sound, Heinlein presents it as a Utopia. The military rulers of this global system are described as the best and wisest rulers in human history, leading to unprecedented freedom and prosperity for all, including the vast majority, who have never served in the military.

The main military conflict in *Starship Troopers* involves a war between the Federation and a race of alien "Bugs," whose Communal ideology is virtually identical to Western Cold War visions of Communism and the Soviet Union, though their alienness considerably simplifies the Us vs. Them terms of the Cold War. Meanwhile, the book also includes direct (but misleading and misinformed) critiques of Marxism, as when one character claims that Marx's labor theory of value implies that human labor can transform anything into anything else, like some sort of alchemy. He further interprets Marx as believing that any human action always increases the value of whatever is being acted upon. Given this kind of radical misinterpretation, perhaps it is little wonder that Marx is described in the book as a "disheveled old mystic . . . neurotic, unscientific, illogical, this pompous fraud" (Heinlein 1987: 92).

Noting this use of the Bugs as stand-ins for Communists, David Seed suggests that "political difference is thereby naturalized into the threatening alien" (Seed 1999: 37). Heinlein, through his protagonist Rico, makes the connection to Communism explicit. Describing the willingness of the Bugs to expend huge numbers of troops, Rico concludes, "We were learning, expensively, just how efficient a total Communism can be when used by a people adapted to it by evolution; the Bug commissars didn't care any more about expending soldiers than we care about expending ammo" (Heinlein 1987: 152–3).

Later science fiction novelists would challenge the extremity of Heinlein's vision in *Starship Troopers*, and at least two popular science fiction novels, Harry Harrison's *Bill, the Galactic Hero* (1965) and Joe Haldeman's *The Forever War* (1974, winner of the Hugo and Nebula Awards), were written partly as parodies of Heinlein's book, though both can also be taken as critiques of the American involvement in Vietnam and of militarism in general. Still, Heinlein's virulent anti-Communism seemed less extreme in the 1950s than it would later. Similarly, the anti-Communist paranoia that informs so many science fiction films of the 1950s must also surely have seemed more serious as a theme at the time than it does now. One might consider here a film such as Lee Sholem's *Tobor the Great* (1954), which featured evil Communist agents trying to steal our technology (à la the Rosenbergs). Other films, including such truly crazed productions as *Invasion U.S.A.* (1952) and *Red Planet Mars* (1952), overtly thematized the 1950s paranoid fear (and hatred) of Communism.

In addition, alien invasion films such as *Invasion of the Body Snatchers* (1956) have routinely been viewed as allegorizations of the perceived threat of Communist invasion during the 1950s. In this classic the-aliens-are-already-among-us statement (based on Jack Finney's 1954 novel of the same title but also reminiscent in many ways of Heinlein's *The Puppet Masters*), Dr. Miles Bennell (Kevin McCarthy) returns home to the small California town of Santa Mira after a trip to a medical convention, only to find that the citizens of the town are being replaced by replicant pod people from outer space. He finally manages to escape to a neighboring town, where he is initially thought insane and hospitalized, until supporting evidence finally convinces the authorities to mobilize against the alien invasion.

But *Invasion of the Body Snatchers* is ultimately more troubling than reassuring. The replicants, who look the same as everyone else but feel no emotion and have no individuality, directly echo the era's most prevalent stereotypes about Communists. Thus, the repeated assurances given Miles by the replacements that his life will be far more pleasant if he simply goes along with the crowd and learns to live without emotion can be taken as echoes of the supposed seductions offered by Communist Utopianism. On the other hand, Biskind concludes that the film is ultimately a right-wing assault on the political center that largely uses its apparent attacks on Communism as cover to avoid being labeled as extremist (Biskind 1983: 144).

Other notable alien invasion films of the period include *The Thing from Another World* (1951), *Invaders from Mars* (1953), Byron Haskin's *The War of the Worlds* (1953), and *I Married a Monster from Outer Space* (1958), which Cyndy Hendershot describes as a "feminine analogue" of *Invasion of the Body Snatchers* (Hendershot 1999: 56). All of these films could be interpreted as dramatizations of the dangers faced by Cold War America in a world populated with sinister foreign enemies. Other films, rather than urging increased vigilance, urged increased understanding. Robert Wise's superb *The Day the Earth Stood Still* (1951) is the classic case of such films. Rather daring for its time, this film insists that we had better learn to get along with the Soviets, along the way making reference to a number of contemporary figures and issues, the most obvious of which is its inclusion of an admirable scientist figure, Professor Barnhardt (Sam Jaffe), who is quite transparently based on Albert Einstein, at that time a rather controversial figure through his pleas for détente. Ultimately, the wise alien of the piece, Klaatu (Michael Rennie), issues a simple warning: the Earth will be destroyed if it seeks to extend its violent ways beyond Earth. Translation: the Americans and the Soviets had better learn to get along or their animosity will eventually destroy the planet.

If films such as *The Day the Earth Stood Still* warned against anti-Communist fanaticism, there were also numerous science fiction novels in the 1950s that counseled against Cold War hysteria. One of the most important of such novels is Frederik Pohl and Cyril Kornbluth's *The Space Merchants* (1952), a satirical critique of many elements of Western Cold War culture. *The Space Merchants* presents a vivid picture of a future world dominated by huge multinational corporations, the most powerful and influential of which are media and advertising firms. In this sense, the book strikingly anticipates the direction of the next fifty years of world history, presenting a future world system much along the lines of that analyzed by Fredric Jameson and other contemporary Marxist theorists as "late capitalism" (Jameson 1991). The protagonist of the novel, ad executive Mitch Courtenay, works for the huge Fowler Schocken advertising conglomerate, which has used bribery and other political manipulations to gain exclusive rights to the colonization of the planet Venus. Courtenay's job is not only to oversee the development of the technologies that will make this colonization possible, but also to develop an advertising campaign that will make colonists want to go to Venus, where the whole planet can then be turned into a new source of profit for Fowler Schocken.

In the course of his efforts, the former organization man Courtenay learns a great deal about the corruption of the consumer capitalist society that surrounds him and about the exploitation of the working class (largely relegated to the Third World, but collectively referred to in this consumer capitalist society as "consumers") on which this society is built. He is also contacted by a secret organization of "Conservationists," or "Consies," who are working worldwide to try to prevent environmental destruction of the earth by industrial capitalism. In the end, the Consies manage to load the only Venus rocket with their people and to blast off with the hope of building on Venus a new world free of the greed and corruption that capitalism has spread across the Earth.

The Space Merchants effectively satirizes both the overall direction of consumer capitalism as a system and on the specific political climate of the USA in the early 1950s. The Consies (although somewhat reminiscent of the modern Greenpeace organization) are rather transparent stand-ins for Communists, and their role in the book serves as part of an effective satire of the anti-Communist oppression of the McCarthy era in which the book was written. Even more striking, however, are the depictions of the negative consequences of the growing power of consumer capitalism and the increasing dominance of media and advertising in enforcing uniformity in the thoughts and desires of people around the world. These depictions are effective in the best tradition of literary satire – seemingly exaggerated in sometimes comical ways, they turn out on reflection to be much closer to reality than one might first have imagined. Thus, Fowler Schocken's marketing tactics seem extreme until one compares them with tactics already in use in the 1950s. One of their favorite techniques is to employ subtle forms of subliminal suggestion so that consumers will associate their products with sexual attractiveness and success and the products of their rivals with sexual frustration or deviance. Meanwhile, one of their most lucrative accounts involves the marketing of a drink called "Coffiest," which is laced with an addictive chemical to ensure that consumers will be hooked for life.

Ben Barzman's *Twinkle, Twinkle Little Star* (1960, published in the UK as *Out of This World*), is even more overt in its critique of the Western Cold War mentality. Described by Alan Wald as a "Marxist science fiction classic" (Wald 1994: 72), *Twinkle, Twinkle Little Star* is a whimsical and entertaining piece (somewhat reminiscent of the earlier novels of Kurt Vonnegut) which nevertheless addresses some important political issues. The main narrative revolves around a scientific research project that results in the establishment of a transport beam between Earth and another planet that is its double. These two Earths are physically identical, though certain historical developments have led to social differences. In particular, the second Earth was able to avert the rise of fascism and therefore did not experience the Second World War. As a result, this alternative world has developed a far more advanced civilization than our own, free of economic injustice and of the competition and social hostilities to which that inequality inevitably leads. Contact having been established, the other Earth considers sharing its advanced technology with ours, only to conclude that, given the climate of the Cold War, our planet is obviously too primitive and warlike to use that technology properly.

Though this conclusion may be somewhat predictable, the narrative is in general an engaging one that keeps the reader's interest while making a number of subtle political points about racism, economic injustice, McCarthyism, and the Cold War. The book is thus a good example of the attempt of many leftist writers in the post-Second World War period to reach a larger audience by writing in popular genres. It also demonstrates the way in which such writers sought to convey their political messages with a light touch given the climate of anti-Communist hysteria in which they were forced to work.

Of course, the quintessential Cold War writer of serious messages with a light, or at least whimsical, touch was probably Philip K. Dick, who wrote a whole series of Cold War fictions, including such postapocalypse narratives as *The World Jones Made* (1956), *The Man Who Japed* (1956), *Vulcan's Hammer* (1960), *The Penultimate Truth* (1964), and *Dr. Bloodmoney* (1965). Of these, only the last makes any serious attempt realistically to depict conditions that might prevail after a nuclear war. Most of them are, instead, satirical fictions that use their postapocalypse settings merely to provide a fresh perspective from which to critique the already dystopian character of contemporary American capitalist society. In fact, even *Dr. Bloodmoney* is intended largely as a defamiliarizing commentary on America at the end of the long 1950s, as Dick suggests in his 1980 afterword to the book.

Dr. Bloodmoney is unique among Dick's postapocalypse novels, especially in that it includes important Utopian elements. In point of fact, *Dr. Bloodmoney* is a complex combination of Utopian and dystopian elements. For example, the nuclear war of the book wipes out many of the negative characteristics of modern corporate capitalism, but the conditions that prevail after the war are hardly ideal. In fact, despite its satirical and fantastic elements, the book provides some of the most realistic (and horrifying) visions of all of the postapocalypse fictions of the long 1950s. Nevertheless, *Dr. Bloodmoney* does suggest that the postholocaust societies that arise over the seven years following the bombing have many Utopian aspects. This is especially true in the West Marin County (California) Community, where the citizens gather in public meetings to make genuinely democratic decisions in the interest of the public good, in a mode somewhat reminiscent of Kim Stanley Robinson's later attempt to envision a future Utopian California Community in *Pacific Edge* (1988), a novel that combines with a postapocalyptic vision in *The Wild Shore* (1984) and a dystopian vision in *The Gold Coast* (1988) to form Robinson's unique "California Trilogy," which in a sense tops off the tradition of Cold War narratives in American science fiction.

One could, however, already see the beginning of the end of that tradition in the 1960s, when the original *Star Trek* series (1966–9) broadcast its compelling vision of a hopeful future, while the British television produced a lasting hit with *The Avengers* (1961–9), an espionage thriller (with strong science fiction elements) that turned Cold War fear into cool 1960s camp. Meanwhile, Dick, in *The Zap Gun* (1967) lampooned the whole notion of the arms race by depicting a Cold War situation in which the East and West maintain a precarious balance of power by competing to develop increasingly intricate weapons that work only in simulations. This situation triggers a major crisis when aliens invade the Earth, which is left to defend itself without any functioning advanced weaponry. Works such as Pohl's *The Cool War* (1979), in which Cold War tensions have degenerated into international dirty tricks campaigns run by operatives essentially free of government control, similarly satirized the earlier apocalyptic rhetoric of Cold War fiction.

Of course, Dick, with *Dr. Bloodmoney*, had already begun to give the postapocalypse narrative comic undertones, and the full title of that book, *Dr. Bloodmoney, or How We Got Along after the Bomb*, points directly to Stanley Kubrick's similarly titled 1964 film, *Dr. Strangelove, or, How I learned to Stop Worrying and Love the Bomb*. The parallel titles call attention to the fact that Dick's novel shares with Kubrick's film a postmodernist sense of the absurdity of the Cold War arms race. Kubrick's film, which satirizes the craziness of the "mutually assured destruction" mentality of the Cold War, is one of the most memorable in film history. Strangelove, himself, a crazed ex-Nazi, is only one of numerous American functionaries whose fanaticism ultimately leads to an unprovoked nuclear bombing of the Soviet Union, which will trigger the release of a Soviet Doomsday Machine, enveloping the planet in a cloud of radioactive dust and destroying all life.

Dr. Strangelove joined (though in a very different, satirical vein) other such cautionary films as John Frankenheimer's *Seven Days in May* (1964, written by *Twilight Zone* maven Rod Serling) and Sidney Lumet's tense thriller, *Fail-Safe* (1964) as reminders of the dangers inherent in the Cold War arms race. But Kubrick's film so effectively portrayed the craziness of Cold War hysteria that it virtually eliminated the postapocalypse science fiction film from Western popular culture for some time. Postapocalypse films and narratives did continue to appear, however, and the film *A Boy and His Dog* (1975, based on a story by Harlan Ellison) became something of a cult hit. The genre made a brief comeback in the 1980s, ushered in by Russell Hoban's linguistically innovative *Riddley Walker* (1980) and including such novels as David Brin's *The Postman* (1985). This decade was marked by the appearance of graphic on-screen depictions of the effects of nuclear war in a series of postapocalypse films that included *The Day After* (1983), *Testament* (1983), and *Threads* (1985), the latter a British entry. The 1980s also saw the continuation of the cycle of films that began with *Mad Max* (1979) and extended through *The Road Warrior* (1981), and *Mad Max Beyond Thunder Dome* (1985), though these films focused more on action and adventure in a postapocalypse world than any commentary on the conditions leading up to the apocalypse itself. Slightly more details about the cause of the apocalypse (runaway computer technology) were provided in the most successful of all postapocalypse cycles, though James Cameron's *Terminator* sequence, which began in 1984, takes place (thanks to a time travel motif) mostly before the apocalypse, which the major characters scramble to prevent. In Cameron's *The Abyss* (1989), however, benevolent aliens once again step in to end the arms race on Earth, preventing apocalypse and providing a bookend that closed the Cold War era in film much as *The Day the Earth Stood Still* had opened it.

REFERENCES AND FURTHER READING

Biskind, Peter (1983) *Seeing Is Believing: How Hollywood Taught Us to Stop Worrying and Love the Fifties*. New York: Pantheon.

Booker, M. Keith (2001) *Monsters, Mushroom Clouds, and the Cold War*. Westport, CT: Greenwood Press.

Clute, John, and Peter Nicholls (eds) (1995) *The Encyclopedia of Science Fiction*, 2nd edn. New York: St. Martin's.

Evans, Joyce A. (1998) *Celluloid Mushroom Clouds: Hollywood and the Atomic Bomb*. Boulder, CO: Westview Press.

Franklin, H. Bruce (1980) *Robert A. Heinlein: America as Science Fiction*. New York: Oxford University Press.

Freedman, Carl (2000) *Critical Theory and Science Fiction*. Hanover, NH: Wesleyan University Press.

Heinlein, Robert A. (1987) *Starship Troopers* (1959). New York: Ace-Berkley.

——(1990) *The Puppet Masters*. New York: Del Rey-Ballantine.

Hendershot, Cyndy (1999) *Paranoia, the Bomb, and 1950s Science Fiction Films*. Bowling Green, OH: Bowling Green University Popular Press.

Henriksen, Margot A. (1997) *Dr. Strangelove's America: Society and Culture in the Atomic Age*. Berkeley: University of California Press.

Jameson, Fredric (1991) *Postmodernism; or, The*

Cultural Logic of Late Capitalism. Durham NC: Duke University Press; London: Verso.

Robinson, Kim Stanley (1984) *The Novels of Philip K. Dick*. Ann Arbor, MI: UMI Research Press.

Seed, David (1999) *American Science Fiction and the Cold War: Literature and Film*. Edinburgh: Edinburgh University Press; Chicago: Fitzroy Dearborn.

Sobchack, Vivian (1997) *Screening Space: The American Science Fiction Film*, 2nd edn. New Brunswick, NJ: Rutgers University Press.

Sontag, Susan (1966) "The Imagination of Disaster." *Against Interpretation and Other Essays* New York: Farrar, Straus and Giroux, 209–25.

Wald, Alan M. (1994) *Writing from the Left: New Essays on Radical Culture and Politics*. London: Verso.

PART III
Genres and Movements

12
Hard Science Fiction
Gary Westfahl

In its very name, science fiction announces a special concern for, and a special connection to, science. Repeated campaigns to eliminate or de-emphasize that concern and that connection by renaming the genre "speculative fiction" have met with ignominious failure; and a broad range of commentators have agreed that, at the very least, science fiction must display a basic respect for the principles and laws of science. Works that utterly fail to meet this standard – by depicting, say, a breathable atmosphere on the Moon or rapid spaceflight to other stars without reference to the limitation of the speed of light – are universally castigated and delegitimized as science fiction.

Approaching the task of defining "hard science fiction," one might begin by calling it a form of science fiction that displays an especially heightened concern for, and an especially heightened connection to, science. Precisely how one might characterize works in that category, predictably, is a matter of ongoing debate. Undoubtedly, certain features in a text would seemingly qualify it as hard science fiction: thorough explanations of scientific facts and/or lengthy expository passages providing evidence of a scientific thought process at work. This is the essence of Allen Steele's commonsensical definition of hard science fiction: "the form of imaginative literature that uses either established or carefully extrapolated science as its backbone" (Steele 1992: 4).

In addition, some would identify a certain sort of narrative voice – detached, objective, cold, clinical – as a defining characteristic. These are the grounds on which David G. Hartwell idiosyncratically classifies J.G. Ballard as a hard science fiction writer, arguing that "hard SF is, then, about the emotional experience of describing and confronting what is scientifically true" (Hartwell 1994: 31).

Finally, my own efforts to define hard science fiction primarily appeal to extratextual evidence: texts can be considered hard science fiction if their authors energetically promote themselves as hard science fiction writers, if they are published in venues known to favor hard science fiction, such as the magazine *Analog: Science Fiction/Science Fact* or publisher Baen Books, and/or if they become the basis for discussions between authors and readers regarding the soundness of their scientific ideas and reasoning (Westfahl 1996).

Just as there are disagreements about the best way to define hard science fiction, there are disparate views regarding the subgenre's value and significance. Aficionados often describe hard science fiction essentially as a stimulating but frivolous "game," as writers enjoy the process of developing imaginary but scientifically valid concepts and readers enjoy the process of analyzing and critiquing the fruits of their labors. Looking especially at hard science fiction stories set in the near future, one might also defend the subgenre, in the manner of Hugo Gernsback, as a productive database of ideas for possible future inventions – the premise of the European Space Agency's recent Innovative Technologies from Science Fiction Project, which hired scholars to examine hard science fiction stories searching for possible initiatives that the ESA might undertake in the future. From such prosaic and utilitarian perspectives, hard science fiction stories might be viewed more as intellectual exercises than as literary works, equivalent to the narrativized mathematical puzzles by Martin Gardner that once appeared regularly in *The Magazine of Fantasy and Science Fiction.*

At the other extreme, some see the scientific foundation of hard science fiction as an effective way to develop and project a uniquely inhuman perspective on the universe and humanity's place in that universe. This virtue in some science fiction stories was recognized by C.S. Lewis:

> It is sobering and cathartic to remember, now and then, our collective smallness, our apparent isolation, the apparent indifference of nature, the slow biological, geological, and astronomical processes which may, in the long run, make many of our hopes (possibly some of our fears) ridiculous. (Lewis 1966: 66)

As John W. Campbell, Jr. explained in a 1956 article, science fiction can provide not only the opinions of people, but "the opinion of the universe" (Campbell 1956). The story Campbell employed to make his point, Tom Godwin's "The Cold Equations" (1954), has since that time been frequently advanced as the archetypal hard science fiction story, as the human desire of its spaceship pilot to rescue his female stowaway is overridden by the unbending laws of science which require her death. Such principles suggest that hard science fiction, far from being primarily extraliterary or extraneous to the genre, in fact represents the purest, most central form of science fiction, the attitude conveyed by the alternate term sometimes used to described the subgenre, "hardcore science fiction."

Definitions and defenses of hard science fiction are sometimes marred by two tendencies which should be politely but firmly resisted. First, hard science fiction is best approached as a relatively small and distinct subgenre, not as one of two large categories encompassing the entirety of science fiction. Some commentators assume that the existence of "hard science fiction" necessarily requires the existence of an opposing form, "soft science fiction," and that all science fiction can accordingly be classified as either "hard" or "soft." Yet this is about as logical as classifying all science fiction as either "space opera" or "non-space opera," or "Cyberpunk" or "non-Cyberpunk." In fact, few if any authors have ever described themselves as "soft science fiction writers," and there has never existed anything resembling a community of soft science fiction writers or an audience clamoring for soft science fiction. Instead, the texts that fall outside the parameters of hard science fiction are numerous, diverse, and badly mischaracterized as monolithic or unified in their nature.

It is also disquieting to see the term "hard science fiction" employed not as a description, but as criticism or praise. Some tend to associate hard science fiction only with makeshift plotting, cardboard characterization, and clumsy prose style, as if all literary considerations were being sacrificed for the sake of scientific content – a description that might work for, say, George O. Smith or Robert F. Forward but is nonsensical when applied to Gregory Benford or Octavia E. Butler. In truth, vastly differing qualities of writing are found both within and outside of hard science fiction. Conversely, others present hard science fiction as the most rigorous and intellectually demanding form of science fiction, implying that those who do not produce it are somehow failing to realize the true potential of science fiction. This is objectionable as well; writers like Chad Oliver and Ursula K. Le Guin, for example, bring to their writing a background in anthropology that makes their extrapolated aliens and future societies every bit as fascinating and intellectually involving as the technological marvels and strange planets of hard science fiction. Because anthropology is a social science, not a natural science, it is hard to classify their works as hard science fiction, but one cannot justly construe this observation as a criticism. In addition, there is much hard science fiction that reflects little in the way of deep thought. Overall, both unfavorable and favorable generalizations about hard science fiction rarely withstand thoroughgoing examination.

Even in the absence of a clear consensus regarding how to properly define and defend hard science fiction, commentators are usually in agreement as to which authors best represent the subgenre; the names of Hal Clement, Arthur C. Clarke, Larry Niven, and Gregory Benford come up most frequently in critical discussions, and any number of authors – Poul Anderson, Ben Bova, Jerry Pournelle, Charles Sheffield, Octavia Butler, Robert L. Forward, David Brin, Greg Bear, Joan Slonczewski, and others who emerged in the 1980s and 1990s – have been universally accepted as exemplars of the subgenre. One might say, as has been said of science fiction as a whole, that hard science fiction is difficult to define in abstract terms but easy to recognize in particular cases.

In attempts to trace the origins and development of hard science fiction, one irony becomes apparent: all the authors most strongly identified with hard science fiction became prominent in the 1950s or later decades, yet all the critical ideas that are central to hard science fiction were promulgated much earlier. Hard science fiction, then, is a subgenre created by critical commentaries, as future authors exposed to those commentaries matured with a determination to produce science fiction that actually practiced the serious devotion to scientific laws and thought that the genre's advocates had long been preaching.

Arguably, one can trace the priorities of hard science fiction back to two of the field's most celebrated pioneers, Jules Verne and H.G. Wells, who contributed key principles. While Verne famously criticized Wells in a 1903 interview, he described his basic techniques, in contrast to Wells' techniques, more respectfully and usefully in a later interview:

> I have always made a point in my romances of basing my so-called inventions upon a groundwork of actual fact, and of using in their construction methods and materials which are not entirely without the pale of contemporary engineering skill and knowledge. . . . The creations of Mr. Wells, on the other hand, belong unreservedly to an age and degree of scientific knowledge far removed from the present, though I will not say entirely beyond the limits of the possible. (cited in Jones 1904; ellipses mine)

This attentiveness to current progress in a given area, and this impulse to cautiously envision how it might be advanced in the near future, would later lie at the heart of hard science fiction set in the near future, meticulous portrayals of space stations, moon colonies, and expeditions to Mars.

As for Wells, though he spoke disparagingly about his science fiction in later years, he did convey a desire to follow a process of logical extrapolation and develop his ideas in detail. In his 1921 "Preface" to *The Sleeper Awakes*, he says:

> The present volume takes up certain ideas already very much discussed in the concluding years of the last century, the idea of the growth of the towns and the depopulation of the country-side and the degradation of labor through the higher organization of industrial production. "Suppose these forces to go on," that is the fundamental hypothesis of the story. (Wells 1980: 238)

And in his 1933 "Preface" to *The Scientific Romances*, he notes that in imaginative fiction "touches of prosaic details are imperative" (Wells 1933: viii). These principles of extrapolation and detailed development would later govern the more extravagant and futuristic forms of hard science fiction, visions of bizarre worlds, massive constructs in space, and remarkable scientific advances.

Still, having acknowledged their contributions, one cannot appropriately classify Verne and Wells as hard science fiction writers, since science was so visibly neither man's chief interest. Both wrote novels emphasizing broader social and political concerns (often obscured in Verne's case by expurgated translations), and neither worried a great deal about detailed scrutiny of the validity of their scientific projections. Verne did not expect or receive readers' letters criticizing flaws in the engineering of his moon cannon in *From the Earth to the Moon* (1865), just as Wells did not expect or receive readers' letters questioning the scientific logic of his antigravity element Cavorite in *First Men in the Moon* (1901).

An author who did make science his chief interest, Hugo Gernsback, would in the 1920s create a true genre of science fiction by editing the first science fiction magazine, *Amazing Stories*, and by describing the characteristics of science fiction in editorials. Science fiction, he asserted, was a combination of narrative, explanations of scientific facts, and predictions of future inventions (see Westfahl 1998) – a definition that seemingly would lead naturally to stories that were both scientifically researched and rigorously reasoned. Yet Gernsback's own stories, and those he published, rarely met such expectations. While stories did include presentations of scientific knowledge, to make science fiction educational, and imagined inventions, to make science fiction prophetic, the two features did not have to be closely connected to each other. Gernsback's typical strategy was to first explain current progress in an area, then announce the future discovery of some element or ray with almost magical properties – "Arcturium," "F-9 rays," and so on – and describe how this miraculous material or radiation enabled scientists to achieve a breakthrough. He made no effort, then, to carefully extrapolate from known science to unknown science in the manner that would later characterize hard science fiction.

Similar procedures were followed to varying extents by the popular authors who dominated the early science fiction magazines, such as E.E. "Doc" Smith, Campbell, Jack Williamson, and Edmond Hamilton. Their works, though sometimes laden with scientific or pseudoscientific jargon, epitomized another distinctive subgenre of science fiction, space opera, offering thrilling adventures in space but displaying little evidence of disciplined scientific thinking.

At one point, Gernsback did attempt to identify and celebrate stories that adhered very closely to current scientific progress, stories that would later be considered one variety of hard science fiction. In a 1930 editorial, "Science Fiction vs. Science Faction," he defined "science faction" as:

> science fiction in which there are so many scientific facts that the story, as far as the scientific part is concerned, is no longer fiction but becomes more or less a recounting of fact.
>
> For instance, if one spoke of rocket-propelled fliers a few years ago, such machines obviously would have come under the heading of science fiction. Today such fliers properly come under the term science *faction*; because the rocket is a fact today . . . the few experimenters who have worked with rocket-propelled machines have had sufficient encouragement to enable us to predict quite safely that during the next twenty-five years, rocket flying will become the order of the day. (Gernsback 1930: 5; ellipses mine).

Such stories were contrasted with standard science fiction, in which "the author may fairly let his imagination run wild" (Gernsback 1930: 5). Needless to say, there were precious few stories in Gernsback's magazines, or other magazines of the day, that would have qualified as "science faction," and the term never became popular.

However, one important precedent was established during the 1930s: the role of magazine letter columns in responding to and debating scientific issues raised in stories. This was particularly evident in the "Brass Tacks" letter column of *Astounding*

Stories, edited by F. Orlin Tremaine. In 1934, for instance, Campbell published a story using the pseudonym Karl Van Kampen, "The Irrelevant," which described a pur-ported method for evading the law of conservation of energy; during the next year, "Brass Tacks" printed numerous letters attacking the story's logic, met by fiery responses from its author. Campbell's ideas could not bear close examination, but the whole experience made a point: there was indeed an audience of science fiction readers who were eager to read and argue about innovative scientific ideas. Soon, authors would be striving to provide them with meatier material for their informed analysis.

When Campbell became editor of *Astounding Stories* in 1937 and renamed it *Astounding Science-Fiction*, his editorials placed more emphasis on science fiction gen-erated by scientific extrapolation, insisting in theory upon the thought process of hard science fiction. Initially, however, the new authors he discovered and promoted did not entirely fulfill this agenda: writers like Robert A. Heinlein and Isaac Asimov were attentive more to exploring future social developments than to devising future inven-tions, while others like A.E. van Vogt and Henry Kuttner flaunted a wild, unfettered imagination that had little to do with scientific thinking.

Still, there were signs throughout the first decade of Campbell's editorial career of authors attempting to build stories upon sound scientific principles. Ross Rocklynne pioneered the form that became known as the "scientific problem story," mimicking the structure of the detective story, in three adventures featuring space policeman John Colbie and criminal Edward Deverel joining forces to reason out the answer to some scientific puzzle, such as how to get off the surface of a huge frictionless mirror. George O. Smith wrote a series of stories about a space station equidistant from Venus and Earth, named Venus Equilateral, to explore the problems of communication across space. And space opera veteran Williamson, using the pseudonym Will Stewart, offered his own contributions in this vein, several stories involving antimatter, termed contra-terrene matter or "Seetee." The results were not always scientifically flawless – Rocklynne's "At the Center of Gravity" (1938) falsely posited that people inside a hollow sphere would be attracted to its center, while George O. Smith needlessly over-complicated the difficulties involved in sending a radio message to a spaceship – but they came closer to the ideals of hard science fiction than previous stories.

Astounding in the 1940s also published early stories by two authors, Hal Clement and Arthur C. Clarke, who would become central figures in hard science fiction. Clement's "Fireproof" (1947), for example, hinged upon the previously unrecognized principle that a fire could not be sustained in space under weightless conditions, while Clarke's "Hide and Seek" (1949) cleverly demonstrated that a man running across the surface of the Martian moon Phobos could plausibly outmaneuver a pursuing space-ship. All the editorials about the importance of science, and all the readers' letters complaining about sloppy or dubious science, were starting to have an effect on the stories published in the magazines alongside those editorials and letters.

Nevertheless, only in the 1950s did the texts that would truly define hard science fiction finally appear. Not surprisingly, each was widely known and highly popular in its day, and each was accompanied by an influential article from its author, published in *Astounding*, explaining how the work was created. What is surprising is that one of the texts was not a story or novel, but rather a film.

Destination Moon (1950) was directly inspired by an important event outside the realm of science fiction: the establishment of an American space program after the Second World War, initially headed by the German scientists who had built the V-2 rockets, and devoted to the announced goal of human flight into outer space. Suddenly, what was then science fiction's most prominent trope – space travel – loomed as a real possibility in the near future; and this naturally inspired writers like Heinlein to ponder how space travel might actually be achieved, and to create narratives that were sufficiently grounded in current research to qualify as plausible predictions of future space flights. Thus, although Heinlein was originally hired to write a film script based on his juvenile novel *Rocket Ship Galileo* (1946), he and producer George Pal quickly decided to abandon its silly plot – two boys help their uncle build a rocket, fly to the Moon, and discover renegade Nazis plotting to establish the Fourth Reich – and instead make a film that would depict a first flight to the moon in a painstakingly realistic manner. Now, the Moon rocket would be constructed by teams of industrialists headed by a retired general, not an isolated genius and his nephews, and moon explorers would battle only the harsh conditions of space, not contrived villainy.

When the film was released, Heinlein published an article in *Astounding*, "Shooting *Destination Moon*," which described the priorities and activities of everyone involved in producing the movie:

> By the time the picture was being shot the entire company – actors, grips, cameramen, office people – became imbued with enthusiasm for producing a picture which would be scientifically acceptable as well as a box office success. Willy Ley's "Rockets and Space Travel" was read by dozens of people in the company. [Chesley] Bonestell and Ley's "Conquest of Space" was published about then and enjoyed a brisk sale among us. Waits between takes were filled by discussions of theory and future prospects of interplanetary travel.
>
> As shooting progressed we began to be deluged with visitors of technical background – guided missiles men, astronomers, rocket engineers, aircraft engineers. The company, seeing that their work was being taken seriously by technical specialists, took pride in turning out an authentic job. (Heinlein 1950: 7)

Heinlein also emphasizes that "realism is compounded of minor details" and that "most of creating the illusion of space travel lay . . . in constant attention to minor details" (Heinlein 1950, 16; my ellipses). Writers and readers could sense from Heinlein's article how exciting and rewarding it might be to be meticulously attentive to all aspects of science in crafting near-future narratives.

Heinlein's film and article, as it turns out, had little influence on Hollywood: while a few other films aspiring to the documentary-style realism of *Destination Moon* were released, like *Riders to the Stars* (1954), *Conquest of Space* (1955), and Heinlein's own *Project Moonbase* (1953), science fiction films generally turned to more colorful and escapist stories featuring aliens, robots, and monsters. But science fiction writers energetically responded to the challenge of portraying humanity's future space ventures carefully and scientifically in prose, rather than on film, leading to the first real outpouring of hard science fiction. One of the most prominent and capable chroniclers of humanity's early steps into space was Clarke. In 1951, he published the first novel about a pioneering flight to the Moon that matched the persuasive authenticity of *Destination Moon*, *Prelude to Space*, and later wrote another serious depiction of a first lunar expedition, "Venture to the Moon" (1958), as well as realistic portrayals of life in space stations (*Islands in the Sky* [1952] and "The Other Side of the Sky" [1958]), lunar colonies (*Earthlight* [1955] and *A Fall of Moondust* [1961]), and Martian settlements (*Sands of Mars* [1952]). Countless authors provided similar stories, often in novels aimed specifically at juvenile audiences: veteran writers Murray Leinster and Lester del Rey, for example, each produced trilogies of juveniles that successively described building a space station, flying to the Moon, and colonizing the Moon (Leinster's *Space Platform* [1953], *Space Tug* [1953], and *City on the Moon* [1957]; del Rey's *Step to the Stars* [1954], *Mission to the Moon* [1956], and *Moon of Mutiny* [1961]). Engineer G. Harry Stine, writing as Lee Correy, emphasized the nuts and bolts of space travel in a series of stories published in *Astounding* during the 1950s. Other hard science fiction writers who debuted at that time, often in the pages of *Astounding*, included Dean McLaughlin, Alan E. Nourse, and Gordon R. Dickson. Overall, while historians of science fiction in the 1950s generally emphasize the emergence of satirical science fiction in *Galaxy*, and of a more literate brand of science fiction in *The Magazine of Fantasy and Science Fiction*, most stories and novels of the decade probably fell into this category of near-future hard science fiction – works largely forgotten because they were overlooked by contemporary critics and rarely examined by later scholars.

A second, more ambitious form of hard science fiction came to the forefront in 1953 with the appearance of Clement's *Mission of Gravity*. He also wrote an article about his novel for *Astounding*, "Whirligig World," which began by describing its creation as a "game":

> Writing a science fiction story is fun, not work. . . . The fun, and the material for this article, lies in treating the whole thing as a game. I've been playing the game since I was a child, so the rules must be quite simple. They are: for the reader of a science fiction story, they consist of finding as many as possible of the author's statements or implications which conflict with the facts as science currently understands them. For the author, the rule is to make as few such slips as he possibly can. (Clement 1953: 102; my ellipses)

This is probably the first description of the friendly but combative relationship between careful authors and nitpicking readers – regularly referred to as "the game" by hard science fiction writers like Anderson and Benford – which would always be closely associated with hard science fiction stories.

The article goes on to describe how Clement, building upon recently discovered evidence of a large planet circling the star 61 Cygni, crafted a huge, rapidly-spinning, pancake-shaped world, named Mesklin, that became the unique setting of *Mission of Gravity*. Never before had an author described developing an imagined world in such extreme scientific detail. At one point, after Clement decides that he must provide his world with moons and a ring, he says:

> I checked the sizes of the rings against the satellite orbits, and found that the inner moon I had invented would produce two gaps in the ring similar to those in Saturn's decoration. The point never became important in the story, but it was valuable to me as atmosphere; I had to have the picture clearly in mind to make all possible events and conversations consistent. (Clement 1953: 109)

He also recounts how Asimov helped him develop the methane-based aliens that would necessarily inhabit this strange planet, giving readers a glimpse of the collaborative thought process often involved in hard science fiction, and he emphasizes the unexpected and creative results that can stem from the process: "The rest of the detail work consists of all my remaining moves in the game – finding things that are taken for granted on our own world and would not be true on this one" (Clement 1953: 113). The result was one of the stunningly original environments ever seen in science fiction: a world of wildly varying gravity, inhabited by small crustaceans with shells hard enough to resist the powerful gravity at its center, yet a sort of world that scientists would have to concede might actually exist. Also, as would become characteristic of such creations, scientifically trained readers carefully examined Clement's work and discovered flaws: as he later reported in an interview:

> I was a little unhappy when the MIT science fiction people buckled down and analyzed Mesklin and found that I was wrong, that it would actually have come to a sharp edge at the equator. (cited in Hassler 1982: 21)

This variety of hard science fiction – demanding writers with a strong scientific background, infinite patience, and a mind constantly open to unexpected consequences – proved harder to emulate than the near-future realism of *Destination Moon*, so there were initially fewer authors who endeavored to follow in Clement's footsteps. But some were up to the challenge. Poul Anderson made himself an expert in the art of concocting imaginary but scientifically plausible planets; later in his career, he first created a planet he called Cleopatra as an exercise to illustrate his techniques for an essay, "The Creation of Imaginary Worlds: The World Builder's Handbook and Pocket Companion," then employed that same world as the setting for his novel, *A World Named Cleopatra* (1977). Another writer who regularly published in *Astounding* during the 1950s, Frank Herbert, presented a landmark achievement of world-building in his novel *Dune* (1965) and its sequels. While some were not impressed by the novel's derivative palace intrigues, everyone could admire its setting, the magnificently developed and hauntingly austere desert world of Arrakis. In 1975, Herbert was asked by

Harlan Ellison to join other hard science fiction writers, including Clement, Anderson, and Larry Niven, in collaboratively creating a distinctive alien planet to serve as the setting for some original science fiction stories, later published in Ellison's anthology *Medea: Harlan's World* (1985).

This is not to say that the construction of innovative worlds was the only sort of extravagant speculation figuring in hard science fiction. Clement, for example, had distinguished himself before *Mission of Gravity* with another novel, *Needle* (1950), which presented a strange protoplasmic alien, capable of entering into and communicating with a human body, who visits Earth searching for an escaped criminal from its home world. Another unusual alien, an immense sentient cloud that drifts toward the Earth, appeared in the first of several novels by astronomer Fred Hoyle, *The Black Cloud* (1957). Clarke dusted off an early novel about a city in Earth's far future, *Against the Fall of Night* (first published in *Startling Stories* in 1948), and rewrote it as *The City and the Stars* (1956), beefing up the scientific underpinnings while retaining its boldly imaginative portrayal of humanity's eventual destiny. He also garnered critical acclaim for *Childhood's End* (1953), in which an alien race conquers Earth and prepares humanity to evolve into a group intelligence. Anderson played with expansive ideas in *Brain Wave* (1954), which posits a future Earth that emerges from a cosmic intelligence-dampening cloud, transforming humans into vastly superior intellects, and in *Tau Zero* (1970), which takes a spaceship traveling near the speed of light countless millennia into the future until it survives through the end of our universe and a second Big Bang that launches a new universe. in 1959, James White launched a series of imaginative stories involving medical mysteries at a far-future hospital in space, Sector General, first collected in *Hospital Station* (1962); the series continued into the 1990s, eventually totaling twelve volumes of novels and linked stories.

As more and more works of hard science fiction appeared, a term was needed to describe them. Throughout the 1940s and 1950s, several terms for forms of hard science fiction were proposed – the aforementioned "scientific problem story," "gadget story," "heavy science story," "engineers' story," "Campbellian science fiction" (see Westfahl 1996: 8–9) – but like Gernsback's "science faction," none of these terms became common. It was not until 1957 that P. Schuyler Miller, then the book reviewer for *Astounding*, properly christened the subgenre. One priority Miller brought to reviewing was a determination to identify the subgenre to which a work belonged, so readers who liked a particular type of science fiction could be guided to what they liked and could avoid what they did not like; as one consequence, he constantly needed terms to describe various subgenres of science fiction. He became the first person to use the term "hard science fiction" in his column "The Reference Library" in the November, 1957 issue of *Astounding*, while reviewing Campbell's recently republished novel, *Islands of Space*:

> It was a world-beater in those days [the 1930s]. Although it has been carefully modernized, it's old-fashioned now. It is also very characteristic of the best "hard" science fiction of its day. (Miller 1957: 143)

In applying the term to what would now be regarded as a colorful space opera, not a controlled work of hard science fiction, Miller reflected what would become a recurring fallacy in later discussions of hard science fiction: namely, the notion that hard science fiction was the typical sort of science fiction seen in the 1920s and 1930s and not a more recent invention. In subsequent reviews, Miller kept featuring the term, and by the 1960s other commentators like James Blish, Ellison, Fritz Leiber, and Algis Budrys were also using it.

A key development in the growth of hard science fiction came in 1960, when editor Campbell changed the name of *Astounding* to *Analog: Science Fact/Science Fiction*, announcing an intent to divide the magazine equally between science articles and science fiction stories. While that plan was abandoned – the magazine was soon retitled *Analog: Science Fiction/Science Fact* and reverted to *Astounding*'s policy of only one or two science articles per issue – Campbell's magazine had been officially designated as a publication emphasizing science, and throughout the turmoil of the British New Wave and its aftermath, it remained a safe haven for hard science fiction writers devoted to careful scientific speculation and uninterested in literary experimentation. When Campbell died in 1971, *Analog* was taken over by Bova, who was already making a name for himself as a hard science fiction writer with near-future thrillers like *The Weathermakers* (1965), and he maintained the magazine's focus on science, as did his successor Stanley Schmidt. Almost all the authors of the 1960s, 1970s, and 1980s who earned the label of hard science fiction writer did so by virtue of contributions to *Analog*; even Orson Scott Card, now better known for space operas and fantasies, was initially pigeonholed as a hard science fiction writer after publishing stories in the magazine.

During the 1960s and 1970s, translations were gradually increasing awareness of scientifically interesting texts being written outside of North America and Britain: from Japan, Kobo Abe's *Inter Ice Age 4* (1959), a complex story of scientists confronting the anticipated submersion of Japan; from Poland, Stanislaw Lem's *Solaris* (1959), an evocative portrayal of an enigmatic sentient planet; and from Russia, Arkady and Boris Strugatsky's *Roadside Picnic* (1971), a striking account of an investigation of puzzling alien debris. But the major English-language hard science fiction writer to emerge in this era was Larry Niven, whose early works included both documentary-style space adventures ("The Coldest Place" [1964] and "Becalmed in Hell" [1965]) and a number of stories set in a well-developed future universe called Known Space. The greatest work in this series, and another milestone in hard science fiction, was the novel *Ringworld* (1970), which envisioned a huge inhabited ring circling a star, somehow constructed by ancient aliens. Incredibly, Niven could demonstrate that it was all technically feasible, and despite some resistance to its mind-boggling concept – Niven published the novel as a paperback original, unable to get it accepted as a magazine serial or hardcover – the novel won the Hugo Award and Nebula Award as the best science fiction novel of 1970. Niven's construct also inspired an unprecedented torrent of reactions from readers anxious to critique and expand upon the basic design, as Niven later reported in his 1990 anthology *N-Space*:

A Florida high-school class determined that all of the Ringworld's topsoil will end up in the oceans in a few thousand years. . . . In Philadelphia, a member of the audience pointed out that, mathematically, the Ringworld can be treated as a suspension bridge with no endpoints. Simple in concept; harder to build. . . . At the 1970 World Science Fiction Convention, students in the halls were chanting, "The Ringworld is unstable! The Ringworld is unstable!" Yeah, it needs attitude jets. Ctein and Dan Alderson, computer wizards working independently, took several years to work out the *exact* instability. Ctein also worked out data on *moving* the Ringworld. (*Yes*, for fun. Isn't that how you have fun?). . . . Dan Alderson, making proper use of playground equipment, designed a system with four Ringworlds. Three are in contact with each other, spinning orthogonally to each other on frictionless bearings. But the fourth was built by Mesklinites (see Hal Clement's *Mission of Gravity*). It's the size of Jupiter's orbit (Mesklinites like it cold) and to maintain hundreds of times Earth's surface gravity, it spins at an appreciable fraction of lightspeed. (Niven 1990: 123–4; ellipses mine)

Niven's novel perhaps qualifies as the quintessential work of hard science fiction precisely because it proved capable of sparking such creative responses, some of which influenced Niven's sequels to the novel, *The Ringworld Engineers* (1980) and *The Ringworld Throne* (1996).

Ringworld also inspired a new sort of hard science fiction, devoted to developing and describing what critic Roz Kaveney called "Big Dumb Objects." Many of these massive structures were directly derived from the work of professional scientists. Freeman Dyson envisioned advanced aliens constructing a huge sphere to entirely enclose a star – called the Dyson Sphere – and such a structure was the centerpiece of Bob Shaw's *Orbitsville* (1975). The space habitats designed by Gerard O'Neill – huge hollow spheres or cylinders rotating to simulate gravity for people living on the interior side of their surfaces – became settings for countless novels, such as Ben Bova's *Colony* (1978), Mack Reynolds' *Lagrange Five* (1979), and Robert Heinlein's *The Cat Who Walks through Walls* (1985); Clarke contributed a similar structure functioning as a mysterious alien starship in *Rendezvous with Rama* (1973), which later engendered three sequels cowritten by Gentry Lee. In 1979, space elevators – the concept developed independently by Yuri Artsutanov and John Isaacs of an immense tower physically linking the surface of Earth to a space station in orbit – burst upon the scene in two novels, Clarke's *The Fountains of Paradise* and Charles Sheffield's *The Web Between the Worlds*. But hard science fiction writers could add their own ideas as well; Clarke, for example, concluded *The Fountains of Paradise* by envisioning six space elevators positioned around the Equator with terminal bases connected by long structures in space to form an inhabited "Ring City" around the Earth.

Throughout the 1960s and 1970s, new authors kept stepping forward to fill the pages of *Analog* with hard science fiction. Some, like Donald Kingsbury, P.J. Plauger, Tom Purdom, and W.T. Quick, never achieved prominence outside the magazine, but others like Vernor Vinge and Dean Ing soon made names for themselves. Jerry Pournelle was best known for his collaborations with Niven, including *The Mote in God's Eye* (1974), a space adventure studded with scientific ideas, and *Lucifer's Hammer*

(1977), a near-future thriller about a large comet that strikes the Earth with disastrous consequences. Pournelle's solo works included a series of stories about political intrigues in Earth orbit that were collected in *High Justice* (1977). Benford, also a physics professor at the University of California, Irvine, published numerous stories and an impressive juvenile, *Jupiter Project* (1975). John Varley, after earning praise for several stories collected in *The Persistence of Vision* (1978), launched a trilogy about a vividly realized, and intelligent, artificial world with *Titan* (1979), first serialized in *Analog,* to be followed by *Wizard* (1980) and *Demon* (1984). James P. Hogan published an intriguing novel about scientists examining evidence of ancient aliens, *Inherit the Stars* (1977), which inspired three sequels about actual alien encounters: *The Gentle Giants of Ganymede* (1978), *Giants' Star* (1981), and *Entoverse* (1991).

In 1979 and 1980, several landmark publications served in a way to signal hard science fiction's coming of age. After Clarke's *The Fountains of Paradise* earned both the Hugo Award and Nebula Award in 1979, Benford won the Nebula Award in 1980 for *Timescape,* an involving portrait of scientists at work in an imperiled future who manage to send a warning to scientists in the past by means of tachyons, particles that travel faster than light. Correy was maintaining the tradition of near-future space adventures with *Shuttle Down* (1980), involving the problems faced by a space shuttle which makes an emergency landing on Easter Island, while Clement returned to prominence with *The Nitrogen Fix* (1980), an impressively nuanced portrayal of a future Earth with a poisoned atmosphere.

However, newer writers were also having an impact. Sheffield's *The Web Between the Worlds* established him as a noteworthy new voice, and George Zebrowski drew upon the visionary ideas of Dandridge M. Cole to produce *Macrolife* (1979), an expansive saga of humanity gradually evolving, by means of space colonies constructed out of asteroids, into an enormous collective intelligence. Scientist Forward made an impressive debut with his novel *Dragon's Egg* (1980), daringly and persuasively positing strange life forms living on the surface of a neutron star. First novels by two other hard science fiction writers, Bear's *Hegira* (1979) and Brin's *Sundiver* (1980), attracted less attention, but both would become major figures after publishing acclaimed works in the 1980s: Bear's *Blood Music* (1985), in which genetic engineering gone awry chillingly transforms humanity into a group intelligence, and Brin's *Startide Rising* (1983), a rousing saga of spacefaring humans accompanied by the animals they have endowed with intelligence, or "uplifted." And, showing that hard science fiction was not necessarily a man's game, women writers were also starting to produce their own carefully extrapolated scientific visions, such as Butler's *Wild Seed* (1980), Slonczewski's *Still Forms on Foxfield* (1980), and C.J. Cherryh's *Downbelow Station* (1981).

Around this time, then, there was a growing feeling that hard science fiction had risen to a higher level, as an exciting subgenre distinguished by fresh ideas and an improving literary style. Even authors who had previously disdained the form began to express interest in joining the game; for example, Brian W. Aldiss, known as a New Wave writer in the 1960s, successfully ventured into scientific world-building with his well-received Helliconia trilogy (*Helliconia Spring* [1982], *Helliconia Summer* [1983], and *Helliconia Winter* [1985]).

Despite signs of its growing stature, however, hard science fiction in the early 1980s had still not risen to the highest level of science fiction, as its writers rarely received extended critical attention or recognition as major talents. It would require another new generation of hard science fiction writers, mostly British, with their own distinctive styles, to further advance the reputation of hard science fiction.

References and Further Reading

Anderson, Poul (1974) "The creation of Imaginary Worlds: The World Builder's Handbook and Pocket Companion," in *Science Fiction: Today and Tomorrow: A Discursive Symposium*, (ed.) Reginald Bretnor. New York: Harper and Row.

Benford, Gregory (1987) "Effing the Ineffable," in *Aliens: The Anthropology of Science Fiction*, (eds.) George Slusser and Eric S. Rabkin. Carbondale, IL: Southern Illinois University Press, 13–25.

Bridgstock, Martin (1983) "A Psychological Approach to 'Hard' Science Fiction." *Science Fiction Studies* 10, 50–7.

Campbell, John W. Jr. (1956) "Science Fiction and the Opinion of the Universe." *Saturday Review* 39 (May 12), 9–10, 42–3.

Clement, Hal (1976) "Hard Sciences and Tough Technologies," in *The Craft of Science Fiction: A Symposium on Writing Science Fiction and Science Fantasy*, (ed.) Reginald Bretnor. New York: Harper and Row, 37–52.

——(1953) "Whirligig World." *Astounding Science-Fiction* 51 (June), 102–14.

Gernsback, Hugo (1930) "Science Fiction vs. Science Faction." *Wonder Stories Quarterly* 2 (Fall), 5.

Hartwell, David G. (1994) "Hard Science Fiction," in *The Ascent of Wonder: The Evolution of Hard Science Fiction*, (eds.) Hartwell and Kathryn Cramer. New York: TOR Books, 30–40.

Hassler, Donald M. (1982) *Hal Clement*. Starmont Reader's Guide 11. Mercer Island, Washington: Starmont House.

Heinlein, Robert A. (1950) "Shooting *Destination Moon*." *Astounding Science-Fiction* 45 (July), 6–18.

Jones, Gordon (1904) "Jules Verne at Home." *Temple Bar* 129 (June), 664–71. Available

online at http://jv.gilead.org.il/ evans/Gordon_Jones_interview_of_JV.html.

Lewis, C.S. (1966) "On Science Fiction," in Lewis, *Of Other Worlds: Essays and Stories*, (ed.) Walter Hooper. New York: Harcourt Brace Jovanovich. Text of a lecture presented in 1955.

Miller, P. Schuyler (1957) "The Reference Library." *Astounding Science Fiction* 60 (November), 142–9.

Niven, Larry (1990) "Introduction to an excerpt from *Ringworld*," in *N-Space*, Larry Niven. New York: Tor Books, 122–4.

Park, Paul (1991) "The Shadow of Hard Science Fiction." *New York Review of Science Fiction* No. 38 (October), 1, 3–4.

Pierce, John J. (1993) "The Literary Experience of Hard Science Fiction." *Science Fiction Studies* 20, 176–83.

Samuelson, David N. (1993) "Modes of Extrapolation: The Formulas of Hard Science Fiction." *Science Fiction Studies* 20, 191–232.

Slusser, George, and Eric S. Rabkin (eds.) (1986) *Hard Science Fiction*. Carbondale, IL: Southern Illinois University Press.

Spinrad, Norman (1988) "On Books: The Hard Stuff." *Isaac Asimov's Science Fiction Magazine* 12 (March), 177–91.

Stableford, Brian (1994) "The Last Chocolate Bar and the Majesty of Truth: Reflections on the Concept of 'Hardness' in Science Fiction. *New York Review of Science Fiction* No. 71 (July), 1, 8–12, and No. 72 (August), 10–16.

Steele, Allen M. (1992) "Hard Again." *New York Review of Science Fiction* No. 46 (June), 1, 3–5.

Wells, H.G. (1933) "Preface" to *The Scientific Romances*. London: Gollancz, 1934.

——(1980) "Preface" to *The Sleeper Awakes* (1921) in *H.G. Wells's Literary Criticism*, (eds.) Patrick Parrinder and Robert M. Philmus. Brighton: Harvester Press, 238–9.

Westfahl, Gary (1996) *Cosmic Engineers: A Study of Hard Science Fiction*. Westport, CT: Greenwood Press.

——(1998) *The Mechanics of Wonder: The Creation of the Idea of Science Fiction*. Liverpool: Liverpool University Press.

13

The New Wave

Rob Latham

Most writers, critics, and fans of Anglo-American science fiction believe that something significant happened to the genre during the 1960s, and the term "New Wave,"
which emerged at the time, remains the prevailing designation for this event. Yet
there is widespread disagreement regarding the New Wave's makeup and influence –
whether it was a coherent movement or a shapeless coalition, whether its intent was
revolutionary or merely reformist, whether it radically split and transformed the field
or caused only minor scars and surface adjustments. A number of key figures associated with the New Wave, such as Michael Moorcock and Damon Knight, have
rejected the label as a description for their work (see Walker 1978) or else, like Harlan
Ellison, have claimed it never referred to a cohesive faction (Ellison 1974). Some critics
have alleged that there were two distinct, if overlapping, New Waves, one British and
one American (Dozois 1983). Others have complained that the term is so sketchy and
liable to misuse that it is perilously close to signifying nothing (Delany 1980). The
New Wave has been seen as both elitist (Spinrad 1990) and deeply engaged with
popular culture (Disch 1998), both an innovation in content (Grobman and Grobman
1982) and all about style (Taylor 1990). In terms of legacy, it has either served to
refresh a moribund genre (Merril 1967a), ushered SF into the realms of serious literature (Moorcock 1979), afflicted the field with a hobbling pessimism (Benford 1984),
or petered out due to its trendy vacuity (Del Rey 1979). It is at once "the single most
important development in science fiction" (Priest 1978: 164) and "boring, miser-
abilist, depressing crap" (MacLeod 2004: 14).

Even the provenance of the moniker is in dispute: while most commentators agree
it was coined in echo of the *nouvelle vague* in French cinema (the pathbreaking work
of Resnais, Truffaut, and Godard), there is uncertainty about what the analogy implies
and who first invoked it. Damien Broderick nominates Christopher Priest (Broderick
2003), while Mike Ashley favors Charles Platt (Ashley 2004). Most concur, however,
that Judith Merril deserves the lion's share of the credit – or the blame, depending
on one's perspective – for popularizing what she called the "New Thing" through her

labors as an editor, book reviewer, and all-around literary impresario. Merril's annual anthology of the *Year's Best S-F*, published through 1967, increasingly emphasized the work of writers who came to be associated with the New Wave, and her review column for *The Magazine of Fantasy and Science Fiction* (*F&SF*), which appeared from May 1965 until February 1969, provided a highly visible platform from which to elevate favorites and chastise rivals. By the mid-1960s, her reputation as a New Wave evangelist was so firmly established within the field that she expressed bemusement at finding herself "the publicly appointed Defender of an undefined Faith" (Merril 1967a: 28) – a disingenuous posture given how assiduously she had cultivated the role. As John J. Pierce has tartly remarked, the "alleged adherents" of the New Wave often feigned shock at being lumped into this category, "even while they endorsed most of each other's works, denounced the same alleged reactionaries and their works, and otherwise behaved like partisans in a common cause" (Pierce 1989: 89).

Judith Merril and the Mainstreaming of SF

Merril's emergence as chief advocate for the New Wave was the result of her own complicated evolution within the genre (see Cummins 1995). She had been writing SF for decades, her first short story, "That Only a Mother" (1948), appearing in the hallowed pages of John W. Campbell's *Astounding* and soon becoming a classic in the field, enshrined in canonical anthologies alongside work by Robert A. Heinlein, Isaac Asimov, Lester Del Rey, and other leading lights of what, by the 1960s, had become the science fiction Establishment. Though never prolific, she published steadily throughout the 1950s, but seemed to find her true calling as an editor, taking advantage of the burgeoning book market, as well as a growing public appetite for SF, to initiate her series of "Year's Best" compilations in 1956. The first four volumes were released by a speciality press and largely featured reprints from the SF magazines, but the fifth annual saw a move to Simon and Schuster, a prestigious literary imprint. Suddenly, the contents began to get more eclectic, including stories by the likes of Bernard Malamud, Muriel Spark, and André Maurois, poetry by John Dos Passos and Conrad Aiken, and Merril's own increasingly bold and searching editorial summations. In the seventh annual, published in 1962, she maintained that SF no longer deserved to be seen as a compartmentalized district within the larger province of modern fiction; rather, it was swiftly being "reabsorbed" into the literary mainstream, an outcome she heralded with gratitude and pride (Merril 1962: 391). In later volumes she rejected the term "science fiction" altogether as a description for her selections, preferring the more catholic umbrella "speculative fiction," a shifty moniker capable of endless amendment and fluid application (see Merril 1971).

Meanwhile, throughout the 1950s, Merril, along with fellow SF authors James Blish and Damon Knight, had taken the lead in promoting higher literary standards and a greater sense of professionalism within the field by establishing an annual series of writers conferences, named for their collective hometown of Milford, Pennsylvania.

Manuscripts were workshopped at these avid gatherings, thus encouraging more care in the planning and construction of stories, and a sense of solidarity was promoted, eventually leading to the formation, in 1965, of the Science Fiction Writers Association (SFWA), with Knight as first president. New outlets for SF were rapidly opening up, including mainstream venues as diverse as *Playboy* and *The Saturday Evening Post*, and the Milford Conferences and SFWA gave writers the tools, in terms of improved craftsmanship and professional support, to capitalize upon them.

These developments stood in marked contrast to the situation that had prevailed during the 1940s, when a handful of editors, most centrally John Campbell, had controlled the marketplace, and writers had been forced to tailor their personal visions and methods of storytelling to narrow ideological and aesthetic tenets. This set-up had proven particularly inhibiting for authors whose work was in any way idiosyncratic or stylistically ambitious, such as Theodore Sturgeon and Ray Bradbury. Campbell's stranglehold had already been broken at the start of the 1950s with the establishment of two major new magazines: *Galaxy*, which featured more social-critical perspectives than Campbell would have favored, and *F&SF*, which encouraged a broader view of the literary horizons by blending SF with other forms of non-mimetic writing and which also emphasized stylistic accomplishment as a prerequisite for successful stories. These magazines had ushered in a wealth of new talent, including Alfred Bester, Philip K. Dick, Philip José Farmer, and Cordwainer Smith, who developed distinctive and striking bodies of work. In the late 1950s and early 1960s, another generation of writers was shepherded into the field, primarily by Cele Goldsmith, editor of *Fantastic* and *Amazing*, and Frederik Pohl, editor of *Galaxy* and *Worlds of If*. If anything, this cohort was even more individualistic and stylish, including several figures who would soon be prominently associated with the New Wave, such as Thomas M. Disch, Roger Zelazny, R.A. Lafferty, Joanna Russ, and Ursula K. Le Guin.

The evolution of Merril's career thus deserves to be seen within the context of this growing diversification and "mainstreaming" of SF, a trend that helps explain both the rise of the New Wave movement and Merril's role as its main champion. The resistance the New Wave provoked, especially among defenders of Campbell's legacy, was also prefigured in the occasional grumblings that had accompanied this trend within the genre. The Milford Conferences, at first welcomed by the authorial community, came to be seen by some as promoting a party line that valorized "fine writing" over against more basic storytelling values; for writers tutored by Campbell, individual style was always secondary to ideational content, logical extrapolation, and scientific literacy. Disaffected authors began griping about a "Milford Mafia" that was endangering SF's unique virtues by imposing literary standards essentially alien to the field (see Del Rey 1979).

An excellent index to the conflicts dividing SF writers on the eve of the New Wave is provided by *PITFCS: Publications of the Institute for Twenty-First Century Studies*, a newsletter that circulated among authors between 1959 and 1962. *PITFCS* featured contentious exchanges on a number of topics, often centering on the literary potential of SF and the writer's role as a creative talent. While Merril and Knight emerged as forceful advocates for the view that genre writers should be confident artists and dedicated professionals, able to express their personal visions without editorial interference, others challenged this model, arguing that the appeal of SF was its essential amateurism, that editors (and even fans) had the right to shape stories, and that authors ought to be more concerned about the caliber of their ideas than of their prose (see Cogswell 1992). With the advent of the New Wave, these simmering disagreements regarding the nature of SF's aesthetic commitments exploded into wider awareness, as what had been bantering shoptalk in the pages of *PITFCS* became ugly public polemics that shattered friendships and damaged reputations.

Michael Moorcock and the New Worlds Experiment

The trigger that ignited this explosion was a seemingly innocuous event that took place on the other side of the world: the longtime editor of the British SF magazine *New Worlds*, E.J. Carnell, retired in 1964, handing the journal over to a young, energetic successor named Michael Moorcock. *New Worlds*, founded in 1946 on the hard-SF model of Campbell's *Astounding*, had been for two decades the principal British outlet for science fiction; over the years, Carnell had cultivated a reliable stable of native talent, such as Brian W. Aldiss, John Brunner, Colin Kapp, and James White, whose work was generally competent if not exactly trailblazing. A change in ownership prompted Carnell's exit for the greener pastures of book editing, and Moorcock's revamped *New Worlds*, sporting a new pocket-size format and a more pugnacious editorial policy, debuted in the Spring of 1964.

Moorcock had previously placed a handful of stories with Carnell, mostly brooding sword-and-sorcery tales for *New World's* sister publication, *Science-Fantasy*; but he was also a highly visible agitator who had often castigated the genre, in the pages of fanzines, for being safe and stale, for lacking commitment to higher literary values. In a guest editorial published in *New Worlds* in April 1963, Moorcock claimed that SF had enormous potential "for the presentation of the human drama" but had been betrayed by "lazy writers or bad writers or downright stupid writers [who] find it impossible to stimulate the mind and the emotions at the same time" (Moorcock 1963: 3). In a scathing assessment of what contemporary SF lacked, Moorcock listed "passion, subtlety, irony, original characterization, original and good style, a sense of involvement in human affairs, color, density, depth and, on the whole, real feeling"; most SF writers, he claimed, were essentially "boy-author[s] writing boys' stories got up to look like grown-ups' stories" (Moorcock 1963: 123). Even readers who recalled these furious musings, however, were likely surprised by the transformations Moorcock was soon to visit on their beloved *New Worlds*.

For the first two years, he remained cautious, continuing to feature a number of Carnell regulars and couching his scorn toward traditional science fiction under his book-reviewer pseudonym, James Colvin (who often blasted Campbell stalwarts such as Heinlein and Poul Anderson). But in February 1966, responding to complaints from "hard-core" fans that "modern SF writers and publishers ha[d] betrayed the spirit of the Golden Age," he unleashed this fusillade:

> these attacks come, it appears, from people who read very little fiction other than science fiction and are unable to form true standards because of this. . . . The half-baked, ill-considered, poorly-informed notions of most of those 'Golden Age' SF writers tell us next to nothing about human character or the human condition and the pulp-derived styles they used often makes the writing itself unreadable. (Moorcock 1966a: 2–3).

There was, in short, an Old Guard of SF authors and fans who simply *didn't get it and never would*, and Moorcock brusquely wrote them off as inconsequential dullards. By contrast, his magazine was addressed to those forward-looking types who (as he had put it in his March 1965 editorial) "believe that since SF is growing up it must slough off some of its more sensational and spectacular aspects; they believe that the form must be reshaped and new symbols found to reflect the mood of . . . present-day society" (Moorcock 1965: 2–3). Moorcock thus balanced his combative negativity, his eagerness to scold the genre for its timidity and backwardness, with optimistic calls for the activation of what he saw as its immense, if dormant, potential.

On the one hand, his overall position merely restated the complex of notions that Merril and the "Milford Mafia" had been pressing stateside for years: that SF – which stood for *speculative* fiction, a wide and noble lineage – could and should be a genuine art, told with skill and passion, addressing the most serious issues and themes in a way that the genre, with its potent vocabulary of image and metaphor, was uniquely suited to do. On the other hand, Moorcock, a young man who had not developed within the American magazine system and thus owed it no loyalties, was willing to take on the field's sacred cows with more uncompromising vigor and dismissive contempt than the Milford cabal dared to muster. His strategy was to prod and provoke rather than to coddle and cajole.

Moreover, while the larger field of speculative literature to which Merril had referred in her annuals was more or less safely middlebrow, Moorcock's lined up with a tradition of avant-garde extremism that extended from Alfred Jarry through the Surrealists up to William S. Burroughs. *New Worlds* during his tenure often featured articles on these and other radical modernists, with his very first editorial, entitled "A New Literature for the Space Age," praising Burroughs' collage novels as the models for "a kind of SF which is unconventional in every sense" (Moorcock 1964: 3). When *New Worlds* changed its layout again in July 1967 to a large-format glossy, its range of reference to the experimental arts grew even broader, with illustrated essays on the likes of M.C. Escher and Eduardo Paolozzi. The thematic and stylistic options open to the genre were thus considerably broader in Moorcock's prospectus and the challenge to conventional modes of storytelling as a result more sharply pointed.

Finally, Moorcock's calls for greater "relevance" in SF writing marked a *generational* split with the Old Guard, an ethico-political commitment to exploring fresh experiences; when he insisted, in an editorial entitled "Symbols for the Sixties," that SF should "use images apt for today" and feature "characters fitted for the society of today," he was demanding an engagement with the emerging counterculture, the militant attitudes and experimental lifestyles of contemporary youth (Moorcock 1965: 3). Moorcock's own fiction often played up this connection, especially his stories featuring sardonic superhero Jerry Cornelius; with his hipster lingo, ultra-Mod wardrobe, and decadent tendencies, Jerry became something of an informal mascot for the magazine, as other hands took up the picaresque chronicle of his wayward adventures. While a few older SF authors, such as Fritz Leiber and Edgar Pangborn, might have flirted with counterculture themes, the genre at the time was fairly staid, which gave a distinctly Oedipal flavor to the *New Worlds* rebellion. Moorcock's alter-ego Colvin rejected Heinlein not simply because he was a bad writer, but because he was "reactionary," an evil father-figure to be arraigned and condemned.

J.G. Ballard and the Shift to Inner Space

Moorcock's disdain for what he saw as the genre's endemic failure expressed only one side of his complex editorial persona; however, in a more constructive vein, he championed the work of a handful of writers who, in his view, broke the ossified moulds of conventional SF. Some of these – like Langdon Jones, Charles Platt, David I. Masson, and M. John Harrison – were his own discoveries; others were Carnell holdovers such as Aldiss and Brunner who seized the opening Moorcock provided to push their fiction in bold new directions. But always at the forefront was J.G. Ballard.

Moorcock's first issue as editor featured a substantial section of Ballard's powerful and enigmatic novel *Equinox* (released in book form as *The Crystal World* [1966]), along with his enthusiastic profile of Burroughs as a quasi-SF visionary. Over the next several years, the magazine tracked and warmly hailed Ballard's restless evolutions, culminating in the publication of his incendiary series of "condensed novels" – harsh, fragmentary montages strongly influenced by Burroughs – that began appearing in the April 1966 issue (and which were eventually gathered into his 1970 book, *The Atrocity Exhibition*). In his October 1966 editorial, Moorcock praised Ballard as "the first clear voice of a movement destined to consolidate the literary ideas . . . of the 20th century," thus giving birth to a new form of SF "that is genuinely speculative and introspective" (Moorcock 1966b: 2). Affirming Ballard's status as *New World*'s standard-bearer, Moorcock declared that "there now exists, centered around this magazine, a group of writers and critics who understand and enthusiastically support the work Ballard is doing" (Moorcock 1966b: 3) – one of the first public statements of a cohesive faction rising within the field, mobilized by Moorcock's editorial program and inspired by Ballard's fearless example.

Unlike Burroughs, Ballard was an SF insider and thus harder for the genre Establishment to ignore. He had begun placing stories with Carnell's magazines in 1956, and by the early 1960s was widely seen as the most original young talent in British

SF. While his fiction could be seen to fit within the social-satirical mold pioneered by *Galaxy*, it was nonetheless distinctive in its range of reference to modern litera-ture and culture, from Kafka and Freud to the Surrealists, whose psychological insights often formed the speculative core of his tales (as opposed to the physical and sociological sciences that had dominated SF's modes of extrapolation to that time). Witty, lyrical, and evocative, his early stories – coming to a peak of achievement in "The Voices of Time" (1960) – were propelled by a powerful undercurrent of obses-sion, often featuring haunted or half-mad characters struggling with internal demons in near-future settings marked by social breakdown and spiritual malaise. A clutch-ing sense of entropic dissolution prevailed, with his protagonists obscurely complicit in their own ruination, a scenario amplified in his 1962 novel *The Drowned World*, where the main character's response to a disastrous rise in the ocean levels is virtually to worship this return of a tropical Eden.

As the American space program got underway in the early 1960s, Ballard launched a series of stories centered on astronauts, beginning with "The Cage of Sand" (1962); but rather than treating these figures in classic Campbellian fashion as brave cosmic voyagers, he limned them as troubled anti-heroes, locked in psychotic delusion or – in a characteristically perverse twist – stupefied with nostalgia for the glory days of space that had long since passed away. That these tales were intended as ironic comment on the genre's cherished vision of spaceflight as humanity's high destiny was made clear by the guest editorial Ballard penned for Carnell's *New Worlds* in May 1962, entitled "Which Way to Inner Space?" Baldly asserting that "space fiction can no longer provide the main wellspring of ideas for s-f," not only because the result was "invariably juvenile" (Ballard 1962: 3) but also because the actual achievements of the space program had eclipsed the genre's fantasies, Ballard called for a turn inward, toward the realms of experimental and aberrant psychology:

> I'd like to see more psycho-literary ideas, more meta-biological and meta-chemical con-cepts, private time-systems, synthetic psychologies and space-times, more of the somber half-worlds one glimpses in the paintings of schizophrenics, all in all a complete spec-ulative poetry and fantasy of science. (Ballard 1962: 118)

The goal, he made clear, was not merely to update the genre's corpus of available themes, but to improve its literary quality, bringing SF in line with the avant-garde impulses of "painting, music and the cinema . . . , particularly as these have become wholeheartedly speculative, more and more concerned with the creation of new states of mind, new levels of awareness." In order to accomplish this, SF would have to "jet-tison its present narrative forms and plots" (Ballard 1962: 117), inherited from the pulp-fiction past, and become instead a truly mature and *modern* genre in synch with the changing times.

If Moorcock's concurrent polemics bemoaning SF's decadence expressed a desire for more challenging styles of writing and more forceful engagements with the "human condition," Ballard's essay provided the first glimmerings of a specific topical and aesthetic approach, a program of renovation that would shift the genre's focus from the soaring vistas of interstellar space to the convoluted mental landscapes of an encroaching modernity. It is thus not surprising that, upon Moorcock's accession to editorship of *New Worlds*, Ballard was often summoned as its resident visionary, his "inner space" agenda providing a loose rationale for the new trajectories pursued by the magazine.

It is perhaps also not too shocking that Judith Merril, always searching for fresh phenomena that would support her brief for a budding speculative fiction, would come to latch upon Ballard as the propitious "New Thing" that proved her cause. She had been the first editor to introduce Ballard to American readers, reprinting his stories "Prima Belladona" (1956) and "The Sound Sweep" (1960) in her "Year's Best" volumes. In 1965, when the World Science Fiction Convention was held in London, she got her chance to experience the undiluted enthusiasm of Moorcock's *New Worlds* experiment first-hand. Reporting on the scene in her *F&SF* column, she spoke of "a feeling of excitement, a ferment of interest and creative activity" that reminded her of the halcyon days of the early 1950s, when new magazine markets had transformed the field (Merril 1966a: 39). Part of the sense of possibility was "the comparative absence of an active Old Guard (either of authors or editors)" such as prevailed in the USA, but mostly it was the artistic boldness and fertility of imagination of young British writers, who seemed animated by a genuine "purpose in their work" (Merril 1966a: 38–9). The leader of this lively cadre was Moorcock, who hosted a continuous salon in his London flat, but its intellectual spearhead was clearly Ballard.

Merril devoted her August 1966 column to a review of Ballard's work to date, offering a penetrating analysis of his "unique and persuasive inner landscape" (Merril 1966b: 62) and defending him warmly as "an intensely conscious and purposeful speculative writer" (Merril 1966b: 64). By that time several of Ballard's novels and story collections had appeared on US shores, and American SF readers had begun to grapple with the provocative and often forbidding perspectives of his fiction. Merril's column provided a sympathetic guidebook to its characteristic themes and obsessions, and as a result she came to be seen as the main stateside advocate of Ballard's work and of the ongoing "Inner Space" revolution in SF. This position was cemented with the appearance of her 1968 anthology, *England Swings SF* (titled in homage to another British pop-culture invasion), which gathered 28 innovative stories, most of them published previously in *New Worlds*. By this time, Merril had fully yoked her long-standing defense of speculative fiction to the Ballard-Moorcock bandwagon.

Old Guards and New Markets

As Merril put it in her November 1967 *F&SF* column, "the only general agreement" genre readers seemed to have regarding the "New Thing" in SF was "that Ballard is its Demon and I am its prophetess" (Merril 1967a: 28). The rueful tone of her comment, and the somewhat defensive tenor of her entire piece, indicate that a quarrel had broken out with American followers of the "Old Thing" (as Merril here calls the Campbell tradition). On the one hand, Merril attempted to defuse the controversy by arguing that the "New Thing" was not an alien incursion but rather continued a trend of stylish speculation that extended well back into the 1950s; on the other hand, perhaps fired by Moorcock's eagerness for battle, she denounced the "highly selective sort of blindness that afflicts the members of Establishments," preventing Old-Guard fans from perceiving how desperately SF needed to move beyond the conventional styles and "gadget-and-gimmick ideas" of its Golden Age (Merril 1967a: 30–1). Science fiction, after all, was the literature of change, so why resist this transformation?

One of those who deeply resented the polemical posturing of the New Wave cohort was Donald A. Wollheim, chief SF editor at Ace Books. In his 1971 study *The Universe Makers*, Wollheim excoriated the *New Worlds* group for what he saw as their trendy nihilism, their rejection of SF's core values in favor of an embrace of chic apocalypses. He chastised Ballard for abandoning space, the only appropriate setting for genuine SF, and accused Moorcock of mounting a "crusade" to convert benighted fans to a fiction at once hedonistic and downbeat, filled with "shock words and shock scenes, hallucinatory fantasies, and sex" (Wollheim 1971: 102–5). The scandalized tone of these remarks pointed to the growing generation gap within the genre, with the *New Worlds* experiment being lumped alongside other fashionable 1960s provocations by Old-Guard fans. Wollheim also expressed a view that came to prevail among a number of American critics of the New Wave: that this movement was not truly part of the continuum of SF because of its essential pessimism, its deliberate denial of the technological progress celebrated by Campbell and his heirs. Even sympathetic commentators have sometimes acknowledged the validity of this charge: Peter Nicholls refers to the New Wave's "sometimes miasmic gloom" (Nicholls 1993: 867), and the title Colin Greenland chose for his history of Moorcock's *New Worlds*, *The Entropy Exhibition*, underlines the magazine's policy of willful catastrophism.

The irony in Wollheim's indictment, however, is that he was actually influential, as an editor, in promoting the New Wave cause. Ace Books brought out the paperback edition of Merril's *England Swings SF*, with an unsigned promotional preface (doubtless penned by Wollheim) talking up the New Wave controversy. Earlier in the decade, he had published several young writers who would become major figures within the American New Wave, such as Samuel R. Delany; and the "World's Best SF" series Wollheim coedited with Terry Carr from 1965–71 took up where Merril's lapsed annuals left off in mediating the *New Worlds* scene to American readers. Wollheim also tabbed Carr to edit a line of "Ace SF Specials" that included some of the high-water marks of the New Wave in America, such as Le Guin's *The Left Hand of Darkness* (1969), Lafferty's *Fourth Mansions* (1969), and Russ' *And Chaos Died* (1970). Similarly, Frederik Pohl, another Old-Guard figure who protested Merril's dubious "New Thing" (and who had once been married to Merril), was responsible, as an editor during the 1960s and 1970s, for spreading its gospel through the fiction he chose to publish (see Dozois 1983). What this trend suggests is that, by the late 1960s if not earlier, a new market for SF had developed in the USA, likely made up of younger readers drawn to the New Wave for its stylistic energy and its striving for social relevance, and canny Old-Guard editors, whatever their personal qualms about the movement, seemed happy enough to cater to it.

One of the cornerstones of this new market was the original anthology, which emerged as a powerful competitor to the traditional magazines. In 1966, founding member of the Milford Mafia Damon Knight inaugurated an anthology series entitled *Orbit*, which featured inventive stories that blended cutting-edge styles of the 1950s with the emergent New Wave; like a conventional magazine, *Orbit* developed a regular stable of authors – including Lafferty, Russ, Gene Wolfe, James Sallis, and Kate Wilhelm – whose efforts, in terms of theme and style, often pushed the boundaries of what would have been acceptable in the current market. Other series eventually appeared – Terry Carr's *Universe*, Harry Harrison's *Nova*, Robert Silverberg's *New Dimensions* – and quickly became seeding-grounds for fresh New Wave talent. But the highest-profile of the lot, at least in terms of its keenness for controversy, was Harlan Ellison's *Dangerous Visions* (1967), often viewed as "the starting gun of the War of the New Wave in America" (Dozois 1983: 13).

Ellison has sometimes been cited as a competitor, with Merril, for the mantle of New Wave's chief sponsor, a nomination he has stoutly rejected (Ellison 1967). Yet he clearly capitalized on the energy generated by Moorcock's shake-up of *New Worlds* to mount his own assault on the "constricting narrowness of mind" of current SF writing and to trumpet a call for "new horizons, new forms, new styles, new challenges in the literature of our time" (Ellison 1967: xxiii, xix). As Merril pointed out in her review of the book, Ellison's taboo-smashing agenda had more to do with the promotion of controversial content – explicit sex, extreme violence, unapologetic atheism – than with genuine stylistic experiment (though Philip José Farmer's contribution involved a delirious extended riff on late Joyce). While praising some of the stories, Merril complained about Ellison's constant editorial posturing and his substitution of "shock for insight" (Merril 1967b: 33) – a negative judgment generally shared by the *New Worlds* crowd. Brian Aldiss has referred to the "thunderstorm of mock controversy" surrounding the book, "like shocking your maiden aunt with ribald limericks" rather than truly "reshaping the materials and attitudes of the genre" as Moorcock's magazine had (Aldiss 1986: 297–8).

Whatever one may think of these verdicts, the publication and reception of *Dangerous Visions* proved two important points. First, it suggested that Moorcock's impudent methods, his eagerness to spur controversy in the name of transforming the field, were beginning to catch on in the USA, especially among aggressive authors such as Ellison who had always chafed under editorial constraints. Second, it showed that such a confrontational approach could, ironically, pay off handsomely: despite Ellison's often shrill indictment of the genre as blinkered and philistine, *Dangerous Visions* – along with its 1972 follow-up *Again, Dangerous Visions* – was showered with awards by SF authors and fans. Amid all the noise and smoke, the New Thing seemed to be winning.

A Cluster of Controversies

One way to grasp the contours of the New Wave in the USA, as the flap over *Dangerous Visions* suggests, is as a series of interlinked controversies, of varying size and duration, that consumed the field over the next decade. Unlike Great Britain, where *New Worlds* provided a high-profile hub for dissent, the American New Wave, as Merril acknowledged, was "less cohesive as a 'school' or 'movement'" but was, as a result, also "more widespread" (Merril 1967b: 28). SF's Old Guard was thus forced to fight the rebellion on a series of shifting and overlapping fronts.

One strategy the New Wave's enemies developed involved attacking any beachhead achieved by *New Worlds* in America, especially the insidious influence of Ballard on younger writers. In a notorious review published in *Galaxy* in December 1966, Algis Budrys laid into Thomas Disch's *The Genocides* (1965) as a pretentious mimicry of Ballardian models. A bleak disaster story, the novel chronicles the gradual extermination of the human race by implacable aliens; it also, according to Budrys, copies Ballard's irrationalist fatalism in the face of world catastrophe. *The Genocides* reduces its characters to the status of "dumb, resigned victims" and thus constitutes an affront to the Campbellian tradition, to "the school of science fiction which takes hope in science and in Man." To his credit, Budrys went on to acknowledge that, although "unflaggingly derivative," the novel "demonstrates the vitality and strength" of the Ballardian mode "whether you like it or not" (Budrys 1985: 92). He also predicted more such efforts from young writers in the future, a sensible prophecy given how many fledgling American talents – Disch, Zelazny, Sallis, Norman Spinrad, John Sladek – had begun to establish strong personal and professional links with the *New Worlds* scene. Many of these authors found their true voices in Moorcock's pages; Disch, for example, has claimed that his 1968 novel *Camp Concentration* (serialized in *New Worlds*) would not have been half as artfully audacious absent the inspirational charisma of Moorcock, "the P.T. Barnum of the New Wave" (Disch 1998: 109).

Another writer who came under suspicion of Ballard's dissolute influence was Barry N. Malzberg, specifically for his 1972 novel *Beyond Apollo*. By this time, as Colin Greenland has pointed out, the antiheroic figure of the "Mad Astronaut," pioneered by Ballard, had become something of a New Wave cliché (Greenland 1983: 49). In Malzberg's scathing psychoanalytic treatment of the theme, a failed expedition to Mars comes to reveal, lurking beneath the space jockey's macho exterior, a confused welter of pathological ambition, paranoid self-doubt, and suppressed homosexuality. Obviously, such a depiction was calculated to vex SF's Old Guard, but what particularly infuriated them was that the novel was selected, by a panel of academics and authors, to receive an award named in memory of John W. Campbell, who had died in 1971. In October 1973, Poul Anderson wrote a letter of protest to *Analog* magazine (formerly edited by Campbell) in which he lambasted the award committee for honoring a book so "gloomy, involuted, and technophobic," qualities Campbell would never have tolerated in the fiction he published (Anderson 1973). *Analog's* new editor, Ben

Bova, would in later years be forced to defend his own Campbellian credentials when the magazine's readers, likely fearful of New Wave contagion, began complaining about the sexual explicitness of some of the stories he chose to run.

The growing acceptance of such "offensive" content, which would have been anathema in the magazine culture of the 1950s and early 1960s, was another area of concern for SF's Old Guard, who saw it as the fallout of New Wave amorality. The cultural politics of the New Wave was, as noted above, strongly shaped by the experimental ethos of contemporary youth; as Disch has testified, Ballard's "Inner Space" catchphrase was widely perceived, by both partisans and opponents of the New Wave, as "shorthand for sex, drugs, and rock 'n' roll" (Disch 1998: 108). Controversies swirled around a number of New Wave texts that pushed the boundaries in their exploration of erotic and psychedelic futures – what Aldiss has famously labeled "lifestyle SF" (Aldiss 1986: 290–1). Spinrad's sprawling *New Worlds* serial *Bug Jack Barron* (1969) was frequently cited as evidence of what Lester Del Rey disgustedly called the "rash of sex in science fiction, along with [the] 'daring' use of four-letter words" (Del Rey 1979: 260). The novel, a satirical take on (among other things) the sexual ethics of corporate media culture, almost cost *New Worlds* an Arts Council grant when its racy prose drew the scandalized attention of a Member of Parliament; it definitely cost Moorcock his chief British distributor, who refused to carry the offensive issues, delivering an economic blow to the magazine from which it never quite recovered (Moorcock 1979).

Representations of drug use also featured in New Wave fiction, perhaps nowhere more brilliantly than in Aldiss' "Acid Head Wars," a series of stories (published in *New Worlds* and later gathered as *Barefoot in the Head* [1969]) set in a near-future Europe pixilated by bombardments of weaponized hallucinogens. Treatments of the topic by New Wave authors were not always sympathetic: Ellison's "Shattered Like a Glass Goblin," published in Knight's *Orbit* series in 1968, depicts a scarifying descent into addiction, while Philip Dick's "Faith of Our Fathers" (in *Dangerous Visions*) contains the chilling drug-induced revelation of a cannibal god who feeds on human agony. Still, the Old Guard continued to mutter about "the overthrow of all standards and morals" that had seemingly afflicted the genre (Wollheim 1971: 104), brought on in part, no doubt, by *New Worlds'* persistent invocations of that notorious literary junkie, William Burroughs.

Probably the most pointed confrontation between Old Guard and New Wave occurred in the pages of *Galaxy* in June 1968 when competing ads appeared, signed by major SF authors and editors, supporting and opposing the war in Vietnam. Because of the presence of Golden Age doves like Sturgeon and Asimov on the antiwar list, the correlation of political stance with generational affiliation is not quite exact; the prowar list, however, contains only one figure clearly linked with the New Wave – R.A. Lafferty. Sociologist William Bainbridge has argued that the New Wave was always "noticeably on the left," associated "with liberal political views, in contrast with the conservatism" of Campbellian hard SF (Bainbridge 1986: 109–10). Throughout the Vietnam conflict, New Wave writers, on both sides of the Atlantic, produced a number of significant stories criticizing contemporary militarism and the neo-imperialist agenda of US foreign policy, a trend that reached its peak in Joe Haldeman's *The Forever War* (1975). Written expressly to contest the jingoistic xenophobia of Heinlein's *Starship Troopers* (1960), Haldeman's powerful novel swept the major awards bestowed by the genre – a testament to how successful the New Wave's ideological platform had been.

Backlash and Assimilation

Despite these successes, the legacy of the New Wave, according to Gardner Dozois, remains inconclusive. By the mid-1970s, it was fairly clear that the battle was over, but "neither side could claim a clearcut or unambiguous victory: both Young Turks and Old Pros were still around, neither had been driven from the marketplace" (Dozois 1983: 14). This is, in fact, not quite true: some writers did disappear, most obviously Ballard, who was elevated into the mainstream as a major surrealist in the wake of his 1973 novels *Crash* and *Concrete Island*. In later years, Moorcock too became a literary novelist, and some of the key authors of the American New Wave, such as Le Guin and Delany, were canonized by academic critics. In a way, these various escapes from the field achieved precisely what Merril had been seeking all along: the acceptance of speculative fiction as serious literature. Yet at the same time, the putative ghettoization of SF continued to be protested by a number of writers, such as Ellison and Robert Silverberg, who claimed to feel trapped by the genre. Silverberg, an older author who had, like Aldiss and Brunner in the UK, used the New Wave as a vehicle to expand his own vision, became so convinced that SF readers "don't want literary quality, they want space adventure" that he angrily retired (Thompson 1975: 7).

He eventually returned, but his noisy departure signaled concerns among a number of New Wave figures that their bold experiments might have fallen on deaf ears. Disch in 1976 alleged that SF was no more than a branch of children's literature, dominated by wish fulfillment and power fantasy (Disch 1976); soon he had moved on to other sorts of writing. Delany continued to defend SF as an aesthetic enterprise, although he basically stopped producing it in the late 1970s, as did Malzberg and Russ. A new generation of authors and fans had entered the field, and an "interval of integration and bruised armistice" began (Broderick 2003: 58). Backlash against the New Wave could perhaps be perceived in the late-career bestsellers enjoyed during the 1970s and 1980s by Golden Age heroes like Heinlein and Asimov; but, though younger writers tended not to announce themselves quite so bravely as "artists" any longer, their work showed enough evidence of New Wave leanings, at least in terms of sexual frankness and social consciousness, to give the Old Guard pause.

As with so many rebellions, the New Wave was partially rejected and partially assimilated by the genre. Clearly, SF's repertoire of themes was powerfully expanded, its affective register enriched, its stylistic range boosted immeasurably; but it never became an avant-garde literature and those who felt it ought to do so were compelled to take their business elsewhere.

REFERENCES AND FURTHER READING

Aldiss, Brian W. with David Wingrove (1986) *Trillion Year Spree: The History of Science Fiction.* New York: Atheneum.

Anderson, Poul (1973) "Letter to the Editor." *Analog* 92, 167.

Ashley, Mike (2004) *Transformations: The History of the Science Fiction Magazine, Volume 2: 1950–1970.* Liverpool: Liverpool UP.

Bainbridge, William Sims (1986) *Dimensions of Science Fiction.* Cambridge, MA: Harvard UP.

Ballard, J.G. (1962) "Which Way to Inner Space?" *New Worlds* 118, 2–3, 116–18.

Benford, Gregory (1984) "In the Wave's Wake." *Foundation: The International Review of Science Fiction* 30, 5–9.

Broderick, Damien (2003) "New Wave and Backwash: 1960–1980," in *The Cambridge Companion to Science Fiction*, (eds) Edward James and Farah Mendlesohn. Cambridge: Cambridge UP, 48–63.

Budrys, Algis (1985) *Benchmarks: Galaxy Bookshelf.* Carbondale: Southern Illinois UP. (Gathers reviews published in *Galaxy* magazine between 1965 and 1971.)

Cogswell, Theodore R. (1992) *PITFCS: Proceedings of the Institute for Twenty-First Century Studies.* Chicago, IL: Advent.

Cummins, Elizabeth (1995) "Judith Merril: A Link with the New Wave – Then and Now." *Extrapolation* 36:3, 198–209.

Del Rey, Lester (1979) *The World of Science Fiction, 1926–1976: The History of a Subculture.* New York: Ballantine.

Delany, Samuel R. (1980) "Reflections on Historical Models of Modern English Language Science Fiction." *Science Fiction Studies* 21, 135–49.

Disch, Thomas M. (1976) "The Embarrassments of Science Fiction," in *Science Fiction at Large*, (ed.) Peter Nicholls. New York: Harper & Row, 139–55.

——(1998) *The Dreams Our Stuff Is Made Of: How Science Fiction Conquered the World.* New York: Free Press.

Dozois, Gardner (1983) "Beyond the Golden Age – Part II: The New Wave Years." *Thrust – Science Fiction in Review* 19, 10–14.

Ellison, Harlan (1967) "Thirty-Two Soothsayers," in *Dangerous Visions*, (ed.) H. Ellison. Garden City, NY: Doubleday.

——(1974) "A Few (Hopefully Final) Words on 'The New Wave,'" in *Science Fiction: The Academic Awakening*, (ed.) Willis McNelly Shreveport, LA: College English Association, 40–3.

Greenland, Colin (1983) *The Entropy Exhibition: Michael Moorcock and the British "New Wave" in Science Fiction.* London: Routledge & Kegan Paul.

Grobman, Monika K. and Neil R. Grobman (1982) "Myth, Cultural Differences, and Conflicting Worldviews in New Wave Science Fiction." *Extrapolation* 23:4, 377–84.

MacLeod, Ken (2004) "Does Science Fiction Have to Be About the Present?" *New York Review of Science Fiction* 185, 14.

Merril, Judith (1962) "Summation: S-F, 1961," in 7th *Annual Edition The Year's Best S-F*, (ed.) Judith Merril. New York: Dell, 391–3.

——(1966a) "Books." *Fantasy and Science Fiction* 30:1, 39–45.

——(1966b) "Books." *Fantasy and Science Fiction* 31:2, 57–69.

——(1967a) "Books." *Fantasy and Science Fiction* 33:5, 28–36.

——(1967b) "Books." *Fantasy and Science Fiction* 33:6, 28–34.

——(1968) *England Swings SF: Stories of Speculative Fiction.* Garden City, NY: Doubleday.

——(1971) "What Do You Mean: Science? Fiction?" In *SF: The Other Side of Realism*, (ed.) Thomas D. Clareson. Bowling Green, OH: Bowling Green University Popular Press, 53–95. (Originally published in 1966 in *Extrapolation*.)

Moorcock, Michael (1963) "Play with Feeling." *New Worlds* 129, 2–3, 123–7.

——(1964) "A New Literature for the Space Age." *New Worlds* 142, 2–3.

——(1965) "Symbols for the Sixties." *New Worlds* 148, 2–3, 25.

——(1966a) "Onward, Ever Onward . . ." *New Worlds* 159, 2–5.

——(1966b) "Ballard: The Voice." *New Worlds* 167, 2–3, 151.

——(1979) *"New Worlds*: A Personal History." *Foundation: The International Review of Science Fiction* 15, 5–18.

——(1983) *New Worlds: An Anthology.* London: Flamingo.

Nicholls, Peter (1993) "New Wave," in *The Encyclopedia of Science Fiction*, (eds) Peter Nicholls and John Clute. New York: St. Martin's, 865–7.

Pierce, John J. (1989) *When World Views Collide: A Study in Imagination and Evolution.* Westport, CT: Greenwood.

Priest, Christopher (1978) "New Wave," in *Encyclopedia of Science Fiction*, (ed.) Robert Holdstock. London: Octopus, 162–73.

Spinrad, Norman (1990) *Science Fiction in the Real World.* Carbondale: Southern Illinois UP.

Taylor, John W. (1990) "From Pulpstyle to Innerspace: The Stylistics of New-Wave SF." *Style* 24:4, 611–27.

Thompson, Donald C. (1975) "Spec Fic and the Perry Rhodan Ghetto." *Science Fiction Review* 15, 6–10.

Walker, Paul (1978) *Speaking of Science Fiction: The Paul Walker Interviews.* Oradell, NJ: LUNA.

Wollheim, Donald A. (1971) *The Universe Makers: Science Fiction Today.* New York: Harper & Row.

14

Cyberpunk

Mark Bould

Reflections on "Cyberpunk"

The word "Cyberpunk" was coined by Bruce Bethke for the title of a story published in *Amazing* in 1983, but it came to prominence when Gardner Dozois appropriated it in his 1984 *Washington Post* article "SF in the Eighties" to describe fiction by William Gibson, Bruce Sterling, Lewis Shiner, Pat Cadigan, and Greg Bear. The self-identified core Cyberpunk group consisted of Gibson, Sterling, Shiner, John Shirley, and Rudy Rucker. They were also dubbed the Movement, the "mirrorshades group" and the "outlaw technologists"; their fiction was sometimes called radical hard SF. As "Cyberpunk" circulated more widely following the success of Gibson's debut novel *Neuromancer* (1984), it accreted fresh meanings and applications. To paraphrase Gibson's famous dictum about human relationships with technology, the street (and the culture industries) found its own uses for "Cyberpunk." It became an ever-expanding term for any slightly edgy artistic or cultural practice concerned with computers and/or the relationships between technology and the body, a synonym for "computer hacker," the name of a role-playing game and even the title of a Billy Idol album.

Although usually considered to refer to a movement, subgenre or an idiom, "Cyberpunk" was also an undeniably commercial label, attracting a lot of attention from readers, writers, journalists, critics, and marketing people. It spawned numerous derivative terms, including "cowpunk," which described a revitalized western fiction (and had already been applied to the music of the Meat Puppets, whose name Gibson borrowed to describe prostitutes with neural blocks); "elfpunk," which described post-Tolkien fantasy with attitude; and "ciderpunk," a variety of pub rock from England's West Country. The more significant derivatives were "steampunk," a kind of techno-logical fantasy set in Victorian Britain, exemplified by Tim Powers, James Blaylock, and K.W. Jeter as well as Gibson and Sterling's *The Difference Engine* (1990) and Rucker's *The Hollow Earth: The Narrative of Mason Algiers Reynolds of Virginia* (1990); "splatterpunk," extremely gory horror fiction written by Clive Barker, Joe Lansdale and sometimes Shirley; and "ribofunk," Paul Di Filippo's term for his own biotech-nology fictions. In the 1990s, "technogoth" was (perhaps jokingly) announced as a rival to Cyberpunk, although the fiction was undistinguished and indistinguishable, and "bad grrrl Cyberpunk," a term echoing riot grrrl punk, grouped together Cyber-punk by female writers, including Misha, Lisa Mason, and Melissa Scott – by which time, "sci-fiberpunk" was already circulating as a derogatory catch-all for poor Gibson imitations.

Bethke said that he intended to "invent a new term that grokked the juxtaposi-tion of punk attitudes and high technology" and so "took a handful of roots – cyber, techno, et al – mixed them up with a bunch of terms for socially misdirected youth, and tried out various combinations until one just plain sounded right" (Bethke). "Cyber" was taken from cybernetics (the Greek root of which means "to steer"), a term coined in 1948 by Norbert Wiener to describe a new science devoted to the study of communication and control systems in animals and machines. It was usually taken to signify the computer networks and cyborging technologies which constituted the essential furniture of Cyberpunk futures. Typical of Cyberpunk's vaguely countercul-tural and romantically antiauthoritarian politics, control was generally envisioned not in cybernetic's neutral descriptive sense but in terms of inherently repressive social structures and institutions, of the "mechanized control of social life, of the body itself" and "the hardening and exteriorization of certain vital forms of knowledge, the crys-tallization of the Cartesian spirit into material objects and commodities" (McCaffery 1991: 185–6). This was not inappropriate: the French "cybernetique" was coined in 1834 to describe the art of governance.

"Punk" came from punk rock, although earlier usages concerned with worthless-ness, marginality, youthfulness, hooliganism, criminality, and homosexual prostitu-tion resonated with Cyberpunk's socially excluded, often criminal, characters living in the ruins and in the shadow of multinational capital. Punk can be seen as urban political disaffection expressed through incoherent outbursts against accepted author-ity, whether musical, social, or political. It has been interpreted as a stylization of revolt, a perspective that has in turn resulted in a frequently naïve celebration of inci-dents of resistance as an alternative to revolutionary praxis. Sterling suggested that Cyberpunk was returning SF to its roots, divesting all its excrescences and accretions just as punk "stripped rock and roll of the symphonic elegances of Seventies 'pro-gressive' rock" (Sterling 1988: viii).

Whether or not Sterling's comparison holds, Cyberpunk did celebrate punk's DIY aesthetics. Shirley was a member of various punk bands, including The Panther Moderns. Sterling, under the pseudonym Vincent Omniaveritas, produced and circu-lated the 'zine *Cheap Truth* (1983–6), in which he launched frequently *ad hominem* attacks on the state of current SF and formulated the manifesto for a revolution in the genre; Shiner contributed pseudonymously as Sue Denim. Rucker used information theory to define both punk and Cyberpunk in terms of their complexity and logical depth before describing a bricoleur's "Garage Music notion of SF," in which he would "start with some fairly standard SF notions – robots, weird drugs, space colonies –

and . . . then think and think about these notions until the final product is very highly exfoliated" and "keep going back to the beat old clichés, back to the robots and the braineaters and the starships, and . . . reinvent the field from that, by thinking harder and harder about what it can do" (Rucker 1991: 462). Sterling's "Green Days in Brunei" (1985) and Shiner's *Slam* (1990) celebrate the opportunities that First World garbage provides for the bricoleur. Gibson repeatedly depicted forms of bricolage: *Neuromancer* refers to dub music, Cornell boxes have an important role in *Count Zero* (1986), and the performance artist Mark Pauline of Survival Research Laboratories appears thinly disguised as Rubin in "The Winter Market" (1986) and as Slick Henry in *Mona Lisa Overdrive* (1988). And Gibson's fiction is that of a bricoleur. In *The Difference Engine*, "[v]irtually all of the interior descriptions, the descriptions of furnishings, are simply descriptive sections lifted from Victorian literature" and "sort of air-brushed . . . with the word-processor" (Fischlin 1992: 9), while *Neuromancer*'s traces of Dashiell Hammett, Raymond Chandler, Nelson Algren, J.G. Ballard, William Burroughs, Robert Stone, Howard Hawks, and John Carpenter are suggestive of postmodernism's "random cannibalization of all the styles of the past, the play of random stylistic allusion" (Jameson 1991: 18). Moreover, *Neuromancer*'s Molly is clearly cobbled together out of Wolverine and Cyclops from Marvel Comics' *X-Men* as well as many of the strong and sexy women with a taste for S&M fetishism found in popular culture, including SF characters in Fritz Leiber's "Coming Attraction" (1950), *The Avengers* (1961–9), Eleanor Arnason's "The Warlord of Saturn's Moon" (1974), and Joanna Russ's *The Female Man* (1975).

Bethke's coinage of "Cyberpunk" itself depended upon a mechanistic form of bricolage. He recombined word-fragments to produce a new word which was sufficiently different from existing words to be distinguishable yet, in uniting unanticipated paradigms (cybernetics and rock), sufficiently familiar to be comprehensible. While Bethke's "until one just sounded right" appears to be a human decision alone, it was dependent upon pre-existing linguistic systems and cultural codes for its construction and acceptance. Lacking the more comprehensively randomizing element of William Burroughs's cut-up method of prose collage, Bethke's coining technique is arguably typical of Cyberpunk. Despite resemblances to Burroughsian collage, Cyberpunk was always concerned with "sounding right"; with reconciling such techniques with the demands of conventional narrative; with disciplining, controlling and incorporating these punkish outbursts; with "airbrushing" over the cracks.

Major Authors and Texts

At the centre of Cyberpunk, both as it developed and in retrospect, is the fiction of William Gibson. He was born in 1948 and emigrated to Canada in 1968. His first story, "Fragments of a Hologram Rose," was published in *Unearth* in 1977; another early story, "Hippie Hat Brain Parasite," was published in *Modern Stories*, a semi-prozine edited by Shiner. Gibson's early stories, most of which are collected in *Burning*

Chrome (1986), hothoused key Cyberpunk images and ideas as well as his distinctive prose style. "The Gernsback Continuum" (1981) reduces politics to style and replaces critique with semiotic analysis, mingling modernist architecture and moderne stylization with cable TV and porn movies so as to depict an America composed of the ruins of previous Utopian dreams, suggesting that at least our contemporary dystopia avoids the totalitarianism implied in H.G. Wells' Utopias and Frank R Paul's illustrations. Two other stories sketched the future Gibson would develop in *Neuromancer* and its sequels. "Johnny Mnemonic" (1981) – Gibson later wrote the screenplay for Robert Longo's 1995 film adaptation – offers a memorable analysis of street tough style, and introduces Molly Millions, a street-samurai with retractable scalpel blades beneath her fingernails and surgically implanted mirrorshades. "Burning Chrome" (1982) introduces Gibson's vision of cyberspace as a virtual realm of abstract geometries, colors, and shapes in which criminals avoid ICE – Intrusion Countermeasures Electronics – while raiding corporate databases. The melancholy of its final paragraph would recur at the conclusion of *Neuromancer*.

From its opening sentence, in which Gibson compares the sky with the color of a dead TV channel, *Neuromancer* marked the emergence of a major new voice, confidently launching the reader into a near-future world in which the natural and the authentic have become meaningless categories. But it was not a modernist vision of efficient machines for living in, as in Aldous Huxley's *Brave New World* (1932), *Things to Come* (Menzies 1936), or *THX 1138* (Lucas 1971). Rather, Gibson's imagined future of ubiquitous digital communication and media technologies, artificial intelligences, biotechnological body-modifications, and copies without originals owed more to shabby dystopias – like those in George Orwell's *Nineteen Eighty-Four* (1949), *Alphaville* (Godard 1965), and the fiction of Philip K. Dick and William Burroughs – in which marginalized characters make lives in the detritus and try to avoid institutions of social control. As in *Escape from New York* (Carpenter 1981) and *Blade Runner* (Scott 1982), some kind of apocalypse involving social and ecological systems seems to have already happened, and governments and states have become irrelevant. Despite being partly set in the USA, the *Neuromancer* trilogy does not mention it by name.

Neuromancer inaugurated the SF of multinational capital and corporate globalization, its depiction of information circulating in cyberspace a potent metaphor for the global circulation of capital. Bearing traces of American anxieties about the rapid growth of the Pacific Rim economies in its Japanese iconography of yakuza and sararimen, Kirin beer and pachinko parlors, *Neuromancer* postulates a world in which power resides with corporations and the key role of any nation lies in the cachet its name can lend to commodities: Russian prosthetics and Chinese nerve splices are notoriously shoddy, but Brazilian dexedrine, Japanese hypnotics, Mexican silver, German steel, Italian suits, and French fatigues are valued, as much for what they signify as what they do. One of Gibson's key innovations was to introduce a new kind of specificity to SF. His descriptions of artifacts recognize that technology takes the form of specifically designed commodities, made by corporations and identified by logos: his is a world of Braun coffeemakers and Sony monitors, a world in which one does not switch on a computer but jacks into an Ono-Sendai Cyberspace 7. This fascination with commodities and mediated images recalls Ballard; their rapid obsolescence and decay, Dick.

Neuromancer is also Gibson's most robustly plotted novel, a crime caper drawing together a group of misfits into shifting, temporary, and uneasy alliances as they pursue their own agendas and an ambiguous goal – the potential liberation and merging of two artificial intelligences, one of which has been manipulating them all along. Gibson builds in numerous cliff-hangers as short sections of text alternate between multiple characters, propelling the reader through a disorientating world which the narrator does not always explain. Neologisms and other unfamiliar linguistic fragments and conceits abound.

Neuromancer was followed by two loosely related sequels, *Count Zero* (1986) and *Mona Lisa Overdrive* (1988), in which the world became more familiar as the narratives grew more attenuated. Molly is made over into a respectable – and maternal – businesswoman while the consequences and implications of *Neuromancer*'s denouement fade in significance. After *The Difference Engine*, Gibson wrote another loose trilogy of thinly plotted novels – *Virtual Light* (1993), *Idoru* (1996), and *All Tomorrow's Parties* (1999) – set in a Cyberpunk future which more closely resembles our own world. This blurring of imagined future and present day is taken a step further in *Pattern Recognition* (2003), an SF novel about a marketing consultant with an unusual sensitivity to logos (and thus an insight as to their likely success) set in the present day. Gibson has retained the eye for the specificity of objects and the ear for the language of commodities and the poetry of idiolects which made his early fiction so distinctive.

Bruce Sterling was born in 1954. His first story, "Man-Made Self," was published in the anthology *Lone Star Universe* (1976). His first novel, the planetary romance *Involution Ocean* (1978), barely hinted at what would follow. Although his next novel, *The Artificial Kid* (1980), also ultimately resolves into a planetary romance, it was – as its almost-synonymic title suggests – well on the way to being Cyberpunk. It opens with a sequence describing a camera viewpoint as it zooms in from orbit above the planet Reverie to focus on the island city of Telset, on "a single block, a single street, a single person, me, and my own image swells to fill the screen" (Sterling 1985: 1). The eponymous narrator is a combat artist, and this is the title sequence for each of his tapes. A style-obsessed and media-savvy celebrity street-fighter, the Kid is chemically fixed in prepubescence, and never goes anywhere without his cameras circling around, filming him. However, unknown to him, the Kid is a new personality occupying the brainwiped body of an ousted politician. He is accompanied through his adventures by a multisexual combat artist, the resurrected founder of Reverie and a celibate with an unrequited passion for the brainwiped politician. Such Cyberpunk staples as exotic pharmaceuticals, semi-sentient technologies, body-modifications, stylized violence, fashion, glamour, media-awareness, mediated images, an ambivalence towards transcendence, and incomprehension in the face of politics are all on display.

Sterling's major contribution to Cyberpunk fiction is *Schismatrix* (1985) and the five associated "Shaper/Mechanist" stories collected in *Crystal Express* (1989). Rather than the near-future cislunar setting of *Neuromancer*, Sterling postulates a future history of expansion across the solar system as two posthuman factions – the Shapers, who utilize bioengineering, and the Mechanists, who utilize prosthetics to reshape themselves to their new environments and desires – compete for supremacy; his most obvious model was John Varley's *The Ophiuchi Hotline* (1977) and related "Eight Worlds" stories. Computers are largely absent from *Schismatrix*, and instead there is a focus on the physical transformation of humans into multiple daughter species or "clades," a term derived from Ilya Prigogine's nonlinear dynamics or chaos theory. The Shaper/Mechanist conflict can be seen as an unwitting Cold War allegory (by attempting to avoid such parallels, Sterling rejects the stereotypical Manichaean image of nations divided by irreconcilably different social systems and ideologies). *Schismatrix* treats capitalist economics as being as immutable as the laws of physics, and the Shaper/Mechanist conflict resolves into competing neoimperialist expansions concealed behind an apparent politics of life-style choices and the micromanagement of the self. As with *Neuromancer*, almost anything about human existence can be transformed except for a contingent economic system, but unlike Gibson, Sterling does not find this cause for despair. Rather, he projected the myth of guaranteed individual diversity within an unchanged economic system – which became a central plank of 1990s "Third Way" politics – centuries into the future several years before Francis Fukuyama argued that *soi-disant* liberal democracy and free markets constituted the end of history.

Cyberpunk was sometimes criticized for the superficiality of the futures it depicted, as if fascination with surfaces ruled out substance. Sterling's *Islands in the Net* (1988) was perceived as a revisionary text concerned with trying to extrapolate – in a manner reminiscent of John Brunner's *Stand on Zanzibar* (1968), *The Sheep Look Up* (1972), and *The Shockwave Rider* (1975) – a Gibson-esque future from the present moment. Both *Islands in the Net* and *Holy Fire* (1996) pay greater attention to the operations of power in the global economic-electronic order. That Sterling's *Heavy Weather* (1994) and *Distraction* (1999) appear rather conventional is testimony to the rapidity with which Cyberpunk was normalized, co-opted, absorbed. That *Zeitgeist* (2000) and the short stories in *Globalhead* (1992) and *A Good Old-Fashioned Future* (1999) retain some of the freshness of the original burst of Cyberpunk is testimony to Sterling's global sensibility constantly finding that Earth is the alien planet.

Sterling's importance to Cyberpunk goes far beyond his fiction. If Gibson was Cyberpunk's stylist, Sterling was its propagandist, announcing its arrival and declaring its demise. The most significant piece he wrote in this respect is the preface to *Mirrorshades: The Cyberpunk Anthology* (1986), which he also edited. Conscious of the furore in SF circles produced by Cyberpunk rhetoric about overthrowing outmoded SF forms and replacing a geriatric Old Guard, the preface announced the revolutionary newness of Cyberpunk while simultaneously situating it in "the sixty-year tradition of modern popular SF" (Sterling 1988: viii), and allied it with both the New Wave and hard SF while finding precursors in both visionary SF and the mainstream: Harlan Ellison, Samuel Delany, Norman Spinrad, Michael Moorcock, Brian Aldiss,

Ballard, Olaf Stapledon, H.G. Wells, Larry Niven, Poul Anderson, Robert Heinlein, Philip José Farmer, Varley, Dick, Alfred Bester, and Thomas Pynchon all rub shoulders in Sterling's prestigious Cyberpunk lineage (he made up for the omission of Jules Verne by recasting him as a kind of punk rebel in a 1987 *Science Fiction Eye* column). What is significant about this list is not its transparent attempt to reassure readers that Cyberpunk was a natural development of SF bringing together what was best or most important from all previous types of SF, but the omission of female writers. In the retrenching 1980s, Sterling voiced a peculiarly male conception of what constituted SF. Intentionally or not, he distanced the media-obsessed Cyberpunk from a media SF which was more commonly associated with female audiences and female fandom, while also denying the more truly radical and overtly political feminist SF of the 1960s and 1970s, certain examples of which – James Tiptree's "The Girl who was Plugged In" (1973), Joanna Russ's *The Female Man* (1975), Marge Piercy's *Woman on the Edge of Time* (1976) – have good claim to predecessor status. Sterling also situated Cyberpunk at the centre of 1980s pop culture, along with rock video, the hacker underground, hip-hop, scratch music, and synthesizer rock – a list which sounded dated even then. After all, 1986 was also the year in which *Cheap Truth* declared that the revolution was over. Sterling's preface was also a eulogy.

The short life-span of Cyberpunk is best illustrated by Lewis Shiner. Born in 1950, he published his first story, "Tinker's Damn," in *Galileo* in 1977. His first and only ineluctably Cyberpunk novel was *Frontera* (1984). Following near-future apocalyptic convulsions, Earth's social and economic order has been restructured, ceding power and influence to corporations, one of which – Pulsystems – sends a mission to Mars to seize technologies developed by an abandoned colony. This is not the Mars of planetary romance or hard SF: protagonist Kane had "expected something that looked like the future, and what he saw reminded him of a shopping mall in decay: cramped, faded, lived-in" (Shiner 1985: 90). Unaware of the mission's true goal, Kane – in a neat piece of self-reflexive anxiety – has been fitted with a brain implant that forces him to act like a hero as codified by Joseph Campbell. Anticipating Gibson, Shiner then turned to fiction set in the present. Sharing Sterling's global sensibility, *Deserted Cities of the Heart* (1988) is a fantasy with magic realist aspirations (and some SF props) set in a contemporary, or perhaps parallel, Mexico being torn apart by US imperialism and indigenous revolution. *Slam* (1990) records life on the margins in Texas, replacing the cod-transcendence of cyberspace with the exhilaration of skateboarding and urging the reader to learn to skate the future. Whereas the *Neuromancer* trilogy tends to depict the marginalized as being capable only of short-term, *ad hoc*, goal-specific collectivism and being limited to theft and bricolage as means of unprogrammatic resistance, *Slam* proposes developing this into a kind of anarchist-libertarian praxis. *Glimpses* (1995) and *Say Goodbye: The Laurie Moss Story* (1999) pay tribute, respectively, to pre-punk and post-punk rock, the former allegiance evident in the title of the antiwar anthology Shiner edited, *When the Music's Over* (1991). Some of his short fiction is collected in *Nine Hard Questions about the Nature of the Universe* (1990) and *The Edges of Things* (1991).

John Shirley was born in 1954. His first story, "The Word 'Random,' Deliberately Repeated" appeared in the anthology *Clarion* (1973). His earliest novels are either surrealist SF – *Transmaniacon* (1979), *Three-Ring Psychus* (1980) – or horror – *Dracula in Love* (1979), *The Brigade* (1982), *Cellars* (1982) – or sharecropped survivalist fiction – between 1984 and 1987 he wrote up to ten novels in the *Traveler* series as by D.B. Drumm. Of his early novels, *City Come A-Walkin'* (1980) is the most significant. Its grim and violent vision of urban life and its plot anticipate *Neuromancer*, albeit with a supernatural manifestation of the city playing the part Cyberpunk would give to an AI. In addition to several short stories, including "Sleepwalkers" (1988), and "Wolves of the Plateau" (1988), and his punk rock credentials, Shirley's major contribution to Cyberpunk was his *A Song Called Youth* trilogy. *Eclipse* (1985), *Eclipse Penumbra* (1988), and *Eclipse Corona* (1990) depict a world in upheaval following a third world war. Thriving on the chaos, the neofascist Second Alliance strives for global supremacy. The only coordinated opposition coming from the ragtag but technologically savvy New Resistance. Ambitious in scope, and replete with such Cyberpunk staples as media-manipulation, invasive technologies, drugs, and fashion, the trilogy often falls back into the rough-edged hackwork of his sharecropped novels and lacks the hallucinatory intensity and visceral imagery of his best writing. Although it is not free from Cyberpunk's political naïveté, the trilogy nonetheless clearly demonstrates a troubled awareness of the rise of the new right and its obeisance to multinational capital and corporate power. Whether SF or horror, his later novels – *A Splendid Chaos: An Interplanetary Fantasy* (1988), *In Darkness Waiting* (1988), *Wetbones: A Novel* (1992), *Silicon Embrace* (1996) – display a sense of impatience, both with genre divisions and with writing. He remains a better short story writer than novelist, but in his collections – *Heatseeker* (1988), *New Noir* (1993), *The Exploded Heart* (1996), *Black Butterflies: A Flock on the Dark Side* (1998), and *Really, Really, Really, Really, Weird Stories* (1999) – a growing conservatism can be discerned.

Rudy Rucker was born in 1946. "Faraway Eyes," his first short story, appeared in *Analog* in 1980. Much of his short fiction – the most comprehensive collection is *Gnarl* (2000) – and most of his novels – including *White Light, or What is Cantor's Continuum Problem?* (1980), *Space-Time Donuts* (1981), *The Sex Sphere* (1983), *Master of Space and Time* (1984), *The Secret of Life* (1985), and *The Hacker and the Ants* (1995) – are exuberant semi-autobiographical comedies concerned with mathematics and/or computers, written under the influence of Edwin Abbott, Lewis Carroll, and Robert Sheckley. Consequently, if Cyberpunk is something more than just five writers from the same generation who emerged at the same time and became friends and collaborators, then Rucker is the most difficult of the initial group to think of as being a Cyberpunk. The "bopper" novels – *Software* (1982), *Wetware* (1988), *Freeware* (1997), and *Realware* (2000) – incorporate a number of Cyberpunk tropes, including sentient machines, downloaded personalities, drugs, biotechnology, genetic engineering, cyborgs, and attempts at technologically achieved transcendence, into the familiar Rucker blend, albeit with a future setting. Rucker calls his robots "boppers" and sets some of the action in the lunar crater Maskelyne; *Gravity's Rainbow* refers to robobopsters and the same crater. But despite foregrounding Pynchon as an influence, the novels are still rather closer to Dick's *ad hoc* philosophical slapstick than to Pynchon or, indeed, to the Cyberpunk of Gibson or Sterling. As with the other Cyberpunks, the music to which Rucker pays tribute is from a pre-punk generation, arguing that if you were a hippie "for the right reasons – a hatred of conformity and a desire to break through to higher realities" (Rucker 1991: 459) then you would also like punk. However, he is the oldest of the Cyberpunks and his fiction has always seemed to be from a slightly older generation, not least in its preference for cannabis and marijuana over heroin and speed and its enthusiasm for transcendent experiences about which the other Cyberpunks – especially the youngest, Shirley – are rather more ambivalent.

Pre-Cyberpunk, Fellow-Travelers, Post-Cyberpunk

Early commentators often evoked Cyberpunk precursors. Missing from those named above are Bernard Wolfe's cybernetic dystopia *Limbo* (1952); Frederik Pohl and Cyril Kornbluth's *The Space Merchants* (1953) and *Wolfbane* (1957); Anthony Burgess's yob dystopia *A Clockwork Orange* (1962); John Sladek's *The Müller-Fokker Effect* (1970), a metafiction about a downloaded personality, dehumanization, and the nature of narrative; Mick Farren's protopunk SF; Alvin Toffler's futurological speculations; and Gregory Benford's "Doing Lennon" (1975), Algis Budrys's *Michaelmas* (1977), and Vernor Vinge's "True Names" (1981), all of which preempted much of Cyberpunk's furniture but demonstrated little of its style or attitude. *Rollerball* (Jewison 1975) envisioned a future dominated by corporations and, like *Death Race 2000* (Bartel 1975), a population media-narcotized by spectacular violence. Grim futures of perpetual Thatcherism and social breakdown dominated the British comic *2000AD* from its inception in 1977; this was echoed in *Brazil* (Gilliam 1985) and in *Max Headroom* (Morton and Jankel 1985), which transformed into something more Cyberpunk-ish with *The Max Headroom Show* (1987). *Alien* (Scott 1979) anticipated Cyberpunk's capitalist future and its fascination with physical transformation. *Videodrome* (1983), the most accomplished of David Cronenberg's ironic interrogations of the visceral, featured shady corporations, global conspiracies, cyborging technologies, body-modifications, and mutilations produced by the media itself and a self-conscious narrative incoherence. It also provided the Cyberpunk mantra, "Long live the new flesh." *Tron* (Lisberger 1982) contained the first comprehensive attempt to imagine a computer's virtual dataspace. *Alphaville* successfully blended dystopian SF with *film noir*, as did *Blade Runner*, a movie from which Gibson is reputed to have fled because it too closely resembled the world he was imagining. Although it does not give computers the prominence they would receive in Cyberpunk fiction, *Blade Runner*'s fascination with corporations, posthuman life-forms, the fragmentation of society into identity-groups and, above all, the retrofitted architecture and accreted detritus of urban life renders it the most influential visual evocation of a Cyberpunk future. Other filmic precursors include *Westworld* (Crichton 1973), *Demon Seed* (Cammell 1977), and *Brainstorm* (Trumbull 1983) as well as the punkish "postfuturist SF" (Sobchack 1991) of *Born in Flames* (Borden 1983), *Liquid Sky* (Tsukerman 1983), *The Adventures of Buckaroo Banzai Across the Eighth Dimension* (Richter 1984), and *Repo Man* (Cox 1984).

Cyberpunk was related to a number of non-SF authors who demonstrated varieties of science-fictional sensibility. Joseph McElroy's dense and poetic *Plus* (1976) recounts the coming-to-awareness and rebellion of a dead engineer's brain which has been transplanted into an orbiting communications satellite. Ted Mooney's *Easy Travel to Other Planets* (1981) is a preapocalyptic tale about information sickness. Don DeLillo's *White Noise* (1985) powerfully evokes a world lost in simulations and simulacra, the desert of the real. William T. Vollmann's *You Bright and Risen Angels: A Cartoon* (1987) is an hallucinatory, improvised phantasmagoria about industrialization, sexual desire, and the war between the bugs and the inventors of electricity. Mark Leyner's *My Cousin, My Gastroenterologist* (1990) collects comic hyperreal fragments, patchworks of medical, scientific, and literary-critical discourses, allusions to popular culture and occasional hints of plot; on some level, each story is about the density of information and the speed at which it circulates in postmodernity. Kathy Acker's *Empire of the Senseless* (1988) incorporates passages from Gibson, while Marge Piercy's *He, She, and It* (aka *Body of Glass* 1991) is a more obviously feminist, if also rather conservative, revision of Cyberpunk's central tropes.

Other SF authors soon became associated with Cyberpunk, most immediately Pat Cadigan, whose "Rock On" (1984) and "Pretty Boy Crossover" (1986), collected in *Patterns* (1989), imagine computer-assisted cyborging developments in the popular music scene. Her first novel, *Mindplayers* (1987), reworks the central conceit – a psychotherapist entering patients' psychic landscapes – of Roger Zelazny's *The Dream Master* (1966). *Synners* (1991) was a more accomplished attempt to flesh out a Gibson-esque future, focusing on a group of hackers, video artists, and simulation creators as a virus is unleashed into the global computer network, threatening to bring it all to an end. The more economical *Fools* (1992) put questions of identity firmly at the centre of its headlong, disorientating narrative. *Tea from an Empty Cup* (1998) and its sequel *Dervish is Digital* (2000) are less substantial returns to a Cyberpunk milieu, but Cadigan's grasp of the economics of life online is nowhere more clearly stated. In Greg Bear's *Blood Music* (1985), a scientist transforms human DNA cells into computers, not anticipating that they will develop individual and collective consciousness. Accidentally unleashed, they restructure much of the planet's biomass into a single transcendent consciousness. The novel, which echoes Arthur C. Clarke's *Childhood's End* (1953) and John Sladek's *The Reproductive System* (1968), negotiates between more traditional hard SF and the emergent Cyberpunk imagery of networked artificial intelligences. More straightforwardly Cyberpunk-ish are Bear's *Queen of Angels* (1990), featuring a police procedural and the coming-to-consciousness of an AI in a world transformed by nanotechnology, and its sequel / (aka *Slant* (1997). K.W. Jeter's *Dr. Adder* (1984) anticipated Cyberpunk's blasted urban arenas and body-modification technologies; written in 1972 and long-championed by Dick, it went unpublished for over a decade and thus always seemed belated. His *Death Arms* (1987) and *Farewell Horizontal* (1989) are unexceptional, but *The Glass Hammer* (1985) successfully reworks *Death Race 2000* and Zelazny's *Damnation Alley* (1969) as a Cyberpunk exploration of mediation and transcendence incorporating Dick-ian concerns with epistemology, theology, and ontology. Jeter has also written three sequels to *Blade Runner* and Dick's *Do Androids Dream of Electric Sheep?* (1968), the most Dick-ian being *Blade Runner 3: Replicant Night* (1996).

Cyberpunk quickly attracted comic treatment. Marc Laidlaw's virtual reality comedy *Dad's Nuke* (1985) satirizes gated communities, Christian fundamentalism, the arms race, and other forms of conspicuous consumption. Richard Kadrey's *Metrophage* (1988) rewires Cyberpunk by returning to its hard-boiled roots in Hammett and Chandler; its black comedy teeters on the brink of parody. Kim Newman's *The Night Mayor* (1989) lays bare one part of Cyberpunk's ancestry, imagining a virtual dream-space constructed from *film noir* imagery. Other comic revisions include Thomas Pynchon's *Vineland* (1990), Bethke's *Headcrash* (1995), Neal Stephenson's *Snow Crash* (1992), *The Diamond Age; or, the Young Lady's Illustrated Primer* (1995), *Cryptonomicon* (1999), and Tricia Sullivan's *Maul* (2003).

Misha's *Red Spider White Web* (1990) intensifies Cyberpunk attention to detail into the kind of surreal density more typically found in comic books by Moebius, Howard Chaykin, Katsuhiro Ôtomo, or Warren Ellis, whereas George Alec Effinger's *When Gravity Fails* (1987) and its sequels were more conservative, relocating Cyberpunk to a not-so-near-future North Africa populated by more rounded characters. Jack Womack's *Ambient* (1987) and its prequels and sequels depict the collapse of the present into a nightmare future of urban disintegration and corporate domination; time-travel into that future's alternative pasts suggest that it is the best of all possible worlds. Jeff Noon's *Vurt* (1993) and *Pollen* (1995), set in south-central Manchester, reimagine virtuality in terms of reality-shuffling hallucinogens. By emphasizing physical sensation both within and without virtual environments, Lisa Mason's *Arachne* (1990) and Melissa Scott's *Trouble and Her Friends* (1994) foreground the embodiedness of the virtual subject that Gibson, or at least his characters, denied, while Candas Jane Dorsey's "(Learning About) Machine Sex" (1988) lambasts Cyberpunk's inherent phallocentrism. Gwyneth Jones's *Escape Plans* (1986), retooling an older anti-Utopian tradition, reminds the reader that posthumanity and other forms of technological transcendence will, like all commodities, be produced for the few by exploiting the many – a lesson reiterated in Jeter's grimly Gothic *Noir* (1998).

As the diversity of the above examples indicates, the ideas and imagery that Cyberpunk brought to the fore impacted upon SF with astonishing speed, producing much that was innovative and fresh as well as the merely imitative. Other writers, such as Michael Blumlein, Jonathan Lethem, Maureen F. McHugh, Lucius Shepard, and Michael Swanwick, had only a tangential relationship to Cyberpunk fiction but in some sense seemed to be enabled by it. The influence of Cyberpunk can be detected on a whole generation of British SF writers, including Neal Asher, Steve Aylett, Eric Brown, Richard Calder, Jon Courtenay Grimwood, Peter F. Hamilton, Simon Ings,

Gwyneth Jones, Roger Levy, Paul McAuley, Ken MacLeod, John Meaney, Richard Morgan, Alastair Reynolds, Justina Robson, Michael Marshall Smith, and Charles Stross. As the bloatedness of *Total Recall* (Verhoeven 1990), *Strange Days* (Bigelow 1995), the *Matrix* trilogy (Wachowski and Wachowski 1999, 2003, 2003) and the *RoboCop* and *Terminator* sequels attest, the Anglophone movies that most nearly approximate Cyberpunk tend to be either relatively low-budget or relatively independent productions, such as *The Terminator* (Cameron 1984), *RoboCop* (Verhoeven 1987), *Hardware* (Stanley 1990), *Wax, or the Discovery of Television Among the Bees* (Blair 1991; reissued as *Waxweb*, a hypermedia version (1999), *Cube* (Natali 1997), *New Rose Hotel* (Ferrara 1998), *Dark City* (Proyas 1998), *Pi* (Darren Aronofsky 1998), *Teenage Hooker Became Killing Machine in Daehakno* (Nam Gee-woong 2000), and *Cypher* (Natali 2003). The impact of Cyberpunk on non-Anglo-American SF is harder to judge, although in Japan a Cyberpunk imaginary quickly became evident in both *manga* and *anime*. Indeed, the nearest thing to an unequivocally Cyberpunk cinema comes from Japan, in *anime* like *Akira* (Ôtomo 1988), *Patlabor 2* (Oshii 1993), and *Ghost in the Shell* (Oshii 1995), and live-action movies like *Gunhed* (Masato Harada 1989), *Tetsuo: The Iron Man* (Tsukamoto 1989), *Tetsuo 2: Bodyhammer* (Tsukamoto 1991), *Tokyo Fist* (Tsukamoto 1996), *Avalon* (Oshii 2000), and *A Snake of June* (Tsukamoto 2002).

Critical Responses

The SF community greeted Cyberpunk with mixed feelings. George Turner and Gregory Benford mocked its pretensions to hard SF. In a pair of columns in *Isaac Asimov's Science Fiction Magazine* in 1986 and 1989, Norman Spinrad demonstrated considerable ambivalence, finding much that was familiar in Cyberpunk novels by Gibson, Shirley, Bear, Sterling, Rucker, and Shiner, and launching an attempt to rename the Cyberpunks as "the neuromantics" (presumably intended as an insult, punning on the New Romantic music which followed punk). In articles in *Asimov's* in 1986 and *Science Fiction Eye* in 1987, Michael Swanwick and John Kessel grouped themselves together with Connie Willis, Pat Murphy, James Patrick Kelly, and Kim Stanley Robinson as authors who could be seen to be building on a tradition of humanist SF writers – including Dick, Thomas Disch, Theodore Sturgeon, Ursula Le Guin, Walter Tevis, and Gene Wolfe – and to offer a humanist alternative to Cyberpunk.

If all this interest was only to be expected in the SF community, the academic response to Cyberpunk was unprecedented. *Science Fiction Studies* published its first article on *Blade Runner* in 1987, and its first article on *Neuromancer* in 1990; but between these two pieces the journal had also hosted an exchange between John Fekete, who offered a poststructuralist critique of Marxist representationalism, and Marc Angenot and Darko Suvin, who identified the politically debilitating nihilism of such a position. The tide, however, was with Fekete, as varieties of poststructuralism and postmodernism came to dominate cultural criticism – and *Science Fiction Studies* – throughout the 1990s. The new critical paradigms derived from the work of Jean Baudrillard on simulations and simulacra, Judith Butler on the performativity of identity, Guy Debord on the spectacle, Donna Haraway on cyborg subjectivity, Fredric Jameson on the cultural logic of late capitalism, Arthur Kroker on panic culture, and Jean-François Lyotard on the death of metanarratives seemed to share perspectives and concerns with Cyberpunk. (And the traffic went both ways – in 1990, Sterling wrote an essay on Baudrillard for *Monad*, and his contribution to Arthur and Marilouise Kroker's *Digital Delirium* [1997] precedes Baudrillard's; Tom Maddox's *Halo* [1991] focuses its Cyberpunk apparatus on the nature of artificial intelligence, but also quotes Baudrillard and Haraway.) It was this conjunction that led to the critical apotheosis of an SF subgenre.

Commentary on Cyberpunk was not restricted to SF journals like *Extrapolation* and *Foundation*. There were special issues of *Critique*, *The Mississippi Review*, and *The South Atlantic Quarterly* (see Dery 1994), as well as extended laudatory treatment in glossy magazines like *Omni* and *Wired*. Whereas the *Fiction 2000* conference (see Slusser and Csicsery-Ronay), cosponsored in 1989 by the University of Leeds and the University of California at Riverside, drew upon the SF academic community, the *Virtual Futures* conferences at the University of Warwick in the mid-1990s brought together a much wider variety of academics and practitioners but effectively ignored SF, reduced Cyberpunk to *Blade Runner* and *Neuromancer*, and subsumed it – along with techno, body-modification subcultures, various online communities, and experiments in virtuality, and performance artists like Orlan, Stelarc, and Survival Research Laboratories – into a broader cultural movement or moment or trend also sometimes called, confusingly, Cyberpunk (see Dixon and Cassidy).

The critical response to Cyberpunk fiction saw many exaggerated claims about its nature and significance. Allucquere Rosanne Stone divided the history of the Western world since the mid-1600s into four epochs, each initiated by a technologically generated "change in the character of human communication" (Stone 1991: 85), with *Neuromancer* marking the beginning of the fourth epoch, that of virtual reality and cyberspace. Timothy Leary argued that Gibson's fiction was proleptic not only of changes in the nature of communications and society but also in the nature of what it means to be human, claiming that *Neuromancer* was "nothing less than the underlying myth, the core legend, of the next stage of human evolution" (Kellner 1995: 298). Such hyperbole made Jameson's suggestion that Cyberpunk represents "the supreme *literary* expression if not of postmodernism, then of late capitalism itself" (Jameson 1991: 419) seem understated.

While George Slusser dubbed Cyberpunk "literary MTV" (McCaffery 1991: 334), Brian McHale treated it as emerging from feedback relationships between SF and a "postmodernist mainstream fiction which has already been 'science-fictionalized' to some degree" (McCaffery 1991: 315). Csicsery-Ronay, Jr. described Cyberpunk as "implosive" SF about hallucination and derangement which located "SF problematics not in imperial adventures among the stars, but in the body-physical/body-social and a drastic ambivalence about the body's traditional – and terrifyingly uncertain – integrity" (McCaffery 1991: 188). Veronica Hollinger contended that Cyberpunk's cyborging posthumanism "radically decenters the human body, the sacred icon of the essential self, in the same way that the virtual reality of cyberspace works to decenter conventional humanist notions of an unproblematic 'real'" (McCaffery 1991: 207). Joan Gordon found in Cyberpunk's "motif of the journey to the underworld" the possibility for a covert feminist SF to "acknowledge our full female identity" (McCaffery 1991: 200–1), whereas Nicola Nixon argued that Cyberpunk relegated SF's political potential "to a form of scary feminized software," creating "an alternative, attractive, but hallucinatory world which allows not only a reassertion of male mastery but a virtual celebration of a kind of primal masculinity" (Nixon 1992: 231).

A decade later, Carl Freedman excoriated Cyberpunk for its tedious cynicism, sentimentality, conservative reassurances, and nostalgia, its acceptance "of an ultracommodified global totality increasingly difficult to comprehend and increasingly resistant to the counter hegemonic projects of praxis" and its "banal, cringing surrender before the same actuality so lyrically celebrated by the apologists of capital" (Freedman 2000: 197, 198). In contrast, reviewing *Pattern Recognition*, Jameson noted a convergence between Gibson and "the 'Cyberpunk' with which he is often associated, but which seems more characteristically developed" in Sterling's "Hunter-Thompsonian global tourism" fiction (Jameson 2003: 105, 107). In Gibson and Sterling, "technological speculation and fantasy of the old Toffler sort takes second place to the more historically original literary vocation of a mapping of the new geopolitical imaginary," and together they constitute "a kind of laboratory experiment in which the geographical-cultural light spectrum and bandwidths of the new system are registered" (Jameson 2003: 107).

Between them, Freedman and Jameson demonstrate that there is still no consensus reply to the question Darko Suvin posed in 1991: "*is Cyberpunk the diagnostician of or the parasite on a disease?*" (McCaffery 1991: 364).

REFERENCES AND FURTHER READING

Bethke, Bruce Foreword to "Cyberpunk" at http:// www.users.zetnet.co.uk/iplus/stories/cpunk.htm

Butler, Andrew M. (2000) *Cyberpunk*. Harpenden: Pocket Essentials.

Critique Studies in Contemporary Fiction 33.iii (Spring 1992) Issue on Postmodern Science Fiction.

Dery, Mark (ed.) (1994) *Flame Wars: The Discourse of Cyberculture*. Durham, NC and London: Duke University Press.

——(1996) *Escape Velocity: Cyberculture at the End of the Century*. London: Hodder and Stoughton.

Dixon, Joan Broadhurst and Eric J. Cassidy (eds) (1998) *Virtual Futures: Cyberotics, Technology and Post-Human Pragmatism*. London and New York: Routledge.

Featherstone, Mike (ed.) (1995) *Cyberspace/ Cyberbodies/ Cyberpunk: Cultures of Technological Embodiment*. London: Sage.

Fischlin, Daniel (1992) "'The Charisma Leak': A Conversation with William Gibson and Bruce Sterling." *Science Fiction Studies* 56, 1–16.

Freedman, Carl (2000) *Critical Theory and Science Fiction*. Hanover: Wesleyan University Press/ University Press of New England.

Gray, Chris Hables (ed.) (1995) *The Cyborg Handbook*. London and New York: Routledge.

Hayles, N. Katherine (1999) *How We Became Post-Human*. Chicago and London: University of Chicago Press.

Heuser, Sabine (2003) *Virtual Geographies:*

Cyberpunk at the Intersection of the Postmodern and Science Fiction. Amsterdam and New York: Rodopi.

Jameson, Fredric (1991) *Postmodernism, or, The Cultural Logic of Late Capitalism.* London: Verso.

——(2003) "Fear and Loathing in Globalization." *New Left Review* 23, 105–14.

Kellner, Douglas (1995) *Media Culture: Cultural Studies, Identity and Politics between the Modern and the Postmodern.* London: Routledge.

Kraus, Elisabeth, and Carolin Auer (eds) (2000) *Simulacrum America: The USA and the Popular Media.* Rochester, NY and Woodbridge: Camden House.

Kraus, Elisabeth (2000) "Real Lives Complicate Matters in Schroedinger's World: Pat Cadigan's Alternative Cyberpunk Vision," in *Future Females, The Next Generation,* (ed.) Marleen S. Barr. Lanham, MD and Oxford: Rowan & Littlefield, 129–42.

McCaffery, Larry (ed.) (1991) *Storming the Reality Studio: A Casebook of Cyberpunk and Postmodern Science Fiction.* Durham, NC and London: Duke University Press, 334–42.

Minnesota Review (1994/5) Cyberpunk issue. 43/44.

Nixon, Nicola (1992) "Cyberpunk: Preparing the Ground for the Revolution or Keeping the Boys Satisfied?" *Science Fiction Studies* 57, 219–35.

Rucker, Rudy (1991) "What is Cyberpunk?" In *Transreal!* Englewood: WCS, 457–63.

Shiner, Lewis (1985) *Frontera* (1984). London: Sphere.

Shirley, John (1987) "Cyberpunk or Cyberjunk? Some Perspectives on Recent Trends in SF." *Science Fiction Eye* 1.i (Winter), 43–51.

Slusser, George and Istvan Csicsery-Ronay, Jr. (eds) (1992) *Fiction 2000: Cyberpunk and the Future of Narrative.* Athens, GA: University of Georgia Press.

Sobchack, Vivian (1991) *Screening Space: The American Science Fiction Film.* New York: Ungar.

Sterling, Bruce (1985) *The Artificial Kid.* Harmondsworth: Penguin.

——(ed.) (1988) *Mirrorshades: The Cyberpunk Anthology* (1986). London: Paladin.

——(1991) "Cyberpunk in the Nineties." *Interzone* 48 (June), 39–41.

Stone, A.R. (1991) "Will the Real Body Please Stand Up? Boundary Stories about Virtual Cultures," in *Cyberspace: First Steps,* (ed.) Michael Benedikt. Cambridge, MA: MIT Press, 81–118.

15

Science Fiction and Postmodernism

Veronica Hollinger

Recent scientific and technological breakthroughs demonstrate that the gap is being bridged between science fiction and science fact, between literary imagination and mind-boggling technoscientific realities.

There has been intense speculation and research concerning black holes, worm holes, parallel universes, ten-dimensional reality, time travel, teleportation, antigravity devices, the possibility of life on other planets, cryogenics, and immortality. Moon and Mars landings, genetic and tissue engineering, cloning, xenotransplantation, artificial birth technologies, animal head transplants, bionics, robotics, and eugenics now exist. At the same time, weighty questions are being raised about how many "realities" and "universes" might simultaneously exist, whether or not nature is "law-like" in its fundamental dynamics, and just how exact scientific knowledge can be. (Best and Kellner 2001: 103)

Science Fiction becomes Postmodern

In virtually every description of "the postmodern" developed in the past two decades, the increasingly pervasive influence of science and technology on human life has been cited as one of its constitutive features (Haraway 1989; Baudrillard 1991; Jameson 1991; Best and Kellner 2001). While, arguably, every corner of the global community is now subject to the slow but steady diffusion of technoscientific development, its immediate pressure is most apparent in contemporary Western hi-tech societies, where, for example, fraught ethical and ideological battles surround current research into reproductive technologies, biomedical engineering, artificial intelligence, communications technologies, and military control-and-command systems. The term "technoscience," used by science critics such as Bruno Latour and Donna Haraway, suggests that, in today's environment of transnational capitalism and globalized politics, the traditional distinctions between "pure" science and "applied" technology no longer hold. Knowledge is intertwined with power, and technoscience is a political and cultural practice, neither "objective" nor "value-neutral." This perceived collapse of the separation between science and technology is only one of many such "implosions" whose implications, taken together, constitute one broad understanding of the postmodern.

Given the inescapable impact of technoscience in our lives today – for both good and ill – it is not surprising that *science* fiction (SF) has increasingly become an object of attention for readers and scholars seeking to develop some adequate understanding – in Fredric Jameson's terms, seeking to develop some form of "global cognitive mapping" (Jameson 1991: 54) – of our radically complex present moment. As the epigraph by Best and Kellner suggests, developments in technoscience are rendering our lives more and more science fictional, and the case has often been made that the term "science fiction" now refers not only to a popular narrative genre, but also to an increasingly widespread mode of cultural description and analysis. Science fiction has become "an aspect of the quotidian consciousness of people living in the postindustrial world, daily witnesses to the transformations of their values and material conditions in the wake of technological acceleration beyond their conceptual threshold" (Csicsery-Ronay, Jr. 1991: 389; see also Benison 1992). This, arguably, is the postmodern condition of science fiction itself and it suggests intriguing questions about the on-going cultural function of this future-oriented narrative genre. (Some critics have concluded that the ultimate expression of the technological postmodern is to be found, not in print SF at all, but in the spectacular effects of science fiction film. See the discussions of film elsewhere in this collection.)

"Postmodern"

Like so many critical/theoretical concepts introduced into discursive circulation in the past several decades – for example, "subject," "queer," "postcolonial" – the meaning of "postmodern" has been and continues to be energetically contested. What sets "postmodern" apart, arguably, is that the very contested nature of all these terms and concepts can be understood as *symptomatic* of postmodernity itself; in other words, even those positions that deny any affiliation to "the postmodern" have been shaped *within* its overarching framework. Expressive as it is of a wide array of understandings about social, political, economic, and cultural relations, "postmodern" functions as a kind of umbrella term incorporating within itself the features of a fragmented and hybridized way-of-being in a world that is itself understood to be random, chaotic, and open to multiple and contradictory interpretations. "Postmodern" has been used to refer to – among other things – a particular sociocultural condition shaped by multinational capitalism (Lyotard 1984; Baudrillard 1991; Jameson 1991); a complex of hegemonic global technopolitics demanding resistance and opposition from the margins (Haraway 1989; Latour 1993; Best and Kellner 2001); a network of ironically self-reflexive aesthetic forms and themes (Hutcheon 1989; McHale 1992). Efforts

to pigeon-hole individual theories or texts too narrowly into any of these possible currents, however, always risk negating the complexities of their models, as well as the
complexities of "the postmodern condition" itself.

I agree with Jonathan Benison that "the *postmodern* as such . . . [is] a social condition marked by a shift in the reception of culture" (Benison 1992: 141). As *social condition*, "postmodern*ity*" or "the postmodern condition" is often read as a philosophical
and/or political break with, or swerve away from, the long project of Enlightenment
modernity, a project whose origins are historically associated with the eighteenth-
century rise of the sovereign subject of humanism in the context of political liberalism, secularism, and the triumph of scientific method (see Lyotard 1984). As *cultural
expression*, "postmodern*ism*" has been taken to refer to recent imaginative responses to
this historical shift, suggesting a wide variety of aesthetic, formal, and thematic experiments expressed in a broad range of cultural products, including architecture, dance
and music, painting and sculpture, and, of course, fiction.

Postmodern*ism* tends to be historically located on this side of the modernist cultural projects of the second half of the nineteenth century and the early decades of the
twentieth. In this particular historical understanding, postmodernism signals a broad-
based cultural shift that begins to occur sometime after the Second World War. For
Best and Kellner, for example, Thomas Pynchon's manic and magisterial novel,
Gravity's Rainbow (1973), set at the end of, and immediately after, the Second World
War, is exemplary of the turn toward textual representations of a postmodern condition marked by technological, political, and economic crisis on a global scale (Best
and Kellner 2001: 23–56). Not coincidentally, *Gravity's Rainbow* is considered to have
been a major influence on some of the first science fiction writers to be identified with
postmodernism, including Pat Cadigan, Walter Jon Williams, Lucius Shepard, Bruce
Sterling, and William Gibson (McHale 1992: 231–3).

Postmodernist Self-Reflexivity

The problematic prefix "post" should perhaps be understood less as indicating a radical
break with earlier (modern) systems and perspectives than as a critical problematiza-
tion of the foundational assumptions underlying those same systems and perspectives.
Put another way, the "postmodern condition" is an inherently self-conscious condition,
denoting a series of transformations in how we have come to perceive and define aspects
of contemporary reality. This in part explains the self-reflexive nature of so many postmodernist texts: whatever else these texts are "about," they are also about themselves
as narrative texts. As a genre, science fiction is not much given to this kind of self-
reflexivity; that is, it is rarely openly "metafictional." But as soon as a genre has been
around long enough to have developed identifiable tropes and conventions, it becomes
a suitable target for this kind of playful and/or critical reassessment.

One early examination of SF "in the postmodern era" argues that "postmodern SF
writers are parodists, playing with and within the genre they have chosen to cham-

pion, self-consciously questioning the rules that their forerunners simply accepted without thinking, . . . creat[ing] works *of* science fiction that are also *about* science fiction" (Everman 1986: 25). Among the texts discussed in this early analysis are several examples from the New Wave of the late 1960s and 1970s, a writerly "movement" devoted, in part, to the development of science fiction's literary potential. These include Samuel R. Delany's *The Einstein Intersection* (1967), whose narrative is interspersed with excerpts from the journal that Delany kept while writing *The Einstein Intersection*; Philip José Farmer's intertextual "Riders of the Purple Wage" (1969), whose title refers to Zane Grey's classic Western, *Riders of the Purple Sage* (1912), while its story parodies James Joyce's classic modernist novel, *Finnegans Wake* (1939); and Norman Spinrad's *The Iron Dream* (1972), which presents readers with a violent and pulpish science fiction novel, *Lord of the Swastika*, penned by a little-known author named Adolf Hitler in an alternative time-stream in which the Second World War never took place.

To turn to a more recent example of science fiction self-reflexivity, consider John Kessel's time-travel story, "Invaders" (1991), which is structured around a series of juxtaposed temporal sites. In 1532, Pizzaro and his priests and soldiers have invaded Peru and will soon complete the destruction of the Inca empire; in 2001, apparently friendly and funny aliens, the Krel – a name Kessel lifts from the classic 1950s film, *Forbidden Planet* – arrive in the middle of a Washington Redskins' football game; in a third time-stream, "Today," a science fiction writer, whose description exactly matches that of the "real" John Kessel, sits at his desk writing the story we read. In a key fragment set in "Today," the writer contemplates the act of reading – and writing – science fiction:

> It's not just physical laws that science fiction readers want to escape. Just as commonly, they want to escape human nature. In pursuit of this, SF offers comforting alternatives to the real world. . . .
>
> Like any drug addict, the SF reader finds desperate justifications for his habit. SF teaches him science. SF helps him avoid "future shock." SF changes the world for the better. Right. So does cocaine. . . .
>
> [But] I find it hard to sneer at the desire to escape. Even if escape is delusion. (Kessel 1993: 848)

In "Invaders," the construction of the "author" as a character in his own fiction – who watches himself in the very act of writing that fiction – not only demonstrates a typical postmodernist interplay between different levels of reality (different ontological levels), but also tells us something about the ironic self-consciousness of postmodern subjectivity.

Kessel's story also exemplifies the realization that representational practices are never simply transparent mirrors "reflecting" the real world back to us, but that representation in all its forms – scientific, linguistic, visual, textual – "cannot avoid involvement with social and political relations and apparatuses" (Hutcheon 1989: 3), even as it necessarily serves to shape our understandings of ourselves and of our world.

This awareness that our representations are as much constructions as they are descriptions is an important facet of the postmodern tendency toward self-referentiality, impelling fiction in the context of the postmodern to pay attention to its own status as textual representation. Russell Hoban's postapocalyptic *Riddley Walker* (1980), for example, is a self-conscious postmodernist novel written *in the mode of science fiction* as a way of commenting, in a displaced way, on aspects of contemporary reality. It is written in a carefully constructed "illiterate" dialect that never allows readers to forget that they are decoding a fictional text. The text itself is Riddley's highly entertaining first-person account of his far-future travels through the primitive but fantastical wasteland that used to be England: "Walker is my name and I am the same. Riddley Walker. Walking my riddels where ever theyve took me and walking them now on this paper the same" (Hoban 1982: 8).

Readers are implicated in Riddley's struggle to solve riddles through their own struggle for meaning in a text which, as signifying system, does not readily yield to decoding. As his tribe's "connexion man," Riddley's purpose is to read the unreadable "and get a good look at how the woal thing ben bilt" (Hoban 1982: 57) – in other words, to develop some kind of adequate "global cognitive mapping" of his world. The quest for such a totalizing meaning, however, is one of the targets of the novel's satire, since the "grand narratives" which once served to explain this world are exactly those that have been definitively discredited – I am tempted to say exploded – through the nuclear destruction of a world that once invested in them. Approaching *Riddley Walker* as allegory, we can read its nuclear apocalypse as a metaphor of the postmodern condition as a radical break with the values and traditions of an earlier historical moment now forever lost to us.

Cyberpunk and Other Denaturalizations of Human/Nature

More often than not, signs of the postmodern in science fiction are more readily recognized in the details of its imagined worlds than in the relatively rare instances of its formal self-referentiality. Science fiction "officially" became postmodern in 1984, with the publication of William Gibson's now-classic Cyberpunk novel, *Neuromancer*. As a result of the attention generated by Gibson's novel in particular and the Cyberpunk "movement" in general, many critics and scholars from outside the field turned to Cyberpunk during the latter half of the 1980s and the early part of the 1990s as a particularly privileged textual expression of "the postmodern condition" at the turn of the millennium (Jameson 1991; McHale 1992; Bukatman 1996). Novels such as *Neuromancer*, Lewis Shiner's *Frontera* (1984), Bruce Sterling's *Schismatrix* (1985), Lucius Shepard's *Life During Wartime* (1987), and Pat Cadigan's *Synners* (1991) seemed especially accurate in their imaginative representations of life in the context of transnational technoscience and global mediatization.

At the same time, spurred in part by Jameson's compelling reading of Cyberpunk as "the supreme *literary* expression if not of postmodernism, then of late capitalism itself" (Jameson 1991: 419, n.1), many science fiction scholars discovered in postmodern theory a new and exciting framework through which to understand the relationship between science fiction and its sociocultural moment (Hollinger 1991; McCaffery 1991; Bukatman 1996). Gibson's cyberspace – the vast and complex web of data into which we are projected through the screens of our computers – was welcomed as an imaginative representation of the new postmodern spatial consciousness identified by Jameson, as well as a convincing construction of the (mediated) *virtual* realities that are increasingly replacing our experiences of an (unmediated) material world. Gibson's cyborgs, artificial intelligences, and clones, presented in a flatly neutral manner that neither celebrated nor condemned their "posthuman" ways of being in the world, became exemplary of the inevitable coevolution of human beings and their proliferating technologies (see Hayles 1999; Graham 2002).

In this view, Cyberpunk is read as expressing, through the fictional constructions of its (for the most part) near-future hi-tech worlds, one way in which conventional ideas about "the human" have been disrupted in the context of the postmodern, an era and a condition that regards "man," that is, the conventional Enlightenment Subject, to be – in Michel Foucault's phrase – "an invention of recent date. And one perhaps nearing its end" (Foucault 1973: 387). Arguably, some of the impact of Foucault's observation about the impending "end of man" derives from the way in which it philosophically "de-naturalizes" everyday understandings about "the human" as a stable and unchanging category. Cyberpunk's stories about the implosions of organic nature and inorganic technology imagine processes of denaturalization in which "the human" is *literally* transformed into the posthuman (we might consider this a more radical version of "defamiliarization," the "making the familiar strange" that is often considered to be the essence of SF's interactions with "the real world").

Linda Hutcheon has argued persuasively that "the postmodern's initial concern is to de-naturalize some of the dominant features of our way of life . . . (they might even include capitalism, patriarchy, liberal humanism). . . . Even nature, postmodernism might point out, doesn't grow on trees" (Hutcheon 1989: 2). In Cyberpunk, the implosion of organic and inorganic often spills over into the natural world as well, as is cleverly suggested in the metaphors of *Neuromancer*'s very first sentence: "The sky above the port was the color of television, tuned to a dead channel" (Gibson 1984: 3). This denaturalization of both "human" and "nature" continues in some (but by no means all) strands of contemporary hard SF, sometimes referred to as "radical hard science fiction." In the very far future of Greg Egan's novel *Diaspora* (1997), for example, posthuman subjects exist in a variety of embodied and digital states, many of which do not appear to be "human" in any recognizable sense of the term. Only a few "fleshers" still inhabit conventional human bodies. Some organically based subjects are "exuberants" whose bodies have been radically transformed for efficiency and longevity. Other individuals inhabit nonorganic bodies called "Gleisner robots." *Diaspora*'s central characters are disembodied, intelligent software systems called "shapers" who live within the virtual environments of the "polises," digital communities whose safety is assured through the creation of multiple back-up copies stored in locations scattered all over the solar system. Ultimately, the carnivalesque chaos of subjectivities in Egan's far future amounts to the disappearance of any significant opposition between embodied reality and digital verisimilitude.

Not surprisingly, Philip K. Dick has long been considered SF's undisputed maestro of postmodern defamiliarization, and a crucial influence on Cyberpunk. In part, this is because of the paranoid extremity with which he dramatized the potential of postmodern technoculture to function as an all-encompassing system incorporating both the human world and the natural world. His short story, "The Electric Ant" (1969), for example, raises the specter that the self may literally be a fake, a mere imitation of the human, a programmed machine that mistakenly believes in its own autonomous subjecthood. In this story, Dick's protagonist Garson Poole accidentally discovers that he is "really" an "electric ant," that is, an organic robot constructed to be an imitation human being. As one of the other characters tells him, his conviction that he is human is exactly the result of his lack of authenticity and agency: "You never guessed because you were programmed not to notice" (Dick 1992: 227). Poole, "the electric ant," begins to question everything he has previously taken for granted, including the reality of his coworker, Sarah: "You're not real," he tells her. "You're a stimulus-factor on my reality tape. A punch-hole that can be glazed over" (Dick 1992: 237). In the end, he is driven by the desperate desire to break through illusion into the realm of the true, the real, the authentic: "What I want, he realized, is ultimate and absolute reality, for one micro-second. After that it doesn't matter, because all will be known; nothing will be left to understand or see" (Dick 1992: 236). Poole cuts the tape that inputs his programming. He "dies." Shortly after, Sarah notices that "through her legs the carpet showed, and then the carpet became dim, and she saw, through it, farther layers of disintegrating matter beyond" (Dick 1992: 239).

It is appropriate, in a postmodern way, that Philip K. Dick's career in science fiction has continued on after his death in 1982. In 1985 he made an appearance in K.W. Jeter's "experimental" Cyberpunk novel, *The Glass Hammer*, in the character of the visual artist Bischofksy; and in 1987 he turned up as Philip K. Dick, an amnesiac writer, in Michael Bishop's *The Secret Ascension; or Philip K. Dick is Dead, Alas*, an *hommage* to Dick written as a pastiche (or parody) of Dick's own stylistic and thematic concerns. And, in what is perhaps the most ironic fate of all for a writer of Dick's political commitments, his novels and stories continue to provide the plots elements for a series of ever more spectacular films produced at the cusp of multinational capitalism and cutting-edge technoscience – from *Blade Runner* (1982) to *Screamers* (1996) to *Total Recall* (1990) to *Minority Report* (2002) to *Paycheck* (2003).

Theory: Lyotard and Jameson

While it is impossible, within the confines of this brief discussion, to trace all, or even most, of the relevant scholarship on the postmodern, several analyses stand out because of the frequency with which they have been applied to (re)readings of the SF genre.

Jean-François Lyotard's influential analysis of "the postmodern condition," first published in French in 1979, does not directly examine popular culture forms, but it has definite implications for SF as a generic project. For Lyotard, to be postmodern means to have lost faith in the master-narratives that have guided and legitimated Western development since the Enlightenment (Lyotard 1984: xxiv); these grand narratives include "Religion," "History," and "Progress," as well as "Science." In this view, "Science" is the ultimate tool of the sovereign humanist Subject in its accumulation of knowledge about and mastery over the natural world; the efficacy of "Science" is posited upon an absolute categorical distinction between observing Subject and observed object. In part, Lyotard's particular construction of "the postmodern" is concerned with epistemological possibilities, that is, with the ways in which we come to know what we know about ourselves and our world(s).

Lyotard also identifies the increasing commodification of knowledge in the global economy as definitive of contemporary postmodernity, and, in this, his views intersect directly with Fredric Jameson's important neo-Marxist analysis of "postmodernism" as "the cultural logic of late capitalism." This is the title of Jameson's 1984 essay in which he first outlined an anxious postmodern condition marked by the shaping forces of multinational capitalism, the pervasiveness of lowest-common-denominator (American) media culture, and the inescapable grip of commodity fetishism. For Jameson, postmodernism is our contemporary "cultural dominant" (Jameson 1991: 4), the force shaping *all* cultural expression today. Postmodernist culture can be identified by, among other things, its attention to surface style (in contrast to the "depth" models of characters and worlds constructed by earlier realisms and modernisms), its lack of emotional affect, and its loss of any sense of historical continuity. Given this particular model, it is not at all surprising that, for Jameson, Cyberpunk was the quintessential fictional representation of postmodernity and *Neuromancer* the quintessential Cyberpunk novel.

More recently, Jack Womack's series of near-future novels, set in a violent and crumbling world in which the Dryden Corporation (Dryco) is far more powerful than any other political or economic body and in which media obfuscation and economic oppression are the order of the day, has continued to explore aspects of the kind of future originally suggested by Cyberpunk (although Womack's world is much more lo-tech than the average Cyberpunk future). Most interesting, perhaps, is Womack's gradual construction over the course of these novels of an increasingly opaque future discourse that, although not as "hip" as the street slang of Gibson's *Neuromancer*, nevertheless (like the language of Hoban's *Riddley Walker*) functions as the textual marker of "futurity" in Womack's fictional world, a future that bears obvious resemblances to both Lyotard's and Jameson's versions of the postmodern.

Womack's *Elvissey* (1993), for example, is an ironic examination of the continuing power of Elvis Presley's hold on the popular imagination. In this satirical critique both of the power of grand narratives and the human potential for self-delusion, the majority of the population belongs to various sects of the C of E – the Church of Elvis – and they await "His" return as the new Messiah who will spiritually "regood" their decaying world. As Isabel, Womack's protagonist, tells herself: "If Dryco could regood itself – regood, therefore, our world – there was naught to believe that my husband and I would not eventually regood ourselves as well, in like manner, to life effect. This we told ourselves, timeover time, until we almost believed it" (Womack 1993: 13). Isabel is sent by Dryco to an alternate 1950s world to kidnap its version of Elvis Presley; Dryco will offer Elvis the riches of this world if he agrees to play the part of its commodity-messiah, ensuring Dryco's control over the millions of Church of Elvis believers. In an ironic parallel to the Biblical temptation of Christ by Satan, Isabel's instructions are to "Cliffside him, and show him his awaiting cities. Hold any carrots you have close to his nose" (Womack 1993: 50–1). But this is an alternate Elvis, very different from the "authentic" one – and, in any case, even the "real" Elvis has always been the construction of his fans and believers. Appropriately, *Elvissey* is also an ironically self-reflexive text: the alternate Elvis, befuddled by the chaotic reality of the world into which he has been kidnapped, can find no other means of expressing his confusion than to conclude that "It's all science fiction" (Womack 1993: 248). The Dryco executives who wish to manipulate "E"'s power over his followers fear that his penchant for pulp SF "contributes nothing to the image" (Womack 1993: 171).

Jameson was one of the first to identify another significant postmodern implosion in the perceived waning of the once sacrosanct distinctions between "high" (literary, modernist) culture and the products of "low" (popular, generic) culture, including such frequently denigrated forms as science fiction. Alas for Jameson, this "aesthetic populism" (Jameson 1991: 2) is not a positive development, leading as it does in his view to the devaluation and commodification of our most sacred (high) cultural icons. Many students of the postmodern, while taking their cue from his arguments, have nevertheless welcomed this as a democratizing development. For one thing, it has helped to draw critical attention to previously marginalized cultural forms such as science fiction.

One increasingly noticeable result of this weakening of the boundaries between "high" and "low" culture is the frequent incorporation (some would call it "appropriation") of SF images and ideas into "literary" texts written *in the mode of science fiction* – *Riddley Walker* is one good example – which remain more or less distinct from "traditional" genre texts. Other examples include Angela Carter's baroquely poetic postapocalyptic novel, *Heroes and Villains* (1967), Douglas Coupland's "postgenre" novel of suburban apocalypse, *Girlfriend in a Coma* (1997), and Margaret Atwood's eccentric vision of a future wasteland transformed by out-of-control genetic engineering, *Oryx and Crake* (2003). In these postmodernist speculative fictions, SF functions less as an extrapolative narrative genre than as a mode of metaphorical discourse about the present, "one way of talking about certain recent developments in advanced industrial society" (Benison 1992: 139). Many of these texts are postapocalyptic stories of forlorn futures cut off from their pasts and they seem to echo, in fictional form, Jameson's description of a critical postmodern condition marked by the loss of any sense of historical continuity.

"The SF of Theory": Baudrillard and Haraway

As a mode of cultural description and analysis, science fiction has directly influenced some theoretical writings about the postmodern, resulting in what Istvan Csicsery-Ronay, Jr. has termed "the SF of theory" (Csicsery-Ronay, Jr. 1991). In the late 1970s and early 1980s, for example, Jean Baudrillard, sociophilosopher of the "hyperreal," published a series of influential commentaries on postmodernity as a condition of science-fictional simulation. In his model, the hi-tech world of transnational capitalism and globalized multimedia is virtually defined by the endless multiplication and circulation of images and pseudoevents which have gradually erased all signs of "the real." Simulation replaces authenticity and the copy erases the original. This is not unlike the "society of the spectacle" described in James Tiptree, Jr's feminist proto-Cyberpunk story, "The Girl Who Was Plugged In" (1973), in which media stars are managed by representatives of big business and employed as living advertisements to sell products in a future of rampant consumerism which has banned direct advertising. This is the same world we recognize in many Cyberpunk novels, in which the image is often more powerful than material reality, and where physical embodiment is abandoned by characters such as *Synners'* Virtual Mark in favor of disembodied digitalized existence.

According to Baudrillard, "classic" SF, notable for its extrapolative approach to world-building, is now an impossibility: "We can no longer imagine other universes . . . Classic SF was one of expanding universes: it found its calling in narratives of space exploration and colonization indigenous to the nineteenth and twentieth centuries." He concludes that, in all probability, "the 'good old' SF imagination is dead, and that something else is beginning to emerge . . ." (Baudrillard 1991: 309). For Baudrillard, science fiction that responds to the contemporary disappearance of "the real" would be an especially significant form of cultural representation or "cognitive mapping." "SF of this sort is no longer an elsewhere, it is an everywhere" (Baudrillard 1991: 312), he argues, noting both Philip K. Dick's satirical fantasy of simulation, *The Simulacra* (1964), and J.G. Ballard's techopornographic novel, *Crash* (1973), as particularly cogent dramatizations of the hyperreal present. From now on, Baudrillard insists, the "real" exists only as an object of nostalgia. Constructing a model of the postmodern as a condition of ironic – but fascinated – paralysis in the grip of the hyperreal, he leaves us trapped in irreality like characters lost in the cyberspace of some grim present-day Cyberpunk novel.

One result of the waning influence of the grand narratives analyzed by Lyotard, however, has been a widespread movement of decentering, so that "voices" historically relegated to the margins of discourse have come to the foreground (including the voices of popular culture forms such as science fiction). The proliferation of SF by women writers provides an excellent example of this, and the many feminist revisions in recent decades of SF's conventionally masculinist stories is one very positive outcome of the crises of authority which, in part, have defined the postmodern. The

very nature of the feminist project – as radical theoretical rethinking and deconstructive practice – links it to the postmodern.

In 1985, Donna Haraway published her now-classic "A Manifesto for Cyborgs," a
critique of Western technoscience and imperialist politics which she describes as "an
ironic political myth faithful to feminism, socialism, and materialism" (Haraway
1989: 173). The "Manifesto" introduces the figure of the cyborg – techno-offspring
of the SF imagination and the military-industrial complex – as a relational and "post-
gender" subject that refuses the Judeo-Christian master-narratives of origin-fall-sal-
vation, a subject that "was not born in a garden; it does not seek unitary identity and
so generate antagonistic dualisms without end (or until the world ends); it takes irony
for granted" (Haraway 1989: 203). Haraway's "Manifesto" introduced issues of gender
politics – as well as the politics of environmentalism and forms of community activism
– into the all-too-often apolitical discourses of the postmodern. For Haraway, "Late
twentieth-century machines have made thoroughly ambiguous the difference between
natural and artificial, mind and body, self-developing and externally designed, and
many other distinctions that used to apply to organisms and machines" (Haraway
1989: 176). Her cyborg, inspired in part by the work of feminist SF writers, is a
valorization of postmodern border crossing and boundary breakdown: "The cyborgs
populating feminist science fiction make very problematic the statuses of man or
woman, human, artifact, member of a race, individual identity, or body" (Haraway
1989: 201).

Haraway's "manifesto" suggests possibilities for resistance and political challenge
from the margins of the social world. For her, politically engaged science fiction can
be a significant imaginative intervention. "I am indebted," she states, "to writers like
Joanna Russ, Samuel Delany, John Varley, James Tiptree, Jr., Octavia Butler, Monique
Wittig, and Vonda McIntyre. These are our storytellers exploring what it means to
be embodied in high-tech worlds. They are theorists for cyborgs" (Haraway 1989:
197). As also are newer writers such as Geoff Ryman (*The Child Garden* [1989]), Amy
Thompson (*Virtual Girl* [1993]), Melissa Scott (*Trouble and her Friends* [1994]),
Shariann Lewitt ("A Real Girl" [1998]), and Laura J. Mixon (*Proxies* [1998]).

Postmodern (and politicized) denaturalization is not confined, of course, to hi-
tech worlds and cyborged bodies. In her award-winning novel, *White Queen* (1991),
Gwyneth Jones offers a radically revised version of the first-contact scenario. In *White
Queen*, the arrival on Earth of a group of hermaphroditic aliens known as "Aleutians"
poses a radical challenge to the gendered perspectives of Jones' human characters,
threatening to destabilize the already fragile political and economic balance of their
near-future world. The action in *White Queen* is set against the backdrop of the "gender
wars," one of a number of conflicts – including political and economic rivalries, and
ethnic and religious hostilities – that have fragmented this world. For readers of the
novel, the Aleutians' comically skewed views on gender difference – in all their apparent illogicality and contingency – strongly suggest the same lack of logic and necessity in the constructions of human gender, which owes at least as much to culture as
it does to nature. Given the hermaphrodite nature of Aleutian individuals, their ideas

about gender have nothing to do with sexed bodies; in fact, one of the aliens considers how differentiation by gender is "an idle, gossipy game":

> Feminine people . . . are the people who'd rather work through the night in the dark than call someone who can fix the light . . . The kind of people who can't live without being needed but refuse to need anything from anyone. Masculine people, on the other hand, can never leave well enough alone, break things by way of improving them, will do absolutely anything for a kiss and a kind word . . . (Haraway 1989: 121)

Not surprisingly, the Aleutians have great difficulty appreciating the basis of human gender difference. The Aleutian Clavel tries to explain it in this way: " 'There are two nations. . . . One bears the others' children for them. They get called "Feminine"; and the obligate-parasites "Masculine." ' . . . A division into parasites and child-bearers was another peculiarity to add to [humans'] obsession with religion [and] their horrid food" (Haraway 1989: 117).

Signs of the Postmodern

Like "postmodern," "science fiction" is a tendentious term notoriously open to definition and redefinition. The case can nevertheless be made that, as a genre developed in the context of the nineteenth century's commitment to ideals of Reason, Science, and Progress – a genre, moreover, whose nearest formal relative is the realist novel – science fiction has tended to pay at least lip-service to these particular grand narratives. Even as it works through the construction of imaginary fictional worlds, it is also aligned with the values attached to scientific accuracy, intellectual rationality, and the self-evident materiality of the physical universe. The great figures of first-generation postpulp American SF – Isaac Asimov, Robert Heinlein, Arthur C. Clarke – have come to represent a "Golden Age" during which scientific method was translated into its fictional analogue, demonstrated in the aesthetics, formal features, and themes of their writing: unselfconscious and transparent prose style, linear cause-and-effect narrative development leading to logical resolutions, thematic commitment to human intellect and rationality, and a more-or-less optimistic faith in humanity's ultimate triumphant expansion beyond the confines of Earth.

From this perspective, science fiction is an unlikely candidate for postmodernization. In fact, genre SF is rarely also postmodernist fiction, although significant examples appeared especially in the 1970s, a decade that saw an explosion of postmodernist writing which spilled over even into popular genres such as science fiction. Important instances include Samuel R. Delany's muliplex "heterotopian" novel, *Triton* (1976; aka *Trouble on Triton*) and Joanna Russ' classic feminist satire, *The Female Man* (1975). The world within Delany's text – one of SF's earliest attempts to express the sheer complexity of contemporary reality – is reflected in the density and intricacy of the language through which Delany creates it: this is a far-future society in which advances in technology have rendered sex changes commonplace, so that bodies are "worn" like clothes; the social body recognizes many more than only two genders; the number of available subject identities and life choices is absolutely dizzying; and the very environment – a city on a moon orbiting Neptune – is an entirely technoartificial construction. *The Female Man* is a formally postmodernist metafiction, self-consciously structured through a narrative that fragments a single female subject – "J" – into four diverse personalities existing in parallel worlds: Joanna (the "author" of the novel), Jeannine (her extreme "feminine" version), Jael (murderous agent in an ongoing battle between Manland and Womanland), and Janet (envoy from the Utopian all-woman planet of Whileaway).

While formally experimental science fiction continues to be rare, other signs of SF "postmodernization" are everywhere, for instance in the frequency with which SF writers revise, "quote," parody, and otherwise explore earlier generic conventions. Although science fiction has always been "intertextual" – that is, its writers have always tended to borrow (and revise) each other's ideas and conventions – many of today's writers have grown up *within* science fiction and are keenly aware of their genre history. Consider, for example, Kim Stanley Robinson's brilliantly self-conscious revision of the alternate-history novel as Utopian project in *The Years of Rice and Salt* (2002), or the current revival of space opera – the New Baroque Space Opera, as it is sometimes named – in texts whose vast and complex far-futures are inhabited by hosts of wildly divergent posthuman characters (not coincidentally, these texts are often associated with the "radical hard SF" of writers like Greg Egan and Paul J. McAuley). Bruce Sterling's far-future Cyberpunk novel, *Schismatrix* (1985), is one of the earliest examples of this revival, followed more recently by novels such as Dan Simmons' *Hyperion* (1989), Colin Greenland's *Take Back Plenty* (1990), Iain M. Banks' *Consider Phlebas* (1992), Alastair Reynolds' *Redemption Ark* (2002), and Charles Stross' *Singularity Sky* (2003). These texts are contributing to a self-conscious revival, in new directions, of one of SF's oldest (and most denigrated) subgenres, constructing futures that – quite cheerfully, for the most part – reflect back to us the incredible complexity of the technoscientific present. Here, for example, is a passage from Stross' short story, "Halo" (2002):

> Half a lightyear away, tired Earth wakes and slumbers in time to its ancient orbital dynamics. A religious college in Cairo is considering issues of nanotechnology . . . (If the mind of one of the faithful is copied into a computing machine's memory by mapping and simulating all its synapses, is the computer now a Moslem? If not, *why not*? If so, what are its rights and duties?) Riots in Borneo underline the urgency of technotheological inquiry. (Stross 2003: 205)

Given the ongoing border traffic between postmodernist fiction and science fiction, the situation is equally interesting at the margins of the genre, which is virtually exploding with textual "hybrids," by which I mean texts that both are and are not science fiction. It is worth noting that, while the 2003 Hugo Award went to Robert J. Sawyer's very conventionally plotted novel, *Hominids* (2002), the 2002 Hugo was won by Neil Gaiman's "weird fiction" novel, *American Gods* (2001), in which human characters interact with contemporary manifestations of the old Norse gods. The borders of genre have become porous, impossible to police against the constant incursions of texts that are not quite the "real thing."

Science philosopher Bruno Latour has argued persuasively that the ongoing efforts of the modern (Enlightenment) world to categorize, to distinguish, to differentiate, and to label the various bodies and objects and relations in the world have inevitably resulted in "the proliferation of exceptions" (Latour 1993: 50). Examples of such "exceptions" abound in science fiction today, texts composed of various mismatched features that, like Frankenstein's Creature, are neither one thing nor the other and which, in the eyes of purists, should probably be driven out of the genre community altogether. (Nor is this a new situation for science fiction. At various times, for example, purists have made the case that "soft" SF – which foregrounds the social sciences instead of the physical sciences – is not "real" SF; or that New Wave SF – with its primary commitment to literary aesthetics – is not the real thing; or that "feminist" SF, or black, or lesbian, or gay, or "ethnic" SF – openly committed as each is to a particular politics – is not the real thing.)

Under the sign of the postmodern, it is the "exceptions" that are courted and that begin to constitute, in effect, a new kind of "norm." One of the most acclaimed recent "hybrid" texts is China Miéville's massive fantasy/science fiction/horror novel, *Perdido Street Station* (2000). Nominated for both fantasy and science fiction awards, the text's generic hybridity is a formal "reflection" both of the diversity of its characters – ordinary humans, insectoid humans, technological intelligences, and a host of other possible and impossible creatures – and of the inconceivable complexity and randomness of New Crobuzon, the fantastical city that they all inhabit. In a similar manner, the collection of "weird fiction" recently edited by Peter Straub in *Conjunctions* 39 (2002) includes short stories and novel excerpts which self-consciously explore the potential of genre "implosions" on the borders of SF, fantasy, and horror (see Wolfe 2002).

By now those borders are crowded with texts that, like Hoban's *Riddley Walker* and Womack's *Elvissey*, are recognizably science fictional but whose self-consciously "literary" (formal, linguistic, stylistic) features, as well as their dialogue with the other fantastic genres, situate them at a distance from the "center" of the genre. These include novels such as James Morrow's *Towing Jehovah* (1994), Jeff Noon's *Pollen* (1995) and *Nymphomation* (1997), Jonathan Lethem's *Amnesia Moon* (1995) and *Girl in Landscape* (1998), Archie Weller's *Land of the Golden Clouds* (1998), Adam Roberts' *Salt* (2000), Nalo Hopkinson's *Brown Girl in the Ring* (1998) and *Midnight Robber* (2000), and Carol Emshwiller's *Carmen Dog* (1988) and *The Mount* (2002). While it may be all too easy to discount Baudrillard's lament that "the 'good old' SF imagination is dead," it is nevertheless true that "something else is beginning to emerge" (Baudrillard 1991: 309) at the margins of the genre. Under the sign of the postmodern, the exceptions continue to proliferate and, in the process, they continue to transform science fiction in all manner of rich and strange new directions.

One of the most significant of these "postgeneric" transformations is suggested in the latest novel by William Gibson, whose *Neuromancer* had such a key role in the initial postmodernization of science fiction. *Pattern Recognition* (2003) is a realist novel about the future-present. Everything in its fictional world of technologies and commodities – the hi-speed technologies of travel and communication, the esoteric and labyrinthine practices of multinational businesses, the virtual computer-mediated relationships through which much of the action develops – is already a part of our contemporary technocultural environment. *Pattern Recognition* dramatizes for us how the present has already been invaded by the future, has already become the stuff of science fiction. SF as mode of description and analysis blurs here into SF as narrative genre in what may be, for science fiction, the ultimate postmodern implosion:

> . . . we have no future. Not in the sense that our grandparents had a future, or thought they did. Fully imagined cultural futures were the luxury of another day, one in which "now" was of some greater duration. . . . We have no future because our present is too volatile. . . . We have only risk management. The spinning of a given moment's scenarios. Pattern recognition. (Gibson 2003: 57)

References and Further Reading

Baudrillard, Jean (1991) "Simulacra and Science Fiction." (1981) (trans.) Arthur B. Evans. *Science Fiction Studies* 18.3, 309–13.

Benison, Jonathan (1992) "Science Fiction and Postmodernity," in *Postmodernism and the Rereading of Modernity*, (eds) Francis Barker, Peter Hulme, and Margaret Iversen. Manchester: Manchester University Press, 138–58.

Best, Steven and Douglas Kellner (2001) *The Postmodern Adventure: Science, Technology, and Cultural Studies at the Third Millennium*. New York: Guildford Press.

Booker, M. Keith (2001) *Monsters, Mushroom Clouds, and the Cold War: American Science Fiction and the Roots of Postmodernism, 1946–1964*. Westport, CT: Greenwood.

Bukatman, Scott (1996) *Terminal Identity: The Virtual Subject in Postmodern Science Fiction*. Durham, NC: Duke University Press.

Butler, Andrew M. (2003a) "Postmodernism and Science Fiction," in *The Cambridge Companion to Science Fiction*, (eds) Farah Mendlesohn and Edward James. Cambridge: Cambridge University Press, 137–48.

——(2003b) *Postmodernism*. Harpenden: Pocket Essentials.

Csicsery-Ronay I. Jr. (1991) "The SF of theory: Baudrillard and Haraway." *Science Fiction Studies* 18.3, 387–404.

Dick, Philip K. (1992) "The Electric Ant" (1969), in *The Collected Stories of Philip K. Dick*. Vol. 5:

The Eye of the Sibyl. New York: Citadel Twilight, 225–39.

Egan, Greg (1997) *Diaspora*. London: Millennium.

Everman, Welch D. (1986) "The Paper World: Science Fiction in the Postmodern Era,"in *Postmodern Fiction: A Bio-Bibliographical Guide*, (ed.) Larry McCaffery. Westport, CT: Greenwood, 23–38.

Foucault, Michel (1973) *The Order of Things: An Archeology of the Human Sciences* (1966). New York: Vintage.

Gibson, William (1984) *Neuromancer*. New York: Ace.

——(2003) *Pattern Recognition*. New York: Putnam.

Graham, Elaine L. (2002) *Representations of the Post/Human: Monsters, Aliens and Others in Popular Culture*. New Brunswick, NJ: Rutgers University Press.

Haraway, Donna (1989) "A Manifesto for Cyborgs: Science, Technology, and Socialist Feminism in the 1980s." (1985) In *Coming to Terms: Feminism, Theory, Politics*, (ed.) Elizabeth Weed. New York: Routledge, 173–204.

Hayles, N. Katherine (1999) *How We Became Posthuman: Virtual Bodies in Cybernetics, Literature, and Informatics*. Chicago: University of Chicago Press.

Hoban, Russell (1982) *Riddley Walker* (1980). London: Pan.

Hollinger, Veronica (1991) "Cybernetic Deconstructions: Cyberpunk and Postmodernism." (1989) In *Storming the Reality Studio: A Casebook of Cyberpunk and Postmodern Science Fiction*, (ed.) Larry McCaffery. Durham, NC: Duke University Press, 203–W18.

Hutcheon, Linda (1989) *The Politics of Postmodernism*. London: Routledge.

Jameson, Fredric (1991) *Postmodernism or, The Cultural Logic of Late Capitalism*. Durham, NC: Duke University Press.

Jones, Gwyneth (1992) *White Queen* (1991). London: Victor Gollancz.

Kessel, John (1993) "Invaders" (1990), in *The Norton Book of Science Fiction: North American Science Fiction, 1960–1990*, (eds) Ursula K. Le Guin and Brian Attebery. New York: Norton, 830–50.

Latour, Bruno (1993) *We Have Never Been Modern* (1991), (trans.) Catherine Porter. Cambridge, MA: Harvard University Press.

Lyotard, Jean-François (1984) *The Postmodern Condition: A Report on Knowledge* (1979), (trans.) Geoff Bennington and Brian Massumi. Minneapolis: Minnesota University Press.

McCaffery, Larry (ed.) (1991) *Storming the Reality Studio: A Casebook of Cyberpunk and Postmodern Science Fiction*. Durham, NC: Duke University Press.

McHale, Brian (1992) *Constructing Postmodernism*. New York: Routledge.

——(1997) "Science Fiction," in *International Postmodernism: Theory and Literary Practice*, (eds) Hans Bertens and Douwe Fokkema. Amsterdam: John Benjamins, 235–9.

Palmer, Christopher (2003) *Philip K. Dick: Exhilaration and Terror of the Postmodern*. Liverpool: Liverpool University Press.

Science Fiction Studies (1991) Special issue on "Science fiction and postmodernism." 18.3.

Stross, Charles (2003) "Halo" (2002), in *The Year's Best Science Fiction: Twentieth Annual Collection*, (ed.) Gardner Dozois. New York: St. Martins, 184–211.

Wolmark, Jenny (1994) *Aliens and Others: Science Fiction, Feminism and Postmodernism*. Hemel Hempstead: Harvester Wheatsheaf.

Wolfe, Gary K. (2002) "Evaporating Genre: Strategies of Dissolution in the Postmodern Fantastic," in *Edging into the Future: Science Fiction and Contemporary Cultural Transformation*, (eds) Veronica Hollinger and Joan Gordon. Philadelphia: University of Pennsylvania Press, 11–29.

Womack, Jack (1993) *Elvissey*. New York: Tor.

16

The Renewal of "Hard" Science Fiction

Donald M. Hassler

My topic here is firmly located in the time and place of the final decade of the twentieth century as it, in turn, has been reflexive of the long century of hard science fiction that reaches from high point to high point back to the original scientific romances of H.G. Wells. To be more accurate, I might label the historical moments as low points since I see the literature often as reaction or response to historical stress points. In other words, this topic deals with "renewal" of elements and effects in a long generic tradition. Scholars of the British Enlightenment, the group that nurtured my academic work originally and who are, I think, an appropriate set of ancestors for modern science fiction, like to refer to the "long eighteenth century" that extended from the Restoration to the French Revolution. I borrow the notion here in order to evoke hard science fiction from 1895 when Wells published his first scientific romance, *The Time Machine,* to our historical present or, at least, to that awful moment of September 2001.

This focus, then, on renewal and reflexiveness clearly falls short of a Utopian or revolutionary reading of hard science fiction. In his major review of the anthology that may have suggested in the first place the need to identify hard science fiction in the 1990s, Russell Blackford praises the highest, most philosophic fictions of this category that appeared during this decade. These include the several novels of Greg Egan, the concept in Nancy Kress' novella "Beggars in Spain" (1991), the speculations on artificial intelligence in the work of Vernor Vinge, and the new thinking of the veteran hard science fiction writer Gregory Benford that, like the others above, pushes against the edges of our scientific thinking about human nature and about inner space. Like Blackford, I find that recent work so original and so scientific even that, indeed, it moves toward the "no place" of Utopian writing.

But those ideas are not my topic here. I am interested in exploring "renewal" in the genre as opposed to the more philosophic topic of what may be genuinely revolutionary in some of the work. Perhaps this important distinction for me can be illustrated by labels that we use in creative writing classes for modes of writing, the distinction between verse and prose. Verse turns back on itself, is reflexive and renewing. Prose is linear and, hence, capable of moving on toward infinity. Like scientific hypothesis, prose literally can push outward toward the "no place" of Utopian thinking. The renewed vitality of hard science fiction in the final decade of the twentieth century includes some exciting Utopian thought, even scientific thought. But as a literary genre, it has seemed to me more like the turning of verse. It harks back to important echoes from twentieth-century science fiction as it has attempted to be rational and rigorous in thinking about nature and about future possibilities, and these echoes go back to when the British Empire was still intact and when gaslight and electric lights were still vying in the marketplace to see which would illuminate our lives. I think this is a wonderful genre topic about the long twentieth century and about the part that science fiction has played in popular culture during that time, culminating in this renewal of the 1900s.

Blackford's review of *The Hard SF Renaissance* (2002), also labels nicely the reflexive turning I am interested in exploring here, ". . . the technolibertarian and/or promilitarist stance of more traditional hard science fiction" (Blackford 2003: 12). Traditional hard science fiction, despite its commitment to whatever is current in scientific thinking, has clearly been built on images that feature invention and gadgets, on libertarian attitudes of the idiosyncratic and individualist inventor and vigilante, as well as on a haunting xenophobia that calls for pre-emptive military action at times. Further, I suggest that in science and philosophy one does not repeat, or return to, a trek of discovery or exploration. The scientist moves on always to the new place or the Utopian "no place", whereas the power of the artist often lies in the ability to echo familiar sounds, tropes, topics, locations. Hence the sense of renewal in a set of genre characteristics may be more appropriate to notice and to map than the outlying innovations that are moving away from the old genre. Maybe the renewal that I write about here is the end of a long and tortuous century filled with the tropes of hard science fiction. Maybe the writing is changing radically so that the Vinge "singularity" about human nature that Hartwell and Cramer describe well in the prefatory note to his story in *The Hard SF Renaissance* foreshadows what is to come in the literature (Hartwell and Cramer 2002: 743). But in the renewed hard science fiction at the end of the century some of the old haunts return, and they return with an appealing, amusing, and palliative self-consciousness. I think these literary effects need to be described even though they may represent the end of the genre. Perhaps as "end" they may even be a culmination or fulfillment.

So another reason not to ignore the older effects is that, as a final fulfillment, they may help us to purge the haunts that lie beneath them. Old and traditional literary effects sometimes are just that – old and stuffy and devoid of blood and guts. I think of the old, century-long tradition of the heroic couplet that I toyed with in my early work on Erasmus Darwin. Blood and guts did exist in his holding up of that artistic shield in his work; but that is a much older, though analogous, story of art helping out with life and science. In twentieth-century science fiction writing, the blood and guts implications in the literary effects, the repeating genre characteristics, are still very much with us to disturb us. Hard science fiction, going back to Wells' xeno-phobia about tripodic Martians, developed originally to face some of the worst haunts of the long twentieth century; and we have used fiction, or art, to deal with those haunts ever since. In the case of the original invading Martians depicted in *The War of the Worlds* (1898), the haunt may have been a mix of anti-Semitic racism and colo-nialism represented in part by the Dreyfus affair and social Darwinism. Overall, two of the most virulent of these haunts from the start have been racism, or eugenics (the Satanic temptation to purge, purify, and then recreate human nature along the Frankenstein model of the Superman) and then the more fundamental haunt of a prag-matism that questions any essential outlines to our humanness. A belief in the second of these haunts opens the floodgates for experimentation with the first.

Thus, before I turn to the familiar libertarian, adventure, militarist, and xenopho-bic tropes in the fiction from Wells through Heinlein to the renewals in the 1990s, I need to emphasize the ambivalence in tone one might expect in the presence of such haunting historical specters. My 1982 book *Comic Tones in Science Fiction* treats this ambivalence and relates it to similar tonal effects found in some eighteenth-century writers of the Enlightenment. In others words, I think the twentieth-century agonies expressed well in hard science fiction are part of a larger "modern" story. Recently what I had attempted in my book as a description of an ambivalence of tone in the face of harsh realities has been done with more detail in a book on post Civil War trauma among American pragmatist thinkers, especially William James, Charles Sanders Peirce, and John Dewey. This fine study by Louis Menand barely touches the twentieth-century agonies such as racism, militarism, and libertarianism, nor the science fiction use of them that will consume the rest of this essay; but it does describe the key role of Oliver Wendell Holmes, Jr. in supporting the famous 1927 United States Supreme Court case that upheld the constitutionality of the Virginia eugenic sterilization law. Holmes was another of the post-Civil War group of thinkers who briefly called themselves "The Metaphysical Club," also the title of the book. Menand seems to me forceful enough, however, in his statement about the loss of belief in belief that inspired these thinkers to warrant using his formulation here:

> They all believed that ideas are not "out there" waiting to be discovered, but are tools – like forks and knives and microchips – that people devise to cope with the world in which they find themselves. . . . And they believed that since ideas are provisional responses to particular and unreproducible circumstances, their survival depends not on their immutability but on their adaptability. . . . It made [them] lose [their] belief in beliefs. . . . *This* idea [they] stuck to, with a grimness and, at times, a cynicism that have occasionally repelled people. (Menand 2001: xi, 4)

I believe that such profound skepticism leads to an ambivalence of tone as well as a nostalgia for "antebellum" beliefs that governs much that follows in the literature I will discuss here.

One thing about ambivalence of tone that science fiction writers discovered early while working, and have not forgotten, is that ambivalence of tone is entertaining and amusing. I love the pressure of the marketplace on these important cultural ideas because those pressures, clearly, represent another way in which the genre, the one renewed here, is far from being remotely Utopian and grounded in the highest "no places" of thought. I am mapping here hard realities of artistic and genre effects that have had to survive commercially. Also, the contingent and always-reactive pragmatism that Menand describes fits well with the literary effects often evoked to dismiss science fiction as literature. It is called merely a gadget literature. The gadget of Wells' original time machine is not much more than a very fancy bicycle because he did not know much about wormholes or other exotic means of transport. But thanks to Thomas Edison, the Wright brothers, Henry Ford, George Westinghouse, and a myriad of other individualist inventors, gadgets became much more interesting to write about almost as quickly as the historical trauma points multiplied in the long twentieth century. Menand's focus on the challenge to belief in the American Civil War is certainly well taken, and the new technology of improved mechanisms for warfare and for killing played no small part in that challenge. But many similar challenges to belief, or historical stress points, followed rapidly – from *The Mauve Decade* that produced Wells to the Clinton years a century later as prelude to terrorism. At each moment, new gadgets, new technological wonders, worked to fascinate and to tantalize us with possible remedies and simultaneously added to the trauma. And the ambivalence, I suggest, has also been continually that somehow we long to go back, to reaffirm what Menand calls antebellum certitudes about belief at the same time that we move forward with the pragmatic tools.

Almost like a relieving ointment that stings a little as it heals, a major cultural tool, as we have thought about and learned to cope with the warlike stress points in the long twentieth century, has been hard science fiction itself and its repeating tropes that extrapolate from what we know and that only deceive us in terms of emphasis and tone. Long before the Manhattan Project actually produced what we called then "the atom bomb," one could read stories about weapons of mass destruction, about death rays, about incredibly lethal devices invented by Edison which would take care of the Martians or which would quickly end the Great War (Davis 2003: 303). I am not quite old enough to have noticed in their original form the popular stories about Edison's fantastic weapons, but I do remember wandering home from elementary school terrified, with my buddies, that the atom bomb would vaporize our Midwestern home town. And then I read and had my mind distracted by pulp atom bomb stories. Anything that interesting, I thought, must be part of the same plan, God's plan, that I was being told about in Sunday School. This effect was real, practical ambivalence of tone that somehow did help us all get through the atom bomb moment in the long twentieth century. The effect, of course, is much like the effect from horror literature; but even more ambivalence comes from the knowledge that the horror is extrapolated from harsh and present facts of nature.

One trope that seems particularly healthy and useful as it keeps cropping up, even when we think that science fiction does not need more of it, is the Mars image. Our neighbor in the solar system is named, of course, for the god of war; and later I will contrast the appropriateness of war on Mars to love on Venus in the overall scheme of hard science fiction. But for the moment it is the renewed interest in stories about the war planet at each moment of stress in our history of wars from the Great War of 1914, when Burroughs was beginning, to the current war on terror that seems significant. Weinbaum and many others in the 1930s, Heinlein and Bradbury in the Cold War, (even C.S. Lewis, who exhibits sadly no ambivalence of tone at all and so is never what I would call a hard science fiction writer but rather a true antebellum anachronism) – so many extrapolators have made use of the reliable image from Wells of the red planet. Recently, I was amused to discover Brian Stableford's glib dismissal of Mars as he writes in the 1979 version of the reliable Nicholls and Clute encyclopedia:

> Within that [Mars] mythology have been written some of the most fascinating and most enduring of sf's literary products, but it seems that it has now run its course. There is little more to say now that Mars stands revealed for what it really is. (Nicholls 1979: 383)

It seems to me that Stableford's logical assumption makes my point about the vitality and mystery of artistic renewal, the "verse" in hard science fiction as a palliative art form for our time, as opposed to linear logic. Mars is clearly back as a trope for hard science fiction because there is a renewal of hard science fiction in our time.

Mars: Renewed Image and Heroic War

Even though a cursory look at the short fiction in the Hartwell and Cramer anthology as well as important new novels from those by Ben Bova to Alastair Reynolds will show that Mars has proven Stableford wrong, my own reading recently has uncovered two novel-length gems that illustrate my argument here and that reaffirm my love of hard science fiction effects. Both books have been relatively underrated or, at least, they have not received the awards and attention during this renewal period that Kim Stanley Robinson's central Mars trilogy has; but I think that both are superb and, furthermore, nicely illustrative of the effects of genre renewal and of tone that interest me here. Another element that I have only implied thus far is the appeal in hard science fiction of the sensawonder adventure tale; but as we turn to this Mars section of the discussion it will be clear how strong is the sense of adventure in the fiction, even heroic adventure. And true to the other effects under discussion, the adventure tales echo back through our century of adventure. The set of novels by Robinson emphasize the extrapolative terraforming of the Red Planet, and I think it is no accident that Robinson himself during the 1990s traveled to expedition bases in Antarctica and then wrote an important fiction/nonfiction book about the continent that most resembles the planet Mars in its cold, harsh conditions. Similarly, in both the Mars novels that fascinate me here as well as in the recent, and sadly, the final pieces of hard science fiction by Hal Clement, who always can be in our minds as we read about tough treks over alien terrain, we can find literary allusions to the hard treks of Captain Robert Scott and Sir Ernest Shackleton, which were a kind of wakeup call just prior to the Great War of what was to come in the twentieth century. So even in this small detail of allusion to history the sense of renewal and return in thinking back to heroic moments in the long twentieth century is strong.

But it is the pointing back not so much to historical events as to familiar science fiction tropes that make these works appear as renewal and strongly refreshing works for me, although Hiroshima, Hitler, Antarctic exploration do figure. Allen Steele published *Labyrinth of Night* in 1992; the title is the English for *noctis labyrinthus*, a prominent feature on the surface of Mars. Geoffrey A. Landis published *Mars Crossing* in 2000. Both writers are included in Hartwell and Cramer as bonafide hard science fiction writers. Steele has produced a number of other hard science fiction novels during the last fifteen years or so, the most recent of which is *Chronospace* (2001), an interesting time travel tale that brings some focus to Hitler during his rise to power in the 1930s and to the crash of the Hindenburg dirigible in 1937. The Landis novel is his first, and he has won awards for his short fiction. Both books gain much of their power from extrapolative details, gadget details, and about how strange it is to move around in unusual environments – the nausea and sexual adjustments humans have in microgravity, the flight problems in the thin atmosphere of Mars, and always the alien terrain itself. Landis solves the problem of Mars flight with a spindly, huge-winged aircraft. Steele uses a massive dirigible named the *Akron*. In both novels, the resonance is with gadget fiction and with twentieth-century history where one thinks of Akron, Ohio in the 1930s and our clever inventors competing with the cleverer Nazi inventors on dirigible design. The Nazi ship crashed and burned in 1937; so does the *Akron* in the novel. But the greater resonance is with fictional trekking over tough and challenging terrain and in tough atmospheres. Any avid reader of hard science fiction is continually reminded of the difficulty of movement and flight across a tough planet, such as the planet Mesklin in the work of Hal Clement. And in these novels both the terrain and the means of coping with it represent plausible, strange, and hence slightly funny measures all at the same time. It is sad, and yet fulfilling, to learn of the death of Hal Clement just as I am writing these lines about clever and difficult treks over an extrapolated Mars in 2003. The fulfillment is that his work helped to teach hard science fiction writers to make such extrapolations, such tough treks. In the nonliterary history of the twentieth century, Clement also flew many tough missions against Nazi Germany.

In the Landis novel, there are no aliens – other than the hard, alien universe itself. But for Steele the importance of xenophobia is both central to his story and comic. A robotic and insect-like alien civilization in the novel (the bugs in Heinlein) has cleverly left a sort of spider-like trap on Mars epochs ago in order to lure mankind to their assistance once we have developed "nuke" capability. I find that Steele is ingenious in his linking these clever plot moves to our historical adventures at Hiroshima and to the great racist haunt of the twentieth century in which genocide became a pragmatic tactic to make changes in the world. The heroine in the Steele novel had grandparents living in Hiroshima when it was bombed, and so the novel is able to conjoin the "atom bomb" haunt with the racist haunt as it extrapolates from twentieth-century history. At the same time, Steele devises a successful move by his "cootie" Heinleinesque buggy aliens to utilize the twentieth-century nuke power of the humans to propel themselves back to their own remote corner of the universe. It is wonderfully complex, resonant both of literature and of history, and funny. Here is what Steele writes at the front of the novel about his pragmatic use of ideas – a sort of comic removal of himself from the seriousness of the ideas and from the real science about Mars:

> For the purposes of this work, the Face and the City are treated as if they do indeed exist, but this should not be misconstrued as wholehearted endorsement of the "Face on Mars" theories; the author neither claims to be a believer nor a disbeliever. This is intended as a work of science *fiction*, nothing more nor less. Your acceptance of the underlying premise, or your skepticism of the same, are both welcome. (Steele 1992: vii)

In other words, he is saying to his readers just to buy the book and both to laugh at and to marvel at the strange science and at our strange century.

Finally, the echo all the way back to Wells, a century before NASA, is very funny also when, in the course of exploration, the Japanese heroine exclaims that the nanotechnology (itself an interesting 1990s extrapolation) of the insect-like aliens is producing huge, three-legged machines. "H.G. Wells was right, " she said. "There *are* tripods on Mars" (Steele 1992: 301). It is the human conflict, however, between the Satanic, Hitleresque military xenophobe who wants to nuke the aliens (ironically when he does that the move falls right into the trap prepared by the aliens) and the James Bond type hero, another military undercover agent on Mars named August Nash, that drives the plot. The two of them die together in the action ending on the failing dirigible. Finally, Nash is the lonely hero who still believes in spite of himself; and he utters a prayer as he is falling in the deep ravines of the *noctis labyrintus*. This loneliness is echoed in one of the final sentiments of the book as the alien robots hurdle away home:

> . . . they waited for a reply, watching the terminal screen for a change in pattern, an alteration in the interplanetary static. A sign that they cared. None came. As before, the human race was left only with themselves. . . . No farewells, no promises to return. No comfort from a hard, remorseless universe. Only the memory . . . falling through the labyrinth of night. (Steele 1992: 340)

I think that Steele's book is large-scale space opera adventure with good gadgets and interesting echoes to other science fiction as well as to the harsh realities of nature and of history so that is a fine example of the effects of hard science fiction. The novel is one those long narrative developments of the famous story "The Cold Equations" (1954) by Tom Godwin.

But I think the Landis novel succeeds even more at conveying the sense of the lonely, isolate character (the lonely inventor perhaps) left to stand heroically against a cold universe. One of the space agency rules that is more multinational in the novel of the near-future version of NASA is that no astronaut on the Mars expedition may be a married person. In a similar vein, Landis published a short Mars story in *Analog* two years after his novel titled "Falling onto Mars" in which he conceives of the planet as a very genealogically complex prison colony. The story ends with the cryptic statement, "There are many stories from the days of the first refugees on Mars. None of them are love stories" (Landis 2002: 139).

So what we find in these several Mars fictions of "the renewal" are characterizations that emphasize something like the lonely Byronic hero. In Landis, also, we find provocative efforts to explore what is two-dimensional, changeable, and very adolescent about the lonely hero. Perhaps all Byronic heroes are adolescent. One member of the expedition that has to cross Mars is both an adolescent and an imposter. He has switched identity with his test tube twin back on earth. The twins are identical, but three years apart in age; hence in order to join the expedition the younger one has to assume the identity of the older to meet the age requirement. He dies on Mars in a sort of cold equation death when he is lost out in the open during the cold Martian night. Another skillful wrinkle of characterization in the Landis novel is that the military hero leader of the expedition – an echo of the Nash hero in Steele and of many Heinlein military heroes – has had to escape a tough, cyberpunk, adolescent gang upbringing in order to become the squeaky-clean astronaut ace of the story. But he carries with him considerable baggage of guilt because his brother had had to go to jail for him in order for him to escape the ghetto.

I suspect that each of these space-hero human characterizations is secondary to the interesting conceptual schemes about loneliness in pragmatic space and about the need to be self-reliant and a bit of an adolescent in order to be flexible enough, even two-dimensional enough, so that one can survive in alien environments. In other words, I think the concept is that there are, indeed, no love stories in future space; and this may mean no complex family romance such as we usually expect to see depicted in the romance novel or, for that matter, in any novel other than science fiction. A recent reviewer in *The New Republic* quotes the following pronouncement by Wallace Stegner, ". . . if fiction isn't people it is nothing" (Smith 2003: 33). Further, a new novel by Timothy Zahn, who usually writes hard science fiction, attacks this problem of characterization in science fiction writing directly by creating a symbiosis of a human adolescent hero and an alien symbiont. The alien has the capability to flow into a liquid crystal sort of film and so can become invisible as a nearly two-dimensional layer on the back of his human. This is a clever and forceful set of images to make the argument that adolescent personality, with all of its flux and vitality, as well as the two-dimensional character are perfectly appropriate for the purposes of science fiction. In any case, the conclusion of *Mars Crossing*, after all the good gadgets and the accurately described terrain cleverly coped with, seems to me particularly Byronic, poignant, and grimly comic. I find the clash of Byronic sentiment and harsh reality comic, even in Byron. The heroine chooses to remain alone at the Martian North Pole; someone has to stay due to problems of weight just as in Godwin. I quote first the narrator's general statement and then, at the end, three grimly little lines of dialog:

> Alone between the ice and the sky, [she] felt free to be nobody at all. . . .
> "I'm done with that. . . .
> "I decided, I don't care if I go back. I don't need it. . . .
> "I want to be alone." (Landis 2000: 318, 330)

Time Travel and Genre

To be left so much alone, even in a sublime universe that is conceptualized as hard reality, does seem unacceptable, in the final analysis, and even morally self-indulgent. We know that we ought to try, at least, to imagine a sense of community, a family, something or someone to love and conditions where we can live out our lives fully rather than constantly bemoaning our loneliness. So a final element that has been present in hard science fiction from the beginnings with Wells and that may be consistent with what nature actually offers us, like all the gadgets and military toughness, is time travel. And the fictions about time travel that have appeared in the last decade of the long twentieth century, again following Wells in his famous bicycle trip through time to see the evolution of the Eloi, Morlocks, and beyond, have often been stories about the vast ranges suggested in the ideas of Darwin. A series of novels on human evolution by the Canadian Robert Sawyer is getting a lot of attention. The British writer Stephen Baxter, who is skilled at gadget fiction about space, has written his own Mars novel (*Voyage*, 1996) and has produced some powerful tales about evolution that make use of time travel to help the reader feel connected. Most recently, Baxter has begun a set of novels in collaboration with Arthur C. Clarke who, along with Fred Pohl, is now one of the few remaining survivors from the great traditions of hard science fiction that came before this end-of-century renewal. In *Time's Eye* (2004), which I have seen in proof, Clarke and Baxter actually permit their readers to meet Rudyard Kipling in the future. The book is, also, a story about the military – Kipling, of course, started out as a military journalist – and the motivation of the mysterious aliens, called the Firstborn, who introduce time travel into the plot figures prominently in the thinking of Clarke and Baxter. Strangely, this motivation seems to have less to do with community than with science itself. One explanation is that, as experimenters, the Firstborn simply want to observe our most imperial sort of warfare just as human scientists like to observe the behavior of chimps. I listened recently to a talk by a well-known anthropologist who claims that, with artificial means of reproduction, we should be capable soon of breeding early hominid species so that we may observe them in cages. Maybe we will find out more about the motivations of the Clarke/Baxter Firstborn in the sequels to come, and the motivations may be communal as well as objective. In any case, the pragmatic science that undergirds so many of the adventure tropes and loneliness tropes and tones of hard science fiction also may provide the most plausible means to satisfy our need for community – time travel.

In this discussion, I have barely touched on the many other accounts of the origins and nature of hard science fiction. As Gary Westfahl, especially, has pointed out that the commercial ingenuity of Hugo Gernsback represents the great model for clever writers such as Steele, working to sell their books and to sell their readers on plausibility. Many of the writers and theorists who comment on hard science fiction, also, are scientists themselves and in recent decades have worked in the space industry. Landis and Baxter are examples. But finally, as I have argued, for the works of the 1990s and the early years in the turn of the century to be thought of as a genuine renewal we need to imagine a generic location of ancientness so that, almost like time travel itself, the evocation of the generic or family characteristics in that ancestor provides the sense of return as opposed to raw innovation. The power innovation, of course, is always present. Wells himself wrote the strange and overly ambitious literary innovation that he titled *A Modern Utopia* (1905). But he also set down some more solid roots in his scientific romances. It is amazing for me to see these roots renewed with a sense of genre in the hard science fiction a century later. Perhaps a huge singularity of newness in science fiction writing is among us with works like those of Vinge and Egan. In the meantime, however, we can amuse and comfort ourselves with the renewal of conventions that seem particularly appropriate to our needs at the end of a long century where, as Coleridge writes in his masterful poem "Kubla Khan" and I modify here just a bit, *ancestral voices prophesied war.*

REFERENCES AND FURTHER READING

Baldwin, Neil (2003) *Henry Ford and the Jews.* New York: Public Affairs.

Blackford, Russell (2003) "Review of *The Hard Science Fiction Renaissance.*" *The New York Review of Science Fiction* 178, 11–14.

Beer, Thomas (1926) *The Mauve Decade.* New York: Knopf.

Burroughs, Edgar Rice (1917) *A Princess of Mars.* New York: McClurg.

Clarke, Arthur C. and Stephen Baxter (2004) *Time's Eye.* New York: Del Rey.

Davis, L.J. (2003) *Fleet Fire: Thomas Edison and the Pioneers of the Electric Revolution.* New York: Arcade.

Hartwell, David G. and Kathryn Cramer (2002)

The Hard Science Fiction Renaissance. New York: Tor.

Hassler, Donald M. (1982) *Comic Tones in Science Fiction.* Westport, CT: Greenwood Press.

——(1982) *Hal Clement.* Mercer Island, WA: Starmont.

Heinlein, Robert A. (1959) *Starship Troopers.* New York: Putnam.

Landis, Geoffrey A. (2002) "Falling onto Mars." *Analog* July/August, 136–9.

——(2000) *Mars Crossing.* New York: Tor.

Menand, Louis (2001) *The Metaphysical Club.* New York: Farrar, Straus, and Giroux.

Nicholls, Peter (1979) *The Science Fiction Encyclopedia.* New York: Doubleday.

Robinson, Kim Stanley (1993) *Red Mars*. New York: Bantam.

Sawyer, Robert J. (2002) *Hominids*. New York: Tor.

Slusser, George E. and Eric S. Rabkin (1986) *Hard Science Fiction*. Carbondale, IL: Southern Illinois UP.

Smith, Zadie (2003) "The limited circle is pure." *The New Republic* November 3, 2003, 33–40.

Steele, Allen (2001) *Chronospace*. New York: Ace.

——(1992) *Labyrinth of Night*. New York: Ace.

Weinbaum, Stanley G. (1974) *A Martian Odyssey and Other SF Tales*. New York: Hyperion. (Title story originally published 1936.)

Wells, H.G. (1905) *A Modern Utopia*. London: Chapman and Hall.

——(1895) *The Time Machine*. London: Heinemann.

——(1898) *The War of the Worlds*. London: Heinemann.

Westfahl, Gary (1996) *Cosmic Engineers: A Study of Hard Science Fiction*. Westport, CT: Greenwood Press.

PART IV
Science Fiction Film

17

American Science Fiction Film: An Overview

Vivian Sobchack

As a film genre, science fiction dramatizes the social consequences of imaginary science and technology in speculative visions of possible futures, alternate pasts, and parallel presents. The genre's breadth of thematic material and settings includes the exploration and colonization of outer and inner space, apocalyptic world cataclysms and their aftermath, invasion of the Earth by superior extraterrestrials or destructive and monstrous creatures, time travel as well as space travel, human and alien cultures meeting in novel circumstances, and the extension and transformation of human beings through technological and biological manipulation and accident. Visual by nature, SF film is less contemplative and analytic and more spectacular and kinetic than its literary counterparts. Thus, its emphasis is on dramatic action, a markedly wondrous *mise-en-scène* that defamiliarizes this world as it envisions others, and a foregrounded use of "special effects."

SF did not emerge as a distinctive American film genre until the 1950s. This decade saw the production of a large number of narrative features that, through imaginative displacement in space and time, speculatively mapped the future (or lack of it) of a postwar world transformed forever by major technological innovation and new forms of energy and communication. However, although historically unique, the SF film's first "Golden Age" (1950–1960) had its origins in the popular culture of earlier decades. The genre drew loosely on the visionary novels of Jules Verne and H.G. Wells and also on the American literature of individual entrepreneurship and technological invention that sparked the popular imagination of the first quarter of the century. Furthermore, the 1920s and 1930s saw the rise of both popular journalism devoted to science and technology and pulp magazines devoted to "science fiction," a term often credited to Hugo Gernsback, who, in 1926, began *Amazing Stories* which, despite the magazine's lurid covers, sought technical plausibility and "hard" scientific fact in its speculative fiction, its overall tone signaling a general belief that modernization achieved through technology was the very essence of democracy. *Astounding Stories* followed in 1934 and, edited by John Campbell, published SF more concerned with the

impact of radical technological change on society, culture, and human and alien subjectivity than with high-tech hardware and adventures in outer space. These decades
also gave Americans quasi-SF comics with superheroes like *Superman* (1938), who promoted American individualism and democratic ideals through special extraterrestrial
powers or futuristic technologies.

It was in this context that the first American SF films appeared during the mid-
1930s – most "serials" that owed more to comic strips and pulp SF magazines than
to the growing body of serious SF literature. Indeed, throughout the 1930s and 1940s,
there were few SF features and other than a rather loony SF "romantic comedy" – *Just
Imagine* (1930), its futuristic vision of New York City in 1980 clearly borrowed from
Fritz Lang's *Metropolis* (1926) – most of them figured the dire consequences of scientific inquiry and technological invention. Subsumed by the horror genre so popular
in the 1930s and 1940s, quasi-SF films such as *Dr. Jekyll and Mr. Hyde* (1912, 1920,
1932, 1941), *Frankenstein* (1931), and the more urbane *The Invisible Man* (1933), were
focused on nineteenth-century "mad scientists" who challenged the "proper" order of
things, and had themes committed more to the preservation of traditional social and
moral values than to the radical transformation of society through scientific discovery and new technology.

Prior to the Second World War then, American SF film meant low-budget serials.
Made for young audiences, their plotting was simple and their perspective was generally xenophobic. The comic strip hero Flash Gordon appeared in 1936's *Spaceship to
the Unknown* to do battle with an orientalized tyrant, the Emperor Ming of the planet
Mongo and, in 1938, the year that Martians invaded Earth in the Mercury Theater
radio adaptation of H.G. Wells' *War of the Worlds*, *Flash Gordon's Trip to Mars* was also
theatrically serialized. In 1939, the opening year of the future-oriented New York
World's Fair, Buck Rogers made his initial appearance in *Destination Saturn*. And in
1940, the first year of the Second World War, theatres screened *Flash Gordon Conquers
the Universe*. Conquest of the universe, however, became a more ambiguous enterprise
after the Second World War. The menace was "Red" rather than an orientalized yellow
and it hailed from the Communist Soviet Union. Furthermore, the greatest "special
effect" the world had ever seen – atomic destruction – demonstrated that expansionist dreams, invasion fantasies, and high technology could well result in apocalypse
right here on Earth. The last of the SF serials, released during the early years of the
Cold War and reflecting their "atomic" moment, included *Radar Men from the Moon*
(1952), and *Canadian Mounties vs. Atomic Invaders* (1953). Serialized SF disappeared in
the mid-1950s – not only because of changes in theatrical exhibition practices but
also because of the new technology of television. Indeed, television provided what
seemed a "natural" conjunction of "futuristic" serial SF with a "futuristic" technology
– resulting, appropriately enough, first in *Captain Video* (1949–53), and then in *Space
Patrol* (1950–3), and the anthology series, *Tales of Tomorrow* (1951–3).

The sudden appearance of the SF feature film in the 1950s is thus not so surprising as might first appear. The genre emerges as a symbolic response to an America
transformed by heightened public recognition of the vast power and sociopolitical

consequences of rapid advances in science and technology; a new consciousness of the relativity of spatial and temporal distance and the planet as a connected global community; and by a lived sense of political enmity and geophysical vulnerability. The Cold War period is marked ambivalently – both by the historically unique threat of nuclear annihilation and the domestic promise of new technologies such as television and the computer. Politicians urged technological superiority in the "arms race" and school children went through "duck and cover" civil defense drills while consumers bought "modern" home appliances, wore "miracle" fabrics, and lived "better through chemistry." The SF film poetically dramatized and gave visibly concrete and novel form to the hopes and fears generated by these new conditions of existence. Indeed, the two key films that initiated American SF film's first "Golden Age" are exemplary in symbolically figuring the positive and negative attitudes about the technologized future that informed both the culture at large and the genre in particular.

Destination Moon (1950) was big-budget, its Technicolor narrative of a manned space mission optimistic about an expansionist future enabled by the cooperation of hard science, high technology, and corporate capitalism. In images filled with shiny futuristic technology, a sleek spaceship (created by a rocket designer), the beauty of limitless outer space (provided by an astronomical artist), and "special effects," the film visually went "where no man had gone before." However much marked by the ideology of its present, the film's creation of awesome moonscapes, its extraterrestrial perspective on Earth, its grounding in current scientific knowledge, and its privileging of human curiosity presage later visionary SF such as *2001: A Space Odyssey* (1968) and *Close Encounters of the Third Kind* (1977). The moon its destination and "special effects" technology its means of transportation, *Destination Moon* promised its audiences a progressive, expansionist, and shiny new future.

The Thing (1951), however, was pessimistic about both rational science and the future. Low-budget and black-and-white, the film's narrative about a murderous alien creature on an Arctic military outpost was xenophobic and antiscience, privileging technology only for the weapons it provided against alien attack. Indeed, with its dark *mise-en-scène* and caution against obsessive scientific curiosity, *The Thing* harkened back to earlier horror films whose moral was "there are some things man is not meant to know." Claustrophobic, creating danger in off-screen (and outer) space, it presaged not only its own remake in 1983, but also the wary and confined vision of the *Alien* films (1979, 1986, 1992, 1997). *The Thing* envisioned the future not in terms of limitless space and scientific progress, but in terms of merely staying alive and safe. Its paranoid last warning was: "Keep watching the skies!"

These two films set the boundaries and tonal range of the first period of SF's popularity as a genre. They also dramatized the period's essential ambivalence about the new Cold War conjunction of science, technology, the military, and corporate capitalism. But for some few exceptions like *War of the Worlds* and *Invaders from Mars* (both 1953) which were Earth-bound Technicolor nightmares of alien invasion, the legacy of the big-budget, effects-laden *Destination Moon* were films that, even when cautionary, celebrated technology as progressive and the American future as expansive in awesome and poetic displays of graceful, glittering new machinery and startlingly beautiful extraterrestrial landscapes and spacescapes. Nonetheless, perhaps because of production costs or the prevalence of fear over hope, there were far fewer Technicolor SF films like *When Worlds Collide* (1951), *Riders to the Stars* (1954), *The Conquest of Space* (1955), and *Forbidden Planet* (1956) than black-and-white films that shared the paranoia of *The Thing*.

This negative vision of the future developed in several directions: "creature features," alien invasion fantasies, and films about the fear of radiation and nuclear apocalypse. "Creature features" foregrounded atomically awakened or mutated creatures that embodied the present threat of nuclear annihilation in "prehistoric" figures. Stomping cities and chomping their inhabitants, primal beasts and giant insects caused mass urban chaos and, through special effects, brought to visibility what Susan Sontag called the "imagination of disaster" and the "aesthetics of destruction." *The Beast from 20,000 Fathoms* (1953), *Them!* (1954), *Tarantula* (1955), *It Came from Beneath the Sea* (1955), *The Deadly Mantis* (1957), and *The Black Scorpion* (1957) give us creatures who condense in their gigantic size, primitive biology, and acts of mindless and outsize destruction not only the affective charge of an annihilating energy run amok, but also the suggestion of humanity's postapocalyptic future as a regression to prehistory and the primal sink. At the same time, however, these primitive creatures drew attention away from the advanced science and technology that gave rise to them – thus allowing scientists and the military to use that science and technology to "save" humanity (just as they had in the Second World War). Hardly regarded as works of art or social commentary, these films were nonetheless culturally significant. Ritualistic in their simple plotting and repetitive structure, they were mythic in function – narratively resolving intense and contradictory feelings about scientific rationalism and advanced technology, and their historically novel destructive (and military) applications.

The alien invasion films dramatized another cultural anxiety: the popular fear of Communism as a dehumanizing political system bent on destroying individual subjectivity, committed to world conquest, and proficient in frightening new forms of "invasive" and "invisible" domination like "brainwashing." These films disguise (sometimes only thinly) Cold War nightmares about being "taken over" by powerful, inhumanly cold (and rational) others, who would radically flatten human emotion and transform (American) consciousness into a collectivity, but they do so in two quite different forms.

Like the creature films, one type of invasion film features the "aesthetics of destruction" and an urban America under attack – but here from aliens, whose superior weapons blast distinctly American landmarks like the Washington Monument at the same time the invasion is seen through newspaper and television montage as global in scope. *War of the Worlds* (1953) and *Earth vs. the Flying Saucers* (1956) dramatize radical xenophobia, fear of planetary annihilation through high-tech weaponry, and a contradictory yearning for both a United Nations fantasy of peaceful global coalition and another morally clear-cut – rather than ambiguously "cold" – world war. Only

The Day the Earth Stood Still (1951) took a critical view of the period's xenophobia, its extraterrestrial (if humanoid) protagonist speaking out against irrational fear and knee-jerk militarism, and emphasizing the cosmic consequences of nuclear power. Even this film, however, used the threat of planetary destruction (by the technologically superior extraterrestrials) as the solution to the threat of planetary destruction (by technologically inferior humans). Its singular critical intelligence and plea for world peace was thus ultimately informed by the very structure of Cold War *détente*.

The second type of alien invasion film dramatized cultural anxieties about the more "invisible" threats of Communism: infiltration of America by a subversive "fifth column" and ideological "brainwashing." *Invaders from Mars* (1953), *It Came from Outer Space* (1953), *Invasion of the Body Snatchers* (1956), *I Married a Monster from Outer Space* (1958), and *The Day Mars Invaded the Earth* (1963) locate themselves in the ordinary and familiar worlds of small-town and suburban America where aliens "take over" the bodies of family members, cops, doctors, workmen, and lovers. These low-budget films created a paranoid style (and spectatorship) in which alien "difference" was marked not by special effects but by the wooden demeanor and small failures of the human-looking aliens to respond appropriately in ordinary human situations: not blinking at the sun, not responding maternally to a child or passionately to a kiss. Yet, in *Invasion of the Body Snatchers*, those "taken over" tell those still human: "Love, desire, ambition, faith. Without them, life is so simple." Expressing Cold War fears about a "soul-less" alien social system and emotional fatigue at the complexity of global politics, these invasion films gained additional power from their location in American suburbia – for the 1950s of the Eisenhower years were also marked by ambivalence and critique of the rise of the gray-suited "organization man," the cookie-cutter sameness of tract housing, and of "creeping conformity" (a domestic equivalent to alien "collective consciousness," whether Martian or Soviet).

SF postapocalyptic fantasies played out anxieties of yet another kind. Fear of radiation's effects on the human body were poeticized in extreme dramas of scale like *The Incredible Shrinking Man* and *The Amazing Colossal Man* (both 1957), while visions of life after nuclear apocalypse were set in recognizable urban contexts, now ghost towns emptied of people but for a few survivors. Structured around loss and absence, both elegiac and cautionary in tone, *On the Beach* and *The World, the Flesh and the Devil* (both 1959) starred significant Hollywood actors and were received less as SF than as serious adult drama. Other low-budget films like *Five* (1951) or the later *Panic in the Year Zero* (1962) also foregrounded moral questions of the period about what "survival of the fittest" might mean in actual postapocalyptic practice.

At the end of the 1950s, SF film went into major decline, the reasons linked to dramatic changes in both the motion picture industry and American society. The 1960s saw the final throes and economic collapse of the monopolistic Hollywood studio system and major changes in production and exhibition that virtually did away with the low-budget "B" picture and "double features" (on both of which the existence of most SF film depended). Television was also providing audiences with a major entertainment alternative, offering SF in well-written series such as *The Twilight Zone*

(1959–64), *The Outer Limits* (1963–9), and *Star Trek* (1966–8). Although, in response, the film industry introduced wide-screen and experimented (unsuccessfully) with 3-D films such as *It Came from Outer Space*, there was now little theatrical place for the "low" genre of SF. During its first "Golden Age," most SF films were made on shoe-string budgets, some so impoverished (in plot as well as budget) that, over time, they became enshrined in popular culture as unintentionally funny "cult" classics. *Robot Monster* (1953), for example, featured an alien invader costumed in a gorilla suit and diving helmet, and *Cat Women of the Moon* (1954) peopled Earth's satellite with a society of seductive women in black leotards. However, the most laughable films emerged toward the decade's end as the genre's relevance and popularity precipitously declined, the most famous and beloved of them *Plan 9 from Outer Space* (1958), with an aged Bela Lugosi, cardboard sets, and a complete lack of plot continuity con-tributing to the film's reputation as the worst picture ever made.

The cultural taste for SF clearly changed in the 1960s. Life in the nuclear shadow became normalized and "new" technologies no longer quite so exciting. Other than during the Cuban missile crisis in 1962, most Americans were less concerned with nuclear annihilation than with domestic problems – "alien threat" coming not from the USSR or outer space but from black Americans demanding their civil rights; flower children rejecting parental values and "spacing out" on drugs; angry feminists; and protesters against the war in Vietnam. For those still interested in outer space, the Cold War relocated there (and on television) in an explicit "space race" – that, in the early 1960s, America was losing to the Soviets. Against the "real thing," and the "right stuff" evidenced by the 1969 Apollo II moon landing, the futurism of SF film and cinematic special effects seemed outdated. Furthermore, looking toward the stars and for "new frontiers" (after President Kennedy was assassinated in 1963 and Martin Luther King in 1968) seemed increasingly irrelevant in a decade faced with the Earthbound gravity of civil unrest, political assassinations, bloody demonstrations, interrogation of social institutions from government to the family, and an ambiguous and nonnuclear jungle war in South-East Asia that belied high-tech SF fantasies about colonial expansion and American military pre-eminence.

Although the SF film did not disappear between the 1960s and 1977 (the year of the genre's "renaissance"), it did recede in popular consciousness. Exceptions were Stanley Kubrick's *Dr. Strangelove: or How I Learned to Stop Worrying and Love the Bomb* (1964), a black comedy about the onset of nuclear war, and *2001: A Space Odyssey* (1968), a critically acclaimed epic that set new standards for cinematic effects and ironically foregrounded the increasing banality of technologized human being against the grandeur and possibilities of an unknown universe. 1968 also saw release of the very popular *Planet of the Apes*, which combined a postapocalyptic theme with space and time travel to displace and explore contemporaneous American race relations. And, a year after the Environmental Protection Agency was founded, *Silent Running* (1971) extended the period's dystopic mood with a focus on Earth's ecological future; featuring the latest sophisticated cinematic technology, the narrative took place on a dilapidated "greenhouse" spaceship where a lone crew member and three little robot "drones" fight (unsuccessfully) to preserve the last of Earth's trees and plants from human destruction. Even our leisure entertainments were suspect insofar as they had become overly technologized and frighteningly complex. For example, in *Westworld* (1973) a futuristic theme park (a "fantasy land" for adults) runs amok – a theme that will return in the 1990s with Spielberg's *Jurassic Park* (1993).

Indeed, it may well have been SF's narrative inability to sufficiently transform and displace contemporaneous terrestrial concerns in post-1968 American culture that kept viewers away. More adult, socially relevant, and mainstream than it had been previously, between 1970 and 1977, SF was hardly escapist, dealing with overpopulation, food shortages, urban blight, and aging in films like *Soylent Green* (1973) or with the consequences of corporate capitalism and media violence in films like *Rollerball* (1975). Certainly, between 1969 and 1974, the years of Nixon's presidency (ended by the Watergate scandal and Nixon's ignominious resignation), space travel and extraterrestrials seemed irrelevant to a future threatened more by domestic political corruption, reckless consumption, and corporate greed than by the possibilities of alien attack.

Yet, in 1977 (a year after the American bicentennial), it was precisely space travel and extraterrestrials that marked the inauguration of SF's second "Golden Age." Indeed, the statement that began Gerald Ford's short presidency (1974–77) – "Our long nightmare is over" – seemed fulfilled by its end in two extraordinarily popular, big-budget, effects-laden, and visionary and benign SF fantasies: George Lucas' *Star Wars* and Steven Spielberg's *Close Encounters of the Third Kind*. Radically different from their more baleful SF predecessors, *Star Wars* was an epic space adventure and coming-of-age film set in a mythic past "long, long ago," but realized futuristically in a galaxy "far, far away"; and *Close Encounters* was an epic domestic adventure about an ordinary man's search for "something important" and "wonder-full" that culminates in a spectacular and joyful encounter and communication with child-like yet technologically advanced extraterrestrials. Both films were positive and enthusiastic about the future of human beings (and special effects) and envisioned alien life forms as potentially friendly allies in adventure. Made by cinematically literate "movie brats," both were also playful, often comic, and reflexive about their own generic existence and history. And, more radically, both films transformed SF's "objective" and rational vision of a high technology promoted through special "effects" into a "subjective" and emotional expression of new technological "highs" and special "affects." (Indeed, to realize this new technological "sublime," Lucas founded his appropriately-named Industrial Light and Magic effects company, a pioneer in the cinematic use of computer-generated imagery.) Most significant, both films were huge commercial successes and made SF "mainstream" entertainment – *Star Wars* particularly striking as a cultural "event" that generated millions of dollars globally not only in ticket sales and years' worth of sequels and "prequels" (1980, 1983, 1999, 2002) but also in the mass sale of ancillary toys, lunch boxes, pajamas, bed sheets, and video games.

What in the American cultural milieu of the late 1970s accounted for this sudden change in popular attitudes toward the genre – not just these two inaugural blockbusters but the large number of mainstream SF films that followed through the 1990s? Informed by bicentennial nostalgia and a rhetoric of integrity, gentleness, and political openness, the first two years of Jimmy Carter's presidency (1977–81) were a time of national "healing" and middle-ground compromise. As "losers" in Vietnam, popular culture reinvented Americans as valiant "underdogs" and, in a paradoxical turn, identified with the "little guys" against big "Evil Empires." American culture began to sentimentalize the recent past (now "long, long ago"), seeking alternatives in spiritually inflected and escapist SF fantasies that promised something better "far, far away." First wave feminism's interrogation of gender roles (*Ms.* magazine was founded in 1972) as well as military defeat also prompted popular reappraisal of "masculinity" and traditional notions of patriarchal power in fantasies figuring alien "born-again" males dropping naked, sensitive, and without "mach " baggage, into the earthly *mise-en-scène*. (*The Terminator*, *Starman*, and *The Brother from Another Planet* were all released in 1984.) Thus, it was no accident that Princess Leia was "bossy" or that, in *Alien* (1979), Ripley (written for a male actor) was a fiercely intelligent and independent female protagonist embraced by women not only in the audience but also in the academic community. In sum, for the first time since the 1950s, when women in SF film may have screamed a lot but often had PhDs in biology, the genre began to recognize and reflect the (somewhat) changed position of women in American society.

In 1981, an increasingly bad economy ceded the Carter presidency to Ronald Reagan. Promoting big business and America as a world power, the former actor served until 1989, rearticulating the historically regressive terms of the Cold War in science fictional rhetoric. Indeed, in 1985, Reagan explicitly connected his plans for a satellite defense system to *Star Wars* and told America, "The force is with us." It was a decade of corporate expansion, high technology, and media fiction – and the height of the SF film's renaissance. But all was not well in the body politic and the body proper. Supply-side economics, massive deregulation of greedy corporations, and an enhanced military budget led to an increasing national deficit; furthermore, first diagnosed as such in 1981, AIDS became epidemic and, connected to homosexuality, was popularly conceived as an "alien" disease. Thus, parallel to (and eventually overtaking) the more sanguine SF of the decade such as the enormously popular *E.T.: The Extra-Terrestrial* (1982) and *Back to the Future* (1985) were films from the "dark side" of the "force." Thus, the aesthetically influential "tech noir" *Blade Runner* (1982) and poignant *Robocop* (1987) seemed responsive to postindustrial pollution and corporate deceit, while *Lifeforce* (1985) and *The Fly* (1986) visualized horrible (and AIDS-related) bodily transformation and decay. There were, as well, less mainstream films like *Repo Man* (1984) and *Uforia* (1986) that ironically figured contemporary American culture as habitually alien-ated and science fictional.

The renaissance of SF film in the late 1970s, and its heightened success in the 1980s and 1990s through the Reagan, Bush Sr., and Clinton administrations owed a great deal to concurrent – and extraordinary – advances in a domesticated computer technology that not only made special effects more spectacular and "seamless" than ever before but also inaugurated an increasing extension of the media and spectatorship. The scope and kinesis of SF-related electronic games and play-stations; CD-ROM and DVD technologies; the rise of the Internet and "interactivity"; the increase of 3-D "virtual reality" simulations in both theme parks and arcades – all inculcated the sense of not just seeing but actually living (for good or ill) in an increasingly "naturalized" science fictional world. The "natural" world was also transformed by advances in the biological sciences: DNA and the mapping of the human genome; cosmetic surgery; reproductive technologies and genetic cloning – all suggesting (for good or ill) an unprecedented surveillance of our bodies, matched only by new communications technologies' (and business and government's) unprecedented surveillance of our preferences and activities. The SF films of the 1980s and 1990s refract and figure this world in three major – and overlapping – cinematic "maps."

Prevalent in the early 1980s, and certainly influenced by Spielberg's *Close Encounters* and *E.T.*, the first map charts cultural longing for a simpler and more innocent world, one in which technology is generally benign and often emotionalized, in which "alien" others are sentimentalized, spiritual mentors who are kinder, gentler, and more enlightened than humans. This sanguine and emotionalized strain of mega-budget mainstream SF not only coincided with the more "upbeat" spiritual rhetoric and rampant consumerism of the Carter and Reagan years, but also could be sold as "family" entertainment: its hardware and special effects to men, its new sentimentality to women, its spectacle to "children of all ages." Films such as *Star Man* (1984) and *Cocoon* (1985), in which aliens were figured as innocent lovers and spiritual friends, seemed to fulfill the culture's need to escape a complex and heterogeneous world that refused both moral and ideological simplification. This cultural desire for a return to the innocence and simplicity of childhood found its apotheosis in Spielberg's hugely popular *E.T.* (1982). The story of a suburban boy's friendship with a small and cuddly alien was SF with a "heart light," and had an emotional appeal more to do with resolving family problems than with the rational science and high technology previously associated with the genre. (The same could be said of 1985's *Back to the Future* in which Marty McFly time travels to ensure the union of his own parents.) Nonetheless, most of the regressive nostalgia in the films of this first mapping were also reflexively aware that the innocence and wonder they promoted were less a fact of life than a figment of popular media imagination. Thus, many were "remakes" of previous movies and television series, a strategy that seemed hermetically safe for the spectator and financially "safe" for the conservative industry (and foreshadowed the massive "recycling" to come). This was SF at its most white, middle-class, and family themepark clean. (During this decade, Disneyland opened its simulated ride, "Star Tours," and Universal Studios took visitors back to a simulated future.) It was also the basis for major "branding" and "franchising": the *Star Wars* trilogy (initially 1977, 1980, 1983, with "prequels" in 1999 and 2002); the *Superman* films (1978, 1980, 1983,

1987); the *Star Trek* movies (ten of them between 1979 and 2002); the *Back to the Future* trilogy (1985, 1989, 1990); as well as the darker *Alien* series (1979, 1986, 1992, 1997).

Like the aliens, technology had also became increasingly domesticated, both in – and out of – the new SF film. By the late 1970s and early 1980s, consumer electronics were a part of everyday American life and science fictional items such as digital watches, microwave ovens, and VCRs were commonplace. The large computers initially associated with the secretive military-industrial complex became small, affordable, "user-friendly," and "personal." Nonetheless, however familiarized, the wedding of electronics with popular entertainment kept much of its military and SF flavor in Reagan's America – not only in everyday life but also in the cinema and a burgeoning electronic games market. In the late 1970s, companies like Atari, Sega, and Nintendo were inspired by the space battles in *Star Wars*. In the early 1980s, in Disney's *Tron* (1982) transforms a video game designer into a computer program to successfully battle an evil corporate empire and its "master program"; the teen hero of *Wargames* (1983) "hacks" his way into a computer game called "Global Thermonuclear War," only to find out it's not a game at all; and *The Last Starfighter* (1984) is a teen video game champ whose skill enables him to save the universe. These "family" SF films ended happily but figured not only the proliferation of electronic gamesmanship, but also Reagan's Cold War brinksmanship and the rhetoric that zapped Americans into and out of "real" space and "game" space, "game" space and outer space.

In the mid-1980s, this "domestication " of SF led also to a second – and overlapping – map, quite different in tone and terrain from the first. A significant number of low-budget, independent, "quasi-SF" films emerged on the margins of the genre as a counter-cultural critique. Using visibly cheesy special effects, *Liquid Sky* (1984), *Strange Invaders, Brother from Another Planet, Repo Man, Night of the Comet* (all 1984), and *Uforia* (1986) dramatize American culture as pervasively "science fictionalized" and "alien-ated" – indeed, more anthropologically bizarre than anything mainstream SF could dream up. In these films, extraterrestrial aliens are easily "integrated" into black Harlem, run up against the drug subculture and punk scene, and are confronted with their image in the *National Enquirer*. Their SF "plots" are also played out in the familiar yet estranged spaces of convenience stores, suburban shopping malls, and supermarkets celebrating "Hawaiian Days." Often called "postmodern" because of their use of irony and pastiche, these films played up their own "B" movie status – although there were no more "B" movies – and many went quickly to video stores and cult status. Nonetheless, their parodic mode and ironic tone (although not their cultural critique) were highly influential in the decades to come.

Indeed, mainstream SF films also began to use pastiche and parody. The media-savvy *Explorers* (1985) featured aliens who spoke like Groucho Marx and Marilyn Monroe from watching old Earth movies, and a human protagonist at a loss to explain to them the difference between televised SF films and "real" American history – and Tim Burton's parodic remake of *Invaders from Mars* (1986) borrowed the earlier film's pie-plate spaceships in an extremely broad comedy. This new ironic or comic tone – based primarily on the bald recycling and recognition of generic conventions – informed any number of extremely popular SF action films in the next decade, most notably *Independence Day* (1996), whose bug-eyed aliens unsuccessfully attempt to invade Earth; *Starship Troopers* (1997), a militarist "blast-em-up," pitting humans against giant insects; *Men in Black* (1997), whose "secret agents" often and explicitly confuse illegal extraterrestrial aliens disguised as humans with "illegal" Mexican aliens; and *Galaxy Quest* (1999), in which a group of has-been actors from a cancelled SF television series are conscripted by extraterrestrials to save their planet from evil alien invaders.

From its beginnings, however, the second "Golden Age" of SF film also had a dark side. Thus, the third map of the genre ignores benign suburban landscapes and starry spacescapes – and paranoia, schizophrenia, and anxiety outweigh parody (although not homage to earlier films). Urban clutter and blight or confined and claustrophobic spaces set the *mise-en-scène* not only for remakes of several 1950s films such as *Invasion of the Body Snatchers* (1979), *Body Snatchers* (1994), and *The Thing* (1982), but also for historically particular cinematic responses to the rampant consumerism of the Reagan years; the downward economic spiral of the Bush Sr. years; and, during the Clinton and Bush Jr. years, to the immense power of "invisible" multinational corporations and to increasing surveillance in every sector of society. At the beginning of SF's renaissance, the extremely popular and frightening *Alien* (1979) did a contemporary turn on *The Thing*, its dark, claustrophobic spaceship and multicultural crew threatened as much by multinational corporate greed as by the rapacious alien creature that stalks the ship. There were other films in the same paranoid vein, among them *Lifeforce* (1985), *Predator* (1987), and *Predator 2* (1990). By the beginning of the Clinton administration in 1993, however, the paranoid fear of alien creatures and predators had become the tamer and contained "thrill" of the CGI dinosaurs in *Jurassic Park*, a theme park ride of a movie about a theme park – soon to be simulated outside the theater in a theme park.

Much more troubling, perhaps, than predatory creatures (alien or terrestrial) were more domestic and intimate threats to human being and the quality of contemporary existence. Thus, this third, and darkest, SF map, although harkening back to earlier and pessimistic social visions of the genre, traced a historically unique – and "postmodern" – ambivalence about what was perceived as a degraded future. Perhaps best characterized by *Blade Runner* (1982), these films both criticized and eroticized the urban blight in which they were set, finding peculiar beauty in garbage, decay, industrial exhaustion, and a cityscape saturated by both by acid rain and advertising. In these films, "new" technology and "modern" architecture look "recycled" and shabby. Thus, dark in tone, filled with highly atmospheric pollution, *Escape from New York* (1981), *Blue Thunder* (1983), the extremely popular *Terminator* films, *Robocop* (1987), and *Total Recall* (1990) stand as celebratory monuments to the consumer culture of late capitalism (and the Reagan years) even as they ironically lament it.

Here it is important to remember that, during the 1980s and early 1990s, the world geopolitical situation radically changed. While Reagan celebrated American moral right and militarism for two terms against "Evil Empires," during George Bush Sr.'s administration (1989–93), the threat of foreign enemies seemed to dissipate. In 1989, the Berlin Wall was dismantled by civilians; the USA quickly liberated Kuwait from Iraqi invasion in the "mediatized" (and sanitized) Gulf War of 1990; and the Soviet Union collapsed from within in 1991. Thus, popular consciousness turned inward – the peril facing Americans coming less from "aliens" than from the transformation (and perceived loss) of those qualities seen as essential to human being: subjectivity, memory, personal identity, privacy, and agency (all which could now be easily extroverted, manipulated, and "hacked.").

The Internet, biotechnology, "artificial" intelligence and robotic/prosthetic technologies, and media simulation (and dissimulation) tied to information, commerce, politics, and entertainment made the nature of human "identity" and "reality" highly ambiguous and spatially and temporally diffuse. Tracing this ambiguity across the decade and owing much to (and often borrowing from) the paranoid literary SF of Philip K. Dick, films such as *Blade Runner* and *Videodrome* (both 1982), *The Terminator* and *Dreamscape* (both 1984), *Robocop* (1987), *The Hidden* and *Total Recall* (both 1990) emphasized a growing confusion of the real with its simulation and immediacy with mediation – and they figured memory, identity, and experience as vulnerable not only to commodification and manipulation but also to theft and erasure. Traditional subjectivity seems to lose sight of itself amid an excess of things and media images. Old forms of identity are "terminal" in an age of media simulation, microchips, biotechnology, cosmetic surgery, and body-building. In *Videodrome*, a man inserts a videocassette into his body and his television set pulsates from pornography as if it were alive. *Blade Runner's* genetically manufactured "replicants" are "more human than human," valuing existence more than do their exhausted human counterparts. *The Terminator* is a killing machine made of flesh and chrome while *Robocop* is a cyborg policeman with residual flesh and human subjectivity. The protagonist of *Total Recall* is never sure his memories or identity are truly his own. Indeed, in the early 1990s, the ambivalently figured (if darkly funny and gender-bending) "human" shape-shifting of the hedonistic alien in *The Hidden* and the liquid fluidity and boundless CGI "morphing" of the chilling and relentless antagonist in *Terminator 2* (1991). These films dramatize malaise, euphoria, and irony about the transformed nature of human consciousness, identity, memory, and embodiment – all of which were recognized popularly as, in various ways, subject to the mediation and manipulations of technology.

Although inaugurated in the 1980s, this paranoid strain of SF has became particularly dominant in the late 1990s and has continued into the present years of the twenty-first century. Insofar as human subjectivity, memory, and identity have become visibly unstable, insecure, and mutable, so too has our sense of "reality." Indeed, it is significant that, in 1998 and 1999, no less than six films interrogated not only the slippery (and always mediated) boundaries between our perceptions of "illusion" and "reality" but also the increasingly slippery boundaries between our perception of generic science fiction and mainstream cinematic drama. In 1998, *Dark City* affectively "effects " the complete SF ungrounding and destabilization not only of space and place but also of human memory and identity through formal and narrative "warping" and "morphing" – while the mainstream *The Truman Show* created an equally artificial and manipulated world wrought not by aliens but by television. 1999 saw the release of *The Thirteenth Floor*, which figured "ordinary" reality as a manufactured illusion; *EXistenZ*, which blurred the boundaries for both characters and spectators between "real" life and virtual game life; the extraordinarily popular *The Matrix*, of course, which posited "real" life the creation of a computer program and real "real life" as a passive and unconscious existence – and, again blurring the boundaries and thematics of SF and mainstream drama, *Fight Club*, in which male passivity and consumerism meet in ambiguous space. These critical thematics and confusions continue to the present day, not only in the *Matrix* sequels (both *Reloaded* and *Revolutions*, 2003), but also in *Solaris* and *Minority Report* (both 2002), and *Paycheck* (2003).

In the last years of the twentieth century and the first years of the twenty-first, the more sanguine strain of the SF film has also become diffused – this, on the one hand, because of the boundless possibilities yet "naturalization" of CGI cinematic effects and, on the other hand, because of a more general sense of play, kinesis, and wish fulfillment created by the "flattening" of real life "gravity" and computergraphic "grace." Special effects technology is no longer linked to rationalism or science and its disassociation, to great extent, explains the slippage of SF "proper" into quasi-SF/fantasy comic book films or its subsumption by fantasy. Thus, in the present period, the SF genre is matched by "superhero" films such as *X-Men* (2000) and *X2: X-Men United* (2003); *Spider-Man* (2002) and *Spider-Man 2* (2004); and *Hulk* (2003) – and countered by fantasy films such as *Harry Potter and the Sorcerer's (Philosopher's) Stone* (2001), *Harry Potter and the Chamber of Secrets* (2002), and *Harry Potter and the Prisoner of Azkaban* (2004); and the extraordinary *Lord of the Rings* trilogy – the *Fellowship of the Ring* (2001), *The Two Towers* (2002), and *The Return of the King* (2003).

Nonetheless, SF continues as a popular American film genre, paradoxically no longer confined to the theater screen. Video games, CD-ROMs, and DVDs; interactive movies and television; and SF adventures in the perceived depth and motion of virtual space in arcades and theme parks – all promise the film genre a future that exceeds the very mechanisms and industry that gave it birth. In sum, from 1950 to the present day, the SF film continues to give concrete narrative shape and visible form to America's changing historical imagination of technological progress and disaster, and to the ambiguities of being human in a world in which advanced technology has altered both the morphology and meaning of personal and social existence. The genre thus functions to imaginatively map a spatial and temporal history of popular American consciousness and experience. It is symbolic not only of the terrain of our possible futures, but always also of our grounding in the realities of the present.

References and Further Reading

Booker, M. Keith (2001) *Monsters, Mushroom Clouds, and the Cold War: American Science Fiction and the Roots of Postmodernism.* Westport, CT: Greenwood Press.

Brosnan, John (1978) *Future Tense: The Cinema of Science Fiction.* New York: St. Martin's Press.

Bukatman, Scott (1993) *Terminal Identity: The Virtual Subject in Post-Modern Science Fiction.* Durham, NC: Duke University Press.

Hendershot, Cynthia (2001) *I was a Cold War Monster: Horror Films, Eroticism, and the Cold War Imagination.* Bowling Green, OH: Bowling Green State University Popular Press.

King, Geoff and Tanya Krzywinska (2001) *Science Fiction Cinema.* London: Wallflower Press.

Kuhn, Annette (ed.) (1990) *Alien Zone: Cultural Theory and Contemporary Science Fiction Cinema.* London: Verso.

——(1999) *Alien Zone II: The Spaces of Science-fiction Cinema.* London: Verso.

Landon, Brooks (1992) *The Aesthetics of Ambivalence: Rethinking Science Fiction Film in the Age of Electronic (Re)production.* Westport, CT: Greenwood Press.

Luciano, Patrick (2002) *Smokin' Rockets: The Romance of Technology in American Film, Radio and Television, 1945–1962.* Jefferson, NC: McFarland.

Newman, Kim (ed.) (2002) *Science Fiction/Horror: A Sight and Sound Reader.* London: British Film Institute.

Penley, Constance, *et al.* (eds) (1991) *Close Encounters: Film, Feminism, and Science Fiction.* Minneapolis, MN: University of Minnesota Press.

Redmond, Sean (ed.) (2004) *Liquid Metal: The Science Fiction Film Reader.* London: Wallflower Press.

Sardar, Ziauddin and Sean Cubitt (eds) (2002) *Aliens R Us: The Other in Science Fiction Cinema.* London: Pluto Press.

Seed, David (1999) *American Science Fiction and the Cold War: Literature and Film.* Edinburgh: Edinburgh University Press.

Slusser, George and Eric. S. Rabkin (eds) (1985) *Shadows of the Magic Lamp: Fantasy and Science Fiction in Film.* Carbondale, IL: Southern Illinois University Press.

Sobchack, Vivian (1997) *Screening Space: The American Science Fiction Film.* New Brunswick, NJ: Rutgers University Press.

Sontag, Susan (1967) "The Imagination of Disaster," in *Against Interpretation, and Other Essays,* (ed.) Susan Sontag, London: Eyre and Spottiswood.

Springer, Claudia (1996) *Electronic Eros: Bodies and Desire in the Postindustrial Age.* Austin, TX: University of Texas Press.

Telotte, J.P. (1995) *Replications: A Robotic History of the Science Fiction Film.* Urbana, IL: University of Illinois Press.

——(2001) *Science Fiction Film.* Cambridge, UK: Cambridge University Press.

18
Figurations of the Cyborg in Contemporary Science Fiction Novels and Film

Christine Cornea

In science fiction novels and films, ideas about human subjectivity and identity have most often been established in a comparison between self (human) and Other (non-human) characters. So, in terms of the genre's codes and conventions, it is possible to see how the alien or robot of science fiction may provide an example of Otherness, against which a representation of "proper" human subjectivity is worked through. Images of Otherness in science fiction can be understood as a metaphor for forms of Otherness within society, or between societies, which have traditionally been built upon gendered divides or upon distinctions based on racial differences. Indeed, a recognition of how science fiction operates on this metaphorical level has allowed critics and theorists alike to take the genre seriously, to look at what it might tell us about various definitions of the human subject and about the fears and anxieties surrounding a given society's Others. However, in recent years, a new and important figuration called the cyborg has become prominent in both science fiction novels and films. This is a figuration that manifestly challenges the dichotomous model of self/Other that the genre has previously relied upon. As Claudia Springer puts it, whereas in past science fiction robots have represented "the acclaim and fear evoked by industrial age machines for their ability to function independently of humans, cyborgs incorporate rather than exclude human, and in so doing erase the distinctions previously assumed to distinguish humanity from technology" (Springer 1991: 306).

In the cyborg we have the literal melding of what were previously seen as separate and divided: the human/machine, the human/nonhuman, the human self/Other. Therefore, the cyborg can not only be understood to mark a possible shift in the very structures that underlie the science fiction genre, but can also be seen as a potent threat to much of Western philosophy's reliance upon Cartesian-inspired dualisms (mind/body), or the binary dichotomies that underpin dominant patriarchal society – self (white male)/Other (female, nonwhite male, etc.).

What is the Cyborg?

Manfred E. Clynes and Nathan S. Kline originally coined the term "cyborg" in 1960 (by combining the words "cybernetic" and "organism") to describe how man (sic) might be amalgamated with machine, in order to survive the adverse conditions of space travel. However, the word cyborg also refers back to the advent of an earlier scientific discipline known as cybernetics, which was founded by Norbert Wiener (1948). In brief, Wiener's theoretical system was born of the marriage of communications theory with other scientific disciplines, and aimed at developing "a common explanatory framework to talk about animals, machines, and humans by considering them as information processors" (Hayles 1995a: 82).

In recent years, the term cyborg has come to allow for a very broad description of cyborgian being; spreading liberally to encompass practically any living organism that is altered by, or interacts with, mechanical and biotechnologies. For instance, in looking at the human/machine cyborg, N. Katherine Hayles makes the case that:

> About 10% of the current U.S. population are estimated to be cyborgs in the technical sense, including people with electronic pacemakers, artificial joints, drug implant systems, implanted corneal lenses, and artificial skin. A much higher percentage participates in occupations that make them into metaphoric cyborgs, including computer keyboarder joined in a cybernetic circuit with the screen, the neurosurgeon guided by fiber optic microscopy during an operation, and the teen game player in the local videogame arcade. (Hayles 1995b: 322)

This broad list alludes to the current potency of the term and even though Hayles creates a distinction between "technical" and "metaphorical," the cyborg can also be understood as simultaneously "a creature of social reality as well as a creature of fiction" (Haraway 1991: 149). The idea of the cyborg as both a material production and concept has opened up a highly contingent space in which various cyborg imaginings can be conceived and contested – a space from which it is possible to challenge traditional/dominant ideas of "proper" human social/material arrangements. In fact, past definitions of what counts as human subjectivity now appear so deficient that this has led theorists like Hayles to consider the notion "that the age of the human has given way to the *posthuman*" and to argue that the cyborg stands "at the threshold separating the human from the posthuman" (Hayles 1995b: 321–2). Hayles' statements can be understood in a variety of ways, but in looking at the various representations of this new form of being in science fiction, it seems that this figure is used in written fiction and films to either recuperate and/or to reconfigure a sense of human selfhood in a rapidly changing, technological world. Taken this way, the site of the cyborg offers not only the hope of a form of human survival, but also the chance to rewrite what counts as human subjectivity. Certainly, it is my hope that the brief analyses to follow will make apparent how questions of human beingness and personhood are currently being fought out over the fused body of the cyborg in both science fiction literature and film.

Cyborg Narratives and Theory

In the 1980s, rewriting what it means to be human in today's world was being busily undertaken by a number of science fiction authors. With roots that can be traced back to novels like Philip K. Dick's *Do Androids Dream of Electric Sheep?* (1968; the novel upon which the film *Blade Runner* [1982] was based), J.G. Ballard's *Crash* (1973) and Joanna Russ' *The Female Man* (1975), the Cyberpunk subgenre emerged. Writers such as William Gibson (the *"Neuromancer"* trilogy [1984, 1986, 1988] etc.), Bruce Sterling (Cyberpunk writer and editor of the *Mirrorshades* collection [1986], etc.), Pat Cadigan (one of the few female writers within the genre: *Synners* [1991], etc.) and Marge Piercy (whose *Woman on the Edge of Time* [1983] and *Body of Glass* [1991] owes much to Cyberpunk) tackled this issue as a primary concern within their narratives. These writers presented the reader with a number of central cyborg characters whose interaction with technology was illustrated in a variety of different ways. For instance, there is a great difference between the kind of technological melding undertaken by Cadigan's "Visual Mark" character and that of "Sam-I-Am" – both of which appear in the novel *Synners*. Visual Mark strives to become completely immersed within a virtual environment and eventually succeeds in downloading his conscious-ness into a computer world, thereby leaving the material world forever. Sam-I-Am, however, relies upon her body to literally power her customized technological enhancements and interfacing system to the Net, thereby remaining firmly connected to the material world. A further example can be taken from Gibson's *Neuromancer* in which his "console cowboys" work side by side with characters like Molly Millions: Molly's body is cybernetically enhanced, giving her increased physical prowess, whereas Case (our main console cowboy), spends most of his time with his mind "jacked" into a computer created world called the Matrix, through which he directs his desires. So, each of these novels appears to extrapolate from today's metaphorical and technical cyborg to give the reader a range of cyborgian forms of being.

Not only is Cyberpunk concerned with exploring emerging forms of Being; it also succeeds in commenting upon the way in which the human subject is losing its primacy and, to a certain extent, centralized control in the world. The human char-acters of Cyberpunk no longer reign supreme but, as cyborgs, interact with a dense network of alternative agents/actants. Indeed, the profusion of central characters in many Cyberpunk novels, in part, adds to the confusing of what might be understood as human and nonhuman characters. If compared to detective fiction (which is heavily referenced in Cyberpunk), where the narrative most often unfolds from the point of view of a single character, it is often the case in Cyberpunk novels that:

> The enigma is not solved by the actions and thoughts of a single person, piecing it together like a detective. Instead, the characters [often] do not even know each other. However, collectively, knowingly or not, they move the narrative forward and solve the enigma. (Chernaik 1997: 73)

This diffusion does not necessarily lead to a lack of agency (conscious or otherwise); agency simply appears spread between characters. These characters may not have ultimate control over the world around them, or, indeed, the narrative, but they do negotiate with their environment and are therefore able to effect change, push the boundaries and exert a kind of will.

In her seminal piece, *A Manifesto for Cyborgs* (1985; collected in *Simians, Cyborgs, and Women*, 1991), Donna Haraway uses the figure of the cyborg to suggest how feminists might engage with contemporary technological society in a way that can be considered empowering: for Haraway the cyborg offers up a possible path away from the oppositional deadlock of gender politics. She explicitly engages with the importance of fictional writing in the conceiving of, what she calls, "political imaginations" and mentions academic and political theorists, alongside writers of science fiction, as influential in the formulating of her own ideas. As if to illustrate this point, in her later work, *Modest_Witness@Second_Millennium*, Haraway borrows the character of Nili, from Marge Piercy's *Body of Glass* and uses this cyborg as the inspirational model through which she articulates her own position as a theoretical writer, scientist, and feminist critic. Nili is situated in both the semiotic space of a virtual reality Matrix as well as in the material space of the diegetically real world in *Body of Glass*, thereby encapsulating the way in which Haraway views her own situation. She backs up this approach by stating that "[f]igurations are performative images that can be inhabited" (Haraway 1997: 11). For Haraway, "the imaginary and the real figure each other in concrete fact" and the actual and figural are both "constitutive of lived material-semiotic worlds" (Haraway 1997: 2). In this way, she sees herself as working within a kind of "situated" interzone, between what is perceived as real/material and what is understood as imagined/fictional.

So, for Haraway the cyborg becomes a provocative and potentially powerful figuration through which she can work to transform and articulate her own sense of being. However, she has deliberately chosen to borrow a figuration here from a known feminist writer and activist and it is well to bear in mind that although Cyberpunk novels may offer inspirational models of being, not all may be considered as inherently progressive texts. For instance, Gibson's novels have been criticized for their masculinism and have been read as very conservative texts – certainly in terms of the way in which gender is configured in his characterizations. As Claudia Springer has deftly pointed out, "while popular culture texts enthusiastically explore boundary breakdowns between humans and computers, gender boundaries are treated less flexibly" (Springer 1991: 308). In fact, Springer goes on to point out that there is an exaggeration of traditional gender oppositions in much Cyberpunk. Although her examples, at this point, are drawn from comic books, in which the visual compositions predominate (her definition of Cyberpunk extends to a variety of mediums and is not confined to the written novels), the same criticism has been made of Cyberpunk novels (Wolmark 1994). It certainly seems that while much Cyberpunk writing might offer up unconventional representations in comparison with more traditional depictions of gender identity, oppositions based upon sex/gender are still kept firmly in place in many of these texts. For instance, if I were to compare Gibson's characters, Molly and

Case, in *Neuromancer*, this might clarify the point. Molly, previously a sexual object sold for the gratification of male clients, becomes newly configured as a powerful fighting force; she was a "working girl" before she became a "fighting girl." Even though she appears to have transgressed gender boundaries in using her body as a fighting tool, she remains defined by it in terms of the role she performs within the narrative. Then there is Case, who at first glance seems to challenge a traditional model of masculinity in the simple fact that he embraces his cyborgian existence. This may not be a conventional representation of masculinity but his constant desire to transcend his "meat" (his body) and become pure consciousness (mind) can be read as a reaction to this female reconfiguration. Instead of creating a closer affinity between the sexes Case disengages himself from "her world" and marks himself firmly apart by entering his own world in the Matrix.

Anne Balsamo, in looking at the apparent gendered oppositions in Cadigan's *Synners*, states that "the female body is coded as a body-in-connection and the male body, as a body-in-isolation." However, she reads this divisionism as "an alternative narrative of cyberpunk identity that begins with the assumption that bodies are always gendered and always marked by race" (Balsamo 1993: 692). In this sense, she argues that the cyborgian bodies in *Synners* relate to current gendered and racial identities in a way that signals a political awareness of material-semiotic construction. Perhaps Balsamo is simply putting a more positive spin upon the way in which Cyberpunk appears to uphold the binary oppositions associated with gender or perhaps the cyborg carries with it the shadow of the past in this respect? I would say that Cadigan foregrounds her own gendered constructions in *Synners* in such a way that she highlights the theatrical; gender is performed in *Synners* and is central to the characters' performance within the cyber-spatial world of the narrative. This becomes particularly evident when Sam-I-Am starts to wonder about the gender of an AI (artificial intelligence) called Art Fish. Sam is initially unconcerned by Art's gender, but gradually becomes aware that she has assumed Art to be masculine and even finds herself flirting with this AI. It is unclear as to whether Art's "personality" or later screen appearance actually does change or whether this is simply a projection of Sam's libidinal desires (Sam articulates an awareness of both of these possibilities). Sam's desire to see Art as masculine or, perhaps, Art's decision to become an object of desire for Sam may be interpreted as a conscious performance of heterosexuality on the part of the two characters.

So in Cyberpunk novels it appears that a gendered divide remains. On the one hand, this could indicate that the binary opposition of male/female or masculine/feminine still provides a foundation upon which other oppositions are built. On the other hand, it could be that in some of these texts a self-consciously created opposition based upon gender becomes a manifest reference to the very dualisms that the cyborg challenges.

The Celluloid Cyborg

The sort of gender divide prevalent within Cyberpunk writing is even more obvious when looking at the way the cyborg has been configured in films. This is particularly evident in mainstream Hollywood films of the 1980s; however, in sharp contrast to Cyberpunk's "disappearing" masculine body, the films of this period presented the viewer with visions of an excessively masculine cyborg body. Samantha Holland, looking at a number of examples released in the 1980s–early 1990s, has commented that in these films:

> The cyberbodies are represented in such a highly gendered way to counter the threat that cyborgs indicate the loss of human bodies, where such a loss implies the loss of the gendered distinctions that are essential to maintaining the patriarchal order (which is based on exploiting difference). (Holland 1995: 159)

These images presented the viewer with highly exaggerated versions of masculine subjectivity and critics had much to say about the hypermasculinized heroes and anti-heroes that rampaged through these films. Susan Jeffords, in a scathing critique of these muscle-man cyborgs, relates these figurations specifically to "the Reagan Era" in America. Jeffords (1994) argues for links between a 1980s conservative "backlash" and the sheer number of highly muscular, male heroes seen in mainstream Hollywood cinema during this period. She backs up her case in charting the apparent modifications made to the representation of masculinity in films of 1980s through to the 1990s. One of the examples she uses is the shift in how the cyborg is represented in the first *Terminator* film (dir. James Cameron, 1984) compared with *Terminator 2: Judgment Day* (dir. James Cameron, 1991). She argues that, in the first film, the cyborg's "hard body" stood for the aggressively militaristic and defensive business strategies of this period in American politics. With the advent of the "softer" Bush administration, Jeffords contends, the terminating cyborg was refashioned into a protecting father figure (Jeffords 1994: 156–75). While there is certainly a point to be made here, Jefford's sometimes bases these arguments on an overly simplistic model of the relationship between text and context, often bordering on a reading of these figures as a direct and unmediated reflection of the social context from which they may well have emerged. For instance, I would contend that the sight of the Terminator body provides such a hyperbolic visual metaphor that it may well exceed the kind of narrative intent that Jeffords assumes. In this sense, the excessively muscular body of the Terminator comes to represent a performance of masculinity clinging to residual notions of gender and can therefore be taken as kind of political critique of the period.

Other analyses of some of the cyborg heroes/antiheroes of this period have revealed a more ambivalent picture than Jefford's reading suggests. For example, the very fact that these spectacular male bodies are set up for visual scrutiny can be seen to problematize traditional gendered identity – particular bearing in mind the more conventional cinematic viewing constructions that position the female/feminine body as that which is to be openly gazed upon (Tasker 1993). Whilst in some of these science fiction/action films there are moments when a passive display of the male cyborg body appears offset by demonstrations of extreme violence (Neale 1983), the majority of these early cyborg films encourage a very consistent gazing upon the body in question. Surely, an invitation to gaze is hard to contest when, for instance, in both *The Terminator* and *Universal Soldier* the central male cyborgs are featured naked. In this way, the male body can be thought of as feminized within traditional Hollywood conventions. Of course, the cyborg status of these male characters may well serve to underline a certain sexual/gendered ambiguity. In other words, their status in these films not only marks them as transgressive figures, but can also be seen as the "excuse," the justification, for such an open invitation to gaze, because they are not fully human subjects in a comparison with the other characterizations featured in the films. The fact that most of these cyborgs were played by white Europeans also suggests that, in some subtle way, race was an issue in their casting: these cyborgs could therefore be read as not fully human subjects because they were not American (see below for further discussion on issues surrounding race and the cyborg).

Gender Blending and the Female Cyborg

Although super-masculine, male cyborgs were certainly the order of the day during the 1980s, this does not mean that female cyborgs were altogether absent in films.

In fact, one of the first examples of the cyborg to hit the screens is female and can be found in the Science Fiction/Horror film *Demon Seed* (dir. Donald Cammell, 1977). This female cyborg is the progeny of a human mother, Susan, who is raped by the masculine computer AI called Proteus. In an effort to persuade Susan to nurture and care for this creation, Proteus creates a copy of Susan's deceased daughter. However, in the closing moments of the film the copied child speaks the words "I'm alive" with the male voice that has been associated with Proteus throughout the film, thereby signaling that although this child's body might be female, the mind inside is masculine. This child's composite nature, as literal melding of human and machine, is therefore manifestly echoed in her composite gendered being.

The cyborg child is featured alongside all the visual trappings associated with the horror genre: the birthing room becomes saturated in a watery sludge that oozes from Proteus' artificial womb and the child's body is covered in a gelatinous substance. Slime, gunge, and goo are prevalent in horror films and any substance that "leaks" through the boundaries of a given body becomes horrific and abject within this genre's conventions (Carroll 1990) and it is notable that these same visual tropes are employed in a number of following films that featured the female cyborg (e.g., *Alien: Resurrection* [dir. Jean-Pierre Jeunet, 1997], *Star Trek: First Contact* [dir. Jonathan Frakes, 1996]). Barbara Creed has argued that within patriarchal society it is the reproductive female body that is understood as horrific, as monstrous, as abject, as "leaky vessel" (Creed 1993). So, this marriage between the female cyborg and the codes of the horror genre could indicate that the fear and horror of fusion, of boundary breakdown evoked by the concept of the cyborg, are displaced onto the female in these films.

Perhaps a more emancipatory figuration of the female cyborg can be found in looking at the recent advent of the "female hero" to American science fiction/action cinema. The "female hero" emerged to full prominence in the mainstream cyborg films with the reconfiguring of the "Sarah" character from the first *Terminator* film into a muscled warrior in *Terminator 2*. Given the codes of the action genre, this would seem to suggest that a gendered divide was being eroded here and that this erosion was, in some ways, being celebrated in this film. But, upon closer inspection it becomes apparent that Sarah is "out-performed" by the Terminator; her newly acquired physique is placed within a hierarchy of muscularity in which the Terminator is figured as more powerful. In addition to this, Sarah is predominantly characterized as fighting *for* patriarchy, particularly in her function as vessel for the birth of a future male savior. However, a more obscure cyborg film offers an interesting comparison here. The "direct to video" *Nemesis* series of films (dir. Albert Pyun, 1993–6) presents us with a far more startling and potentially radical form of female hero, which can be usefully read alongside the muscled and athletic "female hero" displayed in many mainstream films of the mid-1990s period and beyond. Alex (Sue Price), the central "female hero" in both *Nemesis 2: Nebula* (1995) and *Nemesis 3: Time Lapse* (1996), is a genetically altered female created to oppose the "mechanical" form of cyborg that has overrun an America of the future. Echoing *The Terminator* films, Alex is transported back in time to the relative safety of East Africa in 1980. She is taken in by a local African tribe and we see her adult life begin as she is about to undertake a "rites of passage" ritual to attain warrior status. Before performing this role, Sue Price, was a "heavy weight" bodybuilder. Therefore she presents an especially spectacular and excessive version of the built up female body which is more on a par with the Schwarzenegger-type physique. The first views of Alex in *Nemesis 2* are a sequence of close body and face shots in which it is hard to detect her sex. None of these shots expose her as female and it may be quite a shock to the viewer when her sex is finally revealed. This introduction seems designed to foreground the ambiguities present in "the redefinition of the sexed body that is worked out over the muscular female body of the 'action heroine'" (Tasker 1993: 141). It is as though this opening sequence were intended to undermine the viewer's expectations not only in terms of what to expect of a central action hero (that they be male), but also what to expect from the muscularity achievable upon a female body. The similarities in plot and action between *Terminator 2* and *Nemesis 2* invite an intertextual reading. For example, it would be interesting to imagine what *Terminator 2* would have looked like had Sue Price played the Sarah role: a simple commutation test surely reveals the recuperative tactics displayed in *Terminator 2*.

Further examples of the "female hero" would include Jane (Dina Meyer), in *Johnny Mnemonic* (dir. Robert Longo, 1995), and Trinity (Carrie-Anne Moss), in *The Matrix* series (dirs. Wachowski brothers, 1999–2003). Both of these characters are physically active and possess the bodily strength and expertise to triumph against male and female opponents. However, Jane primarily functions as Johnny's "love interest" as well as his paid bodyguard hired to protect him. Trinity, though, is a member of the rebel group attempting to free humanity from the supposed illusion of the Matrix, but, like Jane, although she is shown to be physically/mentally skilful, she is also romantically partnered with Neo (Keanu Reeeves) and believes him to be the savior, born to lead the rebels in a battle with the virtual "agents" that protect the Matrix. So, the mere "borrowing," by a female character, of what are understood as masculine traits does not necessarily lead to a representation of "equality" between the sexes. As these examples show, the visual threat presented by the "female hero" is often ensnared within a narrative that strongly upholds patriarchal values.

Again, it is illuminating to look at *Nemesis 3* (1996) as an alternative example. Here Alex is pursued by another cyborg, Farnsworth 2 (Tim Thomerson), who is sent back to a 1980s Africa in an attempt to return her to his future. He is particularly concerned with whether or not she has procreated, as the mechanical cyborgs from the future wish to recuperate heirs, to bring their powers back within the patriarchal boundaries of their own future. Alex has not had children and fights against Farnsworth's attempts to impose his will upon her. In fact, in this film, Alex seems to stand outside of the film's narrative and this is underlined in those moments when its linear flow becomes severely disrupted and jumbled, thereby placing emphasis on Alex's present actions. The narrative of this film represents a patriarchal imprisonment that she refuses to accept; narrative and spectacle being literally opposed in this film. What I am suggesting is that whereas the spectacle of Sarah seems to serve the overall narrative in *Terminator 2*, the spectacle of Alex takes centrality from the narrative in this film. Although, in many ways, the *Nemesis* series might be considered "poor," these two films can operate to disrupt and question the kind of gendered arrangements found in their mainstream counterparts.

Mind Over Matter

What we might call the mainstream cyborg film has "evolved" since the 1980s/early 1990s, from those films that can be read in alignment with the most basic codes of the action film or the horror genre to those that may be more accurately described as "cyber-thrillers" (Springer, 1999). Whilst many earlier cyborg films displayed an engagement with the same themes that were being dealt with in Cyberpunk, the "cyber-thrillers' have more in common with a Cyberpunk aesthetic in a variety of ways. For instance, with the emergence of "cyber-thriller" came a shift from the earlier "hard bodied" male cyborg to the image of the slimmed down, "jacked in," male cyber-savior; made particularly evident in the featuring of Keanu Reeves in both *Johnny Mnemonic* and *The Matrix* series. It is also common to have a range of featured cyborg figurations in these more recent films, to the extent that in the *Matrix* series practically all the characters can be read as cyborgian beings. However, whilst oppositions may not strictly be displaced onto the human/cyborg (as was the case with so many of the 1980s films) these "cyber-thrillers" do appear to pit one *kind* of cyborg against another in ways that underline divisions based upon sex or race. *Johnny Mnemonic* provides one example. In this film our eponymous male hero is cyborgized due to the prostheses implanted into his brain, which enables him to carry vast quantities of data and also to "jack" directly into the Net. Conversely, like Gibson's Molly, his "female hero" partner (Jane) is marked as a cyborg because of the technologies that enhance her bodily strength and skill. This film was based upon a short story written by Gibson and the mind (male)/body (female) divide apparent in his Cyberpunk writing is accentuated here – with Johnny standing for "mind" and Jane for "body."

Racial differences are also heavily marked in many of the later cyborg films. Although these films seem quite liberal, given the sheer variety of ethnic or ethnically mixed races on display, in terms of casting and character centrality, distinct self/Other dichotomies are still at play. This is particularly evident in the way that African, Afro-Caribbean, or West Indian-American characters are represented. For example, in *Virtuosity* (dir: Brett Leonard, 1995) a white/black racial opposition is ostensibly upheld through the figuring of the cyborg hero and villain of the film. The film's ex-lawman, Parker (Denzel Washington), sports a cybernetic prosthesis that replaces his previously damaged arm (heavy metaphorical references here to his lost status as lawman), whereas the villain, Sid (Russell Crowe), has been literally constructed from the human memories of several white serial killers. Therefore, once again, racial difference is mapped onto a mind/body dichotomy in the figuring of these two cyborg adversaries. In *Strange Days* (dir: Kathryn Bigelow, 1995) not only is a white/black opposition upheld, but this is mapped onto an opposition based upon sex. Here the central male hero, Lenny (Ralph Fiennes), resembles the countercultural, hacker characters ("console cowboys') of Cyberpunk writing, through his consistent use of an immersive cybernetic technology called "squid." His athletic and physically skilled, female cohort, Mace (Angela Bassett), is signaled as more fully human because she consistently refuses to engage with this technology. There is a long history of black characters being represented in both novels and films as more primitive than their white counterparts and, in some ways, their appearance in these films as more human than their white counterparts is simply an updated version of this old stereotype. For instance, although Mace can be seen as a female hero figure she can also be read as a modern day "noble savage," who, within this highly technologized society, operates as a reminder of a more "authentically" human past.

Borderline Cases

Taking *Strange Days* and *Virtuosity* again, as examples here, there are moments in both of these films when the use of highly interactive technologies is associated with the "oriental." In *Virtuosity* it is an orientalized space that Parker finds himself within during his opening, virtual battle with Sid in cyberspace. Also, in *Strange Days*, there is a scene in which Lenny attempts to sell the Squid technology to a Japanese businessman. It is then revealed that the businessman already possesses the latest model of "player," putting him at the cutting edge of this technology. Although both these moments are brief they do serve to indicate a pervasive suturing of interactive/cyborgian technologies with the "oriental," which has developed into a common trope in many recent cyborg films. Of course, this kind of orientalization was a feature of cyber-punk writing (i.e., the Yakuza characters in Gibson's novels) and, as far back as *Blade Runner* (Dir: Ridley Scott, 1982), "oriental" figures have been represented as inti-mately allied with new technologies in science fiction cinema, but "orientalization" is now far more prevalent in the recent spate of "cyber-thrillers."

In *Blade Runner* an oriental underclass are seen to be the makers/producers of tech-nologies surrounding the manufacture of the Replicants, although it is a Western male who plays the part of the "overlord/creator" in charge of the whole operation. At the time of *Blade Runner's* release certain Eastern economies were growing fast and coun-tries like Japan and Korea were well known for their manufacture of computer com-ponents and other cutting edge technologies. For a while these Eastern nations were understood as suppliers for the West, but over the course of the 1980s it became apparent that these countries were fast moving from being the copiers/providers of Western led technology to becoming the inventors/initiators of new technologies. This shift was echoed in the prominence and popularity of video and computer games pro-duced by these countries; an emerging, interactive form of entertainment that not only offered a potentially more direct engagement with the kind of cyberspaces fea-tured in Cyberpunk narratives, but also threatened to eclipse cinema as we know it.

The Hollywood film industry answered to this economic, technical, and cultural shift by producing films based upon some of the most popular games. Even though spin-off games had been created alongside earlier cyborg films (e.g., *The Terminator* series, *Star Wars* series, etc.), the significance of Hollywood's expansion into this market became particularly evident when films like *Mortal Kombat* (dir. Steven De Souza, 1995) and *Streetfighter* (dir. Paul Anderson, 1994) were produced; both of which were based upon pre-existing games. In these films the audience is presented with a markedly fictional, exotic space; a space that can be understood as corresponding to the cyberspace in which the games are played. So, cyberspace is represented in these films as a kind of virtual orient in which the " 'tourist' can be freed from western ratio-nalism and taste the 'mystical essence' of the East" (Cornea 2004). Although there are Asian and Asian-American characters present in these films, aspects of a now popu-larized oriental culture are appropriated by the Western characters, which is particu-larly obvious in their consistent use of martial arts in the action sequences of the films. Offering a more decentered image of the fighting body, increasingly, the martial arts content of a Hollywood science fiction film has become a kind of free floating signi-fier of the interaction between human and computer technologies; a signifier of a cyborgian state of being.

A more recent and rather telling example of this trend can be found in *Lara Croft Tomb Raider: The Cradle of Life* (dir. Jan de Bont, 2003), in which Lara battles with a Chinese crime syndicate to regain control over Pandora's box. Although the box brings with it a kind of "nuclear" threat, it can also be read as representing the power asso-ciated with computer technology (it is not uncommon for new computer technol-ogies to be referred to as "black box" technologies). But this development reaches its zenith in the *Matrix* series, where the somewhat hyperbolic use of martial arts sequences, in conjunction with the latest computer graphics technology, indicates that these characters have been orientalized as well as cyborgized in becoming immersed in such technologies. What is, therefore, most notable is that rather than representing an opposing and "authentic" Otherness, as in the case of black characters in the cyber-thrillers, here we have a sort of "in between" figure; a figure that can be understood as connoting a hybrid/cyborgian identity in terms of race, gender, culture, and technological interaction. For instance, knowledge of Reeves background and his star persona are drawn upon to underpin his cyborgian status. Not only is Reeves' sexual persuasion kept deliberately enigmatic in the marketing of him as a star performer, but much is made of the fact that he was born of a British mother and Chinese-Hawaiian father. He can therefore be understood as a kind of literal hybrid in terms of his racial heritage and, perhaps, a suitable representative of the postmodern, hybrid subject in America.

Just how we might read this "in between" figuration is currently open to debate. For example, David Morley and Kevin Robins have also noted how representations of "postmodern technologies" are often sutured to oriental imagery. By drawing upon the seminal work of Edward Said, they coin the term "Techno-Orientalism" to describe, what they see as an ongoing orientalist practice in the West (Morley and Robins 1995: 147–73). However, I believe that, in some cases, it is possible to read this kind of "in between" characterization in alignment with certain strands of postcolonial theory, in which ideas of hybridity and hybrid identities are being proposed as a positive next step, as a way of "elud(ing) the politics of polarity" (Bhabha 1994: 39) when looking at issues of race, culture, and postcolonial identities. In a recent article I again looked at examples of the cyborg film taken from the direct to video market of the early-mid 1990s (Cornea 2004). I found that many were made by Asian-American filmmakers and, in comparison with the mainstream Hollywood films of this time, they more often featured central Asian-American characters. Of course, these films can be taken as exploitation movies and it is possible that some of these Asian-American filmmakers and performers were attempting to break into a more mainstream market by "cutting their teeth" on these lower budget films. However, although these films do draw upon the codes and conventions common to the Hollywood science fiction film and can hardly be considered particularly progressive or oppositional, they frequently carry out a kind of dialogue with the mainstream; a dialogue that effectively refocalizes the narratives of their mainstream counterparts and brings racial issues to the fore. Films like *Grid Runners* (Dir: Andrew Stevens, Prod. and Presented: Ashok Amritraj, featuring: Don Wilson, 1995) and *TC 2000* (Dir: T.J. Scott, featuring Bolo Yeung and Billy Blanks, 1993) appear to utilize the figure of the cyborg to provide a rather more complex picture of racial/cultural hybridity than had previously been seen in the revamped stereotypes of their mainstream forerunners. Yes, these films draw upon certain racial stereotypes, but given the authorial control that the low budget film more readily allows for, it is also possible that some of these filmmakers attempted to articulate the specificity of their own racial/cultural hybridity.

As has become apparent throughout this account of the cyborg in contemporary novels and films, it appears that great efforts are frequently made to "contain" any threat posed by this hybrid, composite, cyborg figuration. On one level, the apparent commercialization of the Cyberpunk aesthetic (particularly in recent films), could indicate that the transgressive implications of this figuration are held in check. So, has the figure of the cyborg lost its political and philosophical clout as a potentially transformative figuration? It is hardly surprising that mainstream Hollywood films present such conservative images of the cyborg, but analysis reveals that more provocative and alternative visions of the cyborg are there to be found. Alternative visions could be seen, for a brief time, in the "direct to video" films mentioned, but they can also be found in films like Cronenberg's *Crash* and his later *eXistenZ* (Cornea 2003), which, within the confines of this article, it has not been possible to discuss. Of course, we might have to search for alternative images more actively in future, if the latest marketing strategies are anything to go by. For example, both the *Matrix 2* and *3* films act like epic "teasers' for a multitude of games and spin-off video films/DVDs released at the same time as the films – effectively squeezing out the possibilities for an "exploitation" market. Whilst this may make financial sense, I cannot help wondering if there is also an attempt to forestall or control the kind of intertextual commenting and reading encouraged by the lower budget films. The more revolutionary challenges presented by the very concept of the cyborg might not be played out in full in many popular cultural texts and there may an attempt to hermetically seal up cyber-spatial imaginings; however, it is my contention that this figuration still presents the viewer/reader with opportunities to question and contest the premises of what it means to be human.

REFERENCES AND FURTHER READING

Balsamo, Anne (1993) "Feminism for the Incurably Informed," in *Flame Wars: The Discourse of Cyberculture*, (ed.) Mark Dery. Durham, NC and London: Duke University Press.

Barnett, Chad, P. (2000) "Reviving Cyberpunk: (Re)Constructing the Subject and Mapping Cyberspace in the Wachowski Brothers' Film 'The Matrix'." *Extrapolation* 41: 4, 359–74.

Bhabha, Homi (1994) *The Location of Culture.* London and New York: Routledge.

Bukatman, Scott (1993) *Terminal Identity: The Virtual Subject in Postmodern Science Fiction.* Durham, NC and London: Duke University Press.

Carroll, Noel (1990) *The Philosophy of Horror: Or, Paradoxes of the Heart.* London and New York: Routledge.

Chernaik, Laura (1997) "Pat Cadigan's 'Synners': Refiguring Nature, Science and Technology." *Feminist Review* 56, 61–84.

Cornea, Christine (2003) "David Cronenberg's *Crash* and Performing Cyborgs." *Velvet Light Trap* 52 (September), 4–14.

——(2004) "Techno-Orientalism and the Postmodern Subject," in *Screen Method: Comparative Readings in Screen Studies*, (eds) Jackie Furby, Karen Brandt. London: Wallflower Press.

Creed, Barbara (1993) *The Monstrous Feminine: Film, Feminism, Psychoanalysis.* London and New York: Routledge.

Greco, Diane (1995) *Cyborg: Engineering the Body Electric.* Watertown, MA: Eastgate Systems.

Haraway, Donna (1991) *Symians, Cyborgs, and*

Women: The Reinvention of Nature. London: Free Association Books.

——(1997) *Modest_Witness@Second_Millennium. FemaleMan©_Meets_OncoMouse™: Feminism and Technoscience.* London and New York: Routledge.

Hayles, N. Katherine (1995a) "Making the Cut: The Interplay of Narrative and System, or What Systems Theory Can't See." *Cultural Critique* 30, 71–99.

——(1995b) "The Life Cycle of Cyborgs: Writing the Posthuman," in *The Cyborg Handbook*, (ed.) Chris Hables Gray. New York and London: Routledge, 321–35.

Holland, Samantha (1995) "Descartes Goes to Hollywood: Mind, Body and Gender in Contemporary Cyborg Cinema," in *Cyberspace, Cyberbodies, Cyberpunk: Cultures of Technological Embodiment*, (eds) Mike Featherstone and Roger Burrows. London: Sage Publications.

Jeffords, Susan (1994) *Hard Bodies: Hollywood Masculinity in the Reagan Era.* New Brunswick: Rutgers University Press.

Morley, David and Kevin Robins (1995) *Spaces of Identity: Global Media, Electronic Landscapes and Cultural Boundaries.* London: Routledge.

Neale, Steve (1983) "Masculinity as Spectacle: Reflections on Men and Mainstream Cinema." *Screen* 24: 6, 2–17.

Piercy, Marge (1992) *Body of Glass* [US title *He She and It*]. Harmondsworth: Penguin.

Romney, Jonathan (2003) "Everywhere and Nowhere." *Sight and Sound* 13: 7, 24–7.

Rorvik, David M. (1975) *As Man Becomes Machine: The Evolution of the Cyborg.* London: Sphere.

Springer, Claudia (1991) "The Pleasure of the Interface." *Screen* 32: 3 (Autumn), 303–22.

——(1999) "Psycho-Cybernetics in Film of the 1990s," in *Alien Zone II: The Spaces of Science Fiction Cinema*, (ed.) Annette Kuhn. London and New York: Verso, 203–18.

Tasker, Yvonne (1993) *Spectacular Bodies: Gender, Genre and the Action Cinema.* London and New York: Routledge.

Telotte, J.P. (1990) "The Doubles of Fantasy and the Space of Desire," in *Alien Zone: Cultural Theory and Contemporary Science Fiction*, (ed.) Annette Kuhn. London and New York: Verso, 152–9.

Wiener, Norbert (1965) *Cybernetics: or Control and Communication in the Animal and Machine*, 2nd edn. Cambridge, MA: MIT Press.

Wolmark, Jenny (1994) *Aliens and Others: Science Fiction, Feminism and Postmodernism.* London: Harvester Wheatsheaf.

——(ed.) (1999) *Cybersexualities: A Reader on Feminist Theory, Cyborgs and Cyberspace.* Edinburgh: Edinburgh University Press.

19
British Television Science Fiction
Peter Wright

Literary science fiction often provides "not only a reflection of but also on reality" (Suvin 1979: 10). British television science fiction (TVSF) intended for an adult audience is little different. In fact, for most of its history, it avoids simply reflecting the shifting political, social, and scientific anxieties of its national context in order to constitute a mode of cultural criticism. This consistent engagement with its milieu is a key characteristic in maintaining British TVSF's distinct Britishness. Where it is less preoccupied with reacting to its sociopolitical environment, it derives an equally apparent identity from its relationship with British anti-Utopian writing and literary SF. It is only in the 1990s, following the growth of global television and facing increased competition from American productions, that British TVSF begins to lose some of its coherent identity.

The foundations for British TVSF's political content were laid on 11 February, 1938, when the BBC broadcast a truncated adaptation of Czech writer Karel Čapek's play *R.U.R.* (1920). *R.U.R.* had enjoyed considerable success in London and New York since premiering in Prague in January 1921 and various companies had performed the play in regional theatre. After the BBC began scheduled transmissions from Alexandra Palace on 2 November, 1936, part of its programming included photographed stage plays, either broadcasts of live theatre or restaged extracts from West End productions (see Jacobs 2000: 25–48). *R.U.R.*'s popularity and uncomplicated staging is likely to have ensured its translation to television.

Importantly, *R.U.R.* is also instructive, providing a parable of dehumanization, mass production, and the abuse of power in its dramatization of an android revolt that destroys humanity. For the BBC, following the moral ideology of public service broadcasting established by John Reith, its first Director General, *R.U.R.*'s ethical message probably influenced its transmission as much as its popularity. Regrettably, with no means of telerecording the play or the full versions based on Nigel Playfair's "adaptation for the English stage" broadcast twice in 1948 (see Cooper 1998; Hayes 2002) comparatively little is known of the productions.

Although *R.U.R.* is the first instance of SF on British television, an example of British SF was not broadcast until January 1949, when Robert Barr staged his live version of Wells' *The Time Machine* (1895). Unlike *R.U.R.*, with its claustrophobic interiors intended for the theatre, Wells' novel follows a time traveler from Victorian London, through an inhuman future society descended from the class system, to the heat death of Earth. In reworking the novel, Barr and his designer Barry Learoyd made extensive technical demands to ensure an adequate representation of Wells' vision. The hour-long production, which employed filmed inserts and back-projection, became the first TVSF to acknowledge the narrative potential of special effects (see Glenn 1991: 28–30).

Like *R.U.R.*, *The Time Machine* could not be preserved. However, its production is significant, since it demonstrated the BBC's readiness to include SF in its postwar schedules. It also consolidated the practice of adapting SF texts for television that continued through to the 1990s. More importantly, Barr's teleplay confirmed the BBC's commitment to SF with social or political overtones; and it placed the figure of the scientist – the Time Traveler – in a central narrative position. These last two characteristics were highly influential until the mid-1970s.

The Time Machine's technical experimentation signaled the need for "updating" what drama producer Rudolf Cartier perceived in 1952 as the "stagy" qualities of BBC drama (Jacobs 2000: 1). Cartier's fervor for narrative and stylistic innovation led to the wellspring of British TVSF: Nigel Kneale's technically ambitious *Quatermass* trilogy. In its reflection of contemporary British scientific endeavour, its postwar settings, characterization, Cold War ambience, and associations with indigenous literary science fiction, the *Quatermass* trilogy is the epitome of British TVSF.

Kneale shared Cartier's impatience with theatre-like dramas that failed to exploit television's technical potential and with the suggestion that television should foster a reassuringly intimate relationship between producer and consumer. "Cartier and Nigel Kneale . . . [wanted] . . . to invigorate television with a faster tempo and a broader thematic and spatial canvas, and it was no coincidence that they turned to science fiction" (Jacobs 2000: 133–4). Unhampered by the restrictions of realism, SF could confront viewers with dramas to challenge their perception of a changing medium and a changing world. Hence, the title of Kneale's *The Quatermass Experiment* (1953) connotes both to the teleplay's subject matter and its creative approach to television drama.

Kneale's adaptation of Charles Irving's *Number Three* (1953) anticipates the *Quatermass* trilogy by focusing on scientists and the implications of new technology and in challenging the "cosy" nature of British television. Each *Quatermass* drama is a variant on the theme of an alien invasion uncovered by Professor Bernard Quatermass. Eschewing spectacle in favor of invasion by stealth, Kneale captures the fear and suspicion prevalent in the early 1950s. In an interview in 1996, he reflects on how "That decade has sometimes been called one of paranoia, which means abnormal, sick attitudes and irrational fears. I don't think it was irrational to be fearful at that time: there was a lot to be frightened of and stories like mine were a sort of controlled paranoia, inoculation against the real horrors" (Pixley and Neale 2003). In short, while challenging the expectations of television audiences, Kneale was also sublimating their fears of earthly conflict.

Like John Wyndham's *The Day of the Triffids* (1951) and *The Kraken Wakes* (1953), Kneale's trilogy addresses contemporary disquiet. As Nicholas Ruddick points out, "The fundamental anxiety underlying Wyndham's catastrophe fiction is that of being superseded" (Ruddick 1993: 139). It is a fear reflected in both *The Quatermass Experiment*, where an amorphous alien attempts to transform all organic matter on Earth into alien tissue, and in *Quatermass II* (1955), a "take-over" narrative that parallels Jack Finney's *The Body Snatchers* (1955). Kneale's invasions clearly reflect the insecurity felt in postwar Britain as it entered a new "Cold" War. In *Quatermass II*, the alien's gestalt, "Communist" intelligence (Quatermass describes it as "A group creature . . . a countless host, a thousand billion individuals if you like . . . with one single consciousness" (Kneale 1960: 90), its diction and Quatermass' decision to use his atomic-powered rocket as a nuclear device expose the drama's Cold War subtext and the fear of supersession through infiltration. Like Wyndham's novels and Wells' seminal *The War of the Worlds* (1898), Kneale's teleplays show "the fear of human extinction at the hands of some more advanced or ruthless species" (Ruddick 1993: 139). That such a species substitutes for the threat posed by Soviet Russia illustrates Kneale's efforts to sublimate contemporary fears as British scientific ingenuity and the British bomb (here repackaged as a rocketship) save the day.

Such reassurance is absent from *Quatermass and the Pit* (1958–9), in which Quatermass discovers human aggression is the consequence of evolutionary tampering by ancient, antagonistic Martians. "If we cannot control the inheritance within us," warns Quatermass at the conclusion, "this will be their [the Martians'] second dead planet." With this polemic speech, delivered straight to camera, Quatermass strips away the earlier teleplays' sublimatory strategies to engage the audience directly with the harsh political realities of the 1950s. The fact it is spoken by – albeit – a fictional scientist gives the warning extra weight.

Throughout the 1950s, the British scientific community and scientific endeavour were becoming increasingly conspicuous following the progressively technologized conflict of the Second World War. In 1951, the Festival of Britain "made a spectacular setting as a showpiece for the inventiveness and genius of British scientists and technologists" (Morgan 2001: 110) and succeeded in alleviating the sense of austerity and gloom presiding over Britain from the late 1940s. The *Quatermass* trilogy draws further attention to the importance of science to Britain's postwar recovery and security. Indeed, there is a distinct development in the central character's representation across the trilogy. In *Experiment*, Quatermass is an ambiguous figure. The alien invades Earth through Quatermass' rocketry experiments; it is defeated only by the power of his rhetoric. *Quatermass II* is less ambivalent, casting its protagonist as a savior. In *Quatermass and the Pit*, he has become the voice of reason. Scientific ventures no longer force a crisis of conscience as they did in *Experiment*. Rather, Quatermass is exonerated from any complicity in future conflict or disaster in a script that attributes strife to an augmented, but controllable, human nature. Quatermass becomes a social commentator for whom the scientific project is morally neutral, providing those who control its products exercise restraint. Being addressed by such a figure through the "intimate medium" would have ensured audiences recognized the power of television not merely to entertain but to alarm or provoke.

Kneale was no novice to writing disquieting television. His Cartier-produced 1954 version of Orwell's *Nineteen Eighty-Four* (1949), provoked angry responses and sparked a House of Commons debate. Kneale's adaptation exploits the rationing and ruin of postwar Britain to capture the mood of Orwell's novel and transforms Cold War fears into a terror not only for, but of, the future. Rather than sublimating his audience's anxieties, Kneale exploits those fears, showing a British totalitarian state emerging after an atomic attack. Consequently, he simplifies Orwell's narrative and endorses the political ideology of the Cold War, where Britain's atomic bomb is framed implicitly as the only viable (i.e., comparable) defense against the advent of Big Brother. Just as Quatermass' rocketship-bomb saves Britain so, by extension, Britain's nuclear deterrent – the exercising of armed restraint – preserves it from the predations of totalitarianism (see Jacobs 2000: 139–55).

Importantly, whilst Kneale reaffirms his audience's faith in one form of technology, he suggests the mechanics of totalitarianism may already exist in the presence of another. When Big Brother glares from the play's telescreens, he glowers from the television itself, identifying viewer with subjugated character. Using this artful composition, Kneale questions the possibilities of television itself. As such, the play is a doubly unsettling experience seldom paralleled in its ability to disturb.

Much TVSF of the 1950s shared Kneale's concerns with the Cold War, including John Lett's dystopian *One* (1956), Christopher Hodder-Williams' *The Voices* (1955), Charles Morgan's morality tale *The Burning Glass* (1956), J.B. Priestley's typically pro-CND *Doomsday for Dyson* (1958), Jimmy Sangster's *I Can Destroy the Sun* (1958), and James Forsyth's *Underground* (1958). Others were variously topical, like Kneale and Cartier's *The Creature* (1955), an account of the Yeti, which followed Edmund Hillary's conquest of Everest; or Michael Pertwee's ethical *Man in a Moon* (1957); or thought experiments in time travel (Charles Eric Maine's *Time Slip* [1953]) or cryogenics (Evelyn Frazer's *The Critical Point* [1957]).

As the 1950s drew to a close, the twin characteristics of British TVSF – the centrality of the scientist and the theme of nuclear conflict – remained fundamental, but their dramatic presentation was changing. The misleadingly titled *H.G. Wells' The Invisible Man* (1958–9) transforms the scientist from an academic into an action-oriented secret agent and Marghanita Laski's *The Offshore Island* (1959) is more openly critical of Cold War American influence on Britain than earlier dramas, adopting an antiestablishment stance that anticipated much of the TVSF produced in the 1960s.

A for Andromeda (1961), for example, is bold in its condemnation of the political and military conscription of science and scientists. Where such criticism was implicit or personalized in *Quatermass*, *A for Andromeda* shows a scientific community distrusted by and accountable to Whitehall. Written by astronomer Fred Hoyle and scripted by

BBC producer John Elliot, the six-part serial recounts the consequences of constructing a supercomputer following plans received from the Andromeda galaxy in 1970. By showing Europe negatively as America's frontline under a state of siege, the series addresses Cold War politics while restating the incorruptibility of the inviolable scientist. Pitting the idealistic scientist John Fleming (Peter Halliday) against the seemingly hostile alien supercomputer, a myopic British government, the unscrupulous multinational corporation Intel, and a US general intent on selfishly safeguarding "aircraft-carrier Britain," *A for Andromeda* re-emphasizes the moral and intellectual superiority of scientists over politicians first established in *Quatermass*. Whether Hoyle and Elliot were reacting critically to the Labour Party's efforts to court scientists and the professional classes in the early 1960s by suggesting "socialism was 'about science'" – and which led to the publication of "Labour and the Scientific Revolution" in 1963 (Morgan 2001: 231–2) – is conjectural. However, their criticism of "earthly politics," of short-termism, economic incompetence, and political exploitation is sustained throughout. In the sequel, *The Andromeda Breakthrough* (1963), the critique shifts from the politics of science in relation to military and economic matters to censure science and scientists involved in the capitalist enterprise. The series concludes with the promise of a new renaissance masterminded by a Wellsian-derived scientific technocracy.

The notion of a salvatory scientist as a politically and socially critical figure is fundamental to the characterization of the itinerant and eccentric protagonist of *Doctor Who* (BBC1, 1963–89). In *Doctor Who: The Unfolding Text* (1988), Tulloch and Alvarado note how the Doctor "has consistently adopted that liberal populist role in criticizing 'sectionalist' forces of 'Left' and 'Right', and in rebuking the 'official' and the powerful in big business, the military, government or militant unions" (1988: 54). In short, he continues the work begun by Fleming in the *Andromeda* dramas. As a liberal, the Doctor, like Fleming, occupies neutral ground from which he can criticize socially, morally, and aesthetically, the mores of his contemporary audience. The Doctor's critical role reflects the BBC's self-professed liberal political and social agenda, which make the Doctor an extension of their own programming policy.

Partly conceived to assist the teaching of science and history to children, *Doctor Who* is informed intermittently by explicit and implicit pedagogic discourses. As Tulloch and Alvarado argue, it draws on the soft science of its Wellsian model to investigate alternate cultures and advocate "a responsible cultural perspectivism" (1988: 41). Additionally, it promotes "a liberal discourse of 'tolerance' and 'balance' against the militaristic tendencies of the Bug Eyed Monster (BEM) syndrome" (1988: 41–2). This form of "responsible entertainment" is perceived as inherently British as a consequence of the BBC's commitment to national education.

Doctor Who was initiated by Sidney Newman, the motivating force behind ATV's *Armchair Theatre* and ABC's acclaimed anthology series, *Out of this World* (1962), thirteen plays that dramatized stories by John Wyndham, Isaac Asimov, and Philip K. Dick under the guidance of story editor Irene Shubik. The development of *Doctor Who*, with its flexibility and critical potential, and the quality of *Out of this World*, meant that many contemporary drama serials appeared rather conservative in comparison, including the BBC's invasion scenario *The Monsters* (1962), ATV's alien subversion story, *Undermind* (1963), and *Adam Adamant Lives* (BBC1, 1966–7), in which the eponymous Edwardian adventurer-scholar is frozen in 1902 and revived in 1966 to defend an outdated morality.

The reactionary *Adam Adamant Lives!* contrasts sharply with ATV's *The Prisoner* (1967–8). Created by and starring Patrick McGoohan, *The Prisoner* unites the paranoid uncertainties of espionage narratives with British New Wave SF's interest in psychology and altered states of consciousness to produce a provocative political and philosophical discourse on the nature of freedom. Previously Nicholai Soloviov, a trapped cosmonaut in ABC's *Man Out There* (1961) and spy John Drake in *Danger Man*, McGoohan plays Number Six, a former secret agent gassed, incarcerated, and interrogated in The Village, a bizarre amalgamation of holiday resort and detention center for the politically inconvenient. Here, he enters a battle of wits with a series of Number Twos, The Village's de facto administrators, determined to uncover why he resigned, and begins a quest to find Number One, the mastermind behind his imprisonment. The series is notoriously ambiguous as it problematizes the cultural ferment of the 1960s. At times, it seems to subscribe to the decade's antiestablishment, libertarian values; on other occasions McGoohan's political conservatism underpins an attack on such values and their representatives, particularly in "Fall Out," the surreal final episode. Indeed, the revelation that Number Six *is* Number One undermines the program's peculiar "psychedelic realism," suggesting that the series is a visual metaphor for Number Six's internal debate over his motives for resigning. Whatever the solution, *The Prisoner* eloquently dramatizes the dilemma of understanding and safeguarding one's individuality in an increasingly clandestine world. As such, it is a uniquely ingenious series which exerts little influence over subsequent productions, although *Sin With Our Permission* (ATV, 1981) recaptures its paranoid ambience in an intelligent critique of New Town uniformity, mass observation, and social control.

In addition to *The Prisoner*, *Doctor Who*, and the *Andromeda* series, the 1960s saw an abundance of single dramas. Some, like *Night of the Big Heat* (1960) and *The Friendly Persuaders* (1969), were retrograde alien invasion scenarios. Others remained firmly engaged with Cold War politics. *The Poisoned Earth* (1961), for example, complicates the debate surrounding disarmament by contrasting the economic benefits to a small town of a neighboring weapons-development facility with the larger political concerns of proliferation and conflict. *Course for Collision* (1962) and *Danger* Zone (1963) are more sensational treatments of nuclear politics whereas Nigel Kneale's *The Crunch* (1964) invokes supernatural aid to save London from the Bomb. The increasing tempo of the space race informed *Countdown at Woomera* (1961) and both *The Test* (1961) and *Campaign for One* (1965) examine the psychological effects of scientific research and space travel. *The Devil's Eggshell* (1966) follows the *Andromeda* series in casting its scientists as conspirators attempting to overthrow tyrannical politicians. Fittingly, sex was central to the decade's most controversial play, Kneale's *Year of the Sex Olympics* (1968). Borrowing ideas from Orwell and Huxley, Kneale anticipates the twenty-first century fascination with "reality" television by creating a dystopia where mass voyeurism is used to control the audience's emotional drives.

Throughout the 1960s, adaptations remained intrinsic to British TVSF. Robert Sheckley's satirical "Seventh Victim" (1953) became the *Murder Club* (1961) and Asimov's *The Caves of Steel* (1954) was screened in 1964 on *Story Parade*, becoming BBC2's first SF production. It is possible that *The Caves of Steel* influenced *The Girl Who Loved Robots* (1965), a thriller that also unites conventions from SF with the detective genre. Subsequently, British TVSF returned to its origins to produce *Days to Come* (1966), a version of Wells' novella, which anticipates Aldous Huxley's savage anti-Utopian *Brave New World* (1932) and *The Metal Martyr* (1967), a *R.U.R.*-derived drama of robot revolution. The BBC televised Huxley's own satirical postnuclear narrative, *Ape and Essence* (1948) in 1966.

Following her success with *Story Parade*, Irene Shubik went on to produce the acclaimed BBC anthology series *Out of the Unknown* (1966–71), which offered 49 plays either adapted from stories by such notables as John Wyndham, Isaac Asimov, Ray Bradbury, Kate Wilhelm, and Frederick Pohl, or written specifically for the screen. With Shubik's departure at the end of Season Two, which marked a shift from SF towards supernatural thrillers, the practice of producing SF anthology series came to an end.

The rejection of such series by both BBC and ITV regions anticipated the decline of the SF play throughout 1970s. With the exception of Donald Jonson's *A.D.A.M.* (1973), which bears a striking resemblance to Dean Koontz's *Demon Seed* (also 1973), the plays produced showed a growing concern with environmentalism. John Fletcher's *Stargazy on Zummerdown* (1978) rejects industrialization for a rural society in which twenty-third-century Britain is sustained by advanced but ecologically sound technology. *Alternative Three* (1977) by David Ambrose is more alarming. Introduced as part of Anglia's *Science Report* series, *Alternative Three* is as accomplished a hoax as *Ghostwatch* (BBC, 1992) or Orson Welles' radiobroadcast of *The War of the Worlds* (1938). It professes to expose a global conspiracy in which American and Soviet officials concluded that the removal of Earth's elite was the only means by which humanity would survive an impending environmental catastrophe. Broadcast on June 20, few viewers noticed the copyright date was April 1. Anglia was flooded with concerned callers. Though such a response suggests the gullibility of television audiences, it also demonstrates that members of the British public recognized human activity on Earth may already have been cataclysmic.

Human influence on the environment was a defining theme of *Doomwatch* (BBC1, 1970–2), which follows the efforts of a government department to safeguard environmental and public safety from scientific, military, or corporate negligence. Created by *Doctor Who* script editor Gerry Davis and environmentalist Dr. Kit Pedler, the series responded to a growing scientific concern for pollution, resource depletion, and ecological mismanagement that culminated in *Only One Earth: The Care and Maintenance of a Small Planet* (1972), a report commissioned by the Secretary-General of the United Nations Conference on the Human Environment.

The BBC had explored similar ground with *R3* (1964–5), which followed the publication of Rachel Carson's *Silent Spring* (1962). However, the overtly critical *Doomwatch* is not simply an expression of its creators' distrust of scientific developments; it is also an appeal for an interrogation of scientific practice and establishment complicity. Its main character, Dr. Spencer Quist (John Paul) is a driven man. Occupying a desk opposite a glowering triptych of nuclear test photographs, Quist seeks redemption for his part in the Manhattan Project and absolution for the death of his wife from leukemia. By challenging government and corporations alike, Quist is a symbolic figure, reminding the audience that whilst they, like him, have lived under the shadow of the Bomb, the world is being poisoned by less spectacular but equally catastrophic means. Accordingly, the single-minded Quist is a further example of the BBC's antiestablishment, salvatory scientist made popular in the *Andromeda* serials and *Doctor Who*.

The Doctor himself underwent significant revisions in the early 1970s. Where the first six seasons of *Doctor Who* offer historical adventures, alien worlds, temporal voyages, and stories of extraterrestrial invasion, seasons 7–11 deal with more politically and socially pertinent material. Banished to Earth, the Third Doctor (John Pertwee) joins the United Nations Intelligence Taskforce (UNIT) to combat threats to British national security. Although part of the establishment, Pertwee's Doctor is notably more critical of his contemporary context than either of his predecessors (played by William Hartnell and Patrick Troughton). Indeed, he is unfailingly disparaging of the establishment and its metaphorical substitutes, commenting on Britain's entry into the Common Market ("The Curse of Peladon" [1972]), industrial pollution ("The Green Death" [1973]), and difficult industrial relations ("The Monster of Peladon" [1974]). Disapproving of bureaucracy, militarism, and despotic capitalism, the Doctor's role as a social and moral critic is never more obvious, nor as concerned with the state of contemporary Britain, than during Pertwee's tenure.

Like *Doomwatch* and *Doctor Who*, LWT's dystopian *The Guardians* (1971) is discomforting in its engagement with contemporary politics. Set in the near future after the specters of British politics – mass unemployment, a general strike, and raging inflation – force the collapse of a coalition government, the series shows the alarming consequences of a ruling body dedicated to the preservation of order at all costs. In hindsight, *The Guardians* seems remarkably prophetic, anticipating the economic and social upheavals under Jim Callaghan's Labour government and the early Thatcher administration. More critical of British politics in the 1970s is William Greatorex's Orwellian *1990* (BBC2, 1977), which targets "the burgeoning bureaucracy of the 1970s" (Fulton 1995: 276) in a series that is part dystopian critique, part adventure thriller.

Clearly, throughout the 1970s, British TVSF demonstrates a growing disillusionment with domestic politics and an increasing parochialism that reflects Britain's waning influence on world affairs, its economic weakness, and a withdrawal from the implications of its entry into the EEC in 1973. This mounting inwardness explains, in part, why Gerry Anderson's first live action series, *UFO* (1970–73), and its successor, *Space 1999* (1975–6), proved unpopular. Produced when Britain no longer shared an equal relationship with America, Anderson's American-modeled and financed series, appear too abstracted from British cultural life. Although both series reflect the somber mood of Britain in 1970s, the future they show is not a British future; neither provides anything beyond derivative space opera with the pace, if not the charm, of Anderson's earlier puppet series.

In contrast, *Moonbase 3* (BBC1, 1973) dramatizes the hazards of venturing into an inhospitable environment. Conceived by Barry Letts and Terrance Dicks, the producer and script editor for Pertwee's Doctor, *Moonbase 3* is a realistic, extrapolative vision of lunar living. Its scientific accuracy is attributable to James Burke, principal commentator on the BBC's Apollo coverage and presenter of the popular science program, *The Burke Special*, who served as scientific advisor. *Moonbase 3*'s appeal to realism resulted in a disquieting sense of claustrophobia and isolation that undermined the optimism of its premise and captured the general mood of insularity felt (and often desired) in Britain during the early 1970s (see Morgan 2001: 342).

A comparable insularity is found in Terry Nation's *Survivors* (1975–7), in which the remnants of British society struggle to rebuild civilization after a plague kills 95% of the world's population. The series explodes the myth of cosy, middle-class self-sufficiency popular in the 1970s (and typified by the sitcom *The Good Life*) to expose the difficulties of returning to a less industrialized existence. Its focus on middle-class characters in crisis, together with its tone of cautious optimism and its combination of political modeling and social criticism, borrows from Wyndham and the tradition of British disaster fiction, yet its avowedly nationalistic, isolationist politics seem a direct reaction against Britain's involvement in Europe. The disaster is the means by which England re-emphasizes its sovereignty. The penultimate episode, "Long Live the King," exposes the series' conservatism and emblematizes an apparent need to restate traditional communal and cultural values at a time when industrial confrontation and violence seemed poised to overthrow conventional British stability and government attachment to Brussels constituted a "greater detachment of the community from the processes of administration" (see Morgan 2001: 353–5).

Nation's *Blake's 7* (1977–81) adopts a similar political stance, advocating traditional values over the amoral mechanics of an assimilative bureaucracy. Reclaiming the conventions of space opera for a British context, Nation's series follows a rebellion by a group of criminals led by idealist Roj Blake (Gareth Thomas) and cynic Kerr Avon (Paul Darrow) against the despotic activities of Earth's Federation. Here, however, Nation is less concerned with contemporary politics than with restating his opposition to totalitarianism, which had previously informed his conception of the Daleks for *Doctor Who*. Taking inspiration from the anti-Utopian writings of Orwell and Huxley, Nation produced the antithesis of Gene Roddenberry's *Star Trek*. *Blake's 7* replaces the camaraderie of Roddenberry's series with hostility and distrust; the seemingly benign United Federation of Planets is countered with the militaristic Federation; and heroic individuals are supplanted by ambivalent characters with ambiguous motives. Where *Star Trek* advocates triumphant expansionism, Nation's dystopian space opera chronicles a series of hollow victories and bitter defeats. The climax of Blake's ineffective rebellion, which sees all but one of the rebels killed, reflects the sullen mood of a Britain beset by economic decline, mass unemployment, civil unrest, and the dictatorial premiership of Margaret Thatcher.

When Quatermass returned in 1979, Kneale addressed the contemporary political and social malaise afflicting Britain directly. Set in a decaying, anarchic England, where street gangs rule the inner cities and New Age hippies wander the countryside waiting to be taken to the stars, *Quatermass* is unrelentingly grim. It shows an almost complete loss of faith in a youth either intoxicated by violence or by the promise of salvation. Only Quatermass and a group of aging scientists offer any hope of salvation from a vast alien structure harvesting the hippies whenever they gather in sufficient numbers around the world. When Quatermass and his granddaughter sacrifice themselves in a nuclear blast that damages the alien vessel and saves the world, Kneale's teleplay betrays its essential conservatism. By advocating self-sacrifice in the face of hardship as the only way to rescue society from ruin, Kneale attempts to reinstate nobility in an act that, for many, had already proved unacceptable. After the economic "sacrifices" expected by Callahan's government had given rise to the Winter of Discontent, Kneale's sentiment seems as anachronistic as his vagrant hippies.

The Conservative victory in May 1979 provoked varied responses from British TVSF. P.J. Hammond's *Sapphire and Steel* (1979–82) presented Thatcher's premiership as the triumph of Conservative order over social chaos in a somber, deeply symbolic series. The program synthesizes tropes from the Gothic and the English ghost story with the rational, investigative processes of science fiction and the Golden Age crime novel to structure a conflict between the metaphorical representatives of perceived contemporary social malaise – militant groups, "wet" or ineffective politicians, immigration, faceless bureaucracy – and the eponymous Thatcherite protagonists. Authoritarian and uncompromising, Sapphire (Joanna Lumley) and Steel (David McCallum) are guardians of the social and temporal order. After the miserable Winter of Discontent, it is perhaps unsurprising that Sapphire and Steel were accepted as heroic figures despite their obdurate, misanthropic attitude.

Other dramas were more critical of Thatcher, particularly of her rapport with Ronald Reagan and their "cooperative" defense policy. Thatcher's willingness to allow US Cruises missile into Britain and the gradual upgrading of the Polaris submarine system to Trident provoked widespread condemnation while providing CND with a new impetus for action. Thatcher's antipathy towards the Soviet Union, Reagan's "evil empire," led to a new chilling of the Cold War, a renewed attention to civil defense in Britain, and a concomitant growth in public concern over the prospect of nuclear conflict. British television responded with a provocative intersection between mainstream drama, documentary, and science fiction: Barry Hines' *Threads* (1984).

Threads formed part of a series of dramas and documentaries addressing nuclear war screened by the BBC throughout 1984 and 1985, including an adaptation of Robert C. O'Brien's *Z for Zachariah* (1974) and the belated broadcast of Peter Watkins' previously banned *The War Game* (1966). Directed with harrowing verisimilitude by Mick Jackson, *Threads* focuses on the events leading up to and following a nuclear attack on Britain. Seen through the lives of two Sheffield families, the Becketts and the Kemps, the holocaust becomes an uncomfortably intimate experience that Jackson juxtaposes with bland yet horrifying statistical information. Politically, *Threads* is scathing. It destroys the credibility of the government's *Protect and Survive* guide and exposes the myth of viable Civil Defense. As such, it owes a significant debt to *The War Game*.

Watkins' docudrama had already established a precedent for critiquing government policy towards nuclear weapons. It is, in part, a response to the decision by Harold Wilson's Labour government to abandon its policy of unilateral disarmament and develop a new nuclear weapons program. Since there was no discussion of the consequences of a nuclear exchange, Watkins addressed the subject himself. Using neorealist cinematography, nonprofessional actors, and natural lighting, Watkins produces a strikingly satirical treatment of a nuclear attack on Kent. Like Jackson, he explodes the notion of a plausible civil defense and mounts a sustained critique of establishment figures in favor of nuclear weapons. As Ronald Garmon observes, after the attack, "Watkins spends the rest of film demolishing several national myths and offending sensibilities wherever found" (Garmon 1998). The BBC banned the film in 1965; when it was released in cinemas worldwide in March 1966, it won the Oscar for Best Documentary.

Following the suppression of Watkins' work, the nuclear subject remained largely absent from British television for almost twenty years. *Salve Regina* (1969), a claustrophobic drama scrutinizing the interactions of four survivors in a department store basement, is notable for being the first treatment of the subject to be aired successfully. Strategically broadcast on the eve of the Apollo 11 moon landing, the drama was overshadowed and is now virtually forgotten.

The BBC's antinuclear programs are certainly indicative of its opposition to Thatcher's policies and imply a socialist bias within the Corporation. Where the BBC had banned *The War Game* to ostensibly protect Wilson's pronuclear policy, *Threads* seemed intended to damage a comparable Conservative position and support Labour's unpopular unilateralist position. Indeed, the BBC's antinuclear stance extended to the nuclear industry itself; Troy Kennedy Martin's critically acclaimed *Edge of Darkness* (1985) is both intelligent and direct in its critique of the secrecy and duplicity surrounding nuclear power and weaponry. Like Steven Poliakoff's play *Stronger than the Sun* (1977), *Edge of Darkness* exposes the inherent dangers – environmental, political, and personal – of nuclear power. However, Martin's ecodrama is more politically motivated in its critique of the clandestine interactions between the secret powers of the state and the equally covert operations of corporate business. Displaying the gothic gloom of *Sapphire and Steel*, *Edge of Darkness* is embedded in the context of the 1980s, balancing what Martin sees as "political pessimism" with "moral optimism" (Martin 1990: x) in its juxtaposition of idealism and materialism, environmentalism and exploitation, morality and deceit.

Unrelenting pessimism was the defining tone of the BBC's *Play for Tomorrow* (1982), six specially commissioned plays offering chill visions of a Thatcherite future of overcrowded prisons (Caryl Churchill's *Crimes*), political oppression (*Bright Eyes* by Peter Prince), nuclear defense (Tom McGrath's *The Nuclear Family*), mass unemployment (*Shades* by Stephen Lowe), and Anglo-Irish relations (Graham Reid's satirical *Easter 2016*). Only *Cricket*, Michael Wilcox's tale of skulduggery in the world of county cricket, lightened the tone of a politically scornful series. The urban and industrial decline of Thatcher's Britain was also the subject of Channel 4's *Max Headroom* (1985), which delivers a wry satire on television culture and public apathy at the hands of unscrupulous advertisers.

Humor is also essential to Douglas Adams' *The Hitch-Hiker's Guide to the Galaxy* (1981). Formerly a Radio 4 drama, Adams' series is conscious not only of the meaninglessness of human existence but also the folly of searching for meaning. Adams understands that humor is the only defense against such a bleak realization. Where other, less successful SF-comedy series, including *Star Maidens* (1976), Kneale's *Kinvig* (1981), *Astronauts* (1981), and *They Came from Somewhere Else* (1984), employ SF tropes to revitalize exhausted sitcom conventions, *Hitch-Hiker's* employs comedy to recount a science fiction story that exposes the general absurdity of the cosmos and articulates a sobering and melancholy misanthropy. In its anarchic plotting, the importance of human existence is undermined, the pettiness of human officialdom mocked, and the scale of human achievement parodied.

When British TVSF disengaged itself from censuring Thatcherism, it seemed inconsequential. *The Flipside of Dominick Hide* (BBC1, 1980) and *Another Flip for Dominic* (1982) were clichéd time-travel fantasies; *The Nightmare Man* (1981) saw a return to Cold War paranoia; and Douglas Livingstone's version of Wyndham's *The Day of the Triffids* (BBC1, 1981) was workmanlike in its faithfulness. Written as six 25-minute episodes, it could not recapture the novel's sense of decline, struggle, and progress, which had, ironically, been achieved with the Wyndham-derived *Survivors*. Although Barry Letts' and Terrance Dicks' treatment of Wells' *The Invisible Man* (1984) was rendered with the integrity usually reserved by the BBC for its Victorian adaptations, it seemed already familiar. Invisibility was longer exceptional and the production could not revitalize or make relevant Wells' condemnation of scientific hubris.

Chris Boucher's *Star Cops* (1987) appears to reflect a burgeoning mood of contemporary optimism as the British economy improved and the worst excesses of Thatcherism seemed in remission. Uniting conventions from crime and science fiction, Boucher recaptures the realist approach of *Moonbase 3* to create a communication-rich future in which the developed nations have permanent bases in orbit, on the Moon and Mars. This positive vision of 2027 is tempered, however, by showing the greed, distrust, manipulation, and ambition characterizing human interaction on Earth transferred to space. The series' cynicism, profanity, and jaded perception of international and personal relationships indicate a loss of faith not only in humanity but also in humanity's capacity for change. *Star Cops* also exposed a lack a faith in science fiction. Aired on BBC2 and cancelled after nine episodes, its demise is indicative of a gradual decline in British TVSF throughout the 1980s. The most accomplished productions – *Sapphire and Steel*, *Threads*, *Edge of Darkness* – were only marginally SF. There were no new series to follow *Doomwatch*, *Survivors*, or *Blake's 7* as the BBC gradually withdrew its support from mainstream science fiction drama. The cancellation of *Doctor Who* in 1989 is symptomatic of this retraction.

After its political phase in the early 1970s, *Doctor Who* enjoyed considerable commercial success throughout Tom Baker's term as the Fourth Doctor. With Philip Hinchcliffe as producer, seasons 13 and 14 drew on the Gothic tradition for moodier, more horrific stories; under Graham Williams, the series became increasingly pantomimic; and when Jonathan Nathan Turner began his tenure as producer, *Doctor Who* obtained a stylish quality it had previously lacked. Although style often triumphed over substance, Peter Davison's exploits as the Fifth Doctor are notably imaginative. Following Davison's departure, *Doctor Who* was beset with problems: poor writing, Michael Grade's antipathy, a disagreeable Doctor (Colin Baker), and scheduling against *Coronation Street*, all contributed to a marked decline. Sylvester McCoy survived three foreshortened seasons as the Seventh Doctor before the series was finally cancelled at the end of season 26.

The cancellation of *Doctor Who* meant the end of a popular cultural phenomenon, but not the demise of British TVSF. It did, however, signal a gradual decline in production as the BBC, in particular, seemed content to import and repeat increasing numbers of American series, including *Star Trek* and its sequels, *The X-Files*, *Quantum Leap*, *Sliders* and the genre related telefantasies *Buffy the Vampire Slayer* and *Lois and Clark*, which all supplanted indigenous SF. Nevertheless, as *Doctor Who* declined in corporate support, BBC2's SF sitcom *Red Dwarf* (1988–99) was attracting a significant audience. Unlike *Goodnight Sweetheart* (BBC1, 1993–9), which uses time travel to facilitate a largely conventional sitcom about infidelity, Rob Grant and Doug Naylor's *Red Dwarf* derives much of its humor from situations arising from science fiction conceits: sentient moons, alternative worlds, virtual reality environments, and advanced technology. Like *The Hitch-hiker's Guide*, it resists denigrating generic conventions to mere devices to enliven standard comedy situations. However, where *The Hitch-hiker's Guide* parodied bureaucracy, human hubris, and the notion of ultimate knowledge to offer a wry account of humanity's shortcomings, *Red Dwarf*'s humor is more intimate, deriving from personal, class, and masculine conflict between its characters. In a highly persuasive article, Elyce Rae Helford argues that the program's predominantly male cast gives rise to a "postpatriarchal space" in which the politics of gender, representation, masculine anxiety, and male desire take centre stage (see Helford 1995: 20–31). As such, it is the most perceptive of British SF-comedies. It is also one of the few examples of British TVSF to retain a political edge into the 1990s.

Throughout the decade, only Malcolm McKay's drama *Yellowbacks* (BBC1, 1990), Stephen Gallagher's *Chimera* (ITV, 1991), Ben Elton's *Stark* (BBC1, 1993), and David Pirie's play *Black Easter* (BBC2, 1995) retained British TVSF's characteristically reflective stance towards contemporary events. *Yellowbacks* is a dystopian vision of a Britain succumbing to panic as a sexually transmitted virus spreads across the country. In characterizing "Positives" as pariahs, it critiques the social segregation of AIDS victims and the politics of moral panic. Alternatively, *Chimera* questions the ethics of genetic engineering. Inspired by "a report made by the Rand Corporation in America which suggested that . . . production-line sub-humans [would be available] as workers by the year 2025" (Lane 1991: 9), Gallagher's original novel traces modern genetic engineering back to concentration camp experiments and thereby implies, and denounces, the parallels between capitalist exploitation and Nazi atrocity. Although the teleplay removes this theme, it retains its critique of a government intending to further disenfranchise its people of economic self-determination by manufacturing subhuman workers. Clearly, the drama would have been more politically resonant if it had been screened immediately after the novel's publication in 1982. As it stands, it is a disturbing view of what the cooperation between capitalism and science could achieve.

Stark, Ben Elton's adaptation of his 1989 comic novel, is more contemporaneous in its criticism of capitalist complicity in environmental catastrophe. In pitting ecoactivists against the corporate-backed Stark conspiracy, Elton acknowledges the rise of the Green Party (which performed well in the Euro-elections in June 1989) and the challenge a growing ecological awareness posed to "the message of Thatcherite consumption and wealth creation" (Morgan 2001: 502). In contrast, Pirie's *Black Easter* is relentlessly bleak. Set in 2000, it shows Western Europe inundated by refugees of civil war in Russia and a German homicide detective's (Trevor Eve) efforts to solve the murder of a Danish nurse. The climax of the play, a chilling vision of genocide, not only reflects the uncertainty of a Europe in transition following the collapse of the Soviet Union but also anticipates the discovery of ethnic cleansing and mass graves in the former Yugoslavia.

With these exceptions, British TVSF in the 1990s is characterized by either marginal SF series or revisions of earlier dramas. *Bugs* (BBC1, 1995–9), for example, follows an investigative team as they counter high-tech crimes in the near future. Using fantastic gadgets or conceits – miraculous foodstuffs, gold-eating microbes, voice-activated bombs – to drive its action-orientated narratives, *Bugs* eschews political comment in favor of attributing the world's troubles to lunatic individuals. As such, it is light entertainment akin to Anthony Horowitz's punningly titled *Crime Traveler* (BBC1, 1997), in which Holly Turner (Chloe Annett) uses her father's time machine to assist renegade police officer Jeff Slade (Michael French) to solve various crimes. Given the obviously limited dramatic potential of the concept, the Rules of Time provide convenient dilemmas to what would otherwise be mini-adventures.

When *Doctor Who* returned as a telefilm in 1996, it exemplified not only the depoliticization of British TVSF but also the loss – possibly inevitable in an increasingly global entertainment market – of the form's quintessential Britishness. Coproduced by the BBC, its Worldwide division, Universal, and Fox Television, *Doctor Who: The Movie* avoids the original series' "liberal populist" politics in favor of producing a "globalized" or "Westernized" Doctor reinvented by writer Matthew Jacobs and producer Philip Segal to occupy a point of sociocentrality. Revisionist intertexts, transformations of character, and generic shifts bring the production into line with the homogenized productions of the satellite – or at least international – television age. It is bland, uncontroversial (from a conservative perspective), and superficial.

ITV's four-part *The Uninvited* (1997) is equally lackluster as it returns doggedly to the theme of alien subversion to exploit the popularity and paranoid plotting of *The X-Files*. The introduction of an environmental theme fails to distinguish the series from its sources as its complete lack of a political subtext denies it *The X-Files*' anti-establishment sensibility.

Invasion Earth, a six-episode mini-series coproduced by BBC Scotland and the Sci-Fi Channel, is also derivative, failing to conceal the paucity of its ideas behind a significant budget. Revisiting the definitive SF cliché – the alien invasion – it attempts to recapture the mystery and suspense of the early *Quatermass* stories. It succeeds only in offering a dreary tale of Earth being caught in a war between the benign Echoes and the malevolent nDs, who plan to invade Earth. Borrowing character dynamics from the UNIT years of *Doctor Who*, imagery culled from *Alien* (Ridley Scott, 1979) and *Predator* (John McTiernan, 1987), and the notion of aliens harvesting humans from *Quatermass* (1979), *Invasion: Earth* is distinguished only by its apocalyptic climax, which fails to invigorate its formulaic narrative. The presence of American Fred Ward as Maj. Gen. David Reece and the involvement of the Sci-Fi channel indicate that *Invasion: Earth* is aimed, like *Doctor Who: The Movie*, at an international market. Regrettably, like *Doctor Who*, it epitomizes the worst quality of much popular cultural production: an intellectually numbing, politically complicit, and culturally stagnant sameness.

Despite being unimaginative in borrowing from Forde Beebe's *Buck Rogers* (1939), Nation's *Survivors*, and the British disaster tradition, Matthew Graham's six-part *The Last Train* (ITV, 1999) is a refreshingly understated vision of doomsday. Disdaining nuclear conflict, the series deploys the most recent trend in apocalyptic scenarios – an asteroid collision – to wipe out most of humanity. A group of survivors, seemingly representative of multicultural Britain yet still characterized stereotypically (Mick, played by Treva Etienne, is black and a criminal), are preserved when their train from London to Sheffield enters a tunnel at the moment of impact. Frozen cryogenically by the contents of a canister carried by one of the passengers, the survivors regain consciousness and emerge from their tomb almost fifty years after the event. The series chronicles the quest they undertake from a shattered Sheffield (clearly a homage to *Threads*) to the catastrophe-survival shelter ARK. Unlike *Deep Impact* and *Armageddon* (both 1998), *The Last Train* explores catastrophe intimately and without sentiment, dramatizing the difficulties of finding fresh water, food, and shelter in a world remade by disaster. This intimacy is developed further as the series asks, through dialogue, subtext, and event, what drives individuals to survive? The answers form the trajectories of each character as they move across the blighted landscape.

With its thoughtful juxtaposing of delusion and optimism, tenderness and cruelty, the mundane and the extraordinary, *The Last Train* repudiates the global and

American influences affecting *Doctor Who: The Movie, The Uninvited* and *Invasion: Earth* to create a different, yet no less distinct, form of British TVSF. Although it does not engage with its political context, or respond distinctly to indigenous literary SF, it proclaims its Britishness in its impressively apocalyptic location work. It reminds the viewer that, at the end of the twentieth century, Britain is a product of its sociopolitical past, a place of contrasts where industrial blight and natural beauty coexist. As such, *The Last Train* can be read as a celebration and a condemnation of what it means to be British. Through its representative characters – selfish, single-minded, altruistic, deluded, uncertain, confused, and hopeful – it shows a nation divided against itself yet able to survive and prosper. The birth of a child in a wash of lambent white light at its conclusion certainly overplays the series' essential optimism but *The Last Train* nevertheless marks a return of TVSF that at least considers its cultural milieu.

Unlike Graham's survivors, British TVSF has not endured into the twenty-first century. The growth of cable, satellite, and digital channels has permitted easy access to recycled British and American series and new US shows. Coupled with the tendency of British terrestrial television companies to favor imported programs over investment in indigenous science fiction, this has resulted in the relegation of British TVSF to history. The disappearance of new series is symptomatic of a wider extinction. British television drama now rarely seems to interrogate the British establishment; to an increasingly apolitical nation it offers apolitical entertainment. At a time when there is a particular need to scrutinize the practices of government, either directly or metaphorically, British TVSF is absent. Whether the likely return of *Doctor Who* or the possible resurrection of *Blake's 7* will answer this deficiency remains to be seen. Until then, a significant mode of British cultural criticism is mute.

References and Further Reading

Carrazé, Alain and Helene Oswald (1995) *The Prisoner: A Television Masterpiece*. (trans.) Christine Donougher. London: Virgin Publishing.

Cooper, Nick (1998) "British Telefantasy Began in 1963 . . .. Part I and II." http://www.625.org.uk/pre1963/pre1963.htm (October 18, 2003) and http://www.625.org.uk/pre1963/pre19632.htm (October 18, 2003).

Fulton, Roger (1995) *The Encyclopedia of TV Science Fiction*. London: Boxtree.

Garmon, Ron (1998) "Peter Watkins Blows Up the World: The War Game Revisited." http://picpal.com/peterwatkins.html (January 4, 2004).

Glenn, Edward (1991) "Fantasy Flashback: *The Time Machine*." *TV Zone* 17, 28–30.

Greenland, Colin (1983) *The Entropy Exhibition: Michael Moorcock and the British "New Wave" in*

Science Fiction. London: Routledge and Kegan Paul.

Hayes, Paul (2002) "British Telefantasy: As It Began." http://www.the-mausoleum-club.org.uk/RUR/rur_paul_hayes.htm (October 18, 2003).

Helford, Elice Rae (1995) "Reading Masculinities in 'Post-Patriarchal Space' of *Red Dwarf*". *Foundation: The International Review of Science Fiction* 64 (Summer), 20–31.

Hoyle, Fred and John Elliot (1975) *A for Andromeda* (1962). London: Corgi Books.

——(1974) *The Andromeda Breakthrough* (1964). Manchester: Ensign Books.

Jacobs, Jason (2000) *The Intimate Screen: Early British Television Drama*. Oxford: Oxford University Press.

Johnson-Smith, Jan (2004) *American Science Fiction*

TV: Star Trek, Stargate, and Beyond, Middletown, CT: Wesleyan University Press.

Kneale, Nigel (1979) *Quatermass and the Pit* (1960). London: Arrow Books.

——(1979) *The Quatermass Experiment* (1959). London: Arrow Books.

——(1960) *Quatermass II*. Harmondsworth: Penguin.

Lane, Andrew (1991) "*Chimera*." *TV Zone*. 22 (September), 8–11.

Martin, Troy Kennedy (1990) *Edge of Darkness*. London: Faber and Faber.

Morgan, Kenneth O. (2001) *Britain Since 1945: The People's Peace*. Oxford: Oxford University Press.

O'Brien, Daniel (2000) *SF: UK How British Science Fiction Changed the World*. London: Reynolds and Hearn.

Pixley, Andrew and Nigel Kneale. "Nigel Kneale–Behind the Dark Door." http://www.geocities.com/TelevisionCity/8504/kneal.htm (November 21, 2003).

Ruddick, Nicholas (1993) *The Ultimate Island: On the Nature of British Science Fiction*. Westport, CT: Greenwood Press.

Segal, Philip and Russell, Gary (2000) *Doctor Who: Regeneration: The Story Behind the Revival of a Television Legend*. London: HarperCollins-Entertainment.

Stevens, Alan and Moore, Fiona (2003) *Liberation: The Unofficial and Unauthorised Guide to Blake's 7*. Tolworth, Surrey: Telos Publishing.

Suvin, Darko (1979) *The Metamorphoses of Science Fiction*. New Haven: Yale University Press.

Tulloch, John and Manuel Alvarado (1988) *Doctor Who: The Unfolding Text*. London: Macmillan Press.

PART V
The International Scene

20

Canadian Science Fiction

Douglas Barbour

Various kinds of fantastic writing have existed in Canada, or rather what would become Canada, from the very beginning. Nevertheless, most of what we now call early Canadian literature is dependent upon British, or French, literature of the time, and is clearly colonial, and it is only in the mid-twentieth-century that Canadian literature achieves sufficient weight and individuality to be identified as such throughout the world. From one point of view, a history of science fiction might look a lot like a history of invader/settler nation literatures, say Australian or Canadian. That is, although histories of science fiction now point to early proto-SF works, such as *Frankenstein*, science fiction only emerges as a separate genre in the twentieth-century – or the late nineteenth, if we accept Wells and Verne as definite SF writers. Alternatively, if, as Peter Nicholls suggests, science fiction is anyway "an impure genre" (Clute and Nicholls 1993: 567), then early fantastic or Utopian works can at least be included as proto-science fiction.

In that case, for Canada, James De Mille's *A Strange Manuscript Found in a Copper Cylinder* (1888), still considered a classic, is the first major work in this impure field. It was published in the USA, as were the many fantasy adventures, polar worlds stories, and other internationally popular turn-of-the century genre fictions written in Canada. The most distinguished were by Charles G.D. Roberts, whose *Earth's Enigmas* (1896) and *In the Morning of Time* (1919), the latter a prehistoric romance, are still considered important contributions to the field. The specific lure of the Arctic inscribed particularly Canadian overtones on some of these fictions, but the important influences came from Britain and the USA.

Science fiction, as a pop genre unto itself, emerges with *Amazing Stories* in 1926. As pulp fiction, however, it also created a kind of literary ghetto. While in the USA SF writers tended to write only SF, British and European writers continued to turn their hands to any kind of fiction. And it seems that attitude held in Canada, where Frederick Philip Grove could turn from his usual naturalistic novels to *Consider Her Ways* (1947), about a society of ants exploring the mores of North

American civilization. Similarly, writers in Québec, whose literary influences came mostly from Europe, often turned to the "fantastique." Generally speaking, the works of such mid-century writers as Yves Thériault, Gilles Vigneault, Jacques Ferron, Antonine Maillet, Anne Hébert, and Jacque Godbout fall under the rubric of fantasy, and in every case are but one of the many kinds of fiction they wrote. This occasional turn to what might be called speculative fiction also occurs with some of English Canada's best-known writers.

But when we think of science fiction, per se, most Canadian writers of SF grew up on the American variety and wrote for the American markets. Winnipeg-born A.E. Van Vogt, for example, one of the stars of the so-called "Golden Age of SF" in the 1940s, early discovered a method for turning out pulp blockbusters like *Slan* (1940), and *The Weapon Shops of Isher* (1941). Van Vogt wrote much of the work for which he is remembered before moving to the USA in 1944. His talent for creating gothic horror in alien environments, temporal disjunctivities, ESP supermen, and a highly individualist politics, made him a perfect adventure writer for the new *Astounding* under John W. Campbell. Van Vogt's patented method of adding a new twist to a plot every 500 words or so guarantees that his dream-like narratives pulse with energy and drag the reader pell-mell along. Although born in Canada, both H.L. Gold, who became the first editor of *Galaxy*, and Gordon R. Dickson are essentially pure products of America. For a writer like Van Vogt (and other long-forgotten pulp names), as for A. Bertram Chandler in Australia, there were simply no markets in Canada. Even today, when there are some magazines and occasional anthologies in both countries, the better USA markets pay much higher than anything at home.

The Beginnings of Truly Canadian SF: Phyllis Gotlieb

In his major history of *Canadian Science Fiction and Fantasy* (1992), David Ketterer argues that Canadian SF emerged in the years 1959–83. This makes sense, given that Canadian literature finally achieved national and international recognition during the same period. Its progenitor is Phyllis Gotlieb, whom Robert J. Sawyer has called "the grande dame of Canadian SF." He is not alone in seeing her importance to the genre in this country. Gotlieb published "A Grain of Manhood" in *Fantastic* in 1959, and other stories followed in the early 1960s. Her first novel, *Sunburst* (1964) stands as the precursor of a new Canadian SF, a North American kind of writing, but showing a complexity of character and a social and cultural attitude somewhat different than that found in US SF.

Sunburst made Gotlieb a name in the field, especially for its stunning exploration of ESP and psi powers and its moving representation of its protagonist's difficult adolescence as a brilliant and curious outsider. In most SF, psi powers such as psychokinesis or telekinesis, teleportation, pyrolysis, and mind-control are represented as generally good to have. The wild children of *Sunburst* have all these powers but lack ethical control. Shandy Johnson, the protagonist, has none of them; she is instead impervious to such powers, an "Imper," and it is on this distinction that the novel's interrogation of the superman theme turns.

Gotlieb was already a recognized poet when she turned to SF, and had written poems on the need for society to acknowledge its children in all their manifestations. *Sunburst* argues the same case for the children of Sorrel Park, although almost all the ones with psi powers seem psychopathic, and definitely a danger to the public at large. But, as the unforeseen results of an explosion at an atomic power plant, they are also someone's responsibility.

An extremely well-read poet, Gotlieb piles up the allusions in *Sunburst*, many of them explicitly attached to Shandy's wide reading, for although she is only thirteen she is also a genius. Both David Ketterer and Elizabeth A. Lynn argue that *Sunburst* appears to be a conscious interrogation of the kind of ESP superman found in such novels as A.E. Van Vogt's *Slan*, a figure much more often represented in SF than the quiet, unassuming one that Shandy discovers she may be.

The government facility eventually notices Shandy because she has brought *no* notice upon herself. Nevertheless, she demonstrates fairly quickly to the people she comes to care for there that she does possess a moral sensibility. A decided loner, she soon befriends Jason, the good ESPer, Marsh, the old scientist, and Dr. Urquhart, the psychiatrist who tries to work with the kids, or at least to understand what made them what they are. All she had needed was a group of people she could admire in order to want to join the loose family they create among themselves.

There are two intertwined narratives in *Sunburst*: one a thriller having to do with the escape and then recapture of the ESPers, the other, much subtler, concerning Shandy's attempts to discover her purpose in life. Part of the pleasure of the second narrative line comes from Shandy's obsessive questioning of everybody she meets, and her surprisingly mature reason for doing so: that she knows she is different. She comes across as both very intelligent and youthfully naive. That Gotlieb manages to catch this double aspect of her protagonist is one of the reasons the novel still reads so well some forty years on.

Shandy's personal quest provides the real intellectual excitement of the novel, and here Gotlieb contributes something new to the superman theme. Having read widely, if with little discipline, in sociology, psychology, and anthropology, Shandy is a subtle observer of life and people. Collating all her data, she constructs a theory that is not only intrinsically interesting but also deliberately at odds with every psi story since *Odd John* in its argument that ESP is really "primitive," and that civilization exists because of language and other technologies. This stands against a lot of conventional SF, including perhaps Gotlieb's own later work.

In her understated fashion, Gotlieb shows us a Shandy who realizes that she has a long way to go to discover her purpose in life, and that it may be a lonely road she has to follow. This novel, typically for Gotlieb, refuses absolute closure. It is worth remembering that it appeared in 1964, while Ursula K. Le Guin's first novel appeared in 1967 and Joanna Russ's in 1968. Yet, like their work, it still stands up today, and remains perhaps her most important contribution to the genre.

Until the 1980s, Gotlieb almost was Canadian SF, as Ketterer and others have observed. Most of her later works, both novels and short stories, are set in a coherent future history Galactic Federation, in which a kind of galactic UN tries to keep the peace among a number of worlds and species. Humans are just one of these, and not the most powerful, the kind of insight we might expect from a Canadian federalist. Her most recent trilogy, *Flesh and Gold* (1998), *Violent Stars* (1999), and *Mindworlds* (2002), is a complex interstellar thriller, in which ESP is, for some species, a sign of civilization at its best.

Along with her other works, *Sunburst* stands as a paradigmatically Canadian fiction – in its insistence on the primacy of community over the individual. This pattern, of seeking communal solutions rather than individual ones, will emerge again and again in later Canadian SF.

Immigrants and Home-Grown Writers: 1970–85

The 1970s and early 1980s saw the slow development of a popular literature in a Canada where, for too long, writers had sought only to write "the great Canadian novel." One reason for this was the growing power of popular culture, especially that of the USA. Another was the influx of people who had lost faith in US foreign policy, especially as it manifested itself in the Vietnam War. One of the most important immigrants was the already famous SF writer, Judith Merril, who also brought her huge personal library of SF to Toronto in 1968, where it eventually became the core collection in the Spaced Out Library. A wonderfully rambunctious personality, Merril became a catalyst for new writing in Canada, editing the first *Tesseracts* anthology of new Canadian SF (1985). She once pointed out that such basic themes as isolation and dangerous environments found in Canadian literature, as defined by Northrop Frye and Margaret Atwood, almost perfectly matched those of science fiction – hence her feelings of being at home when she moved to Canada from the USA. She was not alone: Spider Robinson, Robert Charles Wilson, and most famously, William Gibson, all came to Canada in the 1960s and early 1970s. Earlier, Donald Kingsbury came to teach mathematics at McGill University. Except for Robinson, all began to write SF after they came to Canada, and I would argue that the mores of their adopted country can be felt in their fiction.

Spider Robinson, of course, is well known for the ongoing series of fun tales set in *Callahan's Crosstime Saloon* (1977), of which there are many volumes now. He won one of his many Hugo Awards for *Stardance* (1979), written with his dancer wife Jeanne, the first volume of a trilogy about humanity moving into outer space. His work, he is happy to admit, is in the tradition of Robert Heinlein's SF, and he remains one of the most popular authors in the field.

The older Donald Kingsbury is a fascinating figure. Born in 1929, he came to Canada in 1948 to teach at McGill. Although he published his first story in 1952 in *Astounding*, he wrote relatively little till near his retirement in 1986. *Courtship Rite*

(1982) is an exuberant, and socially provocative, planetary epic, full of anthropological speculations and finely wrought characterizations. Full of well-conceived background detail, it also explores kinship, marriage, and ecological necessity as a ground for culture as part and parcel of its adventure plot. *The Moon Goddess and the Son* (1986) is set in the near-future, and is full of hard-SF speculations about the construction of space stations designed to dock space-faring freighters. His latest novel takes a somewhat different turn: *Psychohistorical Crisis* (2001) takes on concept of psychohistory, as promulgated in Isaac Asimov's *Foundation Trilogy*, and opens it up to interrogation. A complexly structured narrative, set some two millennia after the end of Asimov's epic, *Psychohistorical Crisis* tells of one young genius whose mathematics eventually undermines some of "the Founder's" ideas, and of the hidden revolutionary group which has constructed a slightly contrary psychohistory to fight against what they see as a tyranny of the elect. It is both intellectually stimulating and a grand epic dependent upon a vast historical context. Although not prolific, Kingsbury has produced a handful of major SF novels.

Although born in the USA, Robert Charles Wilson has lived in Canada since he was nine, and began publishing his well-received novels in the early 1980s. His work is often understated, his protagonists ordinary people, his plots inventive variations on various SF conventions. Gateways to other worlds, parallel universes, time travel, the disastrous overlap of one time or world with our own, a series of huge monoliths from the future that insist a now unknown leader will conquer the world: these are the contexts in which his characters must struggle to live and grow. Wilson has published a novel every two years or so for over two decades now, and they are almost all of high quality, especially in terms of characterization. *Mysterium* (1994), in which a whole town is suddenly transported to an alternate, theocratic, Earth, won the Philip K. Dick Award. *Darwinia* (1998) offers a science fictional explanation for the kinds of horrors usually found in H.P. Lovecraft's dark fantasies. That in itself is quite an achievement, but *Darwinia* is also a complex human story of an alternate twentieth century on an Earth that may only be a form of corrupted information in a Galactic Archive. And in *Chronoliths* (2001), the narrator must come to terms with his personal demons even as the world seems to be descending into a terrible war it cannot prevent. Wilson's ability to keep his readers' empathy for ordinary people caught in epic struggles they often cannot comprehend marks his SF as deeply humanistic.

Of course, the most famous immigrant is William Gibson, who, despite his still noticeable South Carolina accent, is as Canadian as "American" in his artistic vision. He came to Toronto at the age of 20 in 1968, married, eventually moved to Vancouver, took a B.A. in English at the University of British Columbia, and got involved in the fannish community there. Thus, widely varied cultural contexts fed into his own SF, and it is that mixed inheritance of both high and pop culture that eventually allowed him to forge a style seldom found in the genre. "Fragments of a Hologram Rose" appeared in 1977; other stories slowly followed. But it was his first novel, *Neuromancer* (1984), that established him as one of SF's new stars. It, and the whole Sprawl trilogy, are possibly the most analyzed books in the field, and the commentaries continue to pile up. Although Gibson did not invent either the term or the concept of "Cyberpunk," there's no doubt that *Neuromancer* is the central work of the subgenre; as one scholarly wag put it, for many critics "Cyberpunk = Gibson = *Neuromancer*."

Neuromancer exploded onto the scene in 1984, winning all three of SF's major awards, the Hugo, the Nebula, and the Philip K. Dick. Its influence was and remains tremendous. *Neuromancer* is so well known that little needs to be said about it here. What sets it apart is its language, the concepts imaged so thoroughly and in metaphoric depth, and, possibly, the way in which it does not quite follow through on the conventions it utilizes. As it, and his later novels demonstrate, Gibson is "the genre's premier *bricoleur*" (Bukatman 1993: 171). A master of borrowing and mixing, he owes as much to the texts he studied in university as he does to the various popular arts he came in contact with on the street. Certainly, his writing displays signs and portents of his reading in both the great moderns and contemporary Canadian literature (as the sly references that only someone who knows Canadian literature can pick up show). It is Gibson's powerful imagery, in collaboration with the many intertexts, that fuels his glittery, nervous, always cutting style, and it is that style that identified him immediately as a major emerging talent. His "controlled use of collage" (McCaffery 1991: 281) accounts for the thick sense of palimpsest in all his fictions, right up to the present day. Gibson's early work took certain extreme images of far futuristic body adaptation and prosthetic engineering and dropped them into a world changed only slightly from our own, where multinationals oversee "a deranged experiment in social Darwinism," a vision perhaps even more relevant in the 2000s than it was in 1984.

One of the many ironies attached to *Neuromancer* and the other novels of the trilogy is the way so many scientists took its apparent distaste for "the meat" nonironically, and set out to construct the "cyberspace" Gibson so clearly represented in ambivalent terms. *Count Zero* and *Mona Lisa Overdrive* turned toward a more humanistic vision, one in which the social Darwinism of late-capitalism more and more exposed its dark underside. That vision emerges, as well, in his collaboration with Bruce Sterling, *The Difference Engine*, an alternate history offering readers a glimpse of the British Empire in an 1855 where Charles Babbage managed to build a steam-driven calculating machine in the 1820s. But, despite its wonderfully realized historical and cultural context, the novel never quite coalesces into a coherent narrative.

Gibson's "Bridge" trilogy, set closer to our own time, in the early twenty-first century, has all the stylistic verve of his earlier work, but it asks some tougher questions, explores character more deeply, and savagely interrogates our star-obsessed society. Gibson has assumed the growing importance of biotech as well as the increasing power of the media to control peoples' perception of the world. As in the Sprawl trilogy, a few powerful corporations exercise immense political power, and Gibson continues to twist thriller paradigms. Gibson's latest novel, *Pattern Recognition* (2003), although a wholly contemporary story, set in the year following the fall of the towers in New York, recognizes that the present is as weirdly science fictional as any of the futures he constructed in his earlier works. The world we live in is a maze, and, in this age of the world wide web, multinational corporate logos (and logic), and the post-September 11, 2001 never-to-end War Against What, it is a huge and constantly changing puzzle, the patterns of which most of us never fully grasp. Cayce Pollard, *Pattern Recognition*'s protagonist, has her very nerve-ends embedded in the detritus of contemporary culture, and she has at least some sense of what is going on as she makes her way through the maze. Hired to trace the maker of eerily powerful film clips on the web, Cayce eventually discovers how art can still transcend business and political power. Gibson has, once again, proven that he is a master manipulator of contemporary pop culture icons. We recognize the world through which Cayce must find her way, yet it also has a sheen of strangeness that makes it all the more glamorous and enticing. Where Gibson will turn next is anyone's guess, but he has already created a formidable SF oeuvre.

SF-oriented Work from the Canadian Mainstream

As mentioned earlier, writers in Canada, like those in Europe, have felt free to experiment in many genres, and some of our best-known novelists have written fantastical fiction, and even pure science fiction of one sort or another. Margaret Atwood has become one of Canada's most famous writers, internationally recognized as a poet and novelist. Her novels reveal her interest in the Gothic, and she has published two which have been received as SF. *The Handmaid's Tale* (1985) won both the Governor-General's Award and the first Arthur C. Clarke Award. In this near-futuristic dystopia, in which ecological disasters have rendered most women sterile, an oddly askew fundamentalist military has taken over part of the USA and captured fertile women to act as "handmaids" bearing children to their masters. A highly popular work, it was made into a film that simplified the original. An opera, music by Poul Ruders, libretto by Paul Bentley, has been performed in Europe and England in 2002 and 2003. Despite some flaws in terms of its science fictional extrapolations, *The Handmaid's Tale* has all the usual Atwood attributes, including sharp ironies, a masterful use of tone, and an awful playfulness in its construction. Her second SF novel, another ecological and biotech disaster, narrated by the last unaltered human, *Oryx and Crake* (2003) was nominated for the Booker Prize, the Giller Prize, and the Governor-General's Award. Both a biological thriller and the story of a three-way love, *Oryx and Crake* is a deliberately frightening "what if?" tale of human-made destruction, based on contemporary trends in biotechnology, and, as usual with Atwood, it bites. Interestingly, Canada's foremost pro-science SF author, Robert J. Sawyer, attacked Atwood for being both un- and anti-scientific in a negative review in Canada's National magazine, *Maclean's*. Other SF reviewers have suggested its speculations seem dated, as if she had no idea of the directions taken in the genre in the past decade or so.

Timothy Findley, whose work has always been based on moral outrage, especially against the forces usually called fascist, has written both fantasy, *Not Wanted on the*

Voyage (1984) and *Pilgrim* (1999), and SF of a kind, *Headhunter* (1993). *Not Wanted on the Voyage*, a feminist revisioning of the Noah story, is pure fantasy, as is *Pilgrim*, the titular figure of which seems to have lived through major moments of European history since at least the time of the Pharaohs. Findley's great fictional coup is to make Pilgrim's memoirs the basis of Carl Jung's theory of archetypes and a common unconscious. On one level, *Headhunter* is a fantasy too, as it contains a figure who can bring fictional characters into the world, and who one day in the near future lets Kurtz escape from page 92 of *Heart of Darkness*. But it is SF in that the near future in which Kurtz becomes the dangerous head of psychiatry at a Toronto hospital is already falling victim to a new plague, clearly, as in *Oryx and Crake*, the result of biotechnological experimentation. In all of these novels, Findley is more interested in the human interactions, the opportunities for people to act out of love or to fail to do so, than he is in scientific or historical speculation. They are fascinating stories, and part of that fascination depends upon the alternate worlds in which the characters make their human way.

Perhaps because of the popularity of "magic realism" worldwide, Canadian versions of this genre began to appear in the 1970s and 1980s. It could be said that this began with Leonard Cohen's *Beautiful Losers* (1966), which at least took its phantasmical literary alchemical metamorphoses into its future. Gwendolyn MacEwen's *Julian the Magician* (1963) shares Cohen's poetic vision, while her *King of Egypt, King of Dreams* (1971) provides a mystical reconstruction of Akhenaton's rule. Such well-known authors as George Bowering, in *Burning Water* (1980) and *Caprice* (1987), Robert Kroetsch, especially in *What the Crow Said* (1978), Leon Rooke, Audrey Thomas, Hiromi Goto, Margaret Sweatman, Thomas King, Larissa Lai, Thomas Wharton, and others have ventured beyond the limits of realism without really entering the fields of traditional fantasy or conventional science fiction. Still, one might argue that public receptiveness for such fictional playfulness made it easier for younger writers to enter into SF itself while still feeling they were a part of the Canadian literary scene.

The Good New Stuff: Canadian SF since 1985

Nevertheless, if one wanted to write SF as such, it was necessary to turn south and publish in the USA. Wayland Drew's ecological postdisaster trilogy, *The Memoirs of Alcheringa* (1984), *The Gaian Expedient* (1985), and *The Master of Norriya* (1986), presents a tale of a secret group striving to preserve something of the natural environment from planetary destruction. The final novel's quiet despair, a refusal of individual heroism saving the day, perhaps marks the trilogy as Canadian, or at least un-American. The other direction a writer might take was toward Britain, and that is what short story writer H.A. Hargreaves did, publishing almost all his short fiction in the *New Writings in SF* anthologies. They were eventually collected in *North by 2000* (1975).

In some ways, Drew was a precursor to the growing number of Canadian SF writers who began to publish in the 1980s and 1990s. First and foremost among these, at least in terms of international popularity, is Robert J. Sawyer, whose novels have over the years won almost every SF award going. He comes across as a 1990s version of Isaac Asimov, with his wide reading in and knowledge of contemporary science, and the ability to make it clear to the average reader. Like Asimov, he has terrific ideas and the ability to develop interesting stories around them, making the processes of scientific investigation the central narrative facts of his novels. *Golden Fleece* (1990) marked him as a "hard-SF" author to be watched. The "Quintaglio Ascension" trilogy about a world of reptilian "humans" entering an age of scientific discovery, *Far-Seer* (1992), *Fossil Hunter* (1993), *Foreigner* (1994) established his reputation in the SF world. But when *The Terminal Experiment* (1995) won the Nebula Award, he achieved an international success that has continued to the present. *Starplex* (1996), *Frameshift* (1997), and *Illegal Alien* (1997) followed quickly, then *Factoring Humanity* (1998), *Flashforward* (1999), *Calculating God* (2000), and *End of an Era* (2001). The titles alone suggest the range of Sawyer's speculative interests. With *Hominids* (2002), Sawyer started another trilogy, continued with *Humans* (2003), winner of the Hugo Award, and *Hybrids* (2003); in it scientists from an alternate earth in which Neanderthals superseded homo sapiens cross over to our world. The series as a whole allows Sawyer to explore questions of evolution and humanity's relationship to the environment. Sawyer has succeeded by presenting science, the processes of scientific investigation, as the central narrative facts of his novels.

Other writers who have gained a reputation in SF through publication with major US or British publishers include Michael Barley, Julie E. Czerneda, Candas Jane Dorsey, Dave Duncan, Leslie Gadallah, James Alan Gardner, Terence M. Green, Monica Hughes, Scott McKay, Karl Schroeder, Alison Sinclair, Peter Watts, and Andrew Weiner; there are many more, but even a survey like this cannot cover them all. Duncan has written mostly fantasy, and highly successfully too, but *Strings* (1989) and *West of January* (1989) work his particular magic in a science fictional context. Andrew Weiner's short stories, some very witty indeed, were collected in *Distant Signals* (1990). McKay's two novels, *Outpost* (1999) and *The Meek* (2001), are solid and thoughtful hard-SF adventures, the first with a new twist to time-travel, the second with an interesting take on genetic adaptation to Mars and the moons of the outer planets. Czerneda is the author of two popular series, "Web Shifters" and "The Trade Pact Universe," and the intriguing *In the Company of Others* (2001), an odd first contact novel with fine characterizations. Gardner began his career with *Expendable* (1997), and quickly followed that up with *Commitment Hour* (1998), *Vigilant* (1999), *Hunted* (2000), and *Ascendant* (2001), all entertaining adventures set in the same future history of the Technocracy. Michael Barley's *Jackal Bird* (1995) offers a dangerous colony planet where generations clash. Leslie Gadhallah writes solid SF adventure.

Terence M. Green has written a range of SF, from the hard edged future police procedural of *Barking Dogs* (1988) and *Blue Limbo* (1997), through the temporal and ecological speculations of *Children of the Rainbow* (1992), to the quietly intense time travel explorations of family and personal history in *Shadow of Ashland* (1996), *A Witness to Life* (1999), and *St. Patrick's Bed* (2001). In these latter works, which cast a fond but not sentimental gaze back over the early twentieth century, Greene achieves something unusual in SF, a quietly beautiful meditation on family, honor, and love.

Monica Hughes wrote young adult SF of the highest quality for more than thirty years, published in Britain and the USA. Probably her best-known and most profound work in the field is the Isis Trilogy, *The Keeper of the Isis Light* (1980), *The Guardian of Isis* (1982), and *The Isis Pedlar* (1982), a brilliant exploration of personal and community isolation on a environmentally dangerous planet. In all her novels, Hughes mixes intriguing SF speculation with the kinds of moral challenges that attract young readers.

Karl Schroeder and Alison Sinclair have taken up the far future, intellectual, space opera in their works, and their novels are both exciting and challenging. A biochemist, working in the field of structural molecular biology, Sinclair has explored, in *Legacies* (1995), *Blueheart* (1996), and *Cavalcade* (1998), questions of human engineering, alien/human interaction, ecological interventions, and the ethical complexities these involve. Highly complex mysteries and ethnographic studies of adaptive humanity, her novels are also moral interrogations of science and technology's sometimes overweening aspirations. Sinclair builds intricate alien worlds, and peoples them with characters whose complexity depends upon thoughtfully constructed cultures grounded in their environments.

In his two major novels so far, *Ventus* (2000) and *Permanence* (2002), physicist Karl Schroeder demonstrates a similar ability to think up new worlds and new methods of communication and interstellar travel. Set in a far future, galaxy spanning civilization, when science is so powerful it seems like magic, *Ventus* manages to offer a planet still under construction by a nanotechnology gone awry, so that its human inhabitants are forced to live in near-medieval circumstances, a galaxy-wide war with AIs. The lively coming-of-age story *Permanence* is equally inventive, with its sublight speed stellar civilization, the Cycler Compact, slowly crumbling now that FTL (faster than light) flight has been attained, its new Rights Economy worlds where late capitalism run amok is the rule, its alien artifacts, and another tale of someone coming into her own sense of entitlement in a challenging environment. With these two novels alone, Schroeder has become a major new hard-SF writer.

Peter Watts is a marine biologist, and it shows in his best known and most compellingly pessimistic vision of the near-future, the paired novels *Starfish* (1999) and *Maelstrom* (2001). What grew into *Starfish* began as his first published story, "A Niche," which appeared in *Tesseracts 3*. A savage, bitter, and often blackly comic vision of the near future and the bureaucrats who will run it, both original story and novel tell of the remarkable, wounded human beings who "volunteer" for surgical alteration in order to service power stations at the bottom of the ocean. Of course, SNAFUs occur, and *Starfish* moves inexorably toward its cataclysmic conclusion. The world does not quite end, however, and *Maelstrom* explores the possible biological disaster that the protagonist of *Starfish* brings to the upper world in her quest for revenge and under-standing. Watts writes with savage wit, a scientifically grounded rage at what human-ity is doing to what is still its only environment, and a prophet's desire to make us see and change. *Starfish* and *Maelstrom* are major additions to the great dystopian visions of our near future.

Candas Jane Dorsey first made her name through a group of feminist interventions into Cyberpunk, especially the title story of her first collection, *Machine Sex and Other Stories* (1988). Although she took on Cyberpunk tropes, she also created a lovely quiet, if self-reflective, pastoral futuristic tale that seemed archetypically Canadian in tone. Her first novel, the award-winning *Black Wine* (1997), is a multigenerational fantasy with SF overtones in its invented world's various technologies, that shows her com-mitment to the kind of sociocultural speculation associated with writers like Samuel R. Delany. Her next novel, *A Paradigm of Earth* (2001), is one of the most intriguing first-encounter novels in years. Set in her home province of Alberta, only slightly altered for the worse in a truculently far right near-future, it explores questions of community, communication, and love. In this variant on the theme, the aliens have come to Earth, but they seek no political contact with its governments. Instead, they have provided them with a number of blue humanoids, whose intellects are those of a newborn baby, and informed them that these figures are there to be taught to be human and then report back to their clearly technologically superior masters.

The Canadian government sets up its alien facility in Edmonton, and that is where a wounded soul, Morgan, meets the alien who then chooses her as its facilitator. Morgan has just inherited a huge house where she has welcomed some of the social misfits of her so-called civilization. As she, the alien, and they slowly learn to get along, the government representative turns out to be more sympathetic than might be expected, a possibly Canadian take on this kind of fiction. *A Paradigm of Earth* con-firms Dorsey as a master of character and emotional complexity, someone whose every book will ask tough questions in a deeply humanistic manner.

Another critically successful writer is Sean Stewart, whose first novel, *Passion Play* (1992), was published in Canada and won awards as both best first SF novel and best first mystery. His excellence being immediately recognized, he soon had a US pub-lisher and a highly successful series of novels, including two intriguing fantasies and the magic-realist feminist fiction, *Mockingbird* (1998). *Resurrection Man* (1995), *The Night Watch* (1997), and *Galveston* (2000), the latter the winner of the first Sunburst Award (a juried award named in honor of Phyllis Gotlieb's first novel) and cowinner of the World Fantasy Award, make up an alternate universe trilogy covering about 100 years. When magic returns to the world after the Second World War, and then interacts with and contests science and technology in a fragmented polity, groups of people in various places, now cut off from the rest of the world, find ways to live with the strange changes that alter both human and inhuman life. Stewart's characters are complex and moving, striving to survive in the midst of contradiction.

Nalo Hopkinson's award-winning first novel, *Brown Girl in the Ring* (1998), with its wonderful use of Caribbean-Canadian English, brings a different touch of postcolonialism to Canadian speculative fiction. It too explores the negative possibilities of late capitalism run amuck in a future Ontario turned far right, while also speculating on what might happen, in such circumstances, to the most "multicultural" city in the country, Toronto, now a walled off ghetto. Mixing futuristic speculation with voodoo mythography, it achieves a complex refusal of racial determinism, as does the far-future science-fantasy, *Midnight Robber* (2000), with its feminine hero, its powerfully evoked posthuman Caribbean culture, and its other world of "new" slavery. She further explores many similar questions in her collection of short stories, *Skin Folk* (2001), which won the 2003 Sunburst Award.

A Note on Québec Fiction

Although this essay is mostly concerned with English-language SF, a number of highly regarded writers from Québec have added their own twist to the genre. Influenced by various forms of European theory, especially feminism, and other forms of nonrealist fiction, many of these writers have gained reputations in Europe as well as Québec, and, as their works have been translated, in the English-speaking world, as well. One of the most important and influential Québec novels is Louky Bersianik's *L'Euquélionne* (1976), translated as *The Euquelion* (1996), a rich mixture of feminist theory, allegory, parody, and speculation. Its winding narrative concerns a "sister from another planet" who comes to Earth in search of "a male of her species." What she discovers, instead, is the bizarre state of gender relations here, and so she leads, through various comic forms of deconstruction, a rebellion against patriarchal language, law, literature, indeed the whole Western philosophical tradition. Elisabeth Vonarburg is a much purer SF writer, whose stories and novels have garnered many awards in France and Canada. Those translated into English include *The Silent City* (1988), *In the Mother's Land* (1992), *Reluctant Voyagers* (1994), *Dreams of the Sea* (1996), *Slow Engines of Time and Other Stories* (1999). Her work is noted for its feminist themes and fine characterization.

Joël Champetier was fiction editor of the Québec magazine, *Solaris*, where many of Québec SF authors first published. His stories, like those of many other Québecoise authors, have been translated for the *Tesseracts* series, but most of his novels are only available in French. A singular exception is *The Dragon's Eye* (1999), a fast-paced spy thriller set on New China, the fifth inhabitable planet in a double star system. What sets it apart is Champetier's marvelously complete rendering of this new world. Like other Québec SF, Champetier's work suggests the field is alive, well, and wonderfully adventurous in that province.

Award-winning poet, Heather Spears has written a fascinating trilogy, *Moonfall* (1991), *The Children of Atwar* (1993), and *The Taming* (1996), set in a far future where humans are Twins, two heads and personalities sharing one body, and have constructed a complex culture based on this change. The trilogy is both a subtle study of an alternate psychology and a powerful evocation of a new mythology, something new to science fiction yet clearly of it.

Canadian Fantasy

Although this is essentially an introduction to Canadian science fiction, it seems necessary to at least mention the number of Canadian fantasy writers too. Not least because some of the finest among them are engaged in world-building that certainly challenges that of the best SF writers. Such writers seek to test and transcend genre boundaries, and perhaps the most important of these is Guy Gavriel Kay, whose trilogy *The Fionavar Tapestry* – *The Summer Tree* (1984), *The Wandering Fire* (1986), *The Darkest Road* (1986) – sets new standards for post-Tolkien high fantasy. His later works, *Tigana* (1990), *A Song for Arbonne* (1992), *The Lions of Al-Rassan* (1995), and the two volumes of *The Sarantine Mosaic* – *Sailing to Sarantium* (1998) and *Lord of Emperors* (2000) offer political, psychological, and aesthetic insights often missing in the genre. More recently, Steven Erikson has begun a massive ongoing epic, *The Malazan Book of the Fallen* – *Gardens of the Moon* (1999), *Deadhouse Gates* (2000), *Memories of Ice* (2001), and *House of Chains* (2002) – in which a ravaged empire at war is the setting for a study of politics, history, and tragic racial interaction. Writers like these are doing something new in fantasy, and applying anthropological and ethnographic insights to their invented cultures. Charles De Lint, one of the inventors of modern urban fantasy, has written one SF novel *Svaha* (1989), in which Native American technology has superseded that of the invader/settler culture. Many of his fantasies play technology off against various forms of magical thinking, often aboriginal. Some of Sean Russell's historical fantasies also deal with the clash between magic and science. And a new young writer, R. Scott Bakker, has, with *The Darkness that Comes Before* (2003), begun a trilogy in which philosophy is treated with scientific exactness, and war perceived through an anthropological lens.

An Inconclusive Conclusion

Perhaps a fitting way to conclude this survey is by recalling that John Clute, although he lives in England, is a Canadian. One of the foremost critics of SF, and the coeditor of *The Encyclopedia of Science Fiction* (1993) and *The Encyclopedia of Fantasy* (1997), he has recently brought his vast knowledge and theoretical understanding of the field to bear on the construction of one of the most encyclopedic and theoretical fictions the genre has ever seen: *Appleseed* (2001). A bravura performance, a complex comic reimagining of space opera through the lens of post-Cyberpunk far future SF, *Appleseed* is, as Damien Broderick has suggested "a puzzle palace, a memory palace, a cryptic crossword, a map of the world carved up into small, absurd pieces and scattered so that its gestalt recovery in the mind's eye urges theophany, or its simulation" (2002: 13). It manages to utilize all the languages of science fiction to renew the codes of the genre, and to play the fantasy game of Story in a fully SF context. It is both literary and paraliterary, and, like many of the literary works now being written at the margins of empire, it may be a perfect example of how they are unsettling the canon and setting new terms for the future of the art.

References and Further Reading

Broderick, Damien (2002) "*Appleseed* by John Clute." *The New York Review of Science Fiction* 15:4 (December): 12–14.

Bukatman, Scott (1993) *Terminal Identity: the Virtual Subject in Post-Modern Science Fiction.* Durham, NC and London: Duke University Press.

Clute, John, and John Grant (eds) (1997) *The Encyclopedia of Fantasy.* London: Orbit.

Clute, John, and Peter Nicholls (eds) (1993) *The Encyclopedia of Science Fiction.* New York: St. Martin's Griffin.

Hartwell, David, and Glenn Grant (eds) (1994) *Northern Stars: the Anthology of Canadian Science Fiction.* New York: Tor Books.

——(1999) *Northern Suns: the New Anthology of Canadian Science Fiction.* New York: Tor Books.

Ketterer, David (1992) *Canadian Science Fiction and Fantasy.* Bloomington and Indianapolis: Indiana University Press.

Lynn, Elizabeth (1978) "Introduction," in *Sunburst*, Gotlieb, Phyllis. Boston: Gregg Press, v–xv.

McCaffery, Larry (1991) "An Interview with William Gibson," in *Storming the Reality Studio: a Casebook of Cyberpunk and Postmodern Fiction*, (ed.) McCaffery, Larry. Durham, NC and London: Duke University Press, 263–85.

Van Belkom, Edo (ed.) (1998) *Northern Dreamers: Interviews with Famous Science Fiction, Fantasy, and Horror Writers.* Kingston, ON: Quarry Press.

——(1999) *Aurora Awards: An Anthology of Prize-winning Science Fiction and Fantasy.* Kingston, ON: Quarry Press.

21

Japanese and Asian Science Fiction

Takayuki Tatsumi

Warming Up with the Science Fictional "Asia"

What is "Asian" science fiction? Given that science fiction is a byproduct of Western modernization, is it possible for us to clearly sketch the originality and legitimacy of "Asian" science fiction? Are we Asians in an ideal position to objectify something Asian within Asia itself? To speculate upon Asian science fiction now is to construct the self-reflexive strategy for narrating "Asia" as well as "science fiction." Therefore, I begin by meditating upon the science fictional "Asia" in the post-*Blade Runner* age, instead of historicizing Asian science fiction itself.

For example, the year 2002 saw the publication of two works of alternate history especially intriguing for those interested in Asian science fiction: Kim Stanley Robinson's *Years of Rice and Salt* and Gavin Menzies' *1421: The Year China Discovered America*. It is noteworthy that both drew on Louis Levathes' *When China Ruled the Sea* (1994) and both explore the way China achieves world hegemony and comes to discover the New World. Robinson covers the seven centuries of alternate world history, in which Europe is wiped out by plague in fourteenth century and China surpasses Islamic and Buddhist nations in its process of modernization, going on to discover what we now call America. Levathes documents the way the enormous Chinese "treasure" ships, under the command of emperor Zhu Di's loyal eunuch admirals, especially his close friend Zheng He, not only discovered American continent in 1421 but also left their traces all over the world. It is the post-9/11 cultural milieu that helped both works to carry a powerful impact. Most striking is the epigraph that Robinson culled from Chinese classic science fiction *Journey to the West*:

TRIPITAKA: Monkey, how far is it to the Western heaven, the abode of Buddha?
WU-KONG: You can walk from the time of your youth till the time you grow old,
and after that, till you become young again; and even after going through such a cycle
a thousand times, you may still find it difficult to reach the place where you want to

go. But when you perceive, by the resoluteness of your will, the Buddha-nature in all things, and when every one of you thoughts goes back to that fountain in your memory, that will be the time you arrive at Spirit Mountain. (in Robinson 2002: epigraph)

It is very easy to consider this epigraph as a symptom of Orientalism peculiar to a kind of West Coast Anglo-American writers who came of age in the late 1960s, the heyday of the counterculture. Historically speaking, however, while Japan has somehow failed in the projects of space aeronautics and only boasts of anime arts and technology (some of recent Japanese cinema works like Oshii Mamoru's *Avalon* [2000] could not have been produced without what Mark Driscoll designates "anime eye"[1999]) satisfying the imperatives of postmodern Orientalism, China, as if transgressing the limit of such naïve exoticist discourses, so rapidly modernized itself that 2003 saw the success of the first Chinese-manned space mission. Previously unknown, astronaut Yang Liwei became an instant celebrity on October 15, 2003 as the first human to be sent into space under the Chinese space program. Liwei was launched from the Jiuquan desert launch site and orbited the Earth only 14 times in 21 hours, touching down his Shenzhou five spacecraft on the grasslands of Inner Mongolia as a crisp dawn broke, that is, at 6:3 am. Since only the USA and Russia have ever been capable of sending humans into space before this year, this news excited the whole Earth. On the very day, China revealed more details of their space program: to have additional human launches, a space station, probes to the Moon, and eventually humans on the Moon. Thus, in alluding to *Journey to the West*, Robinson must have been conscious of the rapid progress of Chinese modernization.

In retrospect, we could also recall a Japanese SF writer Eisuke Ishikawa's masterpiece *SF Saiyuki* (*Journey to the West: SF Version*) published in the period of Japan's high growth (1970), as well as a famous Native American writer Gerald Vizenor's *Fugitive Poses: Native American Scenes of Absence and Presence* (1998), which has so deeply imbibed the spirit of *Journey to the West* as to construct its own "post-Indian" narratology. Vizenor's global imagination made possible the analogy between Wu Kong and the native trickster Naanabozho. Given the post-9/11 discourse requiring us to radically question the Anglo-American frame of reference, Robinson, very plausibly following the example of Vizenor, pays homage to *Journey to the West* to make his alternative history highly realistic. Developing the Eastern idea of temporality as spelled out by Wu Kong in the epigraph, Robinson gives priority to the cyclical and mythic structure of time over the linear and historical one, and revives key figures with such initials as "K" and "B" very regularly. In a particularly revealing scene, Fromwest, a.k.a. Busho, a descendent of Japanese Samurai, negotiates with sachems of the league of what we now call Native American tribes; he aims to seek military help from the Hodenosaunee in defeating the Chinese, who have invaded Japan in this alternate history. Here Robinson skillfully foregrounds at once the similarity and the difference between Asian peoples.

This latest Anglo-American view of the yellow races will paradoxically help reconstruct the idea and history of Japanese and Asian science fiction. It is widely accepted that science fiction came into being and developed as a literary subgenre as the imperative of modernization accelerated the progress of capitalism. When Fredric Jameson reformulated the periods of literary history in relation to the phases of capitalism (realism coinciding with market capitalism, modernism with monopoly [imperial] capitalism, and postmodernism with multinational [postindustrial] capitalism), he must have had in mind the evolution of science fiction. As is clear from Jameson's argument, this famous periodization was inspired by Ernest Mandel's *Late Capitalism* (1978), which had spelled out three such fundamental breaks or quantum leaps in the evolution of machinery under capital (Jameson 1991: 35–6). To put it simply, since science fiction could not have been possible without the decadent flowering of capitalism, the same is true for Japanese and Asian science fiction. While Anglo-American writers undertake to create a totally different picture of the world from their Orientalist perspective, Japanese and Asian science fiction learns much from western modernization and recreates the tradition of science fiction from their Occidentalist viewpoint.

The Making of Japanese Science Fiction

It is evident that science fiction has insistently served as an indicator of modernization. If you want to know the extent to which a nation is modernized, you have only to read its native science fiction. At this point, Donald Hassler's view of the reciprocity between SF and nationalism sounds very helpful. Re-examining the pulp genre in the 1930s and 1940s, he redefines it as "escapist, idealist, nearly fascist in its yearning for a fresh, universalized, purer narrative of heroes (if not heroines) and of Utopian possibilities for the future" (1999: 213). For Hassler, the fiction from Edgar Rice Burroughs through the early pulp writers "sought images of escape and were a response to the materiality and complexity posited by scientism and positivism. . . . Many of us are able now – I would argue even that we are obliged now – to look back on a cultural adolescence and a personal adolescence in which universalized hopes for a more 'escapist' adulthood haunted our dreams" (Hassler 1999: 213–14).

Hassler's argument works well for Western science fiction. However, Japanese science fiction not only digested the best fruits of Anglo-American science fiction, but also radically reorganized them. While Western science fiction has long projected a linear development for modernization and paradoxically linked escapism and fascism, Japanese science fiction, deeply afflicted with the side-effects of fascism, had to start by giving up the sense of linearity in the wake of the Second World War, ending up with a sensibility of "creative masochism," through which the traumas of military defeat and Hiroshima, is transformed into a postwar cultural energy. This transformation could be illustrated through a variety of world-famous Japanese science fiction heroes such as Godzilla, Astro Boy (Tetsuwan Atomu), and Nausicaa, who could not have come into being without the complete defeat of Japanese imperialism and the construction of postwar democracy. In relation to this postwar sensibility, Sakyo

Komatsu, one of the founding fathers of postwar Japanese science fiction, responded to the interviewers from *Science-Fiction Studies* in 2002 as follows:

> My generation witnessed America develop the atomic bomb and saw it build missiles using Germany's V1 and V2 rocket technology. We were raised in an atmosphere where any day the world might be destroyed. And in Japan, we had actually experienced the Bomb. So when I wrote, even though I was writing in Japan, I wanted to write about something more – civilization. And it was just at that point that American SF entered Japan. The title of my first story, "Pacem in Terris" came from something that happened two years before the *SF Magazine* contest. In 1958, Angelo Roncalli of Bergamo ascended to the papacy and became Pope John XXIII. His first encyclical was "Pacem in Terris" – "Peace on Earth," and I used that as my title. It depicted a fictional world in which the war did not end in August 1945, but continued. (Komatsu 2002: 334–5).

By the twenty-first century, it is impossible to conceive of Japanese science fiction without recalling a variety of works produced out of the visual media, works ranging from *Godzilla*, *Astro Boy*, and *Nausicaa*, to *Japan Sinks*, *Yamato*, *Akira*, *Ghost in the Shell*, *Neon Genesis Evangelion*, *Ramma 1/2*, *Patlabor*, *Princess Mononoke*, and *Final Fantasy*, as is discussed in detail by specialists like Christopher Bolton, Livia Monnet, Susan Napier, and Sharalyn Orbaugh in the "Japanese SF issue" of *Science-Fiction Studies*. We should not forget that our science fiction artists could not have created these popular works without the culture and tradition of Japanese science fiction formed over several generations.

Like their Western counterparts, the precursors of Japanese science fiction were all aware of the works of Edgar Allan Poe, Jules Verne, and H.G. Wells. The first half of the Meiji Era (1867–1912), which signaled the beginning of Modern Japan, saw the publication of translations of Western canonical works such as Verne's *Le Tour Du Monde En Quatre-vingts Jours* (*Around the World In 80 Days*, 1873), which was translated into Japanese by Tadanosuke Kawashima between 1878 and 1880. Responding to the spirit of the times, Japanese pre-science fictional writers started predicting the future in the form of political fictions, coinciding with Edward Bellamy's extrapolative novel *Looking Backward, 2000–1887* (1888). One of these novels, *Secchubai* by Suehiro Teccho (1882), carries a preface by Yukio Ozaki, who wanted to promote the concept of "Kagaku Shosetu," that is, "science fiction," if translated very literally. Ozaki's concept anticipates by decades Hugo Gernsback's coinage of "science fiction" in 1926.

The mid-Meiji era saw the first science fictional controversy, which also served as the first literary controversy in modern Japan. The journalist Ryukei Yano ignited this controversy by publishing a Utopian SF novel called *Ukishiro Monogatari* (*A Tale of the Ship "Ukishiro!"* [Floating Castle]) in 1890. The plot is very dramatic, but highly problematic from today's postcolonialist viewpoint. For Yano describes how an orphan called Seitaro Kamii from the Ohita Prefecture in Kyushu happens to join the project of a couple of colonialists, Yoshifumi Sakura and Katsutake Tachibana, who plan to occupy Madagascar and central Africa to establish an independent nation there. This "Utopian" novel gained huge audiences, taking the place of Verne's adventure stories, which had lost popularity by the late 1880s. Ogai Mori, the representative of Meiji literature, praised *Ukishiro Monogatari* enthusiastically, while other serious writers like Roan Uchia attacked the story scathingly, pointing out the limit of Yano's characterization. This controversy did not have solely negative results, though. Learning much from it, Shunro Oshikawa, sometimes nicknamed the "grandfather of Japanese science fiction," published the masterpiece *Kaitei Gunkan* (*Undersea Warship*, filmed as *Atragon/Kaitei Gunkan* [1963]) in 1900, a future-war novel about a conflict between Japan and Russia, far preceding the actual Russo-Japanese War (1904–5). Creating his own science fiction, Oshikawa continued his critique of imperialism thereafter in his subsequent works.

The heyday of H.G. Wells coincides with the rise of Meiji literature, the first wave of Japanese "modern," if not modernistic, writings. Therefore, even the writers of mainstream fiction naturally responded to modernization and unwittingly incorporated science fictional ideas into their works. For instance, it is very difficult to reconsider the narrator of Soseki Natsume's masterpiece *Wagahai wa Neko de Aru* (*I am a Cat*, 1906), who is a cat endowed with linguistic and literary competence, without recalling the biotechnologically humanized animals as described in Wells' novel *The Island of Dr. Moreau* (1896). The Taisho era (1912–26) saw a number of writers of adventure and fantasy, among which Fuboku Kosakai was most remarkable for his engagement with the ambiguities of scientific progress. It is noteworthy that his short story "Jinko Shinzo" (The Artificial Heart), the first hardcore science fiction in Japan, was published in the first issue of the magazine *Taishu Bungei* (*Popular Literature*) in 1926, the very year Hugo Gernsback launched the first science fiction magazine in the world, *Amazing Stories*.

The works of these precursors established a basis for the Showa era (1926–88), which saw the generic formation of Japanese science fiction. Early Showa, especially from the late 1920s through the 1930s, saw the emergence of Juza Unno, the father of Japanese science fiction, who not only published masterpieces like *Chikyu Tonan* (*The Stolen Earth*, 1936) and *Yojigen Hyoryu* (*Marooned in the 4-D World*, 1946), but also was committed to popularization of this new literary subgenre. In 1933, Rampo Edogawa, a formative figure in Japanese detective fiction who started his career by imitating and recreating Edgar Allan Poe (his pseudonym Edogawa Rampo itself is a pun on Poe's name), called Unno's works "Kuso-Kagaku Shousetsu" (Fantastic Science Fiction). Nonetheless, as Yasuo Nagayama spells out, it is also true that in prewar Japan science fiction was not fully comprehended, but just considered as a variant of detective fiction. The writers well known for science fiction mystery include Shiro Kunieda, Mushitaro Oguri, Kyusaku Yumeno, Keisuke Watanabe, and Udaji Kinoshita.

The market for Japanese science fiction was developed in the postwar period. Publishers such as Muromachi Shobo, Sekisen-sha, Gengen-sha all launched their respective science fiction series, mainly translating leading Anglo-American works in that genre. Hence the publication of the first science fiction magazine called *Seiun* (meaning "nebula") from Mori-no-Michi-sha Publishers in 1954. Although this magazine soon collapsed, it is remembered through the annual "Seiun" award named after this magazine, an award that has served as the Japanese equivalent of the Hugo since its establishment in 1970.

Science fiction as an organized movement in Japan could well be traced back to the publication of the first successful fanzine, *Uchujin* (*Cosmic Dust*, 1957–), and the first successful commercial magazine, *Hayakawa's SF Magazine* (1960–). *Uchujin* was founded by the writer-translator Takumi Shibano, and proved to be the maturing ground for most of the current major science fiction writers, while *SF Magazine* was founded by the editor-writer Masami Fukushima of Hayakawa publishers in order to promote native Japanese science fiction as well as translations. At an early stage, then, an economic training system was set up for native writers: promising fan-writers of *Uchujin* were automatically selected for *Hayakawa's SF Magazine* as professionals. In 1980 the Science Fiction and Fantasy Writers of Japan (SFWJ), which was established by Fukushima, began presenting its Nihon SF Award (the Japanese equivalent of Nebula) for the year's best work, whether in fiction or in any other medium.

With prewar writers like Shunro Oshikawa, Kyusaku Yumeno, and Juza Unno as the distinguished precursors and with styles ranging from scientific fantasy down to sociopolitical extrapolation, the genre of Japanese science fiction in the twentieth century was established through four generations of writers:

(1) "The First Generation Writers," the formative figures of the 1960s, who were so deeply influenced by Anglo-American SF of the 1950s as to write outerspace-oriented science fiction (Kobo Abe, Osamu Tezuka, Aran Kyodomari, Tetsu Yano, Shin'ichi Hoshi, Sakyo Komatsu, Yasutaka Tsutsui, Ryu Mitsuse, Taku Mayumura, Ryo Hammura, Takashi Ishikawa, Eisuke Ishikawa, Aritsune Toyota, Kazumasa Hirai, and Yoshio Aramaki).

(2) "The Second Generation Writers" of the 1970s, who so positively assimilated the New Wave of the late 1960s and the early 1970s, that they drew on science fiction for depicting reality more precisely (Akira Hori, Koji Tanaka, Masaki Yamada, Moto Hagio, Junya Yokota, Chiaki Kawamata, Izumi Suzuki, Yuko Yamao, Takeshi Kamewada, Kaoru Kurimoto, Hiroshi Aramata, Kiyoshi Kasai, etc).

(3) "The Third Generation Writers" from the 1980s, who are mostly contemporaries of the Anglo-American post-New Wave/pre-Cyberpunk writers, and are in a position to consume the cultural milieu and generic heritage of science fiction (Baku Yumemakura, Motoko Arai, Katsuhito Morishita, Azusa Noah, Chohei Kambayashi, Koshu Tani, Mariko Ohara, Makoto Shiina, Keigo Misaki, Ryo Mizumi, Hiroyuki Namba, Koh Hiura, Saori Kumi, Hiroe Suga, etc).

(4) "The Fourth Generation Writers" (the late 1980s–the 1990s) who take for granted the postmodern modes of Cyberpunk, cyborg feminism, and "Yaoi poetics" (the Japanese equivalent of the taste for K/S [Kirk/Spock] fiction and

Slash Fiction) as well as the science fictional tradition generally; and testify to the hyper-capitalist coincidence between Japanese and Anglo-American science fiction (Norio Nakai, Waku Ohba, Jin Kusakami, Goro Masaki, Yumi Matsuo, Hiroyuki Morioka, Miyuki Miyabe, Hideaki Sena, Osamu Makino, Hosuke Nojirii, Yusaku Kitano, Aki Sato, Tetsuya Sato, Koji Suzuki, Hiroki Taniguchi, and Ryotaro Yoshikawa).

Although we cannot yet portray the whole range of a fifth generation of science fiction writers, sometimes nicknamed "JSF" writers, who made their debut around the turn of the century, Toh Ubukata should be named, whose hardboiled SF *Maru-dokku Skuranburu* (*Mardoch* [sic] *Scramble*, 2003) won the 24th Nihon SF Award, as well as Issui Ogawa, whose hard SF *Dairoku Tairiku* (The *Sixth Continent*, 2003) helped revive interest in space exploration.

The critical moment for Japanese science fiction came in the mid-1970s. Following the example of the Kobo Abe, who made a debut as a mainstream writer but whose hard science fiction *Dai-Yon Kampyoki* (1959, translated as *Inter-Ice Age 4*, 1970) has also appealed to a science fiction audience, Sakyo Komatsu speculated about the destiny of the universe and about humanity's position in it, and became the major voice in contemporary Japanese science fiction with his bestselling novel *Nippon Chimbotsu* (1973; translated as *Japan Sinks*, 1976), which sold four million copies. Since the mega-hit of *Nippon Chimbotsu* was immediately followed by the boom of SF film announced by the advent of *Star Wars* in 1977, the latter half of the 1970s saw an explosion of science fiction magazines; *Kiso-Tengai* (*Fantastic*, 1975–90), Tokuma Shoten's *SF Adventure* (1979–93), Kobunsha's *SF Hoseki* (*SF Jewels*, 1979–81), Asahi Sonorama's *Shishioh* (*Lion King*, 1985). In addition, magazines of science fiction criticism began to appear: *SF ISM* (1981–5) and *SF no Hon* (*The Book of SF*, 1982–6).

The era of "Pax Japonica" brought a deep, if exoticist, interest abroad in Japanese science fiction as well as in Japanese culture. This produced the first translations of Japanese science fiction into English. The results of this interest can be seen not only in the anthologies like John Apostolou and G. Martin Greenberg's collection *The Best Japanese Science Fiction* (1988; reprinted 1997) and Alfred Birnbaum's *Monkey Brain Sushi* (1993), but also in the special "New Japanese Fiction" issue of the *Review of Contemporary Fiction* (2002), which was compiled and edited by Takayuki Tatsumi, Larry McCaffery, and Sinda Gregory. Although the number of science fiction novels in translation remains small, the short stories in such collections brought Japanese science fiction to a wider international readership. Up until this point Japan had been an importer of SF to the point of excess; from this period onwards Japan has moved into the export business.

What should not be neglected here is that the extreme popularity in 1996 of Hideaki Anno's directed anime *Neon Genesis Evangelion* triggered the 1997 controversy over "Who Killed Science Fiction?" Indeed, this very anime would not have been possible without earlier developments in Anglo-American hard science fiction. Nevertheless, some critics and even some writers wanted to consider this anime boom as symptomatic of a decline in the print media of science fiction narratives. What is more, the 1990s saw the rise of Japanese slipstream which deconstructs the boundary between mainstream and science fiction, and whose precursors include one of the first-generation science fiction writers, Yasutaka Tsutsui. In this decade a number of contemporary mainstream writers such as Haruki Murakami, Ryu Murakami, Masahiko Shimada, Jugi Hisama, Yoriko Shono, and Rieko Matsuura all started incorporating science fictional and/or magic realistic elements into their slipstream narrative methods. Even the Nobel Prize winner Kenzaburo Oe published in the early 1990s the science fictional diptych of "Chiryo-to" ("The Healing Tower"), which was clearly inspired by Arthur C. Clarke, Stanislaw Lem, and the Sturgatsky brothers, and which deconstructed the boundary between serious fiction and popular fiction. For mainstream writers to survive in this decade it became necessary for them to employ science fictional devices and Japanese fiction was enriched as a result. During the 1990s, science fiction spread throughout the media, and permeated our reality so deeply as to become almost invisible. It is ironic that the more universal science fiction becomes in the culture, the less force its specific genre seems to carry. This issue will be examined in the final section of this chapter to show how Japanese "slipstream" literature has increased the originality and expanded the possibilities of not only Japanese but also "Asian" science fiction.

Aspects of Chinese Science Fiction

A number of Japanese fanzines, including my own, translated short stories of Chinese science fiction in the 1980s. In addition, the special "Global Science Fiction" issues (79 and 80) of *Science-Fiction Studies* (1999–2000) and the Hong Kong 2001 Conference: Technology, Identity, and Futurity, East and West, in the Emerging Global Village (held at the Chinese University of Hong Kong in January 4–6, 2001) all helped reveal the range of contemporary Chinese science fiction, whether from mainland China, Hong Kong, or Taiwan.

According to Mikael Huss, science fiction was first introduced to mainland China when the famous author Lu Xun translated Jules Verne's *From the Earth to the Moon* (*Journey to the Moon*) and *Journey to the Centre of the Earth*, either in 1902 or 1903. As Jie Lu explains, Lu Xun is the most important writer of the early twentieth century, whose pungently satirical works like *Diaries of a Madman*, *The Authorized Bibliography of Ah-Q*, and *The Medicine* established perceptions of social illness and national idiosyncrasies in China (Jie Lu 2000: 219).

Lu Xun simultaneously published an article "On *Journey to the Moon*," (1902 or 1903) in which he attempts to define and praise the principle and possibilities of SF literature, designating this genre as "kexue xiaoshuo" (science novels) before the term "science fiction" had yet come into use in Anglo-America. As already pointed out in the previous section, it was the Japanese writer Yukio Ozaki who first employed the term "kagaku shosetu" (science fiction) in 1886. Asian writers had already invented a term equivalent to "science fiction" around the turn of the century, preceding Hugo Gernsback by 40 years. These terms reflected the writers' hopes of transmitting scientific knowledge to the public through the medium of science fiction.

What, then, is the first Chinese science fiction story? Wu Dingbo locates the earliest one in the 1904 serialization of Huangjiang Diaosuo's "Yueqiu zhimindi xiaoshuo" ("Tales of Moon Colonization") in the magazine *Portrait Fiction*. Huss also stresses the significance of three works published after this date. First, "Shi Nian Hou de Zhongguo" (China in Ten Years) published in *Xiaoshuo Shijie* (*Novel World*) in January 1923, where a future China develops lightweight but effective laser weapons to drive back imperialist aggressors. Second, Lao She's *City of Cats*, published in 1932, a dystopian novel about catlike Martians. Third, the Chinese equivalent of Hugo Gernsback, Gu Junzheng's *Heping de Meng* (*A Dream of Peace*) published in 1940, sometimes considered the first real work of Chinese science fiction. Both Wu Dingbo and Mikael Huss agree that Lao She and Gu Junzheng were very influential figures.

Yet little science fiction was written in China in the first half of the twentieth century because, as Guo states, industrialism was not sufficiently advanced. Since the foundation of the People's Republic of China in 1949, Soviet science fiction as well as Jule Verne's works have been translated into Chinese. However, it is true that especially during the ten years of the notorious "Cultural Revolution" (1966–76) not a trace of science fiction could be found in China (Guo 1997: 217). With the end of the Cultural Revolution, Chinese science fiction went through a golden age (1978–1983), which roughly corresponds with that of Japanese science fiction. Chinese writers and critics visited and reported on TOKON VIII, the 1982 Japanese national convention held in Tokyo. Furthermore, Hisayuki Hayashi, the Japanese authority on Chinese literature, had already started translating Chinese science fiction by 1980. From up to 1000 titles, leading works included Jin Tao's *Yueguangdao* (*The Moonlit Island*, 1980), Zheng Wenguang's *Reixiang Renmazuo* (*Forward to Sagittarius*, 1979), Ye Yonglie's *Heiying* (*The Black Shadow*, 1981), Meng Weizai's *Fangwen shizongzhe* (*Calling on the Missing People*, 1981), and among others Ton Enzheng's *Shanhudao shang de siguang* (*Death Ray on a Coral Island*, 1978). All these novels received high acclaim and were made into popular films. As in Japan, China witnessed an abundance of science fiction magazines such as *Kehuan Haiyang* (*SF Ocean*) from Beijing, *Zhihui Shu* (*Tree of Wisdom*) from Tianjin, *Kexue Shidai* (*Age of Science*) from Heilongjiang, and *Kexue Wenyi* (*Science Art and Literature*) from Sichuan [sic, see Huss 2000: 94]. Wu Ye states that these magazines had hundreds of thousands of readers, with Ye Yonglie, Tong Enzheng, and Zheng Wenguang emerging as popular writers (Huss 2000: 11). What matters here is that in this golden age science fiction writers became aware that they had entered the "postutilitarian" era, which, unlike the period between 1902 and 1979, spread not only scientific knowledge but also a scientific view of life (Huss 2000: 94).

Here we should not neglect the achievements of *Science Fiction World* which started as a monthly in 1979 and now boasts a circulation of about 400,000 to half a million. As far as its marketing power is concerned, *Science Fiction World* is undoubtedly the most widely read science fiction magazine on the globe. *SFW* carries stories by up-and-coming writers such as Xing He, Wang Jinkang, and Han Song; it provides a forum for all the SF readers in China (Huss 2000: 95). As Jie Lu points out, although Chinese science fiction has often been regarded as juvenile literature, and although *SFW* has mainly attracted teenagers, the magazine nevertheless aims to produce adult literature. Establishing the "Milky Way Writing Award," the highest quality SF prize in China and the means for many SF writers to become prominent stars among China's SF fans, *SFW* then hosted the 1991 meeting of the WSF, the World SF Organization, and organized the 1997 Beijing International SF Conference (Jie Lu 2002: 222).

The demonstrations in Tian'anmen Square in May and June of 1989 with their notorious suppression together with the crisis in the Eastern bloc in 1989–90 both had their impact on Chinese SF. *SFW* caught up with the new subjects and in 1996–7 published stories about virtual reality, nanotechnology, cloning, gene therapy, and gigong (Chi Kung; martial arts) masters who communicate telepathically with aliens (Huss 2000: 97). Accordingly Chinese SF seems to have entered a more experimental stage, in which stories overloaded with trendy technological terms enjoy abundance, paying no attention to narratology and characterization. Thus, SF in China has undoubtedly become not only a literary subgenre but has also developed its own subculture, not unlike its Anglo-American counterparts. This process can be seen in the post-Cyberpunk phenomenon in Taiwan championed by Wei Ke-fung, whose story "Inane" centers around a girl working in a florist shop helped by a computer programmer whose physical being has already been transferred into virtual reality, much like Dixie Flatline in William Gibson's *Neuromancer*.

Let us now see what is happening in SF in Hong Kong and Taiwan. For Hong Kong SF, it has been argued that stories dealing with time travel to the Chin Dynasty (221–207 BC), works such as Ni Kuang's *Huo Yong* (*A Live Terracotta Warrior*, 1977), Li Bihua's *Ching Yong* (*A Terracotta Warrior of Chin*, 1989), and Huang Yi's *Xun Chin Ji* (*The Search for Chin*, 1995), embody the best and the worst, the glory and the grotesque of Chinese culture – building the Great Wall, creating the terracotta warriors, and searching for the "pill of immortality." Temporal dislocation felt by each traveler is analogous to the perplexity that the Chinese now have in facing the challenge of modern Western science and technology. We are immediately reminded of William Gibson's post-Cyberpunk novel *Idoru* (1996), in which nanotechnology beautifully dislocates the Walled City from Hong Kong into Tokyo. This techno-hybrid image is further developed by the young American-Chinese SF writer Ted Chiang, whose "Seventy-Two Letters" (2000), the finalist for a Hugo award, has been acclaimed as a type of alchemy punk, and also by the Indian American writer Amitav Ghosh, whose novel *The Calcutta Chromosome: A Novel of Fevers, Derilium, and Discovery* (1996), the winner of the Arthur C. Clarke Award, exotically constructed a kind of cyberspace within malarial fever. This is the point when Asian science fiction joins forces with post-Cyberpunk narrative to exhibit its own dialogic imagination.

From Slipstream to Asian Science Fiction: Keizo Hino's *Hikari*

To conclude, I would like to consider the late Keizo Hino, a practitioner of Japanese slipstream literature, whose consciousness of the interaction between nature and the city has been apparently inspired by the works of J.G. Ballard. Hino's works will give us clues to comprehending the originality and possibility of "Asian" science fiction.

By coincidence, while Ballard was born in Shanghai in 1930 and grew up there, Hino was born in Tokyo in 1929 but grew up in Korea as a child. He spent ten of his primary and secondary school years in Japanese-occupied Korea and returned to Japan after the Second World War. While Ballard first came to the UK in 1946 and later read medicine at King's College, Cambridge without taking a degree, Hino graduated from the sociology department of the University of Tokyo in 1952. Moreover, while Ballard started writing speculative fiction in the 1950s by attacking American outer space-oriented science fiction, Hino, from 1952, had consistently worked for the prominent newspaper *Yomiuri Shimbun*, first as a literary critic in the 1950s and then as a wartime correspondent in Vietnam in the mid-1960s. It was his unique experience in Vietnam that inspired him to start writing fiction in 1965, leading him to win in 1974 the 72nd Akutagawa Prize for *Ano Yuhi* (*That Evening Sun*).

Although Hino died of cancer on October 14, 2002, his work has received a thorough posthumous reappraisal. In particular, we should not forget the way Hino's penultimate novel *Hikari* (1995), which literally translated means "light," and which was originally entitled "Interzone," has been transformed into a fabulous opera, with Yasunari Takahashi as librettist and Toshi Ichiyanagi as composer, which was performed on January 17–19, 2003, at the New National Theatre Tokyo.

The story of *Hikari* begins in the courtyard of a psychiatric infirmary on the outskirts of Tama City, near Tokyo, where the protagonist Mitsuda, who is called Mr. Seki in the original novel, sits gazing at the red, setting sun. After returning home from a mission to the Moon, this former astronaut had been struck by "retrogressive amnesia," and subsequently institutionalized and largely forgotten. His only regular visitor is Ishida, a section chief in the Space Resources Development Agency, who suspects – in contrast to the agency's director, who cannot believe that Space Age astronauts would fall victim to a mental disorder – that something in outer space may have caused Mitsuda's illness. While taking a walk around a nearby train station plaza with his Chinese nurse Hwang, Mitsuda comes to the top of a long flight of stairs. He stops and says, "I sense that I once made an important decision of some kind, here at the top of the stairs" (1995: 45). Mitsuda seems to have his memories of his past sparked by Huang's recollections of her home village of Taishan in China. In search of his own identity, Mitsuda escapes from the hospital to wander round an area near Shinjuku inhabited by homeless people.

Eventually the illness of the protagonist turns out to have been actually caused by what he witnessed on the Moon, that is, the intensity of light, which is not at all the benign and inspiring force Emerson describes in *Nature*. In space Mitsuda becomes unable to tell light from darkness. This recognition constitutes the critical moment of epiphany in the novel. More striking, however, is the author's analogy between the Moon Mitsuda went to and the China the nurse Hwang came from. Just as the hero's transcendental experience takes place in the neutral territory between outer space and inner space, so the nurse always dreams of the beach of the Hwang Ho, that is the Yellow River, in her home country, which is located not only between nature and the city, but also between Hwang's own outer space and inner space. In the conclusion to the novel, her description of the Yellow River will reveal the nurse's deep feelings towards the ex-astronaut:

> Up the Yellow River the forests on both side of the river start fading away, getting mostly invisible, with the huge surface of the water indistinguishable from the sky. The beautiful sky is so enormous that we feel like imagining that it is out of this expanse that the big river flows. Having recovered his memory, that ex-astronaut seems once again interested in going up above the sky. And yet, his sky is closely connected with my river. (Hino 1995: 410)

This striking representation of the Yellow River will immediately bring to mind J.G. Ballard, who also spent his childhood in China (recorded in his 1984 novel *Empire of the Sun*), and who has frequently explored the subject of the failed astronaut in stories collected in *Memories of the Space Age* (1988). Indeed, in one of the stories in this collection, returned astronauts suffer "fugues" not unlike Mitsuda's illness. In his famous literary manifesto, "Which Way to Inner Space?" (1962), Ballard argues as follows: "The biggest developments of the immediate future will take place not on the Moon or Mars, but on Earth, and it is inner space, not outer, that needs to be explored. The only truly alien planet is Earth" (Ballard 1996: 197). What is more, we should recognize Ballard's obsession with summer resorts and beaches as the best locations between dream and reality. Indeed, he once wanted to write the first and ideal speculative fiction about "a man with amnesia lying on a beach and looking at a rusty bicycle wheel, trying to work out the absolute essence of the relationship between them" (1996: 198).

In the 1970s, Ballard went on to rebuild inner space within what he terms the technological landscape, that is, the "technoscape," which he reconsiders the emergent form of nature, as he represented in the technoscape trilogy consisting of *Crash* (1973), *Concrete Island* (1973), and *High-Rise* (1975). Hino began his own speculative fiction writing career by reinvestigating the Ballardian inner space of the "technoscape," as he illustrated it with the novels like *Yume no Shima* (*Dream Island*) and *Hikari* as I have just outlined. Yet sharp differences distinguish Hino's works from Ballard's, and these merit careful attention. Whereas Ballard designated inner space as the central setting of New Wave science fiction, Hino redefined it as an ideal locale for nature writing. Here we may find Hino's paradoxical statement very helpful: "The truly emergent and artificial is perfectly compatible with the wilderness of nature" (1990: 102).

Rereading this passage, we may recall Thoreau's *Walden*, in which the author is sitting rapt in a reverie and then, penetrating his woods like the scream of a hawk, the whistle of the locomotive is heard. The very idea of technoscape as promoted by Ballard and Hino is not incompatible with Leo Marx's concept of the "machine in the garden." Furthermore, reading Hino as a nature writer will also enable us to redefine Thoreau as a speculative fictionist. Consider the following dramatic passage from the last sequence of *Walden*:

> Be rather the Mungo Park, the Lewis and Clarke and Frobisher, of your own streams and oceans; explore your own higher latitudes, – with shiploads of preserved meats to support you, if they be necessary; and pile the empty cans sky-high for a sign. Were preserved meats invented to preserve meat merely? Nay, be a Columbus to whole new continents and worlds within you, opening new channels, not of trade, but of thought. Every man is the lord of a realm beside which the earthly empire of the Czar is but a petty state, a hummock left by the ice. (Thoreau 1985: 578)

At this point, we feel convinced of the impact of the Thoreauvean idea of "Whole Earth" upon the Ballardian concept of this alien planet, and Hino's philosophy about technoscape as another form of wilderness, which we can witness either on the Moon or in Tokyo's shantytown of the homeless. It is when Hino's image of the Yellow River merges not only with the Ballardian inner space, but also the whole Earth, that we vividly comprehend the originality of possibility of "Asian" science fiction.

REFERENCES AND FURTHER READING

Apostolou, John L. (1984) "Japanese Science Fiction in English Translation." *Extrapolation* 25.1: 83–6.

Apostolou, John L. and G. Martin Greenberg (eds) (1997) *The Best Japanese Science Fiction*. New York: Barricade.

Ballard, J.G. (1996) *A User's Guide to the Millennium*. New York: Picador.

Birnbaum, Alfred, (ed.) (1993) *Monkey Brain Sushi: New Tastes in Japanese Fiction*. Tokyo: Kodansha International.

Card, Orson Scott and Keith Ferrell (1997) *Black Mist and Other Japanese Futures: And Other Japanese Futures*. New York: New American Library.

Clute, John and Peter Nicholls (eds) (1993) *The Encyclopedia of Science Fiction*, 2nd edn. London: Orbit.

Driscoll, Mark (2002) "From Kino-Eye to Anime-Eye/Ai: the Filmed and the Animated in Imamura Taihei's Media Theory." *Japan Forum* 14.2: 269–96.

Fukami, Dan (1986) *Japanese Science Fiction in Translation: A Bibliography, 1964–1985*. Tokyo: Taihei.

Galbraith, Stuart IV (1994) *Japanese Science Fiction, Fantasy and Horror Films*. Jefferson, NC: McFarland.

Guo, Jianzhong (1997) "Prospects for SF in China", *Zhongguo Kehuan Xiashuo Fazhan Qianjing* [Essay collection from 1997 Beijing International Conference of Science Fiction] Chengdu: SFW, 104–8.

Hassler, Donald (1999) "The Academic Pioneers of Science Fiction Criticism, 1940–1980." *Science Fiction Studies* 26.2: 213–31.

Hayashi, Hisayuki and Masaya Takeda (2001) *Chugoku Kagaku-Gensou Bungakukan*. {The Museum of Chinese Fantasy and Science Fiction}. Tokyo: Taishukan, 2001.

Hino, Keizo (1990) *Monolith*. Tokyo: Treville.

——(1995) *Hikari (Light)* Tokyo: Bungei Shunju.

Huss, Mikael "(2000) Journey to the West: SF's Changing Fortunes in Mainland China." *Science Fiction Studies* 27.1: 92–104.

Jameson, Fredric (1991) *Postmodernism, or, The Cultural Logic of Late Capitalism*. New York: Verso.

Komatsu, Sakyo (2002) "An Interview with

Komatsu Sakyo." Conducted by Susan Napier, Takayuki Tatsumi, Mari Kotani and Junko Otobe. *Science Fiction Studies* 29.3: 323–39.

Lu, Jie (2002) "Science Fiction in China: A Report on the World's Largest SF Magazine." *Extrapolation* 43.2: 219–25.

Robert, Matthew (1989) *Japanese Science Fiction: A View of a Changing Society*. London: Routledge.

Robinson, Kim Stanley (2002) *The Years of Rice and Salt*. London: HarperCollins.

SFWJ (Science Fiction and Fantasy Writers of Japan), (ed.) (2001) *SF Nyumon*. [*Introducing Science Fiction*]. Tokyo: Hayakawa Publishers.

Sterling, Bruce (1989) "Slipstream," *Science Fiction Eye #5* (July): 77–80

Tatsumi, Takayuki (1993) *Japanoido Sengen* [*A Manifesto for Japanoids: Reading Japanese Science Fiction*]. Tokyo: Hayakawa Publishers.

——(2000) "Generations and Controversies: An Overview of Japanese Science Fiction, 1957–1997." *Science Fiction Studies* 27.1: 105–14.

——(ed.) (2000) *Nippon SF Ronsoshi.* [*Science Fiction Controversies in Japan: 1957–1997*]. Tokyo: Keiso Shobo Publishers.

——(co-ed with Larry McCaffery and Sinda Gregory, 2002.) The special "New Japanese Fiction" issue of *Review of Contemporary Fiction* 22.2.

Thoreau, Henry David (1985) *Thoreau: A Week on the Concord and Merrimack Rivers, Walden, The Maine Woods, Cape Cod.* (ed.) Robert Sayre. New York: The Library of America.

"Top Space Stories for 2003," *Universe Today* [December 31, 2003] http://66.102.7.104/ search?q=cache:1FbkSGiB-KMJ:www. universetoday.com/am/publish/space_stories_ 2003.html+Chinese+space+shuttle,+2003&hl =ja&ie=UTF-8&inlang=ja)

Wu, Dingbo, and Patrick D. Murphy (eds) (1989) *Science Fiction from China: Eight Stories*. Westport, CT: Greenwood Press.

Yamano, Koichi (1994) "Nihon SF no Genten to Shiko" [Japanese SF: Its Originality and Orientation]. Trans. Kazuko Behrends. Eds. Darko Suvin and Takayuki Tatsumi. Introd. Darko Suvin. *Science Fiction Studies* 21.1: 67–80.

22
Australian Science Fiction
Van Ikin and Sean McMullen

Australian science fiction has a long history, which includes many firsts in the field and other great achievements, but it was not until relatively recently that systematically researched works have been written on the subject. Australia's output is easily swamped by the sheer volume of work from America and Britain, yet it has always been a part of the field. Being very distant from the international publications centers made matters even worse for a long time, but with the improvement in communications technology in the late twentieth century, Australia's presence in science fiction has become hard to overlook.

Europeans were speculating about Australia long before they discovered and settled the continent. There was thought to be a need for a Great South Land to balance the continents in the northern hemisphere, so even before a European sailor sighted the Australian coastline for the very first time, people were writing about it. Upon settlement, these tales transmuted into romances set in the unexplored parts of the continent. Many are fictional explanations for anomalies and mysteries recorded in the journals of Australian explorers, and some include quasiscientific effects. Although echoing the masculine adventure-romances of Verne and Haggard, these formulaic storylines nevertheless encode hopes and fears acutely relevant to the supposedly "newly discovered" continent.

"Australia Advanced; or Dialogues for the Year 3032" (*Sydney Gazette*, May 1832) by "Mephistopheles the Younger" foresees the construction of two suspension bridges across Sydney Harbor, the "extinction" of indigenous timber, and the construction of "the *Lightning* locomotive engine, which runs (or flies rather) at 60 miles per hour." "The Monster Mine" (1845) by "PGM" celebrates prosperity to be generated by the mining industry, mentions a process for growing wheat with "electricity" to shorten the time-period between sowing and harvest, and concludes with the revelation that the story has been composed using a "phonotypographical chair." In "Oo-a-deen; or, The Mysteries of the Interior Unveiled" (1847), an unknown author pioneered the "lost civilization" motif in Australian SF: Oo-a-deen, "the Unknown Land," is inhabited by a race of Mahanacumans – but the narrator is more interested in finding gold than in understanding this lost culture.

Marcus Clarke, author of the canonical Australian mainstream novel *For the Term of his Natural Life* (1874), produced a body of early speculative stories. In "Holiday Peak" (*Australasian*, January 1873) the Australian bush is a site of sacrifices to Mithra, Isis, and Osiris and conceals a lost mini-civilization inhabited by people of all nations, creeds, and colors. This is "the wondrous Land of Might-have-been" where impoverished Chinese could become wealthy land-owners and where Thackeray lived to finish *Denis Duval*. Other writers saw the bush as concealing only dark rituals or hidden gold mines; Clarke iconoclastically reveals an alternative literary tradition and social equality. "Human Repetends" (*Australasian*, 1872) offers a quasiscientific explanation for the phenomenon of reincarnation ("But there are in decimal arithmetic repeated 'coincidences' called *repetend*. Continue the generation of numbers through all time, you have these repetend forever recurring.") and "The Mystery of Major Moline" (1881) solves the gothic riddle of the Major who becomes possessed by the devil every Thursday: a "calcareous mass" has grown into his Vague nerve, causing hallucinations. Behavior and morality may be a function of biochemistry.

In *The Golden Lake* (1891) by Carlton Dawe, explorers seeking a fabled "Great White City" in Western Australia find artwork suggesting that the original denizens of this land were from China, and in *The Fallen Race* (1892) by Austyn Granville a lost kingdom is found in a hidden oasis of forest in the outback. Its strange animal-human inhabitants are the products of miscegenation between a lost Aboriginal tribe and kangaroos! Other strange creatures – a race of monkey-like subterranean beings known to Aborigines as "jinkarras" – are found in Ernest Favenc's "A Haunt of the Jinkarras" (1894). Favenc led an 1877 expedition to north-west Australia, then used his adventures as credentials for fiction. Like others of his time, Favenc was fascinated by a controversial entry in Sir George Grey's *Journals of Two Expeditions of Discovery in North-west and Western Australia During the Years 1837, 1938 and 1939* (1841) which describes the discovery of ancient rock-carvings of European style and underpins the speculation that this might be the legacy of a race predating Aboriginal settlement. In Favenc's *The Secret of the Australian Desert* (1895) explorers find a lost tribe of Aborigines "wholly unlike any tribes known ever to have existed" and clearly devised in light of Grey's discovery. Grey's speculations also underpin *The Lost Explorer* (1890) by J[ames] F[rancis] Hogan, a thinly-disguised speculation on the fate of the lost explorer Ludwig Leichhardt, who is revealed to be alive and living in Malua, a lost land once ruled by a vanished race of whites who left after ancient volcanic activity turned Central Australia into wilderness.

The mystery of Leichhardt's disappearance fired the popular imagination more firmly than the riddle posed by Grey's rock-art, but so did the fashionable notion that Australia was the site of ancient Lemuria. Could Lemurian culture and customs still exist out in the uncharted territories into which the Leichhardt expedition vanished? The evidence was construed to suggest that it could. *The Last Lemurian: A Westralian Romance* (1898) by G. Firth Scott draws heavily upon Rider Haggard's *She* in a tale involving reincarnation, lost tribes, and a technologically advanced ancient Lemurian civilization using hydrolic energy in the Australian hinterland. It also includes a "bunyip" – a creature curiously absent from most Australian SF.

Robert Potter's novel *The Germ Growers* (1892) more closely resembles the SF of today and is possibly the world's first alien invasion story, produced in Melbourne six years before H.G. Wells' *The War of the Worlds*. Shape-shifter aliens establish bases in wilderness areas of Earth, including north-west Australia, to conduct biological warfare by cultivating and spreading plague-germs. Unlike Wellsian Martians they do not resort to open warfare with superior technology, but use the stealth of airships, invisibility, and biological weapons.

The appeal of the "lost race" romances endured until the Second World War, pre-served in J.M. Walsh's *The Lost Valley* (1921), M. Lynn Hamilton's *The Hidden Kingdom* (1932), and Val Heslop's *The Lost Civilization* (1936), though these latter-day works were little more than nostalgic throw-backs. The earlier works established a debate about attitudes and prospects for the new land, attempting to supply Australia with a ready-made national identity by creating a mythical past for the new continent.

Other writers had no interest in the past, mythical or otherwise, except to throw it off; their concerns were political and their focus was upon the future. Ignoring Aboriginal possession of the land, they saw Australia as a blank slate upon which Utopian social conditions might be inscribed. Utopianism is recognized as a strand of "mainstream" Australian writing by William Lane, Henry Lawson, and Joseph Furphy, who explored the qualities of egalitarianism, loyalty, and "fair go" inherent in the code of bush mateship. Their vision of Utopian potential is summarized in Bernard O'Dowd's poem "Australia" (1903), which asks if Australia is to be yet another land in which corrupt social values rebuild their "fatal nest," or if it is to be the land where discredited ways are overthrown and "millennial Eden" is finally estab-lished. Nan Bowman Albinski describes this as "inferential utopianism" when com-pared with the "prescriptive utopias of social reform" (Albinski 1987:15) represented by Bellamy's *Looking Backward* (1888) or Morris' *News from Nowhere* (1891); they are not what the average SF reader would regard as Utopian fictions. Australia produced its share of fully-fledged visions of radically Utopian societies, and the first Australian science fiction works of international note are amongst them.

Few Australian Utopian fictions portray a possible future for Australia itself; writers choose the Arctic and Antarctic or other worlds as their setting. *Columbia* (1873) by Robert Ellis Dudgeon portrays a South Pacific undersea Utopian city run on tidal energy and inhabited by lost Englishmen who have interbred with local natives. (Dudgeon, a homeopathic doctor, wrote to compete with a book written by one of his patients – Samuel Butler's *Erewhon* [1872]). George McIver's *Neuroomia: A New Con-tinent* (1894) sites its Utopia in a temperate volcano-ringed zone of the South Pole, and remote polar locations feature in Christopher Spotswood's *The Voyage of Will Rogers to the Pole* (1888) and G. Read Murphy's *Beyond the Ice: Being a Story of the Newly Dis-covered Region Round the North Pole* (1894). William Little's *A Visit to Topos, and How the Science of Heredity is Practised There* (1897) weaves Darwinism and Christianity into a system of eugenics, and the anonymous author of *Erchomenon* (1897) – known to be the Reverend Henry Crocker Marriott Watson – predicts the world of 2026 to feature flying machines, democratic socialism, euthanasia, no marriage, and no religion. The First World War largely put an end to belief in political schemes that might lead to Utopia, but Valerie Chick's *Of Things Entire* (1941) offers a Utopian vision of global peace.

Other works hover between Utopia and dystopia. In *The Coming Terror: A Romance of the Twentieth Century* (1894) Sydney anarchist Samuel Albert Rosa has an international labor alliance use Panmort gas to appoint a beloved dictator who leads the nation into a golden age. *The Coming Terror* sold sufficiently well to justify a reprint edition which was retitled *Oliver Spence, The Australian Caesar* (1895), indicating that much of the book's popularity lay in its portrayal of the average man turned social crusader. In Harold Johnston's *The Electric Gun* (1911), revolution by average citizens transforms Australia into a socialist state, then the dream sours, requiring a counter-revolution in which freedom-fighters prevail thanks to acquisition of one of the electric guns used by the police.

One of the most important Australian Utopian novels is Joseph Fraser's *Melbourne and Mars: My Mysterious Life on Two Planets* (1889). Presenting itself as Joseph Fraser's authorized account of Adam Jacobs' diary, the novel provides a realistic and detailed account of life and work at the time, linking *Melbourne and Mars* with the subject-matter and preoccupations of the "mainstream" fictions of the time. It is the only nineteenth-century Australian SF novel to offer such a weight of realism. But the novel departs from mainstream preoccupations when, at the age of 45, Jacobs begins to have strange dreams of a second childhood and it is revealed that he is living a double life on the progressive and Utopian planet Mars, which is progressive not only in technology (flying machines and electricity) but also in social programs such as education.

The other major and better-known Australian writer of Utopian SF is Catherine Helen Spence, whose interest in the exclusively masculine fields of law, economics, and politics propelled her into public life as a pioneer journalist, social reformer, and feminist. An important figure in mainstream Australian literature, Spence is the first (known) female Australian SF author, her contribution being two feminist Utopian works: *Handfasted: A Romance*, written for a literary competition in 1879, and *A Week in the Future* (*Centennial Magazine* 1888–9). Deemed "too socialistic, and consequently dangerous," *Handfasted* was not published in the author's lifetime, the first published edition appeared in 1984. A group of lost Scottish adventurers has been isolated from the wider world since 1745, allowing them to develop the radically alternative society of Columba, which practices trial-marriage or "handfasting." Spence had campaigned against Anglo-Australian laws and attitudes concerning illegitimacy, divorce, and economic dependence, and Columban handfasting is shown to deal with all these problems. The heroine is a young Columban woman, Liliard Abercrombie, who falls in love with Hugh Keith, the Melbourne explorer who discovers their hidden valley. Liliard is so disillusioned with Columba (equating its contentment with complacency and finding that its satisfactions smother her creativity), that she is willing to leave her Happy Valley and return with her handfasted partner to the utterly non-Utopian world of Melbourne. Thus Spence twice breaks ranks with Utopian traditions – first by entertaining the pluralist notion that no set of social customs can be "Utopian" for all individuals, and second by daring to provide an honest account of the fate of Utopian fervor after the characters return to face conventional society. (In Melbourne the couple continue with their handfasting arrangement by living as married, but when society discovers the irregularity of their union they grudgingly succumb to a conventional marriage before their term of handfasting has expired.)

The feminist Utopia envisaged in *A Few Hours in a Far-Off Age* (1883) by Henrietta Dugdale is sited in the land of Alethia, a new continent which has sprung up after "ancient Australia" has sunk beneath the waves after "a long glacial period." Equating male rule with aggression and competition, Dugdale foresees a peaceful and ordered society arising from the political enfranchisement of women. Feminism combines with romance in *A Woman of Mars; or, Australia's Enfranchised Woman* (1901) by Mary Ann Moore-Bentley. The Martian girl Vesta is dispatched to Earth to organize "the emancipation of Woman and the regeneration of the [human] race." Martians have achieved a state of "human [sic] perfection" and regard "the Woman's Right" as "the bedrock foundation upon which a statesman [sic] must seek to establish a happy, progressive, social State."

The 1850s goldrush generated racial antagonism in Australia, and fears of Asian hordes were reflected in novels which can be regarded as science fiction inasmuch as they extrapolate current social trends to their disastrously logical conclusions. In the vitriolic *White or Yellow?: A Story of the Race War of A.D. 1908* (*The Boomerang*, 1888), by William Lane (writing as "Sketcher"), racial tension is sparked by British veto of Australian colonial legislation to restrict Chinese immigration; in *The Yellow Wave: A Romance of the Asiatic Invasion of Australia* (1895) long-serving politician and military commander Kenneth MacKay shows invasion occurring because Britain gives low priority to the defense of Australia; and in *The Australian Crisis* (1909) by C.H. Kirmess, Asians secretly populate Australia's desolate north-west with children born on Australian soil and Britain upholds the right of these "cuckoos-in-the-nest" to be treated as Australian citizens, sparking a war in which British gunboats shell Australian shores. *The Coloured Conquest* (1904) by "Rata" (politician Thomas Roydhouse) contrarily argues that only an alliance with Britain can save Australia in the event of invasion, contending that the discontent of colored races is caused by the overbearing behavior of white Australians. Sax Rohmer's character Fu-Manchu is anticipated not only by the flamboyant German-Chinese halfcaste who leads a Chinese invasion of Australia in *The Celestial Hand* (1903) by Vincent Joyce, but also by Dr. Nikola, the criminal genius cum magician created by Guy N[ewell] Boothby in *A Bid for Fortune* (1895; published in the USA as *Dr. Nikola's Vendetta* [1908]), *Doctor Nikola* (1896), *Dr. Nikola's Experiment* (1899) and *"Farewell, Dr. Nikola"* (1901). More recent novels of racial invasion, less vitriolic and racist, include A.J. Pullar's *Celestalia: A Fantasy A.D. 1975* (1933), Erle Cox's *Fool's Harvest* (1939), John Hay's *The Inva-*

sion (1968), John Hooker's *The Bush Soldiers* (1984), Eric Willmott's *Up the Line* (1991), and most notably John Marsden's best-selling young adult series commencing with *Tomorrow, When the War Began* (1993).

Erle Cox's *Out of the Silence* (1925) unites the racial, Utopian, and lost civilization strands of Australian SF, and appears to disown racialist theories. Earani, the revived survivor from a technologically superior earlier species of humanity, plans to steer humankind toward "Utopia" by annihilating colored races and controlling human breeding. The Aussie hero is initially attracted by this prospect of Utopia, but his more intellectual friends reject it and Earani is killed. With the possible exception of Liliard Abercrombie in Spence's *Handfasted*, Earani is the first nonstereotypical, strongly individualist female creation in Australian SF.

During the 1920s and 1930s several Australians were published in Gernsback's *Amazing Stories*, including Joe Czynski (who also wrote as "H.M. Crimp"), Phil Collas, and Alan Connell (whose "Dream's End" prompted the famous December 1935 Frank R. Paul cover depicting a battleship floating upside down above New York). Connell's Tarzan-style novels *Lords of Serpent Land, Prisoners of Serpent Land*, and *Warriors of Serpent Land* (1945) first proposed the scenario in which dinosaurs develop a technologically advanced civilization, and the stylish *Vandals of the Void* (*Wonder Quarterly*, 1931) by James Morgan Walsh established the now classic theme of an interplanetary alliance with different planetary governments and strange races, trading, intriguing, and coexisting, and Walsh may be the first SF author to have set an aerial dogfight in space. Australian Desmond W. Hall was assistant editor of *Astounding Stories* in 1931–2 and 1933–4; his Hawk Carse series (written as "Anthony Gilmore") did much to establish the space-faring future vision that grew popular in the 1930s.

One of the most significant works of Australian SF is *Tomorrow and Tomorrow and Tomorrow* by M. Barnard Eldershaw (the pseudonym for Marjorie Barnard and Flora Eldershaw, though this novel was written entirely by Barnard). Framed by a story set in the twenty-fourth century and using the device of a novel-within-a-novel, it offers a complex account of political turmoil in the latter part of the twentieth century. First published as *Tomorrow and Tomorrow* in a censored 1947 edition, the original version was restored under its original title in 1983.

A Second World War import embargo curtailed access to overseas SF and isolated the Australian product. This produced a local pulp industry including short novels from Transport Publishing and Currawong Press and magazines such as *Thrills Inc* (1950–2), *Future Science Fiction, Popular Science Fiction* (1953–5) and *Science-Fiction Monthly* (1955–6), which were distinguished mainly by the poor quality of the "scientific thrillers" they favored. Notable amongst these local pulp writers was N[orma] K. Hemming, who became Australia's first female author of hard SF and space opera, exploring relations between humans and various kinds of aliens; her talent had grown considerably at the time of her early death at age 32.

Children's writer Mary Patchett tried SF early in her career, exploiting the lack of good juvenile SF in the early 1950s. Her *Lost on Venus* (1954) might easily have been set in darkest Africa, with the names changed; for the pre-Sputnik audience the science could be minimal. Similarly, Ivan Southall's "Simon Black" series for young adults were Biggles adventures in space. Simon Black – with his partner, Alan Grant, and Rex the Alsatian – made his debut in *Meet Simon Black* (1950) and continued adventuring until *Simon Black at Sea* (1961). In addition to being an ace airman (like his ex-RAAF creator), Simon Black was an aeronautical genius who invented a series of technological wonder aircraft including the space-going *Firefly 3*.

As airmail became cheaper and more reliable, Australians who had kept abreast of developments in science and in international SF began to sell their work in Britain and America. Frank Bryning's career commenced in the 1950s and revived in the 1970s. His "Commonwealth Satellite Space Station" stories emphasize character and realism, weaving suspenseful plots around the astronauts' humdrum daily life in space; his cycle of "Aboriginal" stories celebrate Aboriginal culture and mythology by bringing it into ironically triumphant contact with supposedly "superior" white technology, showing Bryning to be the first Australian SF writer to take an on-going interest in the Australian Aborigines. The career of Wynne Whiteford was also consolidated in the 1950s, with stories in *Amazing*, *Science Fiction Adventures*, and *New Worlds*, then revived in the 1980s with *Breathing Space Only* (1980) and other novels; his work explores alien contact and maintains optimism about the value of technology used for peaceful purposes.

English seaman A. Bertram Chandler began writing SF in the 1940s and came to Australia in 1956. Best known for his Rimworlds novels featuring Commander Grimes, Chandler used his seafaring knowledge (gained as a ship's master) as a basis for spacefaring SF stories and novels combining genial stylistic simplicity with exotic locations and a liberal outlook. Towards the end of his career he wrote more works with an Australian setting, most notably *Kelly Country* (1983) an alternate history in which the iconic outlaw Ned Kelly wins the battle of Glenrowan and eventually takes over the government of Australia.

Neville Shute's *On the Beach* (1957) prompted the 1959 Stanley Kramer's film starring Gregory Peck, Ava Gardner, and Anthony Perkins. With the northern hemisphere poisoned by nuclear war, people in Melbourne await their death as the radioactivity spreads south; the well-crafted characters die one by one, and the story concludes without offering hope for the world at large.

Chandler and Shute represented the summit of what Australian SF achieved in the 1950s, even though both were mature age recruits from Britain; their writing was identifiably Australian, with just the right balance of credible characters, plausible adventure, and interesting ideas.

In the 1960s, British editor E.J. Carnell took an interest in Australian writers, and at one stage Australian stories in ten *New Worlds* outnumbered American contributions. Readers' polls suggest that Australian works were as well regarded as those by the British. By 1968 local mainstream publishers were publishing locally written SF novels at a profit, the first Australian SF collections and anthologies had been published, and the Australian fan community launched the Australian Science Fiction Achievement Awards, the Ditmars. In one decade Australian SF had made an extraordinary recovery from its long isolation. Unfortunately, local writers were now confronted with shrinking markets as television eroded the popularity of the story, and literary tastes shifted. Financed by Sydney businessman Ron Graham, the magazine *Vision of Tomorrow* was launched in 1969, edited and published in Britain by Philip Harbottle, and won the 1970 Ditmar Award for Best International SF Publication. The best-known *Vision* stories include "Dancing Gerontius" by Lee Harding (December 1969) and "The Bitter Pill" by A. Bertram Chandler (June 1970), and "Anchor Man" by Jack Wodhams (August 1969). Australian artist Stanley Pitt painted two superb covers for *Vision* (the July and September 1970 issues) before the distributors got the better of Ron Graham's patience and *Vision* ceased publication.

John Baxter's two *Pacific Books of Australian Science Fiction*, published in 1968 and 1971, were the first-ever Australian SF anthologies, gathering Australian SF's best work for the two previous decades and making it available to a public that had not known Australian SF existed. Both have had multiple reprints, and together provide the only easily accessible view of Australian SF in the 1950s and 1960. Magazine fiction has usually launched careers for authors ranging from Walsh and Whiteford in the 1930s to Dowling and Egan in the 1980s, offering intense but transitory exposure; many talented Australian SF authors have passed into oblivion because their work is now confined to rare surviving copies of magazines in a few research libraries.

Lee Harding became a major and popular young adult author after *Displaced Person* (1979) won a Children's Book Council Award for its study in urban alienation and paranoia, the main character's predicament striking a chord with teenagers experiencing identity crises.

Melbourne hosted Aussiecon (the 33rd Worldcon) in 1975, and the period between Aussiecon and Aussiecon 2 (in 1985) saw the publication of one or more anthologies per year, worldwide success for Australian genre films (such as *Mad Max* and *Picnic at Hanging Rock*), three writers' workshops run by famous international authors, and a proliferation of semiprofessional magazines including *Void* (edited by Paul Collins), *Nexus* (edited by Elizabeth Close), *Futuristic Tales* (edited by Ray Maulstaid), *Crux* (edited by Michael Hailstone), and *The Cygnus Chronicler* (edited by Neville J. Angove). Each magazine had distribution problems and folded when the editors lost enthusiasm, but they were valuable venues for Australian beginners to practice.

Throughout the 1960s and 1970s Australians established reputations as accomplished SF critics, gaining six Hugo nominations, two of which were for John Bangsund's *Australian SF Review* (1966–9), one of the best critical fanzines in the world. Serious Australian SF criticism culminated in the encyclopedic works of Don Tuck and Peter Nicholls. Tuck received a "special Committee Hugo Award" for *The Handbook of Science Fiction and Fantasy* in 1962, and a decade later began his three-volume work, *The Encyclopedia of Science Fiction and Fantasy* (1974, 1978, 1983), winning a 1984 Hugo for the third volume. The first Australian work to win a Hugo Award was *The Encyclopedia of Science Fiction* (1979), under the general editorship of Peter Nicholls. A second edition, produced in 1993 (with John Clute, the associate editor of the original work), also won a Hugo. Bruce Gillespie's *SF Commentary* (1969–) and Van Ikin's *Science Fiction: A Review of Speculative Literature* (1977–) are currently the most long-standing Australian forums for the discussion of international and Australian SF.

Australian SF films had their genesis in the mid-1970s. Peter Weir's *The Cars that Ate Paris* (1974) involves an outback town where travelers are attacked by adolescents who strip the cars to turn their own vehicles into Heath Robinson-style fighting machines. The three highly successful Mad Max films – *Mad Max* (1979), *Mad Max 2* (also known as *The Road Warrior*) (1981), and *Mad Max Beyond Thunderdome* (1985) – were more overtly SF, being set in a postnuclear apocalypse future. With stars like Mel Gibson and Tina Turner, and exciting chase and action scenes on a par with the contemporary US film *The Terminator* (1984), these movies pointed to a promising future for Australia in media SF.

Mainstream authors also began to take an interest in SF during the 1970s and early 1980s. Peter Carey's career began in the mid-1970s with SF and fantasy stories that ultimately led him to an unchallenged eminence as an Australian mainstream writer. David Ireland won the Miles Franklin Award for *A Woman of the Future* (1979), concerning an Australian adolescent growing up in a near-future Australia. *The Plains* (1982) by Gerald Murnane is a speculative fable which inverts Australian cultural history by dealing with a young film-maker in an Australia with a rich cultural life in its vast hinterland; this was the most successful book published by Norstrilia Press. It is sometimes forgotten that George Turner was an award-winning mainstream novelist before turning to writing SF novels with *Beloved Son* (1978).

Turner began his SF career with a loosely linked trilogy of *Beloved Son* (1978), *Vaneglory* (1981), and *Yesterday's Men* (1983), which are set in a world recovering from a collapse brought about by genetic engineering disasters and limited nuclear war. Turner's postulation of a "noninterference" political ethic in the recovering society parallels the present-day suspicion of products and organisms produced via genetic modification. His best work, *The Sea and Summer* (1987, *The Drowning Towers* in USA), won the Arthur C. Clarke Prize for its treatment of the then relatively new theme of greenhouse warming. Like Egan, Turner was well regarded for his ability to extrapolate current technological trends to build plausible future scenarios.

Launched in 1981, *Omega Science Digest* was similar in format to *Omni*. *Omega* reserved two spaces per issue for original SF by Australian authors and paid better rates than most overseas magazines. Its circulation was an unprecedented 40,000, and it operated at a profit until publishing industry wranglings forced it to close in 1987. *Omega* stories won two Ditmar Awards from five nominations, and nine of the 65 original stories were reprinted. *Omega* launched several careers, but its first and most spectacular find was Terry Dowling. After a series of award winning stories in the 1980s, Dowling's linked-story collection *Rynosseros* (1990) formed the first installment of a consistent vision of a future Australia in which European and Aboriginal cultures peacefully coexist. The detailed mythology, technology, geography, and anthropological speculations are extended in *Blue Tyson* (1992) and *Twilight Beach* (1993), and are described in lyrical prose, all of which earned Dowling a string of fiction awards and a reputation as one of Australia's foremost genre authors.

In 1985, Australia's second World SF Convention, Aussiecon 2, was held in Melbourne. Three books of fiction were launched there: Kurt von Trojan's novel *The Transing Syndrome* (1985), and the anthologies *Strange Attractors* (1985), edited by Damien Broderick, and *Urban Fantasies* (1985), edited by David King and Russell Blackford. During Aussiecon 2, Peter McNamara of Adelaide decided that Australia needed a good SF magazine with a professional finish which published more than *Omega*'s two stories per issue, and within six months *Aphelion* magazine was launched, providing a professional market for beginning authors. *Aphelion* folded within weeks of *Omega*'s demise in early 1987, a year which saw local markets for short SF publish just nine stories – the second lowest annual total since the 1940s. Nevertheless, newcomer Greg Egan established his reputation in the British *Interzone* while newcomer Sean McMullen did likewise in the American *Fantasy and Science Fiction*. In a talk titled "Measures of Success" at the Zencon II Science Fiction Convention in October 1988, McMullen asserted that although the local market was enduring one of its worst recessions ever, there was the potential for a massive boom in local genre publishing if only local commercial publishers could tap into the huge Australian market for overseas SF.

That was precisely what happened, for 1990 marked the beginning of a boom in Australian commercial genre publishing. *Aphelion* re-emerged as Aphelion Publications, winning more awards for its books than any other Australian small press, and establishing the careers of Terry Dowling, Sean McMullen, and Sean Williams. Pan Australia began publishing fantasy trilogies by Martin Middleton, Tony Shillitoe, and Dirk Strasser, following with SF by Shannah Jay and Richard Harland. Perth enthusiasts founded *Eidolon* magazine (1990–2002) and in Melbourne *Aurealis* magazine (1990–) achieved newsstand distribution and the larger circulation that this made possible. In the 13th of his *Year's Best Science Fiction* anthologies, Gardner Dozois cited *Aurealis* and *Eidolon* as two of the three best semiprozines in the world, and considered *Eidolon* to have the best fiction. In 1995, HarperCollins Australia achieved enormous sales with fantasy trilogies by Sara Douglass, then ventured into SF with Sean Williams, Shane Dix, Simon Brown, and Joel Shepherd, only to conclude early in the new century that sales of SF were too small in relation to the huge market for fantasy. In 1995 there were two other important developments. *She's Fantastical*, edited by Lucy Sussex and Judith Raphael Buckrich, offered the first anthology of Australian women's speculative writing. Endeavoring to establish recognition for Australian works other than the Ditmar Awards (voted by fans attending the national SF conventions), *Aurealis* magazine established the Aurealis Awards (using panels of well-read expert judges), which have acquired considerable credibility among commercial publishers. During the 1990s the market for young adult genre fiction also grew considerably, most notably with Gillian Rubinstein's award-winning *Space Demons* trilogy, which depicts young people resolving their problems and frustrations without aggression and Gary Crew's *Strange Objects* (1990), which blends SF, fantasy, and horror in multiple narratives concerning present-day repercussions of the 1629 wreck of the Dutch vessel *Batavia*.

The increase in published Australian fiction was accompanied by greater recognition. Stories by Sean McMullen and Greg Egan were voted onto the Nebula Awards Preliminary Ballot in 1989 and 1990 respectively, and Turner's *The Sea and Summer* was included in the 1990 final ballot by the Nebulas committee – thereby becoming the first Australian work to receive a Nebula nomination. Greg Egan's stories were winning readers' polls in *Interzone*, his novel *Permutation City* won the 1995 Campbell Award, and many of his stories were selected for Dozois' *Year's Best Science Fiction* series. Terry Dowling won the Readercon Award for *Wormwood* (1991) and "Breaking Through to the Heroes" (1992). American author Jack Dann migrated to Australia in 1994, in 1997 becoming the first Australian resident to win a Nebula Award with his novella *Da Vinci Rising* (*Asimov's SF Magazine*, May 1995). Although Australians had won several Hugos for nonfiction over three decades, it was not until the 1999 World SF Convention that Greg Egan's "Oceanic" (*Asimov's Magazine*, August 1998) won the Hugo for Best Novella. No Australian novel has made it to the Hugo shortlist, although Egan's *Teranesia* and McMullen's *Souls in the Great Machine* tied for 10th place in the 2000 Hugo nomination, indicating that such recognition is probably not far off.

By the early 1990s there was a pressing need to assemble the best Australian SF stories into anthologies accessible to students and general readers. This led to *Mortal Fire: Best Australian SF* (1993), edited by Terry Dowling and Van Ikin, which covered a twenty-year period. With *Metaworlds: Best Australian Science Fiction* (1994), editor Paul Collins refined the notion of a "best" collection to stories less than five years old. Both anthologies were economically successful, inducing Collins to edit several more. *Alien Shores* (1994), edited by Peter McNamara and Margaret Winch, Aphelion Publications reversed the trend toward reprinted "best of" anthologies by using only seven reprints out of 29 stories. By the late 1990s there was sufficient original material being published annually to fill a "year's best" collection of Australian SF, and in 1997 *Eidolon* editors Jonathan Strahan and Jeremy Byrne selected *The Year's Best Australian Science Fiction and Fantasy Volume 1*, followed by another *Year's Best* anthology in 1998. Representing the best in Australian genre short fiction at the end of the decade, the anthology *Dreaming Down Under* (1998), edited by Jack Dann and Janeen Webb, won the World Fantasy Award for Best Anthology in 1998.

In the 1990s, a new group of writers consolidated their careers. Simon Brown, Stephen Dedman, Richard Harland, Sean McMullen, Sean Williams, and several others all came to earn significant money from SF writing, and in some cases enough to live comfortably as full-time authors. Sean Williams and Shane Dix impressed George Lucas sufficiently with their novels that they were recruited as authors of *Star Wars* spin-off novels. Statistically the members of this new group of SF authors are predominantly male, while Australian fantasy is dominated by women. Several male authors cross genres into fantasy, but it is very rare for female fantasy authors to write SF (McMullen 2002: 52).

McMullen, like Egan, achieved early success in Britain, America, and Australia with his short fiction, then won two awards from six nominations for his "medieval Cyberpunk" Greatwinter trilogy. Set in a technically regressed, but very elegant and baroque future, the novels feature strange but workable computers, transport systems, forms of government, and in the third novel even an original method of spacecraft propulsion. The highly romantic and comic nature of his novels allowed him to move easily into fantasy with his Moonworlds series, which feature a mixture of romance, black comedy, and scientifically rigorous magic.

Mark Shirrefs and John Thompson produced a series of SF novels originating from their innovative *Spellbinder* television series (1993–4, 1997), becoming among the most commercially successful of Australia's SF writers. Both television SF and young adult SF are very important component of Australian SF in the 1980 and 1990s, and economically they have surpassed adult Australian SF. The Aurealis Awards recognize the importance of young adult writing with a separate category, while television and film SF have been honored many times in industry awards.

By the late 1990s, Damien Broderick was not only the great survivor of Australian SF but also its longest running success story. He published a story collection in 1965 at age 20, then produced novels, short stories, and books of literary and cultural criticism, as well as editing anthologies and writing children's and young adult fiction. He holds a PhD in the semiotics of science, literature, and science fiction, and works such as *The Architecture of Babel: Discourses of Literature and Science* (1994), *Reading by Starlight: Postmodern Science Fiction* (1995), *Theory and its Discontents* (1997), and *Transrealist Fiction: Writing in the Slipstream of Science* (2000) have earned him the reputation as Australia's most internationally respected SF critic and theorist. *The Dreaming Dragons* (1980) is a complex exploration of time travel, evolution, and causality, earning Broderick runner-up position in the Campbell Awards, and *Striped Holes* (1988) offers comic relief in the mode of Sheckley or Sladek. His best novel, *The White Abacus* (1997), is an ambitious reworking of Shakespeare's *Hamlet* in a separate future reality, remaining so faithful to Shakespeare that close equivalents can be found for characters and situations. A serious point underlies the wit, for the novel seeks to forge a new conclusion to the same Shakespearian pattern of events, thus demonstrating that science and humanistic enlightenment can alter the supposedly inevitable tragedies of human affairs. The diverse intellectual sweep of Broderick's writing includes feminism, literary theory, particle physics, biochemistry, and cognitive science, marking him as an astonishingly talented polymath amongst SF writers. Yet despite Broderick's unparalleled achievements, Greg Egan is by most measures the most successful SF author Australia has yet produced, achieving overseas recognition with highly innovative and ruthlessly logical fiction, characterized by intricate reasoning and powerful, unexpected denouements.

The 1990s have been the greatest decade ever for every type of achievement in Australian SF. However, SF has largely been dragged along in the backwash of the really serious performer in commercial terms, Australian fantasy. The majority of the blockbuster titles have been either fantasy, or SF that is indistinguishable from fantasy. For the SF titles that have been published locally, the best sales have been around

5000, while comparable fantasy novels have averaged over double this figure in the relatively small Australian book market. The watershed was the 1990 publication of the fantasy "blockbuster" *Circle of Light* by Martin Middleton. It sold 15,000 copies over three printings, yet the author lacked the traditional apprenticeship in short fiction. The novel was nominated for no awards and was given a chilly reception by fan reviewers, yet its sales demonstrated the existence of a large Australian genre market independent of organized genre fans.

The triumph of fantasy was not absolute, however. For the first half of the 1990s commercial fantasy was virtually absent from even shortlists for awards, which were still dominated by SF that varied from the borderline SF-fantasy of Dowling, to the hard SF of Egan and McMullen. In 1997, fantasy works by Sussex and Blackford won Ditmar Awards, and in 2003 a fantasy novel by McMullen made the Locus magazine annual readers' poll shortlist, but Australian SF still dominates the Ditmar awards, is regularly published overseas, and generally gets more acclaim. If Australian SF is flourishing, however, why is it not more commercially successful within Australia? One problem is that SF is regarded in Australia (perhaps inconsistently) as both juvenile in appeal and technically difficult. Literate adults who would buy a complicated detective thriller or a retelling of the King Arthur legend would seldom contemplate a work on genetic engineering or computer hacking. Similarly, although television SF is booming in Australia, virtually all of it is targeted at young adult viewers.

One last factor in Australian SF is its own history. Until the 1990s, only convention handbooks, fanzine articles, anthology introductions, and encyclopedia entries provided brief accounts of the subject, whose accuracy varied considerably. In 1998, Melbourne University Press published *The MUP Encyclopedia of Australian Science Fiction and Fantasy*, edited by Paul Collins, and this brought entries varying from accounts of individual authors, histories, or awards, and genre artwork together under one cover for the first time. *Strange Constellations: A History of Australian Science Fiction* by Russell Blackford, Van Ikin, and Sean McMullen followed in 1999, and was the first structured and comprehensive account of Australian SF's history. Both books won the William Atheling Award for SF Criticism. It fell to the meticulous and dedicated collector Graham Stone to have the last word and complete the story of the subject; *Notes on Australian Science Fiction* (2001) includes detailed accounts of rare, marginal, pre-European Utopian, newspaper, and mainstream magazine Australian SF up to the mid-1950s.

References and Further Reading

Albinski, N.B. (1987) "A Survey of Australian Utopian and Dystopian Fiction." *Australian Literary Studies* 13, 15–28.

Blackford, Russell, Ikin, V. and McMullen, S. (1999) *Strange Constellations: A History of Australian Science Fiction*. Westport, CT: Greenwood Press.

Collins, Paul (ed.) (1998) *The MUP Encyclopedia of Australian Science Fiction and Fantasy*. Melbourne: Melbourne University Press.

Ikin, Van (1981) "The Role of the Literature Board in Australian SF Publishing". *Science Fiction: A Review of Speculative Literature* 7, 4–6.

——(ed.) (1982) *Australian Science Fiction*. St Lucia, Qld: University of Queensland Press.

——(1985) "Futurities: Identity and Science Fiction." *Island Magazine* 24, 32–6.

——(1988) "Dreams, Visions, Utopias," in *The Penguin New Literary History of Australia,* (ed.) L. Hergenhan. Ringwood, Vic: Penguin Books, 253–66.

——(1992a) "Australian Science Fiction: On the Road to Recognition?" *Journal of Myth, Fantasy & Romanticism* 1(3), 24–31.

——(1992b) "Here there be Monsters: Some Idiosyncrasies of Science Fiction Bibliography in Australia." *Bibliographical Society of Australia and New Zealand Bulletin* 16(4), 149–53.

Ikin, Van, Sean McMullen and Graham Stone (1991) "Science Fiction Magazines in Australia." *Australian and New Zealand Journal of Serials Librarianship* 2(1), 3–34.

McMullen, Sean (1991) "Going Commercial and Becoming Professional." *Eidolon* 6, 54–62.

——(1992) "Australian SF Art Turns Fifty." *Eidolon* 7, 45–55.

——(1992) "Far from *Void*: A History of Australian SF Magazines. *Aurealis* 7, 60–9.

——(1992) "Showcase or Leading Edge: Australian SF Anthologies 1968–1990." *Aurealis* 9, 49–58.

——(1993) "Protection, Liberation, and the Cold, Dangerous Universe: The Great Australian SF Renaissance. *Aurealis* 11, 51–60.

——(1996) "The Golden Age of Australian Science Fiction." *Science Fiction: A Review of Speculative Literature* 36, 3–28.

——(2002) "Science Fiction in Australia." *Locus* 492, 52.

McMullen, Sean, with Nick Stathopoulos (1991) "Not in Print but worth Millions: Non-print SF in Australia." *Eidolon* 5, 36–42.

Stone, Graham (2001) *Notes on Australian Science Fiction*. Sydney: Graham Stone.

PART VI
Key Writers

23

The Grandeur of H.G. Wells

Robert Crossley

"Gee! What a mind!" Charlie Chaplin is supposed to have exclaimed about H.G. Wells, as quoted by George Caitlin in a 1935 letter to Wells; "It must be grand to have a mind like that." The plenitude of his conceptions, the visualizing power of his imagination, the sheer grandeur of his mind as it played over things unattempted yet in prose or rhyme constitute Wells' legacy to the new literary form he helped build. Most of his indelible contributions to what he called "scientific romance" were the product of his first decade as a professional writer, from the mid-1890s through the first years of the twentieth century. But the inventions of Wells' youth made a durable impression on many other writers not usually identified with science fiction. T.S. Eliot, for one, called his story "The Country of the Blind" and the depiction of sunrise as seen from the lunar surface in *The First Men in the Moon* "quite unforgettable" (Parrinder 1972: 320). For Hilaire Belloc, who would later fight with Wells over the Darwinian orientation of his *Outline of History*, the experience of reading "The Crystal Egg" was harrowing: "It is like a death," he wrote to Wells in 1909. Joseph Conrad was so moved by *The Invisible Man* that he told the author, "your diabolical psychology plants its points right into a man's bowels." Years later he praised *The War in the Air* for its "extraordinary force and picturesqueness and a distinct grandeur of aspect" (Conrad 1898: II, 127; 1908: IV, 149).

As science fiction developed its distinctive literary character throughout the twentieth century, writers followed the trails Wells had blazed, and their imaginations were tutored by the great sequence of early Wellsian narratives: *The Time Machine* (1895), *The Island of Dr. Moreau* (1896), *The Invisible Man* (1897), *The War of the Worlds* (1898), *When the Sleeper Wakes* (1899), *The First Men in the Moon* (1901), and dozens of short stories that displayed a mind so rich in ideas that they spilled out of his fiction and into the fertile brains of other writers. Some imitated Wells, and others parodied him; some wrote fictional replies to his stories, some composed sequels, some adapted them to the media of film and radio. So pervasive was Wells' influence on the evolution of science fiction that in 1931, shortly after publishing the future history titled

Last and First Men, Olaf Stapledon offered this tribute to Wells, whom he had not then met and had not explicitly acknowledged in his book: "a man does not record his debt to the air he breathes in common with everyone else" (Crossley 1982: 35). Later in the same decade C.S. Lewis, in his 1938 anti-Wellsian journey to Mars *Out of the Silent Planet*, had his protagonist credit the power of Wells' conception of Martian and lunar monstrosities to shape twentieth-century fantasies and nightmares about other worlds:

> His mind, like so many minds of his generation, was richly furnished with bogies. He had read his H.G. Wells and others. His universe was peopled with horrors such as ancient and mediaeval mythology could hardly rival. No insect-like, vermiculate or crustacean Abominable, no twitching feelers, rasping wings, slimy coils, curling tentacles, no monstrous union of superhuman intelligence and insatiable cruelty seemed to him anything but likely on an alien world. (Lewis 1965: 35)

Wells' youthful scientific romances established the gold standard for science fiction through the first half of the twentieth century. By the century's second half they were no longer the sole model for the genre, but they remained powerful and popular works that never went out of print and were available in multiple editions. Three of Wells' novels – *The Time Machine*, *The Island of Dr. Moreau*, and *The War of the Worlds* – have appeared in scholarly, annotated "critical editions," a distinction accorded to no other science fiction writer. In J.R.R. Tolkien's posthumously published "Notion Club Papers," a discussion-fantasy set in the 1980s and 1990s, some science fiction enthusiasts self-consciously label themselves as "post-Wells," unable and unwilling to get away with such Wellsian devices as an antigravity propellant or the "ridiculous transport" employed by the Time Traveller. But they still revere Wells as one of "the forgotten Old Masters" whose stories rise splendidly above the limitations of their premises (Tolkien 1992: 165–6). Leading practitioners of science fiction throughout the century – among them, Kim Stanley Robinson, Ursula K. Le Guin, Christopher Priest, Brian Aldiss, and Stanislaw Lem – paid homage to Wells' originality, celebrated his early romances as artistic and conceptual touchstones, and exhibited his impact on their own work. Le Guin, introducing a twenty-first-century reprinting of *The First Men in the Moon*, observes the prescience of Wells' inquiry into the consequences of his lunar beings' control over their own biological evolution: "This is a question we, a hundred years later, watching corporate science blithely alter genetic codes in plants, animals, and human beings, are just beginning to ask" (Wells 2003: xiii).

The response of other writers to Wells' scientific romances helps explain why he is *the* indispensable figure in the history of science fiction, even though he neither originated the form nor called it by the name we now know. Mary Shelley created the prototypes of some central themes and icons in science fiction: the responsibilities of the scientist and the figure of the alien (in *Frankenstein*) and the image of the future and the end of civilization (in *The Last Man*, a more ponderous production than her first novel). Later in the nineteenth century Jules Verne added other motifs to Shelley's: travel through outer space, the subterranean journey, exploration of the ocean's depths. His *Voyages Extraordinaires* took the wandering adventures of Odysseus and Sindbad into the industrial era. By the time Wells came on the scene in 1895 some conventions of scientific romance were already in place, but the accepted name for the new form did not get invented until the mid-1920s, by which time there were numerous examples of the genre. The name was conferred by an American editor and writer of limited imaginative gifts named Hugo Gernsback, who reprinted (without authorization) Wells' fictions from the 1890s in his pioneering magazine *Amazing Stories*. With Wells' by-then famous works as his Exhibit A, Gernsback devised the clumsy term "scientifiction," later revised to the more pronounceable "science fiction," and still later reduced by academic theorists to "SF" and by patronizing journalists to "scifi." Shelley, Verne, and Gernsback notwithstanding, Wells was the decisive shaper of the new form, its godfather if not its natural parent. He gave science fiction amplitude, vision, intellectual weight, moral texture, grandeur.

In 1826 in *The Last Man* Mary Shelley wafted Romantic readers, by way of a Sibylline fantasy, into the twenty-second century. Wells' first major work – barely longer than a novella – got readers into the future by technological rather than mystical apparatus. It took readers on a bold ride, on a machine resembling a souped-up stationary bicycle, first into the year 802,701, and, in the climactic chapter of *The Time Machine*, to the year 30 million and the end of life on Earth. The central events of Wells' first masterpiece depict the devolution of humanity into two degenerate semihuman subspecies, Eloi and Morlocks, who represent the logical outcome of the divisions between the leisured and the laboring classes as Wells knew them in 1895. Ursula Le Guin commented nearly a century later that science fiction is neither predictive nor prescriptive but descriptive; it may be set in an imaginary place or a distant future but it is essentially a revelation of the present. "Science fiction," she asserts, "isn't about the future" (Le Guin 1992: 153).

The Time Machine puts that principle into brilliant operation in Wells' depiction of underworld Morlocks preying on languid Eloi in a reversal of the behavior of their Victorian ancestors. The rich who once (metaphorically) devoured the poor become in future time (literally) the food of their former victims. The anonymous inventor who travels through time undergoes something he had not anticipated: the political and moral education of his imagination. Expecting to discover the unfamiliar, he instead confronts familiar, though previously unexamined, realities in every future setting through which he moves: the decadence of privilege in the Eloi, industrial degradation in the Morlocks, the fragility of culture in the Palace of Green Porcelain, the inexorability of the second law of thermodynamics on the deserted beach of the world's end. *The Time Machine*'s grand spectacles and exotic visions promote judicious reflection on self, society, and the universe. As Wells' biographer David Smith has pointed out, the great achievement of his early fiction was not simply the incorporation of scientific talk into his invented worlds but the deployment of new scientific understandings in critically assessing how much progress human civilization was actually making (Smith 1986: 57). The reader begins the journey into the future, just as the Time Traveller does, as a tourist, but in the process of reading becomes an inquirer into the nature of history and civilization, into the prospects for human community, into the ultimate destiny of our species. With good reason Wells made the book's central symbol of this narrative a sphinx – whose image appeared on the dust jacket of the first edition. Paralleling the monstrous Sphinx of ancient myth, Wells' sphinx embodies the riddle of the future: who are these half-witted Eloi, and who are these skulking Morlocks? And the answer to that riddle, just as in the Sphinx's riddle in the Greek story, is "Man." Having framed *The Time Machine* in myth, having shaped it into a modern myth in its own right, Wells in his first major work of science fiction demonstrated the genre's potential for conceptual grandeur.

Now almost universally recognized as the watershed event in the history of science fiction, the publication of *The Time Machine* established the template for Wells' distinctive kind of fiction: the use of technologically ingenious, if not strictly plausible, premises; plots that are as much adventures in ideas as flights of fancy; protagonists who represent, for better and for worse, the modern scientific ethos; and narratives that function as Swiftian parables on the cultural practices and pretensions of a self-conscious age of progress. To state Wells' fictional principles in this way makes him sound glumly didactic, but the Wellsian model for science fiction depends for its critical and educative effects on grand and startling visions. And the grandeur is of three kinds: conceptual, moral, and pictorial. And perhaps there is a fourth, too: comic grandeur, most visibly on display in such short masterpieces as "The Man Who Could Work Miracles" and "The New Accelerator" but also ingrained in the texture of all his novel-length scientific romances except the unfailingly gruesome *Island of Dr. Moreau*. In *The Time Machine* we have the perfect illustration of Wells' deployment of all his talents for imagining on a grand scale the workings of the biological concept of devolution, for indicting the moral bankruptcy of the Victorian leisure class by transforming it into the effete and helpless lot of Eloi, and for creating the splendid nightmare of the upstairs-downstairs world of the year 802,701. And then he slips in the mock-grandeur of a farcical love affair between the Victorian gentleman-adventurer and his four-foot-tall girlfriend from the future. That the Time Traveller would grandiosely cast himself as her chivalric protector but that Wells should give his lady the diminutive name of "Weena" is characteristic of the author's comic subversion.

The concepts Wells pioneered are famous – so much so that they are now taken for granted by some readers who may not know who invented them or gave them their first memorable fictional incarnation: time travel, extraterrestrial invasion, animal experimentation, planetary exploration, atomic warfare. Even ancient motifs like invisibility are given stunningly fresh and modern treatments; *The Invisible Man*, one of several of Wells' treatments of another venerable motif – the lunatic scientist – remains a sometimes amusing and ultimately shattering fable about alienation, terrorism, and self-destruction. Wells was never satisfied with a grand concept for its own sake, but subjected it to searching moral examination. Unlike Orson Welles' ballyhooed 1938 radio adaptation, Wells' *War of the Worlds* was far more than what the broadcaster called a Hallowe'en prank intended to give his audience the shivers. Wells wanted to astound his readers into thought – and in particular into thinking about what the experience of being invaded is like. The Martians do to England what the Victorians had done to Africa, Asia, and the South Pacific – and Wells intended that his fellow English imperialists taste a dose of their own medicine. He accomplished that moral chastisement not by sermonizing but by *depicting*. Sometimes the depiction is by darkly humorous analogy, as when the narrator, recalling how he reassured his wife that the English army would quickly dispose of the sluggish invaders, sets his complacency in the context of an earlier historical episode of extermination on Pitcairn Island: "So some respectable dodo in the Mauritius might have lorded it in his nest, and discussed the arrival of that shipful of pitiless sailors in want of animal food. 'We will peck them to death to-morrow, my dear'" (Wells 1993a: 73).

But even more often, Wells relied on spectacle and tableau – the "special effects" of literature – to apply shock therapy to inert minds. His Martian novel is full of such scenes: the sudden, flaming immolation of a deputation of villagers, pitifully and farcically carrying a white flag towards a pair of Martians armed with an unguessed-at laser technology; the sight of three-storey-high Martian fighting machines on articulated legs moving swiftly and at will through the suburban countryside; the unforgettable enactment of the evacuation of six million Londoners, in utter disorder and panic, to the north and the east; the clinical view of Martian anatomy through the eye of the narrator pressed up against a peephole in the wall of a collapsed house; the Martianizing of the English landscape as a fast-proliferating scarlet weed overruns gardens and chokes rivers. It should not be surprising that Wells eventually longed to make his mark in the new century's newest art form (an ambition he finally achieved in old age with quite mixed results in the 1936 film *Things to Come*) because his imagination was scenic and cinematic.

Wells' best fiction always has scenes of startling pictorial grandeur and fluidity, as if the camera in Wells' mind could not rest content with a single perspective. There are the anamorphic beast-men that emerge from the vivisectionist's operating room in *The Island of Dr. Moreau* who look sometimes nearly human and then, from another angle, appear disquietingly like the animals whose genetic inheritance surgery cannot fully eradicate. *The Invisible Man* has a stunning scene of metamorphosis in which we watch the color bleach out of Griffin's skin when he first assumes invisibility; then, even more dramatically, at the story's end the vigilantes who have beaten him to death watch the invisible man's corpse slowly return to visibility, with the terror and suffering of his face fully revealed. Wells was drawn especially to alternative perspectives from the air, to the panoramic shot that could disclose a view both grand and terrifying, that could not be gotten from down below and within a disaster. His account of the mass exodus from London in *The War of the Worlds*, for instance, is succeeded by a description of the entire event as it would appear to a balloonist hovering over the city of London, watching the growing mass of black poisonous gas unleashed by the Martians begin to blot out whole districts of the city map. The balloon gave way to the airplane as Wells' favored vehicle for this kind of cinematic technique: the view of a futuristic city as seen from a fighter plane in *When the Sleeper Wakes*, the aerial bombardment of Manhattan in *The War in the Air*, the dropping of an atomic bomb (a term Wells famously coined) on Berlin, as witnessed by the aviators in *The World Set Free* who feel they are "looking down upon the crater of a small volcano" from which "a shuddering star of evil splendour spurted and poured up smoke and flame towards them like an accusation" (Wells 1988: 71).

The visual grandeur of Wells' fictions is the product of great technical mastery of language and perspective in the service of the cleansing of perception. For all the wealth of his ideas, the first great modern writer of science fiction brought to his compositions a dramatic and even lyrical imagination that animated those ideas and transported readers into an urgent "sense of precariousness" that Brian Stableford has characterized as a hallmark of Wells' fiction (Stableford 1985: 64). Of all Wells' early masterpieces perhaps *The First Men in the Moon* – even more than the better-known *Time Machine* and *War of the Worlds* – most fully exemplifies the craft of his fiction. In his older years Wells tended to disparage his scientific romances, calling *The Time Machine*, for instance, an "undergraduate performance" (Wells 1931: ix). But he remained proud of *The First Men in the Moon*. In the Atlantic edition of his collected works in the mid-1920s he looked back on that romance as one that he had "sedulously polished" (Wells 1924: I, x).

Wells never surpassed the lyricism of *The First Men* in anything else he wrote. The sixth and seventh chapters, describing sunrise on the moon after fourteen days of frigid darkness and the sudden and rapid germination of lunar flora as the icy surface warms up, are the most celebrated instance of Wells' gift for animating a landscape. Vapors bubble and steam as the frozen atmosphere outgasses under the blazing sun; seeds crack open and thrust roots into the thawing ground; buds and spiky leaves swell and shoot up with precipitate speed. As he narrates these wonders the playwright Bedford asks, "How can I describe the thing I saw?" (Wells 2003: 58) And yet he does describe the ineffable – with vivid and energetic precision. "It was like a miracle, that growth. So, one must imagine, the trees and plants arose at the Creation and covered the desolation of the new-made earth" (Wells 2003: 60). Wells read *Paradise Lost* in the 1890s and he must have recalled Milton's account of the six days of Creation in Book VII – and the extraordinary third day, in particular, with grasses and vines and shrubs and trees bursting through the crust of the earth, rising, bristling, flourishing, dancing as the planet turns green. As a teenager Wells dreamed of how reviewers might one day boost his literary productions ("Beats *Paradise Lost* into eternal smash!" read one imagined blurb [Wells 1957: 14]). If the chapters on the lunar sunrise do not quite displace Milton, it is nonetheless true that a Miltonic vibrancy of language and vision energizes Wells' depiction of life on what was thought a dead world. Concluding his description, Bedford celebrates the pictorial splendor of the event. And then he calls specific attention to the unusual angle of vision from which, within a spherical glass spaceship, he has witnessed this miraculous growth. The paragraph is all about visionary grandeur:

Imagine it! Imagine that dawn! The resurrection of the frozen air, the stirring and quick-ening of the soil, and then this silent uprising of vegetation, this unearthly ascent of fleshiness and spikes. Conceive it all lit by a blaze that would make the intensest sun-light of earth seem watery and weak. And still around this stirring jungle, wherever there was shadow, lingered banks of bluish snow. And to have the picture of our impres-sion complete, you must bear in mind that we saw it all through a thick bent glass, dis-torting it as things are distorted by a lens, acute only in the centre of the picture, and very bright there, and towards the edges magnified and unreal. (Wells 2003: 60–1)

Wondrous as these passages of metamorphosis and visionary splendor are, as yet Wells has touched only the surface of the moon. The full implication of the unex-pected preposition in his title – Cavor and Bedford are to be the first men *in* the moon – emerges after the explorers peer down the enormous shaft disclosed when an automated lid slides open inside a lunar crater. They glimpse a world inside the moon, with faint lights and moving shapes far below in a labyrinth of tunnels and bridges, factories and transport systems, caves and towering staircases and an immense central sea. Wells had a fondness for such pits and passageways, as readers of *The Time Machine, The War of the Worlds, When the Sleeper Wakes*, and "The Door in the Wall" can see. And John Huntington has observed that in structuring his moon with a lush garden on the surface and a machine culture belowground Wells has recapitulated the oppo-sitions of day and night, upper-world paradise and lower-world hell of *The Time Machine* (Huntington 1982: 92–4). Here in *The First Men*, however, we have the unusual chance to see Wells pick up on an undeveloped possibility from a previous book. The world of the Morlocks in *The Time Machine* is never fully described. The Time Traveller spends one tantalizing chapter climbing down a vertical tunnel into their subterranean habitat; after a quick and rather unrevealing look around that dark underworld, illuminated only by matchlight, he scampers back up to the surface with Morlocks in hot pursuit. In *The First Men* Wells exploits the opportunity, which he threw away in *The Time Machine*, to describe an interior world in richly inventive detail.

The First Men is a sharply critical work in which Wells exposes not only the coarse-ness of Bedford's mercantile and colonialist interests in lunar exploration and the fail-ures of imagination in the scientist Cavor's singleminded devotion to "pure research," but also the tyranny of the dystopian society of the moon-dwellers – or Selenites, as Cavor at first calls them. In one of Wells' most famous passages of Swiftian two-edged satire Cavor encounters an example of lunar education that horrifies him. Young Selenites being trained for occupations as machine tenders have been packed into urns from which only their forearms protrude; their limbs are nourished intravenously while the rest of their bodies, having no functional purpose, are allowed to waste away. Cavor's discomfort at this sight indicts both lunar and terrestrial civilization:

It is quite unreasonable, I know, but such glimpses of the educational methods of these beings affect me disagreeably. I hope, however, that may pass off, and I may be able to see more of this aspect of their wonderful social order. That wretched-looking hand-tentacle sticking out of its jar seemed to have a sort of limp appeal for lost possibilities; it haunts me still, although, of course, it is really in the end a far more humane proceeding than our earthly method of leaving children to grow into human beings, and then making machines of them. (Wells 2003: 200–1)

The final scenes of *The First Men in the Moon* are brilliantly narrated through Cavor's telegraphed dispatches from the interior of the Moon, after Bedford has managed to escape alone back to Earth. We learn of Cavor's teaching English to the "mooneys," his tour of lunar cities, his observations of the extraordinary variety of insect-like physiology among the Selenites; we meet his tutors, who are also ominously his guards, with the deliciously silly Gilbert-and-Sullivan names of Phi-oo and Tsi-puff; and, most dramatically, we are ushered into the presence of the Moon's ruler, the Grand Lunar. Enthroned like Milton's Satan in blazing light in a vast, darkened chamber, the Grand Lunar is all brain: a colossal mass many yards in diameter and resembling "an opaque, featureless bladder" atop a pair of "minute elfin eyes" and a tiny, residual body of pale, shriveled limbs. The grandeur of this monarch is, as even the slow-witted Cavor can see, inseparable from his grotesquerie: "It was great. Its was pitiful" (Wells 2003: 208). Cavor's several interviews with the Grand Lunar result in disclosures of the history of human irrationality, depravity, nationalism, and conquest. When at last Cavor starts explaining the practice of human warfare the Grand Lunar is both perplexed and incredulous. He tells him to "make me see pictures" to help comprehend this inconceivable phenomenon. Cavor, with all the naive complacency of Lemuel Gulliver standing before the King of Brobdingnag, readily obliges:

> I told him of the first orders and ceremonies of war, of warnings and ultimatums, and the marshaling and marching of troops. I gave him an idea of manoeuvres and positions and battles joined. I told him of sieges and assaults, of starvation and hardship in trenches, and of sentinels freezing in the snow. I told him of routs and surprises, and desperate last stands and faint hopes, and the pitiless pursuit of fugitives and the dead upon the field. I told, too, of the past, of invasions and massacres, of the Huns and Tartars, and the wars of Mahomet and the Caliphs, and of the Crusades. (Wells 2003: 216)

In fact, the more Cavor reveals about human conflict, the more the Grand Lunar requires cooling sprays to be applied to his fevered brain – and the greater jeopardy Cavor creates for himself. Once the Grand Lunar understands that the secret of space travel rests entirely with Cavor and once he makes the logical inference from the history of human voyages of exploration on their own planet to the likely future consequences should more humans come to the Moon, Cavor's fate is sealed. Cavor's last messages are garbled and fragmentary as the Selenites apparently start blocking his transmissions to Earth, and the concluding silence is both inevitable and funereal. The ending of *The First Men in the Moon* bears out Patrick Parrinder's suggestion that in Wells' best works justice is more poetic than scientific or cognitive (Parrinder 1995: 11).

Wells was thirty-five when his lunar fantasy was published and the trajectory of his career was finally beginning to define itself. He would not just be a scientific romancer. In *The First Men*, as in *When the Sleeper Wakes*, there are clear glimpses of the kind of writing that would preoccupy Wells for his remaining forty-five years: discussion novels, cultural prophecy, utopian speculation. The science fiction Wells wrote in the early years of the twentieth century is marked – some would say, is infected – by those new preoccupations. *The Food of the Gods* (1904), *In the Days of the Comet* (1906), *The War in the Air* (1908), and *The World Set Free* (1914) all have more heavy-handed designs on the reader than his earlier fictions. In *The Food of the Gods*, his story of the invention of a "boomfood" that looses giants on the world, Wells' allegorical intent thrusts itself on the reader more crudely than in the finely tuned grotesque romances of *The Island of Dr. Moreau* and *The Invisible Man*. But even here flashes of Swiftian wit persistently light up the narrative, and Wells' brilliance at lurid scene-painting invigorates the ghastly incident in which an unsuspecting London science teacher puts his bare arm into a pond in which the larvae of water beetles, having ingested some of the growth-enhancing food, have metamorphosed into aggressive, muscular, snapping, blood-sucking monsters.

Throughout his long career Wells never really lost his gift for science-fictional imagining, though he chose to use it only infrequently after the first years of the new century. One of his incomparable short stories, "The Door in the Wall" (1906), and a very late screenplay for an unshot film titled "The New Faust" (1936) are reminders of the persistence of fantastic romance in his work. His long futuristic dream-vision of 1933, *The Shape of Things to Come*, became the basis for the visually splendid though rhetorically bombastic 1936 film *Things to Come*, perhaps the most interesting failure in the history of science fiction cinema. As late as 1937 he was still exploring the notion of an invasion from Mars, though this time through a form of psychic "body-snatching" rather than with the machinery and monsters of *The War of the Worlds*. The protagonist of *Star-Begotten* actually allows Wells a moment of mischievous reflexivity, when his earlier and more famous Martian novel is semi-recalled: "Some of you may have read a book called *The War of the Worlds* – I forget who wrote it – Jules Verne, Conan Doyle, one of those fellows" (Wells 1937: 62).

The real joke here is that it is the author of *Star-Begotten* who has largely been forgotten, not the author of *The War of the Worlds*. For readers in the twenty-first century, Wells' great scientific romances, written mostly in the last years of the nineteenth, will continue to haunt and stimulate the imagination. In certain respects they will seem period pieces (village life in *The Invisible Man*, the male clubbiness in *The Time Machine*, the 1890s Mars mania of *The War of the Worlds*), and the scientific premises of most of them will be risible. But even in their own day that was true, as Wells was always ready to acknowledge: he depended on an "ingenious use of scientific patter," he wrote in a preface to a collection of his science fiction, to engage the reader's imagination not in the scientific ideas and issues themselves but in new ways of seeing and assessing human behavior, new angles of vision on familiar shortcomings (Parrinder and Philmus 1980: 241–2). He had a genius for projecting perennial dilemmas about human nature onto Martians or moon-dwellers or Morlocks or invisible men. That is where the grandeur of Wells' writing comes into play. He had some reservations about how long his fiction would, or should, last. And in a famous scene in *The Time Machine* his traveller passes through a library in the far future and observes the books of the past crumbled into dust. But if Wells himself had a skeptical view of all forms of immortality, including literary immortality, there still may be reason to reflect on the verdict of the great Argentine writer Jorge Luis Borges who predicted that the early books of Wells would enter "the general memory of the species and even transcend the fame of their creator or the extinction of the language in which they were written" (Parrinder 1972: 332).

REFERENCES AND FURTHER READING

Bergonzi, Bernard (1961) *The Early H.G. Wells: A Study of the Scientific Romances.* Manchester: Manchester University Press.

Conrad, Joseph (1986–1990) *Collected Letters*, Vol. II: 1898–1902; Vol. IV, 1908–1911. (eds.) Frederick R. Karl and Laurence Davies. Cambridge: Cambridge University Press.

Crossley, Robert (ed.) (1982) "The Letters of Olaf Stapledon and H.G. Wells, 1931–1942," in *Science Fiction Dialogues*, (ed.) Gary Wolf. Chicago: Academy Chicago.

Crossley, Robert (1986) *H.G. Wells.* Mercer Island, WA: Starmont.

Draper, Michael (1987) *H.G. Wells.* London: Macmillan.

Huntington, John (1982) *The Logic of Fantasy: H.G. Wells and Science Fiction.* New York: Columbia University Press.

Le Guin, Ursula K. (1992) *The Language of the Night: Essays on Fantasy and Science Fiction*, revised ed. New York: Harper Collins.

Lewis, C.S. (1965) *Out of the Silent Planet* (1938). New York: Macmillan.

McConnell, Frank (1981) *The Science Fiction of H.G. Wells.* New York and Oxford: Oxford University Press.

Parrinder, Patrick (ed.) (1972) *H.G. Wells: The Critical Heritage.* London and Boston: Routledge and Kegan Paul.

Parrinder, Patrick (1995) *Shadows of the Future: H.G. Wells, Science Fiction and Prophecy.* Liverpool: Liverpool University Press.

Parrinder, Patrick and Robert Philmus (eds) (1980) *H.G. Wells' Literary Criticism.* Brighton: Harvester Press.

Philmus, Robert and David Y. Hughes (eds) (1975) *Early Writings in Science and Science Fiction by H.G. Wells.* Berkeley and London: University of California Press.

Slusser, George, Patrick Parrinder, and Daniele Chatelain (eds) (2001) *H.G. Wells' Perennial Time Machine.* Athens, GA and London: University of Georgia Press.

Smith, David C. (1986) *H.G. Wells Desperately Mortal: A Biography.* New Haven and London: Yale University Press.

Stableford, Brian (1985) *Scientific Romance in Britain 1890–1950.* London: Fourth Estate.

Tolkien, J.R.R. (1992) "The Notion Club Papers," in Christopher Tolkien (ed.) *Sauron Defeated: The History of Middle Earth*, Vol. IX. Boston and London: Houghton Mifflin.

Wagar, W. Warren (2004) *H.G. Wells: Traversing Time.* Middletown, CT: Wesleyan University Press.

Wells, H.G. (1924–1928) *The Works of H.G. Wells* (The Atlantic Edition), 28 Volumes. New York: Scribner.

——(1931) *The Time Machine: An Invention* (1895) New York: Random House.

——(1937) *Star-Begotten: A Biological Fantasia.* New York: Viking.

——(1957) *The Desert Daisy*, (ed.) Gordon N. Ray. Urbana: University of Illinois Press.

——(1987) *The Definitive Time Machine: A Critical Edition of H.G. Wells' Scientific Romance*, (ed.) Harry M. Geduld. Bloomington: Indiana University Press.

——(1988) *The World Set Free: A Story of Mankind* (1914). London: Hogarth Press.

——(1993a) *A Critical Edition of The War of the Worlds: H.G. Wells' Scientific Romance* (1898) (eds) David Y. Hughes and Harry M. Geduld. Bloomington: Indiana University Press.

——(1993b) *The Island of Doctor Moreau: A Variorum Text* (1896), (ed.) Robert M. Philmus. Athens and London: University of Georgia Press.

——(2003) *The First Men in the Moon* (1901). New York: Modern Library.

24

Isaac Asimov

John Clute

There can be no question that, in the years since he died in 1992, the reputation of Isaac Asimov as a central figure of twentieth-century American SF has undergone a serious diminishment. The reasons for this are numerous, both with reference to any just estimate of his interest and stature as a writer, and as well to the increasingly clear fact that what we may call classic SF, which is pre-eminently the kind of SF Asimov wrote, has become an honored part of the history of the genre. In other words, the kind of SF Asimov wrote no longer exists, except in the exiguous form of works written specifically to imitate it – these works, including some recent novels set "in the world of" Isaac Asimov, are of little but nostalgic interest; and many of them are in fact franchise texts, written for hire by "sharecropper" authors for the owners of enterprises like *Star Trek* or *Star Wars*. When as twenty-first-century students of the genre we attempt to read Asimov, our initial perceptions of his work will almost certainly be clouded: by the parched and marmoreal tone of his own late works, which almost read like self-novelizations; and by the great cloud of franchise work in the "style" of classic SF, work written by authors ill-at-ease with their subordinate role in the enterprise, and ill-at-ease in their attempts to recreate a dead mode in a new century.

It is not the case with his great contemporaries and rivals, Arthur C. Clarke and Robert A. Heinlein; but with Isaac Asimov we do have a task of excavation on our hands before we can reach the pure writer, the purveyor of some of the ideas and tropes that fixed SF on its course for two decades or more from around 1940–5 until the poison chalice of Sputnik finally began to discolor the body politic of the genre (at a point when classic SF was beginning to gain more commercial success than it ever enjoyed when it was healthy). Clarke is and was a man-of-the-world, widely traveled, in touch with scientists and fellow writers across the globe; and his sense of the Near Future, though tinged with Scientific Romance melancholy, was detailed and in touch. Heinlein, whose relationship to Asimov was far more difficult (for Asimov), was also a man who clearly knew the world, and knew how to relate to other human beings.

Far more than either of these figures, Asimov was a figure intrinsic to the subculture for which he wrote.

Indeed, it is quite possible to argue that his was the default voice of the genre, the voice of SF speaking to itself during those years when SF was written for those who elected to read it (in 1945, SF was clearly identifiable through market range, through the specific magazines which published it, and through its readers, who for obvious reasons were always aware that they were reading SF, and for similarly obvious reasons knew, often personally, who else was reading SF). The Asimovian voice was denotative, imageless, impersonal, clear, positive, cognitively soothing, and oddly conspiratorial. It was a voice that seemed to convey an underlying security of worldview and vision so persuasive that it sometimes seems to have lain at the heart of American science fiction for most of the twentieth century; in fact, of course, that Asimovian voice of reason (or reasonableness) dominated the genre only for a relatively short period, a span that also marked the prime of his own career as a writer of fiction. These were the year's of science fiction's pomp, the years when its participants felt that important messages about the nature and future of the world could be shared with readers of a like mind. It was a time to advocate a future bigger than the past; and cleaner. It was a time to talk our way into the future.

To those readers, Asimov spoke, for a while, with huge authority. And he spoke clearly. The secrets of his fiction – just like the secrets of the universe itself – could be shared; the talking heads who filled most of his pages were mouthpieces of truths – of patterns of history – greater than they were. What they represented and advocated, what science fiction readers understood when they read Asimov, everyone might understand tomorrow. If there was a conspiratorial tone to his fiction, and to science fiction as a whole, it was an Open Conspiracy, and the only real edge the conspirators gained was of a sort of insider trading: because they were being told things first. Though (unlike Clarke or Heinlein) he did not in fact engage in much near-future extrapolation, Asimov did all the same manage, for the decade or so after the end of the Second World War, to convey a sense that history-to-come was in safe hands.

It is certainly true that Asimov published his most famous story before 1945 – "Nightfall" first appeared in 1941 in John W. Campbell's then-revolutionary *Astounding Science Fiction* – and that the two series which occupied most of his creative energies for most of the rest of his life – the Foundation stories and novels; and the Robot stories and novels – were also initiated around the same time, for the same magazine. But if readers of the twenty-first century are to gain any real appreciation of his work, they will not only have to dig back down through the badlands of contemporary retro-SF; they will also have to concentrate on works written within a narrow chronological band, from 1945 to perhaps as late as 1958. Asimov's first stories are gawky, awkward, pushed, sophomoric; to a reader of today it is all too apparent that they were written by an extremely intelligent but vastly inexperienced, very young man whose understanding of the world was minimal. He was what we now think of as a geek. By his own account (Asimov 1979), he was an immensely ambitious, pushy, loud, intellectually precocious New Yorker; he also, it seems, fought terrors all his life (we will return to the highly significant fact that he was an agoraphobe), perhaps the greatest of those terrors and insecurities (after his fear of the open air and of heights) being his fairly patent inability to understand or to come to terms with the fact that, with all his skill and intelligence and huge energy and assiduity, he never quite became the number one figure in the field.

With his strong New York accent, Isaac Asimov was the very model of an urban American, and the fact that he was born in Russia (in 1920) always seemed ironic. By 1923, however, his family had emigrated, and he was raised in New York City, which he rarely left in later life, at least in part because his adamant refusal to fly (we have already mentioned his agoraphobia in other contexts). Having been raised in a milieu of intense ambition, he was from an early age conscious of the need to establish himself in a genuine career (his family did not think of writing as real work). At Columbia University he took a B.S. in chemistry in 1939, an M.A. in 1941, and the Ph.D. in 1948, after war service. He then became an instructor in Biochemistry at Boston University School of Medicine, becoming an Associate Professor in 1955.

In a "fair" universe, even with a professional career to manage, he might have been the father of modern SF. He lived and loved and wrote SF from his early teens (he never came to SF; he, and modern SF, were born together). He began his long publishing career in 1939, the first year of what has generally been reckoned to be the Golden Age of the genre, at least in its American form. He became almost immediately famous within the field for "Nightfall"; for the invention of a plausible vision of robots as nonmonstrous adjuncts to human civilization; and for the domestication of the rickety empires of earlier space opera in the form of a galactic empire whose history rewrote in large the history of the Roman Empire. By 1945 or so, he was creating his paradigm robot and empire tales (a fact somewhat concealed by the pattern of book publication early genre SF writers had to submit to for several years after the end of the Second World War), and in the 1950s wrote two or three novels that must be read today by anyone who wishes to understand the roots of modern SF.

At about this point he was afflicted by a crisis of ambition. Two decades of producing science fiction had made him famous (though not quite famous enough) in a field looked down upon by his professional colleagues; he had come to the end of the road, as far as he could then predict, of both the Robot stories and the Foundation epic. He published several volumes of short fiction, including *The Martian Way* (1955) and *Earth Is Room Enough* (1957), and his finest single novel, *The End of Eternity* (1955), a singleton given over to a dark-hued narrative analysis of the implications of time travel on the structure and texture of reality – after a complex series of events, the novel climaxes in an atomic war. But here he seemed to stall. In 1958 he decided that he must transform his career, announced his retirement as a writer of fiction, and gave up active teaching at Boston University, receiving no salary but retaining his professorship (he was made a full Professor in 1979, but remained inactive as an academic). Of the hundreds of books he published between 1958 and 1982, only three were novels, though one, *The Gods Themselves* (1972) won both the Hugo and Nebula Awards for that year. The novel itself, with its touchingly antiquated sense of how science might be done in the decades after 1972, has not worn well. The rest of his prolific output – up to ten books a year – comprised a series of works of scientific popularization, which made him a household word in the USA, and which also made him rich. He returned actively to fiction writing in 1982. Though ill-health dogged him from about 1985 (he died of AIDS caught from an infected blood transfusion), his final years were full of honors. By the time of his death he had published nearly 500 books, an astonishing figure, even given the fact that to come close to this total – he published three collections, successively entitled *Opus 100* (1969), *Opus 200* (1979) and *Opus 300* (1984), and he was extremely eager to reach 500 – he had to include a very large number of anthologies of which he was only one of several listed editors.

But Asimov never did become the undisputed father of the modern genre. 1939 was the year in which Robert A. Heinlein began to publish his own first novels and stories, also in Campbell's *Astounding Science Fiction*, and it was Heinlein, with his stylistic flair and his mesmerizing grasp of the potentials of the new form, who became and for half a century remained the father-figure of the field. For those 50 years, Asimov was the younger brother, always somehow in the shadow of the fluent, naturally dominant, highly social Heinlein; brash, boastful, and workaholic, though in fact a solitary man who rarely left his apartment, Asimov seemed always on the verge of displacing his older contemporary as the dominant figure in the tight communal world of SF, but he never quite accomplished the feat. By the time Heinlein died, in 1988, Asimov was far beyond his prime.

The reason for Asimov's failure was almost certainly related to his greatest strength as a writer: the utter clarity with which he told stories in a manner too barren of obscuring imagery to seem quite human. He had no gift of description; landscape – indeed the whole of the outdoors – either bored him or evoked his agoraphobia or both; and from acts of heroism to acts of love, the tangled organon of human behavior and interaction seemed a puzzle to him. It did not sufficiently matter that through the proper exercise of his stylistic and intellectual clarity, he became one of the century's greatest and most prolific popularizers of science and the arts. It did not matter enough that – without ever telling a lie, or avoiding a thorny problem in physics or astronomy or biology or half a dozen other fields – he made everything seem easy; even books in fields unrelated to science, like his *Annotated Guide to Gilbert and Sullivan* (1988), were illuminating. The work that counted in the end, which was the fiction, suffered fatally from chill.

In his nonfiction, then, the impulse was to seek a premise to argue the world from, and elucidate, in clear, the implications of that premise. That this impulse worked seriously less well in fiction may have had something to do with his partial retirement as a creative writer between about 1958 and 1980; and his gingerly attempts to introduce females and sex into his late fiction may have been at least in part inspired by some sense that something was missing from the earlier.

For the first decade of his career, Asimov wrote nothing but stories (Heinlein's instant and remarkable success as a novelist may help explain this particular abstention) but there was no way an ambitious young science fiction writer in 1940 could abstain from confronting the intense and dictatorial presence of the field's dominating father-figure, John W. Campbell Jr, in whose *Astounding Science Fiction* most of the significant work of the 1940s first appeared. Asimov soon became identified as a Campbell writer, and it was Campbell who suggested to him the premise and plot of "Nightfall", the single most popular story ever published by an SF magazine. The story as Asimov developed it embodied the essence of the genre's appeal to the conceptual imagination, but it may be that the undoubted power of its telling, despite some real awkwardnesses in the narrative, comes from the fact that it was an ideal story for an agoraphobe to write: what (Asimov suggested in language which made the idea enticingly legible to his readers) if there were a planet whose complex orbit around a multiple-sun system ensured that it was always day; that there was always some sun shining in the sky. The problem is that civilization on this planet seems cyclical – every 2,000 years something terrible happens, and the world descends into barbarism. We slowly learn that it may be the case that once every 2,000 years an extremely complex eclipse might block all sunlight from the planet, for an hour or two. As the story progresses, the predicted eclipse does occur, bringing darkness and a view of the innumerable stars. Suddenly the inhabitants of the planet realize something of the immensity of the universe, realize how intolerably minute their own lives are; and they all, immediately, go insane, bringing civilization to an end for another cycle. The presumption that a sudden affliction of perspective would drive everyone insane is, pretty clearly, an agoraphobe's privy nightmare; but the story itself remains quite astonishingly powerful.

In its relative concision, and in its raw effectiveness, "Nightfall" was, perhaps, a good example of beginner's luck. Certainly no single tale Asimov wrote over the next few years had a similar impact; what one remembers from this period is not the individual works, whose callowness was not always fully concealed by their tone of triumphant reasonableness, but the overall concepts being gradually unfolded. As already noted, it was at this time (and also in close consultation with Campbell) that Asimov evolved the premises that shaped his two most enduring contributions to the genre, the Robot stories and the Foundation series.

The Robot sequence demonstrates, throughout its long life, an almost infernal ingenuity on the part of Asimov, as it must have become clear to him fairly soon that he had, in a sense, backed the wrong horse. The Near Future, he must soon have guessed, was going to be shaped by the manipulation of information, primarily through the evolution of the computer; not by the relatively simple application of knowledge through the medium of the robot. (The robots that do exist in the twenty-first century are applications of the information revolution; not the other way round.) Asimov gets around his wrong guess in two ways.

The first tactic is very famous. The "Three Laws of Robotics," which Campbell and Asimov formulated in 1940, had little to do with the infant science of robotics, as their actual imprinting into a primitive robot "positronic" brain would have been (and will be for an indeterminate period) inconceivably difficult to enact. Their strength was in fact a story strength; for they worked very effectively to establish some usable literary protocols for the treatment of artificial creatures, and indeed in written science fiction their promulgation sounded the death knell for certain kinds of sensationalism about killer robots and the like. For many years, despite the impossibly huge problem of real-life implementation, the Three Laws underwrote almost all SF discourse on the subject of mobile artificial beings, and whatever their intrinsic scientific worth they have been influential as well in the ferment of thought that generated the field of cybernetics. These are the Laws:

(1)   A robot may not injure a human being, or, through inaction, allow a human being to come to harm.
(2)   A robot must obey the orders given it by human beings except where such orders would conflict with the First Law.
(3)   A robot must protect its own existence as long as such protection does not conflict with the First or Second Law.

From the first, readers tended to concentrate their attention on the Laws and how they were applied. Very effectively, Asimov used their iterations as a kind of abacus for the calculation of possible robot stories, stories that necessarily took the possibility of imprinting these Laws for granted. For half a century, no matter how far one of his tales might seem to stretch them, the initial code always stood revealed, and justified, in the end, no matter how jesuitical the reasoning needed to become to reach that satisfactory conclusion. The mostly early stories collected variously in *I, Robot* (1950) and *The Rest of the Robots* (1964), and the novels of his prime like *The Caves of Steel* (1954) and *The Naked Sun* (1957), all presented an image, or vision, of the artificial being as being involved in a series of ultimately successful negotiations with the iron law of the Laws in order to remain helpful servants of humanity.

It is here that one may examine Asimov's second tactic to box the circle of the wrong guess. From the very first days, much of the actual narrative focus of the Robot stories has not been on robotics at all – not even, for that matter, directly on the Three Laws themselves – but on a long conflict between robots (and those who make and use them) and the very large number of people who irrationally despise and fear them. Story after story is built on this conflict (a conflict contemporary readers may find hard to fathom, partly because of the very success of the Robot series as a demonstration that "good" robots can exist); and in story after story, robots themselves are written in a fashion that asks for sympathetic reader identification.

By the time of the great robot novels of the 1950s, this tactic had matured enormously, and in the figures of Earth detective Elijah Bailey and his robot partner R. Daneel Olivaw we have reached a point where our identification with the "side" of the robots is complete, and the Three Laws become a subtext not deeply examined, beyond rendering Olivaw, in the last analysis, strangely docile. This subordination of Olivaw, and other advanced robots, did not in fact weather particularly well over the years, as advances in the imagining of Artificial Intelligence significantly darkened the reader response of human beings to creatures, whether or not artificial, more intelligent and more capable than we are. When Asimov returned late in life to the question of the Robot in compilations like *Robot Dreams* (1986) or Robot Visions (1990), he tended to hedge his bets. And late novels like *The Robots of Dawn* (1983) or *Robots and Empire* (1985) began cautiously to suggest that humanity might have a greater need for keepers than for servants. It is in these late titles that the long conflict between humans and robots is resolved, and it is only here that the Three Laws receive their ultimate application: superior robots from R. Daneel Olivaw onwards, in order to obey the Laws according to their sophisticated understanding of what the Laws truly demand of them, will need to protect interstellar humanity from itself. In order for this to happen, in order to protect humanity from the horrific consequences of an unmediated fall of the Galactic Empire, the two Foundations will have to be created.

There are no robots in the main Foundation sequence, that series of stories and novellas published during the 1940s, and released in book form as *Foundation* (1951), *Foundation and Empire* (1952), and *Second Foundation* (1953). Known from the first as the Foundation Trilogy, it is the first multivolume sequence to appear in the SF world after the release of E.E. Smith's great Lensman space opera sequence. Set around 60,000 years after our era, the Trilogy immediately established itself as the central SF description of the temporal and physical nature of the human-dominated galactic civilization that has served as a template for innumerable SF stories ever since. But it was only decades after the original stories first saw print that Asimov attempted to conflate his Near-Future Robot stories with the Foundation epic.

The first Foundation stories were written at the same time as the first Robot stories (though they remained, as we have implied, entirely distinct for decades), the earliest tales later assembled in *Foundation* being published in 1942. Just as he made sense of robots in the Robot sequence, in the Foundation and Empire sequence Asimov cast a similarly rational eye upon the traditional world of American space opera, taming its ray-gun, Ruritanian excesses through a sustained and sober use of historical analogy: specifically, he based his long description of the fall of a sclerotic galactic empire as a rewriting of the decline and fall of the Roman empire. The city-planet Trantor is, of course, Rome. The two Foundations, established by psychohistorian Hari Seldon to tweak the laws of psychohistory which state that the coming Fall is inevitable, are an analogue of Christianity, though there is no religious content whatsoever in the Asimovian vision. The tweak they effect upon the course of galactic history effects a reducing of the Interregnum after Trantor falls from many thousand years down to a mere millennium. The first Foundation – ostensibly established to house efforts to write an encyclopedia of the galaxy (Asimov's disinclination to think in terms of information revolutions makes any point in his work where information is manipulated seem unduly quaint) – proves a successful tweaker of the decline, though its representatives have been deliberated excluded by the now-long-dead Seldon from any knowledge of the laws of psychohistory itself, in order to protect their self-esteem, and for other reasons.

But when a mutant human – known as the Mule – makes his presence felt in Foundation and Empire, the First Foundation is comparatively helpless; only the Second Foundation, which exists in a secret location and which houses scholars fully apprised of the laws of psychohistory, will be able to counter the rogue effects of the Mule. Their success in so doing provides the real climax to the trilogy; *Second Foundation*, which comprises two long novellas whose protagonists obsessively seek the true home of the Second Foundation, is a kind of coda. It is better written than earlier volumes, but the long attempts to work out the location of the Second Foundation, through analysis of Seldon's ancient statement that it was located at the other end of the galaxy from the First Foundation, tiresomely echo some of the more intricate logic-chopping exercises in interpretation of the Three Laws. The ultimate solution is simple: the other end of the galaxy from the remote semirural planet that houses the First Foundation is in fact Trantor. This revelation, which ends the trilogy, works well narratively; but in retrospect seems an unduly simple solution to a conundrum that is supposed to have aroused the best efforts of generations of scholars.

Despite its seeming simplicity of analysis, the Foundation Trilogy does offer some remarkably clear-cut speculations on the nature of political and cultural decadence; and in the Foundation/Christianity analogy, Asimov gives a cogent description of the dynamic interplay between a barbarian world and a goal-oriented clerisy. The greatest problem for contemporary readers may be the scientism contained in the concept of psychohistory, whose precepts are never specifically laid down. Asimov's implicit explanation for this failure to state any of these laws is that the only relevant way to express them is mathematically. Whatever intuitive understanding of human behavior Seldon may be assumed to have gained, his wisdom is dramatized in the text solely through fixed appearances of a prerecorded simulacrum who proves that his predictions that certain crises are about to erupt are correct. A second, related problem resides in the nature of the rule of the Foundation itself: making predictions about the working out of history leads inevitably to attempts to preshape events so that the predictions will (as of course they must) come true.

There have been many stories and novels which have reflected the influence of Asimov's quietly told but all the same intoxicating vision of the power of thought over vast realms of empire. Of these, Donald Kingsbury's *Psychohistorical Crisis* (2001) is the most deeply interesting; though Kingsbury was apparently not given permission to set his work directly in the Asimovian creation, there can be no question that the galactic empire he has created, along with scholar-empire that succeeds it, amount to a close analysis of the arguments and assumptions of the famous trilogy. This analysis of the Foundation Trilogy as a thought experiment is clearly conducted with great affection, and constitutes perhaps the most remarkable homage any SF writer has ever received from another SF writer. At its deepest creative level, Kingsbury's novel not only lovingly dissects Asimov's thought; what may be the most remarkable accomplishment of this vast tale is its quite moving replication of the Asimov's style, the default style of which we have spoken: the calm cajoling relentless voice of the SF of half a century ago, when it seemed so tantalizingly possible that that tomorrow was something we could understand; that the future was going to work out.

For Asimov himself, there would be no safe return to that secure world. *The Gods Themselves*, as we have already indicated, displays a deep unease about how to depict the near future; its remoteness from anything like the congestion and multifacetedness of late twentieth-century reality has the effect of forcing readers to understand that Asimov was, in fact, always remote. His talking-head protagonists, calmly dissecting what was about to happen but never seeming to participate in these great events, now seem strangely touching; they seem, to a reader today, despite the slightly complacent tone of reasonableness they convey, deeply evasive of the world.

All the same, in 1982, he returned in full spate to his first love. He had maintained strong personal links with the science fiction world, and when he began writing novels again, he produced work designed to demonstrate both his contemporaneity and an unbroken continuity with the past. To accomplish this, and to take advantage of the marketing revolution which had transformed science fiction from a minor and eccentric genre into a source of bestseller titles, he decided to return to his Robot and Foundation books, and to amalgamate them, through a sequence of large and ambitious sequels, into one giant entity, though which a future history of unparalleled scope might emerge. The late Robot novels, as we have seen, work towards an understanding that, in order to protect humanity from the fall of Empire, something which is effectively the entire Foundation sequence will have to be created. The retrofitting into contemporary texts of this transformation of the Foundation series shapes the remaining Foundation texts, which include *Foundation's Edge* (1982), *Foundation and Earth* (1986), *Prelude to Foundation* (1988), and *Forward the Foundation* (1993). Critical response was mixed, for it seemed that Asimov had retained in old age the remote discursiveness of his prime, but had lost the concision that graced his early work, though he continued to seem to clean the world by thinking about it. Nor was that remoteness restricted to novelist techniques; unlike Clarke and Heinlein, his great contemporaries to whom we have already referred, Asimov saw the world as through a camera obscura. The world he saw was rendered in blacks and whites and grays. He saw the world from deep indoors.

He was a man of ample ego and, despite his reclusiveness, wide friendships. For years all the fiction he had ever written remained in print. The field honored him repeatedly with Hugo and Nebula Awards. Ever since 1958, he had written a monthly science column for a science fiction magazine, without a single break. When it was announced, therefore, that he had been forced in 1990 to abandon work half-way through the composition of the 400th column, a feeling of premonitory sadness swept the field; his death followed soon after. It was, in a way, the death of SF. The speculative fiction that now dominates depicts planets far removed from Isaac Asimov's clean orbs.

References and Further Reading

Selected fiction by Isaac Asimov

The Robot Series
I, Robot (Hicksville, NY: Gnome Press, 1950)
The Caves of Steel (Garden City, NY: Doubleday, 1954)
The Naked Sun (Garden City, NY: Doubleday, 1957)
The Rest of the Robots (Garden City, NY: Doubleday, 1964)
The Robots of Dawn (Garden City, NY: Doubleday, 1983)
Robots and Empire (Garden City, NY: Doubleday, 1985)
Robot Dreams (New York: Berkley Books, 1986)
Robot Visions (New York: Roc, 1990)

The Foundation Series
Foundation (New York: Gnome Press, 1951)
Foundation and Empire (New York: Gnome Press, 1952)
Second Foundation (New York: Gnome Press, 1953)
Foundation's Edge (Garden City, NY: Doubleday, 1982)
Foundation and Earth (Garden City, NY: Doubleday, 1986)
Prelude to Foundation (Garden City, NY: Doubleday, 1988)

Forward the Foundation (New York: Doubleday, 1993)

Other novels and collections
Pebble in the Sky (Garden City, NY: Doubleday, 1950)
The Stars, Like Dust (Garden City, NY: Doubleday, 1951)
The Currents of Space (Garden City, NY: Doubleday, 1952)
The Martian Way, and Other Stories (Garden City, NY: Doubleday, 1955)
The End of Eternity (Garden City, NY: Doubleday, 1955)
Nightfall, and Other Stories (Garden City, NY: Doubleday, 1969)
The Gods Themselves (Garden City, NY: Doubleday, 1972)
Buy Jupiter (Garden City, NY: Doubleday, 1975)
The Bicentennial Man and Other Stories (Garden City, NY: Doubleday, 1976)
The Winds of Change (Garden City, NY: Doubleday, 1983)
The Asimov Chronicles: Fifty Years of Isaac Asimov (Arlington Heights, IL: Dark Harvest, 1989)

Other references and further reading

Allen, Roger M. (1996) *Isaac Asimov's Utopia.* London: Millennium.

Asimov, Isaac (1979) *In Memory Yet Green: The Autobiography of Isaac Asimov, 1920–1954.* New York: Doubleday.

——(1980) *In Joy Still Felt: An Autobiography of Isaac Asimov, 1954–1978.* Garden City, NY: Doubleday.

——(1984) *Asimov on Science Fiction.* London: Panther.

——(1989) *The Asimov Chronicles: Fifty Years of Isaac Asimov.* London: Century.

——(1994) *I, Asimov: A Memoir.* New York: Doubleday.

——(2002) *It's Been a Good Life*, ed. Janet Jeppson. Amherst, NY: Prometheus Books.

Fiedler, Jean, and Jim Mele (1982) *Isaac Asimov.* New York: Ungar.

Goble, Neil (1972) *Asimov Analysed.* Baltimore: Mirage.

Green, Scott E. (1995) *Isaac Asimov: An Annotated Bibliography of the Asimov Collection at Boston University.* Westport, CT: Greenwood Press.

Gunn, James E. (1996) *Isaac Asimov, The Foundations of Science Fiction*, revised edn. New York: Oxford University Press.

Hassler, Donald M. (1991) *Isaac Asimov: Starmont Reader's Guide.* Mercer Island, WA: Starmont House.

Ingersoll, Earl G. (1987) "A Conversation with Isaac Asimov." *Science Fiction Studies* 14 (March), 68–77.

Kingsbury, Donald (2001) *Psychohistorical Crisis*. New York: Tor.

Miller, Marjorie M. (1972) *Isaac Asimov; A Checklist of Works Published in the United States, March 1939–May 1972*. Kent, OH: Kent State University Press.

Olander, Joseph D. and Martin Harry Greenberg (eds) (1977) *Isaac Asimov*. Edinburgh: Paul Harris.

Palumbo, Donald E. (2002) *Chaos Theory, Asimov's Foundation and Robots, and Herbert's "Dune": The Fractal Aesthetic of Epic Science Fiction*. Westport, CT: Greenwood Press.

Patrouch, Joseph F. Jr. (1974) *The Science Fiction of Isaac Asimov*. Garden City, NY: Doubleday.

Portelli, Alessandro (1980) "The Three Laws of Robotics." *Science Fiction Studies* 7 (July), 150–6.

Touponce, William F. (1991) *Isaac Asimov*. Boston: Twayne.

White, Michael (1994) *Asimov: the Unauthorized Life*. London: Millennium

Wilcox, Clyde (1990) "The Greening of Isaac Asimov: Cultural Change and Political Futures." *Extrapolation* 31.i (Spring), 54–62.

25

John Wyndham: The Facts
of Life Sextet

David Ketterer

"JOHN WYNDHAM – Born circa 14 February, 1949." This typescript statement, from one of the several capsule bios that John Wyndham Parkes Lucas Beynon Harris (born on July 10, 1903) prepared (bios now preserved in the John Wyndham Archive at the University of Liverpool), presumably refers to the approximate date (circa St. Valentine's Day) that he decided to attach the name by which he would become best known to the typescript of "The Reluctant Eve." Written on November 22, 1948 and published in *Amazing Stories* in September 1950 as "The Eternal Eve" (an inferior imposed title) this story (aimed to some degree at a female readership) was the first of his titles to use the "John Wyndham" byline. Of course, it was not until the 1951 publication of *The Day of the Triffids* by John Wyndham that the English-speaking world would take notice. *Triffids* is the first published of his extended attempts to separate from Gernsbackian "science fiction" aimed at a fan readership. He would eventually describe them as "logical" or "believable fantasies" for the general reader.

His previous, much less well-known publications, four novels published in England before the war (beginning with the suppressed *Curse of the Burdens* of 1927) and numerous stories published mostly in American pulp SF magazines like *Wonder Stories* (mostly before the war) were mainly attributed (with three published exceptions) to three versions of John Beynon Harris ("John B. Harris," "John Beynon Harris," and "John Beynon"), the selection of names that JBH (as I shall henceforth mainly refer to him) used in his daily life. The published exceptions were "Vivisection," the fragment of a schoolboy story by "J.W.B. Harris" (1919), "Child of Power" by Wyndham Parkes (1939), and "Love in Time" by Johnson Harris (a 1945 republication of the 1933 "Wanderers of Time"). As for the name by which JBH became famous, he explains in his April 3, 1950 letter to Frederik Pohl (his American agent) that "The original idea of John Wyndham was that I was using it for a different style of stuff. . . . not cluttered up with memories of early Wonder Stories. . . . So if you are agreeable, we will adopt John Wyndham [for *Day of the Triffids*], and stick to it" (see the Frederik Pohl Papers, University of Syracuse Library).

Any twenty-first-century appraisal of "John Wyndham's" fiction must confront two standard put-downs: the claim that he was a writer of "cosy catastrophes" and the characterization of him as simply a clone of H.G. Wells (the young Wells that is). It was Brian Aldiss who applied the catchy "master of the cosy catastrophe" phrase in 1973. Aside from an ambience of middle-class Victorian values, what Aldiss had in mind is made more specific in this underwhelming description of *The Day of the Triffids* and *The Kraken Wakes*: "Both novels were totally devoid of ideas but read smoothly, and thus reached a maximum audience, who enjoyed cosy disasters" (Aldiss and Wingrove1988: 315). It is surely odd to describe a 1951 novel which introduced the notion of genetically modified crops to SF and a 1953 novel which anticipates Stanislaw Lem's theme of the utter unknowability of an alien species as "totally devoid of ideas." Furthermore, virtually all of JBH's fiction explores the consequences of a Darwinian explanation of life. It is the contrast between content and style – the iron cruel lessons of Darwinism couched in a velvet novel of manners style – that accounts for the disturbing and often ironic effects that may be implied by the "cosy catastrophe" tag.

Of course, the Darwinian message is one of the things that links JBH's work with Wells'. Certainly, Wells' SF was JBH's most important model. JBH believed that the Wellsian scientific romance had gone down market, that what was called "science fiction" was an unfortunate abberation, and that it was necessary to return to the standards that Wells had established. But in using the Wells model he added so much that was his own, it is quite unfair to dismiss him as a Wells clone. He did not replicate the kind of work that Wells wrote in his lifetime, he wrote the kind of SF novels that the young non-Utopian Wells might have written had that Wells been reborn after his 1946 death and lived through the 1950s. That is to say, "Wyndham" provided a realistically detailed and convincing portrait of an anxious and demoralized postwar, Cold-War era Britain. And more than most writers of that era, he speculated about the possibilities of genetics, something that would have been much more apparent had *Plan For Chaos*, his novel about cloned Nazis and first extended attempt to deviate from Gernsbackian SF (the writing of which overlapped with that of *Triffids*), been published.

But there are other aspects of JBH's life, beliefs, and personality that make his work unique. He was a feminist (albeit of a rather dated romantic kind) and females often have starring roles in his SF (see D'Ammassa 1977 and Clareson 1990). One cannot say the same of Wells' SF. And in three essays I have attended in detail to what I have called the level of "estranged autobiography" in *Stowaway to Mars* (1936), *The Midwich Cuckoos* (1957), and *Chocky* (1968; see Ketterer 2000b, and 2000a). I characterize these three works as examples of estranged autobiography because the autobiographical details amount to more than isolated elements; in each case they make possible new overall readings. No case has been made for the same degree of estranged autobiography in Wells' SF.

My concern in this essay is with aspects of JBH's psychology rather more than biographical events or circumstances that inform the six 1951–60 novels of "Wyndham's" "golden" period: *The Day of the Triffids*, *The Kraken Wakes*, *The Chrysalids*, *The Midwich Cuckoos*, *The Outward Urge*, and *Trouble with Lichen*. Instead of focusing on these novels as reflections of their time – the usual approach – I wish to demonstrate that they form a sequence expressing successively JBH's fear of women, female sexuality, and sexual relations; his fear of children; and his fear of death. In totality they add up to a statement of his fear of life generally. And that is one reason why, after *Lichen*, his creative life was virtually over. His 1968 novel, *Chocky*, an expansion of his 1963 novella (in turn derived from a lost "prewar production" Peter Hebdon, Managing Director at the publishers Michael Joseph, suggests in an October 12, 1967 letter), seems to be the belated expression of an idealized relationship with his lost father, a theme which can be traced back in JBH's work to 1931 (see Ketterer 2000a). Otherwise, his attempts to write novels after *Lichen* – the posthumously published *Web* (1979), which is about poisonous spiders ("The Little Sisters" who fill in for the dangerous sexuality that is so conspicuously absent in the relationship between hero and heroine, even when they are naked together), and the incomplete *Tuey Flower* (a spin-off of the 1955 "Wild Flower") can be understood as a return to the opening fear-of-female-sexuality phase of the sequence that *Lichen* concludes. He could only repeat the cycle. Indeed, *Web* includes a convenient statement of JBH's encompassing theme: "It probably does one good to be brought up against the facts of life now and again – at least it makes one realize that there is a struggle going on . . .". (Wyndham 1980: 62–3).

What might be called the Facts of Life sequence of six novels falls into three groups of two: *Triffids* and *Kraken* express the fear of female sexuality and sexual relations, *Chrysalids* and *Cuckoos* the fear of children, and *The Outward Urge* and *Lichen* the fear of death. JBH characteristically had two goes at a particular theme. The pattern is first apparent with the two unpublished novels which preceded (partially in the second case) *Triffids*. Both *Project for Pistols* (written 1946–7; revised 1948) and *Plan for Chaos* (written 1947–51; revised 1951) treat the theme of resurgent Nazis, first as a spy thriller, then as SF. In dealing with the "double takes" novels in the Facts of Life sequence, I shall, given space limitations, concentrate on the first two novels and the penultimate one (actually a story sequence that can be read as a novel), *The Outward Urge*. There is likely to be little argument that *Chrysalids* and *Cuckoos* express a fear of children and that *Lichen* (which is about life extension) conveys the fear of death.

"The Elemental Fears": *The Day of the Triffids* and *The Kraken Wakes*

It seems reasonable to identify the narrator of *Triffids* with JBH. For one thing the "WM" reversed form (world turned upside down?) initials of the narrator's name, William Masen, were probably suggested by the first and last letters of "WyndhaM." In this near future world (originally dated 1965), Bill has reason to be grateful to the mysterious and threatening perambulating plants called "triffids." Temporarily blinded by a triffid sting, he escapes the permanent universal blindness caused by the green "shooting stars" (Wyndham 1954: 13) – "a cloud of comet debris" which envelops Earth (Wyndham 1954: 12). Awakening in a hospital to darkness, Bill recalls his fear as a child that something underneath the bed would grab his ankle: "The ele-mental fears were still marching along with me, waiting their chance . . ." (Wyndham 1954: 9). This passage sets the reader up not just for the triffids but for the "elemental fears" of JBH's six-novel sequence. Boiled down, in *Triffids* and *Kraken* it is the fear of females and sex. Early newspaper stories about the triffids were handled "with that blend of cautiously defensive frivolity which the Press habitually employed to cover themselves in matters regarding sea-serpents, elementals, thought-transference, and other irregular phenomena . . ." (Wyndham 1954: 39). The cut-down American text of *Triffids*, published before the British one, substitutes "flying saucers" (Wyndham 1951: 31) for "elementals." Presumably, Doubleday thought "elementals" too recher-ché a concept for the average SF reader who would be much happier with the 1950s flying saucer cliché. But the meaning of "elemental" as a manifestation of the four (or five) basic elements or, more generally, a spirit or natural force in physical form, exactly fits the triffids. And whatever the "kraken" may be, it is also a sea elemental.

As it happens, in a submission letter dated January 5, 1932, JBH describes an early, as yet unpublished story, "The House at Hardease" as "having to do with an elemen-tal." That elemental has something in common with the triffids to the extent that it represents a Shavian-style "life force." The last story that JBH published in his life-time was originally entitled "Life-Force"; it appeared under Frederik Pohl's melan-cholic title, "A Life Postponed," in the December 1968 issue of *Galaxy*. To the extent that JBH's women are representatives of a Darwinian nature and mythically imaged as "Furies," they partake of the elemental.

It is clear that the natural force in *Triffids* is female sexuality when Bill recalls his seeing, for the first time, "the curious, funnel-like formation at the top of the [triffid's] stem" and "the tightly-wrapped whorl within" when, as a young boy, his father lifted him "to look inside" (Wyndham 1954: 38). The primal scene here is of two males, the one engendered by the other, looking into an image of the *vagina dentata*. That whorl can unfurl and lash out, becoming "a slender stinging weapon ten feet long" (Wyndham 1954: 42). It is, of course, pretty much inevitable that a good many of the details that make up JBH's description of a triffid would suggest both female and male sexual organs. For example, it ejaculates: its "white seeds shot into the air like steam" (Wyndham 1954: 50). Could the case I am making for the dominance of female sexuality simply be accidental? The build up of evidence suggests not. The monster in the film *Alien* and its successors is similarly ambisexual but there also it is the threat of female sexuality that dominates. The sticky mess from which the triffid whorl emerges traps insects like a spider's web and so the deadly sexuality of the female spider is linked to the triffid threat.

It has not been noted that essential elements in the first eight chapters of *Triffids* are mirrored in the last eight (see the chapter structure chart). There are various ways of accounting for, or justifying this aesthetic feature. Most obviously it implies the imposition, perception, or extraction of pattern and order on, of, or from disorder or chaos. An important suggested Darwinian pattern is that of the descent of humankind accompanied by the ascent of the triffids and – it is at least hoped – vice versa. But the conception of endlessly duplicated images in opposed mirrors represents a *mise en abyme* which might be equated with both the triffid's vagina-like funnel (or "hell-mouth") and Chapter 9, figuratively the central vanishing point chapter at the singularity pit of the mirrored binary chapters. "Evacuation," the title of Chapter 9, most immediately links the main event of that chapter to the Second World War but the word itself has other meanings (e.g., "making void") that (together with a physical location) could be tied to JBH's fearful conception of female sexuality. Of course, "Evacuation" should also be associated with the Second World War reference in the title of Chapter 1 and the "Withdrawal" part of the title of Chapter 17. Thus it is implied that the opening eight-chapter sequence and the closing eight-chapter sequence both "funnel" into the pivotal central chapter.

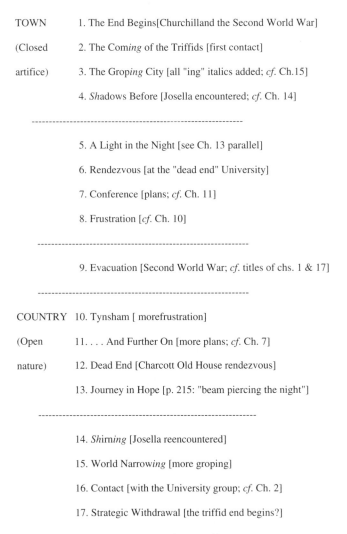

TOWN   1. The End Begins[Churchilland the Second World War]

(Closed   2. The Com*ing* of the Triffids [first contact]

artifice)   3. The Grop*ing* City [all "ing" italics added; *cf.* Ch.15]

     4. *Sh*adows Before [Josella encountered; *cf.* Ch. 14]

----

     5. A Light in the Night [see Ch. 13 parallel]

     6. Rendezvous [at the "dead end" University]

     7. Conference [plans; *cf.* Ch. 11]

     8. Frustration [*cf.* Ch. 10]

----

     9. Evacuation [Second World War; *cf.* titles of chs. 1 & 17]

COUNTRY 10. Tynsham [morefrustration]

(Open   11. . . . And Further On [more plans; *cf.* Ch. 7]

nature)   12. Dead End [Charcott Old House rendezvous]

     13. Journey in Hope [p. 215: "beam piercing the night"]

----

     14. *Sh*irn*ing* [Josella reencountered]

     15. World Narrow*ing* [more groping]

     16. Contact [with the University group; *cf.* Ch. 2]

     17. Strategic Withdrawal [the triffid end begins?]

The mirror (funnel) chapter structure of *The Day of The Triffids*

Triffids seem to have come about as the result of genetic experimentation; they are probably "the outcome of a series of ingenious biological meddlings" in Russia (Wyndham 1954: 27). A Mr Palanguez has not seen a grown triffid but "I have seen a picture, señor. I do not say there is *no* sunflower there at all. I do not say there is no turnip there. I do not say there is no nettle, or even no orchid there. But I do say that if they were all fathers to it they would none of them know their child. I do not think it would please them greatly, either" (Wyndham 1954: 32–3). This implies that the triffid is an illegitimate offspring of wayward sexuality.

What of Bill's sexuality? Like JBH's, it is a little ambiguous. Bill is almost 30 years old and unmarried – "my one attempt to marry had miscarried some years before" (Wyndham 1954: 60). JBH was 48 and unmarried when *Triffids* was published. At age 60, he would marry a schoolteacher named Grace Wilson when she retired at the same age. He had had a relationship with her for about 30 years and she had lived for the past 25 years in a room adjoining his at the Penn Club in Blooms-bury, London (Maxwell 1996: 20). Asked in an interview (two years before his marriage) why he had not married, he replied that he had met the right woman twice but, in both cases, she had met someone righter (Burrows 1961). I have been able to establish that the first of these right women was his beautiful, golden-haired, first cousin, Dorothy Joan Parkes. The skein of evidence is intricate and must await the publication of my lengthy essay "John [Wyndham] Beynon's Case for Rape in *Stowaway to Mars*." The female stowaway in that novel – Joan Shirning – is named Joan because JBH's cousin was known as Joan. And Bill's love interest in *Triffids*, Josella Playton (Joan+Sally+Plato?), who knows an ideal country retreat, a converted and modernized farmhouse in Sussex named Shirning (she+her+yearning?), is a detailed portrait of Joan Parkes.

With Josella (who like himself is not blind), Bill has the idealized relationship that JBH did not have with Joan Parkes. It seems to have been a case of unrequited love. In 1924 Joan married someone more masculine – a businessman named Robert Hamilton Ferguson. One of the barriers to the relationship of Joan and JBH was the fact that they were first cousins. In JBH's time, it was still believed that genetic abnormalities were likely to result from the quasi-incestuous union of first cousins. As it happens, Grace Wilson, the woman whom he eventually married but by whom he did not have children, was worried that she had inherited a genetic defect – Charcot Marie Tooth's disease (or Peroneal Muscular Atrophy). This specific personal anxiety is reflected in *Triffids*. In a chapter entitled "Dead End," Stephen Brennell's impractically small group unnecessarily refortify a manor named "Charcott Old House" (Wyndham 1954: 195, 200, 201) while Bill sets off for the more positively starred Shirning Farm.

Bill and Josella are not first cousins, or related in any known way, and their eventual son David is perfectly normal and healthy. Thus does JBH rewrite his relationship with Joan Parkes. His fear of what might have happened had he married Joan and had a child by her can be deduced from what I have said about the wayward sexuality of triffids with which Josella, the notorious author of *Sex is My Adventure*, is linked. When we first meet a hand-bound Josella, she is "tethered" (Wyndham 1954: 64) – connected by a cord – to a blind man who is beating her. Her state is shared by that of the farmed triffids: in an attempt at control, "the steel stakes to which each was tethered by a chain were in rows" (Wyndham 1954: 46). The verb in common serves to tether Josella to the triffids in terms of the threat of female sexuality. We are not directly told the color of the "head" of a triffid but the hint of sunflower that Palanguez mentions suggests it is yellow and so at least a rough parallel in color with the blonde head of Josella (itself akin perhaps to what is described in a story fragment as Toni Gloriane's "dandelion clock of gold curls"). (For a yellow-headed triffid, see Mark Salwowski's striking cover illustration beginning with the 1987 Penguin edition.) In the 1933 seed story of *Triffids*, entitled by an editor "Spheres of Hell" and retitled "The Puff-Ball Menace" by Wyndham in 1938, it is emphasized that the deadly plant is a "virulent yellow" (Beynon 1933: 232, 138). As an "elemental," the triffid is an horrific, confused manifestation of JBH's and Joan Parkes' sexual union and their vegetable child.

It is the adventurous Josella who instructs Bill that "every man who marries a sighted girl must take on two blind girls as well" (Wyndham 1954: 124). Bill is properly shocked. He realizes that in the interest of procreative survival, Josella is proposing a pragmatic form of free love: he should be willing to have sexual relations with at least three women. When, reunited at Shirning Farm, Bill and Josella do see themselves as "married," he reminds her of her "condition." Her response – "maybe some things haven't fallen out so badly" (Wyndham 1954: 228) – might be regarded as still more shocking given what is unsaid. Presumably Josella is thinking of the two blind women at Shirning – Mary and Joyce. But Mary is married to Dennis and has just become the mother of their sighted baby girl. There is also a fifth female present – the young girl Susan who had accompanied Bill to Shirning. The anarchic sexual possibilities here outside of marriage are unwise, probably disastrous, or beyond the pale. There is a fearful gap in the text here related to sex but we are left to presume that a now much more conservative Josella has retreated from her earlier position. The threatening specter of sexual license and consequent chaos is present but avoided, evaded, or ducked.

It should never be forgotten, however, that the anarchic triffids were originally engineered as a boon to humanity; they are the source of a wondrous oil and but for mass blindness would not have presented a major problem. At the end of *Triffids*, JBH subtly reminds the reader of the relationships between oil, lubrication, fuel, movement, and life and, in terms of the metaphor that I have been exploring, the relationship between sexuality and human survival. Bill fills up a vehicle "from our main petrol supply" (Wyndham 1954: 271) and sabotages a rival's vehicle by pouring "honey" into its tank (Wyndham 1954: 271). To accentuate the point, JBH then has Bill regret that "I had forgotten to oil the shed doors and gave them a curse for every creak" (Wyndham 1954: 272).

The genetic interest and fear of the female theme in *Triffids* would have been much more apparent had JBH's SF thriller *Plan for Chaos* been published. He was writing

Plan for Chaos at the same time as he was writing *Triffids*; his final version of *Plan* was completed by September 1951, seven months after the American *Collier's* serialization of "The Revolt of the Triffids," more than five months after the March 22, 1951 American publication of the abridged *Day of the Triffids*, and a few days after the August 26, 1951 British publication of the complete text. In *Plan*, set in 1974, it turns out that a fearsome blonde woman, a tall Nazi named Marta Dahl (one of JBH's "Furies" – his usual term for aggressive powerful women) has created a group of cloned Nazis (the seeds of a new master race) based on her eggs and the sperm of an unidentified father (possibly Hitler). (JBH's was anticipating Ira Levin's 1976 best-seller, *The Boys from Brazil*.) It is not accidental, in view of JBH's love for his first cousin, that the JBH-style protagonist is in love with his cousin Freda Darl, Marta's earlier, non-cloned daughter. (See also the love relationship between half cousins in *The Chrysalids* and, most importantly, that between first cousins in JBH's early novel, the little read and never reprinted 1935 detective story *Foul Play Suspected*.) *Plan for Chaos* was originally titled *Fury of Creation*. The fearful explanation is provided on page 396 of the typescript: "'Vitality in women,' Shaw once said [in Act I of *Man and Superman*], 'is a blind fury of creation.'" His final title choice, of course, expresses the order/chaos binary that is implicit in the mirror chapter structure of *Triffids*.

In *Triffids* the mobile plants are explained as most probably the result of genetic engineering and the blinding of humanity is also finally attributed to our hand – our satellite weapons may have been to blame. Impacts from comet debris may have released "fissile materials, radio-active dusts, bacteria, viruses . . ." (Wyndham 1954: 247). Josella is somewhat comforted by these explanations because they make things "at least comprehensible" (Wyndham 1954: 248).

Although *The Kraken Wakes* is sometimes dismissed as a rerun of *Triffids* with threatening sea beings replacing the plants, *Kraken* is actually a very different novel. JBH did not like repeating himself and what makes *Kraken* distinct is its world-wide geographical canvas and the narrative strategies that requires plus the key fact that the undersea "invaders" remain incomprehensible. Various hypotheses are proposed but we do not finally know what exactly they are and where they came from. The activities of these truly alien beings might be a form of interplanetary invasion or simply a matter of undersea evolution. JBH had to fight very hard with his American publisher (but not, it would appear, his English one) to retain the incomprehensibility fundamental to his conception.

But *Kraken* is akin to, and a pair with, *Triffids* in one important respect. The "xeno-bathetic intelligences," like the triffids, can be understood as manifestations of the fear of female sexuality. It is proposed that "a state of compromise" should be sought "which will allow both parties [xenobaths and humans] to live peacefully in their separate spheres" (Wyndham 1955: 107). "[S]eparate spheres" refers, of course, to the realms of sea and land but the phrase traditionally refers to the very different worlds of women and men. As the womb of life, the cradle of creation, the sea is coded female and so are the xenobaths. Viscous and slimy, they are associated with a "large, uncertain, oval shape" (Wyndham 1955: 34), with the "curved" (Wyndham 1955: 118,

138), with a "dome-like excrescence" which becomes "spherical" and then opens to eject a vast number of whiplash, sticky "white cilia" (Wyndham 1955: 139–40), with the "round" (Wyndham 1955: 140), with egg-like and "half-egg shapes" (Wyndham 1955: 170), and with "coelenterate bubbles" (Wyndham 1955: 171). All is organic. In a very prescient move, it is hypothesized that what are called their "sea-tanks" "may well be artificial, organic constructions, *built* for a specialized purpose" (Wyndham 1955: 153).

In symbolic terms, the aliens' purpose is castration. They begin by cutting cables and "slicing" "through the hull of a ship with . . . the efficiency of a wire through cheese" (Wyndham 1955: 104–5). It should be noted that the narrator Mike Watson (an M.W. replaces the W.M. of *Triffids*) has a wife named Phyllis, the love interest in the novel; her first name concludes with an "s" sound (picked up by the "s" in Watson) that could, in context, be interpreted as a threatening slicing sound. The xenobaths are the Loretta Bobbits of the deeps. Tellingly, one of JBH's working titles for *Kraken* was the too suggestive *Things Down There*.

The Successor Species: *The Chrysalids* and *The Midwich Cuckoos*

The Chrysalids and *The Midwich Cuckoos* are both about children who are feared because they are different. In the first case, the reader identifies with those children. Postatomic war radiation mutants, they are shunned victims who possess talents that betoken a new stage of human evolution. (Hence the intriguing but mystifying title mentioned nowhere in the text because it was belatedly supplied by Winifred Ashton who edited the Novels of Tomorrow series for Michael Joseph Ltd. and who is best known as the playwright and novelist "Clemence Dane.") In the second case, the reader is encouraged to identify with the "parents" and the older generation. The spooky Midwich children also amount to an evolved version of humanity – a successor species – but they appear to have been seeded by aliens and must (it is argued) be destroyed.

The fear of children which JBH expresses in these two novels goes beyond the specific groups described. JBH applied Darwinian thinking to children and toyed with the idea that all children could be regarded as a successor species. As an Edwardian, he was very aware that change had accelerated in the twentieth century and that the children (of the Western world at least) who came of age in the 1950s and 1960s were very different (and not always in a positive way) from the children of his generation. From quite an early age, JBH and Grace saw themselves as old fashioned, and he regarded his approach to SF as "old hat." At the same time, JBH identified with the different children of both *Chrysalids* and *Cuckoos*. He saw himself as a mutant cuckoo; the feared other, as so often, was the feared self.

Because of space restrictions and because my argument applies to *Chrysalids* and *Cuckoos* in rather obvious ways, I have not supplied detailed analyses. Interested readers are referred to my lengthy essay on *Cuckoos* (JBH's best novel?) and advised that this is the one Wyndham novel that might be best read in its American incarnation. The 1958 Ballantine text contains substantial material that is cut or condensed in all the British editions.

Extinction: *The Outward Urge* and *Trouble with Lichen*

JBH's 1959 story sequence and his 1960 novel do not, at least at first glance, appear to be paired in the same obvious ways as the two preceding paired novels in his Facts of Life series. *Urge* is unlike *Lichen* and the previous novels precisely because it is a story sequence. In this respect, of course, it may be regarded as a microcosm of the Facts of Life sequence; the fifth text in the series, it finally consisted of five stories – a concluding fifth being added in the 1961 Science Fiction Book Club edition. But *Urge* (originally entitled *Man in the Cradle* after Konstantin Tsiolkovsky's notion of Earth as humanity's cradle, and then *Round about Earth* or *The Human Age*) is more particularly unlike the preceding "Wyndham" novels and unlike *Lichen* in that it is a work of hard SF; it deals with the exploration of the inner solar system and is mainly set off Earth. To signal this distinction, JBH provided himself with a cowriter double: *Urge* is the work of John Wyndham and Lucas Parkes, both names extracted from JBH's own full name. Supposedly Lucas Parkes helped out with the technical and scientific details. Actually it was Arthur C. Clarke who performed that role. Enquiring about publishers' interest "in that 'TROON' series of stories," JBH wrote, on October 15, 1957, to Jean LeRoy, his short stories and serial rights agent at Pearn, Pollinger & Higham, that "I can see Arthur is well away – I could just picture him with a towel round the head furiously going to it over the weekend before last. Just his meat, with all the technical stuff at his fingers' ends."

Differences aside, however, *Urge* and *Lichen* are a pair. Together they present a gamut of responses to the fear of aging and death. This is obviously the case with *Lichen* that deals with life extension issues. The biochemist Diane Brackley discovers a lichen that halts the aging process and extends the human life span to over 200 years. One can hang on, like lichen. *Urge* deals with a perhaps more realistic, instinctual solution to the problem of individual death: have children, ideally male children, and make sure that one's genes are perpetuated down the ages. *Urge* also provides a solution to the eventual death or extinction of the human species when, for one reason or another, human life is no longer possible on Earth: journey into space and colonize other worlds. Because *Urge* is an accomplished story sequence which has received no critical attention and because the fear of death in that novel relates quite specifically to JBH's own situation, I shall conclude here by focusing on this penultimate Facts of Life title. As it happens, my essay might have been alliteratively and accurately titled "From Triffids to Troons." The last Troon story was first published in *New Worlds* in November 1960, two months after the first publication of *Lichen*.

JBH, like his younger brother Vivian, his only sibling, did not have children. Their line was doomed to be extinguished with their deaths. As a Darwinist, JBH would have regarded his life as a failure. He had a literary estate to pass on but no children to pass it on to. His solution was, in a rewritten will, to pass it on to the children of Jean Case, the married daughter of his friend Harry "Biff" Barker (Biff's younger daughter Tess was excluded when she became a cloistered nun in 1956). Perhaps JBH has the generation of Troons with which his saga concludes living in Australia because he knew that Australia would soon be (actually in 1964) the permanent domicile of the Cases including his ultimate beneficiaries, Jean's three children. Biff lived in the village of Steep, Hampshire, where JBH had boarded at Bedales School, his idea of the closest thing on Earth to Utopia. JBH regarded Biff's two daughters as his compensatory "children." In *Urge* JBH provides himself with a compensatory family line that stretches into the next two centuries. A glance at "The Troon Line," the genealogical tree with which *Urge* opens, reveals that most of the male Troons are named George. A Brazilian offspring is named Jorge. JBH's solicitor, then barrister, Welsh father was named George. His full name was George Beynon Harris, the initials of which, G.B.H., might well stand for Grievous Bodily Harm given the effects of his marital breakdown on his sons and the very negative role their mother cast him in. (GBH added the distinguished royalist name Lucas, a related family he believed, for snobbish reasons.) GBH's delightful 1911 memoir, *When I Was a Boy* (by Lucas Beynon and dedicated "To Wyndham and Vivian"), opens with these sentences:

> My real name is George. They gave me that name, I am told, because my grandfather's name was George. And because there were several Georges in the family before him – a name, I might say, that I never cared for in the least.
> I often wondered if they were short of names in those days. (Beynon 1911: 1)

By way of compensation, then, GBH provided his first son with six names to choose from. The only name that came from JBH's mother's side of the family was Parkes. The name "Troon" comes from the Welsh word *trwyn*, meaning "(place by the) headland," that land (like the Gower peninsula where GBH was born) that juts and urges outwards.

In an abandoned opening to his short, handwritten memoir of JBH's life, Vivian Beynon Harris writes, "We came from a family that might have been the prototype for the Forsytes." But after their parents' separation, "this idyllic sort of upper-middle class life" was exchanged for "utter social darkness." In the Introduction to *The Best of John Wyndham*, JBH's friend and owner of the Fantasy Book Centre in Bloomsbury, Leslie Flood, describes *Urge* as "a kind of Forsyte saga of the solar system" (Flood 1973: 10).

Like GBH, most of the Troons have three names. The hero of the first story, "The Space Station," is Flight Lieutenant George Montgomery Troon. (Because his initials are G.M.T., he, like "Old Ticker," his grandfather of the same name, is known as "Ticker Troon" [Wyndham 1962: 9–10]. His identification with time provides a link with the fear of aging and death theme. JBH himself would later learn that he had a heart condition – a dodgy ticker from which he would die.) But the parallel between JBH's family and the Troon family is most clearly implied by the 50 year time gap between each of the stories. The first one is set in "A.D. 1994," the second in "A.D.

2044," the third in "A.D. 2094," the fourth in "A.D. 2144," and the fifth in "A.D. 2194." Subtracting 50 years from the first date produces the year 1944, the base line date for the Troon saga. D-Day occurred on June 6, 1944 and five days later Lance Corporal John Beynon Harris of the Royal Corps of Signals began his noncombatant participation in the Normandy invasion. He served as a cypher operator in north-west Europe from June 11, 1944 until September 4, 1946. In "The Space Station," Flight Lieutenant Troon is briefed by the white-haired Air Marshal Sir Godfrey Wilde who recalls "Old Ticker" and drifts "fifty years away" (Wyndham 1962: 10) to the day Old Ticker's aircraft was blown up over Berlin in "August 1944" (Wyndham 1962: 12). The derring-do of generations of thrusting, outward-urged male Troons has an analogous basis in the quiet heroism of the non-thrusting JBH. In *Urge*, the hostility of the Germans in the Second World War becomes the hostility of the Cold War Russians and of the all encompassing hostility of space.

Young Ticker is assigned to help with the assembly of a British space station. (From our present perspective, we are unfortunately in the realm of an alternate history!) Mention is made of Ticker's "premonition" of death (Wyndham 1962: 12) with regard to his earlier than intended marriage, after Sir Godfrey Wilde quotes the concluding lines about the "thin gnat-voices" of stars from an unidentified Rupert Brooke poem ("The Jolly Company"): "He was dead, you know, before he was your age" (Wyndham 1962: 11). ("For All the Night," the title under which this first Troon story was first published in *New Worlds* in April 1958, derives from the opening phrase of the same quote.) During his interview with the Air Marshal, Ticker feels guilty about "the special marriage licence" (Wyndham 1962: 15) in his pocket because, in his dangerous line of work, men are normally required to be bachelors. As it turns out Ticker does die in space as a result of his manoeuvring a smart (radar directed) Russian missile away from "the space-station assembly" and the living quarters known as "the hulk" (Wyndham 1962: 17), presumably because the death-in-life conditions correspond to those aboard England's squalid, disease-ridden, anchored prison ships in the nineteenth century. But a message received before the missile threat – "Happy birthday from Laura and Michael" (Wyndham 1962: 21; an anticipation of the 1968 film *2001*) – means that he died knowing he had a son, the George Michael Troon who will command the British Moon Station in the next story. "He had smuggled himself a family in spite of the regulations" (Wyndham 1962: 22). (JBH might be said to have done the same thing with the Barker daughters.)

The description of exactly how Ticker destroys the missile suggests an analogy with the sexual act that led to George Michael Troon's existence. Ticker manages to sit "astride the nose of the missile" (Wyndham 1962: 39) (an image that anticipates the concluding scene of the 1964 film *Dr. Strangelove*). The nose features "protuberances" or "projections" which he attempts to "unscrew" (Wyndham 1962: 37). "[H]olding on to the projecting knobs" (Wyndham 1962: 41), he then uses his two "pistol-like" hand tubes (Wyndham 1962: 33) to encourage the missile to change its direction but "in space, where every movement is a delicate matter of thrust and counter-thrust, time too is an important factor . . ." (Wyndham 1962: 39). After having "a bash at this short, thick, rod-thing in front of me" (Wyndham 1962: 41), he used his "hand tubes" to slam away "at the short thick rod with all his might." He finally belabors "one of the more slender projections" (Wyndham 1962: 42). (Within the context of this phallic array, it might be noted that the spaceman who survives the entanglement of his line with the missile is named "Nobby" (Wyndham 1962: 32), possibly after JBH's long-time journalist friend "Nobby" Clarke – not Arthur C.) All this phallic action concludes, as one might expect, with an orgasmic explosion. Ticker dies in the explosion but thanks to a previous literal orgasm and ejaculation, a son survives to replace him.

Death is similarly conquered in the four succeeding stories which are set on the Moon, Mars, Venus, and partly among the asteroids respectively. I do not have the space to analyze these stories and must trust that my analysis of the first one is sufficient to make my point. With the publication of *Lichen* in 1960, JBH's Facts of Life series was complete, and so essentially was his life's work. He complained repeatedly about feeling creatively dried up and that, retired in Steep, from August 1963 onwards, I'm turning into a vegetable myself" (JBH to Peter Hebdon, February 27, 1968). He died on March 11, 1969. But on July 10, 2003 the centenary of his birth was celebrated (albeit not as widely as it should have been). He has survived and will continue to do so. His best work, including the Facts of Life Sextet (as I hope I have demonstrated), is built to last.

REFERENCES AND FURTHER READING

Aldiss, Brian W. with David Wingrove (1988) *Trillion Year Spree: The History of Science Fiction*. London: Paladin. Original title *Billion Year Spree* (1973).

Beynon, John [John Wyndham Parkes Lucas Beynon Harris] (1933) "Spheres of Hell." *Wonder Stories* 5 (October): 231–9. Collected as "The Puff-Ball Menace" in John Wyndham writing as John Beynon, *Wanderers of Time* (London: Coronet, 1973), 135–58.

Beynon, John [John Wyndham Parkes Lucas Beynon Harris] (1935) *Foul Play Suspected*. London: Newnes.

Beynon, Lucas [George (Lucas) Beynon Harris] (1911) *When I Was a Boy*. London: Routledge; New York: E.P. Dutton.

Burrows, John (1961) "Living Writers – 4: John Wyndham." *John O'London's* (March 2), 225.

Clareson, Thomas D. and Alice Clareson (1990) "The Neglected Fiction of John Wyndham: 'Consider Her Ways,' in *Trouble with Lichen and Web. Science Fiction Roots and Branches: Contemporary Critical Approaches*, (eds) Rhys Garnett and R.J. Ellis. Basingstoke: Macmillan, 88–103.

D'Ammassa, Don (1977) "Consider His Ways." *Mythologies* 13 (November): 17–30.

Flood, Leslie (1973) "Introduction." *The Best of John Wyndham*, (ed.) Angus Wells. London: Sphere, 7–11.

Harris, John B. [John Wyndham Parkes Lucas Beynon Harris] (1927) *The Curse of the Burdens*; Aldine Mystery Novels No. 17. London: Aldine.

Harris, Vivian Beynon (1999) "[My Brother,] John Wyndham: A Memoir," transcribed and ed. by David Ketterer. *Foundation: The International Review of Science Fiction* 75 (Spring), 5–50.

Ketterer, David (1998) "Plan For Chaos/Fury of Creation: An Unpublished Science-Fiction Thriller by John Beynon/John Lucas (aka John Wyndham)." *Foundation: The International Review of Science Fiction* 74 (Autumn), 8–25.

——(2000a) "John Wyndham and 'the Searing Anguishes of Childhood': From 'Fairy Story' to *Chocky*." *Extrapolation* 41, 85–101.

——(2000b) "'A Part of the Family [?]': John

Wyndham's *The Midwich Cuckoos* as Estranged
Autobiography," in *Learning from Other Worlds:
Estrangement, Cognition, and the Politics of Science
Fiction and Utopia*, (ed.) Patrick Parrinder. Liv-
erpool: Liverpool University Press; Durham,
N.C.: Duke University Press, 146–77.

——(2000c) "'Vivisection': Schoolboy John
Wyndham's First Publication?" *Foundation: The
International Review of Science Fiction* 79
(Summer), 70–84.

——(2004a) "The Questionable Genesis of *The
Day of the Triffids* by John Wyndham." *The New
York Review of Science Fiction* 16 (March) 1, 6–10.

——(2004b) "Questions and Answers: The Life
and Work of John Wyndham." *The New York
Review of Science Fiction* 16 (March), 11–14.

——(2005) "John Wyndham and the Sins of His
Father: Damaging Disclosures in Court."
Extrapolation 46 (Winter).

Maxwell, David C. (1996) *The Penn Club Story: A
Celebration of the First 75 Years of an Independent
Quaker-Based Club in Central London*. London:
The Penn Club.

Moore, Matthew (2003) "Utopian Ambivalences
in Wyndham's *Web*." *Foundation: The International Review of Science Fiction* 32 (Autumn),
47–56.

Stephensen-Payne, Phil (2001) *John Wyndham,
Creator of the Cosy Catastrophe: A Working Bibli-
ography*, 3rd. rev. edn. Leeds: Galactic Central
Publications.

Webster, Owen (1975) "John Wyndham as Novelist of Ideas." *SF Commentary* nos. 44/45,
39–50.

Wymer, Rowland (1992) "How 'Safe' is John
Wyndham? A Closer Look at His Work with
Particular Reference to *The Chrysalids*." *Founda-
tion: The International Review of Science Fiction* 55
(Summer), 25–35.

Wyndham, John (1958) *The Chrysalids* (1955).
London: Michael Joseph; Harmondsworth:
Penguin.

——(1951) *The Day of the Triffids*. New York:
Doubleday.

——(1954) *The Day of the Triffids* (1951). Harmondsworth: Penguin.

——(1955) *The Kraken Wakes* (1953). Harmondsworth: Penguin.

——(1960) *The Midwich Cuckoos* (1957). London:
Michael Joseph; Harmondsworth: Penguin.

——(1960) *Trouble with Lichen* (1963). London:
Michael Joseph; Harmondsworth: Penguin.

——(1980) *Web* (1960). London: Michael Joseph;
Harmondsworth: Penguin.

Wyndham, John and Lucas Parkes (1962) *The
Outward Urge* (1959). Harmondsworth:
Penguin.

26

Philip K. Dick

Christopher Palmer

Philip K. Dick (1928–82) was a prolific writer of science fiction stories and novels from the early 1950s to his death. His life was a very crowded and complicated one – brought up as, in effect, the only child of a single mother (his twin sister died in infancy), married five times; his intense involvements with women, his warm friendships, his ailments, physical and psychiatric, his intake of medicines and drugs; spectacular and much speculated upon experiences (a destructive break into his apartment by persons unknown; an uncanny experience that he felt was a supernatural visitation); all this, and a hectic, varied, and often pressured career as a writer. It is upon the output of this career as a writer, however, that this essay concentrates.

Dick did not only write SF, and his relations with SF were close but complicated, as we shall see. Many of his works are impressive, moving, and illuminating; others are patchy but fascinating, especially for the enthusiast, who can watch Dick's preoccupations recurring and varying from novel to novel; others are a mess. Of his novels, there is a rough measure of agreement that the following (listed in order of publication) are the best: *Time out of Joint* (1959), *The Man in the High Castle* (1962), *Martian Time-Slip* (1964), *The Three Stigmata of Palmer Eldritch* (1965), *Do Androids Dream of Electric Sheep?* (1968), *Ubik* (1969), *A Scanner Darkly* (1977), *Valis* (1981), and *The Transmigration of Timothy Archer* (1982). (The last two are perhaps not SF, but they are productively read alongside Dick's SF.) The present writer also strongly recommends *Clans of the Alphane Moon* (1964), *Lies, Inc.* (1984 – Dick's revision of his earlier *The Unteleported Man*, 1966), *Galactic Pot-Healer* (1969), *A Maze of Death* (1970), and *Flow My Tears, the Policeman Said* (1974), Dick also wrote novels that cannot be classified as SF, though they do not sit easily in other categories such as "realist" or "mainstream"; some of these he wrote early in his career (*Gather Yourselves Together*, c.1950); some later (*Timothy Archer* may be mentioned here), but most fall into the late 1950s , and concern the marital and sexual struggles of ordinary working people in the suburbs or small towns; of these the best is probably *Confessions of a Crap Artist*, the only one published in Dick's lifetime (1975, written 1959). Dick's short stories were mostly written, at a very fast clip, in the early to mid-1950s, though some come later; recommended here, by way of selection, are "The King of the Elves" (fantasy, 1953), "Small Town," "Exhibit Piece" (both 1954), "Foster, You're Dead," "Nanny" (both 1955), and, because they are good stories that have been made – and in some cases very much changed – into interesting films, "Impostor" (1953), "We Can Remember It for You Wholesale" (1966; the story which became *Total Recall*), and "The Minority Report" (1956). (The affinities between Dick's fiction and contemporary films from *Repo Man* to *The Matrix*, and his influence on the "Cyberpunk" SF of the 1980s and since, are topics we have to pass up here.)

So much for recommendations, offered with the caveat that sudden illuminations and poignant moments can be encountered anywhere in Dick's fiction, even, for instance, in a messy and cobbled-together work like *Deus Irae* (written with Roger Zelazny, 1976). What satisfactions and illuminations can a reader expect from this writer? This essay proceeds to answer this question, and then to discuss Dick's relations with SF as a genre, developments and changes in his fiction, and his responses to the history of his time.

Dick is a writer who produces memorable effects. Like most writers of pulp fiction, one thing he is certainly doing is aiming for the sensational and mind-bending, and he works his stories, and sometimes wrenches them, to produce it. What is exceptional about him, however, is the range and intensity of his effects, their dizzying alternations in a single novel or chapter of a novel, and their rich significances. Later we will assess this achievement: does it amount to a vision, is it a thoughtful vision as well as a sensational one, and what is the best way to describe it? Is it better seen as political or as religious in its implications? Dick's preoccupation with matters spiritual is a constant, and intensifies in his last years; the political implications and satirical edge of his work are just as constant. Should it be seen as a complex response to the movement of contemporary society from the modern to the postmodern, or is Dick's response to his own times rather the starting point to a series of compelling fantasies that are not best read as "about" that age? Here we begin by surveying the range of effects.

He can create horror, characteristically as an experience of inertia, entrapment, the encroachment of entropy, the chill of decay and dissolution: a good example is the scene in which Joe Chip struggles to climb the stairs of the old hotel in *Ubik* (ch.13). Another is the episode towards the end of *A Scanner Darkly* in which Bob Arctor experiences the inexorable fading of his sense of self, the departure of what enables him to experience in the first place. He can be funny: an example is the dopers' riff about the man made of hash in *A Scanner Darkly* (ch.12) or Kevin's protest to God on behalf of his dead cat in *Valis* (ch.2). This comedy is often a matter of zany, knotted complication, somewhere between hysteria and an absurd game in which every possible move must be played, as in Arctor's speculation as to whether he forged one of his own cheques (ch.11), or the series of messages the supposedly dead Runciter sends his supposedly living employees in *Ubik* (graffiti, a commercial on TV, a message on a match-folder).

Both these different effects, humor and horror, are underlain by Dick's habitual, almost obsessive interest in transformation, indeed in the dissolution of reality, where reality is defined as the condition that a given character or group of characters had accepted as ordinary and more or less reliable until a few minutes ago. Dick is not the sort of SF writer who introduces his readers to some new, alternative reality and then meticulously and clearly describes it, tracing its ramifications and, perhaps, developments; instead he introduces a new reality, often without pausing to describe it in any orderly way, and then shows it dissolving, and dissolving again, so that even those who are supposed to know it are baffled or terrified, made to envisage strange possibilities or doubt their sanity or decency. Time is put into reverse or its onward movement is frozen (the activities of Pat Conley in the early chapters of *Ubik* or those of Manfred Steiner at the climax of *Martian Time-Slip*, chs.15–16); a celebrity discovers that all memory of him and all signs of his identity have been erased from an otherwise unchanged world (Jason Taverner in *Flow My Tears*); a man experiences recurrent visions of other people as mechanisms (Jack Bohlen in *Martian Time-Slip*); everyone starts to become avatars of the drug lord and intergalactic adventurer *Palmer Eldritch*.

The moods of apparently ordinary and decent characters oscillate so violently as to seem to remake external reality, at least as they experience it. This oscillation may be between abjection and aggression. Dick is unusual among SF writers in plumbing the acrid, mean, and unsavory in ordinary people, Robert Childan in *The Man in the High Castle* for example, and in blurring the lines between normal, neurotic, and psychotic, as happens, for instance, with Louis Rosen in *We Can Build You* (1972). Yet the oscillation may also be between the shameful and the heroic, as with Barney Mayerson in *Palmer Eldritch*.

This can be grim and bleak. We are a long way from the wonder, the sense of expanded possibility in a sublime universe, that is one of the pleasures of SF. Yet Dick's fiction has other sides, just as striking and just as unusual in SF or, arguably, in any fiction. He creates moments of poignancy, transfiguration. The encounter of Barney Mayerson with the telepathic Martian jackal in *Palmer Eldritch* is a good if doleful example (ch.9); the revelation of the situation of the characters at the end of *A Maze of Death*, passing the time on their helplessly marooned spaceship by playing VR games, is another (ch.15); so is the dream of Rachmael Ben Appelbaum that opens *Lies, Inc.* (man as half-rat, half-God). Then again, there are passages not of feverish speculation and calculation, the common coinage of experience and response in Dick's fiction, but of hard-won, sober wisdom: Angel Archer's meditation on the interconnections of Dante, root-canal work and suffering in *Timothy Archer* (ch.9); Phil's thoughts on the difficulties of helping the suicidal and the incurable in the opening chapters of *Valis*; the conversation between Joe Fernwright and Willis the robot on "caritas" in *Galactic Pot-Healer* (ch.10). Dick memorably creates characters of modest virtue – Mr Tagomi in *The Man in the High Castle*, and, in a more comic vein, Lord Running Clam in *Clans of the Alphane Moon*.

This sampling does not exhaust the varieties and intensities of Dick's fiction, and other readers will come up with other selections. It is time to question the shape and significance of this oeuvre. How does it develop and change – can we usefully map its course and shape? What is its relation to SF as a genre, and to the history and society (the USA from the 1950s to the 1970s) of which it is a product and to which it is a response?

Most of Dick's fiction was published and packaged as SF; he was part of the American SF community in one of its most vigorous periods. In his stories we find robots and aliens, space colonies and rocket trips, the full panoply of psionics, and so on. But all this comes with a twist. Dick's relation to SF can be parodic and parasitic; he sends it up, he seems to utilize the range of its devices and tropes without really taking them seriously. Futurist appliances and devices and creatures are often given silly names, vugs and buggies and papoolas, wub fur and Ganymedean slime moulds. Dick can vividly dramatize the operation of advanced technology (for instance, the destruction of the observation satellite in *Lies, Inc.*, ch.7), but he seldom offers sober extrapolation, whereby the possibility of some future development is lucidly teased out. He seems impatient with many aspects of the genre but, rather than ignoring them, he plays with them, exaggerates them, presses them to extremes. It is no surprise that for a period in the late 1950s he tried to abandon SF altogether, though without much success, as the novels he then wrote could not find a publisher at the time. Yet the matter is more complex than this; perhaps we are dealing with an intense love-hate relationship, one whose intensity galvanizes Dick as a writer.

It is a cliché in commentary on Dick to say that he is interested in the human consequences of technology, or – this is a better way to put the case – in the human consequences of any kind of future or imaginary change in social conditions. His novels are intensely social affairs. Their narratives consist of encounters, disputes, confrontations; betrayals, desertions, uneasy reconciliations; philosophical discussions about fundamental issues such as the nature of love or the putative drive to life – or death – that underlies existence; headlong meditations on the part of the point of view character, canvassing radical, dismaying possibilities. The context is always one of radical change and radical changeability, on every level from the condition of one's job or marriage to the state of the universe and the meaning and purposes of God (of some god or other, anyway). It is not only that the conditions of the novel's world and society have changed from what we know. These drastic changes, the result of ecological disaster, mutations, and so on, are not unusual in SF. What is unusual is the degree to which change, often in the form of transformation or dissolution, has entered into the very nerves of the characters. Their oscillations of mood and behavior register this. If SF is premised on the notion that change is the rule in modernity, extending beyond discoveries in science and developments in technology to affect beliefs, cultures, ideologies, and, perhaps, the way people live from moment to moment, then Philip K. Dick is a very thorough-going writer of SF. He is offhand or parodic in his use of features standard to the SF of his time, but he is radical in making narratives out of this modern condition of change.

Yet if he radicalizes (and also sensationalizes) these basic aspects of SF, he also introduces some of the qualities of the realist novel of relationship and point of view into SF. That excursion into novels about ordinary battlers in the suburbs in the late 1950s paid off in the intense depiction of failed marriages, struggling fathers, the betrayals and victories of ordinary people, in SF novels such as *The Man in the High Castle*, *Martian Time-Slip*, and *A Scanner Darkly*. It's not only that the possibilities of SF are expanded by a kind of infusion of the qualities and preoccupations of the realist novel (to use that label by way of shorthand). It is also that what "the real" might be is subjected to radical questioning and painful twisting, as Dick investigates the underlying premises of SF as the literature of modern changeability. The process is restless and dialectical. Later it will be suggested that what fuels it is a response to the movement from the modern to the postmodern in contemporary society.

Let us review the shape of Dick's writing career in the light of this notion of a dialectical to and fro between a radical sense of changeability and a broad sense of the human and ordinary. Dick begins as a writer of short stories, dozens of them, in the period 1952–5 especially. These stories very often make use of the twist in the tale, the solution that dissolves into another puzzle, if possible more dismaying or more weird than the puzzle that dominated the previous part of the story: for example, "Impostor," "The Father-Thing," and "We Can Remember It for You Wholesale" (the twist here is much zanier than in *Total Recall*). Dick never really abandons this effect, which is derived from pulp fiction in general; we can for instance see it at work at multiple levels in the ending of *Do Androids Dream*.

We have the revelation that Mercer, the deity or prophet of the book's religion, is a fake, and then the revelation that at some deeper level he is not, but can still provide spiritual solace. Then we have Deckard's discovery of what he takes to be a real toad, a precious rarity (almost all real animals having become extinct, so that people have to make do with simulated substitutes), then his wife's discovery that it is electric after all, then his recognition that this does not matter ("The electric things have their lives, too. Paltry as those lives are," ch.22). And by the time of *Do Androids*, the effect, and the whole meaning and impact of the ending of the novel, has become a complex one, because Dick has interwoven a series of encounters turning on the overlaps between fake and real, in a context of life and death, since Deckard is a killer.

But the problem of how one might build up an alternative world, so important in SF, does not really press in a short story. Dick's first attempts, in his early novels, are conventional: we have some authority or tyranny which imposes a social order and ideology, and the little guy who is the main character has to resist or, simply, cope. The breakthrough novel here is *Eye in the Sky* (1957), which is set in contemporary America. Here Dick invents a situation that throws normality and reality into a more violent kind of uncertainty. A party of tourists visiting a nuclear installation is irradiated in an accident. It turns out that the effect of the accident is to give reality to the mental worlds of some of the tourists, so that the group passes in succession through the world of a religious fanatic, a prude, and so on, each time learning how to destroy this world by reducing it to absurdity. But there are neurotic people and normal people among the victims, and there seems no good reason why only the neurotics should be able to produce their own realities, subjecting all the others to them for a period. We can infer that the normal people already have their mad reality, in contemporary America itself, as is implied by the last episode, involving the main character's wife and Mcfeyffe the security man (chs 15, 16).

What happens next is that in two powerful and coherent novels of the late 1950s and early 1960s, *Time out of Joint* and *The Man in the High Castle*, Dick builds on what he had discovered chiefly (but not only) in *Eye in the Sky*: the link between neurosis in the ordinary person, and political ideology: their complex mutual interaction, going beyond notions of oppression, of "them" and "us." And it seems very likely that the sympathy for ordinary people that also shapes these two novels, and equally the sustained, rather than sketchy, depiction of ordinary people's circumstances (work, marriages, self-doubts, resentments) comes partly from Dick's recent experience with his non-SF novels, such as *Confessions of a Crap Artist* and *The Man Whose Teeth Were All Exactly Alike* (written 1960, published 1984).

There is a clarity to the structures of *Time out of Joint* and *The Man in the High Castle*. There is a thoughtfulness in the relations between, on the one hand, the personal troubles and circumstances of Ragle Gumm in the first and Ed and Frank and Childan in the second, and on the other the political crises of the wider worlds of the novel (in the first, Ragle's real task, which he and the authorities have elaborately hidden even from himself; in the second, the sinister plans of the Germans against their Japanese allies). These structures are so clear and firm that they can successfully carry such bizarre moments as the reality breakdown at the swimming pool in *Time out of Joint* (ch.3), and that which occurs to Mr Tagomi in the park in *The Man in the High Castle* (ch.14), and such deconstructive textualities as the operation in *The Man in the High Castle* of two further texts, the *I Ching* and *The Grasshopper Lies Heavy*.

So far the shape of Dick's career as a novelist seems clear. He has found a structure firm yet complex enough to express his sense of the instability yet value of ordinary life. But what happens next, throws his fiction onto a different track. We have arrived at Dick's almost manically productive decade, the 1960s. Whatever is going on in novels like *Ubik*, *Palmer Eldritch*, *The Simulacra* (1964), *Clans of the Alphane Moon*, and lots of others, written sometimes at a rate of three a year, it is related to the earlier novels, but hardly a clear development from them. We can say that Dick comes into this period with a set of interests and tropes – reality dissolution, subjectivity intensified almost to madness, an intuition that an "objective" state of affairs is no more normal, or stable, than the mood of the individual. Then we can say that he is inspired by the breakup and efflorescence of the decade's politics and life-styles. That he takes up drugs, with their tendency to blur the boundaries between the objective and the subjective: as avocation, as topic for fiction (for instance in *Palmer Eldritch* and later *A Scanner Darkly*), or as trope (the novel as like a trip for the reader, a given episode as like a trip for the character or characters). And that at a deeper level he intuits that what is involved is not just a set of fashions and movements but a kind of epochal shift, from the modern to the postmodern, from the society of production to that of consumption, from the making and repairing of things (he is always interested in craftspeople and fixers) to the dissemination of signs.

So Dick's typical novel of the 1960s shakes up and pulls apart the comparatively stable structures he had seemed to arrive at. They are not quite abandoned; *Martian*

Time-Slip gives the measure of this. But what emerges is importantly different. The narratives seem less planned than improvised. Joe Chip or Joe Fernwright or Barney Mayerson are pretty much alike, ordinary guy main characters, and their lives are not patiently specified as is that of Tagomi in *The Man in the High Castle*. It is what the artist, or performer, does with them that is spectacular. He seems to challenge himself, to push his control to the limits, or somewhat beyond, through a series of sensational plot shifts and reality dissolves.

It is not simply that these novels are implausible at times, but that they seem to risk implausibility, to seek it. Yet once the plot is well under way, the reader finds herself empathizing with a situation that is on the commonsense face of it quite bizarre. Deckard's joy at finding a real toad in the dreary dust of the novel's northern California, and then his misery when his wife reveals it to be electric (*Do Androids*); the bemusement of Joe Chip and his companions at finding coins not with the face of Castro or the face of Disney, as they expect, but the face of their dead boss Runciter (*Ubik*, ch.8); Joe Fernwright's dilemma as to whether to let himself be absorbed into the "mentation," as well as the giant body, of the deity Glimmung, attempting to raise a sunken cathedral on an alien planet, in *Galactic Pot-Healer*: the reader is absorbed into the situation, moved, and both excited and bewildered that she is moved. The situation is not always completely plausible within the – drastically shifting and unpredictable – terms of the novel; it is hard to connect it to the conditions of our world – though, as will be seen, it is both possible and interesting to do so. This is a radical extension of the experience that any successful fiction offers its reader, and it justifies the lengths to which Dick takes his 1960s novels, as improvisations. (It also explains the pitfalls that await anyone who tries to describe the interest of Dick's fiction to someone who has not read any. Quickly summarized, the extremity of his situations seems merely "zany," silly, or drug-addled, and the way in which the reader is startled and humored and badgered into empathy is hard to capture.)

These novels do seem to be both postmodernist, and concerned with postmodernity as a condition of society, in rich and sometimes troubled ways. They are fascinated with games and with chance. They like to play with the relations or, more likely, the lack of relation, between signifiers and signifieds, and with incidents connected with messages that are mistransmitted or quirky. They are fascinated with fakes and models of all kinds – we can call them simulacra (as Dick himself does in *We Can Build You*, reminding us that "that's the plural, it's a Latin-type word," ch.2). The term catches the postmodern sense in which these are models or fakes that become detached from their origins, or have their own lives regardless of the fact that they are fakes. These novels both play with and are horrified by the instability of reality – environments that are not what they seem or that dissolve abruptly. This can be seen as postmodern instability. And as we have noticed already, the characters caught up in this variety of games and miscommunications, fakes, and reality shifts are themselves very unstable, given to moods, suspicions, depressions, betrayals.

Yet it does not seem adequate to see Dick, in his 1960s novels especially, as a kind of comedian, even a black comedian, of the postmodern. We have not given an adequate account either of the novels or of their author's complicated responses to his own times if we stop there, seeing the instability of 1960s society, its passage from the society of production to one of consumption, as releasing that appetite for zany games and parodies and sensational complications that could be found in Dick from the beginning of his career. It is not only that Dick responds to the new developments in American culture with such enthusiasm that he swerves away from the kind of fiction he had achieved with *Time out of Joint* and *The Man in the High Castle*. He retains in this new phase of his career a set of concerns and values derived from the New Deal liberalism of his youth: a valuation of the solidarity and struggles of ordinary people, especially working males; an interest in work, especially humble hands-on or boring and socially despised work; a sense of the toughness of small scale life; a kind of respect for the small time employer, the boss who still relates closely to his men, and, also, for the beleaguered but conscientious leader (Gino Molinari in *Now Wait for Last Year* [1966] for instance).

All this is interesting because, for all his use of stereotypes, it gives his novels a social richness, that is not always found in SF, and because it complicates his embrace of the 1960s, a decade when social movements turned aside from the earlier interest in and valuation of the ordinary white male. The results are visible in the hectic complexities of Dick's novels of the 1960s. They are not precisely incoherent, they are decentered: here this postmodernist term is useful. Yet they are not simply playful or blackly comic. There are concerns and values which he will not abandon and, as many readers have noticed, the result is a kind of conflict between the radical, postmodern reality-dissolves, and the ethics that the main characters try to live by. Their actions count, they are capable of betrayal, cruelty, cowardice, or of kindness and sacrifice, even in a world in which what is real and what is authentic is both uncertain and constantly changing.

This does not end the story, which, like one of Dick's own novels, is subject to switchbacks and wild swerves. With *A Scanner Darkly*, 1977, Dick writes a very grim finis to the exuberance of 1960s drug culture; yet this is also his most sympathetic and carefully detailed picture of the plight of the modern worker in a postmodern world, and his most thorough depiction of loss of identity in a world in which no one, and especially no authority, can be trusted. *A Scanner Darkly* is also a novel with a clear, if inexorable, structure, and in that respect is something of a return to the form of a novel like *The Man in the High Castle*.

Dick's later novels in certain respects carry on from *A Scanner Darkly*, but to understand the radical formal experiment of, most notably, *Valis*, we have to note that after 1974 and for the remainder of his life he embarked on what was in effect another literary career, as the writer of an immense journal of theological ruminations, almost endlessly speculating, and then questioning his speculations. This journal, his *Exegesis*, was prompted by a kind of mystical or supernatural experience involving a beam of pink light, the miraculous cure of his infant son, and intimations of supernatural messages. Or so he believed, sometimes, and feverishly. The result is to mobilize an interest in theology, especially in esoteric versions of Christianity, which had been explored in several earlier novels – and to push it a good deal further. It is out of this material that he makes his last novels, sometimes giving it a science fictional form, as in *The Divine Invasion*; sometimes an element of the science fictional, as in *Valis*; and sometimes giving it the form of a witty narrative of Californian life with some very uncanny incidents, as in *Timothy Archer*. Of these the most interesting is *Valis*, because in this novel we have the most detailed exposition of the gnostic theology (and speculation about history) that Dick worked on in the *Exegesis*, but also a complex form (whereby the narrator splits into two persons, or personalities, "Phil" and "Horselover Fat") which renarrates the splitting of the individual that had also been a concern of *A Scanner Darkly*.

REFERENCES AND FURTHER READING

Butler, Andrew M. (2000) *Philip K. Dick*. Harpenden: Pocket Essentials.

Carter, Cassie (1995) "The Metacolonisation of Dick's *The Man in the High Castle*: Mimicry, Parasitism and Americanism in the PSA." *Science Fiction Studies* 67 (November): 333–42.

Dick, Anne (1995) *Search for Philip K. Dick, 1928–1982: A Memoir and Bibliography of the Science Fiction Writer*. Lampeter and Lewiston, NY: Edward Mellen.

Freedman, Carl (2000) *Critical Theory and Science Fiction*. Hanover and London: Wesleyan University Press.

Jameson, Fredric (1993) *Postmodernism, or, The Cultural Logic of Late Capitalism*. Durham, NC: Duke University Press.

Levack, Daniel J.H. (1988) *PKD: A Philip K. Dick Bibliography*. Westport, CT: Meckler.

Mackey, Douglas (1988) *Philip K. Dick*. Boston, MA: Twayne.

McKee, Gabriel (2004) *Pink Beams of Light from the God in the Gutter: The Science-Fictional Religion of Philip K. Dick*. New York: UP of America.

Mullen, R.D., Istvan Csicsery-Roney, Jr., Arthur B. Evans, and Veronica Hollinger (eds) (1992) *On Philip K. Dick: 40 Articles from "Science Fiction Studies."* Terre-Haute and Greencastle: SF-TH Inc.

Olander, Joseph D., and Martin H. Greenberg (eds.) (1983) *Philip K. Dick*, New York: Taplinger.

Palmer, Christopher (2003) *Philip K. Dick: Exhilaration and Terror of the Postmodern*. Liverpool: Liverpool University Press.

Pierce, Hazel (1982) *Philip K. Dick*. Washington: Starmont House.

Potin, Yves (1998) "Four levels of reality in Philip K. Dick's *Time out of Joint*," (transl.) Heather McLean, *Extrapolation* 39 (Summer): 148–65.

Rickman, Gregg, (1989) *To the High Castle: Philip K. Dick, A Life 1928–1982*. Long Beach, CA: Valentine Press.

Robinson, Kim Stanley (1984) *The Novels of Philip K. Dick*. Ann Arbor: UMI Research Press.

Rossi, Umberto (2004) "The Game of the Rat: A.E. Van Vogt's 800-word Rule and P.K. Dick's *The Game Players of Titan*." *Science Fiction Studies* 93. 3, 207–26.

Sutin, Lawrence (1989) *Divine Invasions: A Life of Philip K. Dick*. New York: Harmony.

——(ed.) (1995) *The Shifting Realities of Philip K. Dick*. New York: Vintage.

Suvin, Darko (2002) "Goodbye and Hello: Differentiating within the Later Philip K. Dick," *Extrapolation* 43 (Winter), 368–97.

Umland, Samuel J. (ed.) (1995) *Philip K. Dick: Contemporary Critical Interpretations*. Westport, CT and London: Greenwood Press.

Warrick, Patricia S. (1987) *Mind in Motion: The Fiction of Philip K. Dick*. Carbondale and Edwardsville: Southern Illinois University Press.

Williams, Paul (1986) *Only Apparently Real*. New York: Arbor House.

27

Samuel Delany: A Biographical and Critical Overview

Carl Freedman

Life

Samuel Delany was born on April 1, 1942, in New York City, into a relatively pros-
perous African-American family of considerable distinction. For instance, his paternal grandfather, Henry Beard Delany, had been born into slavery but lived to become
a college administrator and an Episcopal bishop (making him the first black American bishop in any predominantly white denomination). Henry Delany's two oldest
daughters, Sarah and Anne Elizabeth Delany – the oldest sisters of the writer's father
– gained considerable fame (thanks to their best-selling book *Having Our Say* [1993],
which was made into a Broadway play and then into a television miniseries) as the
brilliant "Delany sisters," whose lives encompassed almost the entire twentieth
century. Samuel Delany thus grew up in a family environment in which significant
intellectual achievement was common and expected.

The young Delany was educated at private schools and then at the Bronx High
School of Science, at that time the most intellectually renowned public high school
in the USA. He was successful in school, though the earlier years of his educational
career were somewhat marred by severe (and unrecognized) dyslexia, a condition that
plagues him to this day and that some critics feel has left a strong imprint on his literary style. Delany attended classes for part of one year at the City College of New
York, but his diploma from Bronx Science remains the only academic degree ever
earned by this man who today, in addition to his fame as a novelist, enjoys considerable distinction as a scholar and a university professor.

One of Delany's closest friends in high school was Marilyn Hacker, who became
one of the more honored American poets of her generation. In 1961 she and Delany
married, even though Delany's primarily homosexual orientation was clearly known
to both of them. The marriage was marked by emotional complexity, unusual sexual
arrangements (sometimes involving third persons), a great deal of fruitful artistic and
intellectual collaboration, repeated separations and reunions, and, in 1974, the birth

of a daughter, Iva Hacker-Delany. The final separation between Delany and Hacker came in 1975, and the marriage officially ended in divorce in 1980. Since then, Delany's main affectional relationships have been with men, most notably, since 1991, Dennis Rickett, a previously homeless street vendor. Today Delany and Rickett live together in the Upper West Side apartment that has been Delany's primary residence for more than a quarter century.

Though literature has no genuine prodigies in the sense that music and mathematics do, Delany began his literary career about as close to being a prodigy as a writer can come. He completed the manuscript of his first novel, *The Jewels of Aptor* (1962), when he was not quite out of his teens, and then in rapid succession produced another eight science fiction novels, averaging more than a book a year through 1968. These novels – most importantly *Babel-17* (1966), *The Einstein Intersection* (1967), and *Nova* (1968) – established his reputation and remain his most popular works among a significant minority of his readers; several years before his thirtieth birthday, Delany had reached the summit of the science fiction world. He has continued a steady literary output ever since. Though his greatest fame is for science fiction and science fiction criticism, he has also distinguished himself in such fields as historical fiction, contemporary realism, autobiography, letter-writing, and pornography: not to mention the "unclassifiable" (the description is Fredric Jameson's) four volumes of the Nevèrÿon sequence – a complex series of short stories, novellas, short novels, and one long novel – which many readers consider his supreme masterpiece. Delany has received many honors and awards for his writing, including four Nebula Awards (for *Babel-17*, *The Einstein Intersection*, the short story "Aye, and Gomorrah . . ." [1967], and the novella "Time Considered as a Helix of Semi-Precious Stones" [1968]); two Hugos (for "Time Considered as a Helix" and for the autobiography *The Motion of Light in Water* [1988; expanded and republished, 1990]); the Pilgrim Award (for lifetime achievement in science fiction criticism and scholarship); the William Whitehead Memorial Award (for lifetime achievement in gay and lesbian writing); and induction into the Science Fiction Hall of Fame.

As noted above, Delany is a professor as well as an author. His first university job came in the spring of 1975, when Leslie Fiedler (one of the very few major American literary critics, senior to Delany, who took a serious interest in science fiction) arranged a one-semester visiting position for him at the State University of New York at Buffalo. Over the next decade he took a number of other visiting and part-time academic positions, but in 1988 his relationship with the academy became full-time and permanent, as he began an appointment as (full) professor of comparative literature at the University of Massachusetts at Amherst. In 1998, he moved to the poetics program at (again) SUNY-Buffalo, and then in 2000 he moved to Temple University in Philadelphia, where he serves today as professor of English and creative writing. Though writers are often notorious for trying to treat academic appointments as sinecures, Delany has always been known as a hard-working, popular teacher and as a professor who does more than his share of departmental service; he is particularly noted for his support of junior and untenured colleagues. During his academic career

he has sometimes taught workshops in creative writing, but has always taught graduate and undergraduate courses in English literature, comparative literature, and critical theory.

Periodizing the Delany Canon

The division of a writer's output into periods is always somewhat arbitrary, and this
is especially the case when the writer is, like Delany, both highly prolific (he has
authored more than three dozen books to date) and still actively creating new work.
Even so, Delany's literary production thus far can be divided with reasonable convenience into three distinctive chronological groups. The first is clearly the series of nine
science fiction novels that began with *The Jewels of Aptor* in 1962 and ended with *Nova*
in 1968. After *Nova*, no new science fiction novel by Delany appeared for seven years;
but when *Dhalgren* (his longest book so far) was published in 1975, it revolutionized
the field. The second period includes not only *Dhalgren* but also such subsequent substantial masterworks as *Triton* (1976; later reprinted as *Trouble on Triton*), *Stars in My
Pocket Like Grains of Sand* (1984), and the four Nevèrÿon volumes (1979–87). This
period also includes most of the critical work that has established Delany as the only
major science fiction novelist who is also a major critic of the genre. The third period
can be taken to begin after the completion of the Nevèrÿon volumes. This period is
marked by Delany's movement away from science fiction. It thus far includes his
longest autobiographical work, *The Motion of Light in Water*; a great deal of literary
and cultural criticism, mostly (though not exclusively) on matters other than science
fiction; the "pornotopic fantasy," *The Mad Man* (1994; extensively revised and republished, 2002); his highly acclaimed work of realistic fiction, *Atlantis: Three Tales*
(1995); the best-selling *Times Square Red, Times Square Blue* (1999), a combination of
extremely personal reportage with Marxist urban analysis; and a selection of his correspondence, *1984* (2000).

Works: The Early Years (1962–8)

Delany's stature as one of the two or three most consequential innovators in modern
science fiction is so widely appreciated that perhaps the first thing that ought to be
said about the novels from *The Jewels of Aptor* to *Nova* is how deeply rooted they are
in the pulp science fiction of the American magazines as the latter flourished from
the 1920s through the 1950s. This is, indeed, the principal reason that Delany has
always resisted the designation "New Wave," which many commentators have applied
to him. More than once Delany has pointed out that the actual New Wave writers –
a group of British and American-expatriate authors associated in the 1960s with the
London magazine *New Worlds* – were explicitly hostile to pulp science fiction, especially to space opera, and sought to break radically with this tradition of science

fiction. Delany, by contrast, was fond of pulp and especially of space opera; and the evidence of his first nine novels clearly indicates that during this period his project was to rejuvenate the received forms and motifs of pulp rather than to leave them behind. Space opera, with its swashbuckling spaceship captains and its awesome superweapons; the postapocalyptic environment, with civilization struggling to recover from devastating catastrophe; multiplanetary political intrigue; the long and difficult quest journey; contact between human beings and various forms of alien intelligence; the conventional heterosexual love interest – these are among the principal narrative structures and elements that characterize Delany's early work, and all were the common property of his predecessors. All had been familiar in (for instance) the work of the so-called "Golden Age" science fiction authors who wrote for *Astounding* under the editorship of John W. Campbell. For pure space opera, indeed, it is arguable that no finer or more exciting narratives than *Babel-17* and *Nova* have ever been composed.

Despite all that Delany's early work may owe to pulp, it is, however, also clear that, from the very beginning, Delany was never an ordinary follower of Hugo Gernsback and "Doc" Smith, or of Robert Heinlein and Isaac Asimov, or even of Alfred Bester and Theodore Sturgeon, the two science fiction authors in the generation immediately senior to his for whom Delany has always expressed the highest admiration and whose work has left the most pronounced mark on his own. Even in his earliest novels – *The Jewels of Aptor*, the three volumes of the trilogy collectively known as *The Fall of the Towers* (1963–5), and *The Ballad of Beta-2* (1965) – there are hints of the major innovator Delany would soon become. In these books (notably in *The Ballad of Beta-2*) we find a level of interest in language and in the self-conscious process of literary composition almost unprecedented in science fiction, and we also find (notably in the trilogy) a much more sophisticated than usual understanding of politics, an understanding that goes beyond mere intrigue and adventure to encompass economics and complex social conflict. We also find, though somewhat more tentatively, the first signs of the interrogation of received racial and gender roles for which Delany would become famous. Though Delany's first five novels are not generally ranked high within the Delany canon as a whole, they remain important for understanding his development as a writer.

A new standard of innovation and craftsmanship is attained in the next four novels, which raise the achievements of the earlier works onto a higher plane and which constitute the acknowledged masterpieces of Delany's youth. The brilliant short novel *Empire Star* (1966) combines rollicking good space opera with ontological puzzles and with a parable of race and slavery as compelling, perhaps, as any that science fiction has produced – an element of the text clearly rooted in Delany's understanding of his African-American heritage. *Babel-17* offers space battles as well told as any in the genre; at the same time, it features a female starship captain celebrated primarily as a poet, and offers a fascinating engagement with ideas related to the Sapir-Whorf hypothesis about the function of language and its relation to the construction of reality. *The Einstein Intersection* gives us perhaps the most original postholocaust environment that science fiction had yet seen, combined with a remarkably subtle and intricate examination of both race and gender (there are three of the latter). It also represents Delany's first extensive attempt to introduce the formal techniques of literary modernism into science fiction, particularly in its use of myth; it should be noted, though, that, in contrast to most classic modernism, Delany's novel ultimately sets itself *against* myth, which is exposed as irredeemably conservative and regressive. *Nova* (whose protagonist is casually revealed to be black – at that time a nearly unprecedented move in American science fiction) features space opera of unsurpassed excitement and also constitutes (among other things) a sustained, sophisticated meditation on the political and emotional consequences of economic scarcity. Although *Nova*, unlike its two immediate predecessors, won no major award, many readers have always felt that Delany *deserved* a third consecutive Best Novel Nebula for the book.

Works: The Middle Years (1969–87)

Between the publication of *Nova* in 1968 and of *Dhalgren* in 1975, the science fiction world was abuzz with reports and speculations about the new, long novel that Delany was working on. But, when it actually appeared, nearly 900 pages of it in the original Bantam edition, the response was not unanimously favorable. Some fans were disappointed that the literary elements derived from pulp science fiction, so prominent in Delany's previous work, were almost entirely absent from *Dhalgren*; and many also tended to be put off by the novel's bulk and by its passages of modernist (or postmodernist) difficulty. Harlan Ellison, who prided himself on being a propagandist for innovative, cutting-edge science fiction – and who had been an enthusiastic admirer of Delany's earlier books – publicly dismissed *Dhalgren* as boring and trivial, even while admitting that he had not bothered to read most of it. To this day, science fiction readers of the simpler sort still occasionally maintain that with *Dhalgren* Delany ceased to be a real science fiction writer.

But that is a distinctly minority view. Despite the aspects that intimidated Ellison and some others, *Dhalgren* was hugely popular, selling far more copies than any of Delany's prior works and making more money in its first year than any science fiction novel had ever done before. The critical response was also overwhelmingly favorable. Theodore Sturgeon proclaimed *Dhalgren* to be the very best book that science fiction had ever produced, and there are many today who would add that nothing published since has invalidated that judgment. It is now justly regarded as one of the major American novels of the 1970s. Set, apparently, in the 1960s, and in the imaginary locus of Bellona – a large industrial city in the midwestern USA – *Dhalgren* is one of the great fictional explorations of urban America. Owing to some never fully explained cosmic catastrophe, Bellona has been largely (though not totally) cut off from the outside world: most of the population has left (while a few adventurous types have arrived), and normal social structures are deteriorating. The novel explores the social and personal changes experienced in this environment by the unnamed protagonist (known as the Kid) and by a huge cast of supporting characters. *Dhalgren* undertakes by far Delany's most ambitious consideration to that point of race and gender. The Kid is Native American (or, technically, half Native American), most of the other characters are African-American, and racial conflict is a major plot concern; so is the closely related issue of class conflict. Sexual arrangements tend to be experimental, and the book features the first fully explicit representations of homosexual experience in Delany's science fiction. With *Dhalgren*, Delany also went further than any other science fiction author (with the arguable exception of J.G. Ballard) had gone in mastering the techniques of Joycean modernism. It ought to be added, though, that, despite many challenging sections, much of the novel is straightforwardly realistic in presentation – something that is of course equally true of *Ulysses* (1922) itself.

After having made his readers wait seven years for *Dhalgren*, Delany made them wait only one more year for *Triton* (subtitled "An Ambiguous Heterotopia," in clear riposte to Ursula Le Guin's then-recent "ambiguous utopia," *The Dispossessed* [1974]). Superficially, the new novel seems to recall Delany's earlier science fiction – it is set on a moon of Neptune, and contains subordinate elements of space opera – and some readers did see *Triton* as a step backwards from *Dhalgren*. But, in sophistication, in intelligence, in verve, and in sheer readability, *Triton* surpasses even the very best of Delany's early work. It features the author's most intense and sustained examination of sex and gender roles to that point, and in one way inverts the thematic structure of *Dhalgren*: whereas the earlier novel had presented an attractive, sexually emancipated protagonist in the ruins of an oppressive, conformist society, *Triton* offers the hopelessly, if sometimes charmingly, conservative Bron Helstrom and his unhappy attempts to function within a generally liberated, nonsexist world. Humor had rarely been notable among the strengths of Delany's fiction, but *Triton* is, in one of its aspects, perhaps the most brilliant comedy of manners in all science fiction; the elaborate scene of Bron's dinner date with an ardently desired woman friend is worthy of a latter-day Jane Austen. Another innovation is that the book displays Delany's increasing sophistication as a scholar of modern critical theory; with *Triton*, Delany emerges as one of the current masters of the novel of ideas.

He consolidated that position with the four volumes of the Nevèrÿon series that appeared from 1979 to 1987. Here ideas are everywhere, derived from Delany's meditations on the work of Hegel, Marx, Nietzsche, Freud, Saussure, Wittgenstein, Lukács, Adorno, Bloch, Lévi-Strauss, Fanon, Lacan, Foucault, Derrida, Jameson, and a great many other modern thinkers. At the same time, the sequence contains many of the most compelling stories and most richly developed characters in the entire Delany canon – and, stylistically, some of the best writing. Whether the Nevèrÿon books should be classified as science fiction is debatable. The setting – an ancient empire of unspecified time and location – has led many readers to consider the sequence fantasy, while Delany himself has always referred to it as sword-and-sorcery. It is noteworthy that, despite the frequent "feel" of fantasy in its style and manner, hardly anything actually fantastic happens; the Nevèrÿon books contain many swords but little or no sorcery (depending upon how one or two scenes of apparent magic are read). Perhaps the sequence should be seen as alternative history, a well-established variety of science fiction. Or perhaps one should simply be content with Jameson's verdict of unclassifiability.

In any case, the sequence (the only multivolume work Delany has undertaken since *The Fall of the Towers*) is by far his most ambitious fiction yet. It is crammed with almost countless characters and subplots, but is also given unity by the presiding narrative of the dark-skinned Gorgik's successful struggle to abolish slavery in the empire of Nevèrÿon. Once again, slavery and race are central to Delany's vision (a fact that has been recognized only very belatedly by the academic Black Studies establishment). Gorgik is also Delany's first protagonist of primarily homosexual orientation, and with these books gay themes become increasingly central to Delany's writing. Sexual experience is explored with a psychoanalytic shrewdness unprecedented in science fiction, and with a frankness equally unprecedented. Indeed, the unashamed openness with which homosexual life is portrayed in *Flight from Nevèrÿon* (1985), the third volume of the series, created considerable controversy. The series also amounts to the apotheosis, in fiction, of Delany's longstanding interest in the economic basis of society, and is one of the liveliest works in American fiction written under the direct inspiration of Marxist theory. There is also much in the Nevèrÿon books that relates to Delany's interest in language, in the theory of representation, and in much else. Though some excellent critical commentary has already been produced (most notably by Kathleen Spencer), we have only just begun to explore the riches of this extraordinary work.

Stars in My Pocket Like Grains of Sand, a novel of indisputably science fictional character, appeared during the production of the Nevèrÿon sequence. Owing to logically accidental reasons – the fact that it has been long out of print, the fact that an announced sequel has never appeared – the novel is so far the least frequently discussed of the major fictional works of Delany's middle period. Nonetheless, a small but growing number of Delany scholars and critics (which includes Steven Shaviro and me) believes that *Stars in My Pocket* may well be his finest single volume yet. The novel represents a "world" – in the sense of an invented lifeworld, a fictional scene – in which there are over six thousand planets inhabited by sentient species, each one, evidently, roughly as full of biological and cultural diversity as our own Earth. The total amount of variety is thus unthinkably huge. The protagonist, Mark Dyeth, is by profession an "industrial diplomat," someone whose occupation is to make sense, as best he can, of this staggering heterogeneity and to interpret different cultures and species to one another. In this way, *Stars in My Pocket* amounts to the most serious and convincing effort yet made in science fiction to convey what life in a galactic federation (simplistic versions of which are of course a dime a dozen in the genre) might actually feel like. The book's exploration of the interpretive problems involved are a culmination of the concern with language, with artistic construction, with models and representations, and with the fundamental mysteries of communication itself, that Delany's work has always displayed. Then too, the attempt to comprehend unimaginable degrees of diversity has a moral and political as well as an epistemological dimension. The wrestling with species and planetary difference constitutes perhaps the most totalizing effort Delany has yet made to understand human differences of race, of class, of power, of gender, and of sexual orientation – and a totalizing effort made, of course, in full Derridean awareness that achieved totalization is forever beyond reach. Very much a novel of ideas, *Stars in My Pocket* also features the most passionate and convincing love story in the Delany canon. Indeed, in a masterstroke of structural composition, the story of the affair between Mark Dyeth and his lover, the extremely different Rat Korga, is beautifully fused with the overall thematics of social, cultural, and biological difference.

Delany's middle period contains not only his finest science fiction but also most of his science fiction criticism. Though many of the genre's authors have produced critical reflections of genuine interest, only Delany, among science fiction novelists, has written truly major criticism, criticism that would command just as much interest as it actually does even if its author had never written a line of fiction. It is, indeed, difficult to overstate Delany's importance for the field. With the lone exception of Darko Suvin, no other critic did as much as Delany to *professionalize* the study of science fiction, to make it as intellectually rigorous and as theoretically nimble and resourceful as any other field of literary criticism. Probably the most influential of his several books about science fiction is his first, *The Jewel-Hinged Jaw: Notes on the Language of Science Fiction* (1977). As the title suggests, Delany's concern is not to define science fiction (a project he regards as wholly vain), nor, for the most part, to examine science fictional theme and structure in the manner of Suvin, but instead to focus on the level of sentence production itself, to study the genre as a distinctive linguistic and stylistic practice. Whereas earlier science fiction critics had often been limited by not being widely read outside of science fiction itself, Delany brings to bear a remarkably extensive knowledge of the poetry, fiction, and literary theory of the nineteenth and twentieth centuries. In addition to ground-breaking general theorizing, Delany's criticism is noteworthy for close readings of particular texts. Probably the most frequently cited essay in *The Jewel-Hinged Jaw* is "To Read *The Dispossessed*," a meticulous, respectful, and in many ways devastating deconstruction of Le Guin's novel; the essay is, indeed, a kind of companion piece to *Triton*. An even closer reading is found in *The American Shore* (1978), where Delany, in a manner often compared with that of Roland Barthes in *S/Z* (1970), undertakes an intensive book-length reading of a single short story, Thomas Disch's "Angouleme" (1971).

Works: The Recent Years (1988 Onwards)

Though Delany's creative energy has not flagged as regards either the quality or the quantity of his literary output, his most recent period may, in the current context, be dealt with quickly, simply because during these years Delany has published no science fiction (unless one counts *They Fly at Çiron* [1993], a sword-and-sorcery novel based on a story he originally composed in 1962) and relatively little science fiction criticism. It should be noted, though, that much of the major work of the recent years, while not to be counted as science fiction by even the most expansive definitions, does show the imprint of Delany's long career in the genre. For example, "Atlantis: Model 1924," a superb novella in the *Atlantis* volume, is historical realism that seems haunted by the ghost of the science fictional alternative history. Chronology and other factors indicate that the protagonist Sam, who has an encounter with Hart Crane on the Brooklyn Bridge, is directly based on Samuel Delany, Sr., the author's father. But some of the character's attributes appear to link him more closely with the son than with the father: it is almost as though the writer were imagining what might have happened to him had he lived during his father's generation. To take another instance, *The Mad Man* (Delany's longest novel next to *Dhalgren*) presents its story in a super-ficially realistic way. But the author's own description of it as pornotopic fantasy not only explicitly links the book to the Utopian tradition always closely related to science fiction, but also suggests what an attentive reading should make clear: that the text strives not to offer naturalistic reportage about the sexual lives of (mostly homeless) gay men in Manhattan, but rather to perform a quasiscience fictional estrangement of the general sexual practices (heterosexual as well as homosexual) and, even more perhaps, the larger *social* practices of Reaganite and post-Reaganite America. Many science fiction readers wish that Delany would return to the genre. He might perhaps reply that, as the expatriate Joyce said of himself and the city of Dublin, he has never really left it.

Conclusion

Delany's literary reputation has suffered from an abundance of supposedly limiting adjectives: he is described (accurately, of course) as a science fiction writer, a gay writer, an African-American writer. Surely it is high time that he be unanimously recognized as, above all, one of the major *writers* of his era? If we consider, however, his specific place in the history of science fiction, a respectable argument can be made for his actual supremacy within the genre. To list only the most obvious titles: can anyone name another author who has contributed six novels to science fiction equal in impor-tance to *Babel-17*, *The Einstein Intersection*, *Nova*, *Dhalgren*, *Triton*, and *Stars in My Pocket Like Grains of Sand*? Or the matter might be put another way. If a large number of well-informed scholars and critics of science fiction were asked to list the half dozen authors in the genre they regard as having made the most durable contributions to literature, then H.G. Wells' name would appear on more lists than Delany's, and so, probably, would Philip K. Dick's; and so, just possibly, would Le Guin's. But almost certainly no others would (though Olaf Stapledon, Stanislaw Lem, the Strugatsky brothers, and William Gibson would surely be strong contenders). As much as or more than any other author, Delany has made science fiction a literature for adults, a literature that requires no apologies or special pleading. No body of work in the genre is less vulnerable than his to the vulgar charge that science fiction is just limp day-dreaming for adolescent and pre-adolescent boys. Delany has moved comfortably among the most urgent human issues – sexual and psychological, biological and cultural, economic and political, linguistic and philosophical, scientific and technological – and he has always remained alert to the most advanced formal methods in modern literature. Spaceships are hardly more common in Delany's science fiction than are his reflections on the ideas of Wittgenstein or his revisions of the techniques of Joyce. Furthermore, Delany has produced work that is in the best sense *serious* without sacrificing the narrative excitement or the "sense of wonder" that have always been at the basis of science fiction's mass popularity. Delany's large readership and his formal awards – the Nebulas, the Hugos, the Pilgrim – make clear that science fiction has done much for him. But he has done more for it.

References and Further Reading

No other science fiction author (with the exceptions of Wells and, probably, of Dick) has been the object of more intelligent and interesting commentary than has Delany; and the following list is selective. Excluded are the many noteworthy essays about Delany published in journals. But included are all or nearly all of the books devoted, in whole or in significant part, to Delany's work.

Barbour, Douglas (1979) *Worlds Out of Words: The SF Novels of Samuel R. Delany*. Frome: Brans Head Books.

Broderick, Damien (1995) *Reading By Starlight: Postmodern Science Fiction*. London: Routledge.

Carby, Hazel V. (1998) *Race Men*. Cambridge, MA: Harvard University Press.

Freedman, Carl (2000) *Critical Theory and Science Fiction*. Hanover: Wesleyan University Press.

Fox, Robert E. (1987) *Conscientious Sorcerers: The Black Postmodernist Fiction of LeRoi Jones/Amiri Baraka, Ishmael Reed, and Samuel R. Delany*. New York: Greenwood Press.

Jackson, Earl, Jr. (1995) *Strategies of Deviance: Studies in Gay Male Representation*. Bloomington, IN: Indiana University Press.

McEvoy, Seth (1984) *Samuel R. Delany*. New York: F. Ungar.

Moylan, Tom (1986) *Demand the Impossible: Science Fiction and the Utopian Imagination*. New York: Methuen.

Peplow, Michael W. and Robert S. Bravard (1980)

Samuel R. Delany, A Primary and Secondary Bibliography, 1962–1979. Boston, MA: G.K. Hall.

Posnock, Ross (1998) *Color and Culture: Black Writers and the Making of the Modern Intellectual*. Cambridge, MA: Harvard University Press.

Robinson, Paul (1999) *Gay Lives: Homosexual Autobiography from John Addington Symonds to Paul Monette*. Chicago, IL: University of Chicago Press.

Sallis, James (ed.) (1996) *Ash of Stars: On the Writing of Samuel R. Delany*. Jackson, MS: University Press of Mississippi, [includes essays by Russell Blackford, Mary Kay Bray, Ray Davis, Robert Elliot Fox, Jean Mark Gawron, Ken James, Carl Malmgren, David Samuelson, and Kathleen Spencer].

Shaviro, Steven (2003) *Connected, or What It Means to Live in the Network Society*. Minneapolis, MN: University of Minnesota Press.

Slusser, George (1977) *The Delany Intersection: Samuel R. Delany Considered as a Writer of Semi-Precious Words*. San Bernadino, CA: Borgo Press.

Tucker, Jeffrey Allen (2004) *A Sense of Wonder: Samuel R. Delany, Race, Identity and Difference*. Middletown, CT: Wesleyan University Press.

Weedman, Jane (1982) *Samuel R. Delany*. San Bernardino, CA: Borgo Press.

Woodhouse, Reed (1998) *Unlimited Embrace: A Canon of Gay Fiction, 1945–1995*. Amherst, MA: University of Massachusetts Press.

28

Ursula K. Le Guin

Warren G. Rochelle

Ursula Kroeber Le Guin, one of the USA's most critically acclaimed science fiction and fantasy writers of the last half of the twentieth century and now of the twenty-first, was born on October 21, 1929, in Berkeley, California. Named after her patron saint, she is the "youngest child and only daughter of Theodora and Alfred Kroeber." Alfred Kroeber (1897–1960), "internationally known for his anthropological work" among Native Americans, especially those in California, was the founder of what became one of the leading anthropology departments in the country, at the University of California at Berkley (Reid 1997:1). Theodora Kracaw Kroeber Quinn (1897–1979), while always assisting and supporting her husband's work, is respected as a writer and scholar in her own right. Le Guin describes both her "remarkable parents" as "totally nonsexist," with "no difference in expectations for herself and her [three] brothers" (De Bolt 1979: 16). Le Guin feels she "inherited" from her parents, especially her father, "a willingness to get outside [one's] own culture and also a sensitivity to how culture affects personality, which is what [her] father was concerned with" (Le Guin, in Cummins 1990: 2).

The Kroebers were a family of readers and what Le Guin read as a child clearly influenced her adult work. One of her favorite books was Lady Frazer's *Leaves from the Golden Bough*, a child's version of the famous anthropological text (Spivack 1984: 2). Up until her teens, Le Guin read voraciously from myth and then science fiction – abandoning the latter in the late 1940s because it was "all about hardware" (Spivack 1984: 2). Not surprisingly, Le Guin was writing stories at an early age, sending, at the age of 11, a tale to *Astounding Stories*. At 12, when she opened up a copy of Lord Dunsany's 1910 book, *A Dreamer's Tales*, she discovered "people are still making myths . . . Whatever the reason, the moment was decisive. [She] discovered [her] native country" (Le Guin 1992: 21). Le Guin's reading was never, however, confined to science fiction and fantasy. A 1976 list of influences includes: "Shelley, Keats, Wordsworth, Leopardi, Hugo, Rilke, Thomas and Roethke in poetry. Dickens, Tolstoy, Turgenev, Chekhov, Pasternak, the Brontes, Woolf, E.M. Forster in prose.

Among contemporaries, Solzhenitsyn, Boll, Wilson, Drabble, Calvino, Dick" (Reid 1997: 16).

Education and Family and Coming Of Age: 1947–67

The first story for which Le Guin was paid, "April in Paris," a time travel fantasy, was not published until 1962, in *Fantastic*, when she was 32. By then, she had completed her formal education, married, and begun a family. In 1947, she entered Radcliffe College, in Cambridge, Massachusetts, and graduated, Phi Beta Kappa, in 1951. She earned an MA at Columbia in 1952, in French and Renaissance literature, and started doctoral work the same year. In 1953 a Fulbright took her across the Atlantic to study French poetry. On the trip over, on the *Queen Mary*, she met Charles Le Guin, "a tall, handsome scholar of French history from Macon, Georgia." They were married in Paris in December 1953, and Le Guin never finished her doctorate.

In 1954, after returning to the USA, Le Guin worked as a secretary and taught French at Mercer University in Macon, Georgia, while Charles continued his doctoral studies at Emory. By 1956, the couple was at the University of Idaho, where again Le Guin taught French and Charles completed his Ph.D. In 1957, still in Idaho, Le Guin gave birth to her first daughter, Elisabeth. Her second daughter, Caroline, followed in 1959, and the family moved to Portland, Oregon, where Charles began teaching at Portland State. The Le Guins have lived there ever since. The following year, in October, Alfred Kroeber, then in his eighties, died suddenly. Le Guin's last child and only son, Theodore, was born in 1964.

Le Guin describes the years 1959–61 as the time when she came of age as a writer (De Bolt 1979: 17). She rediscovered science fiction – "and a way into print" – in 1960, when "a friend in Portland loaned her some works from his collection, including a copy of *The Magazine of Fantasy & Science Fiction* which contained a story by Cordwainer Smith" (De Bolt 1979: 18). She chose science fiction, besides being able to sell it, because "it has an intelligent readership, and because [she liked] it – [she found] it beautiful" (Le Guin, in Reid 1997: 8). That science fiction is so often dismissed by the literary mainstream as inconsequential genre fiction did not deter her. But even though she feels these attitudes has caused critics to take her work less seriously, Le Guin has been and is "quite loyal to the science fiction community and was one of the founding members of the Science Fiction Writers of America (SFWA)" (Reid 1997: 9).

The discovery of Hain

"April in Paris," was followed by her first paid science fiction story, "The Masters," also published in *Fantastic*, in 1963. She taught herself "the science she needed for this kind of fiction, and she eventually developed a sophisticated understanding of many scientific concepts, although she [favored and still favors] anthropology and psychology" (Reid 1997: 8). The stories that launched Earthsea appeared in *Fantastic* in 1964, "The Rule of Names," and "The Word of Unbinding." These were followed by "three entertaining but undistinguished" science fiction novels, *Planet of Exile* and *Rocannon's World* in 1966, and *City of Illusions*, in 1967. These three novels, which "mix science fiction and fantasy," introduce the Hainish universe, a universe created by Le Guin to "explore her ideas about human society in a metaphorical context." Both the critics and Le Guin consider these "inferior to her later work," as they "haphazardly mix scientific-sounding novelties with mythic elements" (Reid 1997: 9).

Primary Themes and Subjects

Yet, this mix of the fantastic and the scientific, where Le Guin attempted to create worlds with distinct cultures and peoples and mythologies, in a way, bring almost all the primary themes or subjects of Le Guin's to the literary table at the same time. According to Charlotte Spivack, in *Ursula K. Le Guin*, there are "three subjects central to an appreciation of Le Guin's fiction [that] are worthy of a prior introduction: cultural anthropology, Jungian psychology, and Taoist philosophy". To these I would add a fourth, feminism.

Cultural anthropology

Cultural anthropology, as a subject of Le Guin's fiction, is clearly evidence of the influence of her parents, especially her father, Alfred Kroeber. She acquired the "anthropological attitude" necessary for the observation of another culture – or for her, the invention of another culture: the recognition and appreciation of cultural diversity, the necessity to be a "close and impartial observer," who is objective, yet recognizes the inescapable subjectivity that comes with participation in an alien culture. Ethnographic detail, the outsider's perspective, the tension between both objective and subjective – all are part of the anthropological attitude, or what seems to be more appropriate term for Le Guin, the anthropological imagination, the creative gift of world-making. Cultural anthropology as a shaper of her fiction is perhaps the most evident in her protagonists, who are observers, and who often find themselves caught up in cultural confrontation, which they must often mediate.

Jungian psychology and myth

Jungian psychology, with its connections to the mythic, provides a useful tool for both critical analysis of Le Guin's fiction and for understanding her thinking and purpose behind the fiction. Briefly, Jung considered the human unconscious to have two levels, that of the personal and of the collective. The personal is that individual warehouse of repressed or forgotten memories of individual experiences that often appear in one's dreams and are often motivations, unseen and not consciously known, for individual actions. The collective unconscious is formed by the "commonality of human experience – birth, sex, death, loss, hunger, and so forth" (Rochelle 2001: 17). Le Guin defines the collective unconscious as a "vast common ground on which we can meet not only rationally, but aesthetically, intuitively, emotionally" (Le Guin 1992: 75).

Within this collective unconscious one finds the source of the mythic. Here can be found universal human images or symbols, or archetypes, such as the mother, the wise old man, the crone, the Shadow, the Hero, or the journey. Myths are, by Jung's definition, the "narrative elaboration of archetypal images" (Jung 1963: 347). The archetypes "are repeated in all mythologies, fairy tales, religions, traditions, and mysteries. What else is the myth of the night sea voyage, of the wandering hero, or of the sea monster than our timeless knowledge transformed into a picture of the sun's setting and rebirth . . ." (Jacobi 1951: 62)

The mythic permeates Le Guin's fiction. A hero's quest shapes the first three books of the *Earthsea* cycle. Le Guin reimagines the origin of humans, not on Earth, but on Hain, whose people spread our species throughout the Orion Arm, with a history so old that some of it can only be myth. In this Hainish universe Le Guin has created her own mythos. Le Guin sees myth as "an expression of one of the several ways the human being, body/psyche, perceives, understands, and relates to the world. Like science, it is a basic human mode of comprehension' (Le Guin 1992: 69).

Le Guin, however, is adamant that she is not a Jungian "in any sense of the word and dislike[s] being called so," despite her comments on Jung and Jungian thought in her essays, "Myth and Archetype in Science Fiction," and "The Child and the Shadow." According to Le Guin, who admits the common ground, her idea of "the shadow," for example, is one at which she arrived "independently . . . Convergence, not influence" (Le Guin, letter to the author, April 13, 1998).

Taoism

Le Guin was exposed to Taoist philosophy by her parents. Alfred Kroeber's favorite book was the *Tao Te Ching*, which contains the essentials of Taoist beliefs and philosophy. Le Guin, who describes herself as a "congenital non-Christian," felt an instant affinity for Taoism, so much so that it has provided metaphor and structure for much of her fiction, particularly the *Earthsea* cycle. The Tao, or the Way, "refers to the basic moral law which underlies all human behavior. Rooted in nature, it is a fundamental precept underlying all religions." Its key principle is inaction or "what is called the Theory of Letting Alone" (Spivack 1984: 6). This idea of "the virtue of inaction" is adhered to by Earthsea wizards, who only use magic when absolutely necessary. Her anthropologist-observers know the less interference with a native culture, the better for all. The "relativity of opposites" is another key Taoist principle found in Le Guin's fiction, a principle that directly counters the "dualistic philosophy of historic Christianity." Instead of a struggle, light and dark should be reconciled; each needs the other to exist. This interdependence of dualities is one of the dominant metaphors in the *Earthsea* cycle; it is the controlling metaphor of *The Left Hand of Darkness*. The yin/yang symbol, light and dark, light-in-dark, male and female, male-in-female, is given flesh in the ambisexual Gethenians, and coming to understand this Taoist interdependence of male and female is perhaps the greatest epiphany of Ai, one of the novel's observer-narrators.

Feminism

Le Guin's conversion to feminism came relatively late in her life. That Le Guin has always been sympathetic to feminist thinking is evident in *The Left Hand of Darkness*, where masculinity and femininity are clearly presented as social constructs. Barbara Bucknall describes *Left Hand* as Le Guin's "first contribution to feminism" (1981: 9); the "classical feminine coming-of-age process" of Tenar described in *The Tombs of Atuan* might be considered to be the second (Reid 1997: 10). It was not that Le Guin, a member of the National Organization for Women (NOW) and of the National Abortion Rights Action League (NARAL), did not take feminism seriously. Rather, as she explains in her essay, "The Fisherwoman's Daughter," her change was evolutionary and for a long time she was not aware she needed to change: "I was free – born free, lived free. And for years that personal freedom allowed me to ignore the degree to which my writing was controlled and constrained by judgments and assumptions I thought were my own, but which were the internalized ideology of a male supremacist society" (Le Guin 1989: 233–4).

Re-examination of these assumptions came in 1977, when Le Guin was writing *The Eye of the Heron*. It was then she discovered feminist literary criticism, "which questions the lack of women's voices and experiences in the traditional canon." Her daughter Caroline, a feminist and a women's studies specialist, helped Le Guin come to a new awareness of the impact of feminism and feminist thought (Reid 1997: 10).

Maturity: 1967–73

The rise of Earthsea

Cultural anthropology, Jungian psychology and the mythic, Taoism, and feminism – with the latter a more visible subject or theme in her latter works – are the primary threads woven into the fabric of Le Guin's fiction, whether the stories are intended for adults or children. It was a request from Herman Schein, the editor at Parnassus for a book "specifically for the 11–17 audience" that prompted the writing of *A Wizard of Earthsea*, winner of the Boston Globe-Hornbook award, published in 1968. This was the first time she wrote specifically for young people. And as it was, Le Guin feels "The most childish thing about *A Wizard of Earthsea* is its subject: coming of age" (Le Guin, in Reid 1997: 9). Barbara Bucknall considers *Wizard* to probably be Le Guin's "greatest achievement" (Le Guin, in Reid 1997: 9), and Le Guin herself describes *Wizard* as the "best put together [of her] books" (Le Guin, in Reid 1997:

9). It is also the book in which Le Guin begins her questioning some of the givens of the Monomyth – Ged, unlike the default Hero, is a dark-skinned man.

Recognition of Le Guin's own maturity of writer came, however, with her next novel, published in 1969, *The Left Hand of Darkness*. This novel of the already mentioned ambisexual people of Gethen, or Winter – a world in an ice age – who are both sexes and neither, won the 1969 Nebula and the 1970 Hugo, the crown jewels of science fiction. The former is given by the professional members of the SFWA; the latter by the fans at the World Convention of the SFWA. The Taoist idea of the interdependence has already been noted, with the use of the yin/yang symbol by Ai as emblematic of the Gethenians. That this symbol is also one of light and shadow suggests a Jungian connection as well. That Ai collects the myths of the planet's different cultures reaffirms the importance Le Guin places on myth as a tool of cultural understanding.

As also noted earlier, *Left Hand*, while not intentionally feminist, as are later works, does wrestle with one of the key tenets of feminist thought: the social construction of gender. It is through the lens of gender that Le Guin takes on one of the premier questions of science fiction: what does it mean to be human. How much is one's humanity shaped by gender? Indeed, all of Le Guin's primary subjects are present in the texture of this novel. There can be no doubt this novel was and is a "major achievement," an "artistic triumph" (Spivack 1984: 59). Lastly, this novel serves well to introduce Le Guin's notion of the thought-experiment. What if gender could be removed from the social equation? There is no little irony in noting that the same year *Left Hand* was published, Le Guin experienced her first serious sexism as a writer. Le Guin also published "Nine Lives," about, among other things, nine clones without sexual taboos, in *Playboy*, under the name U.K. Le Guin. The editors did not want their readers to know she was a woman. Le Guin agreed, but it "still rankles" (De Bolt 1979: 20).

For Le Guin, publishing *A Wizard of Earthsea* and *The Left Hand of Darkness* marked progress and growth in her career. As she noted of her work up to 1973: "Along in 1967–68 I finally got my pure fantasy vein separated off from my science fiction vein by writing *A Wizard of Earthsea* and then *The Left Hand of Darkness*, and the separation marked a very large advance in both skill and content" (Le Guin, in Bucknall 1981: 83).

Le Guin followed *Left Hand* in 1971 with two novels, the second of the original *Earthsea* trilogy, *The Tombs of Atuan*, and *The Lathe of Heaven*, the latter set in what becomes, in addition to Earthsea and the Hainish universe of the Ekumen, Le Guin's third major locale, the West Coast of the USA. *Tombs* was for some time her only novel with a female protagonist and lead character, Tenar, and the novel is the story of her coming of age. One of Le Guin's secondary themes, names and the power of naming, is central to the story, as Tenar is initially taken from the child to make her the priestess Arha, and is returned to her years later by Ged, as she is discovering herself. (It should be noted that the knowledge of the true names of everything is key to Earthsea's Art Magic.) Philip K. Dick's influence is evident in *The Lathe of Heaven*, particularly his questioning of the nature of reality, as George Orr, the protagonist, who lives in a near-future Portland, has dreams that can change reality.

1972 saw the publication of the third Earthsea novel, *The Farthest Shore*, and the appearance of the novella, "The Word for the World is Forest" in Harlan Ellison's anthology, *Again, Dangerous Visions*. The theme of the first Earthsea novel was coming of age; this, the last of the original trilogy, is about death. The Hero's Journey is complete – Ged, and Arren, the young prince who will be King of All the Isles – travel into the realm of the dead and return, the world saved. And in "The Word for the World is Forest," Le Guin takes a more proactive step towards saving her own world, as her fiction becomes more polemical. The novella is an "allegorical commentary on the horrible impact of the military conflict on the people and land in Vietnam" (Reid 1997: 11). *The Farthest Shore* took the 1973 National Book Award for Children's Literature; "The Word" took was awarded a 1973 Hugo at that year's World Convention of Science Fiction.

The Mid-Years: Calling for Freedom and the Polemics of Utopia, 1973–93

One of Le Guin's most frequently anthologized stories, "The Ones Who Walk Away from Omelas," winner of another Hugo, was published in 1973. Its polemics are clear. Can, Le Guin asks, the many be content in their happiness and wealth and security, if all three are paid for by the suffering of a few – in the story, one tormented and abused child? I read "Omelas" as a political allegory of the USA, and as a Utopian parable: with all our wealth, who is it that is left in the American closet, to suffer to ensure this wealth and all that comes with it, not be taken away? That this story appears in so many high school anthologies and so many first-year composition readers attests to its impact, as argument, as social commentary, as allegory.

In 1974 Le Guin turned from Utopia on the scale of one city, Omelas, to Utopia on the scale of a planet, in *The Dispossessed*, which won, again, both the Hugo and the Nebula. Elizabeth Cummins, in *Understanding Ursula K. Le Guin*, presents *The Dispossessed's* thought experiment thus:

> Let's see what would happen if a theoretical physicist came to maturity in a century-old anarchist society just when it is falling toward a structured government. Let's say further that he needs the stimulation of physicists on other worlds to continue his work, but no travel between worlds has been allowed by his society. (Cummins 1990: 104–5)

But this thought experiment is also a quest – indeed, the novel is "readily and easily identified as a version of the Monomyth, a novel of the Hero and the Quest" (Rochelle 2001: 43). The novel is a work of rhetoric, as Le Guin juxtaposes, through Shevek's journeys, two societies with opposing philosophies. She admits its didacticism: "The sound of axes being ground is occasionally audible" (Le Guin 1992: 109).

It is a feminist Utopia, as Anarresti society is based on full equality and mutual solidarity and cooperation, with its philosophy developed by Odo, a woman.

In 1975–6, two story collections, *The Wind's Twelve Quarters*, and *Orsinian Tales*, and a collection of essays, a book of poems, and a short realistic novel, *Very Far Away from Anywhere Else* are all published. Le Guin has argued that "all fiction has ethical, political, and social weight." Following in 1978, in the wake of *The Dispossessed*, is the novel *Eye of the Heron*, which it fits Le Guin's description of fiction, as it continues her ongoing polemic for human freedom. *Eye*, set on the planet Victoria, has two human societies, the City and the Town, set in political and philosophical opposition, the City the descendants of criminals, the Town, the descendants of peace activists – and spiritually, of those who walked away from Omelas. *Eye* was followed in 1979 by *Malafrena*, set in the fourth of Le Guin's fictional places, the Central European country of Orsinia, in the nineteenth century, in the years when reactionary governments were trying to restore their power after the revolutions of the eighteenth century. Significantly, there are two heroes, the young would-be revolutionary, off to the city to join the struggle, and a young woman, choosing to stay at home. Le Guin is again honored in 1979, the same year her mother dies, with the Gandalf Award, as Grand Master of Fantasy. That same year saw the publication of an essay collection, *The Language of the Night* (a revised version came out in 1992).

The Beginning Place, the tale of two adolescent protagonists and their romance and their coming of age in a fantasy world adjacent and somewhat accessible to our own, came out in 1980. This short novel was followed by two collections of poetry, *Hard Words and Other Poems*, 1982, and *In the Red Zone*, in 1983, and a story collection, *The Compass Rose*, in 1982.

Feminist maturity: 1985–93

Always Coming Home, which Le Guin describes as a truer feminist Utopia than *The Dispossessed*, and perhaps her most unusual book structurally, was published in 1985. It is a fictional ethnography of a people who "might be going to have lived a long, long time from now in Northern California" (Le Guin 1985: First Note). I consider this work a triumph of the imagination as she has lovingly created this future culture of the Kesh, based loosely on that of Native Americans, in intricate detail: their songs (a cassette is included in some editions), children's games, poetry, an excerpt from a novel, histories, death rituals, clothing, and diet, and more. It is a feminist Utopia, neither a matriarchy nor a patriarchy: men and women just are.

1987 saw the publication of another short story collection, *Buffalo Gals and Other Animal Presences*, which again evokes Native American culture and at the time, poses questions about environmental protection and the equality of men and women. Children's books, including the inaugural novel of the *Catwings* series were published in 1988, as well as another poetry collection. While not as well known as her fiction, Le Guin's poetry explores much the same themes and issues, and has evolved as her fiction has evolved, growing more political and polemical and feminist, and with closer examinations of the family and the mysterious and the spiritual. Many of the essays in her collection, published in 1989, *Dancing at the Edge of the World*, "center around feminist issues of power and language" (Reid 1997: 66).

Tehanu: the Last Book of Earthsea, is the 1990 feminist sequel to *The Farthest Shore*. The Monomyth of the Hero and the Quest, as Le Guin explains in her 1993 essay, *Earthsea Revisioned*, has been turned on its head. A novel about dragons and middle age and child abuse, the novel explores the lives of Tenar and Ged, now bereft of his power, lives focused on what has been traditionally considered woman's work: the home, children, the daily, the mundane. More short stories, a collection about the lives of several generations of women, *Searoad: Chronicles of Klatsand*, came out the next year, and chapbooks of poetry and prose in the next two years. In 1993 she edited, with Brian Attebery, *The Norton Book of Science Fiction*, now sometimes used as a text-book in science fiction courses around the USA.

The Later Years: 1994–

The ten years, 1994–2003, have been productive for Le Guin: more poetry, another juvenile, another five short story collections, a translation of the *Tao Te Ching* that was forty years in the making, four connected novellas published in one volume – what Le Guin has called a "story suite" – and two novels, one set in the Hainish universe, the other in the *Earthsea* cycle. The familiar subjects and motifs are still present, as is the overarching political concern for the protection and the nurture of human freedom in all aspects of human life, and for the need for the creation of a true human community. The axes are still, from time to time, audible. But there is still growth, there is still a sense she has not stopped honing the sharp blade of her language – the metaphors and imagery and insight are no less powerful, no less beautiful. The stories are still being told, the myth is still being created, the keen wit is still there.

Suzanne Reid argues, in *Presenting Ursula K. Le Guin*, that in Le Guin's 1994 story collection, *A Fisherman of the Inland Sea*, Le Guin is "questioning the nature of narra-tive and how it changes when we shift viewpoints or allow ourselves to share view-points" (Reid 1997: 97). I would add that she is also examining how knowledge is made, and how we come to know, particularly through story. The stories are, for the most part, set in a somewhat undefined future, except for the title story, "A Fisher-man of the Inland Sea," on O, four light years from Hain. In this story, Le Guin asks the reader to examine what we know and how we know, of human sexuality, as the k'O group marriage assumes bisexuality. *Four Ways to Forgiveness*, published in 1995, as four interconnected novellas, set in the Hainish universe, on the planets Werel and Yeowe, looks at power and the nature of power, through the lens of the master-slave relationship. Reid suggests that this collection is also about feminist thinking and how such thinking can affect and change a society set up in the hierarchy of master and slave, inferior and superior (Reid 1997: 99). Le Guin describes her 1996 story collection *Unlocking the Air* "as not being science fiction, but 'plain realism, or magical realism, or surrealism'" (Rochelle 2001: 172). There is no question these stories push the envelope of what is real and what is not, and at the same time, are, as Le Guin says, "explorations of the mysteries of name and time and ordinary living and ordinary pain" (Le Guin 1996: front cover).

In 2000, Le Guin returned to the Hainish universe in the novel, *The Telling*. Set on the planet Aka, where all old customs and beliefs have been outlawed, with the typical Le Guin outsider observer-narrator, it is a story about stories and storytelling, and the dangerous interplay of politics and religion. 2001 saw what may be the culmination of the *Earthsea* cycle, with the publication of *Tales from Earthsea* and what, as critic Nicholas Lezard argues in *The Guardian*, must be the final book, *The Other Wind*, a novel. In the latter, the dragons again must be confronted, and the very nature of the world is at state. In *Tales*, Le Guin explores both the past and the present of Earthsea, as the question of how the wizards' school on Roke came to be is answered and what happens when the school is forced to change, and women are allowed to enter.

The Birthday of the World, released in 2002, is Le Guin's tenth story collection. Of its eight stories, six are set in the Hainish Ekumen, one is on a distant planet (which *could* be in the Ekumen, Le Guin is not sure), and the last one is definitely not, being placed in some generic future where humans travel to far planets on generational ships, taking years to get there. According to one critic, the driving force here is sex, with the "unifying theme" of "personal isolation within an increasingly communal universe" (Colton 2002).

Her wit is more than evident in 2003's *Changing Planes*, a story collection, which I see as an extended joke, sharpened by Le Guin's sense of satire and social commentary and whimsy. While stuck in an airport, waiting for a delayed flight, Sita Dulip discovers the secret of truly changing planes of existence. Just a short list of the denizens of these other planes should give one a feel for this small collection: a woman whose genome is 4% corn, bearwigs in the walls, a people who mark adulthood by total silence, people who literally never stop arguing, others who migrate like birds (well, they are avian – sort of), and so on. Or, in other words, the diversity of life, of the human experience, and the pain and joy of it all. As Margaret Atwood noted in her review of *The Birthday of the World*, Le Guin is "a quintessentially American writer of the sort for whom the quest for the Peaceable Kingdom is ongoing."

In early 2004, Shambala Press released Le Guin's third major collection of essays and talks, *The Wave in the Mind: Talks and Essays on the Writer, the Reader, and the Imagination*. Here Le Guin again demonstrates the range and depth of her artistry, as this collection includes literary criticism, autobiography, performance art, meditations on sound and rhythm in poetry and prose, and "most centrally her reflections on the arts of writing and reading" (back cover). A young adult fantasy novel, *Gifts*, was released by Harcourt in August 2004. The gifts are what make the families of the Uplands different, and feared as witches by Lowlanders. Each family has its own, passed down from father to son, or mother to daughter, such as the ability to call animals, to twist bodies, to sweep a mind blank, to remove a person's will – and all done "with a glance, a gesture, a word." Guin is again exploring familiar territory when two such gifted children who, as they come of age, decide not to use their gifts. The question is one of power and the consequences of its use and misuse and of choice, choices that echoes those made by the people of Omelas: use the power and accept the cruelty that it brings, or choose another way. Do we make the choices of our parents because we love them, and continue to tell their stories – or not?

There are still more stories to be told, still more answers to how to be truly human – the quest is unfinished.

REFERENCES AND FURTHER READING

Atwood, Margaret (2002) "The Queen of Quinkdom: A Review of *The Birthday of the World and Other Stories*." *The New York Review of Books* 26 September, 2002. *The New York Review of Books Online*. Online. 31 October 2003. Available at http://www.nybooks.com/articles.html

Bierman, Judah (1975) "Ambiguity in Utopia: *The Dispossessed*." *Science Fiction Studies* 2, 249–55.

Bittner, James (1984) *Approaches to the Fiction of Ursula K. Le Guin*. Ann Arbor: UMI Research Press.

Bloom, Harold (1987) *Ursula K. Le Guin's The Left Hand of Darkness*. New York: Chelsea House.

Bucknall, Barbara J. (1981) *Ursula K. Le Guin*. New York: Frederick Ungar.

Colton, Kim (2002) "Science Friction": Review of *The Birthday of the World and Other Stories*, by Ursula K. Le Guin. 3 April, 2002. *Hurry Date* (column) in *Willamette Week Online*. Online. 31 October 2003. Available at <http://www.wweek.com/flatfiles.html>

Cummins, Elisabeth (1993) *Understanding Ursula K. Le Guin* (1990). Columbia, SC: University of South Carolina Press.

De Bolt, Joseph (ed.) (1979) *Ursula K. Le Guin: Voyage to Inner Lands and Outer Space*. Port Washington, NY: Kennikat Press.

Jacobi, Jolande (1951, rev. edn.) *The Psychology of C.G. Jung*. New Haven, CT: Yale University Press.

Jung, Carl (1963) *Memories, Dreams, Reflections*, Aniela Jaffi (ed.), Richard and Clara Winston, (trans.), New York: Pantheon Books.

Le Guin, Ursula K. (1969) *The Left Hand of Darkness*. New York: Walker.

——(1970) *The Tombs of Atuan*. New York: Bantam Books.

——(1971) *The Lathe of Heaven*. New York: Scribner's.

——(1972a) *The Farthest Shore*. New York: Bantam Books.

——(1972b) *The Word for the World is Forest*. New York: Berkley.

——(1974) *The Dispossessed*. New York: Harper & Row.

——(1978) *The Eye of the Heron*. New York: Harper & Row.

——(1979) *Malafrena*. New York: Putnam.

——(1980) *The Beginning Place*. New York: HarperCollins.

——(1985) *Always Coming Home*. New York: Harper and Row.

——(1987) *Buffalo Gal and Other Animal Presences*. New York: Roc Books.

——(1989) *Dancing at the Edge of the World: Thoughts on Words, Women, Places*. New York: Grove Press.

——(1990) *Tehanu*. New York: Bantam Books.

——(1992) *The Language of the Night: Essays on Fantasy and Science Fiction* (1979). New York: HarperCollins.

——(1993) *Earthsea Revisioned*. Cambridge, England: Green Bay Publications.

——(1994) *A Fisherman of the Inland Sea*. New York: HarperPrism.

——(1995) *Four Ways to Forgiveness*. New York: HarperPrism.

——(1996) *Unlocking the Air and Other Stories*. New York: HarperCollins.

——(2002a) *The Birthday of the World and Other Stories*. New York: HarperCollins.

——(2002b) *The Other Wind*. New York: Harcourt.

——(2002c) *The Telling*. New York: Harcourt.

——(2003) *Changing Planes*. New York: Harcourt.

——(2004a) *Gifts*. New York: Harcourt.

——(2004b) *The Wave in the Mind: Talks and Essays on the Writer, the Reader, and the Imagination*. Boston: Shambhala Publications.

——(1968) *A Wizard of Earthsea*. New York: Bantam Books.

Lezard, Nicholas (2002) "A Kind of Magic": Review of *The Other Wind*, by Ursula K. Le Guin. *The Guardian* 27 July 2002. *The Guardian Online*. Online. 31 October 2003. Available at <http://books.guardian.co.uk.html>

Olander, Joseph D. and Martin H. Greenberg, (eds) (1979) *Ursula Le Guin*. New York: Taplinger.

Reginald, R., Slusser, George E. (1996) *Zephyr and Boreas, Winds of Change in the Fiction of Ursula K. Le Guin*. San Bernardino, CA: Millefleurs.

Reid, Suzanne Elizabeth (1997) *Presenting Ursula K. Le Guin*. New York: Twayne.

Rochelle, Warren G. (2001) *Communities of the Heart: The Rhetoric of Myth in the Fiction of Ursula K. Le Guin*. Liverpool, UK: Liverpool University Press.

Selinger, Bernard (1988) *Le Guin and Identity in Contemporary Fiction*. Ann Arbor: UMI Research Press.

Slusser, George (1996) *Between Worlds: The Literary Dilemma of Ursula K. Le Guin*. San Bernardino, CA: Millefleurs.

Spivack, Charlotte (1984) *Ursula K. Le Guin*. Boston, MA: Twayne.

Wayne, Kathryn Ross (1995) *Redefining Moral Education: Life, Le Guin, and Language*. San Francisco, CA: Austin & Winfield.

White, Donna R. (1999) *Dancing with Dragons: Ursula K. Le Guin and the Critics*. Columbia, SC: Camden House.

29
Gwyneth Jones and the Anxieties of Science Fiction

Andy Sawyer

Gwyneth Jones was born in Manchester in 1952 and educated at the University of Sussex. During the late 1970s she and her husband spent several years in Singapore and Indonesia, experiences which colored some of her subsequent fiction. Her first published science fiction novel for adults, *Escape Plans* was written during this period. Before its publication in 1984, however, she had written four children's books beginning with *Water in the Air* (1977), and has since operated a parallel career as "Gwyneth Jones," writer of science fiction for adults, and "Ann Halam" (a name she has used since 1981), a writer of SF, fantasy and ghost stories for children, with her teenage SF novel *The Hidden Ones* (1988) published again as Gwyneth Jones. She has been short-listed for a number of awards for children's and science fiction. *The Fear Man* (1995) won the Dracula Society's Children of the Night award while "The Grass Princess" won the World Fantasy Award for short story in 1996, when *Seven Tales and a Fable* also won the WFA for best collection. "La Cenerentola" won the British Science Fiction Association Award for best short story of 1998. *White Queen* won the 1991 James Tiptree, Jr. award and *Bold as Love*, won the 2001 Arthur C. Clarke award. As a feminist writer, she is interested in how we create an imaginary world and engage with the ideologies that mold this creation. As a critic – reviews have appeared in *Foundation* and *The New York Review of Science Fiction*, and a collection of her reviews and longer essays, *Deconstructing The Starships* was published by Liverpool University Press in 1999 – she is incisive and wide-ranging. As a novelist of British (more specifically, English) life rewriting her times through the medium of SF, she has created a body of work which reflects the formative decades of her life: discovering story and storytelling as a child in the 1950s, the counterculture of the 1960s and the way it was thrust back underground in the 1970s and 1980s. Her engagement with other cultures, however, and the way as a science fiction writer she engages with her *own* culture as containing elements of Otherness and alien strangeness, prevents her from becoming insular even while increasingly turning to British settings and themes.

Two elements of science fiction never cease to worry observers. The particular causes of anxiety, though, oscillate with viewpoint. Even the definition of the "sense of wonder," the factor which is supposed to be the mode's defining characteristic, changes. To some it is SF's *playful* element which is to the fore: world-building, the "what if?" question, the pushing to extremes of imaginative speculation, or, as Gregory Benford puts it, the erotics of playfulness: "effing the ineffable" (Benford 1986/7). This worries those who look to more solid literary qualities such as psychological analysis of character or realism. To others, the defining characteristic is the analytic element. Respondents to early SF focused on, after the example of Hugo Gernsback's policy for *Amazing Stories*, the mode's predictive quality. SF "describes the future" and will even shape it in some form. This *also* worries those who look to solid literary qualities, but it worries science fiction's readers even more. It is still the default "vulgar futurism" which outsiders see as SF's centre and justification. The most frequent "pitch" for a popular program about SF is to consider how so many of our modern technological marvels have in some way already been described, as if this were something wondrous instead of the grindingly obvious phenomenon of a large number of guesses, shaped by a knowledge of technological or social trends, resulting in a proportion of them being more or less right some of the time.

More commonly, though, within the communities of those who write and read it, SF is seen as social comment, or as John Clute has it, a way of "writing" the world: not the world to come, but the here and now. However playful the surface is, at bottom the fiction is our world, our present, for a given value of "our" and "present": whatever the year an SF novel is set in, claims Clute, there is an underlying "real year" (not to be confused as the year in which the book was actually *written*) somehow determining the shape of the future depicted in that novel and from which we can determine how close to a future the tale is truly set (Clute 1995: 349). This, too, seems to be a process fraught with – Clute actually uses the word in the context of how Philip K. Dick moves from a "real year" of 1950 – *anxieties*. In writing the future, the science fiction author is writing forward from the traumas of the present or recent past to the gap between "what is" and "what can be." And when that gap is confronted we see something which, as Mark Bould says of Gwyneth Jones' first SF novel for adults, *Divine Endurance* (1984) "exists in the space between possible interpretations" (Bould 2002: 12).

Gwyneth Jones herself writes in *Deconstructing the Starships*, that "the essence of SF is the experiment" (1999: 4). The very title of her book of collected criticism and reviews is telling. Deconstruction is the most ludic of literary activity, finding meanings in the slipperiness of language, in puns, absences, oppositions, and other ambiguities. Even as Peter Barry describes poststructuralist deconstruction in *Beginning Theory*, moving from "free play of meanings" to Barbara Johnson's "more disciplined and austere textual republicanism," Johnson's own language in the passage he quotes from offers intentional or unintentional double meanings as she describes deconstruction's project as "analysis" rather than "destruction," a kind of *"teasing* out" (my emphasis) of meaning from warring significances in a text (Barry 1995: 67, 71). There is both the experimental analysis of the scientist and the mockery of the licensed clown here, collapsing into the curiosity which asks "What will happen if I pull *this?*" There is this self-awareness of literary playfulness in much of Jones' fiction: those of her aliens in the "Aleutian Trilogy" who use spoken language are called "signifiers" and names like Derrida are dropped almost casually into the text of *Phoenix Café*: "All those structuralists, poststructuralists, semioticists of the pre-contact so forgotten now" (Jones 1997: 195–6). But the cover of *Deconstructing the Starships* actually illustrates an image of constructing a cartoonish model spaceship against a backdrop of stars. There is pleasure in the process of designing an imaginary artifact – like a spaceship, or a story.

Jones' work offers a series of experiments with the "real world." *Divine Endurance* presents an undated and (despite the obligatory map) geographically ambiguous location which could well be read as both extrapolated future and (until the linguistic and geographical clues teach us better) the isolated, unconnected world of Fantasy. Jones remarks, in fact, in an interview, "some bits of *Divine Endurance* seem to me now very naïve, bland, genre fantasy": a comment which seems unfairly self-critical but which hints at the story's underlying fairytale and quest-fantasy elements (Kincaid 1987). Two artificial children, "Worthy To be Loved" (Wo) and "Chosen Among the Beautiful" (Cho) are created in a palace. Wo is given away to a band of nomads and Cho, with the cat Divine Endurance, goes south in search of her brother. The land she comes to is beginning a revolution and Cho becomes an important part of events. It is clear from the outset that Cho, Wo, the Emperor and Empress inhabiting the palace, and Divine Endurance, are artificial beings. It is less clear until Cho encounters the Rulers that she is an "angel doll" designed to grant every human desire, but even by then we have noted that she is bound by rules and permissions and drives encompassed by Asimov's Three Laws of Robotics: "A robot may not injure a human being or, through inaction, allow a human being to come to harm." "A robot must obey the orders given it by human beings except where such orders would conflict with the First Law." "A robot must protect its own existence, as long as such protection does not conflict with the First or Second Law" (Asimov 1968: 8). Jones' use of the Laws – unstated as such throughout the novel – is more complex than their use as sources for "problem" stories in Asimov. The colonial atmospheres of the Peninsula and the feminist explorations of its sociology – women are the dominant gender, only a few men are allowed to reach sexual maturity and the rest remain neutered "boys" – are discourses Jones allows to run through much of her subsequent fictions. ("Boy" is also an address to a subservient male by a colonialist superior.) *Flowerdust*, less a sequel than a sidebar to *Divine Endurance*, presents this scenario much more plainly than the first novel, in which the fairytale irony of "getting what you wish for" weaves in and out of the idea of an advanced technology which echoes another science fictional "Law" – Arthur C. Clarke's Third Law : "Any sufficiently advanced technology is indistinguishable from magic." (Clarke 1999: 2)

The more technologically centered *Escape Plans* (1986) builds Jones' fictional world through acronym and abbreviation. Even by the standards of science fiction, it is likely to be alienating. A reader coming to it "cold" – even one experienced in the proto-cols of reading science fiction where we cannot always assume that the word or phrase in the text means precisely what it does when we encounter it in "real life" – will find difficulties with Jones' uncompromising semiotic slippage. Just as Ray Bradbury introduces a "Mechanical Hound" into *Fahrenheit 451* (1953), Gwyneth Jones' future society uses Distance Order Generators for surveillance and riot control "If vandalism reached a critical level Area Command would send DOGS down to help the cultural police." (Jones 1986: 65). Here we have to hold at least two images in mind at once. Terms like DOGS give us the mental picture of something that is obviously *not* a canine mammal even as it fulfils some of the "guardian" functions of, say a Doberman pinscher or Rotweiller. Elsewhere, words like "sub" and "number" instead of "man" "woman" or "person" offer coded interpretations of what humanity, or a large section thereof, has been reduced to; but it is the code rather than the underlying image which strikes the reader. Yet out of this jargon is a rewarding picture of a dystopian future extrapolated from the control and surveillance systems of our times. As we pick our way through the story, aided by the ironies of the plot and the increas-ingly clear picture of the narrator ALIC (who, despite her much greater skill with the language of this future, is almost as embarrassingly naïve as the reader in her initial ignorance of what is really going on) our own world and its anxiety about power rela-tionships and complicity is rewritten.

There is multiple purpose in an SF text. Bakhtin's concept of heteroglossia is increasingly being seen as relevant to the language of science fiction, just as his "car-nival" is appropriate to comic fantasy writers such as Terry Pratchett (as noted in Butler 2002) and, by extension to other areas of SF. In "Discourse in the Novel" Bakhtin writes "any concrete discourse (utterance) finds the object at which it was directed already as it were overlain with qualifications, open to dispute, charged with value, already enveloped in an obscuring mist – or, on the contrary, by the "light" of alien words that have already been spoken about it." (Bakhtin 1981: 276) The science fiction reader, in this passage, would wonder about the weight placed on the word "alien." By (mis)appropriating Bakhtin's comments one can understand how it is pos-sible to take sentences from *Escape Plans* and read "backwards" to totalitarian trends in our society, and extrapolate them to the future Jones describes. The passage is both a creative use of language and a warning.

This is not to say that the playfulness of SF "has a purpose" as if that is a justifi-cation or excuse, for that is merely shifting into the "SF as didactic preaching" mode. Nor is this, despite the application of currently fashionable cultural theorists, a novel idea. Before the days when writers such as Dick and Gibson were seen to exemplify the "postmodern condition" SF readers were appropriating texts for their own pur-poses. A.E. Van Vogt's *Slan* (1946: serialized in *Astounding Science Fiction*, 1940) is one of the best known examples of fan-rewriting. Brian Attebery, in *Decoding Gender in Science Fiction* is one of many who have noted how *Slan* is seemingly presented for exactly the response that happened when the serial was offered to *Astounding*'s readers: the discovery that this story of an isolated young man who finds himself exploring his differences from his *normal* persecutors speaks directly to them. Harry Warner, Jr., in his history of 1940s science fiction fandom *All Our Yesterdays*, describes how fans recognized themselves. "Fans," the saying went, "are Slans" (Warner 1969: 42, 186). Attebery also uses comments by John W. Campbell, who worked extensively with Van Vogt in creating the story, to create plausible readings for Fans/Slans/"Eggheads" as occupying the same narrative space as other "different" groups such as Afro-Americans or homosexuals or (though neither Campbell in the letters quoted nor Attebery in his gender-focused commentary say) Jews (Attebery 2002: 66–8). Many prominent figures of science fiction's first few decades, such as Isaac Asimov, Stanley Weinbaum, or Hugo Gernsback himself, were of Jewish immigrant origin, and by the time of *Slan*'s book publication the USA had entered the war against Hitler's Germany. This is not a sophisticated reading on the *tabula rasa* of the naïve blank text of popular fiction, but a feature of stories designed for multiple readings. There is no "correct" mapping of "Slan" to "persecuted group" (although all the racial and social groups mentioned are appropriate) because the implied readings are open, constructed by textual clues which the reader may emphasize or de-emphasize at will and which may, or may not, be congruent to further events of the story. The frequent rewriting and extension/deepening of short stories to become "fix-up" novels (again, Van Vogt extensively revised the stories published between 1939 and 1950 which came to make up the novel *The Voyage of the Space Beagle* as published in 1950) is certainly a commercial enterprise. But it is also an investigation of, an adding and extending meaning in, the original texts.

Such designs for multiple readings can, of course, be more sophisticated than others. Gwyneth Jones is a writer of fiction that calls for particularly meaningful dialogue between the reader and the "interior" worlds of the story. *Escape Plans* not only forces the reader to deconstruct Jones' imaginary world along with her protagonist's construction of it, it plays with a range of words and phrases that mean similar-but-different things in the context of the story and in everyday (mundane) discourse and it positions itself with respect to other SF novels of the period. It undermines, for example, the glamour of Cyberpunk's love affair with computers. While Cyberpunk's squalor has the sleazy romance of low-life excitement, Jones' colder version presents a colonized cyber-proletariat engaged in nothing more than a futuristic picture of the repetitious and unfulfilling tasks a managed proletariat has always engaged in: more call-centre wage-slaves than console cowboys. The novel, like *Divine Endurance*, is also set in the Third World. This is a not uncommon location for her fictions: we discover that *Escape Plans* is set in India, while the map in *Divine Endurance* is that of South-East Asia and the Malay peninsula. In common with many British SF writers, when she sets her fiction in her native country it is often within a postcolonial future of decline. *Kairos* (1988), for example – a novel whose title comes from a Greek word for "time" whose theological context to denote the Apocalyptic return of the Messiah resonates with the story's theme of an ambivalent drug-induced breakthrough – takes place in a Britain extrapolated from the Thatcherite years when it was written.

Her most recent sequence, the "Rock and Roll Reich" series, (so far, at time of writing, *Bold as Love* (2001), *Castles Made of Sand* (2002), *Midnight Lamp* (2003) and with at least one further novel, *Band of Gypsies*, scheduled) is certainly on one level a story woven from the imagination of a writer located at a particular stage of the twentieth/twenty-first centuries. It is possible, from the story, to make assumptions about the author's (and readers') class, nationality, tastes in music. The series reworks common fantasy tropes — most notably the Arthurian mythos — as seen through the eyes of a female British writer from a generation which grew up with rock and roll and never ceased to be affected by it. The music played by the fictional bands is music inspired as much by present music as by nostalgia for the author's youth, although the Clutean "real year" is proclaimed by the titles of the series, with their Jimi Hendrix references. If there *is* a default year it may well be 1969, the year of "Woodstock Nation" and Hendrix's explosive and enigmatic version of "The Star-Spangled Banner" during the festival, but there are also elements of the free festivals of the 1970s and the tribal-rave cultures of the late 1980s and early 1990s which, until the passing of the 1994 Criminal Justice Act effectively outlawing free festivals, offered a harder and more threatening postpunk counterculture.

A politically desperate government managing the break-up of the UK strikes a deal with rock-stars and counterculturalists. The fantasy element is mostly played through a series of parallels and correspondences rather than by overt use of magic, although Fiorinda, whose role as both active character and muse/lover echoes that of her namesake in E.R. Eddison's fantasy "Zimiamvia" sequence (*Mistress of Mistresses* [1935], *A Fish Dinner in Memison* [1941], and *The Mezentian Gate* [1958]), seems to have psychic abilities. Like the powers of the Peninsula women in *Divine Endurance* and Catherine in *Phoenix Café*, the "Zen Self" quest for "the point of total perception" expresses the magical quest for changing reality, in pseudoscientific terms "In theory they might be able to manipulate the solid world as if it were the environment of a fantasy game. Like a magician, isn't it?" reflects a character in *Castles Made of Sand* (Jones 2002: 305). Both Fiorinda's power and the technology generating heat and light from ATP (adenine triphosphate) molecules are science fiction literal metaphors about "take[ing] the power into your own hands" (Brown 2002: 9).

Apart from playing with how genre is crystallized out of language, these stories also extrapolate and speculate — what if the counterculture, which throughout its various manifestations from the 1960s to the present insisted that it *was* offering alternatives to the "straight" world, could take charge? What problems, possibilities, even successes, could result? They are also stories which skirt perilously near another of the multiple-voicings of science fiction — that of "slash," that variant of fan-fiction which takes characters from major TV series (or, very occasionally, books) and rewrites them with an emphasis on homoerotic subtexts. As with Van Vogt and *Slan*, it is wrong to suggest that this is somehow arising unknowingly: Jones is too self-reflective a writer to suggest that. The extensive website devoted to the series, the historical and musical parallels which have inspired it, and fanpage-like links to soundtracks and back-story suggest that Jones is in a sense inventing her own slash. If there is not a designed joke in the homage to a band (Guns and Roses, after whose singer Axl Rose the fictional Ax Preston is explicitly named) with a guitarist *called* Slash (the British-born Paul Hudson), it is difficult to think that the author has missed it.

The most sophisticated oscillation of world-building and world-commentary, however, is the Aleutian Trilogy: *White Queen* (1991), *North Wind* (1994), and *Phoenix Café* (1997), in which Jones designs a world in which the very meaning of gender is problematic. If Le Guin in *The Left Hand of Darkness* imagined a world in which gender was not necessary, Jones presents one in which it is both there and not-there, existing, but unmapped upon bodies. Her aliens are "Aleutians" because their first contact with humanity has been from a landing on the Aleutian islands of Alaska, but the name also calls to mind human groups invested with Otherness, such as the Inuit. Themselves nongendered in reproductive terms, the Aleutians recognize character traits which might be classified as "masculine" or "feminine" but which have nothing to do with the mechanics of reproduction, and their mapping of these traits upon the humans they come across has little to do with sexual characteristics. The results are sometimes comic and darkly ironic. In *White Queen* and *North Wind*, humans in contact with Aleutians are requested to wear Man uniforms (with codpiece) and Woman uniforms (emphasizing breasts and buttocks): "Anyone in Aleutian contact work had to be clear about that aspect of their identity: and ready to be open about it" (Jones 1991: 212–3). Gender pronouns like "he" and "she" are frequently used to represent power relationships. This gender-mapping is also related to other constructions of identity. The Aleutians, parthenogenetic serial reincarnators, literally secrete their identities into the world as they exchange "wanderers" or cells which identify their chemical selves. They also construct their identities from past records of themselves. To them, human films and digital archives are something uncanny, ghostly.

Identity, therefore, is something we are forced to read in multiple voices. As Attebery writes, "everything the Aleutians do is familiar" (Attebery 2002: 163). Although they vary in physical shape, they are humanoid to the point that in the first novel Johnny Guglioli in *White Queen* can see one of them as "The mystery girl . . . [with] the bad harelip which left her almost no nose and a split upper lip." (Jones 1991: 10). They explore, trade, make war, eat, drink, defecate, fall in love, joke, create art, and make very human mistakes about sexual signals. But familiarity aids, rather than evades, misunderstanding. Because their biological difference from humanity also consists of the *connection* between individuals in the form of the cellular "wanderers" with which each Aleutian transfers chemical messages of memories, emotions, and information, their concept of "Difference" is not that of ours. What the human characters (and, for a while, we human readers) of the trilogy see as the Aleutian analogue of sex has nothing to do with reproduction or the desire for a romantic Other, but is the ecstatic exchange of information. An Aleutian searches, romantically, for a genetic *Equal* rather than Other: the "trueparent." Both species discover confusion in these similar but incongruent drives. For us, the Alien is different. We read the image of the alien from elsewhere as one of power gradients, mapped by our history of colonial conquest and submission. The Aleutian command of body-language and understanding of how individuals they know will react in certain circumstances is seen by the humans as telepathy because we *know* (from science fiction) that invading aliens will often be telepathic. The Aleutians, however, understand themselves as literally part of the social and biological continuum which exists in human discourse more tentatively as metaphor. Each finds familiarity in the other. Each misinterprets this familiarity.

Consequently, through the lens of their own sociobiology, the Aleutians misunderstand even the fact that humans die, finally, irrevocably; partly because much of our discourse on death is devoted to denial. Believing that humans, as they do, pass identity through generations, they are for a long time unable to understand their error in executing a human. Identities enforced by role, gender, even name, are provisional. Bella in *North Wind* whose inability to produce "wanderers" makes her disabled among his people (the confusion of pronouns is deliberate) is seen throughout the novel as "Maitri's librarian," "Goodlooking," (gendered "male" among Aleutians); "Bella," gendered "female" during her sojourn among humanity with the wannabe Aleutian "Sidney Carton," possibly Johnny Guglioli's daughter and maybe Johnny himself. "Sydney Carton" himself (the spelling differs from Dickens) takes his identity, as is customary among "half-caste" humans who attempt to live like Aleutians, from iconic figures of the past: the reference is to the 1958 film of *A Tale of Two Cities*, with Dirk Bogarde as Carton, rather than the novel. (It is Johnny Guglioli's Carton-like act of self-sacrifice which becomes a more important touchstone towards the novel's end). In introducing an essay on this very question of the Aleutian Trilogy and identity, Sherryl Vint links the formation of the ideological subject, via Althusser, with the acceptance of external recognition, but points out that the subject is formed by sometimes contradictory and certainly competing calls for identity. In recognizing the call of "woman," the subject is unable to answer the call of "man." "Anxiety emerges when the stability of social categories is challenged, and this instability is generally revealed by those subjects who do not easily 'fit' into one category or another" (Vint 2001: 401). A more satirical interpretation of this identity-anxiety is suggested by the way Carton's group of half-castes have "recognized themselves" in famous or fictional characters: Carton himself, Jimi Hendrix (foreshadowing Jones' subsequent series), Mother Theresa, Superman.

Much of the plotting of the Trilogy highlights the anxiety-causing instability revealed by the misconceptions humans and Aleutians impose upon each other as they misread what seem to be obvious aspects of each other's culture. As Vint puts it, humans assume difference while the Aleutians assume similarity (Vint 2001: 404–5). The aliens do not seem to realize the extent of their difference. Humans read the aliens through a lens distorted by a host of assumptions of alien-ness, not necessarily formed by science fiction but suffused by it. Johnny Guglioli is attacked by a "monster," and raped; the aliens apparently have superior technology, including the secret of faster-than-light travel, they possess telepathy and are here, as are all invading alien races, to take over. Apart from telepathy and faster-than-light travel (neither of which the Aleutians really possess) the picture here is that of the "invading alien" which many nations of our human globe know only too well, and whose symbolic appearance in science fiction goes back at least to H.G. Wells' *The War of the Worlds*. Further irony is added by conflict arising through *converging* or at least similar viewpoints. If it is

Aleutians who consider the world a unity maintained by the constant interaction of biochemistry, it is humans who are appalled by the Aleutians' desire, in *North Wind*, to level the Himalayas. While there are ecological and climatic arguments, human outrage is prompted by more than this. The Aleutians miss humanity's symbolic attachment to "dead" matter: "A world can be alive without being saturated with the living cells of its sentient inhabitants. A world can be made sacred, by something other than biology" (Jones 1994: 24).

By imagining aliens "same but different," Jones presents the dynamic between Self and Other, between Language and Silence to the extent that, as she sardonically remarks, "Reinventing the wheel is a commonplace hazard in science fiction. It makes a change to find one has re-invented poststructuralist psychology" (Jones 1999: 118). Jones' characters, especially Bella in *North Wind* and Catherine in *Phoenix Café*, dramatize the anxiety of both socially determined and biological identity. Each, by the end of their respective novels, is not who she thought she was at the beginning; and each reaches this conclusion through oscillations between Aleutian and human viewpoints. This is the result of Gwyneth Jones' experiment: that through the use of science fiction tropes such as genetic manipulation and "alien invaders," she is able to present identities which can plausibly and logically answer competing "calls." This result is not achieved simply through the opposition of human and alien, but the closer examination of human. Throughout the three hundred or so years of the Trilogy (which parallels the time-period of Western Domination of Asia and Africa), humanity is itself in conflict as the Eve Riots of *White Queen* segue into the Gender Wars. Traditionalists and Reformers may be *largely* divided upon the lines of cultural and political relationships between the biological sexes, but each "side" contains many of the other. Jones' "nongendered" aliens may have been crafted to enable the reader to focus on just how problematic the question of gender-specific political and behavioral traits is, but they exist in her fiction against a background in which she deliberately shows exactly that in the human world.

Another anxiety of SF is how far it exists in itself without becoming "contaminated" by other genres – or even if it *can* so exist. This is particularly so in children's science fiction, which frequently speaks the same double-language of science and magic to be found in Jones' adult fictions. Her "Inland" trilogy begins by confidently speaking the language of fantasy. Zanne lives in a post-Collapse world which has exchanged technology for the magical "Covenant": her task is to combat the influence of the machines – computers, power stations, etc. – which remain hidden in Inland and beyond. The sequence begins with *The Daymaker* somewhat in the vein of Le Guin's Earthsea as Zanne discovers her powers and succumbs to the temptation of awakening the "Maker." It becomes clearer, later, that this is the future of a collapsed highly technological society, but only a relatively sophisticated young reader would understand this from the beginning, or make the link between "We have opened another path from the deeps of *between* into the world" (Halam 1988: 210) and the Zen Self "sum of all possible states" concepts taken from quantum theory. The eventual scenario, however, of the "path from the deeps of *between*" is little different from the "quantum" explanations offered in the "Rock and Roll Reich" sequence, which in turn is (as an explanation) gently mocked by Terry Pratchett as "a kind of cosmic 'get out of half-understood explanation free' card" (Pratchett and Briggs 2003: 193). Jones is neither satirizing nor evading the issue, however. She *is* in some respects a "hard science fiction" writer. Her essays "Sex: the Brains of Female Hyena Twins" and "Aliens in the Fourth Dimension" (Jones 1999: 9–107; 108–19) are as rigorous with respect to her own work as, say, Hal Clement's explanatory essay "Whirligig World" on the scientific rationale to *Mission of Gravity* (1954: serialized the previous year in *Astounding Science Fiction*). And when she presents the twin modeling of fantasy and SF in her work, she is both engaged in the "experiment" of genre fusion and adding yet more double-voicing to the question of identity.

Approaching this fusion from a different angle, *King Death's Garden*, a ghost story, considers the ghost story through speaking the language of science fiction. Lonely, asthmatic, unlikeable Maurice continues, desperately, to a "scientific" explanation for the nature of his time-slip experiences in the cemetery, denying the supernatural in the face of all the evidence. These experiences seem to be linked to his encounters with the wild girl Moth, an elemental sprite, or possibly a ghost; and to events described in the diary written by Professor Baxter, who once owned Great-Aunt Ida's house. Although we only see brief quotations, it is clear from Maurice's embarrassed reaction to what he reads that the Professor has been involved in experiences reminiscent of the alleged "Cottingley Fairies." Up to the final pages, after a climactic scene in the cemetery with the shadows almost emerging into full view, Maurice clings desperately to the idea of "chemical patterns. Images from the past, somehow regenerated" (Halam 1986: 114–5) and is unable even to *articulate* the word "dead."

But at the end, the rational explanation does not lie in science. *King Death's Garden* is a subtle, complex story, exploring Maurice's self-centeredness; not only in his own life, but in his fascination with snooping on the memories of dead people. Only at the end does he learn that other people, even dead ones, have a right to respect. No doubt *King Death's Garden* could have been a science fiction novel, with the time-shifts given a scientific explanation and everything neatly explained. It would not be the same; still, a story could have been written in which Maurice's initial "scientific" view prevails – even down to the point where he learns the same moral lessons. A more recent novel by the author, *The Fear Man* (1996) does start out a supernatural story in the M.R. James tradition but places its "solution" in science fiction rationalism in precisely the way *King Death's Garden* does not. More overtly intertextual resonances with classics of science fiction take place with *Dr. Franklin's Island* (2001). The title partly suggests Mary Shelley's *Frankenstein* but also (and location and plot suggest) H.G. Wells' *The Island of Dr. Moreau*. The exaggerated nature of the gene-modifying science might tempt the reader to interpret the book solely as metaphor for our anxieties about genetic engineering, but the exploration of states of Otherness (one character becomes a fish: another a bird) expands the focus. The final questions "Are we monsters? Or are we more than human?" (Halam 2001: 214) are the questions SF is increasingly asking.

References and Further Reading

Asimov, Isaac (1968) *I: Robot* (1950). London: Panther.

Attebery, Brian (2002) *Decoding Gender in Science Fiction*. New York: Routledge.

Bakhtin, Mikhail Mikhailovich (1981) *The Dialogic Imagination*, (ed.) Michael Holquist, (trans.) Caryl Emerson and Michael Holquist, Austin, TX: University of Texas Press.

Barry, Peter (1995) *Beginning Theory*. Manchester: Manchester University Press.

Benford, Gregory (1986/7) "Effing the Ineffable: An Essay." *Foundation: The International Review of Science Fiction* 38 (Winter): 49–57.

Bould, Mark (2002) "Not Writing Cyberpunk: Three Science Fiction Novels by Gwyneth Jones." *Vector* 225 (Sep/Oct), 12–14.

Bradbury, Ray (2001) *Fahrenheit 451* (1953). London: HarperCollins.

Brown, Tanya (2002) "Don't Miss the Fun: an Interview with Gwyneth Jones." *Vector* 221 (Jan/Feb), 8–12.

Butler, Andrew M. (2002) "Theories of Humour." In *Terry Pratchett: Guilty of Literature*, (eds) Andrew M. Butler, Edward James and Farah Mendlesohn. Reading: Science Fiction Foundation, 35–50.

Clarke, Arthur C. (1999) *Profiles of the Future* (1962). London: Gollancz.

Clement, Hal (1953) "Whirligig World." *Astounding Science Fiction* 51 (June), 102–14.

——(2000) *Mission of Gravity* (1953). London: Gollancz.

Clute, John (1995) *Look at the Evidence: Essays and Reviews*. Liverpool: Liverpool University Press.

Eddison, E.R. (1968a) *A Fish Dinner in Memison* (1941). New York: Ballantine.

——(1968b) *Mistress of Mistresses* (1935). New York: Ballantine.

——(1969) *The Mezentian Gate* (1958). New York: Ballantine.

Halam, Ann (1986) *King Death's Garden*. London: Orchard.

——(1987) *The Daymaker*. London: Orchard.

——(1988) *Transformations*. London: Orchard.

——(1990) *The Skybreaker*. London: Orchard.

——(1996) *The Fear Man*. London: Orion.

——(2000) *Don't Open Your Eyes*. London: Orion.

——(2001) *Dr. Franklin's Island*. London: Orion.

James, Edward (1994) *Science Fiction in the 20th Century*. Oxford: Oxford University Press.

Jameson, Fredric (1991) *Postmodernism: or the Cultural Logic of Late Capitalism*. Durham, NC and London: Duke University Press.

Jones, Gwyneth (1984) *Divine Endurance*. London: Allen and Unwin.

——(1986) *Escape Plans*. London: Allen and Unwin.

——(1988a) *Kairos*. London: Unwin Hyman.

——(1988b) "The Profession of Science Fiction, 38: Riddles in the Dark." *Foundation: The International Review of Science Fiction* 43 (Summer), 50–59.

——(1991) *White Queen*. London: Gollancz.

——(1993a) *Flowerdust*. London: Headline.

——(1993b) *Identifying the Object*. Austin, TX: Swan Press.

——(1994) *North Wind*. London: Gollancz.

——(1997) *Phoenix Café*. London: Gollancz.

——(1999) *Deconstructing the Starships*. Liverpool: Liverpool University Press.

——(2002) *Castles Made of Sand*. London: Gollancz.

——(2004) *Bold as Love*. website (http://www.boldaslove.co.uk/)

Kincaid, Paul (1987) "Gwyneth Jones interview with Paul Kincaid." *Interzone* 19 (Spring), 13–15.

Pratchett, Terry and Stephen Briggs (2003) *The New Discworld Companion*. London: Gollancz.

Van Vogt, A.E. (1968a) *Slan* (1946). London: Panther.

——(1968b) *The Voyage of the Space Beagle* (1950). London: Panther.

Vint, Sherryl (2001) "Double Identity: Interpellation in Gwyneth Jones' Aleutian Trilogy." *Science Fiction Studies* 85, 399–425.

Warner, Harry, Jr. (1969) *All Our Yesterdays*. Chicago: Advent.

30

Arthur C. Clarke

Edward James

Sir Arthur C. Clarke has had a unique career in SF. For many readers, wrote Peter Nicholls, he "is the very personification of SF" (Clute and Nicholls 1993: 232). He fulfills an idea of what an SF writer *should* be like. If a science fiction fan of the late 1930s or 1940s had imagined the ideal career for a science fiction writer, it would probably have run like this. The writer would have a scientific training, and preferably be involved in some cutting-edge technology. He (almost certainly "he") would move from fandom and fan writing to publishing in *Astounding*, the leading SF magazine of the day, and would come to the attention of a wider public through his novels. He would be committed to educating the public about science and the future possibilities of science, and write and lecture on the subject. He would become a person of influence, and be regarded as an expert on matters futurological, not just in the USA or UK, but around the world. By his old age he would have seen many of his science-fictional predictions come into existence.

The only writer to approach Clarke as an embodiment of this ideal has been Isaac Asimov (1921–92). Yet Clarke has the edge. Asimov could not equal Clarke as a futurological guru, partly because of Asimov's own somewhat detached attitude to the "real world." The different approach to science fiction taken by the two writers was in a way an extension of their own very different degrees of engagement with the world. Asimov loved intellectual puzzles, and rarely engaged in serious extrapolation of possible futures; Clarke wrestled with important questions of human development and has always been thinking about the impact of current technological ideas on the future. Asimov, for much of his working life, was writing in a room in Manhattan with the blinds pulled down to cut off his view of Central Park. His phobia of airflight meant that once his academic career in Boston was over (in the 1950s) he rarely ventured outside New York; on his only visit to the UK, in 1974, he came by boat. Clarke, however, moved his home from England to Sri Lanka in 1958, and (above all in the years up to 1975, when a change in tax law allowed him to live in Sri Lanka throughout the year) traveled extensively throughout the world. Very few SF writers have had such a close personal knowledge of the world as Clarke, and even fewer have such an internationalist attitude; this has contributed a good deal to his global influence. Asimov's future people feel like Americans; Clarke has a much wider view of human possibilities. Moreover, unlike Asimov, Clarke has been closely associated with the making of a movie – Stanley Kubrick's *2001: A Space Odyssey* (1968) – which brought his vision of past and future to a far wider audience than has been achieved by any other professional writer of science fiction (save perhaps Philip K. Dick). In his lifetime Clarke has received more honors from the world outside science fiction than any other SF writer: the Kalinga Prize from UNESCO in 1961, a shared Oscar in 1968, and a knighthood in 2000, among many others.

Clarke has an international vision and voice, which is very rare among top science-fiction writers. But he also has a very English voice. His optimism about the future may be seen as an American trait; but his doubts, and his frequent reminders that all civilizations are ultimately doomed, seem very English. Unlike other British SF writers who started by writing in the American magazines (like Eric Frank Russell and the early John Wyndham) he never tried to adopt an American persona. It is an accident that his first professional publication was in 1946, the year that H.G. Wells died; but in a very real sense Clarke took over Wells' role as the great English visionary.

Arthur C. Clarke, born in Minehead (Somerset) in 1917, was fascinated by science and science fiction from an early age. Although he was greatly influenced by the British writers H.G. Wells and Olaf Stapledon, he was also an avid reader and collector of American science fiction magazines from the time when he acquired his first – the March 1930 issue of *Astounding Stories of Super-Science* – at the age of thirteen. His first publication in *Astounding* was just eight years later: a letter correcting a mathematical equation in a previous article concerning the exhaust velocities of rockets. By that time he had left school to join the civil service, and had become involved both in science and science fiction. He became the treasurer of the British Interplanetary Society, and was active in its discussions of the best practical method to travel in space; he started writing nonfiction for Britain's first real SF magazine, *Tales of Wonder*, as well as fiction for the short-lived *Amateur Science Fiction Stories*. The war caused a break in this activity, and although Clarke's job freed him from conscription, he did join the Royal Air Force early in 1941. He became a radio operator, and then an instructor in electronics; an article on television in *Electrical Engineering* brought him an invitation to join a team developing a new secret weapon to aid the RAF in its war effort: radar. It was while working there that he wrote three pieces that helped launch his twin career as a science fiction writer and a prophet of future science. Two were stories, published just after the war, in *Astounding*, and the third was an article proposing satellites in geostationary orbit as a solution to world communication problems. This orbit is now known officially as the Clarke Orbit, and his article outlines the principle behind a multibillion dollar industry today. Back in 1945 it was regarded by most as little more than "science fiction"; Clarke earned nothing himself from the idea, and as he himself has often noted, even had patenting the idea been a possibility, the patent would have run out long before the technology was available to make the idea a reality.

After the war Clarke became a student at King's College London, getting a first-class degree in physics and mathematics, and briefly doing graduate work before taking a job as assistant editor of *Physics Abstracts*. All through this period, though, he was writing and publishing science fiction, as well as lecturing and publishing, and he took the first opportunity he could (a commission for a book) to leave his employment and to become a full-time writer. The book was *The Exploration of Space*: his first best-seller, and probably the most widely read nonfiction discussion of the possibilities of space travel in the decade before Sputnik and the Apollo and Gemini missions.

Like all his contemporaries, Clarke began his science-fictional career as a writer of short stories. From the late 1920s to the mid 1950s, the science fiction magazines were not only a major market for short story writers, but were widely read, above all in America. As a direct consequence, short stories were a far more commonly appreciated form than they are today, and writers were still able to make their reputation through them. Isaac Asimov, first published in 1939, was already recognized as a major talent, as a writer of nearly 50 short stories, by the time his first novel was published in 1950. Clarke moved from publication of short stories to novels much more quickly (from the first professional sale of a short story in 1946 to his first novel in 1951), but it was his short stories that initially made his reputation in the science fiction field.

Most of Clarke's short stories date from the period of his greatest productivity as a science fiction writer, from the end of the 1940s to the beginning of the 1960s. In the 18 years between 1946 and 1964 he published 80 short stories (published in book form during that period in five separate collections) and 10 novels (one of which, *Glide Path*, 1963, was based on his wartime experiences, but the rest of which were science fiction). During the same period he published nine books of popular science. In the 40 years since the early 1960s he has not been so prolific, partly as a result of a serious illness in 1962, later diagnosed as polio; partly as a result of his time-consuming collaboration with Stanley Kubrick for the movie *2001* (on which he began work in 1964); and partly because his financial problems diminished with his increasing success. In the forty years since 1964 he has published only eighteen short stories, some of which were slight – although the longest of them, "A Meeting with Medusa" won the Nebula Award in 1972 as the best novella of the year – and only nine more novels, including the novelization of the movie *2001: A Space Odyssey* in 1968, and *Rendezvous with Rama* (1973) which won the four major SF awards for best novel of the year. His last solo novel was the final *2001* novel, *3001: The Final Odyssey* (in 1997); otherwise he has kept himself in the public eye by continuing to publish popular science books and collections of essays, as well as novels written together with writers such as Gentry Lee and Stephen Baxter. Since he may have contributed little more than a plotline to these novels, they are not discussed in this essay.

Even though there was a renewed productivity after the appearance of the *2001* movie, some of this was dependent on his earlier short stories. *2001* was an expansion of "The Sentinel" (1951), and in its turn spawned *2010* (1982), *2061* (1987), and *3001* (1997); *The Songs of Distant Earth*, Clarke's "own favorite novel" (Clarke 2000a: 664), was an expansion of a story of the same name from 1958. It is one of the features of Clarke's career that he developed ideas and plots over long period of time. He began tinkering with *Against the Fall of Night* in 1935; it was published in *Startling Stories* in November 1948, developed into a book in 1953, was totally revised as *The City and the Stars* (1956), and made a final appearance alongside the sequel written by Gregory Benford, as *Beyond the Fall of Night* (1990). In his last solo novel, *3001: The Final Odyssey* (1997), he was still returning to some of those themes he began exploring in 1935.

Clarke in 1956 referred to "Rescue Party" as his first published story (though the epistolary story "Loop Hole" was published one month earlier, in *Astounding* April 1946), and commented that "a depressing number of people still consider it as my best" (Clarke 1956b: I). It is certainly a story in which the ideas of John W. Campbell, Jr., the editor of *Astounding*, perhaps come over as strongly as those of Clarke himself. It does, however, begin the tradition of ironic one-liners as conclusions to stories that are characteristic of some of the most memorable of Clarke's stories. In "Rescue Party" aliens discover that Earth's sun is about to go nova; they send a rescue mission, and find out that, despite Earth's very recently acquired space technology, most of the population of the planet has been put into a fleet of primitive spaceships that are now proceeding to the stars at what appears, to the aliens, to be a snail's pace. They decide to intercept the fleet, and save humans many hundreds of years of flight. They marvel at the ingenuity and determination of humans, and one jokes that they may be a threat even though they are vastly outnumbered by the many alien species. The final sentence: "Twenty years afterward, the remark didn't seem funny" (Clarke 2000a: 55).

Clarke's two most famous short stories also depend on their last lines, but are both stories with serious religious content. In "The Nine Billion Names of God" (1953) two computer engineers set up a computer in a remote Tibetan monastery. The monks believe that creation will come to an end once the nine billion names of God have been recorded, and that the computer will be able to do in one hundred days what the monks would have taken fifteen thousand years to complete. The final sentence, as the computer finishes its run, is: "Overhead, without any fuss, the stars were going out" Clarke 2000a: 422). "The Star" (1955), winner of the Hugo Award for best short story, is about the crisis of faith of a Jesuit who is chief astrophysicist on an exploring spaceship. As in "Rescue Party" there is a nova; this time it has destroyed an entire civilization, except for the vault that it had made to preserve its greatest cultural achievements. The Jesuit discovered that the light of this enormous explosion reached Earth at the beginning of the first Christian millennium. "Oh God, there were so many stars you could have used. What was the need to give these people to the fire, that the symbol of their passing might shine above Bethlehem?" (Clarke 1962b: 183).

Critics have often found it odd that an avowed atheist like Clarke should use religious ideas and images in so many of his stories. Robin Reid has pointed out that when he joined his RAF station he insisted that his religion be listed as "pantheism," and pantheism may account for some of the religiosity in his atheism (Reid 1997: 5). In these two stories it is probably better to say that he is joining in a standard SF project: to make the truths of revealed religions seem petty or implausible when placed in a galactic context. Nevertheless, as has often been pointed out, throughout his writing career Clarke does have his mystical side, and is capable of visions of transcendence alongside the nuts-and-bolts stories of space exploration. In the last ten years it has become fashionable among science-fiction critics to talk about the "posthuman"; the post human has been a constant theme of Clarke's work, from his earliest short stories through to his latest novels. A thorough Darwinist, believing that the human species has evolved from other primates, he consistently asks the question which until recently has been dodged by science fiction writers (except in the wish-fulfillment idea of the appearance of random superhuman powers): what is the next stage of human evolution? Only in his novel *Childhood's End* (1953) does this evolution have religious overtones, and in subsequent years his stance on religion as an institution seems to have hardened. In his last solo novel, *3001*, he offers an open attack on "the psychopathology known as religion": one of the characters was "still famous on Earth for at least two of his sayings: 'Civilization and Religion are incompatible' and 'Faith is believing what you know isn't true'" (Clarke 1997: 141, 113). But he ends the book with an extraordinary apology to his religious friends, who are happy despite their irrationality:

> Perhaps it is better to be un-sane and happy, than sane and un-happy. But it is best of all to he sane and happy.
>
> Whether our descendants can achieve that goal will be the greatest challenge of the future. Indeed, it may well decide whether we have any future. (Clarke 1997: 273)

Much of Clarke's earlier work fitted into two rather loose-knit series, although they were connected by theme and setting rather than by their position in a definitive future history. Some of his stories and novels concerned the development of space flight and the early colonization of the solar system; others were more interested in the evolution of humanity into the posthuman, either in the near future (*Childhood's End, 2001*) or in the far distant future (*The City and the Stars*). What unites both these series is this search for sanity combined with happiness, which is enmeshed with the metaphysical question which recurs from the time of his earliest short stories: what is the purpose of human life? He seems discontented with the standard reply of the atheist, that our existence has no purpose. He is fully aware of the fact that science has the potential to move us much more quickly to our purpose. Science can offer us all that we need, should we ever solve our penchant for human conflict. Science can rid ourselves of poverty, famine and disease; science can supply all the necessities of life, including all our energy needs; science can create a life that would have been regarded as Utopian by any past criteria, yet without any of the menace of totalitarianism that lurks behind many earlier literary Utopias. But is this the purpose of human life? Would we not become mere lotus-eaters if we became the mere recipients of a peaceful and want-free existence?

One of the earliest appearances of this theme, in "The Lion of Comarre," published in *Thrilling Wonder Stories* in August 1949, still offers ideas that are relevant nearly sixty years later. It is a Stapledonian story of a world created by great inventors where their machines were able to keep humans in perfect comfort.

> Men reacted to the new situation in two ways. There were those who used their new-found freedom nobly in the pursuits which had always attracted the highest minds: the quest for beauty and truth, still as elusive as when the Acropolis was built.
>
> But there were others who thought differently. At last, they said, the curse of Adam is lifted forever. Now we can build cities where the machines will care for our every need as soon as the thought enters our minds – sooner, since the analysers can read even the buried desires of the sub-conscious. The aim of all life is pleasure and the pursuit of happiness. Man has earned the right to that. We are tired of this unending struggle for knowledge and the blind desire to bridge space to the stars.
>
> It was the ancient dream of the Lotus Eaters, a dream as old as Man. Now, for the first time, it could be realized. (Clarke 2000a: 126)

Eventually, in the course of this story, these Lotus Eaters, named Decadents, built themselves hidden cities all over the solar system; there was just one on Earth, at Comarre. There the entire population lived in dreams concocted for them by the machines, based on their deepest desires – virtual reality, as we would now call it – solving the eternal problem of Utopias: how to devise a society which would appeal to the varied desires and personalities of humans. In this story each individual's sub-conscious helps in the creation of a Utopia uniquely suited to that individual's desires.

It is not a solution to human problems of which the protagonist of "The Lion of Comarre" approves, any more than does Clarke himself. A character in Clarke's first novel, *Prelude to Space* (1951), complains that gallivanting round space would not solve mankind's problems, and that people should deal with those problems and then "rest and have some peace."

> "The Dream of the Lotus Eaters," [responded Hassall] "is a pleasant fantasy for the individual – but it would be death for the race."
>
> . . . "The Lotus Eaters? Let's see – what did Tennyson say about them – nobody reads him nowadays. 'There is sweet music here that softer falls . . .' No it isn't that bit. Ah, I have it!
>
> '*Is there any peace*
> *In ever climbing up the climbing wave?*'
>
> Well, young man, *is* there?"
>
> "For some people – yes," said Hassall. "And perhaps when space flight arrives they'll all rush off to the planets and leave the Lotus Eaters to their dreams. That should satisfy everybody."
>
> "And the meek shall inherit the Earth, eh?"
> (Clarke 1954: 82–3)

In this novel, at least, Clarke is prepared to end with a traditionally British compromise: Hassall concludes that "there are two types of mind – the adventurous, inquisitive types and the stay-at-homes who're quite happy to sit in their own back-gardens. I think they're both necessary, and it's silly to pretend that one's right and the other isn't" (Clarke 1954: 84).

Most of his novels contribute in one way or another to this debate, including his "Solar System" novels, the sequence begun with *2001*, and the two novels most closely associated with this debate, and the two which are among the most fondly remembered of all his novels: *Childhood's End* (1953) and *The City and the Stars* (1956). "Seeker of the Sphinx" (1951) and "The Songs of Distant Earth" (1958) and the 1986 novel of the same name are all largely about the cultural clash between the Lotus Eaters and the Explorers. The original short story ended rather lamely "And which was better, who could say?" (Clarke 2000a: 686); but the novel version showed that the issues were far more complex than a simple either/or would suggest. From the beginning Clarke recognized the attraction of lotus-eating, even while most of his sympathies were with the Explorers.

By accident, probably, rather than as the result of considerable forward planning, Clarke's "Solar System" stories were published in rough chronological order of his future history from *Prelude to Space* (1951) through to the full colonization of the solar system in *Imperial Earth* (1976). He did not elaborate a Future History in the way that Robert A. Heinlein pioneered, fitting stories and novels into a self-consistent historical framework. He did make some half-hearted attempt at that: the Treaty of Phobos, for instance, which ended human warfare at the end of *Earthlight* (1955), is mentioned in *Imperial Earth* (1976). But each novel really stands alone, and gives a different version of a possible future. *The Sands of Mars* (1951), for instance, introduced the idea of intelligent life forms on Mars, who do not make any appearance in the later solar system novels. The space stations of *Islands of Space* do not play any major part in his other novels. Clarke is also much more concerned to keep up to date with current scientific developments than to complete obsessively the chapters of a consistent Future History. In 1978, for instance, he develops the idea of a sky-hook space elevator as a cheap means of reaching Earth orbit, in his *The Fountains of Paradise*. It was a cutting-edge idea that first reached fiction in 1978, not just in Clarke's book but also in *The Web Between the Worlds*, by another scientifically trained British SF writer, Charles Sheffield. (Kim Stanley Robinson acknowledged their joint achievement in his Mars trilogy (1992–6) by naming the terminals at each end of his Mars-based sky-hook Clarke and Sheffield.)

Prelude to Space documents the first mission to the Moon: launched by a British team from the Australian rocket base of Woomera – a scenario that might still seem plausible in the early 1950s. *Prelude to Space* was written in the same year that the British comic series *Dan Dare* began, featuring a British future for the solar system; Clarke was for a while its scientific advisor (James 1987). The protagonists were motivated as much by Utopian impulses as by scientific curiosity:

The rush to the new worlds would destroy the suffocating restraints which had poisoned almost half the century. The barriers had been broken, and men could turn their energies outwards to the stars instead of striving among themselves.

Out of the fears and miseries of the Second Dark Age, drawing free – oh, might it be forever! – from the shadows of Belsen and Hiroshima, the world was moving towards its most splendid sunrise. (Clarke 1954: 166)

Those words were somewhat premature, as the events of the later novel *Earthlight* (1955) showed. By then the Moon, Mars and the larger satellites of Jupiter and Saturn had been colonized, and a war takes place between the Earth and the Federation of the new colonies. The Battle of Pico was a stalemate; and the Treaty of Phobos was signed: "Never again, as far ahead as imagination could roam, would the human race be divided against itself" (Clarke 1963: 158). Humanity was able to continue expanding; the Explorers could have their way, while the Lotus-Easters at home prospered.

The Solar System novels deal with a universe without powerful aliens: the kangaroo-like aliens of *The Sands of Mars* and the floating giants of "A Meeting with Medusa" would not disturb the human drive to the stars. But Clarke has explored the possibility of humans meeting with powerful aliens who disturb or control human development and evolution. In *Rendezvous with Rama* (1973) a giant alien artifact passes through the solar system: its purpose could not be discovered, but its very presence served both to disrupt and energize those on Earth. (This story is followed up in three sequels, probably largely written by Clarke's collaborator Gentry Lee, published in 1989, 1991, and 1993.) In *2001* and its sequels aliens have been interfering with the evolution of other life-forms for millions of years. Their featureless black monoliths serve both as spurs to evolution (as when a primitive ape-man is inspired to discover murder) and as signals, to warn them of species that are on their way to a higher civilization (as when astronauts discover the monolith on the Moon).

In *Childhood's End* (1953) the alien intervention is far more direct. Alien starships appear over the cities of Earth (in scenes which seem to have directly inspired the movie *Independence Day*, 1996), and aliens take over the control of human affairs. They lead humanity to what appears to be a Utopia; but Utopia is only a stage towards the actual goal, which is to prepare a proportion of the human race for evolution into a state of pure mind – a godlike state which is humanity's true end, and which reveals all humanity's past to have been merely the childhood of the species. The novel has frequently topped polls for the SF readers' favorite novel: in a poll conducted by the British Science Fiction Association, 50 years after its publication, it was only beaten into second place by Orwell's *Nineteen Eighty-Four*. The popularity is interesting in the light of Clarke's own remarkable note, published at the front of the novel: "The opinions expressed in this book are not those of the author." Various explanations have been put forward, but probably the most plausible is Clarke's own (Goldman 1987: 21): that in this novel he presented, unwillingly, the idea that "the stars are not for Man" (Clarke 1956a: 118). Almost all Clarke's other fiction has presented a vision of space exploration and colonization as the most fitting aim for the human race; indeed, so contrary is *Childhood's End* to the dominant ethos of science fiction that it has been called "curiously anti-SF."

That criticism cannot apply to *The City and the Stars* (1956), which remains many readers' favorite Clarke novel, and one that sums up his ethos as well as any other. The City is Diaspar (an imperfect anagram of "Paradise"), a static enclosed world in which almost everyone lives a happy fulfilled life, whether they are children adventuring in virtual reality or serious adults with their scholarly hobbies. Alvin, the protagonist, is dissatisfied; indeed, he has been programmed to be dissatisfied by those whose computer programs have kept Diaspar running for a thousand million years. He escapes from Diaspar, and finds another model for Utopia, in the open countryside near the city: Lys is a rural paradise, inhabited by people who have mastered mental talents such as telepathy. But this too does not satisfy Alvin; Lys is as inward-looking and enclosed a society as Diaspar. Alvin uncovers the truth of Earth's history, and persuades others that true fulfillment for the species will involve going back to the stars. The solar system was dying, "but elsewhere the stars were still young and the light of morning lingered; and along the path he once followed, Man would one day go again" (Clarke 1957: 283). In the 1950s, at the height of his powers as an SF writer, Clarke was able to express the ideology and poetic vision of science fiction better than anyone else.

PRIMARY FICTION BIBLIOGRAPHY (FIRST EDITIONS)

Prelude to Space (New York: Galaxy Novels, 1951)

The Sands of Mars (London: Sidgwick Jackson, 1951)

Childhood's End (New York: Houghton Mifflin, 1953)

Earthlight (London: Muller, 1955)

The City and the Stars (New York: Harcourt Brace, 1956)

A Fall of Moondust (London: Gollancz, 1961)

2001: A Space Odyssey (New York: New American Library, 1968)

Rendezvous with Rama (London: Gollancz, 1973)

Imperial Earth (London: Gollancz, 1976)

The Fountains of Paradise (London: Gollancz, 1978)

The Songs of Distant Earth (New York: Ballantine, 1986)

3001: The Final Odyssey (London: Voyager, 1997)

The Collected Stories (London: Gollancz, 2000)

REFERENCES AND FURTHER READING

Agel, Jerome (ed.) (2000) *The Making of 2001: A Space Odyssey*. New York: Modern Library.

Bruce A. Beatie (1989) "Arthur C. Clarke and the Alien Encounter: The Background of *Childhood's End*." *Extrapolation* 30.i (Spring), 53–69.

Clarke, Arthur C. (1954) *Prelude to Space*. New York: Ballantyne.

——(1956a) *Childhood's End* (1953). London: Pan.

——(1956b) *Reach for Tomorrow*. New York: Ballantine.

——(1957) *The City and the Stars* (1956). London: Corgi.

——(1962a) *Profiles of the Future*. London: Scientific Book Club.

——(1962b) *The Other Side of the Sky*. London: Victor Gollancz.

——(1963) *Earthlight* (1955). London: Pan.

Clarke, Arthur C. (1972) *The Lost Worlds of 2001*. New York: Signet.

——(1984) *1984 Spring: A Choice of Futures*. London: Granada.

——(1985) *Reach for Tomorrow* (1956). London: Victor Gollancz.

——(1997) *3001: The Final Odyssey*. London: Voyager.

——(1999) *Greetings Carbon-Based Bipeds! A Vision of the Twentieth Century as it Happened*. London: Voyager.

——(2000a) *The Collected Stories*. London: Victor Gollancz.

——(2000b) *2001: A Space Odyssey*, special edn. London: Orbit.

Clarke, Arthur C. and Stanley Kubrick (1968) *2001: A Space Odyssey*. New York: Signet.

Clute, John, and Peter Nicholls (eds) (1993) *The Encyclopedia of Science Fiction*. London: Orbit.

Daniels, Keith Allen (ed.) (1998) *Arthur C. Clarke and Lord Dunsany: A Correspondence*. San Francisco: Anamnesis Press.

Foundation: The International Review of Science Fiction, (ed.) Edward James: special issue on Clarke, no. 41 (Winter 1987).

Goldman, Stephen H. (1987) "Wandering in Mazes Lost or, The Unhappy Life of Clarke's *Childhood's End* in Academia." *Foundation: The International Review of Science Fiction* 41 [Arthur C. Clarke issue] (Winter), 21–9.

Hollow, John (1987) *Against the Night, the Stars: The Science Fiction of Arthur C. Clarke*. Athens, OH: Ohio University Press.

James, Edward (1987) "The Future Viewed from Mid-Century Britain: Clarke, Hampson and the Festival of Britain." *Foundation: The International Review of Science Fiction* 41 [Arthur C. Clarke issue] (Winter), 42–51.

Kubrick, Stanley, and Carolyn Geduld (1973) *Filmguide to 2001: A Space Odyssey*. Bloomington, IN: Indiana University Press.

McAleer, Neil (1992) *Odyssey: The Authorized Biography of Arthur C. Clarke*. London: Victor Gollancz.

Olander, Joseph D. and Greenberg, Martin Harry, (eds) (1977) *Arthur C. Clarke*. New York: Taplinger.

Rabkin, Eric S (1979) *Arthur C. Clarke*. Starmont Reader's Guide No. 1, West Line, OR: Starmont.

Reid, Robin Anne (1997) *Arthur C. Clarke: A Critical Companion*. Westport, CT: Greenwood Press.

Samuelson, D.N. (1984) *Arthur C. Clarke: A Primary and Secondary Bibliography*. Boston, MA: G.K. Hall.

Slusser, George E. (1978) *The Space Odysseys of Arthur C. Clarke*. San Bernardino, CA: Borgo Press.

31
Greg Egan
Russell Blackford

In 1983, Australian author Greg Egan (1961–) commenced his career as a science fiction writer with the publication of his first short story, "Artifact." Through the 1980s, he produced a body of work – one novel, and a total of eight short stories – that showed talent and literary promise, combining exceptionally lucid, deceptively simple prose with bizarre storylines that frequently crossed into metafiction or surrealism. This work gained him reprints in major Year's Best anthologies in the fantasy and horror fields. However, he gave the impression of being only a marginal SF writer whose strongest interests were in cinema, horror, and experimental forms of narrative. He appeared likely to have a respectable, but relatively modest, career in the SF genre.

Then, at the start of the 1990s, that changed completely. He altered the subject matter of his work, pursued new thematic concerns, and adapted his flexible and essentially sound literary style to new purposes. From this time on, Egan's work presents extraordinary situations with relentless verisimilitude; its realism of narrative technique places it within the main SF tradition.

This changed approach opened commercial markets, and Egan's published writing became far more prolific. Such was the intellectual intensity and scientific rigor of the stories and novels that he produced in the 1990s, and the sense it created of a writer positioned at the genre's cutting edge, that Damien Broderick was able write with some plausibility that Egan had become "perhaps the most important SF writer in the world" (Broderick 1998: 50).

*

"Artifact" – Egan's debut story – appeared in an Australian small-press anthology, *Dreamworks* (King 1983), and it attracted little immediate attention, although it was reprinted some years later in another small-press anthology (Ikin 1990). It is a rather slight piece, but notable for a sharply focused depiction of the narrator's psychological breakdown during a scientific voyage in interstellar space. In describing the details of travel at relativistic velocities and the characteristics of a mysterious alien object discovered eight light years from Earth, Egan displays a concern for mathematically exact science. However, the story's overall effect is quite unlike that of hard SF in the manner of Arthur C. Clarke, for example, or of Gregory Benford. Instead, it is almost surreal, right from its opening sentences, which describe one of the narrator's troubling dreams.

Egan's first novel, *An Unusual Angle*, appeared in the same year as "Artifact," and from the same Melbourne-based publisher, Norstrilia Press. It is narrated by a high-school student who claims to possess various psychic and similar abilities, including the equivalent of a movie camera within his skull, enabling him to record everything that occurs around him in 35mm cinematography. He can observe and record events from viewpoints outside of his own body, obtain close-ups, mix in other real or imagined footage, and listen to sounds from magnetic recordings without needing a player. He uses these abilities to document four years of inane activity at his school.

The novel's title refers to its narrator's alienated perspective on classes, sports, carnivals, assemblies, and a play production. Each of these is mocked in a dry, learned manner, for the narrator is shown to be precociously erudite in the humanities and sciences, making it seem all the more absurd that he must endure day after day of arbitrary regimentation, irrelevant subject matter, and contrived loyalties. There is some suggestion that the events involving his extraordinary powers should be read at a nonliteral level: perhaps as fantasies or daydreams, or as a kind of magic-realist expressionism. In the final analysis, however, they appear to make coherent sense only if taken literally, with the words on the page amounting to the printed equivalent of a movie that he has spliced together.

In essence, the book is little more than a postadolescent send-up of high school life, but it is written with panache and sharp intelligence – and there are signs of the rigorous SF writer that Egan was to become. The use of a camera viewpoint presages the internal camera used by the protagonist of Egan's fourth novel, *Distress* (Egan 1995b). *An Unusual Angle* also draws heavily upon scientific detail, but mainly as a source of metaphor or to provide distancing effects, as in this zanily hyperbolic description of a school swimming carnival:

> Such tricks as the positioning of large masses so as to increase the path lengths of the other factions' lanes, and the creation of spatially limited back currents isolated to specific lanes by invisible monomolecular viscosity barriers, are common practice. I am one of the few who notice such activities, but they don't worry me at all, as the outcomes of the senseless races mean nothing to me. (Egan 1983: 21)

Like "Artifact," Egan's next two stories appeared in Australian anthologies with relatively small audiences, but he had an initial breakthrough in 1986 with the publication of "Mind Vampires" in the influential British SF magazine, *Interzone* (reprinted in Broderick 1988). More sales to *Interzone* followed, and the association has continued with benefit to both parties. However, his career really took off when he began to sell to the American market.

Egan's first sale directly to the USA was "Whistle Test," which initially appeared in *Analog* in 1989 (reprinted in Egan 1995c). Then came the true turning point: 1990, when eight new Egan stories appeared in print. Of these, the most significant was "The Caress," his first sale to *Asimov's Science Fiction Magazine* (reprinted in Egan 1995a).

"The Caress" is a near-future detective story, depicting the investigation of a murder that takes place in a world of advanced biological and computational technology. The murdered woman leaves behind her a chimera, a creature that genetically melds two different animal forms, in this case a leopard and a human woman. The chimera, Catherine, has been designed to be identical to the leopard-woman in Fernand Khnoppff's Symbolist painting "The Caress," and has been constructed as part of a bizarre artistic performance, into which the detective protagonist is unwillingly drawn.

The publication of "The Caress" began Egan's fruitful association with *Asimov's*, paralleling that which he'd already begun with *Interzone*. A survey of Egan's publications from 1983 to 2002 shows that he published a total of 52 short stories (including those at "novella" and "novelette" length). Of these, 22 first appeared in *Interzone* and thirteen in *Asimov's*, accounting for two-thirds of his output at less than novel length. In addition, *Asimov's* editor Gardner Dozois reprinted many Egan stories in his annual *Year's Best Science Fiction* collections. On four occasions (1991, 1992, 1996, and 1998), Dozois selected two Egan stories from the previous year to be reprinted in his *Year's Best* volume. Egan's associations with *Interzone*, *Asimov's*, and their editors assisted him in obtaining a high profile relatively quickly.

Stories such as "The Caress" made Egan's mark as a hard SF writer who was influenced by the 1980s Cyberpunk movement, but had his own ultralucid, intensely focused style, combined with a deep absorption in the implications of science and technology. His protagonists are often investigators of various kinds, sometimes detectives as in "The Caress," sometimes reporters or epidemiologists. Invariably, their professional investigations – whether of a crime, a lost artifact, or the vector of a disease – lead them far beyond what they ever contemplated. Often, they obtain disturbing or even terrifying kinds of knowledge, as they come to understand aspects of the universe, their societies, or their own identities.

Egan was soon nominated for numerous Australian and international awards, and won more than his share – including the John W. Campbell Memorial Award for his third novel, *Permutation City* (Egan 1994), and a Hugo Award for his 1998 novella "Oceanic," first published in *Asimov's Science Fiction* (reprinted in Dozois 1999).

By the mid-1990s, he was obviously one of the SF field's leading *thinkers*: a hard SF writer with particular expertise in physics, biology, the implications of computer science, and related aspects of modern philosophy. His work was seen by many students of the SF genre as a major development, comparable to the "New Wave" fiction of J.G. Ballard and other writers associated with *New Worlds* during the editorship of

Michael Moorcock in the 1960s, or to the canonical texts of the Cyberpunk movement, such as William Gibson's "Burning Chrome" and *Neuromancer*, in the early
1980s.

                                         *

Any description of the recurrent and significant ideas in Egan's work is likely to over-
simplify, and to express the critic's particular perspective. Nonetheless, at least one
significant element in many of Egan's stories and novels is that the protagonists are
forced to confront disturbing facts about their situations, and, indeed, about themselves. Sometimes they realize that their own choices, actions, and emotions are, in
one sense or another, without intelligible justification. They may find themselves
estranged from their own volitions and emotions, or may have experiences that challenge their sense of any stable or essential self at all. In Egan's work, the self possesses
a troubling (or liberating) plasticity. It can expand, contract, morph, and even
proliferate.

Sometimes it is difficult to discern whether Egan's characters have reached a level
of Sartrean heroism by continuing to live with disturbing knowledge about themselves or their universe, or whether they have rationalized their situations in a manner
that is essentially cowardly. Either way, however, they learn and survive. That in itself
may seem admirable.

For example, the narrator of "Axiomatic," first published in *Interzone* in 1990
(reprinted in Egan 1995a), makes a temporary modification to his own personality.
This allows him to commit a vengeful murder that goes against his everyday principles. As the story ends, his act of vengeance is in the past, but he is about to alter his
personality permanently, in order to regain the certainty he felt while committing the
murder. Here, the narrator's deliberate choice to change himself by using a neural
modification device might seem like a travesty of normal human growth and change
– of the development of character, such as we encounter in own lives or, in a more
stylized form, in traditional kinds of fiction. But perhaps the narrator knows better
than this, since all such changes to the self are ultimately neurophysiological. Perhaps
he is simply more clear-eyed than the rest of us.

The narrator of "The Infinite Assassin," first published in *Interzone* in 1991
(reprinted in Egan 1995a), confronts a very different but equally disturbing situation.
He lives in an infinite ensemble of multiple, splitting worlds in which all his choices
and actions are ultimately predetermined, since his many alter egos make *every* available choice in one world or another. He faces the fact that the particular choices of
any one alter ego appear fundamentally unjustified. At any rate, they all happen,
whether justified or not. Yet, he continues his work of attempting to bring some order
to the ensemble of worlds, participating willingly in the process of choice and action.

Yet another kind of ultimately unjustifiable, yet unavoidable, choice is described
in "Reasons to be Cheerful," first published in *Interzone* in 1995 (reprinted in Egan

1998). The narrator, Mark, finds that advanced neurosurgery has left him with the ability to choose his own motives and tastes, shaping his own character, almost without limit. Once again, he faces such disconcerting knowledge . . . and still makes choices. Mark's final words in the story – to his father, who has questioned his decision to live in an unprepossessing neighborhood – are "I like it here" (Egan 1998: 227). It is not easy for him to live with the continual knowledge of the arbitrariness of choices that actually create identity. Yet, choose he must, and choose he does.

Egan sometimes shows compassion, and sometimes a degree of scorn, for those who cannot embrace his austere vision of a universe that is knowable by rational science, yet ultimately meaningless. Some of his characters, usually relatively minor ones, seek to live with a more anthropocentric understanding of reality, one in which the universe itself somehow bestows meaning on human activity and is responsive to human concerns. As portrayed by Egan, reality is simply not intelligible in that way, though it is open to successively deeper levels of understanding through rational investigation. Living admirably seems to consist in facing the implications of science, whatever those might be, and abandoning the illusion that the universe cares about us, or that our own identities somehow exist outside the naturalistic order.

All of this may sound bleak, but Egan also shows that the rational pursuit of knowledge is immensely rewarding in its own way. See, for example, his 1998 story "The Planck Dive," first published in *Asimov's* (reprinted in Egan 1998). Like much of Egan's work, particularly since the mid-1990s, this is set in a future in which humans have long been superseded by posthuman software beings. One character, Prospero, is presented in a mercilessly satirical way, as he proposes to construct a legendary narrative, something like a far-future *Iliad*, about the scientific investigation of a black hole in distant space. His "legend," steeped in archetypes of human effort and heroism, would confer upon the enterprise, and on the natural world itself, a significance that they just do not have.

Prospero is unable to understand the investigation of nature, carried out for its own sake, and for the beauty that is revealed. By contrast, the story's protagonist, Gisela, "wanted to understand the universe at its deepest level, to touch the beauty and simplicity that lay beneath it all" (Egan 1998: 263). The honest search for this kind of understanding appears to be the closest thing to an absolute value in Egan's work. His most admirable characters are those who live for that search, and achieve that kind of understanding.

*

Egan's novels combine elements of satire, hard-edged scientific speculation, and visionary depictions of future societies, some of them, like that shown in "The Planck Dive," far in the future, with no human beings as we know them. The novels' protagonists often reach points where something about the ontology of the universe itself is revealed to them, as in *Quarantine* (Egan 1992) which provides an increasingly complex picture of the implications of quantum theory.

Published nine years after *An Unusual Angle*, *Quarantine* was Egan's second novel, but the first to use hard science for more than decorative purposes. It begins as a fast-moving Cyberpunk detective tale, but it soon concentrates upon the problems and implications of personality modification technology, such as appears in "Axiomatic" and other Egan stories of this period. The main character, Nick Stavrianos, is a typical Egan protagonist whose experience has brought him to a point of seeing *through* the illusion of an unchanging, essential self. It is revealed that Nick's wife was killed while his mind was primed for police work: altered by neural modification in a way that made him more efficient and prevented him from caring. As he later explains to another character, he was not hurt by her death while his mind was altered. He reacted with what seems like cold rationality, by acquiring another "neural mod" before returning to a state where he could feel grief. The new mod was designed to duplicate the happiness his wife gave him.

Nick (supported, seemingly, by Egan) justifies this shocking course of action on the basis that all of us always try to shape our own identities. What is new about neural mods is not that they allow us to attempt this, but merely that they work. It is not clear that Nick's choice is in any sense cowardly or an evasion of the truth; it may be seen as realistic accommodation to the fact that we are all material beings, our natures the product of evolution, experience, and our own neurophysiology. While Nick may shield himself from grief, he does not attempt to evade understanding of the universe in which he lives, of his place within it, or even of himself.

Permutation City (1994), Egan's third novel, is one of his most complex narratives, with many conceptual twists, as it explores the possibility of software intelligence in a purely virtual environment. Ultimately, that idea is taken to its logical conclusion as Egan portrays an entire virtual universe.

The possibility of uploading characters as "Copies" in virtual reality might be viewed, from one perspective, as an irresponsible fantasy of escape from the limitations of the body, but that kind of criticism would miss the point. The more fundamental issue is that our bodies and our minds are seen by Egan to be part of physical nature, while our neurophysiology is not necessarily unique in providing the kind of complexity that can sustain thought and subjective experience. Nothing need be special about human flesh. If that much is granted, everything else follows. Egan might well see any obfuscation here as showing intellectual weakness or an anthropocentric evasion of the truth.

The main characters of *Permutation City* theorize that the entire universe which we experience is merely one patterned selection out of neutral space-time events in an endless substrate of random, disconnected "dust." Within the dust, an infinity of coherent patterns might be traceable, entailing an infinite number of universes. As the novel proceeds, the dust theory of reality is confirmed, but the proof is not available to flesh-and-blood human beings, only to software Copies who have been created for the purpose of an extraordinary scientific experiment.

The experiment requires an apparatus that runs a pocket universe on computer hardware – for a brief allocation of time. If the theory is true, the Copy will experience an ongoing reality after the time is up, a reality explicable only by the "dust theory." The last third of *Permutation City* is set in just such an emergent reality. In one sense, the dust theory eliminates anything special, not only about our place in the universe but about our universe itself, which is seen as only one of an infinity of coherent possibilities coexisting in an endless, random, neutral substrate. Such a universe has no meaning, and requires no gods or other metaphysical entities. Yet, the feeling conveyed is not one of terror or despair, but of wonder.

The action of *Distress* (Egan 1995b) takes place in 2055, mostly at a conference on fundamental physics, timed to mark the centenary of Albert Einstein's death, and held upon Stateless, an artificial island that has been established as an anarchist Utopia. The narrator, Andrew Worth, is a science journalist whose body cavity is packed with recording and editing equipment to assist him in carrying out his trade. His assignments interweave in the narration, leading (yet again) to a point of extraordinary metaphysical revelation.

Worth's assignment on Stateless is to commence a documentary about a young African scientist, Violet Mosala, one of an elite group of physicists who are working on theories that are the leading candidates for the most elegant and successful Theory of Everything (i.e., a theory that would coherently explain all of the fundamental forces known to physics). By the final chapters, the characters are speculating even further, about the metaphysical foundations of a final physical theory.

Once again, the book depicts characters who use technology to modify themselves. For example, the biomedical technology is available in 2055 for people to have themselves rendered totally sexless. Indeed, one of the main characters, Akili, is a "neural asex," and has no physical or psychological remnants of sex, no sexual characteristics, no drive for sexual experience, or sexual feelings for others. Nor is this extreme choice presented as in some way dehumanizing: from Akili's viewpoint, it is as logical as Nick's choice in *Quarantine* to modify his mind so that he never has to feel the onrush of grief.

Diaspora (Egan 1997) commences in the late centuries of the third millennium, when the solar system is inhabited by three kinds of intelligence, reflecting the varied decisions made by humans hundreds of years before. First are the remaining "fleshers," who are embodied, as the name suggests, in the flesh – although almost all have ceased to be entirely human, having become genetically altered "exuberants." Some appear avian or amphibian in form. Some have engineered out their speech facilities, becoming "dream apes," though such removal of capacities, rather than the development of new ones, is a rare exception. More typical are those of a familiar human appearance who have been genetically engineered with neural structures for handling new concepts, perceptions, and communicative possibilities.

Secondly, there are gleisner robots, or just "gleisners," which are conscious software beings embodied in robotic hardware. Thirdly, there are the "citizens" of the "polises," software beings running within virtual-reality communities (polises) that are maintained by well-protected supercomputers.

This posthuman setting is a thoroughly worked out version of how the various possibilities for altering the human species might reach an equilibrium, but that is only Egan's starting point. He asks what might happen *after* such a stage is reached in future history, and tells a story that takes his main characters, over vast gulfs of time, beyond Earth's solar system to the stars.

Indeed, the characters ultimately find their way beyond four-dimensional Einsteinian space-time itself, leading into an increasingly rich vision of nature's underlying geometry. In the process, *Diaspora* grapples with questions about extraterrestrial contact, the significance of connection with physical reality if posthuman technologies and satisfying virtual worlds are available, and the morality of exponential growth and astrophysical engineering. In the end, as the characters find themselves transcending and outliving every reality that they encounter, the main protagonist, Yatima, finds meaning in continued rational inquiry, in the "Truth Mines" of observation and mathematics.

With *Teranesia* (Egan 1999), Egan literally returned to Earth. As in *Quarantine*, quantum theory turns out to be critically involved in the narrative, but the novel is based around a biological mystery, and it places great emphasis on the viewpoint character's inner development. The story commences in December 2012, when Prabir Suresh is nine years old and his sister, Madhusree, is aged only 15 months. Their parents are Indian scientists investigating a bizarre life form, a biologically impossible species of butterfly, on a tiny Indonesian island.

Egan conveys a convincing picture of young Prabir's mind, largely by direct rendering of the boy's schemes, daydreams, fantasies, and his internal trying on of stances and roles. The full implications of these inner dramatics become clear to Prabir and the reader only much later. The book traces his growth to adulthood in Canada and his traumatic return to the island, following his sister, who has become a biologist like her parents. *Teranesia* is a very impressive book indeed, blending complexity of ideas with painstaking clarity, a fine sense of pacing, the extraordinary scope of Egan's imagination and the stunning detail of his scientific knowledge.

Arching over all this is the vision of a universe that offers no privileged place or role for humanity, and is indifferent to our actions and needs – but is open to rational investigation. The ability of Prabir and Madhusree to overcome the problems that confront them, when the course of biological evolution goes suddenly haywire, is shown to depend not only upon their use of scientific reasoning, but also on the mechanistic – rather than cunning or malevolent – character of the alarmingly morphed and speeded-up evolutionary process. Thus, it is actually comforting when the final words of the book, assigned to Madhusree, are: "Life is meaningless" (Egan 1999: 248).

By contrast with *Teranesia*, *Schild's Ladder* (Egan 2002) moves back into the vastness of space. It is another uncompromising depiction of far-future, posthuman beings, and is undoubtedly Egan's most a daunting book; it requires considerable concentration and effort from the reader to penetrate its tracts of scientific discourse. The action takes place twenty millennia from now, when the galaxy has been extensively colonized by our descendants, whose minds run on quantum level computational devices called "Qusps" ("quantum singleton processors").

These people can live in a disembodied, virtual form or move between different bodies as necessary. What to them is just the continuity of memory and experience, not the physical survival of whatever medium, organic or otherwise, instanciates their personalities at any time. Indeed, in works such *Diaspora*, "The Planck Dive," and *Schild's Ladder*, Egan depicts events in which some characters make multiple software copies of themselves to explore different experiences or solve problems beyond the capacity of any individual "self." Particular copies of their personalities are expendable, and are often placed in situations of extreme danger.

The radical attitude to personal identity shown here appears similar to that of the distinguished British philosopher Derek Parfit (Parfit 1987) and perhaps to Buddhist theories that account for the self as an illusion, or a mere composite of elements. Despite this metaphysical radicalism, *Schild's Ladder* deals with the familiar themes of love, identity, and (of course) the pursuit of knowledge. Its drama commences when an experiment in fundamental physics goes wrong, creating a region of "novo-vacuum" in outer space. The novo-vacuum immediately begins expanding outwards at half the speed of light, engulfing star systems and planets, which have to be evacuated before its destructive edge can reach them.

This unprecedented disaster triggers two main political responses. The "Preservationists" want to save the existing colonized worlds, which would mean stopping the expansion of the novo-vacuum, or even destroying it, whereas the "Yielders" want to save and study it, or even adapt to it. They see the novo-vacuum as a new universe, flowering within the old, offering a much-needed stimulus to their stagnating interstellar civilization. As studies continue, the position of the Yielders appears to be justified. It becomes apparent that the novo-vacuum is not so empty, after all – it has developed its own rich internal structure, including a form of life.

*

The importance accorded by other writers, and by leading SF critics, to Egan's stories and novels goes far beyond that given to many writers with more years of experience, a larger output of work, and greater popularity, as measured in sales. Why, exactly, is Egan so respected? At least three considerations seem relevant.

First, Egan's work is remarkable for its convincing engagement with real science, though this sometimes expressed in so much technical detail that it renders passages inaccessible to those with only a general scientific literacy. Be that as it may, the science is up to date, supported by a professional expertise in mathematics and computing, and molded, whenever necessary, to create entirely fictional, yet uncannily plausible, scientific theories. Egan always seems to be aware of the latest speculation about the impact of postulated scientific/technological developments, and he has an ability to take other people's speculation to the next logical step – then the next. These qualities create the sense that he is a writer of SF for readers who actually care about science.

Second, his work expresses a distinctive and science-friendly worldview. While it explores a vast range of issues, its thematic subtext is something very like a scientifically-informed rethinking of the existentialism of Sartre or Camus. What is at stake is knowledge of the true nature of reality – disturbing though this may be – and of the place in the universe occupied by human beings (or posthuman intelligences). Egan's protagonists are often forced to confront uncomfortable truths not only about the world, but also about themselves. Sometimes the vision seems bleak. Often it is superficially mind-blowing, which must assist the author's popularity. Most importantly, it is also profoundly liberating. Thus Egan offers a body of highly intelligent literature for readers who are fascinated by science and its implications, and reject traditional sources of meaning or value, such as religious faith, or popular substitutes such as New Age spirituality.

Third, for all this, Egan's novels and stories are as accessible as they could be, given their seriousness and the author's commitment to real science. The style and structure of the prose are simplified to the maximum, so that any problems of accessibility derive entirely from the intrinsic difficulties of the concepts. The narrative pacing is almost flawless, and Egan has a sure instinct for creating suspense. Despite its cerebral qualities, his work depicts action, conflict, and satisfying resolutions. He is able to make us care about the fates of his characters, even when they are far-future beings of computer software – not human at all, but our posthuman successors.

In short, Egan engages with science in almost unprecedented depth; he has a scientifically oriented philosophy, attractive to many SF readers; and he can dramatize all of this through character conflict and well-shaped storylines. In many ways, his work has set new standards, especially for the hard SF field. It is likely to be admired and influential for many years to come, even if Egan never attains the mass popularity of some less rigorous, more accessible SF writers.

REFERENCES AND FURTHER READING

Blackford, Russell, Van Ikin, and Sean McMullen (1999) *Strange Constellations: A History of Australian Science Fiction*. Westport, CT: Greenwood Press.

Blackford, Russell (2000) "Hammer blows to the ego: Greg Egan's rational materialism." *Nova Express* 19: 11–15.

Broderick, Damien (ed.) (1988) *Matilda at the Speed of Light*. Sydney: Angus & Robertson.

Broderick, Damien (1998) "The Next Three Millennia." *Australian Book Review* 189: 50.

Dozois, Gardner (ed.) (1999) *The Year's Best Science Fiction: Sixteenth Annual Collection*. New York: St. Martins.

Egan, Greg (1983) *An Unusual Angle*. Melbourne: Norstrilia Press.

——(1992) *Quarantine*. London: Century-Legend.

——(1994) *Permutation City*. London: Orion-Millennium.

——(1995a) *Axiomatic*. London: Orion-Millennium.

——(1995b) *Distress*. London: Orion-Millennium.

——(1995c) *Our Lady of Chernobyl*. Sydney: MirrorDanse.

——(1997) *Diaspora*. London: Orion-Millennium.

——(1998) *Luminous*. London: Orion-Millennium.

——(1999) *Teranesia*. London: Orion-Gollancz.

——(2002) *Schild's Ladder*. London: Orion-Gollancz.

Farnell, Ross (2000) "Attempting Immortality: AI, A-Life, and the Posthuman in Greg Egan's *Permutation City*." *Science Fiction Studies* 80: 69–91.

Ikin, Van (ed.) (1990) *Glass Reptile Breakout and Other Australian Speculative Stories*. Perth: Centre for Studies in Australian Literature.

Ikin, Van (1999) "Tomorrow's Selfhood: Self in the Science Fiction of Greg Egan," in *The Fantastic Self: Essays on the Subject of the Self*, (eds) Janeen Webb and Andrew Enstice. Perth: Eidolon Publications, 295–303.

King, David (ed.) (1983) *Dreamworks: Strange New Stories*. Melbourne: Norstrilia Press.

Parfit, Derek (1987) *Reasons and Persons* (1984). Oxford: Oxford University Press.

PART VII
Readings

32

Mary Shelley: *Frankenstein: Or, the Modern Prometheus*

Susan E. Lederer and Richard M. Ratzan

Mary Shelley's *Frankenstein* (1818) is one of the most indelible literary creations of the last two centuries. Much more than the story of a young man who makes a monster, the novel featured a convergence of several literary genres – the romance, the epistolary novel, the Gothic, travel stories – into which Shelley wove ideas from contemporary scientific workers and developments in physics, chemistry, and medicine. Although there remains disagreement about Shelley's novel as the ur-text of science fiction, no one disputes that *Frankenstein* represented a significant moment in the historical development of the genre. The main protagonist of the novel, the young Victor Frankenstein, as Roslynn D. Haynes notes, "has become an archetype in his own right, universally referred to and providing the dominant image of the scientist in twentieth-century fiction and film. Not only has his name become synonymous with any experiment out of control but his relation with the Monster he creates has become, in the popular mind, at least, complete identification: Frankenstein is the monster" (Haynes 1994: 92). In the nineteenth century, the word "Frankenstein" was deployed by politicians and political commentators in England and the USA to denote processes or people out of control. Reflecting the ascendancy of science in the twentieth century, Shelley's creatures (man and monster) increasingly framed discussions of the implications of medical developments (from cardiac pacemakers in the 1930s to heart transplants in the 1960s) and military power (the atomic bomb and the nuclear battlefield). In the late twentieth century, the prefix "Franken" became ubiquitous in discussions of genetically modified foods (Frankenfarms and Frankentomatoes), potentially threatening organisms (Frankenvirus – genetically modified smallpox), and researchers (Franken + name of scientist). Many such references owe much more to the rhetorical needs of activists and the cinematic transformation of the Frankenstein story than to Mary Shelley's novel. Nonetheless, since 1818 the novel has appeared in hundreds (perhaps thousands) of editions. The seeming insatiable interest in the Frankenstein story has spawned numerous adaptations of Mary Shelley's story, from cartoons, comic books, and computer games to screen treatments and theatricals.

The genesis of the novel may be as well known as the monster itself. During the summer of 1816, the 18-year-old Mary Wollstonecraft Godwin and her lover, the poet and free-thinker Percy Bysshe Shelley, were frequent visitors to the Swiss villa where George Gordon, Lord Byron, was staying with his traveling companion, the physician John William Polidori. Following long evenings of reading aloud "German stories of ghosts," Byron suggested a story competition. Each of the four would contribute a story based on a supernatural occurrence. Two of these stories were eventually published. Mary Shelley, who had married Percy in December 1816, following the death by drowning of his wife Harriet, published *Frankenstein: or, the Modern Prometheus* in 1818. The following year, Polidori published *The Vampyre*.

No author's name appeared on the 1818 edition of *Frankenstein*. Mary Shelley's decision to dedicate her novel to the author of the radical political texts *Enquiry Concerning Political Justice* (1793) and *The Adventures of Caleb Williams* (1794), William Godwin, her father, excited speculation that the book had been written by Percy Shelley. Percy Shelley shared many of Godwin's political ideas, as well as those of Mary's mother, the feminist philosopher Mary Wollstonecraft, who died shortly after her daughter's birth in 1797. He furnished the preface to the 1818 edition, which identified some of the scientific work that Mary Shelley drew upon in creating her story. "The event on which this fiction is founded has been supposed, by Dr. [Erasmus] Darwin, and some of the physiological writers of Germany, as not of impossible occurrence" (Hunter 1996: 5).

In 1831, when Mary Shelley published a revised edition of *Frankenstein*, she added a new preface, in which she credited the lengthy discussions between Byron and Shelley on the principle of life as an inspiration for her story. She explained that she had sought to devise a story that "would speak to the mysterious fears of our nature, and awaken thrilling horror – one to make the reader dread to look around, to curdle the blood, and quicken the beatings of the heart" (Hunter 1996: 171). She recalled how she experienced a waking dream in which she imagined a creature of "imperfect animation:"

> I saw with shut eyes but acute mental vision the pale student of unhallowed arts kneeling beside the thing he had put together. I saw the hideous phantasm of a man stretched out, and then, on the working of some powerful machine show signs of life, and stir with an uneasy half vital motion. Frightful must it be; for supremely frightful would be the effect of any human endeavor to mock the stupendous mechanism of the Creator of the World. (Hunter 1996: 172)

Like her husband's earlier preface, the 1831 preface discussed the speculations of the English physician Erasmus Darwin about the spontaneous generation of living organisms. Shelley recalled hearing that the physician had placed a piece of vermicelli (the worm) in a glass case, which later exhibited voluntary motion. She also noted the excitement caused by galvanism and the potential for reanimating dead tissue. The direct application of electricity or galvanism to revive the dead generated intense excitement among physicians and the public. In the 1790s, the Italian anatomist Luigi Galvani performed an extensive set of experiments in which he applied an electric source to the dissected muscles of a dead frog, producing movement. Galvani concluded that this effect resulted from electricity in the dead frog's body, which he called "animal electricity." Galvani's nephew, Giovanni Aldini, conducted extraordinary public demonstrations throughout Europe in which he administered electrical current to the ears, noses and faces of newly decapitated animals. In 1803, Aldini visited London, where he demonstrated the novelty of galvanic stimulation to the Prince and Princess of Wales; in this case, Aldini applied current not only to dead animals but also to dead humans. After he administered electrical current to the head of a murderer executed at London's Newgate Prison, the muscles of the face reportedly twitched, the jaw began to quiver, and the adjoining muscles were horribly contorted. Such demonstrations continued in England and the USA through the 1840s.

In creating her story of "imperfect animation," Mary Shelley drew on transgressive practices calculated to create fear and disquiet in her readers, including the dissection of a dead body. Victor Frankenstein acquires the raw materials that he uses in making a monster from "the unhallowed damps of the grave, or tortured the living animal to animate the lifeless clay." Shelley describes Victor's visits to the charnel houses, the abattoir, and the dissecting room; her protagonist explains that he experiences no supernatural horror conducting his investigations into the corruption of the human body after it becomes "food for the worm." Mary Shelley knew that some, perhaps many, of her readers would recoil at the passages in which her pale student makes nocturnal visits to acquire flesh and fluids for the creature. Before the revised edition of *Frankenstein* appeared in 1831, the only bodies legally available to physicians and surgeons for anatomical dissection were those of convicted criminals. Unlike Andreas Vesalius, the Italian anatomist and author of the extraordinary text *On the Fabric of the Human Body* (1543), Victor has no relationship with the local authorities to attend the execution of criminals to acquire anatomical specimens. The dearth of legal bodies for dissection sparked a thriving business of grave-robbing. Professional "resurrectionists" procured recently dead bodies from graveyards for a fee for anatomists and medical educators. The notorious 1828 trial of Robert Burke and Robert Hare further stimulated efforts at reform. Rather than disinter bodies in cemeteries and deliver them to the eminent Edinburgh anatomist Robert Knox, Burke and Hare killed some 16 hapless individuals and sold their newly dead bodies to the physician. To overcome the vulgar hostility to postmortem dissection, British philosopher Jeremy Bentham at his death in 1832 donated his own body for dissection to the anatomist Thomas Southwood Smith. Bentham asked that Smith offer a public lecture on the usefulness of the knowledge that accrued from the dissection. That same year, 1832, the British Parliament passed the Anatomy Act, which greatly enlarged the supply of dead bodies by allowing anatomists access to the bodies of the unclaimed poor from workhouses and hospitals.

Shelley's novel opens and ends not with the story of the young Victor Frankenstein, but instead with a series of letters written by another ambitious young man seeking to expand human mastery of the natural world. The explorer Robert Walton writes to his sister Margaret Saville (who shares Mary Shelley's initials) about his exhaustive search for a land of wonders at the North Pole. "I shall satiate my ardent curiosity with the sight of a part of the world never before visited, and may tread a land never before imprinted by the foot of man. These are my enticements, and they are sufficient to conquer all fear of danger or death" (Hunter 1996: 7). Walton's letters convey his determination and preparation for his quest, and his willingness to endanger his crew to achieve his goal. Walton's experiences also serve to expand Shelley's ideas about the pursuit of knowledge – geographical, medical, chemical – and the responsible use of power.

Walton's fourth letter describes the arrival of an emaciated, near-frozen man whose own quest for knowledge and wisdom has resulted in "great and unparalleled misfortunes" (Hunter 1996: 17). The man is Victor Frankenstein, who is persuaded to relate his narrative in the following days to Walton. Frankenstein's narrative constitutes the major portion of the novel. Victor describes his family, his childhood, and his studies in Germany at the University in Ingolstadt. There Victor encounters Professor Waldman, whose lectures on the achievements of modern chemistry make an indelible impression on the young man. The modern practitioners of chemistry, notes Waldman, "have indeed performed miracles. They penetrate into the recesses of nature, and shew how she works in her hiding places. They ascent into the heavens; they have discovered how the blood circulates, and the nature of the air we breathe. They have acquired new and almost unlimited powers; they command the thunders of heaven, mimic the earthquake, and even mock the invisible world with its own shadows" (Hunter 1996: 27–8). Seeking to attain similar and personal control of the natural world, Frankenstein withdraws to solitary labor in his "workshop of filthy creation" (Hunter 1996: 32). He relates how he assembled materials for his creation, his moment of triumph in infusing the spark of life into a lifeless thing, and his emotional rejection of the monstrosity he had created. The horror of imperfect animation – the ugliness of the creature and its convulsive, agitated movements – prompt Victor to flee the scene. When he returns, the monster is gone. Victor learns of the murder of his younger brother William. Despite his certain knowledge that his creature, the result of his "curiosity and lawless devices" is responsible for William's death, Victor remains silent when a local woman Justine Moritz is convicted of the crime and sentenced to death (Hunter 1996: 52).

Frankenstein's narrative is interrupted by his creature's life history. Unlike Frankenstein, however, this creature has only a "father," a father who not only abandons him but fails to give him a name. The creature's namelessness deepens the contrast Shelley draws between John Milton's omnipotent deity and Victor's imperfect parentage. Fostered by no one, the creature lives on berries and plants in the forest, observing a family living in a cottage. He receives an unusual education in the form of a leather portmanteau containing several works: *Plutarch's Lives*, Goethe's *The Sorrows of Young Werter*, and Milton's *Paradise Lost*. As if the lines from *Paradise Lost* Book 10 on the novel's title page is not enough ("Did I request thee, Maker, from my clay /To mould me man? Did I solicit thee /From darkness to promote me?"), Shelley has the creature make his comparison with Adam explicit:

> Like Adam, I was created apparently united by no link to any other being in existence; but his state was far different from mine in every other respect. He had come forth from the hands of God a perfect creature, happy and prosperous. Guarded by the especial care of his Creator; he was allowed to converse with, and acquire knowledge from beings of a superior nature: but I was wretched, helpless, and alone. (Hunter 1996: 87)

The creator's desperate efforts to locate family and friends, to obtain integration into human society, are rejected, and he turns to violence. When he encounters Victor, he demands that Frankenstein provide a creature of another sex, an Eve to his Adam, an equal who will afford him the affections of a sensitive being and an alternative to his profound isolation from the world of men. Although Frankenstein initially agrees to provide this mate, he ultimately rejects the proposal. The monster's rage erupts into the murder of Frankenstein's closest friend, Henry Clerval, and later his bride. Elizabeth Frankenstein is killed on her wedding night by the creature. These events culminate in Victor's frantic search in the Northern seas, his death aboard Walton's ship, and the monster's remorseful promise to end his life in the "torturing flames of the funeral pile" (Hunter 1996: 156).

The first run of 500 copies of *Frankenstein* sold well. Only a few months after the book appeared, a friend of the Shelleys noted that *Frankenstein* was universally known and read. It was not universally loved. John Croker, writing in the *Quarterly Review,* characterized the novel as "a tissue of horrible and disgusting absurdity," which failed to inculcate any useful lesson of conduct, morality or manners (Hunter 1996: 189). But the novelist Sir Walter Scott, who reviewed the book for *Blackwood's Edinburgh Magazine* in March 1818, praised the power and beauty, if imperfect execution, of the "wild fiction;" Scott later praised *Frankenstein* as a "powerful romance" (Williams 1968: 260–72, 326). In June 1818, Mary Shelley wrote to Scott to reveal her authorship of *Frankenstein,* seeking to absolve Percy Shelley of any responsibility for her "juvenile attempt." (Bennett 1980 I:71) Percy Shelley continued for decades to be credited with *Frankenstein*'s novelty and power. "Nothing but an absolute magnetizing of her brain by [Percy] Shelley's," the *Dictionary of National Biography* (1897) noted, "can account for her having risen so far above her usual self as in 'Frankenstein.'" (Stephen and Lee 1897: 29) Until the 1970s, it can safely be said that Mary Shelley was better known for being the wife of Percy Shelley and the daughter of William Godwin and Mary Wollstonecraft than for her own writings, with the exception of *Frankenstein,* which include such novels as *Valperga* (1823) and *The Last Man* (1826), as well as numerous essays and short stories.

Absolute magnetizing aside, Percy Shelley, as the more experienced author, certainly participated in the development of *Frankenstein.* In addition to composing the preface, he made numerous suggestions, "about a thousand in all," which survive in the manuscript pages of the novel (Mellor 1988: 160). Most of Percy Shelley's changes were stylistic; he preferred more learned, less colloquial constructions. Mary Shelley published a new edition of *Frankenstein* in 1831 (she was compelled to support herself and her young son after Percy Shelley's death in 1822). Despite her claim that her alterations were "principally those of style," she significantly revised the novel (Hunter 1996: 173). She wrote a new preface, and altered a number of relationships and descriptions. These changes included a new relationship between Victor Frankenstein and Elizabeth Lavenza (from first cousin in the 1818 edition to no blood relation in the 1831), the role of Clerval and the presentation of the Frankenstein family, a new conception of Nature as mechanistic, and the degree of responsibility assigned to Victor's faults. In the 1818 edition, Victor's sin is his failure to love and care for the creature he fathered; in the 1831 edition, his sin is his hubris in the endeavor "to mock the stupendous mechanism of the Creator of the world" (Hunter 1996: 172) These changes have fostered debate over Percy Shelley's contribution. Whereas James Rieger found Percy Shelley's assistance so extensive that he could be regarded as more of a minor collaborator rather than an editor, David Ketterer among others, has argued that this extreme position is not borne out by the evidence. The differences between the 1818 edition and the 1831 edition have also raised the vexed question of which edition represents the definitive *Frankenstein*.

In the 1970s, feminist critics found much to consider in Mary Shelley's *Frankenstein*. Ellen Moers was the first to advance the idea that the novel was actually a "birth myth," drawing on Mary Shelley's own preoccupations with birth, death, and imperfect animation: "No outside influence need be sought to explain Mary Shelley's fantasy of the newborn as at once monstrous agent of destruction and piteous victim of parental abandonment. 'I, the miserable and the abandoned,' cries the monster at the end of *Frankenstein*, 'I am an abortion to be spurned at, kicked at, trampled on'"(Hunter 1996: 222). The idea that Frankenstein was a "'woman's book' that encodes Shelley's acute anxieties about maternity" became almost a canonical reading of the gender politics of *Frankenstein* (Rose 1995: 813). Following Moers, other critics have interpreted Victor's disgust at the first sight of his creature as symptomatic of postpartum depression, and as a sign of Mary Shelley's profound ambivalence about her pregnancies and the loss of her own mother. In 1816, when Shelley first conceived *Frankenstein*, she had already given birth twice. Her first child, a daughter, died in March 1815. Her second child, a son named William, was born in 1816. Before *Frankenstein* was completed she gave birth to another daughter, Clara, in 1817. Only one of the children born to Mary and Percy Shelley survived infancy to reach adulthood. Clara died of fever in 1818, the three-year-old William succumbed to malaria in 1819, the same year her lone surviving child, Percy Florence was born.

Locating the wellsprings for *Frankenstein* in Mary Shelley's life also turns on the issue of resuscitation. Not only did the resuscitation of the near-dead garner considerable public attention in the late eighteenth and early nineteenth century, but three attempted resuscitations (one successful, two failed) profoundly influenced Shelley's life. The first was her mother's rescue from a 1795 suicide attempt. In a letter written shortly before her attempt, Mary Wollstonecraft expressed the hope that her body would not be insulted by being "snatched from death." But when she plunged into the Thames River and lost consciousness, she was rescued by watermen, taken to a receiving station of the Royal Humane Society, and successfully revived. Humane societies dated from the 1760s when physicians and reformers sought to encourage the revival of the drowned and suffocated. The London Humane Society, formed in 1774 and later renamed the Royal Humane Society in 1787, disseminated information about such techniques as resuscitation bellows, the use of smelling salts, and vigorous rubbing and shaking as methods to revive the unconscious or rescue those near-drowned. By 1796, this society boasted of having revived more than 2,000 people, including Mary Wollstonecraft. In a letter written after her revival, she expressed her resentment: "I have only to lament that, when the bitterness of death was past, I was inhumanly brought back to life and misery" (quoted Williams 2001: 223). Carolyn Williams has argued that Mary Shelley was influenced by her mother's experience and her regrets, which she knew from her father's indiscreet biography of his late wife, *Memoirs, of the Author of a Vindication of the Rights of Woman* (1798).

Williams, like other writers, also points to the implications for *Frankenstein* of the death of Mary Shelley's first child, a daughter born prematurely on February 2, 1815, and found dead in her crib on March 6. The baby was apparently dead for several hours before anyone realized that something had gone wrong. In her journal Shelley recorded a poignant dream in which the baby was revived. "Dream that my little baby came to life again – that it had only been cold and that we rubbed it by the fire and it lived – I awake and find no baby – I think about the little thing all day – not in good spirits" (Feldman and Scott-Kilvert 1987 I: 70). Williams points out that Shelley's maternal dream was no baseless fantasy. In 1816 the Royal Humane Society presented a medal to matron Catherine Wigden for the successful revival of infants at London's Lying-In Hospital, where she used mouth-to-mouth resuscitation, warmth and friction "to recover life from those infants who are apparently still-born" (Williams 2001: 224–5).

The failure of a resuscitation attempt by the Royal Humane Society made it possible for Mary and Percy Shelley to marry. When Harriet Shelley, Percy Shelley's wife, attempted suicide by drowning in a London lake in December 1816, her body, like that of Mary Wollstonecraft, was taken to a receiving station of the Royal Humane Society, where efforts to revive her failed. Despite these failed efforts at resuscitation, the sense of power and possibility was shared by many of the medical Prometheans of Mary Shelley's day, who celebrated the "god-like power of restoring suspended animation" (Lederer 2002: 12) Shelley included some detailed descriptions of restoring the near-dead in *Frankenstein*. In the opening section, when Walton and his men find the nearly frozen Victor Frankenstein, they perform with near textbook-precision the necessary and scientific steps to revive him:

> We attempted to carry him into the cabin, but as soon as he had quitted the fresh air he fainted. We accordingly brought him back to the deck and restored him to animation by rubbing him with brandy and forcing him to swallow a small quantity. As soon as he showed signs of life we wrapped him up in blankets and placed him near the

chimney of the kitchen stove. By slow degrees he recovered and ate a little soup, which restored him wonderfully. (Hunter 1996: 14)

Such passages suggest Mary Shelley's interest in and acquaintance with the ability to restore life to the apparently dead.

Shelley's novel ends, as it began, in the icy waters of the frozen north. Victor Frankenstein lies dying on board the ship of another explorer seeking to pour a torrent of light onto this dark world. After telling Walton his strange and tragic story, Victor Frankenstein bids the explorer farewell and offers this final advice: "Seek happiness in tranquility and avoid ambition, even if it be only the apparently innocent one of distinguishing yourself in science and discoveries. Yet why do I say this? I myself have been blasted in these hopes, yet another may succeed" (Hunter 1996: 152). Another may succeed in the Promethean possibility of bringing life to humankind. The Prometheus myth exerted a profound influence on the Shelleys. In Greek myth, Prometheus created humans out of mud and water; he angered Zeus and the other gods by stealing fire from the heavens and giving it to his creation. As a punishment he was sentenced for eternity to be chained to a rock where an eagle or vulture would daily devour his liver. When Mary Shelley prepared her husband's epic poem, *Prometheus Unbound,* for publication after his death in 1822, she explained in the preface that Prometheus had wielded knowledge as a weapon to defeat evil, "by leading mankind beyond the state wherein they are sinless through ignorance, to that in which they are virtuous through wisdom" (Lederer 2002: 65). Although her protagonist, Victor Frankenstein, failed to act wisely, Mary Shelley's selection of "the modern Prometheus" as the subtitle of her novel suggests the potential for humankind to acquire these virtues to combine power with responsibility.

Frankenstein has exerted extraordinary influence. "There is no such thing as *Frankenstein,*" Paul O'Flinn aptly observed, "there are only *Frankensteins*, as the text is ceaselessly rewritten, reproduced, re-filmed and redesigned" (1995: 22). In his exhaustive survey of the Frankenstein story, Donald Glut reported that by 1982, there were some 130 fictions based on *Frankenstein*, more than 40 film adaptations, over 80 stage productions, and 80 additional films. A decade later, Stephen Jones listed more than 400 films based, more or less, on the novel in *The Illustrated "Frankenstein" Movie Guide* (1994). Although it is tempting to see the popular interest in the Frankenstein story as a twentieth-century development in light of the power of film images, nineteenth-century authors and audiences found the Frankenstein story, shorn of much of Mary Shelley's nuanced characterizations, compelling.

By 1831, Mary Shelley realized that the novel has escaped her control, when she bade what she called "her hideous progeny" to go forth and prosper. In 1823, she had enjoyed the performance she attended at the English Opera House of a play based on her novel. Adapted by Richard Brinsely Peake, *Presumption, or the Fate of Frankenstein* focused on the "fatal consequences of that presumption which attempts to penetrate beyond prescribed depths, into the mysteries of nature" (Lederer 2002: 31) She was especially pleased that in listing the performers, there was a blank space for the name of the creature, noting "this nameless mode of naming the unnameable is rather good" (Bennett 1980 I: 378). She had not foreseen that the name of her pale student would become the name of the creature she fashioned.

Today the name of her composite creation – Frankenstein as maker and monster – is unavoidable in discussions of biomedical innovations. Although the novel *Franken-stein* was apparently banned in South Africa in 1955 as "indecent and objectionable," this did not stop the first recipient of a human heart transplant to invoke the monster in 1967 (Rose 1995; 809). When he awoke from the anesthesia after his surgery, South African patient Louis Washkansky told his nurses: "I am a new Frankenstein" (The Heart). Since that time, the prefix *Franken* has become ubiquitous in discussions of genetically modified foods, plants, and organisms and the use of embryonic stem cells. In 1997, when Scottish researcher Ian Wilmut announced the successful cloning of an adult mammal (Dolly), one reporter noted a major outbreak of the "Frankenstein syndrome," fears that science had unleashed an ungovernable menace to the unsuspecting public. In 2003, when a Manhattan judge dismissed a lawsuit against McDonald's Corporation, he invoked Frankenstein to refer to the unnaturalness of fast foods, labeling Chicken McNuggets "a McFrankenstein creation of various elements not utilized by the home cook" (Weiser 2003). This rubric was immediately recognizable as a cultural short hand for science out of control.

The creation of these hyphenated creatures is a pale echo of Mary Shelley's literary work. One of the most striking features of her novel is the degree to which it is a composite work. *Frankenstein* contains references to and even excerpts from such influential literary works as the Bible, *Paradise Lost*, the works of William Blake, Samuel Taylor Coleridge, Percy Shelley, and William Wordsworth. As Judith Wilt describes it, "*Frankenstein* is a deeply complex and somewhat ambiguous mélange of analogies." (Levine and Knoepflmacher 1979: 18) Many commentators have analyzed the novel as not just a composite, but a hybrid, an intermediate form *between* existing forms. Darko Suvin characterized it as "a revealingly flawed hybrid of horror tale and philosophical science fiction" (Suvin 1979: 127). Mary Lowe-Evans described *Frankenstein* as "a novel whose style and subject stand somewhere between the exotic, egocentric Gothic fiction of the eighteenth century and the community-minded social novels of the Victorian era"(Lowe-Evans 1993: 6). Terrence Holt writes, "Like the construction of the Creature out of dead, disarticulated parts, *Frankenstein* also figures its own construction out of discarded bits of prior literary forms – epistolary and journal and especially the gothic romance"(Holt 1990: 19).

If Mary Shelley's *Frankenstein* is a hybrid, some critics would insist that it is a chimerical monster as well. Lee Sterrenburg has described the metaphorical power of the Monster, as "a hybrid, a cross between two traditions", i.e., the Burkean tradition of horrific, evil monsters and the republican tradition of social monsters" (Levine 1993: 165–6) In doing so, he argues, Mary Shelley created a unique third tradition, a monster with insight and the eloquence to describe what it feels like to be not only a victim (the Burkean tradition) and a rebel (the republican tradition) but a "victim who is a rebel."

To carry the metaphor of *Frankenstein* as constructed hybrid, one might say that Mary Shelley assembled not only a new hybrid novel but delivered an entirely new fictional species. *Frankenstein*, Muriel Spark has written, fused the scientific empiricism of the eighteenth century and the nineteenth century's imaginative reaction, thereby giving rise to "the first important example of that fictional genre which was later endorsed by H.G. Wells and M.P. Shiel" (Spark 1951: 159). This genre, what H.G. Wells called "scientific romance," is what is now called science fiction and within it *Frankenstein* initiated an ongoing tradition of narratives describing the experiment-gone-wrong. With her creation of *Frankenstein*, Mary Shelley, like Victor, was not just constructing an entity from existing and new materials. She was, like Victor, performing an experiment. Mary Shelley was doing research on genre and prose, using the artistic method to analyze the humanistic results of a man amorally using the scientific method.

References and Further Reading

Aldini, Giovanni (1803) *Account of the Late Improvements in Galvanism.* London: Cuthell and Martin.

Anon. (1967) "The Heart: Miracle in Capetown." *Newsweek* (December 18) 86.

Back, K.W. (1995) "*Frankenstein* and *Brave New World* – Two Cautionary Myths on the Boundaries of Science." *History of European Ideas* 20: 327–32.

Baldick, Chris (1987) *In Frankenstein's Shadow: Myth, Monstrosity and Nineteenth-Century Writing.* Oxford: Clarendon Press.

Bann, Stephen (ed.) (1994) *Frankenstein, Creation and Monstrosity.* London: Reaktion Books.

Behrendt, Stephen C. (ed.) (1990) *Approaches to Teaching Shelley's "Frankenstein."* New York: Modern Language Association.

Bennett, Betty T. (ed.) (1980) *The Letters of Mary Wollstonecraft Shelley.* Baltimore, MD: Johns Hopkins University Press. 3 vols.

——(1996) *Mary Wollstonecraft Shelley: An Introduction.* Baltimore, MD: Johns Hopkins University Press.

Bloom, Harold (ed.) (1985) *Mary Shelley: Modern Critical Views,* New York: Chelsea House.

Botting, Fred (ed.) (1991) *Making Monstrous: "Frankenstein", Criticism, Theory.* Manchester: Manchester University Press.

——(1995) *Frankenstein: A New Casebook.* London: Macmillan.

Butler, Marilyn (ed.) (1994) *Mary Shelley, Frankenstein: Or, The Modern Prometheus: The 1818*

Text. Oxford and New York: Oxford University Press.

Feldman, Paula R., and Diana Scott-Kilvert (eds) (1987) *The Journals of Mary Shelley 1814–1844.* Oxford: Clarendon Press. 2 vols.

Feldman, Paula R., Lucy Morrison, and Staci L. Stone (eds) (2003) *A Mary Shelley Encyclopedia.* Westport, CT: Greenwood Press.

Fisch, Audrey A., Anne K. Mellor, and Esther H. Schor (eds) (1993) *The Other Mary Shelley: Beyond "Frankenstein."* New York: Oxford University Press.

Gigante, Denise (2000) "Facing the Ugly: The Case of *Frankenstein.*" *ELH: English Literary History* 67: 565–87.

Gilbert, Sandra M., and Susan Gubar (1984) *The Madwoman in the Attic: the Woman Writer and the Nineteenth-Century Literary Imagination.* New Haven, CT: Yale University Press.

Glut, Donald F. (2002) *The Frankenstein Archive: Essays on the Monster, the Myth, the Movies and More.* Jefferson, NC: McFarland.

Godwin, William (1992) *Enquiry Concerning Political Justice* (1793). Oxford: Woodstock Books.

——(1794) *Things as they Are, or, The Adventures of Caleb Williams.* London: B. Crosby.

——(1990) *Memoirs, of the Author of a Vindication of the Rights of Woman* (1798). Oxford: Woodstock Books.

Haining, Peter (ed.) (1994) *The Frankenstein Omnibus.* Edison, NJ: Chartwell Books.

Haynes, Roslynn D. (1994) *From Faust to Strangelove: Representations of the Scientist in Western Literature*. Baltimore, MD: Johns Hopkins University Press.

Hogle, Jerrold E. (ed.) (2003) *Frankenstein's Dream*. College Park, MD: University of Maryland Press.

Holt, Terrence (1990) "Teaching Frankenstein as Science Fiction," in *Approaches to Teaching Shelley's "Frankenstein,"* (ed.) S.C. Behrendt. New York: Modern Language Association.

Huet, Marie-Helene (1993) *Monstrous Imagination*. Cambridge: Harvard University Press.

Hunter, J. Paul (ed.) (1996) Mary Shelley, *Frankenstein: The 1818 Text*, ed. J.P. Hunter (*Frankenstein: Or, The Modern Prometheus*, 1818), Norton Critical Edition. London and New York: W. W. Norton.

Hustis, Harriet (2003) "Responsible Creativity and the 'Modernity' of Mary Shelley's Prometheus." *SEL: Studies in English Literature* 4: 845–58.

Jones, Stephen (1994) *The Illustrated "Frankenstein" Movie Guide*. New York: Titan Books.

Ketterer, David (1978) "Mary Shelley and Science Fiction: A Select Bibliography, Selectively Annotated." *Science Fiction Studies* 5 (July): 172–8.

——(1997) " 'Furnished . . . Materials:' The Surgical Anatomy Context of *Frankenstein*." *Science Fiction Studies* 24 (March): 119–23.

Lederer, Susan E. (2002) *Frankenstein: Penetrating the Secrets of Nature*. New Brunswick, NJ: Rutgers University Press.

Levine, George (1993) *Realism and Representation*. Madison: University of Wisconsin Press.

Levine, George, and U.C. Knoepflmacher (eds) (1979) *The Endurance of Frankenstein: Essays on Mary Shelley's Novel*. Berkeley, CA: University of California Press.

Lowe-Evans, Mary (1993) *Frankenstein: Mary Shelley's Wedding Guest*. New York: Twayne.

Marshall, Tim (1996) *Murdering to Dissect: Graverobbing, Frankenstein, and the Anatomy Literature*. Manchester: Manchester University Press

Mellor, Anne K. (1988) *Mary Shelley: Her Life, Her Fictions, Her Monsters*. London: Methuen.

O'Flinn, Paul (1995) "Production and Reproduction: the Case of *Frankenstein*," in *Frankenstein: Contemporary Critical Essays*, (ed.) Fred Botting. London: Macmillan, 21–44.

Polidori, John William (1990) *The Vampyre* (1819). Oxford: Woodstock Books.

Preiss, Byron (ed.) (1991) *The Ultimate Frankenstein*. New York: Dell.

Rose, E.C. (1995) "Custody Battles: Reproducing Knowledge about Frankenstein." *New Literary History* 26: 809–32.

Shelley, Mary (1969) *Frankenstein: Or, The Modern Prometheus*, (ed.) M.K. Joseph [1831 text]. Oxford: Oxford University Press.

——(1996) *The Last Man* (1826), (ed.) Nora Crook and Pamela Clemit. London: Pickering and Chatto.

——(2000) *Valperga: Or, The Life and Adventures of Castruccio, Prince of Lucca* (1823), (ed.) Michael Rossington. Oxford: Oxford University Press.

Skal, David J. (1998) *Screams of Reason: Mad Science and Modern Culture*. New York: Norton.

Smith, Johanna M. (ed.) (1992) *Frankenstein: Complete Authoritative Text, etc.* Boston, MA: Bedford Books/ St. Martin's Press.

Spark, Muriel (1951) *Child of Light: A Reassessment of Mary Wollstonecraft Shelley*. New York: Welcome Rain.

Stephen, Leslie, and Sidney Lee (eds) (1897) "Mary Wollstonecraft Shelley." *Dictionary of National Biography*. London: Smith, Elder, Volume 52: 29.

Suvin, Darko (1979) *Metamorphoses of Science Fiction: On the Poetics and History of a Literary Genre*. New Haven, CT: Yale University Press.

Turney, Jon. (1998) *Frankenstein's Footsteps: Science, Genetics and Popular Culture*. New Haven, CT: Yale University Press.

Vasbinder, Samuel H. (1976) *Scientific Attitudes in Mary Shelley's "Frankenstein."* Ann Arbor, MI: UMI Research Press.

Veeder, William R. (1986) *Mary Shelley and Frankenstein: The Fate of Androgyny*. Chicago, IL: University of Chicago Press.

Weiser, B. (2003) "Your Honor, We Call Our Next Witness: McFrankenstein." *New York Times* Jan. 26 4:5.

Williams, Carolyn (2001) " 'Inhumanly Brought Back to Life and Misery': Mary Wollstonecraft, *Frankenstein*, and the Royal Humane Society." *Women's Writing* 8: 213–32.

Williams, Ioan (ed.) (1968) *Sir Walter Scott on Novelists and Fiction*. London: Routledge and Kegan Paul.

Wolf, Leonard (ed.) (1977) *The Annotated Frankenstein*. New York: Clarkson N. Potter.

33

Charlotte Perkins Gilman: *Herland*

Jill Rudd

Written in 1915 as a serial (published separately as a full novel in 1979) *Herland* is Gilman's most popular foray into Utopian writing, although it was not her first (*Moving the Mountain* appeared in 1911). It exemplifies many of the traits associated with both Utopian fiction and books first published in installments, having a straightforward plot and a few, clear, characters who pose and answer questions about the central phenomenon of the book: a country inhabited solely by women. Such simplicity of form means that the story is easily summarized: three male friends join an expedition during which they hear tales of a country in which there are no men. Having ascertained its existence (dye residues in a waterfall provide proof) they resolve to return on their own, to seek it out. This they duly do. A reconnaissance flight reveals signs of cultivation, houses, and good straight roads. This last in particular convinces them that this country must have men; that it is, in short, civilized. Gilman has a good deal of fun with the concept of "civilization" by confronting her rash male explorers with the fact of an entirely female population. The men are captured, treated well, escape, recaptured, and gradually taught the language and customs of this strange land that they call Herland (we never discover what the inhabitants themselves call it). In due course they are reintroduced to three young women (the first people they encountered when they left their plane) and they pair up. Terry, the most macho, finds it increasingly difficult to live in a place in which men hold no special place, except that of potential fatherhood, and finally reaches such a pitch of sexual frustration that an attempted seduction of his partner, Alima, descends into an assault. The event is cataclysmic and Terry is expelled. He and Van, the narrator, return home, leaving Jeff, the third man, happily behind. Van's partner, Ellador, agrees to leave with them to see what a dual-sex world is really like.

This basically linear narrative is clearly told through one character, Van, a sociologist, who recounts the whole thing from memory, having lost his notes for some undisclosed reason. As we might expect, much time is spent explaining the customs of this new country to the detriment of the men's (and our) own. Each chapter tends to deal with a specific topic but, unusually for a serial publication, there are only two cliff-hanger moments and indeed remarkably little in the way of events of any kind. Van comments on this lack as Chapter 5 begins:

> It is no use for me to try to piece out this account with adventures. If the people who read it are not interested in these amazing women and their history, they will not be interested at all. (Gilman 1979: 49: unless otherwise stated, page references are to *Herland*)

With a literary sophistication with which Gilman is rarely credited (even when it is present) this comment parries any criticism on the part of Gilman's own readers. We are made aware of how boorish we will seem if we complain, as Terry does, that nothing ever happens in this country. Our attention is directed firmly towards how *Herland*'s arrangements work so much better than ours, particularly in the realms of child-care, education, and the general wellbeing of its people.

The monthly journal in which *Herland* appeared was *The Forerunner*, which Gilman herself produced from 1901 to 1916. The novel thus shares with all her other novels (each of which appeared first in *The Forerunner*) a wider context of articles, short stories, poems and editorials, all addressing issues Gilman considered worthy of attention. She penned every word herself, including the few advertisements that appeared in the earlier issues. These adverts were both personal endorsements by Gilman of practical products and tacit encouragements to cleaner, healthier, and more honest lives. Thus Calendula was advertised because it "took the pain from a raw wound" and various types of soap and hosiery recommended for their reliability, but no space was given to more frivolous items. The unembellished language of her advertisements was as out of step with the prevailing norm then as it would be now, but is entirely in tune with her serious commitment to improving women's place in society, which she regarded as indicative of the health of society as a whole. She presumed that her readers were conversant with, or willing to be instructed in, new and reformist ideas, such as Lester Ward's theory of women as the "race type" (norm) of the human species, with men being a later aberration required only as sex type," and social Darwinism which understood social development by analogy to Darwin's theory of species evolution). Both of these theories are evident in *Herland*, as Carol Farley Kessler's usefully tailored account of them shows (Kessler 1995: 32–8).

Idiosyncratic, even comic as *The Forerunner's* advertisements seem, they nonetheless carry some interest for us. Their emphasis on clean, simple living and straight talking is a direct reflection of the desire for openness in all dealings that underpins Gilman's vision of a better world. In *Herland* the men are as much flummoxed by this as the elusive commercial sponsors of *The Forerunner*, but Gilman's firm belief that the world would be better for being a good deal more straightforward is evident throughout. Gilman was earnest in her intent; her journal's title, *The Forerunner*, is indicative of the energy and conviction she not only expended herself but expected of others. The future was there to be molded and turn-of-the-century America was the place to do it. All that was needed was the vision to see what was possible and the steady commitment of purpose to such possibilities the reality.

In the hope of providing such vision and eliciting such purpose, Gilman spent her life writing and lecturing; seizing every opportunity to talk to clubs, societies, churches – wherever she was invited in America and Britain – and publishing articles in other papers as well as her own. Her internationally admired book *Women and Economics* (1898) made her reputation as a thinker and was followed in due course by other sociological discussions, each received well in her lifetime and attracting new consideration and respect today. The titles give a good idea of the topics that preoccupied her: *Concerning Children* (1900); *The Home, Its Work and Influence* (1903); *Human Work* (1904); *The Man-Made World: or Our Androcentric Culture* (1911); *His Religion and Hers: A Study of the Faith of Our Fathers and the Work of Our Mothers* (1923) and her autobiography, *The Living Of Charlotte Perkins Gilman* (1935) which was written when she knew she was dying of inoperable cancer and ends with the last line of her suicide note: "I have preferred chloroform to cancer." The possibility of informed choice was of paramount importance to Gilman and lends its weight to the twin themes of work and reform that recur throughout her work. Her arguments are rooted in the centrality of the home, while yet propounding that traditions can be both respected and changed. Old habits may die hard, but they can be overcome, and again we can see this demonstrated in Herland, where laws are constantly revised to ensure they are in keeping with current needs, with the result that most are less than twenty years old.

This introduction runs the risk of making Gilman appear serious to the point of zealous and enthusiastic to the point of hectoring, but such was not the case. Although *The Forerunner*'s avowed purpose was to "voice the strong assurance of a better living, here, now, in our own hands to make" (*Forerunner* 1.1 [1901]: 55) and despite Gilman's own assertions that her reformist agenda took precedence over any other consideration in her writing – she even referred to her poetry as "written to drive nails with" (see Golden 1999) – we do Gilman a disservice to read her fiction solely as a means to an end. Thus Ann J. Lane's 1979 Introduction to *Herland* begins by asserting, not Gilman's renown as a public speaker, economist, and social reformist, but that "*Herland*, is a very funny book" (Lane 1979: v). Not all readers would go as far as Lane in regarding Gilman as a skilled humorist, but there are many amusing moments in *Herland* which become increasingly funny on reflection, even if the laughter is wry with acknowledgement of Gilman's accuracy in social observation. An example is the way the three male explorers automatically envisage the women of an all-female land as nubile young maidens and so are rather ill-prepared for the more mature women who govern the country. As this shows, Gilman's humor is a mixture of the broad and the subtle and her jokes tend to be at the expense of types. Indeed much of the novel relies on her readers sharing some very basic and again fairly broad assumptions, several of which become rather disconcerting if pondered over for any length of time. However, in addition to this overt humor there is a pervasive playfulness, characteristic of all Gilman's fiction, which is a trait she shares with many other female authors of Utopian fiction, although there is little evidence of her being read by any later women SF writers.

Much of the playfulness in *Herland* comes from Gilman's use of the Utopian convention of explorers finding a hitherto undiscovered country in which life seems to be ideal in terms of the contentment and comfort of its citizens. Usually the readers are linked closely with the explorers, whose removal from both new and familiar societies allows for admiration and criticism of both. While this is clearly the case in *Herland*, Gilman adds a twist by encouraging us to smile wryly at her male stereotypes from the start. Terry is a man's man, successful with women, but not the kind of person even his best male friend "was quite pleased to have . . . with [his] sisters" (1979: 9). Significantly, Terry is the one with the money: it is due to his wealth that the expedition can be mounted quickly and easily and in supplying this detail Gilman reveals her pragmatic side, allowing her readers a collusive smile. Jeff, by contrast, is a romantic who "idealized women in the best Southern style" (1979: 9) and here we can detect a degree of distaste as Gilman recognizes that such adoration tends to infantilize women. Interestingly Van, the narrator, describes Jeff as "born to be a poet, a botanist, – or both" (1979: 2) but he is in fact a doctor, thus combining the supposed objectivity of a scientist with the more aesthetic appreciation (arguably equally supposed) of an artist. Van is a sociologist and as such carries the main ironic force of the book. The objectivity hinted at in Jeff's character is clearly undermined not only by the plot, but also by Van's comments on his ready adoption of all the Herlander's ways. The fact that this leads Van to call Jeff "something of a traitor" (1979: 51) merely allows Gilman a sardonic smile at both their expenses.

With these three to carry her readers through the story Gilman is well-placed to explore the notion of a world run by women with no reference to men, as a commentary on the world run predominantly by men with no real reference to women. We do not expect, and do not get, an even-handed discussion of the relative positions of men and women in turn-of-the-century America, but we do get a book which is both in earnest about the ways women's potential is thwarted by society and yet is able to be humorous about the alternatives it offers. Thus, for instance, when the three men attempt to escape from Herland by returning to the plane they so carefully landed in the outreaches of the country, their attempt is foiled by finding the machine (symbol of male achievement) literally sewn up in a cloth bag in an image that show-cases stereotypical female accomplishment (1979: 40). However, such elements remain only suggestions. We never learn how the Herlanders create and maintain their impressive roads or how they manufacture the cloth that bags the plane and from which their eminently sensible clothing is made. What we do learn is that they have evolved a style of garment that is eminently practical, amply supplied with pockets (1979: 73), aesthetically pleasing and readily adaptable to any task (1979: 26). Gilman's subversion of the usual science fiction obsession with technological advances is an example of her playfulness genre expectations. The decision to foil the men's early escape attempt by bagging the plane rather than incapacitating it with some intricate invention, not only serves the plot, but mocks two of the genre's assumptions:

technological advance and adventurous escapades. Yet, although it is tempting to say she simply omits the science from this particular work of fiction, that is not entirely true. Rather she replaces the expected technical information about manufacturing and mechanical developments with information about social processes explaining how the inhabitants are educated intellectually and socially, to become valued members of a single, harmonious race. One might regard this as social science replacing technical science. At every level, Gilman reminds us that we are in a thoroughly female environment, and demonstrates how that changes everything, including the expectations of the book we are reading.

Other elements of Utopian writing are evident, however. The new world entered in *Herland* exists, not in the future or on some distant planet, but a hidden spot of our own contemporary world. Gilman goes to some lengths to provide a credible, if remarkable, explanation of how such a country could have come about invoking physical geography to help her out. Herland, we learn, is the consequence of an earthquake, which led to a freak landslide that sealed the country off from the rest of the world some 2,000 years before the book begins. For Gilman it is important that her fictional world shares some common ground with our own, so the ancestors of the Herlanders lived in a familiar social structure: feudal, slave-owning, patriarchal, and in essence, Western. Having created this distant shared history, Gilman is then free to dispense with the men by burying most of them under the landslide and having the remaining few killed either in the ensuing slave revolt, or by the terrified but feisty women, who defend themselves against the threat of rape and ownership by their former slaves (women slaves here go unmentioned). It is colorful stuff, verging on the sensational, the telling of which takes little space, but the descriptive terms used are worth pausing over. The country is "the hinterland" (*Herland* 1979: 54) of a larger nation which had a coastal strip, "ships, commerce, an army, a king" (1979: 54) in short all the trappings of "the best civilization of the old world" (1979: 54) with which we are assured they must once have had contact. This immediately brings us to an aspect of Gilman's thought that causes us a good deal of trouble today: she is careful to include the fact that the Herlanders are "white." The term is enclosed in inverted commas, because she and Van use the word to denote bloodline, openly acknowledging that it is a poor description of the skin color of her heroines, who are "darker than our northern races because of their constant exposure to sun and air" (1979: 55). The point is unambiguous: "these people were of Aryan stock"; and although in 1915 that term had yet to acquire the particularly distasteful connotations it now carries, there can be no doubt about Gilman's belief in the superiority of the Western world, especially as found in the northern states of America. As a social Darwinist, she did not dismiss all other nations as being incapable of reaching the high standards found in America, simply unfortunately disadvantaged in not having reached them yet. In Gilman's eyes America had its exemplary position to maintain and was honor-bound to continue developing its own civilization so that others might know the right path to follow, and American women were to ensure that the way taken was the best possible.

Such disturbing elements are rightly beginning to receive due attention (see Ganobcsik-Williams 1999 and Weinbaum 2001) but they are not elements that disturbed Gilman herself. Her own, internal, conflicts tended to revolve around less controversial topics and these elements, too, deserve some consideration. Calling the mountain home of the Herlanders the "hinterland" of the previous country suggests that it was regarded as an inhospitable region to which the occupants were driven by the force of their enemies. It was not a place to live by choice. Soon after it is referred to as "this beautiful high garden land" (1979: 55). This describes the country as it is found by the three explorers, some two thousand years after the earthquake that cut off the "hinterland" from the rest of the world. It is clear that the change in termi-nology reflects the deliberate cultivating effort of the women over the course of those intervening centuries; it is less clear whether the choice of term is that of Van alone or whether Gilman is deliberately invoking the notion of a Utopia as an ideal land, reminiscent of the Golden Age or the Garden of Eden. If the latter, it is possible to see here part of the utopian literary tradition in operation, for we would expect such apparent perfection to be somehow deeply flawed and that alone could account for the patronizing tone which is otherwise rather troubling. However, if this is a deliberate ploy, it is extremely subtle, for at this point Herland is being presented in positive terms only. The women who are left after the final massacre of all men (which Gilman mentions with comic casualness) may be, in Van's term, "a bunch of hysterical girls and some older slave women" (1979: 55) but, in typical Gilman phrase, "they set to work" (1979: 55) and the tone here is clearly one of approbation. Van's increasing admiration for this race of women here meets with Gilman's firm belief in the virtues of physical exercise and mental determination.

However, there are more enduring difficulties with the image of the garden world. The term "garden land" is belittling when used of a whole country, limiting the place both in the sense of being a restricted area and in being highly controlled. Similarly, Terry calls the forest "petted" (1979: 13) implying small size and overindulgent care. Both are in fact true of Herland and it may be that the patronizing undercurrents are intended as a dry reflection of the men's several attitudes to this unknown territory. Certainly Van admires what he finds, but the basis for that admiration is perhaps being challenged because it rests on a sense of wonder that mere women could prove capable of such rational effort. Terry's term, used with "restrained enthusiasm," is more obvi-ously condescending, as cultivation is proof of the civilization he is convinced cannot exist without men. Gilman's precise attitude is elusive here: how far are we expected to scoff at these men's reactions, how far share them and how far are we allowed to crit-icize Herland itself? This ambiguity is similar to that surrounding Van's mockery of Jeff's courtly, Southern gentleman style of admiration. Jeff is utterly won over by Herland and its ways, yet we are all too aware of his uncomfortably idealistic view of women and are surely made uneasy by the way he seems to adapt so easily to this all-female world. Somehow it does not quite ring true, and it is hard to tell whether that is a deliberate decision on the part of Gilman or an unintentional effect. What is not in doubt is Gilman's ironic presentation of typical male reactions to her all-female world. Calling their land a "garden" fits perfectly with Van's initial description of the first young women they meet as "frolicsome children" and "big bright birds," "parrots" (1979: 15). Terry goes a step further: "Peaches!," "Peacherinos – apricot-nectarines!" (1979: 15). Where Van is an indulgent adult looking on, Terry is a consumer; neither take this new world seriously and referring to it as a garden betrays a deep-seated attitude that these women, with their highly developed society and successful management of very limited resources, are somehow only playing at government and civilization. Their country is a domesticated leisure ground, a garden to delight and marvel at, but not the real world. Here more insidious associations of women and nature are at work, which reduce the Herlanders to the level of attractive children at play, waiting to be introduced to the adult world by the three men who have stumbled in on them, one of whom is now telling us their story.

Despite such suggestions, Gilman's stance is by no means as radical as that adopted by some latter-day feminist science fiction writers. The Herlanders have a rational and pragmatic approach to the natural world, not the mystic connection with it we see operating in, for example, Sally Gearhart's *The Wanderground* (1985). Faced with the highly limited resources of their little county, they shifted their attention away from wasteful animal husbandry and grass crops to cultivating trees, which furnish food in the shape of nuts and berries as well as building materials in their wood. Even a species of tree that they wished to preserve for its beauty is subjected to nine centuries of experimentation until it is finally made to bear "a profuse crop of nutritious seeds" and so able to justify its continued existence (1979: 75). There are "no wild animals and very few tame ones" (1979: 49). All farm animals have been exterminated and the only domestic animals mentioned are cats, which have been bred to hunt rodents, but ignore birds. Gradually it transpires that the cats seen at large are all female; the toms are kept in secure, but large, areas to prevent there being too many kittens. Van and the highly macho Terry are inevitably taken aback at such treatment of the male but soon become victims of Gilman's sardonic writing as they explain the lot of dogs in America. So, while Gilman is very aware of the issues surrounding human land use, she cannot be recruited easily by the Green cause (but see Graham 1998 and Shishin 1998). In *Herland* she presents a community of women who think of themselves as an entire unit and work for the common good, but that good is indisputably and unashamedly human.

Here we encounter one of Gilman's abiding concerns: throughout her life Gilman believed that women and men should be free to exploit their individual talents to the full, whatever they were, believing that the greatest damage people suffered ensued from thwarted abilities, particularly through enforced domesticity. This is the theme of many of her short stories and it is central, too, to *Herland*. Gilman never satisfactorily resolved the conflicts surrounding motherhood, not even in her Utopian world, but she does go someway towards solving some of the more knotty problems. First of all she explicitly separates bearing children and bringing them up, with the care of infants and the education of children being entrusted to those who have a gift for it. Women whose talents lie elsewhere, but who nonetheless wish to be mothers (and

Gilman does not envisage a woman without maternal desires) are relieved of the destructive guilt Gilman associates with being forced to take on sole responsibility for an utterly dependent being. She does this without challenging the notion of maternal love; the mother–daughter bond is evidently strong, but the potential for frustration is removed. At the same time Gilman eliminates the possessiveness that she sees as underpinning many mother–child relations, and, more dangerously, the majority of male–female ones as well.

This issue is also reflected in naming conventions and domestic architecture. Herlanders have complete records of family trees, but no family name, feeling no need of them: "as to everyone knowing which child belong to which mother – why should she?" (1979: 75). From the start each person is regarded as an individual, an attitude reflected in their houses, which are private spaces made up of "two rooms and a bath" (1979: 125), the outer room being used to entertain friends while the inner one remains a secluded rest room. Significantly, there are no kitchens, thus removing another source of domestic misery. There are communal refectories, or food can be ordered in to houses when preferred. Such lack of possessiveness fosters genuine independence and confidence in each person while also inculcating an automatic assumption that everyone will both desire privacy and individual integrity and expect it in others. It is this that is so catastrophically breached in Terry's assault on Alima. Gilman makes it clear that the attempt is born of frustration not only of sexual desire, but also of the Terry's American social training according to which "she adapts herself to him" (1979: 122) and it is this assumption that she seeks to overthrow. However, despite the alternative offered in the love between Van and Ellador in which sexual relations are finally a part of a wider friendship, some difficulty remains. This must in part be due to Gilman's own personal belief in the power and rightness of female sexual desire, which was frequently a source of personal conflict (see Hill 1980 and 1995) and the result for the novel is that many readers are left rather uneasy about this particular aspect of the Herland Utopia.

Suppressed conflict is a trait of Gilman's writing: as Ann J. Lane puts it, Gilman "struggled to . . . envision a world that relied neither on class violence nor on uncontrolled individualism" (*Herland* x). Significantly, for Gilman the key to a better world lay explicitly in self-control. Herlanders prevent the birth of more children than they can sustain by voluntarily suppressing the "utter exaltation" that presages conception through increased physical and mental activity, including diverting the maternal urge into the care of existing babies (1979: 70). With typical honesty Gilman admits that the flaw in this system lies in those who do not readily comply with the self-control demanded by Herland and it is here that the struggle of imagination is most evident. She attempts a solution to crime by referring to "breeding out" the undesirable character traits where possible by appealing to any remnant of "social duty" in the "girl showing bad qualities" and persuading her to renounce motherhood altogether. Where that does not work, Gilman takes refuge in her belief in the power of education and diverts the discussion to that of child-rearing in general (1979: 82) thus narrowly avoiding the latent and more uncomfortable topic of eugenics.

Throughout the book, Gilman hints that some degree of responsibility for our predominantly "man-made world" lies with the women who marry and rear men in ways that perpetuate rather than challenge the status quo. Van repeatedly declares his conviction that Herland ways have much to recommend them, and readers who question Van's objectivity are led to ponder their own, as we become increasingly aware of the occasions when our estimation of Herland is closer to the men's than we would perhaps like. General unease with the level of control that pervades the country, from pregnancy to the exercise regime to the intensive cultivation of the land, is a case in point. Although this last relies on laudable practices of recycling by which "everything which came from the earth went back to it" (1979: 80), it also coerces every part of this world into the service of the women. Only the birds are free, presumably because they can fly out of the country at will, just as it is only through flight that the men can first enter and then leave Herland. However, the greatest indication of the contradictions surrounding this country lies in its name and the title of the book. The name "Herland" is conferred in jest by Terry, and at first is seems simply ironic that the name that sticks is the one coined by the character who disrupts its society most fully. However, the term is more appropriate than we initially believe. The pronoun indicates alienation (this is no more our country than it is the three men's) but it also indicates possession, the very characteristic that seems most abhorrent to the women. Terry comes up with the name when the three leave the plane and set out to take possession of their new-found land. By making it "hers" he creates the possibility that it could become "his" and so unknowingly seeks to pull the country back down the path of its own history to its distant past of domination and conquest. In the end this name becomes as inappropriate as the others that are so quickly dismissed: "Ladyland" (1979: 10) implies too leisured an existence while "Ma-land" (1979: 146), the final term hurled at its inhabitants by a defiant but defeated Terry, misses its mark by capturing what defines the country, but expressing it (quite deliberately) in exactly the wrong tone. Interestingly, the only name not invented by Terry is the rather unwieldy "Woman Land" which is the term used by Van right at the start of the book when recounting the guide's assertion that such a land exists.

Even this conflict serves a purpose: it reflects Gilman's central intention of highlighting the unequal weight of associations attending "man," "male" and "woman," "female." The whole concept of the book rests on this difference and the decision to envisage the effects of having them reversed. This founding premise is finally articulated by Van considers what Ellador will make of his world.

> When we say *men, man, manly, manhood,* and all the other masculine derivatives, we have in the background of our minds a huge vague crowded picture of the world and all its activities. . . .
>   And when we say *women,* we think *female* – the sex.
>   But to these women, . . . the word *woman* called up all that big background . . . and the word *man* meant to them only *male* – the sex. (1979: 137)

Gilman reiterates these themes in the sequel, *With Her in Ourland* (1916) which showcases the elasticity of the Herlander mind created by their particular education and the distress Ellador suffers due to the pervasive sense of ill-will and lack of brotherly, sisterly and above all maternal feeling in our world's societies. Significantly, the name "Herland" is set aside as Van refers to Ellador as his "wife from Wonderland," thus rewriting the science fiction notion of discovery of a credible alternative world with the less challenging one of a purely fictional and childish realm (the reference to Lewis Carroll is unmistakable). Soon, though, "Herland" reasserts itself as the name of Ellador's country, but by this time Gilman has reached the point of direct social comment (although not satire) housed in a rather plodding report form devoid of the vestiges of science fiction that remain at the end of *Herland*.

Herland itself does not plod because in it Gilman offers an alternative picture; one in which "women were 'the world'" (1979: 137) and she did so in the full knowledge that such a notion would be as "astounding" to the actual women reading her books as it was to the fictional men within it. In 1915, she still retained hopes that women might prove willing to change the world, or at least America, as she believed they could. By the time she died she was disillusioned, remarking "I did expect better things of women than they have shown" (Gilman 1990: 371). Although far more radical visions have been offered by women science fiction writers since, *Herland* still elicits nods of recognition and wry smiles from its readers and as such continues to serve as a playful, yet serious, suggestion we might do things better.

REFERENCES AND FURTHER READING

Ceplair, Larry (ed.) (1991) *Charlotte Perkins Gilman: A Non-Fiction Reader*. New York: Columbia University Press.

Davies, Cynthia J. (2003) "His and Herland: Charlotte Perkins Gilman 'Re-presents' Lester F. Ward," in *Evolution and Eugenics in American Literature and Culture, 1880–1940*, (eds) Lois A. Cuddy and Claire M. Roche. London: Associated University Presses, 73–88.

Ganobcsik-Williams, Lisa (1999) "The Intellectualism of Charlotte Perkins Gilman: Evolutionary Perspective on Race, Ethnicity, and Class" in Gough and Rudd, 1998, 16–44.

Gearhart, Sally M. (1985) *The Wanderground: Stories of the Hill Women*. London: Women's Press.

Gilman, Charlotte P. (1979) *Herland*. London: Women's Press.

——*The Forerunner: A Monthly Magazine* vol 1. McLean, Virginia: IndyPublish.com.

——(1990) *The Living Of Charlotte Perkins Gilman:*

An Autobiography. Madison: University of Wisconsin Press.

——(1997) *With Her in Ourland: Sequel to "Herland."* (eds) Mary Jo Deegan and Michael R. Hill. Westport and London: Greenwood Press.

——(2001) *The Man-Made World*. With an introduction by Mary A. Hill. Amherst, NY: Humanity Books.

Golden, Catherine (1999) "'Written to Drive Nails With': Recalling the Early Poetry of Charlotte Perkins Gilman" in Gough and Rudd 1998, 243–66.

Golden, Catherine and Zangrando, Joanna (eds) (2000) *The Mixed Legacy of Charlotte Perkins Gilman*. Cranbury, London and Mississauga, Ontario: Associated University Presses.

Gough, Val and Rudd Jill (eds) (1998) *A Very Different Story: Studies on the Fiction of Charlotte Perkins Gilman*. Liverpool: Liverpool University Press.

Graham, Amanda (1998) *"Herland*: Definitive Ecofeminist Fiction?" in Gough and Rudd, (1998), 115–28.

Hill, Mary (1980) *Charlotte Perkins Gilman: The Making of a Radical Feminist 1860–1896.* Philadelphia: Temple University Press.

——(1995) *A Journey From Within: The Love Letters of Charlotte Perkins Gilman 1897–1900.* Lewisburg, PA: Bucknell University Press.

Karpinski, Joanne (ed.) (1992) *Critical Essays on Charlotte Perkins Gilman.* New York: G.K. Hall.

Kessler, Carol Farley (1995) *Charlotte Perkins Gilman: Her Progress towards Utopia.* New York: Syracuse University Press.

Lane, Ann J. (1979) *Charlotte Perkins Gilman: Herland.* London: Women's Press.

Rudd, Jill and Gough, Val (eds) (1999) *Charlotte Perkins Gilman: Optimist Reformer.* Iowa City: University of Iowa Press.

Scharnhorst, Gary (1985) *Charlotte Perkins Gilman: A Bibliography.* Metuchen, NJ. Scarecrow Press.

Shishin, Alex (1998) "Gender and Industry in *Herland*: Trees as a Means of Production and Metaphor" in Gough and Rudd 1998, 100–14.

Weinbaum, Alice E. (2001): "Writing Feminist Genealogy: Charlotte Perkins Gilman, Racial Nationalism, and the Reproduction of Maternalist Feminism." In *Feminist Studies* 27:2, 271–302.

34

Aldous Huxley: *Brave New World*

David Seed

Brave New World (1932) is the single most famous science fiction novel to describe genetic engineering and since the 1980s has become a major point of reference in discussions of cloning and related techniques. As Robert S. Baker (1990) and Krishan Kumar (1987) have shown in their excellent commentaries on the novel, *Brave New World* engaged with a whole range of social and scientific issues from the 1920s. Its immediate trigger was the publication in 1924 of J.B.S. Haldane's pamphlet *Daedalus or, Science and the Future* which built on the prophetic optimism found in Wells to evoke a near future where biology has become applied to eugenics so successfully that disease has been eradicated. What Haldane terms "ectogenesis" (the term was coined in 1883 in relation to bacteria and appears in *Brave New World*, signifying the growth of a fetus in an artificial womb) has become universal by the 1950s and 1960s, but exactly how that universality is achieved Haldane does not say. This technique also has its drawbacks, which Haldane hints at by stating: "The effect on human psychology and social life of the separation of sexual love and reproduction . . . is by no means wholly satisfactory" (Haldane 1924: 65). Huxley probably had *Daedalus* in mind when he wrote in 1927 that according to Haldane it would soon become possible to "breed babies in bottles" (Huxley 2000–2 II: 283). This image is woven into *Brave New World* as an early and inadequate expression of the technology the regime has since perfected. Huxley's brother, the biologist Julian, published a damning fictional comment on Haldane's concept in 1927. "The Tissue-Culture King" (which appeared in *Amazing Stories*) describes how an English explorer meets a former researcher at the Middlesex Hospital in the African interior who has developed tissue culture so effectively that he has produced a collection of misshapen "circus freaks." The title and location of this story make clear the colonialist ambitions of its scientist. This latter-day Moreau (the echo of Wells is clear) claims to have simply extended the methods of earlier experimenters. He tells the narrator: "I have merely applied the mass-production methods of Mr. Ford to their results" (Conklin 1962: 161); but the story carries an explicit moral which contradicts this self-denigrating description, namely, to what end is his knowledge directed?

By his own account Aldous Huxley originally planned *Brave New World* to be a "novel about the future – on the horror of the Wellsian Utopia and a revolt against it" (Smith 1969: 348). Initially conceived as a rejoinder to Wells' *Men Like Gods* (1923), Huxley's novel explores satirically many of the issues which emerge in that earlier work: the eugenic regulation of population growth, the applications of "mechanical power" (Wells' phrase), the nature of the scientific state, and the desire to control Nature. Although Huxley moved beyond his initial purpose, there are echoes of *Men Like Gods* in the description of the Reservation; in Wells the visitors to Utopia have to be quarantined to avoid spreading disease. And there may be an echo in Huxley's title of Wells' 1908 speculations on the possibility of a rational socialist state, *New Worlds for Old*. In *Men Like Gods* a group of characters pass from 1920s England through a time warp into a future world which seems to have achieved order and much of the narrative consists of dialogues between the visitors and their Utopian counterparts. *Brave New World*, by contrast, shows a culmination of historical change and Huxley's reduction of dialogue reflects his greater pessimism about how far such change could be understood, let alone controlled.

In 1931, the year that he was writing *Brave New World*, Huxley published an essay that questioned the whole concept of Utopia. Drawing an analogy with drinking wine, in "Boundaries of Utopia" he argues that the mathematical model of increase simply did not work when applied to happiness and democratization. If Utopia enables more and more people to travel, the places visited will gradually come to resemble each other and the point of travel will collapse. Thus, "increase of material prosperity, increase of leisure, increase of liberty, increase of educational facilities are perfectly useless to individuals, in whom every such increase beyond a quickly reached maximum gives diminishing returns of happiness, virtue, and intellectual efficiency" (Huxley 2000–2 III: 128). Huxley never actually says so in the essay, but he probably had Wells in mind when making this criticism of quantification in calculations about the future.

The pivotal experience that shaped *Brave New World* was Huxley's visit to the USA in 1926. In an essay published the following year, "The Outlook for American Culture," he laid the ground for his novel by asserting starkly that "the future of America is the future of the world. Material circumstances are driving all nations along the path in which America is going." Therefore it followed that "speculating on the American future, we are speculating on the future of civilized man" (Huxley 2000–2 III: 185). We shall see some of the consequences of this perception for *Brave New World* in a moment but first we should note that America also had a special importance for H.G. Wells who described it as the leader of material progress in *America and the Future* (1906) and the one country which might lead the West out of the Depression in *The New America, The New World* (1935). The latter title should remind us that *Brave New World* has a specific relevance to the link between the USA and the future, especially in the period following the First World War. Indeed, Peter

Firchow has helpfully demonstrated how Huxley's novel emerged from an ongoing debate on both sides of the Atlantic over the course which was being taken by American culture and reflected Huxley's perception that the USA was the "Harbinger of the final and most profound revolution" (Firchow 1984: 111–2). Despite any misgivings Huxley might have had about this tendency, he took up permanent residence in the USA in 1937 and remained there until his death in 1963.

In *Jesting Pilate* (1926), Huxley's record of travels around the world, we can clearly see the signs of social change which he was to expand in *Brave New World.* He noted the application of advertising techniques to religion, the flappers" ("so curiously uniform") promise of "pneumatic bliss," the accelerated tempo of society, and many other features which suggested to Huxley a "revaluation of values, a radical alteration (for the worse) of established standards" (Huxley 1930: 273). Furthermore, in the American entertainment industry Huxley saw evidence of applied Freudianism where a new categorical imperative ("amuse yourself") was emerging. Anticipating the motto of the World State in his novel, he commented that the new slogan for America should be "Vitality, Prosperity, Modernity" (Huxley 1930: 280).

Brave New World opens with the image of a high-rise building which in the 1930s would have been an unmistakable sign of American culture. Although most of the novel is set in London and the suburbs – yet another glance at Wells' locations – it is a transformed England where the new features that Huxley had found in Los Angeles – cabarets, sky-signs, and so on – are superimposed on a geographical location that has only a notional difference from anywhere else. The hotel in Santa Fe where Bernard Marx and Lenina stay on their way to the Reservation sets a keynote for the landscape of the whole novel. Its electronic features offer comforts that distract the customer from asking where s/he is and in fact Huxley describes a world where American commercial and technological developments have reached their culmination. This marks another difference between Wells and Huxley. For Wells the idea of a World State represented the triumph of political reason, whereas for Huxley it meant the final phase in an economically determined spread around the globe of socioeconomic conditions originating in America. Huxley's names help to make this point. Taken variously from the political right and left, contemporary science and industry, these names encode the suppressed history of Huxley's regime and suggest that all these disparate threads have converged in a process of Americanization. As many critics have noted, Mustafa Mond is named after the then director of ICI, but with an obvious pun on "monde" (i.e., "world"). He speaks for the world, but in the name of Ford.

A number of factors had brought Huxley to this perception of change, not least the impact of Henry Ford's *My Life and Work*, which he had read the previous year. Ford rejects any notion of class or social hierarchy in the name of efficiency. He asserts starkly that "the conception of democracy which names a leveling-down of ability makes for waste" (Ford 1924: 11) and in its place applies the method of industrial mass-production as a model of social organization. Since performance is all in this Utopia, he reintroduces hierarchy through classifications of work as A, B, and C.

Huxley had an ambivalent attitude towards what had become known as Fordism. In the early 1930s he made a number of journeys into "Alien Englands" where he criticized the evident lack of social planning. One startling exception was the massive ICI factory at Billingham which he described as "one of those ordered universes that exist as anomalous oases of pure logic in the midst of the larger world of planless incoherence" (Huxley 2000–2 III: 276). Huxley views the factory partly as an aesthetic construct, partly as an idealized model for the working of society. He was fascinated by Ford's apparent willingness to discard social tradition in order to construct a whole new system linking raw materials, production, and sales. And from Fordism Huxley took his key figure of the machine as a metaphor of unstoppable social process and his new slogan for America: "Business is religion" (Huxley 2000–2 III: 191).

The Fordist style of society in *Brave New World* can be seen in the prevalence of slogans which were written into the manuscript at a late stage. These slogans or catch-phrases have a specific American resonance which dates back to the eighteenth century. Benjamin Franklin promoted his cherished values of thrift and industry through proverbs like "time is money" (one particularly valued by Ford) which combined piety with practical advancement. In Huxley's novel the figure of Ford has displaced the deity ("cleanliness is next to fordliness") and entertainment has replaced industry ("never put off till tomorrow the fun you can have today"). The novel's satire partly invites the reader to recognize how the form of proverbs has been retained, with key terms altered so as to suggest a culture of hedonism and consumerism where some catch-phrases resemble advertisements for the drug soma: "a gramme in time save nine." Such phrases offer their users a technique of warding off the unpleasant. As Krishan Kumar has stated, "there are slogans to handle all situations" (Kumar 1987: 257). More importantly, the currency of these expressions functions as a reassuring ritual, bonding the members of society to each other. Here Huxley anticipates the truncated dialogues that occur in postwar American dystopias like Kurt Vonnegut's *Player Piano* (1952) and Ray Bradbury's *Fahrenheit 451* (1953), where speakers feed cues to each other for expected responses. In all these cases the speech-style of characters reflects an ethos of collectivism and the recurrence of the terms "synthetic" and "surrogate" in naming the goods of this society evokes an endless series of simulations of lost originals now only indicated through their verbal traces.

The production line gives us our determining point of access to the world of Huxley's novel. He avoids the Utopian convention of the visitor from another world by starting with an educational visit where the merits of the Hatchery are expounded to the eager students. As Robert Baker points out, "the tour of the Hatchery itself replicates the birth process" (Baker 1990: 80), but replicates it in such a way that Huxley's account straddles apparently distinct categories. The very term "hatchery" is only applied to nonhuman species; the nurses' style and function resembles a hospital rather than a factory, but the Director explains the process in terms of the prime Fordian values of speed, efficiency, and economy. And since the nurses and other workers were themselves created through this process, we have the bizarre case of a product supervising a production line. This oscillation between the human and the nonhuman is helped by the fact that Huxley retains names. He does not reduce his characters to encoded functions within a system as Zamyatin does in *We*.

Although the reader is positioned close to the students, Huxley draws our attention to aspects of the place that they would miss. By stressing the symbolic interrelation between cold, whiteness, and the north, he suggests that the process of the Hatchery is in fact directed towards a kind of death: "Wintriness responded to wintriness. The overalls of the workers were white, their hands gloved with a pale corpse-coloured rubber" (Huxley 1994a: 1). Response implies dialogue, another standard feature of Utopian exposition, but there is virtually no exchange between the Director and the students. The whole purpose of the tour is to induce admiration for an achieved system, whereas descriptions like the one just quoted invite a skeptical reading of the scene through ironic nuance.

Once Huxley has shown the genetic technology of designer humans, in the following two chapters he depicts social enforcement through conditioning and the internalization of social norms. The application of behaviorism and the technique of hypnopedia are both designed to produce a minimal subjectivity. Huxley could not have had a character narrate his novel, as happens in Zamyatin's *We*, since the very existence of such a subjective consciousness would contradict the collectivist ethic of *Brave New World* summed up in the slogan "everyone belongs to everyone else." Several critics have commented on the line "the air was drowsy with the murmur of bees and helicopters" (Huxley 1994a: 26), as if it opposes Nature to technology, but there is a less obvious symbolism in this and other references to bees. Huxley was familiar with Maurice Maeterlinck's *Life of the Bee* (1901), which compares this creature with humans and which provides an early statement of the hive mind, which is virtually what exists in Huxley's novel. This is why the description of Lenina unzipping her overall and entering the corporate bathroom encapsulates a social ethic. Theodor Adorno has explained the mentality of Lenina and her companions as a loss of mind: "Their inability to perceive or think anything unlike themselves . . . the law of pure subjective functionalism – all result in pure desubjectivisation" (Adorno 1986: 102).

The society of *Brave New World* is a place of apparent plenty where labor-saving devices cater to every need. American technological ingenuity had been celebrated in novels like Hugo Gernsback's *Ralph 124C 41+* (1925) which describes a "hypnobio-scope," a device that imprints texts on the brain while the subject sleeps. Gernsback's equivalent to Huxley's hypnopedia is explicitly designed to save the subject from "wasting" half his/her life in sleep which is a common but unquestioned aim of all the innovations described in America of the year 2660. Huxley too describes a culture devoted to efficiency, but dramatizes how leisure has become a problem. If we backtrack to his first impressions of Los Angeles, that city took on a symbolic importance for Huxley who described it as the "great Joy City of the West" (Huxley 1930: 267). This was a place uniquely devoted to a single purpose: having a Good Time. He saw labor-saving technology as inducing a passivity – in that sense it was "creation-saving" – and also a desire in the consumer for immediate gratification. In Huxley's novel the drug soma is thus the ideal example of a general process: it works immediately and is readily available. Its name ("body" in Classical Greek) suggests a further anti-Wellsian irony in Huxley's novel. In his speculations about physical evolution Wells predicted that the human brain would grow and the body gradually atrophy, but in *Brave New World* the direct opposite has occurred. For the vast mass of the population the mind has declined and the body become even more important. Indeed, the culture of immediate gratification has dissociated pleasure from individual activity and in that respect Adorno is surely right to assert that Huxley cannot tolerate the "neutralization of a culture cut off from the material process of production" (Adorno 1986: 108). Entertainment consists of endless physical distractions and endless consumption. When Edith Wharton registered her enthusiasm for *Brave New World* Huxley returned the compliment by praising her 1927 indictment of upper-class leisure activities in her novel *Twilight Sleep* (Murray 2002: 257). The Westminster Abbey Cabaret which Lenina and Henry Foster visit one night is typical. The huge electronic signs blank out the external darkness. Indeed, the whole place is a carefully controlled environment appealing to sight (the lights), smell (artificial scents), and sound from performing "sexophonists." The "feely" cinema of course adds one more sense to the list: that of touch. The cabaret is an environment where all customers move together in a common dance and the pleasure of the visitors is expressed in terms of "togetherness": "How kind, how good-looking, how delightfully amusing everyone was!" (Huxley 1994a: 68). It is not clear who is thinking this and it does not matter because the whole point of the situation is to induce pleasure from collective participation.

Chapter III of *Brave New World* revolves around the theme of sameness and difference, first bringing home to the reader a possible consequence of Huxley's gloomy perception that liberty in 1920s America had come to mean the enforcing of the will of the majority in order to produce a "general uniformity of habits, customs, and beliefs" (Huxley 2000–2 III.208). Zamyatin had already evoked such an ethos in *We* partly through the application of Taylorist time-and-motion methods, arriving at a social situation where the term "freedom" had taken on an entirely negative meaning. Uniforms in dystopias are one of the most obvious signs of uniformity, identity in the sense of sameness. At this point in the novel Huxley uses a more complex strategy of counterpoint like cinematic montage where he runs three voices together in order to dramatize the internal contradictions within that society. In the following passage, where characters are not named as if they are interchangeable, the first speaker is Mustapha Mond the Controller describing the history of the regime, the second Lenina crowing with pride over her new Malthusian belt, and the third the disgruntled Bernard Marx:

> "All crosses had their tops cut and became T's. There was also a thing called God."
> It's real morocco-surrogate.
> "We have the World State now. And Ford's Day celebrations, and Community Sings, and Solidarity Services."
> "Ford, how I hate them!" Bernard Marx was thinking.
> "There was a thing called heaven; but all the same they used to drink enormous quantities of alcohol." (Huxley 1994a: 47)

The first statement blurs the distinction between sign and referent, between the spiritual and the material. The second is straight oxymoron in referring to a real simulation, but it further implies that religion has not been abolished, only secularized. The statement of solidarity is directly contradicted by Bernard's expression of hatred. Even if we take him as a faulty product rather than a dissident, such a flaw should not exist. The juxtaposition of religion with alcohol supposedly shows the weakness of the old world, but then ignores the function of the drug soma. Apart from inverting Marx so that the opiate becomes the religion of the people, the very existence of this drug undermines the contrast between then and now, and further implies social needs that are not otherwise being addressed.

Huxley ridicules the secular rituals of the state as a degraded imitation of religion. The sign of the letter T visually captures this effect as an incomplete version of the cross. Like the religion of solidarity in Edward Bellamy's *Looking Backward* (1888) and the collectivization rituals in Zamyatin's *We*, Huxley's Solidarity Services are obligatory performances which are neglected at the individual's peril. They parodically combine aspects of American evangelism, infantile regression to games with nursery rhymes, and a jazz-fed sexual orgy. The fact that in the novel the description of one such ritual follows an account of the equally circular dancing at the Westminster Abbey Cabaret gives us a clear hint that Huxley sees one as a continuation of the other, a politically orchestrated form of mass entertainment.

Although Huxley's world state is a millenarian version of the USA, in other words an embodiment of American newness, America also contains the old world in the Reservation. In *We* old and new worlds are separated by a wall; in Huxley by an electric fence given the following symbolism: "the fence marched on and on, irresistibly the straight line, the geometrical symbol of triumphant human purpose" (Huxley 1994a: 94). "Marched" suggests an army, or at least progression, but the ground along the fence is littered with the corpses of animals. This is where its true significance is made clear. The fence is a graphic image of the world state's hostility to Nature, of its imposition of cultural order on Nature's teeming diversity. But, as many critics have observed, Huxley does not use the Reservation like the green world of *We* as a place of freedom. The description of the pueblos and Native Americans is focalized through visitors from the civilized world who only see those things excluded from their own culture: disease, deformity, and squalor. Nor does Huxley leave any space for the "darkness" of response D.H. Lawrence found, say, in the Hopi snake dance described in *Mornings in Mexico* (1927). The category of the "savage" gives place to John Savage, a cultural hybrid, and his mother Linda, another hybrid by displacement from her original culture.

The "shocking" description of Linda's appearance and the Reservation episode generally draw our attention to two aspects of Huxley's novel which are conservative and rarely commented on: gender and race. Consider the culmination of the Solidarity Service. Acting out a pastiche of the mass, groups of twelve celebrants dance symbolically in a circle, working themselves up to a sexual frenzy, which peaks with their expectation that the "Greater Being" is coming. Huxley makes a final comment on the scene: "it was as though some enormous Negro dove were hovering benevolently over the now prone or supine dancers" (Huxley 1994a: 76). On the one hand, he clearly wants to demonstrate how secular rituals replace religion in this new world, and probably also to satirize how these rituals reinforce the totalitarian regimes of the 1930s by infantilizing the participants; at the same time, however, the casual racism of the interwar period shows itself in Huxley's implicit identification between the primitive, jazz, and African-Americans. The cultural category of the savage is not confined to the reservation but also emerges in the London context where the design of human operatives should have made it an irrelevance. Thus some of the menial workers are Africans, others dwarfs, others simply Deltas. Is Huxley suggesting that the new world covertly prolongs old-style colonialism and racism such as he observed in the stratification of American society? The reader cannot be sure.

Secondly, there is the question of gender. Other dystopias of the period like Charlotte Haldane's *Man's World* (1926) and Katherine Burdekin's *Swastika Night* (1937) investigate the ways in which gender informs totalitarian regimes. In the first of these, written by the scientist's wife and almost certainly known to Huxley, a world state has emerged from postwar chaos where the scientist replaces the politician. Unlike Huxley, Haldane describes a society coming into being. Experiments in ectogenesis are being carried out but women are still needed as propagators to continue the race primarily through male offspring. Thus "mother settlements" have been established where women perform this function but they also debate it among themselves. In contrast, *Brave New World* reserves the most complex subjectivity for its male characters. Again despite its ostensible newness, the novel's depiction of women confines itself to the predictable roles of nurse, "pneumatic" magnets to the male gaze, or consumers. June Deery has helpfully identified aspects of the novel that pull against the notional liberation of women from drudgery. Upper-caste men seem to date lower-caste women; there must be upper-caste women but they are scarcely referred to, let alone described; and the senior technicians are always male (Deery 1996: 133–6). In all these examples there is a clear but unexplained disparity between the notional equality of Huxley's new society and the practices he actually describes.

The ideology of Huxley's world state is maintained by a suppression of its own history. As in many dystopias, the state has a vested interest in preserving its own existence, which it does by promoting the general conviction that the current state of affairs is "natural" and has always been so. Mustafa Mond, the Controller, is the regime's ideologue and in the early chapters Huxley gives us glimpses of coercion and conflict which predate the millenarian age of Ford. Hints of wars, passing references to biological weapons, and the treatment of dissent all set up the supposed inevitability of conditioning superseding the techniques of force. And it is exactly as a question of technique that Huxley presents this issue, not as a question of morals or belief. It is ironic that Orwell accused Huxley of leaving no room for opposition in his dystopias because Huxley's depiction of superstate, structured on an economic caste system and run by a supervisory elite actually anticipates James Burnham's description of a managerial revolution in politics which directly influenced *Nineteen Eighty-Four*. The regime signals its own Utopian identity by symbolically closing the museums and forbidding all books except those produced by the state. This closure of the archive attempts to suspend the consciousness of the people in an extended present which means that any reference to the past within this context becomes political. Specifically, it means that, as in Ray Bradbury's *Fahrenheit 451*, the very existence of a satirical novel like *Brave New World* would be impossible within the regime it describes. Thus the many allusions in the text to earlier literature and especially the discovery of an edition of Shakespeare by John Savage, implicitly reopens the archive or collective cultural memory the regime has attempted to suppress. When Mond opens his safe and produces examples of banned books, his action is not as dangerous as it might seem, however, since the vast mass of the population has simply lost interest in earlier literature and, by implication, in thought itself.

When Orwell compared *Brave New World* with Zamyatin's *We* in his 1946 essay "Freedom and Happiness," he declared that "both works deal with the rebellion of the primitive human spirit against a rationalized, mechanized, painless world" (Davison 1998: 14). But are there any rebels in Huxley's novel? The two protagonists are social misfits. Bernard Marx has been misconditioned so that he is saddled with a self-image he hates. The roots of his dissatisfaction are physical (he is just that bit too short, just too hairy) and arise from his perceived failure to measure up to the physical norms of the state which ultimately he does not question at all. The second protagonist is John Savage, as his name suggests, a hybrid figure neither defined by the Reservation nor at home in the "civilized" world. John's story is a Freudian one of ultimately self-destructive masochism. Huxley had attacked Freud for promoting theories that undermined the family and for promoting a desire for self-gratification which he parodies in the entertainments of his novel. Both Bernard and John make possible comic scenes revolving round dialogues of incomprehension, but neither is a match for Mond. In the discussion between Mond and John, Huxley skilfully conveys the impression that the latter's desire for freedom is perverse and irrational. His rousing political speech to a crowd of Morlock-like Deltas sparks off a riot when their soma distribution is delayed and the crowning irony of John's fate lies in his assimilation (through the film *The Savage of Surrey*) into the media industry he has been attacking.

Huxley's other science fiction novel *Ape and Essence* (1949) presents an ironic depiction of the new barbarism ushered in by a nuclear and biological holocaust, the culmination at once of unbridled nationalism and misdirected science. Set in a devastated Los Angeles, the action inverts American history. The USA has to be rediscovered by an expedition from New Zealand and is revealed to be a paranoid culture where any divergence from physical norms is punishable by death. Like John Wyndham's *The Chrysalids, Ape and Essence* uses the fear of mutation in a nuclear aftermath as a metaphor of social intolerance. In Huxley's earlier novel unorthodox behavior was treated as an illness; now the fear of difference reflects a puritanical attempt to escape from the body, from the ape within – hence Huxley's choice of title. And once again any Wellsian optimism in progress is totally undermined by Huxley's description of a collective reversion to tribal cultism.

Huxley's postwar essays and lectures, particularly those collected in *Brave New World Revisited* (1958), make an extended retrospective commentary on his novel and essentially flesh out a perception Huxley expressed to Orwell in 1949: "I believe that the world's rulers will discover that infant conditioning and narco-hypnosis are more efficient, as instruments of government, than clubs and prisons" (Smith 1969: 605). In the early 1950s Huxley read up on studies of subliminal advertising techniques, brainwashing, and advances in political propaganda. He also followed with great interest psychological experiments into the physiology of perception. Speaking at a conference on pharmacology and the study of the mind at the University of California in 1959, Huxley somewhat apocalyptically spoke of a "Final Revolution" in the application of technology to all aspects of human affairs. This revolution he attributed to a general and all-engrossing "Will to Order" which reduces human multiplicity to a manageable uniformity where the individual had becomes a virtual robot. Surveying developments in advertising, the cinema, and other media, Huxley had earlier declared: "Today the art of mind-control is in process of becoming a science" (Huxley 2000–2 VI: 245). Again and again throughout the 1950s Huxley speculates on the imminence of a population that will either love its servitude or at least be totally unaware of it. And, given the American origins of Huxley's extrapolation in *Brave New World*, it is important to note that he felt he was actually witnessing in the USA the emergence of a social ethic whereby, as in his novel, the ultimate crime was unorthodoxy of behavior.

The evocation of a technologically streamlined society in *Brave New World* has exerted a strong influence on postwar science fiction writers such as Ray Bradbury and Kurt Vonnegut. The genetic modification of humans on analogies with other species or to satisfy some specific function like space travel has featured prominently in the novels of James Blish, Philip K. Dick, and others. Similarly, Huxley's Solidarity Services are echoed in the Church of State meetings in David Karp's *One* (1953). James E. Gunn's *The Joy Makers* (1961) pursues Huxley's theme of consumer gratification in the activities of a company, which markets happiness. Hedonics, Inc. makes happiness into an expansive business, offering unlimited service contracts in return for the customer's entire assets. Just as the company takes over individuals, so its ambition is to dominate – to buy up – the USA, which it eventually does. William F. Nolan and George Clayton Johnson's novel *Logan's Run* (1967), with its sequels *Logan's World* (1977), and *Logan's Search* (1980), draw on Huxley to evoke a postapocalyptic America where the young have taken over society. A central computer prescribes the needs for every citizen (including recreational drugs and sex sessions) within a technological environment dedicated to pleasurable consumption. *Logan's Run* was adapted for the cinema in 1976 and for a television series later in that same decade. Brian Stableford has recorded his continuing fascination with Huxley's novel and his essay on "Genetic Engineering" (Stableford 1993) remains a valuable survey of how Huxley's main theme has been treated in Science Fiction. Stableford's survey of contemporary scientific developments, *Future Man* (1984), provides an excellent companion to this fiction.

Haldane continued his speculations about the biological future of humanity after the Second World War and in the course of his discussion took Huxley and John Wyndham to task for doing a "considerable disservice to clear thinking" (Haldane 1963: 340) about the mutants, which might result from a nuclear war. Writing in 1963, he predicted a rebirth of eugenics and the growth of cloning, declaring: "I expect that most clones would be made from people aged at least fifty . . . from people who were held to have excelled in a socially acceptable accomplishment" (Haldane 1963: 353). This possibility of human cloning was further addressed by J.B. Watson, who led Haldane's daughter Naomi Mitchison to write her novel *Solution Three* (1975), published in a decade that saw a marked increase in the number of novels to deal with human cloning. This work describes a new world where the male and female genders persist in image but where the species renews itself through asexual reproduction. The novel's title refers to a Utopian scheme of removing human aggression through a centrally controlled scheme of cloning. The new regime, however, is neither universal nor one without its opponents and Mitchison uses the novel as a forum for characters to debate the nature of maternal love, the ethics of cloning, and encounters between different cultures.

Huxley's title has been reused again and again in works dealing with biotechnology and genetic engineering. Grant Fjermedal's *The Tomorrow Makers: A Brave New World of Living-Brain Machines* (1986) and Roger Gosden's *Designing Babies: The Brave New World of Reproductive Technology* (1999) are only two from many works that routinely express misgivings over the apparent realization of science fiction by technology. The science journalist David Rorvik has commented on these developments in his book *Brave New Baby: Promise and Peril of the Biological Revolution* (1971) and has also described (*In His Image*, 1978) the case of a childless millionaire who, having read Huxley's novel, had a baby cloned from his body cells.

REFERENCES AND FURTHER READING

Adorno, Theodor W. (1986) *Prisms.* Translated by Samuel and Shierry Weber. Cambridge, MA: MIT Press.

Armytage, W.H.G. (1968) *Yesterday's Tomorrows: A Historical Survey of Future Societies.* London: Routledge and Kegan Paul.

Baker, Robert S. (1982) *The Dark Historic Page: Social Satire and Historicism in the Novels of Aldous Huxley, 1921–1939.* Madison, WI: University of Wisconsin Press.

——(1990) *"Brave New World": History, Science, and Dystopia.* Boston, MA: Twayne.

Bedford, Sybille (1973–4) *Aldous Huxley: A Biography.* London: Chatto and Windus.

Berman, W. and J. Berman (eds) (1988) *"Brave New World": International Understanding Through Books.* Perth, WA: Curtin University of Technology.

Bloom, Harold (1996) *Aldous Huxley's "Brave New World,"* New York: Chelsea House.

Bloom, Harold, and Aaron Tillman (eds) (2002) *"Brave New World": Modern Critical Interpretations.* New York: Chelsea House.

Brander, Laurence (1969) *Aldous Huxley: A Critical Study.* London: Hart-Davis.

Brooke, Jocelyn (1968) *Aldous Huxley.* London: Longman, Green.

Brown, E.J. (1976) *"Brave New World," "Nineteen Eighty-Four"* and *"We": An Essay on Anti-Utopia.* Ann Arbor, MI: Ardis.

Burdekin, Katherine (1985) *Swastika Night* (1937). Old Westbury, NY: Feminist Press.

Calder, Jenni (1976) *Huxley and Orwell: "Brave New World" and "Nineteen Eighty-Four."* London: Edward Arnold.

Conklin, Groff (ed.) (1962) *Great Science Fiction by Scientists*. New York: Collier Books.

Davison, Peter (ed.) (1998) *Complete Works of George Orwell. Volume 18: Smothered Under Journalism, 1946*. London: Secker and Warburg.

Deery, June (1996) *Aldous Huxley and the Mysticism of Science*. New York: St. Martin's Press.

De Kosta, Katie (ed.) (1999) *Readings on "Brave New World."* San Diego, CA: Greenhaven Press.

Dunnaway, David K. (1989) *Huxley in Hollywood*. New York: Harper and Row.

Ferns, Christopher S. (1980) *Aldous Huxley: Novelist*. London: Athlone Press.

Firchow, Peter E. (1984) *The End of Utopia: A Study of Aldous Huxley's "Brave New World."* London: Associated University Presses.

Fjermedal, Grant (1986) *The Tomorrow Makers: A Brave New World of Living-Brain Machines*. New York: Macmillan.

Ford, Henry, with Samuel Crowther (1924) *My Life and Work*. London: Heinemann.

Gernsback, Hugo (2000) *Ralph 124C41+: A Romance of the Year 2660* (1925). Lincoln, NE: University of Nebraska Press.

Gosden, Roger (1999) *Designing Babies: The Brave New World of Reproductive Technology*. New York: W.H. Freeman.

Gunn, James E. (1961) *The Joy Makers*. New York: Bantam.

Haldane, Charlotte (1926) *Man's World*. London: Chatto and Windus.

Haldane, J.B.S. (1924) *Daedalus or, Science and the Future*. London: Kegan Paul, Trench, Trubner.

——(1932) *The Inequality of Man*. London: Chatto and Windus.

——(1963) "Biological Possibilities for the Human Species in the Next Ten Thousand Years," in *Man and his Future*, (ed.) Gordon Wolstoneholme. London: J. and A. Churchill, 337–61.

Hillegas, Mark R. (1967) *The Future as Nightmare: H.G. Wells and the Anti-Utopians*. New York: Oxford University Press.

Holmes, Charles Mason (1970) *Aldous Huxley and the Way to Reality*. Bloomington, IN: Indiana University Press.

Huxley, Aldous (1930) *Jesting Pilate: The Diary of a Journey* (1926) London: Chatto and Windus.

——(1949) *Ape and Essence*. London: Chatto and Windus.

——(1962) *Island: A Novel*. London: Chatto and Windus.

——(1994a) *Brave New World* (1932). London: HarperCollins.

——(1994b) *The Human Situation* (1959). London: HarperCollins.

——(2000–2) *Complete Essays*. Robert S. Baker and James Sexton (eds) 6 vols. Chicago: Ivan R. Dee.

Huxley, Laura (1968) *This Timeless Moment: A Personal View of Aldous Huxley*. New York: Farrar, Straus and Giroux.

Jones, Greta (1980) *Social Darwinism and English Thought: The Interaction between Biological and Social Theory*. Brighton: Harvester Press.

Kumar, Krishan (1987) *Utopia and Anti-Utopia in Modern Times*. Oxford: Blackwell.

May, Keith M. (1972) *Aldous Huxley*. London: Elek.

Mitchison, Naomi (1975) *Solution Three*. London: Dennis Dobson.

Murray, Nicholas (2002) *Aldous Huxley: An English Intellectual*. London: Little, Brown.

Rorvik, David M. (1971) *Brave New Baby: Promise and Peril of the Biological Revolution*. New York: Doubleday.

Sion, Ronald T. (2001) *Aldous Huxley: Literary Prophet*. Philadelphia, PA: Xlibris Corporation.

Smith, Grover (ed.) (1969) *The Letters of Aldous Huxley*, London: Chattto and Windus.

Stableford, Brian (1984) *Future Man*. London: Granada.

——(1993) "Genetic Engineering," in *The Encyclopedia of Science Fiction*, (eds) John Clute and Peter Nicholls. London: Orbit.

Thiel, Berthold (1980) *Aldous Huxley's "Brave New World."* Amsterdam: John Benjamins.

Watt, Donald (ed.) (1975) *Aldous Huxley: The Critical Heritage*. London: Routledge and Kegan Paul.

Wells, H.G. (1923) *Men Like Gods*. London: Cassell.

35

Ray Bradbury: *Fahrenheit 451*

Brian Baker

Fahrenheit 451 is, famously, the temperature at which book-paper catches fire and burns. The world of Ray Bradbury's *Fahrenheit 451* is a police state where agents of the government, known as "Firemen," control the populace through the destruction of printed material. Books are publicly burned in spectacular raids on secret caches and libraries maintained by dissident individuals. This burning is a manifestation of censorship and control, a system reinforced by omnipresent radio and television. The narrative of Ray Bradbury's 1953 novel charts the trajectory of alienation of Guy Montag, a Fireman who begins to doubt, then oppose, the system of control of which he was once a part. Montag begins to find value in the books he once burned. Ultimately this leads to his estrangement from the Fireman-state, and his exile: he is hunted by the "Mechanical Hound," a lethal tracking device, while millions in the city watch his flight on television. Montag crosses the river which divides the city from the country, the mechanical from the natural. When the city is destroyed in a nuclear or atomic blast, Montag and the community of men he has found outside the city – each of whom has memorized a book – return to rebuild "civilization."

In *Fahrenheit 451*, opposition to the repression and censorship of a dystopian state is focused on books (representing "high culture"), a locus of repression going as far back in the Utopian tradition as Plato's *Republic*. This is reliant on the preservation of cultural values symbolized by, and contained within, the pages of the books in the Waukegan library frequented by Bradbury in his childhood. The book is, for Bradbury, a repository of those values worth preserving. In a 1967 preface to *Fahrenheit 451*, Bradbury writes of his "great and abiding love of libraries," and this, he explains, was the motivation for writing *Fahrenheit 451*. He writes:

> It followed then that when Hitler burned a book I felt it as keenly, please forgive me, as his killing a human, for in the long sum of history they are one and the same flesh. (Bradbury 1967: 11)

Bradbury refers to the Nazi book-burnings rather than the McCarthyite fires contemporaneous with the publication of *Fahrenheit 451*, but the potency of the images of book-burning cannot have been lost in 1953. The Firemen signify the forces of repression, and Bradbury has himself suggested that he struggled to get "The Fireman," the novella that is the basis for Fahrenheit 451, published. In 1953, the analogy must have been all too clear. The Fireman-state's abhorrence for books is a symbolic disavowal of the liberal humanist "civilization" also threatened by postwar developments in advertising, mass consumption, and television. In *Fahrenheit 451*, the "high culture" of the literary canon is the means by which mass culture, television, and state control can be opposed.

Fire and the Fireman-state are metaphors for the growing conformity of American society in the 1950s, and the domination of television, consumerism, and suburban lifestyles, a domination expressed in cultural homogenization. To read a book, in *Fahrenheit 451*, is also to assert individuality and individual moral action. Books are literally humanized in the novel, to the extent that they actually take human form at the end of the narrative. Little wonder then, that Montag is, in Bradbury's own phrase, "a book-burner who suddenly discovers that books are flesh-and-blood ideas and cry out, silently, when put to the torch" (Bradbury 1967: 12–13). Bradbury's insistence upon the materiality of ideas indicates his conception of books is as central to human experience and human culture. When books are lost, so is humanity. Books, in *Fahrenheit 451*, are transmitters of the ethical knowledge that produces stable and liberal communities. The society of *Fahrenheit 451* is one without this source of moral direction, and therefore with no ethical base. The irony here is that although Montag must reconstitute his moral and authentic self in the course of his alienation from the state, the absence of moral frameworks and communitarian ideas means that society is organized only through culturally reinforced habit (disseminated through the wall-sized television screens) and the repressive action of the firemen themselves. Because there are no books, there is no development of individual morality; because there is no ethical framework, there is no community.

Language and Dystopia

The powerful opening paragraph of the novel emphasizes the centrality of language and linguistic play to both *Fahrenheit 451* and the dystopian form itself. The diminution or destruction of language is a key dystopian trope, such as Newspeak in *Nineteen Eighty-Four*, or *Player Piano*'s mechanized and ritualized language. To control language is to control reality. Beatty, Montag's boss and antagonist, says to the woman whose house he will burn, "You've been locked up here for years with a regular damned Tower of Babel" (Bradbury 1967: 48). This is a fascinating reference for Beatty to make, as the Tower of Babel indicates a myth of an originary and unified language, one that was destroyed in the tower's fall. If a library is Babel, it signifies a linguistic confusion that undermines the ideology of the state. The Library of Babel is then a curiously conflated double symbol, both of a plurality which opposes the language-control of the state, and of a canon or body of texts which provide the means for intellectual resistance. Fire burns and controls books, but books, conversely, threaten fire because they threaten the stability of the official discourse.

The color symbolism of black and white, the colors of fire (red, orange, and yellow), and the spectacle of conflagration, are vividly depicted: Montag "strode in a swarm of fireflies," "[w]hile the books went up in sparkling whirls and blew away on a wind turned dark with burning" (Bradbury 1967: 19). This play of imagery suggests the intoxication with spectacle which is the means of control in the Fireman-state, just as the fragmentation of discourses in the bottling-plant section of Huxley's *Brave New World* signifies both the endless circulation of language, and the deliberate evacuation of meaning from it. *Fahrenheit 451* often has recourse to a highly symbolic language, particularly so in the final pages of the book. The carefully constructed and "literary" imagery and symbolism of *Fahrenheit 451* reveals the extent to which the very textual fabric of the novel is intended to echo the literary culture that the Firemen seek to erase. The text aligns itself with the books that are being burnt by Montag and his colleagues, the artifacts of a humanist "civilization," where a "poetic" complexity of language and meaning compromises the ideology of the state, where, as in Vonnegut's phrase, the "truths were few and simple." In reading *Fahrenheit 451*, then, the reader is opening herself or himself up to the possibility of dissent.

The American 1950s

Fahrenheit 451's critique of postwar American society rests upon the connection between individuality and a liberal (or ethical) community, and in this, Bradbury's text is typical of the American 1950s. Ray Bradbury grew up during the Depression years. Born in 1920, Bradbury spent much of his childhood in Waukegan, Illinois, and the small town is the focus for much of Bradbury's nostalgia. For Bradbury, the small town and its values, placed in opposition to those of corporate capitalism and urban life, become a place of escape from, or avoidance of, the dystopian configurations of mid-twentieth-century culture and society. The crisis in the capitalist system after the Wall Street Crash of 1929, and the Depression years that followed, affected Bradbury personally: in the years 1926–7 and 1932–3, Bradbury traveled with his family to Arizona where his father, laid off, hoped to find work. Bradbury, like Kurt Vonnegut, Frederik Pohl, and the Futurians, is a product of his political era, influenced by the years of Depression, Popular Front politics and the world war that followed. The "progressive" ideals of the 1930s, one which could easily be married to a form of science fiction that imagined the future in terms of the triumph of reason and order, and scientific discovery and its technical applications, become much more cloudy in the postwar period. The reaction against the Utopia of technological wonder and World States, a reaction manifested in Huxley, Orwell and *Fahrenheit 451* (despite Bradbury's small-town, communitarian impulses), was partly produced by the drift away from the politics of the Communist-influenced left towards a centrist and "liberal" consensus. Christopher Brookeman, in his *American Culture and Society since the 1930s*, describes a "disenchantment with communism and explicit ideological commitment that became a hallmark of the 1940s and 1950s" (Brookeman 1984: 2). Socialism itself was identified with Stalinist totalitarianism. Brookeman writes that:

> [t]he problems of sustaining ideological positions and loyalties within the contradictions of world history led many American writers and intellectuals to seek what Arthur M. Schlesinger called the "vital center," a core of agreed basic democratic values that could act as a focus of critical enquiry, not subject to the sudden ravages of history, revolution and ideological schisms. (Brookeman 1984: 3)

Daniel Bell, a political and social theorist described by Brookeman as an "anti-Communist liberal" or "neo-conservative," argued in *The End of Ideology* that this shift away from ideological commitment, towards a nonpartisan or "nonideological" position, was in fact the removal of a distorting and redundant analytical framework. *The End of Ideology* attempted to justify the argument of its title, in suggesting that:

> [i]n the Western world . . . there is today a rough consensus among intellectuals on political issues: the acceptance of a Welfare State; the desirability of decentralized power; a system of mixed economy and of political pluralism. In that sense, too, the ideological age has ended. (Bell 1960: 373)

Bell, writing at the end of the 1950s, defined "ideology" as "the conversion of ideas into social levers" and a "road to action" (Bell 1960: 370). The exhaustion of ideology is, for Bell, largely the exhaustion of Marxism as the motive force behind opposition to, and critique of, the prevailing organization of life in 1950s America.

Spectacle and War

Fahrenheit 451 is set at a time of (Cold) war: jet planes scream overhead, there is a generalized cultural anxiety, and the text ends with the destruction of the city by an atomic or nuclear device. The novel, as noted above, begins with a scene of conflagration, destruction in microcosm: Montag the Fireman sets fire to piles of books. The culture of *Fahrenheit 451* is based on war, economic power, and prosperity being explicitly linked to military might and social repression: "We've started and won two atomic wars since 1960! . . . I've heard rumors; the world is starving and we're well fed. Is it true, the world works hard and we play? Is that why we are hated so much?" (Bradbury 1967: 74). At the end of the text, with the city destroyed, the dissident Granger declares "some day we'll remember so much that we'll build the biggest goddam steamshovel in history and dig the biggest grave of all time and shove war in and cover it up" (Bradbury 1967: 149).

The Fireman-state is a warfare state, one in which, like that of the USA in the immediate postwar years, a "military-industrial complex" tooled for world war, then Cold War, generates an economy of mass consumption and a society of conforming consumers. In contrast to Kurt Vonnegut's *Player Piano* or the dystopian worlds of Frederik Pohl, *Fahrenheit 451* is a world in which consumption occurs apparently without production, and consumption is largely based not on commodities but on spectacle. In fact, work is almost entirely absent from *Fahrenheit 451*. Its world is suburban and middle class, corresponding to social criticism of the time of the corporate and consumerist culture of the American 1950s in texts such as David Riesman's *The Lonely Crowd* (1950) and William H. Whyte's *The Organization Man* (1955). The world of the city, dominated by the television screens, is an unreal world, behind which nature lies. Montag must break through "the seven veils of unreality" (Bradbury 1967: 130) when he crosses the river into the wilderness: "He felt as if he had left a stage behind and many actors . . . He was moving from an unreality that was frightening into a reality that was unreal because it was new" (Bradbury 1967: 129). The unreality perpetuated by the television screens corresponds to a fabricated ideology which hides the true state of the world from its citizens.

For those such as Millie, Montag's wife, an eternally circulating and spectacle-based present completely masks the systematic erasure of "culture." Spectacle is a motif common to many dystopian texts of the 1950s, and is usually linked to a fabricated reality and false ideology disseminated by the mass media. The 1950s was the first decade in the USA in which television played a dominant cultural role; in the dystopias of the period, this is imagined as a means of social and political control. Millie is described as standing in front of the television screen: "Behind her the walls of the room were flooded with green and yellow and orange fireworks sizzling and bursting to some music" (Bradbury 1967: 65). The television screens show representations of fire that are designed to distract, as are the spectacles of mutilation of the White Clowns. Montag is appalled by "three White Clowns [who] chopped off each other's limbs to the accompaniment of immense incoming tides of laughter" (Bradbury 1967: 92). This surface, this lack of content, both replicates and masks a void at the core of official discourse. The process of consumption, aligned with television and the processes of social interaction, is spectacle: "so bring on your clubs and parties, your acrobats and magicians, your daredevils, jet cars, motorcycle helicopters, your sex and heroin, more of everything to do with automatic reflex" (Bradbury 1967: 67). This, of course, is bread and circuses. The spectacle of death is one that keeps the citizens pacified (or perhaps ideologically anaesthetized). At the end of the narrative Montag is chased through the city while the population watch him on their "parlor walls." Montag's struggle for escape and life becomes a spectacle, an entertainment: "so they must have their game out, thought Montag. The circus must go on, even with war beginning within the hour" (Bradbury 1967: 124). Even in his rebellion, he has in one way been reincorporated into the structures of the state. His escape is covered up and his capture and execution faked to satisfy the logic of the state ideology, the desires of the viewers, and the self-containment of the system.

The Authentic Self

Richard Corber has suggested that the emphasis on individuation and selfhood found in texts such as *Fahrenheit 451* was part of a move towards the Cold War liberal consensus: "Cold War liberals . . . sought to shift attention from the material world to the individual's subjective experience of it by defining reality in such a way that it did not lend itself readily to Marxist analysis" (Corber 1993: 53). Many writers of dystopias in the 1950s, Bradbury included, react against an oppressive state organization of life, but their reliance upon individual rebellion betrays a suspicion of all organized political movements or "ideological" positions. Instead, they place a reliance upon the values of the "vital centre," which, for *Fahrenheit 451*, are located in the works of "great literature." Dystopias of the 1950s are organized around a discovery (through alienation) of an autonomous "liberal" self, and an expression of humanist values which oppose the pressures towards conformity and control in a bureaucratized American 1950s. In the dystopias of the 1950s, the protagonist's alienation is married to a search for the "authentic life" that lies behind the ideological "real" of official discourse.

This "authentic self" indicates the extent to which the political critique of 1950s dystopias comes to rely upon the assumptions of liberal humanism and the rhetoric of "core values." Alienation is not figured as political activism, but as spatial exclusion. For these dystopias, there is no way to remake the system from within: flight or escape is the only alternative to oppression. *Fahrenheit 451* shows Montag's alienation both from internal, domestic space of the Firemen, and his flight to the natural world beyond the city's limits. Early in the text, when Montag first leaves the fire station, he walks home, becoming a pedestrian. This aligns him with Leonard Mead of Bradbury's short story "The Pedestrian," as does "The Fireman," an early version of *Fahrenheit 451*, in which Montag is not "Guy" Montag but "Leonard" Montag. In "The Pedestrian," a lone man is arrested because his desire to walk in the night air is marked as deviant by a blankly conforming society. Some of the details of the society and culture clearly place this short text in the same dystopian world as *Fahrenheit 451*: there is a distinction between inside and outside; the soporific nature of the television screens; the destructive nature of the automobile, and the control of public space; binary oppositions between heat and cold, urban and natural, the artificial light of the television and moonlight; emptiness as key signifier of the society; and the immanence of death. In both texts, the notion of walking outside spatializes the key dystopian theme of the protagonist's growing estrangement from his culture. In "The Fireman," Montag walks the city, feeling like ""the only pedestrian in the entire city!"," and he too is stopped:

> So he walked alone, aware of his loneliness, until the police car pulled up and flashed its cold white light upon him.
>   "What're you doing?" shouted a voice.
>   "I'm out for a walk."

"He says he's out for a walk."
The laughter, the cold, precise turning over of his identity cards, the careful noting of his address. (Bradbury 1951: 11)

The emptiness of life is given spatial form in a deserted cityscape, a zone of isolation, control, and death. The world of the pedestrian is an empty one, making the procedures of pursuit and elimination of the outsider much easier for the repressive state. Later, on making his escape from the world of the firemen, Montag has to run across the highway, transformed into a killing zone. The "empty boulevard" is a place where children in stolen cars attempt to run down stray walkers or destroy each other, and Millie tells Montag that Clarisse McClellan has been run down by an automobile. This emptiness signifies a psychological lack of affect, a lack of human empathy that becomes mapped onto the alienating urban space of the city. The city is like a stage set, a "vast stage without scenery" (Bradbury 1967: 115), its emptiness furthering the Firemen's imperatives of control, surveillance, and if necessary, pursuit. The motor-car in *Fahrenheit 451* and "The Pedestrian" are technologies antithetical to human life, symbols of a society heading towards ruin. The society of *Fahrenheit 451*, like the car on the highway, is accelerating towards destruction.

Montag is chased through the city while pursued by the Mechanical Hound towards the end of the narrative, which again spatializes his alienation. The Mechanical Hound, another mechanized and malign transformation of the natural, is an artificial tracking device which corners then dispatches its quarry with a lethal injection. When Montag leaves the suburban environment and crosses the river into a natural wilderness, he cannot be followed, even by the Hound, for the pastoral is a space outside the control and spectacular systems of the firemen. The natural world, like the Green world of Zamiatin's *We* or the deer of Vonnegut's "Deer in the Works," clearly (as exemplified through Montag's escape) signifies an interstitial space in the state's structures of repression, even though the space outside the city is explicitly allowed by the state because it poses no threat. The group of men who live there, the book-preservers, exist, like books, in the interstices or margins of the system.

Gender and Subjectivity

Montag's trajectory from Fireman to book-man is negotiated through key encounters with three male figures of authority. To begin with, Montag's growing resistance to the state is opposed to the cynical rhetoric of Captain Beatty, who outlines the rationale for controlling the population so repressively. Later, Montag pursues Faber, the former professor who helps him in a later dialogue with Beatty, but who is aghast when Montag's resistance turns into homicidal action. Faber's alienation from the state is passive, and ultimately he cannot help Montag in his search for the authentic self. Finally, Montag encounters Granger, the leader of the book-men, in the world outside the city, and who offers a practical program for the restitution of civil society, through the agency of the canonical books the group have internalized. However, it is Montag's relationships to two women – Clarisse McClellan and his wife, Millie – that indicate his personal transformation. That transformation is to shed the signs of performativity, signs associated with his status as Fireman, and rediscover the "authentic self" of childhood.

In the first page of the novel, analyzed in terms of language above, the performativity of Montag's Fireman-subjectivity is indicated: "He knew that when he returned to the firehouse, he might wink at himself, a minstrel man, burnt-corked, in the mirror" (Bradbury 1967: 19). The public burning of books are a spectacle of control *pour encourager les autres*, but the passage suggests that the "fierce grin" Montag wears is a mask: if he does not "remember" to wear it, then a different, and more troubled, persona emerges. (This word is actually used in the text to signify Montag's performance of conformity: a "mask of happiness.") Also associated with a performative subjectivity is Millie: her "family" are the actors she sees on the "parlor walls," the three huge television screens which almost enclose her. Early in the novel, Millie takes part in a "play" in which she acts the part of the "homemaker": "When it comes time for the missing lines" she tells Montag, "they all look at me out of the three walls and I say the lines" (Bradbury 1967: 33). Pathetically, Millie takes this fake interaction to be more real that her life with Montag, although as we have seen earlier in the narrative, Millie actually finds her life so unsupportable that she attempts to commit suicide, but covers this knowledge with a mask of conformity. In the television play, Millie literally *performs* the role of "homemaker" when it is unavailable to her in reality. This artificial subjectivity is encoded in Millie's material being: later in the novel she is described as having "hair burnt by chemicals to a brittle straw," with skin like "white bacon" (Bradbury 1967: 56). While Millie's inability to respond to the books Montag brings home signifies *Fahrenheit 451*'s somewhat conservative gender politics – she even betrays Montag and dies in the destruction of the city – her association with performance indicates the kind of subjectivity that Montag inhabits at the beginning of the narrative, and must reject.

The opening scene, where "minstrel man" Montag winks at himself in the mirror, introduces an image of doubleness. This doubleness, or split subjectivity, is also at the heart of the performance that Millie and Montag must enact. In fact, this split – between the Fireman and the "man" beneath, which Clarisse recognizes when first meeting Montag – is induced by the insupportable contradiction of the state's ideology. For Montag this is particularly urgent, as he comes into contact with, and burns, the very books that represent all that is missing from his and Millie's life. Both Millie and Montag despair, and are empty within, because of the cultural emptiness without. Millie is driven to suicide because she cannot find fulfillment in the "parlor walls," the very thing she uses to keep herself anaesthetized. Montag, however, is driven to resist, and to seek out the very things he is meant to suppress. Montag's split subjectivity is indicated at key points in the narrative. On finding Millie comatose after overdosing on sedatives, the text suggests: "Montag was split in half. He felt his chest chopped down and split apart" (Bradbury 1967: 27), and later in the narrative he finds his own body seemingly acting of its own accord. His hands are described several times as performing without his will: "His hands, by themselves, began to rip the pages from the book"; just before he kills Beatty, "Montag saw the surprise there [in Beatty's eyes] and himself glanced to his hands to see what new thing they had done" (Bradbury 1967: 87; 111). This somatic rebellion indicates a split in Montag between mind and body, between ideological imperatives and the need to fill the emptiness within. The novel signifies this split explicitly: Montag has an "other self, the subconscious idiot that ran babbling at times, quite independent of will, habit and conscience" (Bradbury 1967: 25). The last word of this quotation, "conscience," indicates that the "subconscious idiot" is telling Montag the Fireman things he does not want to hear; it also signifies that "conscience" is exactly what Montag is developing.

All the things that Montag has lost, and must rediscover, find their embodiment in Clarisse McClellan. She is associated with nature; she is independent of thought and action; and most importantly, she represents both culture and childhood. *Fahrenheit 451*'s persistent representation of ethical choice in material terms is evident in the choice Montag must make between Millie and Clarisse. In a sense, as we see Montag walking home from work, thinking of a book he has hidden at home before the novel begins, his choice has been made already. In his flight and rebirth, Montag internalizes the values that Clarisse McClellan represents. *Fahrenheit 451*, like Montag himself, crosses into more symbolic territory when leaving the cityscape, coming into a territory of fantasy, memory, and childhood. Childhood becomes a kind of Utopian zone in the text, a zone of escape. The only child in the text is Clarisse: the dystopian state is signified by the absence of children. "Children are ruinous," says Mrs. Phelps (Bradbury 1967: 94). The rejection (or perhaps erasure) of childhood by the Fireman-state is an erasure of its own future. An idealized childhood is linked strongly with the past and with the pastoral as the ideal states of *Fahrenheit 451*, and freedom is explicitly associated with the familial. Childhood (as memory) is also linked with "reality," with a zone of unmediated experience placed in opposition to the repression of city life. Memory is therefore signified as more "real" than the life of the city: like childhood, more meaningful in its experience and its associations. This is what Montag must, and does, recover, but only after his performative subjectivity has been destroyed in the spectacle of the televised manhunt.

Religious Symbolism

Montag's crossing of the river into the natural world is a symbolic cleansing and baptism. As Montag becomes progressively more alienated from the state, he has been shedding the significations of fire that introduced his character on the first page, and begins to accrue those of water. In a scene where he admits his doubts to Millie, he says: "No, not water; fire. You ever seen a burned house? It smolders for days. Well, this fire'll last me the rest of my life. God! I've been trying to put it out, in my mind, all night. I'm crazy with trying" (Bradbury 1967: 59).

Montag refers to his own alienation as drowning: "It was only the other night everything was fine and the next thing I know I'm drowning" (Bradbury 1967: 121). Montag becomes self-alienated, so far as to become someone else. He has internalized Clarisse's attributes, and in putting on Faber's clothes to avoid the Mechanical Hound, sheds his old identity. Earlier, Montag had fantasized that

> he would not be Montag any more, this old man told him, assured him, promised him. He would be Montag-plus-Faber, fire plus water, and then, one day, after everything had mixed and simmered and worked away in silence, there would be neither fire nor water, but wine. (Bradbury 1967: 100)

The transmutation of water into wine has obvious Christian symbolic importance. While Bradbury confesses no particular religious conviction, it is clear that in the final section of *Fahrenheit 451* Christian symbolism is used to characterize both Montag's trajectory and the apocalyptic end of the city. Montag is baptized, and reborn. Montag brings to the group two Biblical texts, just as he had shown the Bible to Faber as a token of his alienation. He brings Ecclesiastes, and Revelation, where in "The Fireman" he had brought Job. While *Fahrenheit 451* does portray the destruction of the city, the text is reliant upon Christian eschatology to provide its imagery. Nuclear war is only shown in coded, highly symbolic terms.

The ending of *Fahrenheit 451* remains open. There is a balance, a moment of possibility, in which the narrative ends. Montag and the group of bookmen walk towards the city and what remains of "civilization," largely what they carry inside them. The conflation of books with nature, the symbols of the authentic life in *Fahrenheit 451*, opposes the repressive and malign state of the Firemen, but exposes Bradbury's own ideological reliance on the high-cultural artifacts of "Western Civilization." These are themselves not "natural" in terms of the values and life they describe, but are ideologically produced and producing. The Utopian zone in this dystopian text – in *Fahrenheit 451*, nature and literature – is the space in which the author's own ideological premises are revealed.

REFERENCES AND FURTHER READING

Adams, Anthony (ed.) (1975) *Ray Bradbury/ Ray Bradbury*. London: Harrap.

Aggelis. Steven L. (ed.) (2004) *Conversations with Ray Bradbury*. Jackson, MS: University Press of Mississippi.

Bell, Daniel (1960) *The End of Ideology: On the Exhaustion of Political Ideas in the Fifties*. Glencoe, IL: The Free Press.

Bloom, Harold (ed.) (2001) *Ray Bradbury's "Fahrenheit 451": Modern Critical Interpretations*. Philadelphia: Chelsea House.

Bradbury, Ray (1951) "The Fireman." *Galaxy Science Fiction* 1.v (February), 4–61.

——(1967) *Fahrenheit 451* (1953). New York: Simon and Schuster.

——(1971) "The Pedestrian." *The Golden Apples of*

the Sun (1953). Westport, CT: Greenwood Press, 25–30.

Brookeman, Christopher (1984) *American Culture and Society since the 1930s.* London and Basingstoke: Macmillan.

Corber, Robert J. (1993) *In the Name of National Security: Hitchcock, Homophobia, and the Political Construction of Gender in Post-war America.* Durham, NC and London: Duke University Press.

De Koster, Katie (ed.) (2000) *Readings on Fahrenheit 451.* San Diego, CA: Greenhaven Press.

Greenberg, Martin Harry, and Joseph D. Olander (eds) (1980) *Ray Bradbury.* Edinburgh: Paul Harris Publishing.

Johnson, Wayne L. (1980) *Ray Bradbury.* New York: Ungar.

Nolan, William Francis (1975) *The Ray Bradbury Companion.* Detroit, MI: Gale Research.

Reid, Robin Anne (2000) *Ray Bradbury: A Critical Companion.* Westport, CT: Greenwood Press.

Riesman, David. (1950) *The Lonely Crowd: A Study of the Changing American Character.* New Haven and London: Yale University Press.

Seed, David. (1994) "The Flight from the Good Life: *Fahrenheit 451* in the Context of Postwar American Dystopias." *Journal of American Studies* 28:2, 225–40.

Touponce, William F. (1989) *Ray Bradbury.* Mercer Island, Wash: Starmont House.

Vonnegut, Kurt (1992) *Player Piano* (1952). London: Flamingo.

——(1972) "Deer in the Works," *Welcome to the Monkey House* (1968). St. Albans: Panther, 196–208.

Watt, Donald (1980) "Burning Bright: *Fahrenheit 451* as Symbolic Dystopia." In *Ray Bradbury,* (ed.) Martin Harry Greenberg and Joseph D. Olander. Edinburgh: Paul Harris Publishing, 195–213.

Whyte, William H. (1955) *The Organization Man.* New York: Simon & Schuster.

Zipes, Jack. (1983) "Mass Degradation of Humanity and Massive Contradictions in Bradbury's Vision of America in *Fahrenheit 451.*" *No Place Else: Explorations in Utopian and Dystopian Fiction,* (ed.) Eric S. Rabkin, Martin Harry Greenberg and Joseph D. Olander. Carbondale and Edwardsville: Southern Illinois University Press, 182–98.

36

Joanna Russ: *The Female Man*

Jeanne Cortiel

When Sarah LeFanu said, "Joanna Russ is the single most important woman writer of science fiction, although she is not necessarily the most widely read" (LeFanu 1988: 173) she crystallized the complexity and depth of Russ' accomplishment as well as its intellectual and aesthetic challenge. Joanna Russ writes not for quick and facile consumption; she pushes the envelope of genre conventions and literary style, but also of contemporary political thinking, particularly after her move into feminism in the late 1960s. Her fiction takes feminist theory to some of its most radical conclusions, but simultaneously destabilizes its most fundamental assumptions, crossing it with contradictory, indeed opposed theories of social and cultural critique. Rooted in materialist political thinking, it creates a separatist – women-only – Utopian society that also anticipates the explosion of the category "woman" in poststructuralist feminist theory (see Cortiel 1999) and the creation of the "cyborg" as a critique of postindustrial labor practices (see Hicks 1999). Reading Russ is never light work, but always deeply rewarding.

Within Joanna Russ' oeuvre, which runs the gamut of science fiction, fantasy, Utopian, and mainstream fiction through eight novels and countless short stories, *The Female Man* is arguably the most influential work; it is doubtlessly her most critically acclaimed novel. Yet while *The Female Man* (1975, subsequently cited as *Female Man*) clearly merits the critical attention it has received because of its influence in both science fiction and feminism, it is important to acknowledge that Russ' other novels and short stories also hold their own as major contributions to the genre. Especially worth mentioning here is Russ' first novel, *Picnic on Paradise* (1968), which places her popular character Alyx, protagonist of an earlier series of sword-and-sorcery short stories, in a science fictional world where she becomes one of the first genuine female heroes in the genre. Samuel Delany has argued that the Alyx series constitutes Russ' most important work in her early phase before her move into explicit feminism in the short story "When it Changed" (1972), whose Utopian world then became transformed as part of *The Female Man* (Delany 1977: 191), her third novel. Other novels include *And Chaos Died* (1970), *We Who Are About to . . .* (1975), *The Two of Them* (1978), and *Extra(Ordinary) People* (1985).

Beyond her contribution as a fiction writer, Joanna Russ has also had a significant impact as an acute science fiction critic, for which she received the prestigious Pilgrim award in 1988, and as feminist thinker, most recently in the monumental *What Are We Fighting For: Sex, Race, Class, and the Future of Feminism* (1998). Interpretations of Russ' work in science fiction studies and feminist studies alike routinely start out from critical paradigms developed by Russ herself in a number of essays collected in *To Write like a Woman* (1986).

The Female Man has troubled and fascinated reviewers and critics since its publication in 1975, perhaps because of its openness, ambiguity, and structural complexity, but most certainly because of its radical feminist politics and matter-of-fact inclusion of explicit lesbian eroticism. Though justifiably categorized as science fiction novel, *The Female Man* is a textual crossroads of different genre conventions, discourses, and political theories and comes to its full power when read along with these multiple, sometimes contradictory, textual connections. The novel's most significant affiliation is with feminism, but even here the text avoids monologic simplification and intersects with distinct strands or moments within feminism that oppose and destabilize each other. This essay introduces *The Female Man* as a postmodern science fiction novel that strategically interlaces four distinct genres – Utopia, science fiction, alternative history, and "mainstream" postmodern autobiographical writing. The four generic worlds correspond with the four protagonists, Janet, Jael, Jeannine, and Joanna, but these characters importantly also cross generic boundaries to create a text that is both fragmented and coherent. This generic juxtaposition and crossing enables a complex narrative text, whose dominant political vision – in spite of its simultaneous skepticism, scorching critique, and even despair – remains full of hope throughout.

Janet: Programmatic Utopia

In *Picnic on Paradise* (1968), Russ transported Alyx, the protagonist of a series of sword-and-sorcery short stories, into a highly technologized future world, letting her travel not only through time but also across genre lines from fantasy into science fiction. Part of this early novel's charm lies in the incongruity of Alyx's archaic presence in the technologically sophisticated world of the cultures warring over Paradise. In many ways a much more complex novel, *The Female Man* picks up and expands this strategy of crossing genre conventions, wedding it with the science fictional topos that posits an infinite number of parallel universes (see *Female Man* 1:6). *The Female Man* explores four such universes that lie on very close historical strands of probability. Each of these worlds supplies one of the main protagonists: First, the novel introduces Whileaway, a Utopian, all-female world, the home of strong-minded and independent Janet, who is "stupid" by Whileawayan standards with an IQ of 187;

beyond this Utopian world, there are two worlds that simultaneously exist in 1969 – Jeannine's world, in which the Second World War never happened, and Joanna's, the basic narrative world, which represents the USA at 1969; and finally, Jael's world, in which men and women live on separate continents and are in a state of cold war with each other. In addition to supplying a narrative space and distinct historical, material, and social parameters shaping the protagonist that emerges from it, each of these worlds also constitutes a textual universe that follows its own generic rules. Therefore, Janet's home world Whileaway functions as Utopia only in the context of the three non-Utopian textual worlds that are its source and antithesis. In a way, *The Female Man* is so effective as Utopian text precisely because Utopia makes up only part of its narrative (see Bammer 1991: 97). Partly through its juxtaposition to these other worlds, Whileaway becomes an example of what Tom Moylan has called a "critical utopia," enriching the hopeful vision of the good place with a distinctly skeptical edge.

It is this joining of passionate hope with lucid critique and doubt that enabled *The Female Man* to help propel the Utopian tradition out of its dystopian hiatus in the early 1970s (Moylan 1986: 56ff; Albinsky 1988: 159), along with a network of other Utopian novels published in the late 1960s and early 1970s, such as Ursula Le Guin's *The Left Hand of Darkness* (1969), Monique Wittig's *Les Guérillères* (1969) and Dorothy Bryant's *The Kin of Ata are Waiting for You* (1971) (for a comparison of *Female Man* with Piercy and Wittig see Bartkowski 1989; with Le Guin and Bryant see Roberts 1993). Feminist Utopian writing in the 1970s had to work with and against problematic early ancestors such as Mary E. Bradley Lane's *Mizora* (1890), an all-female Utopia of blonde super-women, and Charlotte Perkins Gilman's *Herland* (1915), which also bases its Utopian vision on the assumption that if it were up to (white) women, the world would function perfectly and rationally. The renewed resurgence of Utopianism in a more socially and politically aware incarnation (see Roberts 1993: 76) as "critical utopia" provided the impetus for subsequent writing, much of which was feminist, in the late 1970s and early 1980s (see Moylan 1986: 60). This group of novels includes, among others, Ernest Callenbach's *Ecotopia* (1975), Ursula Le Guin's *The Dispossessed* (1974), Marge Piercy's *Woman on the Edge of Time* (1976), Samuel Delany's *Triton* (1976), Suzy McKee Charnas' *Walk to the End of the World* (1974) and *Motherlines* (1978), and Sally Miller Gearhart's *Wanderground* (1980).

It is significant in this context that *The Female Man* eliminates one of the central features of Utopian writing, the non-Utopian visitor/narrator who reports systematically on the Utopian society as an ethnographer (see Moylan 1986:63). Such an ethnographic account of the Utopian world suggests control over it and echoes colonialist accounts of "foreign" cultures. In Russ' novel, the Utopian character has a voice of her own. Janet Evason introduces herself and her world and sets the stage by assuming the privileged position of claiming the first person pronoun in the novel's initial sentence: "I was born on a farm on Whileaway" (1:1). What is more, however, not only does the Utopian character assume the role of the narrator, but one of the other characters, Alice Jael Reasoner, is by profession indeed an ethnographer as well as a revolutionary and an assassin. The fact that the ethnographer here never enters Whileaway and does not begin to understand the Utopian world other than as it relates to her own objectives adds weight to Russ' critical reevaluation of the Utopian tradition.

While Janet does not make available interpretive control over her world as an ethnographer, she does disclose certain characteristics of Whileawayan society that distinguish the Utopian world from the basic narrative world. Her description of the Utopian world, which also sets it apart from earlier feminist Utopian visions, is more akin to poetry than to methodical ethnography. Instead of laying out a systematic account of Whilewayan architecture, for example, the narrator creates a poetic image of belonging and transition, linking the physical environment to the culture's personality or ambiance:

> Some homes are extruded foam: white caves hung with veils of diamonds, indoor gardens, ceilings that weep. There are places in the Arctic, to sit and meditate, invisible walls that shut in the same ice as outside, the same clouds. There is one rain-forest, there is one shallow sea, there is one mountain chain, there is one desert. Human rookeries asleep undersea where Whileawayans create, in their leisurely way, a new economy and a new race. Rafts anchored in the blue eye of a dead volcano. Eyries built for nobody in particular, whose guests arrive by glider. There are many more shelters than homes, many more homes than persons; as the saying goes, My home is in my shoes. Everything (they know) is eternally in transit. Everything is pointed toward death. (5:12)

The Utopian narrative in *The Female Man* is not about recounting in detail how Whileawayan culture differs socially, economically and sexually from the basic narrative world, even though each of these differences has a significant presence in the text. Nor is the narrative voice stable: Oscillating from being Janet speaking as an insider to being Joanna looking dreamily through Janet's eyes, this changing voice makes Whileaway seem both real and fantastic. Even in the novel's most political moments, the poetry of this Utopian vision captures a dense ambiguity and emotional depth that propels it far beyond the purely programmatic.

Russ' treatment of work on Whileaway is another case in point for the novel's distance from and reformulation of classic Utopian ethnography. According to the Utopian narrator Janet, Whileawayans "work too much" (3:4), they "work all the time. They work. And they work. *And they work*" (3:6). Whileawayan life is indeed structured and defined by work, yet the assessment of what constitutes "too much" work seems to differ substantially from that of the basic narrative world, i.e., that of Joanna's USA at 1969: "Whileaway is engaged in the reorganization of industry consequent to the discovery of the induction principle. The Whileawayan work-week is sixteen hours" (3:12). This casual revelation moves Whileawayan work ethic deeply into a postscarcity, postindustrial economy. Heather J. Hicks has indirectly analyzed this discrepancy, reading *The Female Man* as an important response to the New Left's notion of the increasing obsolescence of work in an automated world and the contemporaneous struggle of liberal feminism to open the workplace for women (Hicks 1999: para 4). Hicks' analysis opens a new perspective in Russ criticism that also makes it possible to analyze the relationship to and influence upon Donna Haraway's conceptionalization of contemporary female workers as "cyborgs." Technology, to Russ, thus has an important function in her Utopian vision and comes with a clearly liberatory potential.

The Female Man thus introduces a new version of Utopianism that is not centered on a monologic critique of society, but rests on uncertainty, speaking with many different voices from a variety of vantage points. While the novel links with a network of other Utopian texts published around that time, its four protagonists, who turn out to be genetically identical, offer a unique vision that effectively links a clear political position, a materialist critique of capitalist patriarchy, with its destabilization. The non-Utopian protagonists and their worlds offer a counterpoint that adds further depth to this destabilized/destabilizing critique.

Jael: Parallel Universe Science Fiction

Jael, the second narrator-protagonist in *The Female Man*, makes a ghostly appearance in part two of the novel as protean figure without a "brand name" (2:1). While the novel, from Janet's perspective, most distinctly taps the Utopian tradition, it affiliates Jael with the parallel universe tradition in science fiction. Distinctly non-Utopian, Jael embodies the liberatory potential of technology and has turned herself into an effective killing machine, a cyborg before the name, with the ruthlessness and deadly skill of a cat. Seeing an analogy to Marge Piercy's dystopian world in *Woman on the Edge of Time* (Bartkowski 1989: 61; Walker 1990: 179), some have argued that Jael's world, a future earth on a different strand of probability, is Whileaway's dystopian other. However, Jael's universe more precisely represents Whileaway's *generic* counterpart, less dystopian than science-fictional. Unlike in Piercy's novel, Jael's world is not history gone wrong, but, in the logic of a historical dialectic, the prerequisite stage that makes the Utopian world possible (see Cortiel 1999: 76–91). Finally, Jael is also an allegorical figure, referencing medieval notions of retribution and anger. It is this combination of divergent discourses that makes Jael so attractive as a model for later characters of Cyberpunk fiction, most prominently perhaps in William Gibson's female assassin in "Johnny Mnemonic" (1981) and his Neuromancer trilogy, Molly Millions (see Wolmark 1993: 116).

More than any other character in the novel, Jael references the painful and violent transition from powerlessness to agency, which is not just the ability to act effectively, but the ability to act as a protagonist in her own narrative. In Jael's world, the "battle of the sexes," another important science fictional motif (Larbalestier 2002), has been externalized: Men and women are separated geographically in "Manland" and "Womanland" and are pitted against each other in a cold war that Jael aims to bring to the point of battle. Whereas Janet's Whileaway is steeped in ambivalence, the major conflict in Jael's story and in her world is based on a simple opposition between good and evil. She is the major protagonist in this science fictional plot line and brings the other women together to enlist their support for her revolutionary war. Her name – perhaps surprisingly in the secular context of the novel – opens a biblical reference, which is continued and confirmed by a direct quote from Deborah's song of victory, in which a woman sings about another woman, Jael, who kills a man and saves her people: "[A]t her feet he bowed, he fell, he lay down; at her feet he bowed, he fell, he lay down dead" (*Female Man* 8: 8; Judges 5: 27). Jael's name thus links two of the agency-constituting acts in the novel, killing a man and telling a story.

Whereas Janet represents hope and spiritual redemption, which corresponds to the undialectical Whileawayan version of history in which the men just died in a plague, Jael is a liberator and revolutionary in a very much this-worldly, material sense, in spite of her biblical affiliations. From Jael's perspective it is her atrocious killing of men that makes Whileaway possible. When Janet refuses to let her establish a military base on Whileaway, Jael bursts out:

> "Disapprove all you like. Pedant! Let me give you something to carry away with you, friend: that 'plague' you talk of is a lie. I know. The world-lines around you are not so different from yours or mine or theirs and there is no plague in any of them, not any of them. Whileaway's plague is a big lie. Your ancestors lied about it. It is I who gave you your 'plague,' my dear, about which you can now pietize and moralize to your heart's content; I, I, I, I am the plague, Janet Evason. I and the war I fought built your world for you, I and those like me, we gave you a thousand years of peace and love and the Whileawayan flowers nourish themselves on the bones of the men we have slain." (9:7)

From Jael's perspective, the Utopian world is paid for by murderous acts that tragically destroy her ability to become part of the Utopia. Although Jael makes Whileaway possible, she can never enter nor even understand it. While the Utopian character Janet can take her agency for granted and encounters men with amused curiosity rather than hostility, the act of killing men is Jael's way to reverse the violence committed against her and other women, establishing women's agency in the genre of science fiction (Cortiel 1999: 56–64).

Jeannine: Alternate History

While Whileaway constitutes a fully fledged Utopia and Jael's world a science fictional vision of war, the third textual space with its central character opens an alternate history tale that asks the science fictional "what if" question in terms of the past. Generically, alternate history is affiliated with science fiction, but follows different rules: instead of basing its speculation on scientific extrapolation, alternate history experiments with changed events in the past, for example to speculate what the world would be like if the South had won the American Civil War, or if Hitler had won the

Second World War, as for example Philip K. Dick's acclaimed novel *The Man in the High Castle* (1962) does. In similar ways as Whileaway transforms Utopia, Jeannine's textual world is an twist on such alternate worlds, in which "Herr Shicklgruber" (1:2) (close but not identical to Hitler) was killed before he could accumulate power, the Second World War never happened, the USA in 1969, the narrated time, is still in the midst of an economic and social Depression and women are even further removed from power.

Accordingly, Jeannine is the weakest of the four main characters in all respects and lives unhappily in a repressive cultural and social regime, in which women wholly depend on their relationships with men. Jeannine is 29 and unmarried, an old maid and failure according to the standards of her world and her family. Having no outlet in the outside world, her creative energy becomes destructive to herself. Similarly ill-fitted for this society's notions of gender propriety, Jeannine's unenthusiastic boyfriend Cal is a failed actor, cross-dresses secretly, and cries when they are having sex.

Jeannine's utter lack of agency is most acutely manifested in her inability to assume the role of the narrator even within the space of a women's text. All of the other pro-tagonists have a voice of their own and therefore control over their participation in genre conventions. Yet while the narrator does channel Jeannine's thoughts in a few instances of personal narration, Jeannine's own voice is confined to the level of char-acter speech – controlled by the narrative voice. Representing the willingness to act that is forced to inaction, Jeannine is nevertheless potentially Janet and potentially Jael. Therefore it is not surprising that it is Jeannine who most willingly enters an agreement with Jael about establishing military bases in her world. At that moment, through this contract she assumes power over her entire universe as its sole represen-tative. It is probably the first decision of any import she has ever made. Ironically, she exerts this great power at a commonplace event in an ordinary place: Thanksgiving dinner in a chain restaurant, Schrafft's, primarily frequented by women. After this crucial assumption of power, Jeannine says "I" for a brief moment as a narrator during the sending off scene at the end of the novel: "We got up and paid our quintuple bill; then we went out into the street. I said goodbye and went off with Laur, I, Janet; I also watched them go, I, Joanna; moreover I went off to show Jael the city, I Jean-nine, I Jael, I myself" (9:7). When Jeannine says "I" here, even if she is speaking with Joanna's voice, she indicates that she, too, has changed. While such a transformation would have been inconceivable within the confines of Jeannine's own textual universe, crossing over to another generic space makes it possible.

Joanna: Postmodern Autobiography

Joanna introduces yet another, nonscience fictional textual level, which affiliates her world with mainstream postmodern autobiographical writing and refers to the USA at the end of the 1960s. Unlike the other generic spaces, Joanna's textual world is steeped in ambiguity, indeterminacy, and uncertainty driven by her imaginary interactions with Janet, Jael, and Jeannine, in all of whom she sees herself. Viewed from the perspective of Joanna's textual universe, the novel constitutes an "inward journey," in which all the other characters are not external alter-egos as in Jael's narrative, or alternate historical versions of the same woman as in Jeannine's, but textual manifestations of Joanna's multiple personalities (see McClenahan 1982: 120); from this perspective, Joanna's imagination serves to make the division – and reintegration – of the narrator-protagonists possible. For Joanna, everything, including her own transformation, takes place between her psyche and the act of narration. Read through this character, the novel is her therapeutic narration, and the other plot lines are her own Utopian dreams, nightmares, or allegorical stories juxtaposed in a postmodern pastiche of feminist vignettes that together constitute a scathing critique of the USA at the cultural moment of 1969.

However, it is important to point out that Joanna represents only one of four perspectives or textual worlds in the novel, whose combined aesthetic and political power hinges upon the interaction between them and their mutual destabilization. There is no point in the novel at which Joanna wakes up from her dream or reintegrates her multiple personalities. Neither does Whileaway ever absorb all four protagonists, nor does Jael manage to take over with her vision of war. Each of the protagonists thus also has four dimensions: Jeannine, for example has a presence as alternate history variation on the genotype that she shares with all the other protagonists; she is also the source and justification of the Utopian vision represented by Janet and the representative of her world in military negotiations with Jael. Read through Joanna's, the modernist/postmodernist perspective, Jeannine represents one Self exploring itself, a potential personality of the main narrator, the creative energy that cannot come to its own. This is the extraordinary feat of *The Female Man*: Each textual world retains its generic integrity although or precisely because it is destabilized through the intersection and interaction with generically different worlds. Therefore, as much as *The Female Man* has been established as an exemplar of feminist postmodern writing, it is crucial to also place the novel in the context of generic fiction as political practice.

Joanna introduces herself matter-of-factly as a woman who is transformed into a man at a cocktail party, "I mean a female man, of course; my body and soul were exactly the same" (1:4). Nevertheless, Joanna does not emerge as a fully-fledged character until she begins to interact with Janet and Jeannine as "visitors" to her personal world. For Joanna, Janet is a glimpse of what she aspires to be, and Jeannine represents the look in the mirror that reflects her own weakness as a participant in the culture that denies women full access to the power to act and signify. Joanna's transformation into a man coincides with Janet's appearance in her world, but while simultaneity suggests an aesthetic or emotional relationship, it does not establish a direct causal link between the two events: "After I called up Janet, out of nothing, or she called up me (don't read between the lines; there's nothing there) I began to gain weight, my appetite improved, friends commented on my renewed zest for life, and a nagging scoliosis of the ankle that had tortured me for years simply vanished overnight" (3:1). At the same time, ironically, Joanna works to transform Janet by teaching her precisely the rules of decorum that make herself see Jeannine when she looks in the mirror.

Joanna as the narrator who shares the author's name moves along the seams between the different textual worlds, gesturing at the multiple generic affiliations of each character: Janet is both a figment of Joanna's imagination and a material visitor from a Utopian world, both a tourist that she politely teaches appropriate social skills, and her own phantasmic invention. Laura Rose Wilding, the teenage daughter of Janet's host family who eventually enters a sexual relationship with the Whileawayan, represents another such textual seam, as she shifts from being Janet's to being Joanna's lover in the final part of the novel. Instead of providing the illusion of coherence, these seams draw attention to the breakages and contradictions between the different textual worlds in the novel that pull its Utopia, science fiction, alternate history, and autobiography apart and generate productive tensions between them.

The Fifth Presence: Framing the Author

With the four different plot lines and generic affiliations exerting such a strong centrifugal force, the question remains what forces operate in the text to keep it together as a novel with recognizable contours. While the textual seams provide important lines of demarcation that both connect and emphasize the separation between the four plot lines, the female body, as Robert Shelton has argued, constitutes another – albeit unstable – source of coherence in *The Female Man* (Shelton 1993: 172). The bodies of the four protagonists, as different as they may be, all share the same genetic information, the same DNA. Their physical interactions, violent as well as erotic, bridge the dividing lines between the textual worlds without dissolving them.

Most significantly, however, the figure of the fictional author in the text generates what Bruce F. Kawin has called a "fifth presence," an open frame around the four narrator-protagonists, Janet, Jeannine, Jael, and Joanna. Foregrounding a sense of healed wholeness and completion potentially created by the authorial presence of "Joanna Russ" as writer in the text, Kawin identifies structural similarities between *The Female Man* and modernist literature, most notably to Doris Lessing's *The Golden Notebook* and William Faulkner's *As I Lay Dying* (Kawin 1982). However, while it is true that there is such a presence in the text, it is not, as Kawin argues, the sum of the protagonists brought together in "wholeness of self and vision" (Kawin 1982: 314ff). It is precisely the novel's refusal to settle with such wholeness that has made it so productive and influential in science fiction and particularly in feminist thinking. Although *The Female Man* is legible as a novel through the forces that pull it together, the text does not depend on or seek closure in unfragmented female subjecthood.

This authorial presence is initiated by the usual framing devices, such as the novel's title page, its dedication, and epigraph, but it asserts its power in metafictional asides to the fictional reader, which draw attention to this important though mostly hidden relationship in *The Female Man*. This authorial voice is much more than the abstract sense of an implied author that every text shares, but the personal presence of "Joanna Russ" as author figure who directly addresses the reader and thus creates and systematically develops this figure as her pedagogical other. The authorial voice variously addresses its counterpart as "Dear Reader" (5:5), creating a figure of an ideal reader who understands and emerges transformed from the act of reading, or as "idiot reader" (8:10), anticipating a reader who imposes his/her generic expectations on the text and finds it lacking. It is on this level of author-reader interaction that Russ' humor reaches its fully subversive, indeed revolutionary power (on humor as structural element in *Female Man*, see Rosinsky 1982). Reading the novel next to William Blake's poetic vision, Catherine McClenahan argues that "like Blake, [Russ] aims to liberate, not enslave, the reader's imagination" (McClenahan 1982: 116). *The Female Man* thus invites multiple reading strategies, generating not only a strong authorial voice, but also conjuring the presence of an active reader. Though this figure of the reader has no body in the text and no voice, the act of reading shapes the movement of the novel.

In a similar vein, Rachel Blau DuPlessis (1979) has read *The Female Man* as a "teaching story" or apologue. If the author assumes the role of the teacher in the apologue, the reader becomes the admiring and attentive student, whose transformation and liberation is the author-character's implied objective: "Remember: we will all be changed. In a moment, in the twinkling of an eye, we will all be free. I swear it on my own head. I swear it on my ten fingers. We will be ourselves. Until then I am silent; I can no more. I am God's typewriter and the ribbon is typed out" (9:7). This relationship between the author and her reader rests on desire that flows in both directions in the act of reading/teaching, and Russ' novel makes this transformative desire intensely political. The book itself as physical object becomes a conduit for this desire. The mediation between the act of reading and the act of writing in the pedagogical interaction – not to be confused with crude didacticism – is absolutely crucial to *The Female Man*.

The lesbian relationship between Janet/Joanna and the young woman Laura echoes this interaction and absorbs its sexual manifestations. This reduplicated erotic relationship between the younger and the older woman ties the level of author–reader interaction and its vision of liberation to the levels of narration and character interaction, straight across its fragmented narrative and polyphony of narrators. With this redemptive intergenerational relationship, *The Female Man* participates in a recurrent motif in Joanna Russ' oeuvre, and in feminism at large, which Russ herself identified as "the rescue of the female child" (see Russ 1986: 142; Spencer 1990; Cortiel 1999). This narrative pattern pulls together fragments of traditional stories of women's bonding, empowerment, and liberation, such as the biblical story of Jael, and appropriates traditionally masculine patterns of initiation, heroism and romantic quest to create a genuinely new tale of a young woman coming to adulthood through her relation not with men but with an older woman.

In spite of the importance of the young woman's personal liberation and sexual development, the women in the novel relate to each other across the full range of human interaction, as enemies, teachers, students, storytellers, readers, friends, lovers, and many others in between. The fabric of the novel enables separation and connection, erotic love and enmity. When the four narrator-protagonists in *The Female Man*, Janet, Jeannine, Jael, and Joanna, meet, the four textual spaces, four generic affiliations, and four interdependent story lines touch each other as well. All participate in each other's stories as characters, and in so doing, they also participate in a generic universe alien to themselves. Furthermore, they represent four distinct, parallel reading perspectives creating an intricate fabric of storylines, an interwoven narrative of possibilities.

With its four protagonists, its tongue-in-cheek authorial voice, and wide-ranging linkages to the literary tradition, *The Female Man* – continuing the legacy of New Wave science fiction – remains stylistically experimental and participates in the serious playfulness of American postmodernism, pushing the limits of genre on the level of plot as well as on the level of individual sentences. In his excellent essay on Russ, "Orders of Chaos" (1985), Samuel Delany celebrates this stylistic virtuosity of Russ' writing, speaking about her work as a whole: "Russ' prose style was from the beginning rigorous, deeply felt, richly envisioned, and with all its riches controlled by not only a verbal but also by a psychological economy that marks her sentences with a pace and precision one associates with writers such as John Hawkes or Vladimir Nabokov" (Delany 1985: 98–9). Importantly, Delany links her stylistic rigor directly with her commitment to political critique: "Russ' insistence, through the years and at all resolutions, on keeping her science fiction perched so precisely at the critical edge may be that ever so important process we respond to so joyously in her work" (Delany 1985: 122). Similarly, Tom Moylan sees the novel's technique of literary montage directly linked to its antihegemonic praxis (Moylan 1986: 83).

As a nodal text, *The Female Man* participates in the major conflicts of her time, anticipating in the early 1970s developments in science fiction and feminism in the 1990s. Drawing from many different literary modes, the novel juxtaposes the science fictional and the Utopian, the lyrical, dramatic and narrative, fable, joke, and parody. It pulls together traditional science fiction, which it critiques, and New Wave experimentation, anticipating and helping to shape later developments, such as Cyberpunk. At the same time, *The Female Man* manages to combine a ruthless commitment to agency and revolutionary political action and an affirmation of the historical dialectic with distrust of clear categorical distinctions. On a level that transcends its immediate historical context of feminism and patriarchal oppression, *The Female Man* ultimately deals with the perennial question of how deep cultural change can be effected, materially, symbolically, and imaginatively. Though rooted in the political and cultural climate of the 1960s, the book remains fresh and electrifying for new readings in the early twenty-first century.

REFERENCES AND FURTHER READING

Albinsky, Nan Bowman (1988) *Women's Utopias in British and American Fiction.* London and New York: Routledge.

Bammer, Angelika (1991) *Partial Visions: Feminism and Utopianism in the 1970s.* New York and London: Routledge.

Barr, Marlene (1992) *Feminist Fabulation: Space/ Postmodern Fiction.* Iowa City: University of Iowa Press.

Bartkowski, Frances (1989) *Feminist Utopias.* Lincoln, NB and London: University of Nebraska Press.

Cortiel, Jeanne (1999) *Demand My Writing: Joanna Russ/Feminism/Science Fiction, Science Fiction Texts and Studies.* Liverpool: Liverpool University Press.

Delany, Samuel (1977) *The Jewel-Hinged Jaw: Notes on the Language of Science Fiction.* Elizabethtown, NY: Dragon Press.

Delany, Samuel R. (1985) "Orders of Chaos: The Science Fiction of Joanna Russ." In *Women Worldwalkers: New Dimensions of Science Fiction and Fantasy*, (ed.) Jane B. Weedman. Lubbock, TX: Texas Tech Press, 95–123.

—— (2004) "Joanna Russ and D. W. Griffith." *PMLA* 19.iii, 500–8.

DuPlessis, Rachel Blau (1979) "The Feminist Apologues of Lessing, Piercy, and Russ". *Frontiers* 4.i, 1–8.

Gardiner, Judith Kegan (1994) "Empathic Ways of Reading: Narcissism, Cultural Politics, and Russ' *Female Man.*" *Feminist Studies* 20.i, 87–112.

Hicks, Heather J. (1999) "Automating Feminism: The Case of Joanna Russ' *The Female Man.*" *Postmodern Culture* 9.iii, 41 pars.

Kawin, Bruce F. (1982) *The Mind of the Novel: Reflexive Fiction and the Ineffable.* Princeton: Princeton University Press.

Larbalestier, Justine (2002) *The Battle of the Sexes in Science Fiction.* Middletown, CT: Wesleyan University Press.

Law, Richard G. (1984) "Joanna Russ and the

'literature of exhaustion'." *Extrapolation* 25, 146–56.

LeFanu, Sarah (1988) *In the Chinks of the World Machine: Feminism and Science Fiction.* London: Women's Press.

McClenahan, Catherine L. (1982) "Textual Politics: The Uses of Imagination in Joanna Russ' *The Female Man.*" *Transactions of the Wisconsin Academy of Sciences, Arts and Letters* 70, 114–25.

Moylan, Tom (1986) *Demand the Impossible: Science Fiction and the Utopian Imagination.* London: Methuen.

Roberts, Robin (1993) *A New Species: Gender and Science in Science Fiction.* Urbana and Chicago: University of Illinois Press.

Rosinsky, Natalie M. (1982) "A Female Man? The 'Medusan' Humor of Joanna Russ." *Extrapolation* 23.i, 31–6.

Russ, Joanna (1986) *To Write Like a Woman: Essays in Feminism and Science Fiction.* Bloomington: Indiana University Press.

—— (1998) *What Are We Fighting For? Sex, Race, Class, and the Future of Feminism.* New York: St. Martin's Press.

Shelton, Robert (1993) "The Social Text as Body: Images of Health and Disease in Three Recent Feminist Utopias." *Literature and Medicine* 12.ii, 161–77.

Spencer, Kathleen L. (1990) "Rescuing the Female Child: The Fiction of Joanna Russ." *Science Fiction Studies* 17.ii, 167–87.

Wagner-Lawlor, Jennifer A. (2002) "The Play of Irony: Theatricality and Utopian Transformation in Contemporary Women's Speculative Fiction." *Utopian Studies* 13.i, 114–34.

Walker, Nancy A. (1990) *Feminist Alternatives: Irony and Fantasy in the Contemporary Novel by Women.* Jackson and London: University Press of Mississippi.

Wolmark, Jenny (1993) *Aliens and Others: Science Fiction, Feminism and Postmodernism.* New York and London: Harvester Wheatsheaf.

37

J.G. Ballard: *Crash*

Roger Luckhurst

The volumes of Helen's thighs pressing against my hips, her left fist buried in my shoulder, her mouth grasping at my own, the shape and moisture of her anus as I stroked it with my ring finger, were each overlaid by the inventories of a benevolent technology – the moulded binnacle of the instrument dials, the jutting carapace of the steering column shroud, the extravagant pistol grip of the handbrake. I felt the warm vinyl of the seat beside me, and then stroked the damp aisle of Helen's perineum. Her hand pressed against my right testicle. The plastic laminates around me, the colour of washed anthracite, were the same tones as her pubic hairs parted at the vestibule of her vulva. The passenger compartment enclosed us like a machine generating from our sexual act an homunculus of blood, semen and engine coolant. (Ballard 1975: 68)

How are we supposed to read a paragraph like that?

Ballard's book, published in 1973, has the rare distinction of causing not one but three separate controversies over the course of 30 years. First, as a novel, the relentless incantation of the sexual possibilities of the car crash, the perverse interpenetration of metal and flesh, listed exhaustively in precise technical prose by a character named James Ballard, prompted the first manuscript reader to report that the author was "beyond psychiatric help." The resolute neutrality of tone, assisted by the conflation of author and character, might well support a reading of *Crash* as a Swiftian satire, but it has also provoked many to assert the moral position they find so woefully lacking in the book. "A writer needs a moral viewpoint, some system of belief," Peter Nicholls complained. Without it, "Ballard is advocating a life-style quite likely to involve the sudden death of yourself or those you love" (Nicholls 1975: 28, 31). Ballard gave no help to confused readers seeking reassurance in authorial intention. In his introduction to the French edition, Ballard claimed that the book was "cautionary, a warning against that brutal, erotic and overlit realm that beckons more and more persuasively to us from the margins of the technological landscape" (Ballard 1984: 98). He then withdrew this claim, "which I have always regretted . . . *Crash* is not a cautionary tale. *Crash* is what it appears to be. It is a psychopathic hymn" (Self

1995: 348). His most illuminating statement was the least helpful in terms of managing intent: the book embodies a "terminal irony, where not even the writer knows
where he stands," he said in response to Nicholls' essay (Ballard 1976: 51). Nicholls'
literal-minded and earnest condemnation of course only gave sustenance to *Crash* as
a cult novel, the little read but notorious final statement of the experiments in stretching the boundaries of genre and taste associated with New Wave SF. The book existed
somewhere between SF's focus on the technological transformation of the human and
a long avant-garde tradition investigating the extremity where sex and death elide.
Marginality became a token of its authenticity.

After a long period of quiet, in which Ballard and even *Crash* were domesticated
by the mainstream success of his autobiographical fiction *Empire of the Sun* (1984), a
second controversy erupted, albeit in a different context. In 1991, the academic
journal *Science Fiction Studies* translated Jean Baudrillard's short essay on *Crash*. Written
in 1976, after the French edition of Ballard's novel appeared, the essay had been left
out of the shortened first English translation of Baudrillard's most famous polemic,
Simulacra and Simulation. In this book Baudrillard, a former Marxist sociologist and
key theorist of postmodernism, declared that we had reached an era where the real
world had vanished into mediation. We now inhabited a *hyper*-real world where there
could be no reference outside television, cinema, or the ceaseless circulation of media
images. The simulacra is a copy whose original is lost: simulations function "as a set
of signs dedicated exclusively to their recurrence as signs, and no longer at all to their
'real' end" (Baudrillard 1994: 21). There was no reference, no truth, no history in
hyper-reality, but there was also no alienation or despair either. Instead, we lived in
a sort of glazed, blissed-out state, enfolded in a self-sustaining mediated fiction. The
opening essay of Baudrillard's book, "The Precession of Simulacra," had become
central to many definitions of postmodernism in the American academy when published separately in the 1980s. To find that *Crash* was one of Baudrillard's few cultural examples of this new logic belatedly placed Ballard's book at the core of
postmodernism. Indeed, Scott Bukatman soon claimed that postmodernism *itself* was
"inconceivable" without Ballard (Bukatman 1993: 46). Baudrillard absolutely
accepted the novel's logic, and quickly dismissed Ballard's cautionary preface. James
Ballard's trajectory towards full acceptance of a "sexuality that is without referential-
ity and without limits," where "this mixture of body and technology is totally immanent – it is the reversion of the one into the other," clearly worked for Baudrillard as
a story of immersion in an artificial hyper-reality, the new order of being delivered by
technologically saturated environments like the motorway (Baudrillard 1991: 314).
The book's fascination with mediation – car crashes are obsessively photographed and
restaged by the "hoodlum scientist" Robert Vaughan and his fellow researchers – produces dizzying moments of recursion, where the sense of original and copy are lost.
In one scene, a test crash is watched in real time, then replayed on film: "The audience of thirty or so visitors stared at the screen, waiting for something to happen.
As we watched, our own ghostly images stood silently in the background, hands
and faces unmoving while this slow-motion collision was re-enacted. The dream-like

reversal of roles made us seem less real than the mannequins in the car" (Ballard 1975: 110). Baudrillard also delights in the refusal of any critical or ethical distance: "is it good or bad? We can't say. It is simply fascinating, without this fascination imply- ing any kind of value judgment whatsoever. And this is the miracle of *Crash*. The moral gaze . . . cannot touch it" (Baudrillard 1991: 319).

Baudrillard's amoral stance provoked a number of SF critics to respond violently in *Science Fiction Studies*. Vivian Sobchack, usually one of the more sophisticated theorists of the conjunction of SF and postmodernism, was sufficiently knocked off balance by Baudrillard's provocation to appeal to the direct experience of her own bodily pain after surgery. "The man is really dangerous," she warned, and wished on Baudrillard some real pain that he might rethink his theorization of the "techno-body . . . that is *thought* always as an *object,* and never *lived* as a *subject*" (Sobchack 1991: 329, 327). This vitriol was nothing compared with Ballard's own horrified reaction to seeing his novel sucked into the academic discourse of postmodernism and critical theory (Ballard 1991). This phobic response was perhaps motivated by suspicion of the professional or institutional intellectual and that *Crash*'s provocation was being reutilized within academic language. Ironically, Ballard's riposte only produced ever more academic discourse dedicated to trying to articulate the precise relationship between Ballard and Baudrillard (see Ruddick 1992; Butterfield 1999; Day 2000).

The third controversy began in 1996, when the film director David Cronenberg showed his necessarily sanitized version of *Crash* at the Cannes festival, to a mixed response of boos and cheers (Ballard enthusiastically supported the film and it even- tually won a Special Prize, reportedly against the wishes of the chair of judges, Francis Ford Coppola). Alexander Walker, the film critic of the conservative London *Evening Standard,* writing from Cannes, declared the film "beyond the bounds of depravity" in its advocacy of "some of the most perverted acts and theories of sexual deviance I have ever seen propagated in main-line cinema" (Walker 1996: 16). The film was demonized in even stronger terms by the right-wing *Daily Mail*. For over a year, the *Mail* campaigned to ban this "sick" film to preserve English decency – and road safety. The Conservative Minister at the Department for National Heritage also advocated a ban without seeing the film, yet the British Board of Film Certification passed the film uncut in 1997 having commissioned research to investigate whether *Crash* might indeed "deprave" its audience or produce the copycat car crashes that the *Daily Mail* darkly foretold. The decision to grant cinema licenses to show the film now devolved to local councils. The staunchly Tory Westminster City Council refused a license, quoting its own psychiatric expert that "sexually inexperienced people may look to the main characters as role models" (cited Barker *et al.* 2001: 8). Neighboring Camden Council passed the film, producing a strange boundary – a crash barrier? – that ran through London's West End. This censorship campaign was conducted in the last months of a failing Tory government and now seems like an opportunistic attempt by a loose alliance of right-wing interests to generate some panic about the "porno- graphy" likely to be unleashed under the (allegedly) more liberal regime of a Labour government.

The film produced a subsidiary academic dispute. A group working on empirical audience reception, led by Martin Barker, received a large grant for a project on *Crash,* and their research detailed how the *Mail* campaign shaped the way the film was viewed even by liberals and libertarians opposed to censorship. The polemical aspect of this project was targeted at the direction of film theory. Whilst a right-wing coalition had materially sought to constrain cultural expression, Barker argued that *Crash* had been discussed in the premier academic film journal *Screen* (in a short "debate" section of four essays in 1998) without interest in the concrete threat to civil liberties, but merely as an occasion to fine tune various critical theories. For Barker, in a rather tortured metaphor, this presented "the unedifying spectacle of abstruse clerks fiddling with their concepts ignoring Nero striking matches to set fire to their house" (Barker *et al.* 2001: 153).

These three *Crash* controversies are striking in a number of ways. Perhaps most notable is the sheer volume of discourse that *Crash* has now produced, a body of commentary that outweighs the original book itself many times over. This reflects the surprising longevity of *Crash,* for the avant-garde strategy of provocation and shock is usually punctual, extremely limited in time and effect. What shocks is either rapidly recuperated into the history of an aesthetic form, or else comes to seem a rather quaint measure of the very constraints of the era the avant-gardist had aimed to offend. Over a period of profound social change, *Crash,* which is framed by a thoroughly 1960s ethos of the liberation of sexual (and deathly) energies, has nevertheless continued to provoke outrage. The text appears to have found a magical way of rejuvenating the shock effect. It might have done this in different contexts – as novel, as postmodernist token, as film – but another striking thing is the repetitive form the argument takes, in which literalists and ironists grapple inconclusively over the icy neutrality of Ballard's prose (or Baudrillard's theory or Cronenberg's film).

It is clearly this key device, Ballard's affectless monologic style, that produces all this supplementary commentary. The text absents itself from making any conclusion about the thesis it remorselessly restates page after page, and this makes it a classic instance of what Roland Barthes termed the *"scriptible"* text – that is, a text that has to be actively completed, to be almost cowritten by the reader if any sense of meaning or closure is to be reached (Cronenberg repeated the effect in the film by resisting explanatory voice-over or the subjective point-of-view). The neutral text therefore invites moral stricture as much as providing sufficient hooks for ironists to detect. This kind of oscillation, the unsettling experience of trying to decide on the tone of the novel, is extremely difficult to convey critically. As the lists of atrocities or perversions pile up in dense paragraphs, the reader (*this* reader, anyway) is caught undecidably between detecting gravity and comedy. Here is just one sentence:

> I think of the crashes of excited schizophrenics colliding head-on into stalled laundry vans in one-way streets; of manic-depressives crushed while making pointless U-turns on motorway access roads; of luckless paranoids driving at full speed into the brick walls at the ends of known culs-de-sac; of sadistic charge nurses decapitated in inverted crashes

on complex interchanges; of lesbian supermarket manageresses burning to death in the collapsed frames of their midget cars before the stoical eyes of middle-aged firemen; of autistic children crushed in rear-end collisions, their eyes less wounded in death; of buses filled with mental defectives drowning together stoically in roadside industrial canals. (Ballard 1975: 12)

On the one hand, this incantation brilliantly conveys dogged obsession, James Ballard's breach of any remaining social constraints on his traumatized imagination. The repetitive clauses intone the catalogue with almost Biblical portent, the stately syntax jarringly at odds with the semantics. On the other hand, little details render this comic: why do *lesbian* manageresses drive *midget* cars and die in front of *middle-aged* firemen? One almost has the sense that these adjectives are scrawled in by another hand, sabotaging the gravitas by pushing the liturgy over the edge and into absurdity. Or is the whole thing intended to be comic, anyway? J.G. Ballard, the good Freudian, might concur with Freud that jokes revolve around "unacceptable" extremes of sex and violence because "the wishes and desires of men have a right to make themselves acceptable alongside of exacting and ruthless morality" (Freud 1960: 110). The novel rails against "the repressive activity of civilization" by invoking every obverse of bourgeois nicety it can command (Freud 1960: 101). Is *Crash* a serious joke? Typically, the reader is left reaching for oxymorons like this: the book is a serious joke told with enervating energy, received with excited boredom, with a smile that might also be a rictus of pain or the start of a headache. But does languishing in neat paradoxes take us any closer to finding a way of reading *Crash*?

Aidan Day has invoked the method of "close reading" for resolving the moral certainty of *Crash*; for me, it only heightens the ambiguity. Yet Day is right that critical work on *Crash* has substantially veered away from reading the close grain of the text. In fact, I would say that much of the academic writing on *Crash* has demonstrated another strange readerly effect – one that might be termed involuntary repetition or discursive mimicry. Jean Baudrillard's essay deliberately sought to elide his theory of simulation with Ballard's novel, largely abandoning analysis for a rhythmic interchange between his own vatic style and long paragraph citations from *Crash*. This was motivated by Baudrillard's sense that a world of simulation abolished the possibility of any genuine critical theory. Social theory had become science fictional, whilst Ballard's fiction was social theory: "*Crash* is *our* world: nothing in it is 'invented'" (Baudrillard 1994: 125). Baudrillard's version of "terminal irony" is what he calls the "fatal strategy," where the object "escapes the analyst everywhere" (Baudrillard 1990: 82). All the critic can do is mimic the object, which might surrender analysis, but at least does so knowingly. Elsewhere, readings inspired by various critical theories repeat the discourse of *Crash* in involuntary ways. These are commentaries written in their own private theoretical languages, monologues entirely isolated from any external reference points, often embracing specific theorists or frameworks with an obsessional, near messianic belief – exactly, of course, like the fanatical project depicted in the novel. Here, *Crash* is not read so much as reiterated in a different register.

The new technologically mediated sexualities depicted in *Crash* can lend themselves very well to explanation through psychoanalytic frameworks. *Crash* not only explores nongenital perversion but also neatly literalizes Freud's later speculations about the existence of a "death drive," a primitive human instinct that might actively wish for the quiescent state of death. Freud's ideas were controversially extended by the French psychoanalyst and poststructuralist Jacques Lacan. Lacan was a notoriously difficult theorist whose work, once translated, was extremely influential on film theory in the 1970s and literary theory in the 1980s. A substantial critical literature on the Lacanian version of *Crash* now exists. Dennis Foster, for instance, suggests that *Crash* demonstrates a failure of paternal phallic authority, unleashing generalized perversity. Foster argues that this Lacanian framework can help articulate the critique that he believes underpins *Crash*: the book "demonstrates less how perversion originates than the way it has become fully interwoven with the forms of advertising and technology that drive contemporary capitalism" (Foster 1993: 527). Other Lacanians seem intent only on transposing *Crash* into the correct psychoanalytic register. In their short entry to *Screen*'s debate on the film, Fred Botting and Scott Wilson helpfully suggest that James and Catherine Ballard's fascination with "Vaughan's dick" is "a quite literal instance of perversion – in the Lacanian sense of a turning towards the father (*père version*) that foregrounds the symptom or object *a* supporting the paternal function" (Botting and Wilson 1998: 187). Botting and Wilson's statement *is* meaningful, but only to readers who share *Screen*'s long immersion in Lacan (I have wondered if their essay might in fact be a parody of the 1970s *Screen* style, in the spirit of Ballard, in which case the joke is on me). The discourse is hermetically sealed and monologic; there is no counterargument, no sense of the substantial body of criticism that argues that *Crash* resists psychoanalytic accounts. This sense of repeating the closed, obsessional world of *Crash* is probably at its most extreme in Parveen Adams' Lacanian rumination about whether *Crash* "belongs to the register of Other jouissance, or even perverse jouissance" (Adams 1999: 61). Towards the end of this weird piece, the theory-mantra is indistinguishable from Ballardian text, even though the novel is referred to nowhere: "Where is the wound in this sequence of crashes and car wash? The answer is that it is both multiple and dispersed. There are many wounds, but the whole scene is a wound . . . The wound is the opening of the gap of the Real. Life ebbs and flows through the wound" (Adams 1999: 68–9).

If Lacan is not to taste, there are other theorized versions of *Crash* that exhibit the same insular tendency. Brian Baker processes the book through the philosophy of eroticism formulated by Georges Bataille, concluding that *Crash* "conforms to the way in which Bataille understands transgression to operate" (Baker 2000: 93). The text can be handily translated into the existential terminology of Martin Heidegger: Vaughan embodies "this *ecstasis* or running ahead, that, for Heidegger, *Dasein* is revealed in its authentic being as futural" (Grant 1998: 184). There has also been a recent surge of interest in reading *Crash* through the lens of the philosopher Gilles Deleuze, which reframes the text in radically antipsychoanalytic terms (Varga 2003). Paul Virilio, another French philosopher and vatic commentator on the apocalyptic consequences of contemporary technological milieux, and particularly the logic of the accident, will surely be along soon.

It is extremely unfair to reduce this body of work solely to a litany of discursive mimicry; these frameworks can and do provide illuminating commentary. Yet it is surely significant that *Crash* can support so many self-sustaining yet entirely contradictory readings. It might be that the studied neutrality of the text cunningly reshapes itself to whatever theoretical approach is thrown at it. But more likely, I think, is something I've not seen acknowledged in this flurry of criticism – that these theoretical interventions are in exactly the same avant-garde tradition as the text they ostensibly strive to "explain." Both Bataille and Lacan formulated their work in the 1920s and 1930s in critical dialogue with the Surrealist movement. Lacan published early work in the Surrealist journal *Minotaur* and, like Ballard, was inspired by the "paranoiac-critical method" of the painter Salvador Dali, in which the world is remade to the shape of a desire whose perversity is positively embraced and amplified. Ballard's essay on Dali was one of his central formulations of the "death of affect" thesis, leaving us to "the excitements of pain and mutilation" and the "moral freedom to pursue our own psychopathology as a game" (Ballard 1969: 25). Lacan and Ballard seem to me to make the most sense if they are understood as writing in the wake of Surrealism. Bataille, whose perversions proved too extreme even for André Breton, the leader of the Surrealists, had a revival in the 1960s when his fiction exploring ecstasy-unto-death in *The Story of the Eye* was finally published in English translation. Ballard's consistent defense of pornography echoes that of other 1960s thinkers finessing ideas of liberation and liberalization: Susan Sontag's "The Pornographic Imagination" is now printed as a postscript to legitimate the avant-garde provocation of *The Story of the Eye.*

Similarly, I think we might understand the affinity of *Crash* with many French poststructuralist thinkers by seeing them as the product of the same extraordinary era. Baudrillard turned savagely against his own commitment to Marxist critique in the mid-1970s, as did other radical philosophers like Jean-Francois Lyotard. The Situationist International, the last direct inheritors of Surrealism, dissolved themselves in 1972. Many alliances and activisms formed in the revolutionary 1960s split apart with acrimony; many wrote disordered books, obsessed with violence, a distant echo of the terroristic solutions chosen by many radical left wing groups in the early 1970s. After the failed revolutions of 1968, Julia Kristeva suggested, the distrust of the "political dimension" grew, and there was a turn inward to psychology, with the aim that the "violence" of the social contract "be conceived in the very place where it operates with the maximum intransigence, in other words, in personal and sexual identity itself" (Kristeva 1986: 194, 209). The aim of *Anti-Oedipus,* cowritten by Gilles Deleuze and Felix Guattari in 1972, followed a parallel logic: it was to smash open the subjectivity held in place by Oedipal psychopathology at the service of capitalism, and return us to that state of potentiality and possibility before the constricting Self was formed. This was a key text of the antipsychiatry movement, in England a project best represented by the practice and writing of R.D. Laing, the rogue psychiatrist who was a constant point of reference for Ballard. Needless to say, I think that there are many distinct parallels between this trajectory of "poststructuralism" and the arrival of *Crash*. The book emerged from the dissolution of an avant-garde, New Wave SF, the group brought into being by Michael Moorcock and J.G. Ballard, which adopted the language of revolutionary transformation, this time in aiming to turn a pulp genre into the vital literature of the age. It pursued its aims as a relatively cohesive group between 1964 and 1970. Ballard's explorations of the new media landscape and its attendant liberation of sexual and violent energies formed one of the core projects of the New Wave. These pieces, uncategorizable hybrids of fiction and social theory, were eventually published as *The Atrocity Exhibition,* a book I have tried at length elsewhere to place in its appropriate avant-garde contexts. The financial collapse of *New Worlds* magazine in 1970, in part the victim of a conservative attempt to curtail the countercultural press in England, produced some truly disordered, violent, and pessimistic books (Christopher Priest's *Fugue for a Darkening Island* or Michael Moorcock's *Breakfast in the Ruins* spring to mind), and acrimonious splits. Moorcock and Ballard are now "rival chroniclers" of the era of New Wave SF, rather hostile to each other, as Iain M. Sinclair shows by intercutting between their versions of events in his book-length meditation on *Crash* (Sinclair 1999: 96). *Crash,* then, is a statement of dissolution, "one of the cultural markers that signaled the end of the 60s" (Sinclair 1999: 8). It is a book that flags the end of the New Wave avant-garde by pushing its logic of violent transformation to exorbitant ends.

This goes some way towards explaining the affinity of *Crash* with so many of the critical theoretical frameworks currently let loose in the academy. I am not convinced, however, that they do much more than translate the language of one avant-garde into another. Yet because many critics treat *Crash* in absolute, Vaughan-like isolation, without reference to the SF and avant-garde contexts of the early 1970s, there is a blindness to these connections and parallels. What, then, would truly start to open a reading of *Crash,* one that would avoid the risks of either forcing a moral commitment on it, or falling into involuntary repetition or discursive mimicry? One answer is a return to history: what Vaughan wants to escape in his endless circulation of the slick, anonymous highways, what the historical avant-garde dismissed as a deadweight, and what many critical readings of *Crash* ignore because they repeat the terms of the text. I would like to see more attention paid to the cultural-historical context of the novel from both long and short temporal perspectives. Jeffrey Schnapp has placed *Crash* suggestively at the end of a two hundred year "anthropology of speed," from the mail coach to the motorcar, where acceleration produces an "expanded sense of selfhood . . . a wakeful hallucinatory or visionary state in which "terror" fuses with 'terrific beauty'" (Schnapp 1999: 22). In much tighter historical focus, *Crash* is evidently trying to make sense of a whole new technological locale: the roads of the West Way and the interchanges around London Airport (not yet named Heathrow). In 1971, Reyner Banham had written ecstatically about Los Angeles as an "autopia" where "the freeway system in its totality is now a single comprehensible place, a coherent state of mind, a complete way of life, the fourth ecology of the Angeleno" (Banham

520   *Roger Luckhurst*

1990: 213). The elevated section of the A40, the West Way, the site of James Ballard's transformative crash at the opening of the novel, had opened in 1970, and brought something of that new "ecology" to England. As Edward Platt details in his history of the A40, this arterial road had been first built in the spirit of Utopianism in the 1930s, part of a wave of optimistic belief that the motorcar would bring into being the Radiant City. By 1970, the urban theorist Henri Lefebvre lamented the end of the democratic *polis* and the rise of totalitarian *urban society,* in part dictated by the car. What strikes me rereading *Crash* now is not the danger of speed but the amount of time the characters spend in traffic jams and queues, their obsessions fuelled by fumes as they inch along in heavy traffic. Ballard's vision takes shape at the very beginning of a new era of motorway transport; in this beginning he gleans its deathly logic and envisages its apocalyptic end.

The task science fiction undertakes, as I see it, is a reflection on the potential for transformation of social and psychic existence by technology. *Crash* is therefore an exemplary science fictional text in this regard. This is a crucial recognition if we are to begin to read it properly, even after 30 years of readings. We have to exit the traffic in off-the-peg critical theories to explain *Crash,* but understand it in all the complexity of its place in science fiction history and the explosive cultural-historical milieux of England in the early 1970s.

References and Further Reading

Adams, Parveen (1999) "Cars and Scars." *New Formations* 35, 60–72.

Baker, Brian (2000) "The Resurrection of Desire: J.G. Ballard's *Crash* as Transgressive Text." *Foundation: The International Review of Science Fiction* 80 (Autumn), 84–97.

Ballard, J.G. (1969) "Salvador Dali: The Innocent as Paranoid." *New Worlds* 187, 25–31.

——(1975) *Crash.* London: Panther.

——(1976) "Two Letters." *Foundation: The International Review of Science Fiction* 10 (June), 50–2.

——(1984) "Introduction to *Crash,*" in *Re/Search No. 8/9: J.G. Ballard,* (eds) Vale and Andrea Juno. San Francisco: Re/Search Publications, 96–8.

——(1991) "A Response to the Invitation to Respond." *Science Fiction Studies* 18, 329.

Banham, Reyner (1990) *Los Angeles: The Architecture of Four Ecologies.* Harmondsworth: Penguin.

Barker, Martin, Jane Arthurs, and Ramaswami Harindranath (2001) *The Crash Controversy: Censorship Campaigns and Film Reception.* London: Wallflower Press.

Barthes, Roland (1975) *S/Z* (trans.) Richard Miller. London: Cape.

Baudrillard, Jean (1991) "Ballard's *Crash,*" (trans.) Arthur B. Evans. *Science Fiction Studies* 18, 313–20.

——(1990) *Fatal Strategies,* (trans.) Philip Beitchman and W.G.J. Nieluchowski. New York: Semiotext(e).

——(1994) *Simulacra and Simulation,* (trans.) S.F. Glaser. Ann Arbor: University of Michigan Press.

Botting, Fred and Scott Wilson (1998) "Automatic Lover." *Screen* 39, 186–92.

Bukatman, Scott (1993) *Terminal Identity: The Virtual Subject in Post-Modern Science Fiction.* Durham: Duke University Press.

Butterfield, Bradley (1999) "Ethical Value and Negative Aesthetics: Reconsidering the Baudrillard/Ballard Connection." *PMLA* 114, 64–77.

Cronenberg, David (1996) *Crash.* London: Faber.

Day, Aidan (2000) "Ballard and Baudrillard: Close Reading *Crash.*" *English* 49, 277–93.

Foster, Dennis A. (1993) "J.G. Ballard's Empire of the Senses: Perversion and Failure of Authority." *PMLA* 108, 519–32.

Freud, Sigmund (1960) "Jokes and their Relation to the Unconscious" [1905]. *Standard Edition of the Complete Psychological Works of Sigmund Freud, volume VIII*, (trans.) James Strachey. London: Hogarth Press.

Grant, Michael (1998) "Crimes of the Future." *Screen* 39, 180–5.

Kristeva, Julia (1986) "Women's Time," in *The Kristeva Reader*, (ed.) Toril Moi. Oxford: Blackwell, 187–213.

Luckhurst, Roger (1997) *"The Angle Between Two Walls": The Fiction of J.G. Ballard*. Liverpool: Liverpool University Press.

Nicholls, Peter (1975) "Jerry Cornelius at the Atrocity Exhibition: Anarchy and Entropy in *New Worlds* Science Fiction." *Foundation: The International Review of Science Fiction* 9 (November), 22–44.

Platt, Edward (2001) *Leadville: A Biography of the A40*. London: Picador.

Ruddick, Nicholas (1992) "Ballard/*Crash*/Baudrillard." *Science Fiction Studies* 19, 354–60.

Self, Will (1995) "Conversations: J.G. Ballard." *Junk Mail*. London: Bloomsbury, 329–71.

Schnapp, Jeffrey T. (1999) "Crash (Speed as Engine of Individuation)" *Modernism/Modernity* 6, 1–49.

Sinclair, Iain M. (1999) *Crash*. London: British Film Institute.

Sobchack, Vivian (1991) "Baudrillard's Obscenity." *Science Fiction Studies* 18, 327–9.

Varga, Darrell (2003) "The Deleuzian Experience of Cronenberg's *Crash* and Wenders' *The End of Violence*." In *Screening the City*, (eds) Mark Shiel and Tony Fitzmaurice. London: Verso, 262–83.

Walker, Alexander (1996) "A Movie Beyond the Bounds of Depravity." *Evening Standard* June, 3 16.

38

Margaret Atwood:
The Handmaid's Tale

Faye Hammill

Science fiction is a way of looking at things, and it's a way of looking at things that is very hard to do in any other kind of fiction. It's a creation of a different kind of metaphor.
Margaret Atwood (Tidmarsh 1992: 24)

The Handmaid's Tale (1985) remains the outstanding success of Margaret Atwood's career, and is the novel that made her an international celebrity. On first publication, it stayed in the *New York Times* best-seller lists for 23 weeks, and received the Arthur C. Clarke Award for science fiction and the Governor General's Award, Canada's highest literary honor, as well as being shortlisted for the Booker Prize. Atwood's subsequent books have achieved both extremely high sales and critical respect, and she has won dozens of literary awards, culminating with the Booker Prize in 2000. But she is still frequently identified by readers, reviewers, and websites as "the author of *The Handmaid's Tale*." The only one of her books that has been made into a film and, more recently, an opera, *The Handmaid's Tale* is also repeatedly selected for school and university literature syllabuses. In the twenty-first century, a new reading of this book is needed: one which places it in the context of Atwood's later science fiction writing. Her two latest novels are the most relevant: *The Blind Assassin* (2000) contains within it a pulp-style science fiction narrative composed by one of the characters; while *Oryx and Crake* (2003) is a dystopian novel which has been compared to *The Handmaid's Tale* by almost every reviewer. In all three books, Atwood creates "a different kind of metaphor" by constructing temporally distant societies whose apparent unfamiliarity only barely disguises their direct relevance to the novelist's present as well as to various earlier periods of human history.

The Handmaid's Tale describes a near-future USA society, the Republic of Gilead, a totalitarian theocracy governed by white, male supremacists. Birth rates have been drastically reduced by epidemics and nuclear and industrial accidents, and women with "viable ovaries" (Atwood 1986: 135) are now routinely removed from their families and compelled to act as "handmaids," or surrogate mothers for the childless wives of the ruling elite. These fertile women are referred to by a patronymic based on the name of the "Commander" with whom they currently live, as in "Offred," the novel's narrator. Appended to her narrative is "a partial transcript of the proceedings of the Twelfth Symposium on Gileadean Studies . . . which took place at the University of Denay, Nunavit, on June 25, 2195" (Atwood 1986: 281), a pseudoacademic commentary on the story of "Offred" and the history of Gildead.

Critics often compare *The Handmaid's Tale* to classic dystopias such as *Nineteen Eighty-Four, Brave New World*, or *Fahrenheit 451*. It has rather more marked similarities to John Wyndham's "Consider Her Ways," the title story in his 1961 short fiction collection, in which the narrator finds herself transformed into a giant breeding-machine, able to give birth to four babies at once, but forbidden to engage in any autonomous or intellectual activity. Atwood herself, while acknowledging the influence of writers such as Orwell and Huxley on her own work, notes that: "The majority of dystopias . . . have been written by men, and the point of view has been male" (Atwood 2003c). She identifies an alternative genealogy for *The Handmaid's Tale*, consisting of female-authored SF texts: "I was self-consciously writing in the tradition of other women that goes right back to *Herland* (1915) by Charlotte Perkins Gilman; Ursula Le Guin, . . . Joanna Russ; etc." (Tidmarsh 1992: 24). *Herland* is a Utopian romance of an all-female society; Le Guin's *The Left Hand of Darkness* (1969) creates a new model of gender based on ambisexuality; and Russ' *The Female Man* (1975) constructs three hypothetical communities on other planets, comprising two dystopian societies and an all-female Utopia. The Utopian elements in the novels cited as the precursors for *The Handmaid's Tale* should alert us to the presence of a Utopian space within Atwood's own text. Raffaela Baccolini argues that many feminist SF novels break down boundaries between Utopia and dystopia by containing both elements at once:

> Traditionally . . . utopia (in the sense of utopian hope) is maintained in dystopia only *outside* the story: it is only if we consider dystopia as a warning, that we as readers can hope to escape such a pessimistic future. This option is not granted to the protagonists of Orwell's *1984* or Huxley's *Brave New World.* . . . Conversely, Burdekin's *Swastika Night* and Atwood's *The Handmaid's Tale* – as well as other novels by Le Guin, Butler, and Piercy – allow readers and protagonists to hope by resisting closure. The ambiguous, open endings of these novels . . . maintaining the utopian impulse *within* the work. (Baccolini 2000: 18)

In fact, *Nineteen Eighty-Four* concludes not with Winston coming to love Big Brother but with a historical note on Newspeak, demonstrating that it has become a thing of the past. This provides a precedent for the "Historical Notes" section at the end of *The Handmaid's Tale*. Winston himself, however, still seems doomed, whereas Atwood permits a greater measure of optimism by leaving open the possibility that "Offred" will escape. Her narrative ends when a van comes for her. It is apparently a police van, taking her to be executed as a subversive, but it may in fact belong to the underground rescue operation. The very existence of the underground movement in

Gilead, together with the Handmaid's success in recording her story, offer hope that the ideology of the regime can be challenged, and transforms the novel itself into a site of resistance against patriarchy and totalitarianism.

Atwood commented in a 1992 interview in an SF fan magazine: "I call *The Handmaid's Tale* speculative fiction. It's not science fiction in the classic sense, that is, there is no time travel, there are no other planets, there are no things we couldn't do now" (Tidmarsh 1992: 24). There are some unfamiliar-sounding pieces of equipment mentioned in the novel, such as the "Compuchek," used to verify people's ID cards, and "Compunumbers" which relate to bank accounts, but these are all based on credit card and identity checking technology that already existed in the mid-1980s. In fact, the futuristic Republic of Gilead is modeled, to a significant extent, on past societies, as is the planet Zycron, the setting for the science fiction tale in *The Blind Assassin*. This is actually consistent with the conventions of the genre: Adam Roberts, summarizing arguments put forward by several critics, writes that "although many people think of SF as something that looks to the future, the truth is that most SF texts are more interested in the way things *have been*" (Roberts 2000: 33). Atwood herself, elaborating on her description of science fiction as "the creation of a different kind of metaphor," explains:

> None of us have actually been to Venus so going to Venus has to be a metaphorical construction. Then you try to figure out what it is conveying, this journey to Venus? . . . Then again, the distant past or future might as well be Venus. (Tidmarsh 1992: 24)

Atwood's conception of time travel, then, does not involve a tardis but an imaginative reconstruction of an unfamiliar society, which may exist in the past or future, or – as in *The Handmaid's Tale* – both at once.

The novel can be related to a range of distinct historical contexts. Most obviously Gilead replicates aspects of the patriarchal social order described in the Pentateuch. One of the epigraphs to the novel tells of the childless Rachel, who said to her husband Jacob: "Behold my maid Bilhah, go in unto her; and she shall bear upon my knees, that I may also have children by her" (Genesis 30: 3). This is the biblical precedent for the role of the Handmaids in Gilead, who are both impregnated and delivered whilst lying between the legs of the infertile wife to whom they have been assigned. Interestingly, the legal provision for a childless wife to use her maid as a surrogate also exists in the Babylonian law system, proclaimed by King Hammurabi. This law is cited by the narrator of the science fiction story in *The Blind Assassin* as one of the inspirations for his imagined city of Sakiel-Norn on Planet Zycron. His lover assumes that the rigidly hierarchical, brutally disciplined society of Sakiel-Norn is a political allegory or dystopia, but he claims: "The culture I describe is based on ancient Mesopotamia. It's in the Code of Hammurabi, the laws of the Hittites and so forth" (Atwood 2000: 17).

These historical precedents may seem too distant to give a genuinely terrifying sense that the events described by Atwood have happened before, and may happen again, but both novels also relate to far more recent history. One of the epigraphs to

The Blind Assassin, taken from Polish writer Ryszard Kapuściński's description of the horrific events at the Persian city of Kerman (now in Iran) in 1794, alerts us to an additional historical model for Sakiel-Norn:

> Imagine the monarch Agha Mohammed Khan, who orders the entire population of the city of Kerman murdered or blinded – no exceptions. His praetorians set energetically to work. They line up the inhabitants, slice off the heads of the adults, gouge out the eyes of the children. . . . Later, processions of blinded children leave the city . . . singing songs about the extermination of the citizens of Kerman.

The children in Atwood's embedded SF story have also lost their sight, through hours of close work embroidering the beautiful carpets for which Sakiel-Norn is famous, as Kerman still is today. The violence of Middle Eastern history is echoed in the cruel treatment of these children, and of the sacrificial virgins of Sakiel-Norn, whose tongues are cut out to prevent protest against their fate. Modern Iran provides a reference point for *The Handmaid's Tale*: one of the historians of Gilead has published a book entitled "Iran and Gilead: Two Late-Twentieth-Century Mono-theocracies" (Atwood 1986: 282). *The Handmaid's Tale* appeared just a few years after the imposition of martial law in Iran (1978) and Ayatollah Khomeini's overthrow of the Shah and establishment of a fundamentalist Islamic republic (1979). The parallels with the Christian fundamentalist state of Gildead are clear. The compulsory identical robes and winged head-coverings worn by women are suggestive of purdah, a practice which developed in Persia and flourished in ancient Babylon, and is adhered to by many modern Muslim communities.

Barbara Rigney, commenting on the Handmaids' red gowns, argues that these women are "personifications of a religious sacrifice, temple prostitutes" (Rigney 1987: 117). This reading of the handmaids connects them to the sacrificial virgins in *The Blind Assassin*. The virgins, in their turn, relate to the lives of Iris and Laura, who are both sacrificed by men in the interests of power and wealth. In order to restore his failing business fortunes, Iris' father marries her off to Richard Griffen, an aspiring politician and successful industrialist. Laura too is sacrificed to Richard: he forces her to sleep with him and she becomes pregnant, which precipitates her suicide. Iris' personal memoir, narrating these events, is interspersed with installments of "The Blind Assassin," a modernist love story supposedly written by her sister Laura, but eventually revealed to be Iris' own work. This novel-within-a-novel itself incorporates the extended SF fantasy told by the male protagonist to his lover. It conforms accurately and self-consciously to the conventions of 1930s pulp SF, yet also comments directly on the interwar Canadian high society recalled by Iris, providing exaggerated reflections of its hierarchies, corruption, and political plotting. Iris witnesses the sleaze and corruption of 1930s and 1940s Ottawa and Toronto at close range, but like "Offred," she endures rather than protesting openly, and thus is vulnerable to accusations of complicity. Yet both Iris and "Offred" defy social dictates by engaging in illicit affairs, and subsequently offer a more effective form of protest through recording their stories.

As well as relating to Hebrew and Middle Eastern theocracies, Gilead has many affinities with the ideologies and behaviors of seventeenth-century Puritans. This context is immediately revealed in the dedication of *The Handmaid's Tale* to Perry Miller, influential historian of the American Puritans, and to Atwood's ancestor Mary Webster, who survived being hung for witchcraft by her Puritan community, and is commemorated in the poem "Half-Hanged Mary" in Atwood's 1995 *Morning in the Burned House* collection. The term "handmaid" comes from the Gospel account of the Annunciation, when Mary accepts her calling as the mother of God by saying "Behold the handmaid of the Lord" (Luke 1: 38), and this phrase was adopted by the Founding Fathers to refer to all women. Many aspects of the Gilead regime are distortions of Puritan teaching, particularly the emphasis on patience, acceptance of one's lot, repression of personal desires in the interests of the common good, continual thanksgiving to God, examination of the conscience, and obedience to authority. These ideals are set out in the writings of the New England Puritans, such as John Winthrop and William Bradford; and are used by the ruling elite in Atwood's novel to maintain their own position and regulate the behavior of the people. Gilead also reintroduces the Puritan practices associated with childbirth (Evans 1994), while the Women's Salvagings, public hangings to punish crimes against the social order, such as adultery, are suggestive of the Salem witch-hunts. The Salvagings – like the impregnation "ceremony," the virtual imprisonment of Handmaids, the destruction of all reading material, and the uniform robes – are part of Gilead's strategy to repress female sexuality, which is perceived as a subversive force.

The attempt to contain female desire and limit women's autonomy is also reminiscent of Victorian thinking, extreme versions of which are discernible in the rules and conventions of Gilead. The ideology of separate spheres is rigidly enforced, with women confined entirely to domestic, reproductive, and maternal functions, and denied any participation in decision-making or public life. Gileadean women cannot own property, which was also the situation of wives in Britain and Canada up until the late nineteenth century; while divorce – which was severely stigmatized in both countries during the Victorian period – is outlawed in Gilead. Women are, however, protected and honored for their role as mothers of the race: "Offred" remarks that handmaids are viewed as "sacred vessels, ambulatory chalices" (Atwood 1986: 128). They are also indoctrinated to perceive protection as more important than freedom – in a key passage, "Offred" remembers jogging in "the time before":

> I never ran at night; and in the daytime, only beside well-frequented roads.
>   Women were not protected then.
>   I remember the rules, rules that were never spelled out but that every woman knew: don't open your door to a stranger, even if he says he is the police. . . . If anyone whistles, don't turn to look. Don't go into a laundromat, by yourself, at night.
>   Now . . . no man shouts obscenities at us, speaks to us, touches us. No one whistles.
>   There is more than one kind of freedom, said Aunt Lydia. Freedom to and freedom from. In the days of anarchy, it was freedom to. Now you are being given freedom from. (Atwood 1986: 24)

The ideas voiced by the Aunts, the female control agency in *The Handmaid's Tale*, read at times like a grotesque parody of the 1870s social purity movement, whose primary aims were the elimination of prostitution and of the sexual harassment and abuse of girls and women. The movement demonstrated "an interesting fusion of feminist impulses within an old fashioned purity agenda" (Jeffreys 1997: 195). Towards the end of the century, some of the new generation of social purity feminists began to inveigh against the abuse of wives by husbands in unwanted sexual intercourse, but this line of thinking was taken to repressive extremes by certain commentators, who "even questioned the necessity of sexual intercourse except for the purpose of creating children" (Jeffreys 1997: 197–8). This last is precisely the approach adopted in Gilead. "Offred" describes the impregnation "ceremony" as follows:

> What's going on . . . is not exciting. It has nothing to do with passion or love or romance or any of those other notions we used to titillate ourselves with. It has nothing to with sexual desire . . . Arousal and orgasm are no longer thought necessary; they would be a symptom of frivolity . . . This is serious business. (Atwood 1986: 89)

The vocabulary "Offred" uses here is a sarcastic parroting of the official discourses of her society. She does not herself believe that love and desire are merely "notions we used to titillate ourselves with," as her devotion to the memory of her husband, and later her passionate response to her lover Nick, clearly demonstrate.

The Republic of Gilead also relates to one further past society: the interwar and postwar years. Aspects of the ideology of the return to the home, and the associated policies and discourses discouraging married women from remaining in paid employment during peacetime, are clearly present. Immediately after the Gilead takeover, all women are fired from their jobs, and the novel's narrator is transformed into a frustrated housewife, whose attempts to submit to the new patriarchal code result in nervous and depressive behavior:

> There were marches, of course, a lot of women and some men. . . . I didn't go on any of the marches. Luke said it would be futile and I had to think about them, my family, him and her. I did think about my family. I started doing more housework, more baking. I tried not to cry at mealtimes. By this time I'd started to cry, without warning, and to sit beside the bedroom window, staring out. (Atwood 1986: 168–9)

Already, the narrator is beginning to conform to the "new" patterns of thinking: her actions are guided by her husband's opinion, she herself asserts that she "had to think about them," and she therefore commits herself more fully to a domestic role. The dismissal of all women employees in *The Handmaid's Tale* is clearly an extreme version of the marriage bar which operated in the first half of the twentieth century. In Britain and the Commonwealth (as well as in numerous other countries) female employees in the public sector were legally required to retire on marriage, and many private companies operated a similar policy, particularly during the period of high unemployment caused by the Depression. The legislation was repealed in Britain in 1946 and in Canada in 1955, but the associated ideology remained influential. The marriage bar was still effectively operational in the 1960s Canada of Atwood's first novel, *The Edible Woman* (1969). The protagonist, Marian, finds that her employer and her fiancé expect her to leave her job when she marries and concentrate on home and family.

The futuristic society of *The Handmaid's Tale* is, then, based on the conventions of various pasts, ranging from the ancient to the recent. But Gilead also represents the logical extrapolation of some of the tendencies of Atwood's present: the 1980s. The influential critic Robert Scholes, in his book *Structural Fabulation*, includes science fiction in a category of "fabulation" which he defines as any "fiction that offers us a world clearly and radically discontinuous from the one we know, yet returns to confront that known world in some cognitive way" (Scholes 1975: 2). *The Handmaid's Tale* confronts its own present in many ways, engaging in particular with concerns about environmental pollution, the increasing surveillance and policing exercised through new technology, the rise of the religious right in the USA, and the failure of the American Equal Rights Amendment legislation which was vigorously campaigned for in the 1970s and early 1980s but has still not been constitutionally ratified. The ideology of separate spheres re-emerged in 1980s America, promoted by the New Right and by fundamentalist Christians. These groups are represented in the novel by the Commander's wife, formerly a gospel television show personality but now trapped and silenced by the very beliefs she used to promote. "Offred" says of her: "She stays in her home, but it doesn't seem to agree with her. How furious she must be, now that she's been taken at her word" (Atwood 1986: 44). As Coral Ann Howells points out, in the voices of "Offred," her rebellious friend Moira, and her subversive shopping partner "Ofglen," Atwood "reinvent[s] those discordant women's voices which ran counter to patriarchal Puritan voices in a fiction which is presented as a historical reconstruction of a future already inscribed in the policies of the New Right" (Howells 1996: 130).

The transcribed lecture at the end of the novel reveals that the handmaid's story has been reassembled, edited, and renamed by male academic historians, and their inaccurate and sexist critique of it might remind us of the partial and distorting nature of our own efforts to reread past societies such as the Puritans or the Victorians. This section of the book also constitutes, as Ann Cranny-Francis has argued:

> A reflexive mechanism designed to obviate the escapist response often associated with the dystopia. Even if readers do finish the tale feeling relieved that they do not live in such a state, the academic rhetoric of the final section of the text demands a response from readers which necessitates . . . a rereading and recognition of the political significance of [Atwood's] text. (Cranny-Francis 1990: 141)

The lecture explains the plummeting birth rates and increasing incidence of genetic deformity in "the immediate pre-Gilead period" (i.e., the 1980s) through reference to AIDS, nuclear accidents, leakages from chemical and biological warfare stockpiles and toxic-waste disposal sites, and the uncontrolled use of insecticides and herbicides (Atwood 1986: 286), demonstrating that the policies adopted in Gilead result directly from global problems existing at the time Atwood was writing the novel. She adopts the technique of defamiliarization: the academics explain our own era to us from the perspective of historical distance, referring to "the serial polygamy common in the pre-Gilead period" and arguing that "racist fears provided some of the emotional fuel that allowed the Gilead takeover to succeed as well as it did" (Atwood 1986: 287). This is a more subtle version of the staple SF technique of the alien perspective on humans, used and manipulated by Atwood in some of her short fiction (such as "Cold-Blooded" and "Homelanding" in her 1992 *Good Bones* collection). The apparently extreme and regressive policies of Gilead frequently prove, on closer examination, to be rooted in the social reality of Atwood's present. For example, the method of naming handmaids is equivalent to the Russian and Greek tradition of deriving a woman's names by combining "of" with her father's name, and subsequently her husband's, or even her son's. This practice is still current in some Greek and Russian families, and is in any case merely a more marked version of the prevalent Western convention of assigning children the surname of their father, and wives that of their husband.

In the lecture that frames the tale of "Offred," the historian of Gilead refers to "a sterility-causing virus that was developed by secret pre-Gilead gene-splicing experiments with mumps, and which was intended for insertion into the supply of caviar used by top officials in Moscow. (The experiment was abandoned . . . because the virus was considered too uncontrollable and therefore too dangerous by many, although some wished to sprinkle it over India)" (Atwood 1986: 290–1). This anticipates the plot of *Oryx and Crake*, in which top geneticist Crake, convinced that overpopulation is the cause of all global problems, manufactures a pill that promises unlimited libido and protection against disease, but actually renders users sterile. He eventually takes more drastic measures, inserting into the pill a virus that eliminates virtually the entire human species.

References to gene-splicing have different effects in the two novels. The 1980s saw a series of significant developments in genetic engineering, including the earliest patents of genetically altered life forms for use as consumer products, and the first field tests of genetically engineered plants. The novelty of this technology at the time when *The Handmaid's Tale* appeared meant that casual references to it created a futuristic feel. Almost twenty years later, the vocabulary of genomics has become familiar through the intensifying public debate about the benefits and dangers of newly available technologies. With the cloning of Dolly the sheep in 1997, the completion of the human genome sequencing project in 2003, and the development of stem cell research, collective media-fuelled fears and fantasies have expanded from the creation of monstrous plants or deadly viruses to the manufacture of genetically modified animals and humans. *Oryx and Crake* both exploits and analyzes these fears, and new technology is a much more significant feature than it was in *The Handmaid's Tale*. Crake's colleagues are working on futuristic-sounding inventions, such as wallpaper that changes color to match your mood; headless chicken "growth units" which produce twenty breasts every two weeks (Atwood 2003a: 202); and a range of sophisticated medical and cosmetic treatments. Yet all these inventions are actually based on ongoing research projects, and the basic premise of the novel is the potentially catastrophic results of existing scientific capabilities. The apparently futuristic society turns out to be terrifyingly similar to the present.

In the novel, scientists have produced various transgenic creatures, including wolvogs, intended for security work, which look like particularly friendly domesticated dogs but are, as Crake explains, "bred to deceive . . . Reach out to pat them, they'll take your hand off. There's a large pit-bull component" (Atwood 2003a: 205). There are also pigoons, designed "to grow an assortment of foolproof human-tissue organs in a transgenic knockout pig host" (Atwood 2003a: 22). Just after the novel reached completion, these creatures became a reality: in October 2002, Italian scientists reported that they had bred a strain of pig containing human genes in their hearts, livers, and kidneys, with the goal of producing organs for transplants. Atwood's protagonist, Jimmy, is afraid that the human DNA in the pigoons means that "if they'd had fingers they'd have ruled the world" (Atwood 2003a: 267). He is also concerned about the wolvogs: "What if they get out? Go on the rampage? Start breeding, then the population spirals out of control – like those big green rabbits?" (Atwood 2003a: 205). The reference to the green rabbits again grounds the novel in current science, acting as a subtle reminder of the fluorescent green rabbit developed in 2000 by French researchers, who used genes borrowed from a jellyfish to make the rabbit glow under special lighting. At the same time, Jimmy's imagined scenarios about the wolvogs or pigoons taking over the world correspond exactly to classic SF plots. This demonstrates what Adam Roberts has described as "the symbolic purchase of SF on contemporary living" (Roberts 2000: 35). Roberts cites several examples, including the popular tendency to describe GM products as "Frankenstein foods," and the way in which discussion about NASA or the International Space Station automatically "inhabits the idiom of SF" (Roberts 2000: 35, 31).

Media debate about genetic engineering is marked by rhetoric relating to the usurpation of the functions of God, and this, too, finds a clear expression in the novel. Crake creates a breed of genetically modified humans, extremely beautiful, immune to disease, and perfectly adjusted to their environment. They grow to maturity in a very few years and are preprogrammed to drop dead painlessly at thirty. The Crakers, or Children of Crake, can be related to non-technological human societies. In an essay on the writing of *Oryx and Crake*, Atwood refers to the inspiration provided by visiting "open-sided cave complexes where Aboriginal people had lived continuously, in harmony with their environment, for tens of thousands of years" (Atwood 2003b). The Crakers are also the literary descendents of a whole tradition of deliberately "created" new species in science fiction and fantasy writing, from Frankenstein's monster to the Uruk Hai strain of Orc bred by Saruman in *The Lord of the Rings*. Atwood's beautiful, peace-loving Crakers seem to be the opposite of the loathsome, murderous Uruk Hai, yet they are in some ways just as frightening, not only because of their difference (Jimmy suspects that other people would view them as savage and inhuman) but because, like Tolkein's cross-bred species, they are completely controlled by the will of their creator. They believe implicitly in everything that Crake says because he has adapted their "neural complexes" so that all the "destructive features" of the human brain are removed, and thus they have no concept of deceit (Atwood 2003a: 305). Even Jimmy, lonely survivor of Crake's biological warfare, used to life in a luxurious hi-tech compound and now living in a semi-animal state, unwashed, dressed in a sheet, and scavenging for food, feels that he has become his friend's creature: "'Crake!' he whimpers. 'Why am I on this earth? How come I'm alone? Where's my Bride of Frankenstein?'" (Atwood 2003a: 169).

The creation of new species also takes place, both literally and metaphorically, in *The Handmaid's Tale,* but the emphasis is different. The transformation of Americans citizens into Gileadeans takes place not through the altering of neural networks but through brainwashing. The narrator remembers the day when she is dismissed from her job:

> I could see out into the corridor, and there were two men standing there, in uniforms, with machine guns. This was too theatrical to be true, yet there they were: sudden apparitions, like Martians. There was a dreamlike quality to them; they were too vivid, too at odds with their surroundings. . . .
>
> It's outrageous, one woman said, but without belief. What was it about this that made us feel we deserved it? (Atwood 1986: 166)

Like Jimmy, "Offred" perceives what is happening to her world in the terms of science fiction. She sees the States being taken over by what appears to her an alien species, and dimly understands that they will try to turn her into one of them. New "species" also emerge through mutation, but whereas this is achieved through deliberate experiment in *Oryx and Crake,* it is accidental in *The Handmaid's Tale:*

> What will Ofwarren give birth to? A baby, as we all hope? Or something else, an Unbaby, with a pinhead or a snout like a dog's, or two bodies, or a hole in its heart or no arms, or webbed hands and feet? There's no telling. They could tell once, with machines, but that is now outlawed. . . .
>
> The chances are one in four . . . The air got too full, once, of chemicals, rays, radiation, the water swarmed with toxic molecules, all of that takes years to clean up. (Atwood 1986: 106)

In Gilead, not only is assisted conception replaced by surrogacy, but the regime has also outlawed the fetus-screening methods that permit a degree of selectivity in reproduction and control over the physical characteristics of the next generation. In *Oryx and Crake,* by contrast, reproductive technology has become alarmingly sophisticated, and Crake confidently predicts that "totally chosen babies that would incorporate any feature, physical or mental or spiritual, that the buyer might wish to select" will shortly be available (Atwood 2003a: 304). The reproductive scenarios in both novels are based on very real dangers present in Atwood's society, yet there is just enough extremity in her representations (babies with two bodies; babies whose spirituality has been chosen) to render them horrific and introduce an element of satire into her texts.

The satiric dimension is explicitly signaled in one of the epigraphs to *The Handmaid's Tale*, taken from Jonathan Swift's "A Modest Proposal" (1729): "But as to myself, having been wearied out for many years with offering vain, idle, visionary thoughts, and at length utterly despairing of success, I fortunately fell upon this proposal . . .". Swift's suggestion that the Irish should avoid starvation by eating their own children was, of course, intended to draw attention to the cruelty of English absentee landlords who were allowing the Irish peasants to starve. Atwood's choice of epigraph suggests that the society depicted in *The Handmaid's Tale* is not an attempted portrayal of a probable future, but rather a theoretical extrapolation of the dangerous tendencies of her age. *Oryx and Crake* is also prefaced with an epigraph from Swift, this time from *Gulliver's Travels:* "I could perhaps like others have astonished you with strange improbable tales; but I rather chose to relate plain matter of fact in the simplest manner and style; because my principal design was to inform you, and not to amuse you."

In *Gulliver's Travels*, what initially seem to be "strange improbable tales" turn out to be simply exaggerations or extrapolations of current trends. The strange lands that Gulliver visits are none other than Britain seen through a number of intensifying or distorting lenses. Similarly, the apparently futuristic, fantastic worlds depicted in Atwood's SF-inspired texts, *The Handmaid's Tale*, *The Blind Assassin,* and *Oryx and Crake*, gradually reveal themselves as distorted versions of past and present human cultures. As Atwood said of *The Handmaid's Tale*: "I wanted people to believe that it was possible and, indeed, it is possible because in different ways we've already done it before" (Tidmarsh 1992: 24).

REFERENCES AND FURTHER READING

Atwood, Margaret (1969) *The Edible Woman.* Toronto: Seal Books.

——(1986) *The Handmaid's Tale.* Toronto and New York: McClelland and Stewart-Bantam.

——(1992) *Conversations.* (ed.) Earl G. Ingersoll. London: Virago.

——(2000) *The Blind Assassin.* London: Bloomsbury.

——(2003a) *Oryx and Crake.* London: Bloomsbury.

——(2003b) Writing *Oryx and Crake.* http://www.randomhouse.com/features/atwood/essay.html

——(2003c) "Orwell and Me." *The Guardian*, 16 June. http://books.guardian.co.uk/departments/generalfiction/story/0,6000,978474,00.html

Baccolini, Raffaella (2000) "Gender and Genre in the Feminist Critical Dystopias of Katharine Burdekin, Margaret Atwood, and Octavia Butler." In *Future Females, The Next Generation: New Voices and Velocities in Feminist Science Fiction Criticism,* (ed.) Marleen S. Barr. Lanham, MD and Oxford: Rowman and Littlefield.

Bloom, Harold (ed.) (2000) *Margaret Atwood: Modern Critical Views.* Philadelphia: Chelsea House.

Cranny-Francis, Ann (1990) *Feminist Fiction: Feminist Uses of Generic Fiction.* Cambridge: Polity Press.

Evans, Mark (1994) "Versions of History: *The Handmaid's Tale* and its Dedicatees." In *Margaret Atwood: Writing and Subjectivity,* (ed.) Colin Nicholson. London: Macmillan; New York: St Martin's Press, 177–88.

Howells, Coral Ann (1996) *Macmillan Modern Novelists: Margaret Atwood.* Basingstoke: Macmillan.

——(2002) "Margaret Atwood's Discourse of Nation and National Identity in the 1990s." In *The Rhetoric of Canadian Writing,* (ed.) Conny Steenman-Marcusse. Amsterdam: Rodopi, 199–216.

Jeffreys, Sheila (1997) *The Spinster and Her Enemies.* London: Spinifex Press.

Nischik, Reingard (ed.) (2000) *Margaret Atwood: Works and Impact.* Columbia, SC: Camden House.

Rao, Eleonora (1993) *Strategies for Identity: The Fiction of Margaret Atwood.* New York: Peter Lang.

Rigney, Barbara Hill (1987) *Macmillan Women Writers: Margaret Atwood.* Basingstoke: Macmillan.

Roberts, Adam (2000) *Science Fiction.* London: Routledge.

Scholes, Robert (1975) *Structural Fabulation: An Essay on Fiction of the Future.* Bloomington: Indiana University Press.

Tidmarsh, Andrew (1992) "Dinosaurs, Comics, Conan – and Metaphysical Romance. Andrew Tidmarsh talks to Margaret Atwood." *Interzone* 65, 23–5.

39

William Gibson: *Neuromancer*

Andrew M. Butler

Why *Neuromancer*?

There is a moment in an introduction to *Burning Chrome* (1986), a collection of
William Gibson's short stories, when Bruce Sterling notes that "SF has not been much
fun of late. All forms of pop culture go through doldrums; they catch cold when
society sneezes. If SF in the late Seventies was confused, self-involved, and stale, it
was scarcely a cause for wonder" (Sterling 1986: 9). Five years later, in the usually
distinctly nongenre annual collection of the English Association, *Essays & Studies*, John
Huntington notes that "In *Neuromancer* we are seeing evidence of a new, perhaps the
final, stage in the trajectory of SF" (Huntington 1991: 71). It needs to be said that
reports of SF's death are greatly exaggerated – the period Sterling discusses was a significant one in terms of feminist SF – and that this had happened before. As Roger
Luckhurst argues: "The history of SF is a history of ambivalent deaths. The many
movements within the genre – the New Wave, feminist SF, Cyberpunk – are marked
as both transcendent death-as-births, finally demolishing the "ghetto" walls, and as
degenerescent birth-as-deaths, perverting the specificity of the genre" (Luckhurst
1994: 43). The ambivalent death, indeed the death instinct as described by Sigmund
Freud and Jacques Lacan, will taken as the guiding metaphor for the structure and
theme of *Neuromancer*.

Gibson was born in the USA in 1948, but moved to Toronto in 1968 and, after
some time in Europe, settled in Vancouver, a Canadian city that can look south to the
USA and west across the Pacific to Japan, an economic power house which
increasingly dominated international capitalism through the 1980s, especially in the
realm of electronics. At SF conventions Gibson met first John Shirley and then
Sterling. The three of them appeared on a panel at the October 1982 ArmadilloCon
in Austin, Texas named "Behind the Mirrorshades: A Look at Punk SF," and, according to Lewis Shiner, in the conversations about "Len Deighton, Nelson Algren,
Burroughs and Ballard . . . rock and roll, MTV, Japan, fashion, drugs, and politics"

(Shiner 1992: 21) there was the sense of a new movement. Editor Terry Carr approached Gibson for his revival of the Ace Specials.

Gibson drew on "Johnny Mnemonic," which introduces Molly Millions, a leather-clad, mirror contact-lensed woman with knives for fingernails, and Mnemonic, a man with rentable computer memory in his brain. In "Burning Chrome" he focuses on console cowboys – computer hackers – who are planning one last caper before retirement, and a virtual realm known as the matrix. The story also includes a fence called the Finn. This is the world which became *Neuromancer.*

Plot Summary

Neuromancer begins with its protagonist, Henry Dorsett Case, as good as dead. In his previous life he was a console cowboy, and had skimmed some of the proceeds of a deal off for himself. His employer punished him by ensuring that his nervous system could no longer link to the matrix. He is rescued from his dejected state in Chiba City, Japan, by Armitage, who is willing reverse this in return for taking part in a caper – ensuring Case's loyalty by sewing sacs of poison into his veins. Case is to help steal a ROM tape of the computerized personality of his mentor McCoy Pauley aka Dixie Flatliner. He will then reprogram an artificial intelligence, Wintermute.

Case is not sure who he can trust, since Armitage has not told him the full story. Armitage used to be Corto, perhaps the sole survivor of a botched secret operation during a brief, half-forgotten war. Case's former associate, Julius Deane, murders Case's girlfriend, Linda Lee. Peter Riviera, a pervert with the ability to induce hallucinations in others, has designs on Molly, who in turn wants to avenge Mnemonic's murder. To make things worse, Armitage's boss appears to be Wintermute.

Postmodernism

Istvan Csicsery-Ronay claims that Cyberpunk is "the apotheosis of postmodernism" (Csicsery-Ronay 1991: 193) and Fredric Jameson argues that Cyberpunk is "the supreme *literary* expression if not of postmodernism, then of late capitalism itself" (Jameson 1991: 419). Randy Schroeder notes that Gibson is "a writer within the historical *periodization* of postmodernism" and is "a writer with postmodern *sensibilities*" who offers "a fictive attempt to *think* the bewildering space of postmodernism" (Schroeder 1994: 155). Jameson, whose article "Postmodernism, or the cultural logic of late capitalism," like *Neuromancer,* was published in 1984, was attempting to form a new cognitive map for this world-space, and outlined an aesthetics of postmodernism: the triumph of commodity fetishism and surface over depth, the simulacrum, the waning of affect, the death of the subject and subjectivity, nostalgia, pastiche, and a new sense of sublime exhilaration.

Neuromancer revels in commodity fetishism, embracing life-styles and auras attached to manufactured and marketed objects, with the many technological toys and brand names that populate the book – various Braun equipment, Ono-Sendai and Hosaka decks for entering cyberspace, Molly's body augmentations, the prosthetic arm of Ratz the Chiba City barman, cosmetic surgery and DNA manipulation available to all who can afford. The brand names are supplemented by a bewildering number of neologisms: deck, ice, joeboy, and so forth. The prose, with its constant yoking of a natural vehicle to a technological tenor (and vice versa), follows the postmodern tendency to elevate style over content.

Take the opening sentence: "The sky above the port was the color of television, tuned to a dead channel" (Gibson 1984: 1984: 3). The unexpectedness of the juxtaposition blinds us to the realization that it is not clear what color is being described; more recently televisions default to a vivid blue color, but in the early 1980s it would be more likely to be some kind of dark gray. For Gibson to have begun, "The sky was gray" would be more downbeat, but also dull. The fact that it is a "dead channel" enables Gibson to set up the image of death, which haunts the novel. The port location nods towards other dangerous *noir*ish transition zones, perhaps San Francisco's docks from *The Maltese Falcon* (1941), *Casablanca* (1942), and those that open William S. Burroughs' *Nova Express* (1964) – but a port is also the socket in a computer which may be jacked into, connecting it to a network or other equipment.

The novel is full of simulacra and models of reality: in the matrix as digital representation of information, in Wintermute's masquerading as the Finn or Julius Deane, and in the scenes that could be told from Molly's point of view but are in fact being witnessed by Case who is piggybacking her senses via an implanted chip of "simstim." Jean Baudrillard describes four levels of the simulacra: (a) the reflection of a basic reality, (b) the perversion of a basic reality, (c) hiding the lack of a basic reality, and (d) the pure simulacrum (Baudrillard 1983: 11). According to Cynthia Davidson, Case and Lee can be linked "to stage one; Molly and Riviera, to stage two; Armitage/Corto, to stage three; Neuromancer, Wintermute, and Riviera's projections to stage four" (Davidson 1996: 191). The images of Case and Lee are straight-forward reflections, whereas Molly and Riviera reality in their augmentations disrupt "expectations generated by their initial appearances" (Davidson 1996: 194) thus misrepresenting reality. Riviera's ability to cause hallucinations in others, apparently unexplained in the novel, anticipates Neo's "real world" powers outside of a computer simulation in *The Matrix Revolutions* (2003). Wintermute's programming of Armitage built onto a foundation of the earlier brainwashing of Corto's military training – so Corto is unlikely to be a real identity. Wintermute and Neuromancer, the eponymous AI, create their own realities within the matrix: simulacra.

The waning of affect, which is to say the end of emotion, empathy and sincerity, and death of the individual as an identifiable subject can be observed in the mention of "Armitage's flatness and lack of feeling" (Gibson 1984: 1984: 203) and his breakdown. It is certainly impossible to work out where Armitage begins and ends as a person, given his programming. Wintermute in turn has been programmed Marie-

France Tessier, the matriarch of the Tessier-Ashpool conglomerate which owns it: "I'm under compulsion myself," it admits (Gibson 1984: 206). Molly, who in her previous job as a kind of high-tech whore, had her memory compartmentalized, and suffers from occasional leakage of identity. "[T]hat's just the way I'm wired" (Gibson 1984: 218), she says at one point, justifying her behavior.

At the same time, for all its trappings of high technology, *Neuromancer* looks back to the pulp crime fiction Raymond Chandler, Dashiell Hammett, and James M. Cain. In their novels and the films based on them, the male protagonist is entirely clear what is happening and often act deliberately to cause chaos to see if that will bring clarity. He is resistant to the demands of authority figures, from either side or the law. At the start of the novel he is often alone, down on his luck, and he may well be no better off by the end. There is usually a woman, a femme fatale, whom he both desires and fears, because of and despite her duplicity. The corrupt and homicidal Tessier-Ashpools resemble a number of troublesome families investigated by hard-boiled private eyes, most notably the Sternwoods in Chandler's *The Big Sleep* (1939), a novel whose ending – "On the way downtown I stopped at a bar and had a couple of double Scotches. They didn't do me any good. All they did was make me think of Silver Wig, and I never saw her again" – seems echoed in *Neuromancer*'s exit for Molly.

The Big Sleep was filmed in 1944 by Howard Hawks, a director acknowledged by Gibson as an influence, especially through the homages of John Carpenter such as *Escape from New York* (1981). Hawks' films broadly split into two groups, one featuring largely all-male groups facing forces of nature and occasionally destabilized by token women – for example *Only Angels Have Wings* (1939) – and the other featuring strong women in battles of wits with weak men, such as *Bringing Up Baby* (1939), with his gangster film *Scarface* (1933) straddling both types. In Hawks' films "The undercurrent of homosexuality . . . is never crystallized though . . . it runs very close to the surface" (Wollen 1972: 88), and I will return to this point in the next section.

Neuromancer perhaps also echoes the film *DOA* (1949, remade in 1988) with a protagonist who has a limited time left to live – as Case does – and perhaps the baroque description of the Tessier-Ashpool mansion echoes the enigmatic description (and visuals) at the start of *L'Année Dernière á Marienbad*. Science fiction is also an influence, of course, with an acknowledgement of Alfred Bester's *The Stars My Destination* (1956) in the line "Stars. Destiny" (Gibson 1984: 268) of the Coda. Molly shares its protagonist Gully Foyle's motivation of revenge and his synaesthesia, both narratives feature sudden leaps between locations, and both plots have to be inferred in retrospect. This structure should fill the reader with a sense of exhilaration – although it risks alienating the reader.

Neuromancer reflects the postindustrial capitalist world which is crucial to postmodernism. Now trans- or multinational corporations cut across national boundaries, rendering the state superfluous: "Power . . . meant corporate power. The zaibatsus, the multinationals that shaped the course of human history, had transcended old barriers. Viewed as organisms, they had assumed a kind of immortality" (Gibson 1984: 203). At the same time, the corporation at the center of the novel is Tessier-Ashpool, very much a family firm, owing as much to the Medicis and Borgias as to contemporary conglomerates; there is a superficial resemblance to some of the family-run companies in Philip K. Dick's novels, such as Rosen Associates in *Do Androids Dream of Electric Sheep?* and Runciter Associates in *Ubik*, especially with a leading board member being temporarily frozen in half life. The homogenization of culture and erasure of difference engendered by international capitalism is noted when Case is staying in yet another Hilton and he looks out the window, "almost expecting to see Tokyo Bay" (Gibson 1984: 88), as he had in the one in Chiba City.

Gender and Sexuality

Some of the debate about *Neuromancer* has centered on perceptions of its attitudes towards gender. The traditional position of women in SF — to the extent that there were any — was to be rescued, but Molly was a woman who was able to look after herself and literally on top when it came to sex. Joan Gordon suggests that "cyberpunk is covert feminist science fiction," and notes Molly approvingly, whilst admitting: "To some extent she's a man in women's clothing . . . the most facile and least thoughtful representation of the liberated woman" (Gordon 1991: 196, 198). It might be facile, but at least she can operate as a kind of role model of the active and capable woman. Samuel Delany claims there was a debt to Jael in Joanna Russ' *The Female Man* (1975) (Delany 1988: 8) in the characterization of Molly, and there is also a hint of Alyx from *Picnic on Paradise* (1968). The former is a book from the precise period Sterling overlooks — although of course Gibson is not Sterling.

Lance Olsen argues that "with Molly, Gibson has ironically imposed stereotypically male traits upon a female character. He has also devalued those traits by implying that they are part of the decadent material world that must be transcended by attaining cyberspace, an area of being to which only males have access in *Neuromancer*" (Olsen 1992: 283). Olsen's reading is based upon a mind/body split which is transferred onto the matrix/meat world split. Molly's modified body represents the meat that console cowboys wish to leave behind when entering a postsex-marked realm. The online world seems an exclusively male one — the Artificial Intelligences, for all their digital origins, end up being referred to as men, and whilst Maelcum the Rasta, Dixie, and other male characters enter the matrix, Molly does not.

Case's masculinity is bolstered through language: he sees himself as jacking into the matrix, a sexualized penetration, and indeed entering into Molly. But it is Molly who enters Case; Amanda Fernbach claims that: "In fact, in the terminology of the electronics industry, Case is the 'feminine' connector and the computer that electronically penetrates his skull for a direct cortical connection is the 'masculine' connector. It is Case who is a sensitive surface, a vulnerable receiver into which information is deposited" (Fernbach 2000: 247). Nicola Nixon argues that the tough-guy masculinity of console cowboys, with (albeit bantering) references to "it'd be like tellin' the boys in the T-A boardroom the size of your shoes and how long your dick is"

(Gibson 1984: 167), returns to earlier mythologizing of the frontier male. Just as the explorers of the frontier are masculine, so the virgin territory is feminine: the word "matrix" is from the Latin for womb. Whilst Molly leaves him – in part because he is not Mnemonic – by the time of *Mona Lisa Overdrive* (1988) she is beginning to behave maternally, especially to her Japanese charge. Case's matrix avatar finds a ready-made family in a version of Linda and a child who resembles Neuromancer and in the real world he settles down with a "girl who called herself Michael" (Gibson 1984: 270), fathering four children by *Mona Lisa Overdrive.*

Given the very 1980s crisis of Case's masculinity, the clearly active sexual role of Molly, the predominance of homo-social relationships, and the eventual unifying of two AIs, both gendered as male, there is potential to queer the narrative. Armitage, with his "special Forces earring" (Gibson 1984: 45) has been seen as "A stock figure of both '80s gay porn, military recruiting posters, and 'straight' bodybuilding culture" (Curtain 1997: 133–4). Julius Deane, Wintermute's mouthpiece for much of what Case learns about Armitage and killer of Linda, is an old queen, picking at crystallized ginger, crying out to be played by Sydney Greenstreet. The (queer old) Deane "triggers what by this point we shouldn't hesitate to call homosexual panic, anger, and hatred in Case" (Curtain 1997: 134), causing Case to kill him.

The Death Instinct

Underlying *Neuromancer* is what Peter Brooks describes as "Freud's Masterplot," in which the narrative reaches towards an inevitable end: cellular, animal, human, and narrative life are all structured according to a (metaphorical?) death drive, instinct, or wish. Theorizing about the death instinct derives from Freud's *Beyond the Pleasure Principle* (1922), where he ranges from clinical to personal experiences, delves into narratives such as Faust, makes comparisons with biology both at the level of the cell and the organism, and anticipates objections by admitting he does not quite believe all this himself. It is a cunning performance designed to convince us of its veracity.

Freud begins by questioning why trauma victims, from the trenches or disasters, relive their experiences so often. Why is there this compulsion to repeat? He compares this to the behavior of a baby with an absentee mother, who repeats this absence through the deliberate loss of a favorite toy and the joyful triumph of its return. Freud sees in all these cases a deliberate compulsion towards displeasure, which cannot be accounted for by the economics of a psyche which has a pleasure principle held in check by the reality principle. There is a force, a kind of death principle, *thanatos* rather than *eros*. Freud goes as far as to say, "*The goal of all life is death*" (Freud 1922: 47), which is to say the *proper* death at the *appropriate* time. There is both an impetus towards this death and a wish to return to an earlier state; there is "*a tendency innate in living organic matter impelling it toward the reinstatement of an earlier condition*" (Freud 1922: 44). The interaction of these two forces are actually survival traits, so the individual paradoxically confronts death in order to persist. When Freud writes "When certain fish undertake arduous journeys at spawning time, in order to deposit the spawn in certain definite waters far removed from their usual habitats . . . they are only seeking the earlier home of their kind" (Freud 1922: 45) this finds its echo in Wintermute's "You know salmon? Kinda fish? These fish, they're *compelled* to swim upstream . . . I'm under compulsion myself" (Gibson 1984: 206). Wintermute wants to return to an earlier state, perhaps prior to the prohibitions placed upon it by Tessier-Ashpool.

In examining the human characters, we see examples of the death instinct at work. Molly wishes to transcend death, as Glenn Grant argues, "metaphorically by *killing* it, by destroying certain ninja assassins, the incarnations of death" (Grant 1990: 42). Armitage/Corto is "obsessively re-running the Screaming Fist operation until he gets it *right*, dying as he 'should' have – with the other 'heroes'" (Grant 1990: 46). He "demands" the right death, and works through permutations until he can achieve it – although whether his actual death actually achieves this is open to question.

It is not just the humans who want to die: Dixie Flatliner, no stranger to death as his nickname suggests, wants to die, or at least to be erased: "This scam of yours, when it's over, you erase this goddamn thing" (Gibson 1984: 106). This is curious given the tendencies of console cowboys to want to leave "the prison of [the] flesh" (Gibson 1984: 6). Dixie has escaped the meat, having already gained the reputation of being the "Lazarus of cyberspace" (Gibson 1984: 78) through his previous flatlines. He may have "been granted a victory over biological death" (Siivonen 1996: 234) but he now seeks total and absolute death.

One death is not enough: it has to be the correct death. Like many of Freud's ideas, the notion of the death instinct was later modified by Jacques Lacan's structural linguistic take on psychoanalysis. The death instinct is discussed in *The Ethics of Psychoanalysis*, in part through a reading of the Marquis de Sade:

> Nature wants atrocities and magnitude in crimes; the more our destructions are of this type, the more they will be agreeable to it. To be of even greater service to nature, one should seek to prevent the regeneration of the body that we bury. Murder only takes the first life of the individual whom we strike down; we should also seek to take his second life, if we are to be even more useful to nature. For nature wants annihilation; it is beyond our capacity to achieve the scale of destruction it desires. (Lacan 1992: 211).

Lacan traces a horrific period "between two deaths" when the subject is dead and yet not-dead, and seeks for total death. This half-life, this undead state, is examined in relation to the Greek tragedy *Antigone* but it relates to narratives involving zombies, vampires, ghosts, demons, and so forth. It is difficult to keep strictly distinct narrative type, but there are the deaths without proper rituals (Antigone, perhaps Dixie?) which need to be supplied; and there are the inappropriate rituals which need to be countered (*The Evil Dead* [1982], *RoboCop* [1987]).

Case offers *Neuromancer*'s clearest example of a character being between two deaths, having been disconnected from cyberspace: "For Case, to be severed from cyberspace is to be dead. And dead to the world is what Case is when the novel begins, since his ability to jack has been destroyed by a disgruntled former employer" (Mead 1991: 354). Case is one of the undead, his sleeping in a "coffin" invoking images of vampires – although the coffin here is a Japanese hotel "room." His actions seem calculated to get him killed: "Ninsei wore him down until the street itself came to seem the externalization of some death wish, some secret poison he hadn't known he carried" (Gibson 1984: 7). Armitage immediately recognizes that he is "trying to con the street into killing you when you're not looking" (Gibson 1984: 28) and Dixie twice tells him not to do something unless he had "a morbid fear" of death (Gibson 1984: 115, 132). But it is too soon for him to die, it is not the proper time, the appropriate rites have not yet been spoken.

Case is himself a bearer of rites, and the Rasta Aerol suspects he "might serve as a tool of Final Days" (Gibson 1984: 110), to mark a shift between the current spiritual death of the world (Babylon) and apocalypse proper. This being Cyberpunk, the rites are computer codes, and on a number of occasions the novel explicitly links linguistic rites with the undead or computers. One of the Turing Police, Michèle, observes that "For thousands of years men dreamed of pacts with demons" (Gibson 1984: 163), with AIs now being the demons, and Neuromancer says "To call up a demon you must learn its name" (Gibson 1984: 243). It seems to be Case's role, in seeking his own death, to bring death to others – to the three people he has killed before the start of the novel, to Dixie and Julius, and apparently to Wintermute and Neuromancer.

Case's death instinct seems to intersect with Wintermute's: "if Wintermute's backing the whole show, it's paying us to burn it. It's burning itself" (Gibson 1984: 131). Wintermute also brings death to people, including Linda, Armitage, and the Turing Police, not to mention those inadvertently killed during the run to retrieve the Dixie construct. Wintermute perhaps inadvertently allies himself with the demonic by his admittance that "I am that which knoweth not the word" which would allow him to "cease" (Gibson 1984: 173) – but also the Word of God. The other AI is also connected with death; Neuromancer says "I call up the dead . . . I *am* the dead, and their land" (Gibson 1984: 244) and, as Paul Alkon (1992: 83) has noted, quotes the Auden poem "As I Walked Out One Evening": "The lane to the land of the dead" (Gibson 1984: 243; Auden 1986: 228). But because of the use of the word, Neuromancer "will die soon, in one sense. As [will] Wintermute" (Gibson 1984: 259).

The two AIs do not die except as individual subjects – they merge as two parts of a whole, the personality of Neuromancer and the decision-making of Wintermute. This moment of sublimity seems to be beyond our comprehension because, whilst the new AI is now in contact (facing a threat from?) AIs in the region of Centauri, this encounter does not feature in *Neuromancer*'s two sequels, *Count Zero* (1986) and *Mona Lisa Overdrive* (1988). Instead it appears that the AI has fragmented and operates as a series of individual "spirits," *loas*, as Gibson appropriates voodoo cultural beliefs. The death instinct is still at work, and the second death has yet to come. In the matrix, Case hallucinates his own critique: "Really, my artiste, you amaze me. The lengths you will go to in order to accomplish your own destruction" (Gibson 1984: 234). Case remains an artiste, in both the actual and virtual realm, although seems to resign from actively seeking death by reinscribing himself in the social order through marriage. He has presumably spoken ritual words.

Conclusion

The parallels between *Neuromancer* and Freud and Lacan's notion of the death instinct are striking, but at the same time I do not want to insist that the instinct really exists, nor that Gibson is consciously modeling his novel on it. It could be argued that Freud is seeking – as he does in dream analysis – to narrativize, and that he is imposing a masterplot of fictional narratives onto life. Brooks argues that the death instinct underlies narrative and "The desire of the text (the desire of reading) is . . . desire for the end, but desire for the end reached only through the at least minimally complicated detour, the intentional deviance, in tension, which is the plot of narrative" (Brooks 1984: 104). Huntington, citing Brooks, notes that "The double dynamic of narrative, simultaneously progressing and retarding, and its relations to the death instinct and to art are all formulated by *Neuromancer*" (Huntington 1991: 66–7).

But that end of narrative, that supposed second death, is not the end. What happens to the AIs, to Molly, to Case? The Matrix trilogy, which repackaged Gibson for cinema-goers, demonstrates a similar tension: *The Matrix* (1999) left many unanswered questions which *The Matrix Reloaded* (2003) and *The Matrix Revolutions* (2003) did little to resolve. In the latter the second deaths of Trinity and Neo mark a sense of closure, but the possibility of resurrection remains. The mummy, the vampire, the spirits of the dead, the slasher may have been returned to the dead through the proper rituals, but the wrong rites may yet recur. Posters for *The Matrix Revolutions* declared that "Everything that has a beginning has an end," but as Brooks notes, "the idea of beginning presupposes the end [but] the end is a time before the beginning . . . Any final authority claimed by narrative plots, whether of origin or end, is illusory" (Brooks 1984: 108).

This is perhaps why, long after Cyberpunk has been declared dead, it can be resurrected. The frequently prophezied end of SF has also failed to come to pass. Roger Luckhurst argues that "SF moves from crisis to crisis, but it is not clear that such crises come from outside to threaten a once stable and coherent entity. SF is *produced* from crisis, from its intense self-reflexive anxiety over its status as literature" (Luckhurst 1994: 47). Luckhurst argues for a move away from the crisis model, to channel creative energies into something more productive than the compulsion to repeat crises – but such crises throw up new Gibsons, and give us new stimulus, rather than allowing us to fall, like perhaps Case has, into a stable marriage of different elements.

References and Further Reading

Alkon, Paul (1992) "Deus ex machina in William Gibson's Cyberpunk Trilogy." In *Fiction 2000: Cyberpunk and the Future of Narrative*, (eds.) George Slusser and Tom Shippey. Athens, GA: University of Georgia Press, 75–87.

Auden, W.H. (1986) *The English Auden: Poems, Essays and Dramatic Writings, 1927–1939.* London and Boston: Faber & Faber.

Baudrillard, Jean (1983) *Simulations.* (trans.) Paul Foss *et al.* New York: Semiotext(e).

Brooks, Peter (1984) *Reading for the Plot: Design and Intention in Narrative.* Oxford: Oxford University Press.

Butler, Andrew M. (2000) *Cyberpunk.* Harpenden: Pocket Essentials.

Csicsery-Ronay Jr, Istvan (1991) "Cyberpunk and Neuromanticism." In *Storming the Reality Studio: A Casebook of Cyberpunk and Postmodern Science Fiction*, (ed.) Larry McCaffery. Durham, NC and London: Duke University Press, 182–93.

Curtain, Tyler (1997) "The 'Sinister Fruitiness' of Machines: *Neuromancer*, Internet Sexuality and the Turing Test," in *Novel Gazing: Queer Readings in Fiction*, (ed.) Eve Kosofsky Sedgwick. Durham, NC: Duke University Press, 128–148.

Davidson, Cynthia (1996) "Riviera's Golem, Haraway's Cyborg: Reading *Neuromancer* as Baudrillard's Simulation of Crisis." *Science Fiction Studies* 23, 188–98.

Delany, Samuel R. (1988) 'Some *real* mothers: An interview with Samuel Delany" [by Takayuki Tatsumi]. *Science Fiction Eye* 1, 5–11.

Fernbach, Amanda (2000) "The Fetishization of Masculinity in Science Fiction: The Cyborg and the Console Cowboy." *Science Fiction Studies* 27, 234–55.

Freud, Sigmund (1922) *Beyond the Pleasure Principle.* (trans.) C.J.M. Hubback. London and Vienna: International Psycho-Analytical Press.

Gibson, William (1984) *Neuromancer.* New York: Ace.

Gordon, Joan (1991) "Yin and Yang Duke it Out." In *Storming the Reality Studio: A Casebook of Postmodern Science Fiction*, (ed.) Larry McCaffery. Durham, NC and London: Duke University Press, 196–202.

Grant, Glenn (1990) "Transcendence Through Detournement in William Gibson's *Neuromancer.*" *Science Fiction Studies* 17, 41–9.

Huntington, John (1991) "Newness, *Neuromancer*, and the End of Narrative." In *Fictional Space*, (ed.) Tom Shippey. Oxford: Blackwell, 59–75.

Jameson, Fredric (1991) *Postmodernism or, The Cultural Logic of Late Capitalism.* London and New York: Verso.

Lacan, Jacques (1992) *The Ethics of Psychoanalysis 1959–1960: The Seminars of Jacques Lacan VII.* London: Routledge.

Luckhurst, Roger (1994) "The Many Deaths of Science Fiction: A Polemic." *Science Fiction Studies* 21, 35–50.

Mead, David G. (1991) "Technological Transfiguration in William Gibson's Sprawl Novels: *Neuromancer, Count Zero*, and *Mona Lisa Overdrive.*" *Extrapolation* 32, 350–60.

Nixon, Nicola (1992) "Cyberpunk: Preparing the Ground for Revolution or Keeping the Boys Satisfied?" *Science Fiction Studies* 19, 219–35.

Olsen, Lance (1992) "Cyberpunk and the Crisis of Postmodernity." In *Fiction 2000: Cyberpunk and the Future of Narrative*, (ed.) George Slusser and Tom Shippey. Athens, GA: University of Georgia Press, 142–53.

Schroeder, Randy (1994) "Determinacy, Indeterminacy, and the Romantic in William Gibson." *Science Fiction Studies* 21, 151–63.

Shiner, Lewis (1992) "Inside the Movement: Past, Present, and Future." In *Fiction 2000: Cyberpunk and the Future of Narrative*, (eds) George Slusser and Tom Shippey. Athens, GA: University of Georgia Press, 17–25.

Siivonen, Timo (1996) "Cyborgs and Generic Oxymorons: The Body and Technology in William Gibson's Cyberspace Trilogy." *Science Fiction Studies* 23, 227–44.

Sterling, Bruce (1986) "Introduction." *Burning Chrome*, (ed.) William Gibson. London: Gollancz, 9–13.

Wollen, Pete (1972) *Signs and Meaning in the Cinema.* London: Secker and Warburg/British Film Institute.

40

Kim Stanley Robinson: Mars Trilogy

Carol Franko

Although Victor Frankenstein, Mary Shelley's doomed or just chronically irresponsible modern Prometheus, gets talkative in the last days of his life, he never debated his Project with others when he was in the midst of creation. In contrast, the scientist-heroes in Kim Stanley Robinson's Martian future history succeed in their projects at least partly because they are forced to debate and revise them. Unlike Shelley's gothically oppressed Victor, the growth and development – the formation – of Robinson's scientists is not frozen at the moment they make spectacular mistakes. The Promethean challenge of terraforming Mars is achieved not without difficulty or opposition. The personal and political naivety of Sax Russell, terraformer extraordinaire, is broken and reformed into a wise innocence by the end of the trilogy. In the opening volume, in a heated argument with Ann Clayborne, purist-geologist (or areologist) and nay-sayer supreme, Sax makes an inspiring speech supporting terraforming, punctuated by his declarations that "Science is creation," is "more" than studying the mineral history of Mars (Robinson 1993: 159), and that terraforming is even a philosophical imperative: thus Sax's Stapledonian "We are the consciousness of the universe, and our job is to spread that around, to go look at things, to live everywhere we can" (Robinson 1993: 159–60). Sax wins this public debate with Ann, since soon after it his terraforming projects are approved by the political and corporate institutions that are running things. Yet Ann's reply to Sax's exalted rhetoric (his "We can transform Mars and build it like you would build a cathedral") is just as eloquent (see Ann's " 'We are not lords of the universe' " [Robinson 1993: 160]). Sax becomes Ann's most attentive listener, and he spends the next hundred years and more trying to understand and to partially accommodate her commitment to a red – non-terraformed – Mars. At the same time he does not forsake the powers that allow for terraforming, and indeed he becomes committed to using such awesome powers, both for "areoforming" human beings and for building a free Mars and a "decent civilization." "And why not?" thinks Sax (Robinson 1996: 52–3).

Robinson delivers a dynamic view of Utopia and a positive view of science as a powerful tool necessary for the creation of a decent human civilization. Although

Robinson conceived of the project as a "single novel" and still thinks of it as one story that became a "triple-decker in the old style" (Seed 1996: 76), it has of course been published in three award-winning volumes – *Red Mars* (1993 Nebula Award), *Green Mars* (1994 Hugo Award), and *Blue Mars* (1997 Hugo Award). This essay will refer to the whole of Robinson's triple-decker Mars novel as his "Mars trilogy."

Robinson's Mars trilogy is a novelistic achievement, both in revitalizing the myth of science and scientist as hero, and in making Utopia seem plausible and desirable: attractively dynamic, humane, joyful, open-ended, and "open-sided" – culturally diverse. Robinson humanizes the heroic, naturalizes, or renders empirical, the supernatural, and historicizes the ahistorical – especially the classical, outside-of-history view of Utopia. Yet there are indeed heroes in the trilogy, however humbled they are by collisions with Mars, history, one another, and death; these heroes verge on the metaphysical in their reflections; and Robinson's dynamic vision of "Utopia" still leaves an unknown space-time in the future – a space that characters speculate might be the true golden age, at last. If these remarks seem gushingly positive, I would partly agree, since I do not assent to all of the trilogy's ideology. Still, the trilogy's "genuinely comic vision" (Dynes 2001: 151) promoted through Robinson's striking "narrative sociability" (Jameson 2001: 219) calls for readers to engage enthusiastically, if non-unanimously, with Robinson's Martian "Modern Utopia."

Utopia emerges as a path for societies and individuals to travel, and humans are at least partly free to choose and to build a human reality where, as Ann Clayborne muses in the conclusion of *Blue Mars*, "Nowhere on the world were people killing each other, nowhere were they desperate for shelter or food, nowhere were they scared for their kids" (Robinson 1996: 609). Ann's reflections are akin to those of Kevin at the end of *Pacific Edge* (1990), Robinson's Utopian novel set in California. Edward James has noted that Robinson's Mars trilogy does not fit as obviously into the Utopian tradition as *Pacific Edge* does (James 1996: 72). And yet, H.G. Wells' *A Modern Utopia*, which Robinson was reading as he wrote *Pacific Edge* (Franko 1994: 209), is also conceptually close to his Mars trilogy.

Robinson maintains that Utopias need to be rescued from their representations "as isolated, static islands in history or in physical space" and redefined as "a road of history" (Seed 1996: 77). This reimagined, historicized Utopia is similar to H.G. Wells' declaration: "The Modern Utopia must be not static but kinetic, must shape not as a permanent state but as a hopeful stage leading to a long ascent of stages" (Wells 1923: 5). Robinson praises Wells' Utopian writings in which, says Robinson, Wells consistently declares *"let's get our priorities straight: first let's talk about social justice and equal rights, and then after that we'll talk about transcendence and metaphysical and ontological problems"* (Foote 1994a: 55; italics in original). Robinson's Mars trilogy shares these priorities. For Robinson, the achievement of social justice requires the replacement of capitalism, a system that he describes as a version of feudalism (Foote 1994a: 57).

Robinson's and Wells' modern Utopias, in addition to historicizing Utopia, also share an emphasis on Utopia as steeped in contingency and change, as a social reality where individualities are fostered in a world state, and as the place/time where humans learn to use the powers of science to build a good life for everyone. The never very tactful narrator of *A Modern Utopia* declares that early-twentieth-century people are just "too stupid" to use the resources and the models of efficient construction that science offers them – resources and models that would allow humanity to realize the plain fact that "There is more than enough for everyone alive" (Wells 1923: 102).

Sax Russell, who shares the view that destructive behavior is best defined as stupidity, is transformed by his role in the environmental and political crises on Mars, and in turn becomes a key builder of the developing Mars Utopia. In "Areophany," a section in *Blue Mars* narrated from his angle of vision, Sax is out roaming Mars sixty years after the failed first revolution on Mars – the "unrest of 2061" and only months after the successful second revolution. Realizations come together: "There was no one to hide from; no one hunting for him. He was a free man on a free planet" (Robinson 1996: 52). Although Sax acknowledges that the current cooperation of various Mars groups may be only temporary, he is absorbed by speculations on how their technological powers could continue to improve the quality of life for everyone:

> Godlike powers, as Michel called them, though it was not necessary to exaggerate them or confuse the issue – they were powers in the material world, real but constrained by reality. . . . [Yet, it] looked to Sax as if these powers could – if rightly applied – make a decent human civilization after all. After all the many centuries of trying. And why not? . . . Why not pitch the whole enterprise at the highest level possible? (Robinson 1996: 52–3)

From the god-like terraforming of a planet to the god-like achievement of a close-enough golden age, Sax's ambitions are not modest. Luckily for him and for the other planners and builders in the story, the operational myth here is not "Hubris clobbered by nemesis" (Aldiss 1986: 26).

Building a Town and a World

Science-fictional mythmaking involving Mars was inspired by the mistranslation of Giovanni Schiaparelli's 1877 observation of *canali*, or channels, on Mars as "canals" – a word that suggests intelligent manipulation of the landscape (Stableford 1993: 777; Baxter 1996: 5–6). American astronomer Percival Lowell seized on the canal idea and in *Mars* (1895) built "an image of a cool, arid, dying world" (Baxter 1996: 6) – an image that led SF writers like H.G. Wells (*War of the Worlds* 1898) and Edgar Rice Burroughs (the Barsoom series, beginning with *A Princess of Mars* 1912) to imagine variations of "Mars as a more ancient and advanced version of earth" (Westfahl 2000: 8). Wells' cold, survival-driven Martians inspired a host of Martian invasion stories, while Burroughs' romantic, lush Mars continues to haunt SF writers even after Mars stories (such as Arthur C. Clarke's *Sands of Mars* 1952) respond realistically to new data about Mars' harsh environment (Stableford 1993: 778–9; Westfahl 2000:

3). Terraforming, argues Gary Westfahl, is a SF trope that reveals the desire of Kim Stanley Robinson and other current writers "to build the [lush] planet that Burroughs once envisioned" (Westfahl 2000: 13). Meanwhile, two recurring themes in SF treating Mars is that of Mars as a locale for building Utopia (James 1996: 64–75) and of Martian societies gaining independence from Earth (Baxter 1996: 8–9).

In Robinson's Martian scenario, the Ares ship leaves Earth's orbit on December 21, 2026 and begins its nine-month journey to Mars. On board are the First Hundred, supposedly, although actually the First Hundred and One, because of stowaway Desmond/Coyote. This group of high-achieving scientists, engineers, astronauts, cosmonauts, politicians associated with scientific institutes, one psychiatrist, and one stowaway, arrive on Mars, build a scientific station that is also a town, explore Mars, and become increasingly divided – not just over the terraforming issue but also over their degree of loyalty to the powers that sent them to Mars. Several of the most engaging characters become engrossed in the possibility of developing both a terraformed Mars and "areo-formed" humans: a new Martian society. Others strengthen their ties to the transnational corporate interests that are truly financing and that fully intend to control developments on Mars. The divisions among the First Hundred help lead to the disastrous first Martian revolution; the synergy of their scientific talents and political and social passions also helps bring about the successful second and third revolutions.

Robinson has described the scope of his epic with understatement, thus: "The novel says that people might go [to Mars] for what are essentially false or bad motives [like nationalistic ambitions or the exploitations of mineral resources]. . . . but then the good motives can eventually overrun them" (Seed 1996: 76, 77). The science-fictional novum of the longevity treatment (discovered on Mars by scientists of the First Hundred and leading to human life-spans of over 200 years) allows this future history and a collective biography of about a dozen of the First Hundred to coincide. It is the planners and builders of terraformed Mars and areo-formed humanity who make up this almost communal protagonist.

Robinson's narration is third-person, occasionally intrusive, and selectively omniscient, with multiple viewpoint characters. We get an inside view of history, since we share the thoughts and the angles of vision of several of the characters who build a human world on inhuman Mars – members of the First Hundred like the disillusioned idealist Frank Chalmers, the genial American astronaut John Boone, the Russian engineer Nadia Cherneshevsky, and the stereotypical lab scientist Sax Russell. Because the point-of-view characters are always reflecting on the on-going social and scientific situation on Mars, the inside views they provide are also "outside," or social. Seven of the First Hundred are distinguished by being the angle of vision in one or more of the long, named sections of the trilogy: Maya Toitovna, Michel Duval, and Ann Clayborne as well the already mentioned Frank, John, Nadia, and Sax. The remaining viewpoint characters in long sections are Nirgal and Zo – both descendents of the First Hundred – and Art Randolph, a Terran who moves to Mars and becomes intimately involved with its evolving society. Although several key members of the

First Hundred are never – or only very briefly – viewpoint characters, the narrative focus on the First Hundred makes them the representative humans in this Utopian epic.

The First Hundred include professional stereotypes, national moments, and personality types or temperaments, as in Michel Duval's semantic rectangles. They represent how people are determined and how they are free. They are types – some of whom also emerge as individuals. As they age (those that survive revolution and other violent death), they become legends to younger characters and family for one another. Their dead live on in electronic recordings (journals) and in the problematic polyphonic memories of the living.

Two characters that die early but still shape the developing Utopia are John Boone and Arkady Bogdanov. In the section "Falling Into History" told from John's perspective, John travels around Mars, gathering insights from various groups sympathetic to a "new" Mars that synthesizes the best of the old, and making enemies among those who are profiting from fitting Mars into the transnational capitalism of Earth. In a key episode, Arkady explains to John his radical socialist analysis of how things are developing on Mars, and we get a sketch of one of Robinson's ongoing preoccupations: how to combine sophisticated technology with "primitive" and ecologically sustainable lifestyles.

The First Hundred are the first to experience on Mars a Utopia that is both ancient and brand new. As Arkady explains it to John, the First Hundred have been living in the latest version of scientific research station as prehistoric Utopia: separated from a money economy, free of ownership, free to "concentrate . . . attention, on the real work, which means everything that is done to stay alive, or make things, or satisfy one's curiosity, or play. That is Utopia, John, especially for primitives and scientists, which is to say everybody" (Robinson 1993: 309).

In his "Introduction" to *Future Primitive: The New Ecotopias* (1994), Robinson urges SF to imagine futures radically different from the ubiquitous "great industrial city-machines" (Robinson 1994: 9) – new futures that "cobble together aspects of the postmodern and the Paleolithic" and where "sophisticated new technologies [are] combined with habits saved or reinvented from our deep past, with the notion that prehistoric cultures were critical in making us what we are, and knew things about our relationship to the world that we should not forget" (Robinson 1994: 11).

In *Red Mars* the question becomes: how can such a life be made available to everyone, not just to the lucky scientists who in any case are now being asked to pay up? Arkady believes that only mass insurrection and revolution will make this postmodern Paleolithic life an option on Mars; to the sorrow of his friends he lives out these beliefs. John does not want revolution and will not live long enough to see its "evolution" on Mars. Meanwhile the biologist Hiroko Ai and her colleagues from the First Hundred are off living the postmodern Paleolithic Utopia, hidden from the powers that now want the scientists to re-enter the money economy. After the disastrous first revolution, other First Hundred-ers, notably Nadia and Maya, will orchestrate alternatives, with the help of science. Such efforts will eventually win out (well enough and for as long as people work to keep them) over the gravitational pull of the non-Utopian past: "Earth: their curse, their original sin" (Robinson 1994: 438).

Beyond Original Sin

Frederic Jameson writes: "the attempt repeatedly to begin history over again . . . is the very subject of [Robinson's Mars trilogy]" (Jameson 2001: 227). History must be restarted so it can veer onto the Utopian path. But the inertia of the old, non-Utopian history constrains the First Hundred (our representative humans) and tends to keep them in line with old paradigms (Robinson 1993: 46). Although ultimately the trilogy is *not* about forsaking "old" Earth for "new" Mars, the characters have to leave Earth and its history behind before they can (in the developments around the second and third revolutions) help Earth with its "universal catastrophe rescue operation" toward a restarted history (Robinson 1996: 63).

"We understand the world through paradigms," remarks a character in *Green Mars* (Robinson 1994: 66). The Judeo-Christian tradition and particularly Christianity emerges as a paradigm that blocks the Mars – "A new creature waiting to be born, genetically engineered for sure" that John Boone and others are fashioning (Robinson 1993: 312). The conflict between a scientific versus a Judeo-Christian world view is reminiscent of another Utopian novel by H.G. Wells: *Men Like Gods*, in which a narrow-minded priest cannot see the value in a beautiful, peaceful, and scientifically adventurous parallel world because the inhabitants do not feel the need for divine salvation. Robinson's Mars trilogy deals with the anxiety of influence of the Judeo-Christian tradition and makes cognitive room for a new syncretic paradigm in various ways that include satire, naturalizing supernatural elements, and revising Christian paradigms with others borrowed from different traditions in Islam.

The First Hundred get into conflicts over religion during the initial voyage to Mars. Filtered through Russian Maya's perspective on the odd preoccupations of Americans, Minnesotan astronaut John Boone gets intensely irritated with geologist Phyllis Boyle who has just celebrated an Easter service with the dozen or so other Christians on board. John cannot believe that a scientist like Phyllis ascribes to a religion founded on miracles, which contradict natural laws. When Phyllis asks if John "really" knows "the [Christ] story" (Robinson 1993: 47), John counters that he was raised a Lutheran but is now aware that the Christ story is indeed a fiction: he summarizes as though factual some claims about the late composition of the gospels and the resulting situation of Jesus as a "literary figure" rather "like Sherlock Holmes, or the Lone Ranger" (Robinson 1993: 48). Phyllis' complacency is impervious to John's skepticism (or his Lone Ranger remark), and she seems to have no content to her beliefs other than sentiments like the universe itself is a miracle. She tells John he just needs to have faith, something that several of the First Hundred find amusing. Cynical Frank Chalmers seems ready to exploit the political advantage of presenting John to the American public as anti-Christian, while calm empiricist Sax Russell remarks that "'Whenever scientists say they're Christian . . . [he takes] it to be an aesthetic statement'" (Robinson 1993: 49).

Later when miners have found industrial metals on Mars, the satire of Phyllis' sentimental Christianity gets sharper. John, increasingly unwilling to see Mars become a copy of capitalist Earth, visits Phyllis, now a key player in the construction of a space elevator that will bring Mars metals "into the Terran market" in a hugely profitable way (Robinson 1993: 274). As he watches Phyllis lecture about the elevator to her allies in transnational business, John satirizes their enthusiasm as a despicable Pentecost, thinking that he can "almost see the tongues of fire flickering from [Phyllis'] mass of auburn hair. There were fortunes to be made, enormous fortunes . . . No wonder Phyllis and the rest of them looked like they were in church" (Robinson 1993: 278).

While Christianity is satirized in the John–Phyllis conflict, its paradigmatic influence is further diluted in ways that include both Hiroko's ritual of the areophany – a Martian holy communion – and the never solved mystery of whether Hiroko is alive or dead at the end of the trilogy – a dilemma for characters like Sax which raises the question of how dependent humans are on "magical thinking" (Robinson 1996: 360), even while it naturalizes the concept of resurrection. Sax never believes that Hiroko has risen from the dead; rather he is almost sure that Hiroko is still alive because she rescued him when he lost his vehicle in a snowstorm on terraformed Mars. He remembers the pressure of her hand on his wrist and chooses to believe the experience was not a hallucination. He discovers this kind of faith is necessary to him.

In the years after Frank Chalmers arranged the murder of his old friend John Boone, Frank is traveling with Bedouin miners on Mars and is spending a lot of time alone thinking and writing:

> "The Arabs don't believe in original sin," [Frank] wrote in his lectern. "They believe that man is innocent, and death natural. That we do not need a saviour. There is no heaven or hell, but only reward and punishment, which take the form of this life itself and how it is lived. It is a humanist correction of Judaism and Christianity, in that sense. (Robinson 1993: 373)

This passage exemplifies what characters often are doing in the trilogy – learning, reflecting – and also points toward what is presumably an authorial purpose of redefining humanity so as to make real-world Utopia imaginable. But it seems ironic that Frank is the one to think approvingly of how "man is innocent, and death natural" when Frank's betrayal and murder of John is the Biblical-like scenario that impels the narrative for several hundred pages in *Red Mars* (compare Abbott 2003: 38). The trilogy opens with a section that could be termed a flash "forward" since it takes place long after the First Hundred have landed on Mars, on a "festival night" when we follow Frank manipulating various Arab groups to believe that John Boone is shutting them out of the new Mars society. Frank manipulates a young man to arrange John's murder and then cleverly and ruthlessly murders the young man as well.

Frank's motives for orchestrating John's death remain obscure. We see the love triangle of John, Maya, and Frank, with Frank the one left out when John and Maya renew their relationship, and we learn that Frank wants to be a major political player on Mars. Yet his motives remain mysterious – deliberately so, it seems. Not long before his death John visits some Sufis: "Qadarite Sufis . . . pantheists influenced by early Greek philosophy and modern existentialism, trying by modern science and the *ru' yat al-qalb*, the vision of the heart, to become one with that ultimate reality which was God" (Robinson 1993: 281). The Sufis debate whether or not Frank Chalmers is John's *nafs* – his evil self, and one of them remarks "It's the love of right lures men to wrong'" (Robinson 1993: 282).

Frank and John's difficult friendship/kinship is thus reset through each character's encounters with and tentative appropriations of Islamic traditions – John with the Qadarite Sufis and Frank with the Bedouins. The Frank who later reflects on Islam as a "humanist correction of Judaism and Christianity" also thinks how ironic it is that John Boone and the Arabs actually had a quite similar view of history (Robinson 1993: 374). Frank and John are portrayed as brothers who love and hate one another and whose destinies are entangled in some larger plan. As Frank becomes a historical figure and a poignant memory to the First Hundred, we see characters like Maya reading biographies, seeking to understand him. No full revelations emerge, but it seems that if Frank's murder of John is not evidence of original sin, it arises from what could be termed Frank's original anger: anger that throughout history people have been selfish and stupid, and in large numbers, oppressed and disenfranchised.

A Scientist as one of the Heroes

Robinson's Mars trilogy revitalizes the myth of science as the powerful, versatile tool that can be used for good and recreates the scientist as humanist hero in the character of Sax Russell. Science (through its servant, Sax) is humbled and politicized while also being celebrated. Science is multiple on Mars, for example: it is ecopoesis (Robinson 1994: 112; Robinson 1996: 72–3); it involves huge, "god-like," robotic-enabled projects, like the making of solar mirrors or Martian oceans; it is an attitude of paying attention to the "this-ness" of the material world. Science can become the "alchemy" that unites science and mysticism, in the view of psychiatrist and philosopher Michel Duval. And science is always asking (as Sax always asks) – "why?" If Frank brings an original anger at the injustice of history, Sax brings the original curiosity that Arkady alludes to in his description of the original Utopia that is for primitives and for scientists – meaning everyone.

Sax begins as the passionate lab scientist who longs to recreate Mars through terraforming but who also longs to convince "red Mars" Ann of the beauty and value of this creation. He becomes a politicized scientist who helps make a society and a world where science can "really" be done. Along the way he becomes an undercover scientist – a spy for the Martian underground that grows up after the first revolution. He almost becomes the murderer of Phyllis but his empathy redirects him (Robinson 1994: 208). After being captured by the military-intelligence forces of the transnationals and rescued by the Martian underground, Sax becomes a survivor of the brain damage caused by what amounted to torture, as the transnational forces tried to pry loose his secrets.

When he is undercover as Stephen Lindholm, Sax attends a scientific conference and realizes that even though their scientific powers on Mars are such that "their reach no longer exceeded their grasp" (Robinson 1994: 181), and even though the conference at first seems like the cozy, bright, protected world of science conference as Utopia, this Utopian freedom and power of science is an illusion. Economic greed is influencing Martian science at all levels, and Sax is thoroughly disillusioned. Coyote/Desmond welcomes him to the revolution (Robinson 1994: 203). Sax's capture, torture, and recovery thus build on an already politicized consciousness.

Sax's interrogation caused a stroke, which caused "nonfluent aphasia. . . . where a subject can't read or write, and has difficulty speaking or finding the right words, and is very aware of the problem" (Robinson 1994: 260). This scientist who in Michel Duval's phrase is one of the "conscious creators" (Robinson 1994: 213) also becomes the creature: he becomes a Frankensteinian "monster" – undergoing experimental brain treatments as well as lengthy probing conversations with his friend and healer, Michel. Sax and Michel form another pair of friends/brothers who complement one another's strengths. Sax is the empiricist and naturalist and Michel the "alchemist" – the one who pushes naturalism toward syncretic mysticism, as in their dialogue in *Green Mars* (1994: 342–7). Poignancy informs such dialogues: while Michel speaks for the "godlike freedom" of humans, with Sax maintaining "We are still physical reality. Atoms in their rounds. Determined on most scales, random on some others" – it is Michel who seems more "determined" in his emotional and physical life, while Sax gets to "shoot free" into a radically changed self that still gets to keep an essential Sax-ness.

The politicized, estranged-from-language Sax is an intriguing social animal with his reverence for all life coupled with his willingness to take on large-scale sabotage for a "free" Mars. However, Sax is backstage for much of the necessary political work that creates the second revolution. Messy civil life combined with moments of elegant, postmodern Paleolithic ritual make possible a Mars populace united enough to withstand Earth's influence. The Dorsa Brevia meeting of various Mars groups (Robinson 1994: 305ff) is crucial: Nadia, Art, and Nirgal are key players in the civic work of drawing up proposals, coordinating workshops, and emphasizing common ground. Hiroko is key to the dramatic making new of ancient rituals, like the ceremony – an "instinctive and yet highly conscious rebirth" – that concludes the Dorsa Brevia meeting (Robinson 1994: 338). This rebirth ceremony bypasses the Judeo-Christian tradition to go farther back into the human past – closer to that primitive Utopia that Arkady spoke of – and into a "Minoan-Crete" past that is matriarchal in orientation rather than patriarchal.

Ingredients that feed into the all-important second revolution – the revolution that brings a "phase change," a "free Mars" and a close-enough Utopia – thus include politicized science, messy yet effective civic life, and self-conscious rituals that accentuate the Martian "difference" from the patriarchal and capitalist past, while offering imaginative links to the deep past of humankind. Another crucial ingredient is what might be termed authorially strategic floods. While *Red Mars* ends with a catastrophic flood caused by the ill-conceived first revolution, *Green Mars* ends with two floods: the first on Earth, with natural causes going back thousands of years (Robinson 1994: 475); the second on Mars, caused by conflict between underground Mars groups and transnational Earth forces. The global flood on Earth (caused by the breaking up of the West Antarctic ice sheet) is gradual enough to lessen the loss of life, but the flood will also have far-reaching effects – pushing Earth toward a socialist world government. The Terran flood also triggers the second Mars revolution.

The Mars flood – the flooding of Burroughs during the second revolution – proves a victory of negotiation and technology over old violent models of revolution. This flood is caused by conflict between the Mars insurgents and the Earth-transnational forces, but loss of life is prevented due to the largely terraformed atmosphere coupled with the new breathing masks that allow a whole city of people to escape the drowned Burroughs by walking away to the train station. The two floods in *Green Mars* seem like liberal floods compared with the radical one of *Red Mars*: here I am thinking of Nadia and Ardady's debate about liberal versus radical methods for achieving social justice (Robinson 1993: 156–7). Nadia and others have been determined that the violence and chaos of the first revolution not be repeated, and so it works out. And Sax's musing in *Blue Mars* about how their god-like scientific powers can help them make a decent civilization is born out by how the technologies and "alchemies" that created the danger of flooding on Mars in the first place can also save people from drowning – a good step toward restarting history.

Mortal Gods

In *Blue Mars*, Sax gives Ann Clayborne a longevity treatment without her knowledge or consent – a treatment that saves her life. After realizing she is going to live, Ann goes from talking with therapist-philosopher Michel and from experiencing her own exploding emotions to being chased by a genetically designed bear across terraformed Mars, and having dinner with the bear's maker. She then counsels Red ecoteurs, talking these ecoterrorists into responsible civic action. At the very end, her understanding of the past transformed by Sax's memory drug, somewhat reconciled to the terraformed planet, and in a loving relationship with Sax, she withstands a heart attack or stroke (the sudden death syndrome that is plaguing the First Hundred). Humans create and mold the Martian environment – are chased by some of those creations – and are capable of political commitments, civic action, and love. Utopia is near, death is near.

Michel Duval, who proclaims humans to be "gods," is humane, limited, always homesick (if on Earth, for Mars and vice versa), and dies, sadly – a victim of the sudden death that the longevity treatments cannot yet prevent. Michel does not live to see the final, most peaceful revolution or to see Ann's reconciliation with terraformed Mars. Although others like Sax and Ann are still living as the golden age approaches, these old ones know that their presumed eventual death will ease a population crisis that is a chief obstacle to the golden age. As for Michel, he loved his First Hundred, and it seems odd for him to speak of humans as gods when he has known human foibles so intimately. But that is the way Robinson's Mars trilogy works: grand claims are filtered through limited, contextualized voices.

Sax goes after the problem of sudden death (why not?) but then decides to focus on the memory problems plaguing the long lived. His concoction of a memory "cocktail" brings the remnant of the First Hundred and One together at Underhill, where everything began, and where there are now few enough of them to share a "single trailer" – those sleeping trailers where they had first gone to bed "weary with the . . . oh-so-interesting work of building a town and a world" (Robinson 1996: 574). Sax and Ann are brought together in this episode, and their pairing is a crucial symbol for the Third Revolution, which is a mysterious, compressed affair of noisy talk, guided by a compassion for Earth's current population crisis. Third Revolution Mars is the better than decent civilization; it has multiple experiments in postmodern Paleolithic living; and it appears to exist in a restarted Utopian path for history.

References and Further Reading

Abbott, Carl (2003) "Falling into History: The Imagined Wests of Kim Stanley Robinson in the 'Three Californias' and Mars Trilogies." *Western Historical Quarterly* 34 (Spring): 27–47.

Aldiss, Brian W, with David Wingrove (1986) *Trillion Year Spree: The History of Science Fiction*. New York: Avon.

Bailey, K.V. (1996) "Mars is a District of Sheffield." *Foundation: The International Review of Science Fiction* 68 (Autumn): 81–7.

Baxter, Stephen (1996) "Martian chronicles: Narratives of Mars in Science and SF." *Foundation: The International Review of Science Fiction* 68 (Autumn): 5–16.

Crossley, Robert (2000) "Sign, Symbol, Power: The New Martian Novel." In *Histories of the Future: Studies in Fact, Fantasy and Science Fiction*, (eds) Alan Sandison and Robert Dingley. Basingstoke: Palgrave, 152–67.

Dynes, William (2001) "Multiple Perspectives in

Kim Stanley Robinson's Mars Series." *Extrapolation* 42.ii (Summer), 150–64.

Foote, Bud (1994a) "A Conversation with Kim Stanley Robinson." *Science Fiction Studies* 21, 1 (March): 51–60.

——(1994b) "Notes on Kim Stanley Robinson's *Red Mars*." *Science Fiction Studies* 21, 1 (March): 61–6.

Franko, Carol (1997) "The Density of Utopian Destiny in Robinson's *Red Mars*." *Extrapolation* 38.i (Spring): 57–65.

——(1994) "Working the 'In Between': Kim Stanley Robinson's Utopian Fiction," *Science Fiction Studies* 21.ii (July): 191–211.

Huston, Shaun (2002) "Murray Bookchin on Mars! The Production of Nature in Kim Stanley Robinson's Mars Trilogy." In *Lost in Space: Geographies of Science Fiction*, (ed.) Rob Kitchin and James Neale. London and New York: Continuum, 167–79.

Jackson, Thomas E. (1998) "Interview with Kim Stanley Robinson," *New York Review of Science Fiction* 10 (May): 14–18.

James, Edward (1996) "Building Utopias on Mars, from Crusoe to Robinson." *Foundation: The International Review of Science Fiction* 68 (Autumn): 64–74.

Jameson, Fredric (2001) " 'If I find one good city I will spare the man': Realism and Utopia in Kim Stanley Robinson's *Mars* Trilogy." In *Learning From Other Worlds: Estrangement, Cognition, and the Politics of Science Fiction and Utopia,* (ed.) Patrick Parrinder. London and Durham, NJ: Duke University Press, 208–32.

Markley, Robert (1997) "Falling into Theory: Simulation, Terraformation, and Eco-Economics in Kim Stanley Robinson's Martian Trilogy." *Modern Fiction Studies* 43.iii (Fall): 773–99.

Michaels, Walter Benn (2001) "The Shape of the Signifier." *Critical Inquiry* 27.ii (Winter): 266–83.

Robinson, Kim Stanley (ed.) (1994) *Future Primitive: The New Ecotopias.* New York: Tor, [Tom Doherty Associates].

——(1993) *Red Mars.* New York: Bantam.

——(1994) *Green Mars.* New York: Bantam.

——(1996) *Blue Mars.* New York: Bantam.

——(1999) *The Martians.* New York: Bantam.

Seed, David (1996) "The Mars Trilogy: An Interview [with Kim Stanley Robinson]." *Foundation: The International Review of Science Fiction* 68 (Autumn): 75–80.

Stableford, Brian (1993) "Mars." *The Encyclopedia of Science Fiction*, (eds) John Clute and Peter Nicholls. New York: St. Martin's Press, 777–9.

Suvin, Darko (2001) "Afterword: With Sober, Estranged Eyes." *In Learning From Other Worlds: Estrangement, Cognition, and the Politics of Science Fiction and Utopia*, (ed.) Patrick Parrinder. London and Durham, NJ: Duke University Press, 233–71.

Wells, H.G. (1923) *Men Like Gods.* New York: Macmillan.

——(1965) *A Modern Utopia.* Introduction by Mark R. Hillegas. Lincoln, NE and London: University of Nebraska Press.

Westfahl, Gary (2000) "Reading Mars: Changing Images of Mars in Twentieth-Century Science Fiction." *New York Review of Science Fiction* 13.iv (December): 1, 8–13.

41

Iain M. Banks: *Excession*

Farah Mendlesohn

If John Clute's suggestion is correct, that the science fiction which told a common narrative of expectation, is indeed dead (Clute 2003: 65), if that future is no longer with us, then this might explain why it was space opera, with its wide spaces, implausible politics, large ships, and extravagant language – in short, the form that departs most enthusiastically from that rationalized future – which came to dominate SF at the end of the twentieth century.

At the beginning of the 1990s Cyberpunk had dominated the external face of science fiction. In a world of fractionalized peace, and a huge displacement of money and power, Cyberpunk reflected the despair of many westerners at the mass exodus of manufacturing jobs to the developing world, and the threat suggested in the rise of computer networks. Cyberpunk was in many ways a betrayal of science fiction: it was pessimistic (postnuclear novels assumed human resilience), it accepted the inevitable victory of the corporatist agenda for the world even while railing against it, and it turned away from the outward-bound project that was SF and into the mind. But Cyberpunk left a legacy of verbal pyrotechnics.

It was in this context that space opera, the despised child of SF, its most juvenile, immature canvas (Westfahl 2003: 201), emerged as the cutting edge of the genre (*Locus* 2003). Space opera had never pretended to the plausible. It is full of hand-waving effects to ensure that a ship can travel thirty million light years in the blink of an eye, but it celebrated the human, and its very lack of concern for a realizable future offered a counterbalance to the all too predictable vision of global decay. Almost falling off the edge of plausible expectation were the revisionist, political, and overwhelmingly *romantic* space opera Utopias of Iain M. Banks.

Banks refused to accept the inevitability of capitalism posited by Cyberpunk and earlier space opera (Csiceray-Ronay Jr. 2003: 231, 236). SF mostly reflects the social and economic mores of the contemporary world – it is actually very difficult to think outside the box – but in this one area, Banks simply disposed of the box. His space operas take place in a postscarcity society which, while currently unavailable to us, is perhaps the one vision that is still within our grasp, tying Banks to that shared future story Clute suggests we have lost.

By dispensing with scarcity, Banks removed most of the motivations that usually power SF and turned space opera in the most unlikely direction. A form that had never been considered particularly sensitive to the depiction of human emotion became, in Banks' work, the stage for obsessive consideration of how sentients might act if eating each day was not the primary concern. Banks wrote tales in which politics is a game of reputation and memory; empire is truly built on the best of all motives, and the genuine goal of the community is to create the best of all possible places for each individual member of society.

The Culture, although Utopian, is not a planned society but a neo-anarchist collection of individuals, some of whom are humanoid, some of other alien species, and others the descendents of artificial intelligences, huge Minds who sail between the stars, inhabit/run/are artificial habitats, space ships, and drones. It is the inter-relations between these individuals which Banks has made the stuff of space opera. The Culture as a whole has a tendency to sound like a hedonistic missionary. The attention to character ensures that each novel has a tremendously romantic drive. It is as if Banks has taken Churchill's assertion – that we remember the great events of history through our personal important happenings – and used it to power, so far, six novels and a novella. The personal is portrayed with the intensity of a Hampstead novel and each inner life is utterly vital to the wider, space opera issues of politics and empire that are also depicted.

However, Banks' "revisioning" (*Locus*, August 2003) is not only of the depiction of the interpersonal in the space opera, nor in his success in swinging the space opera back to the political left. Space opera has long been considered the most romantic of the subgenres of science fiction with its wide-open spaces and emphasis on action adventure, but it has also been considered the most badly written. Gary K. Wolfe cites early space opera as "damning evidence of its [SF's] subliterariness among outsiders" (Wolfe 2003: 98). There is nothing to suggest that this perception has faded, yet since the 1990s, there is clear evidence that space opera is the canvas on which SF's literary experiments are taking place: most recently in John Clute's *Appleseed* (2001) and M. John Harrison's *Light* (2002). While *Excession* is not a pre-cursor in the sense of inspiring either of these writers (both of whom have lengthy and distinguished careers), it was clearly the first of the modern space operas to take into the subgenre the possibilities of language as the cogs and wheels of SF suggested by the work of Olaf Stapledon in *Last and First Men* (1930) and M. John Harrison in his New Wave space opera, *The Centauri Device* (1975) (MacLeod, *Locus* 2003: 41).

While there are other novels that compete for the title of best Culture novel (*Use of Weapons* may be the most politically sophisticated, and its structure the most impressive), *Excession* epitomizes much of what I have outlined above. It is the most *classic*, the most archetypal in its revisioning of space opera; the most ambitious in its portrayal of a complex political society; and the most successful in its linguistic display and reconfiguration of the space opera baroque and in the immersive techniques of extrapolative fiction.

Iain M. Banks likes convoluted and interwoven plots and at least one of the games to be played with *Excession* is to guess the number of stories. There are two supra plots: an "excession" or Out of Context Problem has appeared in a sector of unclaimed space and could potentially pose a climactic threat to the Culture while elsewhere a princess sits in a tower and mourns her lost love and the baby she has decided to keep nestling in her womb – a perfectly plausible option for members of the Culture.

The appearance of the excession triggers other plots: a man called Byr Genar-Hofoen finds himself on a mission to find a stored soul on the eccentric ship *Sleeper Service*. Ulver Seich is recruited to Special Circumstances (the Culture's equivalent of the CIA) to entrap Byr Genar-Hofoen. One group of Minds meets to discuss the excession and is taken over by a second group of much older Minds – the Interesting Times Gang – who have put plans in place for this eventuality several hundred years before; and yet another group of Minds is plotting to persuade a bunch of allied aliens – the Affront – to declare war on the Culture so that the Culture can be persuaded to wipe out the Affront. A rival society called the Elench is on a mission to be absorbed by everything it meets and thus become something else while the AhForgetIt tendency is exploring the wilder reaches of anarchism. And meanwhile, in a strand so powerful that it *must* be important but later turns out to be a red herring, a ship called the *Grey Area* has been tootling along on its own little mission of investigation and retribution. Conspiracy is layered upon conspiracy and everyone is suspicious of everyone else.

But *Excession* defies the archetype of space opera in a number of ways and the first is that there is a serious question as to what this book is actually about.

At the end of *Excession* the Out of Context Problem retreats, taking with it one of the more inquisitive ships – the *Grey Area*. It leaves behind very little information or data, the only kind of "currency" the Culture values. The Minds conspiring to get the Affront into trouble are found out and are either destroyed in action or retreat. The Affront receive a seriously bloody nose but remain an unruly and unpleasant client species, still a bit too powerful to civilize. The two plots that seem most significant in terms of space opera, come to nothing. It is this, I think, that bothers Westfahl when he argues that despite the creativity of the "postmodern" space operas, they ". . . exude the aura of exercises, brilliantly accomplished but lacking the fervent conviction regarding humanity's manifest destiny in the cosmos that distinguished classic space opera" (Westfahl 2003: 207). However, in Banks' work, this conviction is the default position, as taken for granted as air. And as Banks no longer has to argue for destiny, he can get on with the storytelling.

The plot that most receives resolution is the most personal. Byr Genar-Hofoen has been sent on a wild goose chase. The soul he is looking for has already been sent on her way, her purpose within the plot being solely to trigger Byr Genar-Hofoen into action. Ulver Seich has also been tricked. Suspicious Minds, seeing Byr Genar-Hofoen as somehow connected to whatever was going on, had dispatched her to prevent him from reaching the *Sleeper Service*, although they had no idea why the *Sleeper Service* should want him. They, like we, are convinced that Byr Genar-Hofoen is somehow crucial to a conspiracy on a galactic scale.

He is not.

Byr Genar-Hofoen offers the solution to a niggling problem that the *Sleeper Service* wants resolved before it goes off to do its duty. Many years before, when it first became Eccentric, and began posing the hibernating bodies of Culture citizens in tableaux of famous battles, it took on board a woman called Dajeil Gelian. For the past forty years she has sat on the beach or in the tower it created for her and refused to give birth. In desperation it has brought Byr Genar-Hofoen to Dajeil, hoping that the presence of her former lover will bring about some kind of resolution. The *Sleeper Service* wishes to do this because it cast the deciding vote which allowed Byr Genar-Hofoen to accompany Dajeil to the planet 'Ktik where they became lovers and the whole sorry Tragedy – complete with attempted murder and infanticide – was played out.

Excession is a space opera whose conspiracies seem mainly designed to fulfill the romantic nostalgia of a god (the relationship between the Minds and humans is much like that of the Heinlein's *Star Beast* (1954) who, stranded on Earth, takes to "breeding" generations of John Thomas Stuarts). It is as if someone had just dropped Jane Austen's *Emma* into the middle of a battle. Here *Excession* is a novel of romance, of the day to day of lives lived through great events. Each of the main characters is much more concerned with their individualized futures than with the prospective end of the universe. Compare this with the much more typical of SF, *Schild's Ladder* by Greg Egan (2002) in which love takes a very secondary place to the romance of the space.

Yet at the end *we don't mind*. Dajeil gets her baby and a new lover, Byr Genar-Hofoen gets an Affronter body, and the *Sleeper Service* can go off to battle with a clear conscience. It is the classic triangle of the romance novel.

By now one cannot but help have noticed that Banks' plots are linked to the same source of humor as are the names of the ships. Word play and ironic asides – the main reason why Banks has been labeled postmodernist (Westfahl 2003: 206) – litter the nomenclature of the Minds. Bad puns, buried fairy tales and red-herrings frequently form the backbone of the plots (in *Use of Weapons*, even this last phrase is literalized). *Excession* begins with a fairy tale image: "A little more than one hundred days into the fortieth year of her confinement, Dajeil Gelian was visited in her lonely tower overlooking the sea by an avatar of the ship that was her home" (Banks 1996: 3). It invites expectations of *bildungsroman* in both reader and character: Ulver Seich knows how story works, and sulks when it finally occurs to her that she is in someone else's tale.

All of this is a lot of fun, but it works beyond the red herrings, the politics, the joy of bodies that change shape, immortal intellects, and the sardonic humor of ships. One is struck by the sheer effrontery of Banks' reconfiguration of the space opera and his playful use of language. Against extravagant scenery and epic scale, the choice of modes and mood differs for each section of the novel. This is where Banks' revisioning of what space opera is takes place.

Each of the subplots takes place at different sensory time speeds. Dajeil's story is long and slow. Byr Genar-Hofoen's rapid with much crammed into it. The Drone's story is told in short passages but covers long stretches of time; Pace is built in through the three main characters. Each "story" is told in a distinctive diction which shapes our response to certain characters and at times deliberately engenders a creative misprision.

Dajeil's tale is written in a way that distances us from her. We are positioned external to her feelings, and the elegiac quality of the scenes between Dajeil and the Avatar place them as the small still space within the hurricane blowing across the Culture. This stillness registers in the writing of the landscape.

> Steady lines of waves broke on the grey slope of the shingle beach, beating on shattered, ground-up shells, tiny fragments of hollow animal carapaces, brittle lengths of light-blighted sea-wrack, water smoothed slivers of wood, pitted pebbles of foamstone like dainty marbles of porous bone and a general assortment of seaside detritus collected from a handful-hundred different planets strewn across the greater galaxy. (Banks 1996: 3–4)

The marvelous of the minute, connected to the marvelous of the magnificent, renders a sea shore sublime while Banks' deploys much plainer language whenever he wishes to tell us something marvelous. "The light came from a line, not a point in the sky, because the place where Dajeil Gelian lived was not an ordinary world. At dawn, the sun-line would have appeared to rise from the horizon to starboard" (Banks 1996: 3) estranges us almost as completely as does the elaboration of the mundane in that description of the beach. Prosaic observation becomes the vector for grandeur:

> . . . she tried to imagine the ship as a whole in that same trained mind's eye, remembering the occasions when she had viewed the vessel from its remote machines or gone flying around it, attempting to imagine the changes it was already preparing itself for. She supposed they would be unglimpsable from the sort of distance that would let you see the whole craft. (Banks 1996: 10)

This use of bathos to create the visual sublime permeates the text and is at its most effective when Banks comes later to describe the grandeur of space. When the drone Sisela Ythelus 1/2 realizes there is something else out there, its dilemma is described as microcosm: "The insect trapped in the surface tension of the pond would have gone still now, while the water quivered and whatever was advancing upon it – skating across the water's surface or angling up from underneath – approached its helpless prey" (Banks 1996: 95) but at the start of chapter eight Banks describes the hyper-sphere and hyperspace in ways which alternate the mundane with the magnificent.

> Between any pair of universes there was more than just empty hyperspace; there was a thing called an energy grid. It was useful – strands of it could help power ships, and it had been used as a weapon – but it was also an obstacle, and, by all accounts so far –

one which had proved impenetrable to intelligent investigation. . . . There were white holes, too; ferociously violent sources spraying torrents of energy into the universe with the power of a million suns and which also seemed to be linked to the grid . . . but no body, no ship or even information had ever been observed appearing from their tumultuous mouths; no equivalent of an airborne bacteria, no word, no language, just that incoherent scream of cascading energies and super energetic particles. (Banks 1996: 271)

Within one paragraph we twice move from the images we can realize to those we cannot and begin to see the pattern of juxtaposition which structures plot, mood and metaphor in *Excession*. In *Excession* the invader is simply a presence, it does very little, but the description of this very little is imbued with power:

The Excession's links with the two regions of the energy grid just fell away, twin collapsing pinnacles of fluted skein fabric sinking back into the grid like the idealized renderings of some spent explosion at sea. Both layers of the grid oscillated for a few moments, again like some perfectly abstracted liquid, then lay still . . . (Banks 1996: 19)

In contrast to this tension, the *Appeal to Reason*'s drone is all ornamentation, a "gaily adorned thing, its extremities sporting ribbons, flowers and little ornaments . . . It puttered hesitantly towards the Excession, chirpily beaming signals of innocent goodwill" (Banks 1996: 358). The description is as baroque, but the material is chintz rather than brocade. In these lines Banks expresses his vision of the cosmos through the accretion of the spectacular counterpointed by the diminutive voice and the metaphors of the ordinary.

Elsewhere, Banks constructs his images from forms that *accrete*. His worlds are artificial barnacles in space, some brutal: Phage rock is made up of junk, "new bits of systemic or interstellar debris about it as needs required and its population increased, securing the chunks of metal, rock, ice and compacted dust to its still gnarled outer surface in a slow process of acquisition, consumption and evolution" (Banks 1996: 105). In contrast, Tier Habitat, is an "array of mirrors and mirrorfields situated within the staggered cone of the world's axis provided amounts of sunlight precisely timed, attenuated and where necessary altered in wavelength to mimic the conditions on a hundred different worlds for a hundred different intelligent species" (Banks 1996: 200). The result is beauty to match the beauty of the space in which it floats.

Other sections of the book are shaped not by the complexity of accretion but by the deceptiveness of simplicity. In the scenes between Byr Genar-Hofoen and the Affront we see a switch. Distance and elegy are replaced by bluff rudeness, the depiction of the Affront is reminiscent of satirical depictions of the British gentry of the huntin', shootin' and fishin' sort; both matter of fact and oddly domestic:

. . . amongst the people who really mattered it was one of the most frequently voiced objections to the Affront's membership of the informal association of other space-faring species that having to be nice to other, lesser species – rather than giving the brutes a chance to prove their mettle against the glorious force of Affront arms – had resulted in a distinct dulling of the average society dinner.

Still, on really special occasions these days the fights would be between two Affron-
ters with a dispute of a suitably dishonorable nature, or between criminals. Such contests usually required that the protagonists be hobbled, tied together, and armed with
sliver knives scarcely more substantial than hat pins, thus ensuring that the fights didn't
end too quickly . . . (Banks 1996: 35)

The long-winded exposition builds the perception of buffoonery, Ruritanian
romance gives way to the affectionate satire Jane Austen brought to military balls.
Affront names are nature signifiers: "Fivetide"; "Greydawn," "Risingmoon." Banks
deploys the juxtaposition of absurdity to considerable affect.

At times P.G. Wodehouse creeps in: the description of the Affronter on p. 29, with
his demand that Byr Genar-Hofoen admire his new uniform, could be replaced by
any red-faced, overstuffed colonel at a hunt ball. Banks' use of this hale-and-hearty
tone underlines its attraction while signaling the hidden duplicity. The Affront breed
their females to find sex painful. Later, a cheerful and hearty Affronter captain will
take over the habitat of Tier and threaten its inhabitants with torture and mayhem.
That the Affront are amusing is discomfiting. Similarly discomfiting is that Banks
introduces the elegiac when it seems almost outrageously inappropriate. When the
Affronter Commander loses his temper on Pittance (the asteroid housing mothballed
Ships), he, "unholstered one of the external weapons on his own suit and blasted the
small figure into a thousand pieces, scattering fragmenta of frosty pink and white
across the cold floor of the hangar like a small, delicate fall of snow" (Banks 1996:
225). The small figure is a dead body.

Perhaps the most disturbing sections of the book – another red herring – concerns
the hobbies of the ship named *Grey Area* but popularly called *Meat Fucker*. The *Grey
Area* breaks the only real taboo the Culture maintains: it enters the minds of sentients
without permission. The *Grey Area* forces a retired army officer to relive memories of
genocide. The elaborate dream mode disguises how little we learn, we are not told
the cause. The power of this section is in its rhetorical cadence: part legal defense,
part epic narrative. The rhythm of the dream narrative intensifies the horror that the
genocides have cast themselves as victims.

Those we disposed of; their torment lasted a few days, maybe a month or two, then it
was over as quickly and efficiently as we could make the process.
  Our suffering has gone on for a generation.
  I am proud of what I did. I wish it had not fallen to me to do what had to be done,
but I am glad that I did it to the best of my capabilities, and I would do it again.
  That was why I wanted to write down what had happened; to witness our belief and
our dedication and our suffering. (Banks 1996: 49)

In contrast the language of punishment is prosaic, exposing the brutality behind
the rhetoric: the officer is forced to dream several deaths, until finally, "he was in the
hold of a ship, crammed in with thousands of other people in the darkness, surrounded
again by stink and filth and screams and pain. He was already half dead two days later

when the sea valves opened and those still left alive began to drown" (Banks 1996: 52). Banks constructs his images from bathetic juxtapositions. The contrast between these two passages may indicate one way to read this book: be wary of the beauty of language, the real sublime does not need help.

One area where the language of *Excession* is at its most challenging and estranged is in the conversations between the Minds. The communication between the ships is configured as computer code, emulating the package transmission that relays emails from node to node, varying in rhetorical mood, but here emulating US military-speak.

4) [tight beam, M16, relay, received @ n4.28.855.0085]:
xGCU *Fate Amenable to Change,*
    oGSV *Ethics Gradient*
    &only as required
    Developmental anomaly provisionally rated EqT, potentially jeopardising, found here c9259969+5331.
    My Status: L5 secure, moving to L6.
Instigating all other Extreme precautions. (Banks 1996: 16)

At times, these exchanges feel like a window into the Culture's civil service, computer routing functioning in place of exchanges between departments, a bureaucratic sublime if you will:

. . . sometimes after setting up appointments they were absent in Infinite Fun space for a while. Then the Minds had to be casualed up to, or gossip or jokes or thoughts on a mutual interest had to be exchanged before a request or suggestion was put which re-routed and disguised an information search; sometimes these re-routes took on extra loops, detours and shuntings as the Minds concerned thought to play down their own involvement or involve somebody else on a whim, so that often wildly indirect paths resulted, branching and re-branching and doubling back on themselves. (Banks 1996: 231)

Although the shunting instructions and identification codes are soon dropped it is in these sections that Banks demonstrates his versatility. As the participants of this discussion widen, Banks carefully constructs the different "voices" of his Minds in ways that provide indications of character but also heighten the tension of conspiracy. Early in the novel, the *Serious Callers Only* is content to offer cryptic doggerel. "Here, in the bare dark face of night/A calm unhurried eye draws sight/We see in what we think we fear/The cloudings of our thought made clear" (Banks 1996: 119). Later, having adopted the role of amateur gumshoe, the *Sleeper Service* opts for a more hardboiled style:

Take a look at the enclosed bullshit from the AOANL'sA (signal enclosed). I almost hope its been taken over, If this is the way it really feels, I'd feel slightly worse. (original in bold, Banks 1996: 309)

These exchanges between ships are playful, they reek of conspiracy flavored with faux *ennui* and suppressed humor which renders everything the Minds say, even between each other, untrustworthy.

As a general rule, just as the grander and more natural the scenery, the more prosaic the description; the braver and more heroic the action, the greater the level of self-deprecation and humor. Nowhere is this more effective than in the tale of the plucky drone, escaped from the Elench ship captured by the excession in the first few pages, and desperate to get its message out. In this section Banks combines the vastness of space with unexpected emotion.:

> *It can't be over that quickly, can it?*
> Hiding in the darkness, the drone suspected it was already too late. (Banks 1996: 18)

That quiet thought anthropomorphises the drone. The British response to the lost Mars lander, *Beagle 2* on December 25, 2003, proved similarly anthropomorphic and sentimental suggesting one way, not often considered, in which Banks is a very "British" writer. It is interesting that we do not have to be *told* that the drone is sentient. The drone is our representative, it exists in a world made recognizable to us through reference and allusion, and through a surprising shift to the overblown, grammatically strained riff on classic galaxy-spanning E.E. "Doc" Smith prose:

> And in those swallowingly vast volumes, amongst those spaces between the stars, around suns, dwarfs, nebulae and holes it had been determined from some distance were of no immediate interest or threat, it was of course always possible that some danger waited, some peril lurked, comparatively small measured against the galaxy's present active cultures, but capable – through a developmental peculiarity or as a result of some form of temporal limbo or exclusionary dormancy – of challenging and besting even a representative of a society as technologically advanced and contactually experienced as the Elench. (Banks 1996: 19)

The above is all one sentence. In contrast, the drone's humor is short and sharp. "*Damn, might make it yet; just roll with it*" (Banks 1996: 230). Elsewhere, Banks uses flippancy to reduce the Affront to the level of a child with an adult's watch, who "would take the drone to bits to find out how it worked, drain it of all its information, ransom it if they hadn't destroyed it in the process of investigation and inquisition, [and] probably try to put a spy-program into it so that it would report back to them once it was back among the Elench" (Banks 1996: 133).

Throughout, the drone maintains its bravado, "Its last emotion was a mixture of sorrow, elation, and a kind of desperate pride that its plan might have worked . . . Then it died, instantly and forever, in its own small fireball of heat and light" (Banks 1996: 137). With this tone, Banks communicates the preciousness of *honor* which has remained central to space opera: the *Sleeper Service* has set Byr Genar-Hofoen in motion to retrieve its own personal sense of honor. The Interesting Times Gang feels the existence of the Affront damages the honor of the Culture. When the ancient ship the

Attitude Adjuster suicides, it does so because the *Killing Time* has convinced it that it has become dishonored. This is an astonishing piece of writing, a manipulation of the Shakespearean tragic soliloquy. Over five pages (375–80) Banks sends the *Attitude Adjuster* into a spiral of madness:

> . . . if just the thing it had chosen was the right thing to do . . . Had it not just been flattered to be the object of such attention? . . . Had it not always resented being passed over for certain small but prestigious missions in the past . . . (378)
> . . .
>
> Atrocity. Abomination. Gigadeath.
> It was worthless and hateful, despicable and foul; it was wrung out, exhausted and incapable of revelation or communication. It hated itself and what it had done more, much more than it had ever hated anything . . . (380)

When the end comes, it comes with grandeur, "It decoupled its engine fields from the energy grid and plunged those vortices of pure energy deep into the fabric of its own Mind, tearing its intellect apart in a supernova of sentient agony" (Banks 1996: 380). The *Attitude Adjuster*'s death is made perfect in its explosive beauty, continuing a pattern within this book in which death is both tragic and perfect, operatically aesthetic.

Excession, like all the Culture novels, subverts a number of clichés of space opera. The Minds are not waiting to take over the universe – they have better things to do. Nor is there any grand plan (Palumbo 1999). But the novel is most interesting because of Banks' use of language to mirror and intensify the structure of the plot. Banks' use of language in some of the more excessive passages of *Excession* is just this side of bad: juxtaposition is used to both comic and tragic effect; metaphors mislead us into awe; pastiche is used to intensify the most tragic moments; the bathetic supports the baroque. Individual forms used to great effect in his other novels – the studied detachment of *Song of Stone*, the conspiratorial tone of *Player of Games* – here mix to reconfigure the language of space opera and the description of the sublime.

References and Further Reading

Banks, Iain. M. (1968) *The Player of Games.* London: Macmillan

——(1987) *Consider Phlebas.* London: Macmillan.

——(1990) *Use of Weapons.* London: Orbit.

——(1991) *The State of the Art.* London: Orbit.

——(1996) *Excession.* London: Orbit.

——(1997) *Song of Stone.* London: Abacus.

——(2000) *Look to Windward.* London: Orbit.

——"A Few Notes from the Culture": http://www.compsci.bristol.sc.uk/~stefan/culture. html.

Clute, John (2001) *Appleseed.* London: Orbit.

——(2003) "Science Fiction from 1980 to the Present," in *The Cambridge Companion to Science Fiction*, (eds) Edward James and Farah Mendlesohn. Cambridge: Cambridge University Press, 64–78.

Csicsery-Ronay Jr. Istvan (2003) "Science Fiction and Empire," in *Science Fiction Studies* 90, volume 30, Part 2, 231–45.

Egan, Greg (2002) *Schild's Ladder.* London: Gollancz.

Gordon, Joan (2002) "Utopia, Genocide, and the Other: Science Fiction Explores the Truly Monstrous," in *Edging into the Future: Science Fiction and Contemporary Cultural Transformation*, (eds) Veronica Hollinger and Joan Gordon. Philadelphia: University of Pennsylvania Press, 204–16.

Guerrier, Simon (1999) "Culture Theory: Iain M. Banks' 'Culture' as Utopia," *Foundation: The International Review of Science Fiction* (Summer) 76, 28–38.

Hardesty, William H. (1999) "Mercenaries and Special Circumstances: Iain M. Banks' Counter-Narrative of Utopia, *Use of Weapons*," *Foundation: The International Review of Science Fiction*, (Summer) 76, 9–47.

Harrison, M. John (1975) *The Centauri Device*. St. Albans: Panther Books.

——(2002) *Light*. London: Gollancz.

Heinlein, Robert A. (1954) *Star Beast*. New York: Ace Books.

Kincaid, Paul (2000) Review of *Look to Windward*, *Vector; the Critical Journal of the BSFA*. Issue 213, 18–19.

Locus (2003) "The New Space Opera: Revisioning the Final Frontier with Commentary by Stephen Baxter, M. John Harrison, Gwyneth Jones, Ken MacLeod, Paul McAuley, Russell Letson and Gary K. Wolfe," No. 511, Vol. 51, part 2 (August)

Nye, David (1994) *The American Technological Sublime*. Cambridge, MA: MIT Press.

Palmer, Christopher (1999) "Galactic Empires and the Contemporary Extravaganza: Dan Simmons and Iain M. Banks," in *Science Fiction Studies* 26, 73–90.

Palumbo, Donald (1999) "Chaos-Theory Concepts and Structures in Asimov's Robot Stories and Novels: The Positronic Brain and Feedback Loops." In *Foundation: The International Review of Science Fiction* (Spring), 63–77.

Stapledon, Olaf (1930) *Last and First Men*. London: Methuen.

Westfahl, Gary (2003) "Space Opera," in *The Cambridge Companion to Science Fiction*, (eds) James and Mendlesohn. Cambridge: Cambridge University Press, 197–218.

Wolfe, Gary K. (2003) "Science Fiction and its Editors," in *The Cambridge Companion to Science Fiction*, (eds) James and Mendlesohn. Cambridge: Cambridge University Press, 96–109.

Index

Note: Science fiction novels and stories are mostly listed under their authors; those more discussed have their own entries. Films, magazines and anthologies are listed by title.

Blackwell Companions to Literature and Culture